MACROJUSTICE

The main features of the just society, as they would be chosen by the unanimous, impartial, and fully informed judgment of its members, present a remarkable and simple meaningful structure. In this society, individuals' freedom is fully respected, and overall redistribution amounts to an equal sharing of individuals' different earnings obtained by the same limited "equalization labour." This also amounts to general balanced reciprocity, where each individual yields to each other the proceeds of the same labour. The concept of equalization labour is a measure of the degree of community, solidarity, reciprocity, redistribution, and equalization of the society under consideration. It is determined by a number of methods presented in this study, which also emphasizes the rationality, meanings, properties, and ways of practical implementation of this optimum distribution. This result is compared with the various distributive principles found in practice and in political, philosophical, and economic thinking, with the conclusion that most have their proper specific scope of application. The analytical presentation of the social ethics of economics is particularly enlightening.

Serge-Christophe Kolm is the author of more than thirty books and several hundred professional articles concerning, notably, normative economics, public economics, environmental economics, macroeconomics, financial theory, social change, and political and psychological philosophy. He is Professor and Director at the École des Hautes Études en Sciences Sociales, Paris.

MACROJUSTICE

The political economy of fairness

SERGE-CHRISTOPHE KOLM

Institute for Advanced Studies in the Social Sciences, Paris

PUBLISHED BY THE PRESS SYNDICATE OF THE UNIVERSITY OF CAMBRIDGE
The Pitt Building, Trumpington Street, Cambridge, United Kingdom

CAMBRIDGE UNIVERSITY PRESS
The Edinburgh Building, Cambridge CB2 2RU, UK
40 West 20th Street, New York, NY 10011-4211, USA
477 Williamstown Road, Port Melbourne, VIC 3207, Australia
Ruiz de Alarcón 13, 28014 Madrid, Spain
Dock House, The Waterfront, Cape Town 8001, South Africa

http://www.cambridge.org

First published 2005

Printed in the United States of America

Typeface Minion 10.5/13 pt.   *System* LaTeX 2_ε [TB]

A catalog record for this book is available from the British Library.

Library of Congress Cataloging in Publication Data
Kolm, Serge-Christophe.
Macrojustice: the political economy of fairness / Serge-Christophe Kolm.
p. cm.
Includes bibliographical references and index.
ISBN 0-521-83503-8
1. Economics – Moral and ethical aspects.   2. Distributive justice.   3. Income distribution.
4. Political philosophy.   5. Government.   6. Fiscal policy.   7. Taxation.
8. Wealth.   9. Poverty.   I. Title.
HB72.K563   2004
172′.2 – dc22   2003055595

ISBN 0 521 83503 8 hardback

Contents

Presentation

Conflicts among individuals' and groups' needs and desires due to the scarcity of resources are best faced by teaching individuals how to control the birth of their desires and by mutual altruism.[1] These means have additional virtues. The former develops individuals' mental freedom or autonomy, and the second favours the quality of social relations; both are primordial values in themselves. Although progress in these ways should always be sought, these means often do not suffice. The duty of establishing a just distribution then intervenes.[2] Distributive justice thus plays a major role in human societies. It also favours good social relations in providing reasons for distributions and hence for freely accepting one's share.

Distributive justice in society is a pervasive issue. Each time someone benefits or suffers from something, one can ask why the benefit or the pain does not accrue to someone else, directly or through compensations. However, the issues of justice are extremely varied in scope. They are dominated by the issue of *macrojustice*, which concerns the most general rules of society and their application to the distribution of the benefits from the main resources – overall or *global distributive justice*. We will see that the judgments of the members of society imply a solution to this question. They will imply, first, the rule of *social freedom*, that is, individuals' freedom from the forceful interference of others. Practically, this amounts to the classical basic rights – the constitutional basis of "democratic" societies (who often misapply them) – or to the rights to act and benefit from acts without forceful interference. Since this implies free exchange, overall distributive justice will focus on income (general purchasing power). The implied distributive transfers will then be shown to have a remarkable structure, *equal labour income equalization,*

---

[1] See, respectively, my studies *Happiness-Freedom* (1982a) and *The Good Economy, General Reciprocity* (1984a). Controlling the birth of one's desires is better than mastering existing and possibly entrenched desires, which is often difficult or painful. The method is self-awareness, which usually requires the appropriate education and training.

[2] This distribution may differ from that resulting from mutual altruism, notably as concerns the consideration of individuals' capacities to enjoy or endure (this will be discussed in Chapter 6).

1

depending on a degree of solidarity, community, or reciprocity that will be derived. The rest of justice in society constitutes "microjustice." It concerns issues that are specific in nature, object, concerned people, and often time and place.[3]

The method and principle retained for determining the solution is that justice in a given society is what this society and its members think it is: this *vox populi, vox dei* is "endogenous social choice." More specifically, the basic principle will be unanimity, or consensus, of society members. The relevant individuals' views should, of course, satisfy a few obvious conditions. They should be sufficiently informed. They should embody the minimal rationality of being sufficiently reflective and following logic. Moreover, they should abide by the meaning of the concept of justice, which implies impartiality of some kind. Possible external effects concerning individuals outside the considered society should also be taken care of. The considered individuals' judgments can be actual or notional (theoretically derived) or a mix of both. This general principle of endogenous social choice is fully analyzed in Part IV of the present study, whereas the previous parts only apply the aspects of it that are necessary for determining the general structure of the solution.

The solution comes out in a three-level structure: the general rules; the structure of income distribution and transfers that result from it; and the intensity of the implied solidarity. The following sequence of results will be shown. The general rule turns out to be social freedom, or freedom from forceful interference and domination, which is often expressed as the classical basic rights, or as the theory of process liberalism praising process-freedom (freedom to act and to benefit from the intended consequences of one's acts without forceful interference). This implies that the distributive policy should not be based on individuals' acts or their consequences, and hence should only directly distribute rights or values concerning resources given to society, that is, the classical "natural resources," which include given human capacities.

Productive capacities statistically produce, directly or indirectly, by far the largest part of income (and they would produce more with more labour) – moreover, nonhuman natural resources have often been allocated for long (and many of them are allocated by principles of microjustice). Furthermore, capacities to derive happiness from a given income happen to be unanimously considered irrelevant for overall distributive justice (for the income tax, for instance), for reasons related to concepts of privacy and the self. Hence, overall distributive justice should allocate the value of productive capacities. Such a capacity permits obtaining income from labour, or leisure for a given level of earnings. Then, equality – a rational consequence of impartiality – will be shown to imply that the transfers of global distributive justice amount to an equal sharing of the proceeds of the same labour provided by all individuals (with their different productivities). This is the structure of "equal labour income equalization," or ELIE. The labour considered is the

---

[3] Microjustice about corresponds to Jon Elster's (1992) "local justice." A field of "mesojustice" will also be distinguished.

"equalization labour." Practically, each individual receives or yields in proportion to the difference between her wage rate and the average, the proportion being the equalization labour.[4] Hence, a difference in productivity is compensated by a proportional difference in income transfer.

The ELIE structure of distributive transfers also amounts to each individual yielding to each other the product of the same labour: this is general labour reciprocity. The equalization labour constitutes a crucial parameter of a society: it describes the amount of solidarity, equalization, resource commonality, and reciprocity. This parameter also turns out to be a minimal disposable income as a fraction of the average productivity, for individuals who are not responsible for their low earnings. This coefficient is determined, in Part IV, from the consensus of moral views as concerns its level, the set of transfers, or the method for deriving it – cultural analysis can also be used. These views can be actual or notional, and their convergence can result from impartializations and homogenizations of individuals' actual or notional judgments, using a number of complementary methods implying information about others, dialog and communication, ways of discarding self-interest and self-centeredness, the notional building of impartial views from self-interested or self-centered ones, and so on.

The satisfaction of basic needs is guaranteed by the minimum income implied by the obtained distributive scheme. This turns out to respect individuals' dignity, freedom, and responsibility in two ways. First, individuals receive income which they are free to spend for satisfying their needs as they see them. They can also be provided information and advice for helping them in this choice, but this is no constraint. Additional free care of specific needs is possible, but this is an issue belonging to microjustice. Second, the minimum income implied by the scheme happens to be for individuals who can derive no or little income from the market, because of low wage or unemployment, rather than for people who can earn sufficiently with moderate labour.

The transfers of the ELIE scheme are based on given capacities. Hence, they entail no inefficiency-generating disincentives (this base is "inelastic," and we will see that estimating it is more manageable than for other taxes or subsidies).[5]

The obtained distributive ELIE scheme is a directly applicable policy. It aims at constituting the global distributive aspect of public finances. It should thus tend to replace the progressivity of the income tax and the main transfers and assistance schemes.[6] It is particularly simple and produces no (or minimal) inefficiency-generating disincentive or incentive effects. It is financially self-contained and

---

[4] Each individual i faces the transfer $t_i = k \cdot (\overline{w} - w_i)$, where w_i is individual i's wage rate, $\overline{w}$ is the average wage rate in the society, and k measures the equalization labour. If $t_i > 0$, this is a subsidy. If $t_i < 0$, this is a tax of $-t_i$. This very simple structure can take into account the various dimensions of labour, education, involuntary unemployment, and so on. The information necessary for this policy is globally more readily available than that required for present policies. All these points are presented in detail in further chapters.

[5] In Chapter 10.

[6] Its scope constitutes the bulk of the "distributive branch" of public finances, as Richard Musgrave (1959) puts it.

balanced, and it jointly indicates transfers and their financing, from the same rationale. It is to be associated with the implementation of the other functions of public finances, notably the "allocation" role of financing nonexcludable public goods through benefit taxation. Its primary virtue, however, which entails its other properties, is its rational necessity implied by the derivation outlined above and explained in detail in the rest of this study.

Public finances have various functions with different aims and rationales. Distributive justice is one of them. It includes the noted overall distributive justice, which may possibly have to be completed by some other specific measures.[7] The allocative function includes the provision and financing of the relevant public goods, the required correction of external effects, and the like. A stabilization function is also distinguished.[8] The distinction of these various functions constitutes functional finance. This conception is indispensable for the optimization of public finances. Any other approach necessarily entails confusion, waste, misallocation, and injustice. And this optimization constitutes a major part of securing the quality of society since public finances commonly use about half the social product. Practically, taxes and subsidies can be presented in a consolidated form to each citizen (although her information about their various reasons is a condition for democracy in any sense). However, present common practice of overall taxation distinguishes overall receipts and expenditures much more than the receipts and spending corresponding to the realization of each function. This is rather far away from full functional finance. Public finances can go progressively in the latter's direction, in the appropriate fiscal reform. In particular, the progressive introduction of ELIE distribution will be considered, in increasing the "equalization labour," or in transforming present-day fiscal structures such as the income tax, income-tax credits, or other supports to low income.[9] The transition can also focus on the tax side by a partial application of the obtained result that follows the practice of taxing for financing a given overall expenditure, consisting of taxing according to the principle of "equal labour contribution." That is, the individuals contribute the value of their production (their earning) for the same labour, and this labour is chosen so as to obtain the required total amount. People thus contribute with their different capacities to produce and earn with this equal labour. This applies the principle "from each according to her capacities." The treatment of education, effort, and other characteristics of labour will be fully discussed. This scheme exactly becomes ELIE if the total product were equally shared among all individuals. These taxes are not based on total earned incomes, their base is inelastic (independent of individuals' actions), and hence, they induce no wasteful disincentive. Yet, optimal fiscal reform cannot be content with this step and has to move toward functional finance and fully justified taxation.

---

[7] They will be in fields of "microjustice" or "mesojustice," which are discussed later.
[8] Although it can theoretically be related to various "market failures."
[9] See Chapters 7 and 27.

However, at a still more primitive stage of fiscal reform, one of the first steps should simply be to choose less elastic bases for taxes (and subsidies) – to "de-elasticicize" the bases of public measures – for favouring efficiency (and social freedom). In particular, the taxation of earned income should tend to be based on income earned by given labour, and large progress in this direction is easy.

A number of the analyses developed for this derivation probably are valuable in themselves and for other applications. In particular, Part IV presents and applies the theory of endogenous, consensual social choice, and its various methods and branches.[10] The consensual necessity of social freedom and basic rights, their relation with social efficiency, and the distributive implications, described in Part I, have an intrinsic relevance. The question of rights in human capacities and of their relations with the various types of freedom is an important issue (Chapter 3). The actual or proposed distributive policies, and the distributive philosophies, are compared, and compared with the obtained result, in Part III. Finally, Part V extends these comparisons to the analytical presentation of the whole set of social ethics that are and can be developed within the viewpoint of economics, a presentation that also has an interest in itself.

These properties of rationality, automatic and respectful relief of forced poverty, reciprocity, economic and social efficiency, comprehensiveness and financial balance, simplicity, and meaningfulness and understandability, should favour the introduction of this scheme in fiscal structures and reforms. These properties also favour a didactic use of the associated explanations and discussions. The public dialog can focus on the concept and parameter of the degree of community of human resources, solidarity, reciprocity, and guaranteed income – that is, the equalization labour – and can concentrate its discussion around its various meanings.[11] This can promote awareness of the impartial point of view, and of the relevant nature of society, freedoms, and justice. If this helps increasing concern for others and lowering self-centeredness – which may help deflating grasping egos – thinking about justice will have diminished its own necessity – the true mark of success.

---

[10] They are the theories of dialog, "interest-neutral opinions," the "moral or distributive surplus," the "recursive original position," "moral time-sharing," the notional "uniformization of social distances," "formative" and "empathetic" information about others' moral views, etc.

[11] See the theoretical model of dialog in Chapter 20.

PART ONE

BASES: CONSENSUS, FREEDOMS, AND CAPACITIES

1

Macrojustice: An overview of its place, method, structure, and result

1. INTRODUCTIVE SUMMARY

Justice should probably be seen as a palliative to the insufficiency of the deeper human values that are the choice of one's desires and concern for others. Among the multifarious questions of justice raised in society, macrojustice is concerned with the basic rules of society and the global or overall distribution of goods and of the main resources these rules imply. The specific solution for macrojustice will be shown. This will be the solution that is desired by society, in the sense that all its members unanimously want it when they are sufficiently informed, reflective, and impartial (a property of any view about justice). This will turn out to both imply and be implied by the fact that the general rule of society is social freedom, that is, an absence of relation of force between society members: each individual is free from the forceful interference of others individually or in groups or institutions (except possibly for protecting or realizing others' such freedom). Social freedom is generally presented in the form of the classical basic rights – the basis of democratic Constitutions. Social freedom or, more directly, unanimity, will imply that the overall distribution of resources has a very simple and meaningful structure ("equal labour income equalization"). There will, however, remain to determine a degree of equalization or redistribution, about which the interests of some individuals are opposed. The methods for solving this problem again involve some consensus. In particular, individuals' judgments relevant for justice imply a structure of impartiality – be it actual or notionally constructed.

The final result will be very practical and simple. It will for instance take the place or show the form of the redistributive functions of the income tax and of the main transfers. Its structure will result from the noted freedoms and the efficiency they imply, the fact that the main relevant resource is – by far – the human resource (especially as resource whose value is available for overall redistribution), the consensual desire to respect the privacy of individuals' capacities for happiness (for macrojustice), and equality derived from impartiality. These conditions will be shown to imply that the global distribution has a structure of "equal-labour

9

income equalization" or ELIE. This says, for example, "equally share individuals' earnings during one day and a half a week." This equalizes the benefits from the different capacities of the individuals for this notional labour, but only for it. This duration, which can be completed with other characteristics of labour, can vary according to society, and it constitutes a degree of redistribution, solidarity, reciprocity, and community of the society. A number of related and complementary methods permit the derivation of this crucial parameter of societies from the views of society members.

A summary overview of this overall derivation is proposed in this introductory chapter. All concepts and implications will only be sketched here: their full presentation will be the subject of later chapters. I hope that, nevertheless, this overview can provide a useful guideline, showing the intention, method, concepts, implications, and results of this study. Section 2 of this chapter situates justice in social values. Section 3 indicates the method for obtaining a solution. The result for macrojustice is outlined in Section 4. Section 5 shows the network of implications that lead to this structure, and Figure 1 of Section 6 summarizes it. Section 7 notes the family of methods for determining a society's desired degree of redistribution. Finally, Section 8 presents the structure of the rest of the study.

2. THE PLACE: JUSTICE AS PALLIATIVE

If people were sufficiently able to control the birth of their desires, the desires they would choose for avoiding dissatisfaction caused by the scarcity of goods would *ipso facto* elicit no conflicts about scarce goods. However, difficulties in information and formation seriously impair progress in this direction on a large scale in modern large societies.[1] If, as a second best, people sufficiently liked one another, then, again, no conflicts about sharing scarce resources would arise. Modern societies are aware of this latter value, altruism, but sufficient progress toward such a large-scale altruistic "general reciprocity" is again impaired by questions of formation and information.[2] Then, as a third best, distributive justice indicates the appropriate sharing of goods and resources. Note that sharing resources or goods is necessary in all cases, and notably with sufficient altruism, but altruistic sharing and the solution indicated by principles of justice are bound to differ.[3] In other works, I have analyzed the questions of mental freedom and altruistic reciprocity.[4] I have also proposed and analyzed many general and specific properties of the question of justice.[5] My present purpose is more restricted, but it happens to be central: it is to investigate in depth the solution to the core problem

---

[1] See the study *Happiness-Freedom* (*Le Bonheur-Liberté*, 1982a).
[2] See the study *The Good Economy, General Reciprocity* (*La Bonne Economie, La Réciprocité Générale*, 1984a).
[3] Issues of suffering and happiness would play a more direct and more extensive role in altruistic sharing than in macrojustice (see the reference in note 2).
[4] See the references in notes 1 and 2.
[5] Most of these works are noted in the bibliography of *Modern Theories of Justice* (1996a).

of distributive justice, "global or overall distributive justice" in "macrojustice" in a society.[6]

Hence, justice is certainly not "the first virtue of society," as Aristotle and Rawls put it. Resorting to justice only is a third best, making up for the lack of sufficient personal awareness and control, and of other-looking and integrating social sentiments. It even is a more distant value if one considers the place of culture and the respect of cultural and natural heritage. This does not make it less important for societies as they are. Moreover, justice certainly is a necessary condition for progress toward more deeply desired social values and relations. As Aristotle puts it: "if you have friends, you do not need justice, but if you have justice, you want friends in addition."

3. THE METHOD: JUSTICE AS INFORMED, IMPARTIAL UNANIMITY

3.1. The basis: Consensus, freedom, and endogenous social choice

Justice will be taken to be what society thinks it is. The reference will be to consensus or unanimity of the individuals; hence, these views may also normally be called society's.[7] This consensus will be either direct or applied as required by the problem, and it will suffice for defining the solution. Therefore, no particular conception of justice is a priori assumed, suggested, or imposed. No "moral intuition" is proposed. The only exercise will be to observe and find out what society wants about the necessary questions, and to derive the logical conclusion. In a strict sense, this study is not ethics – at least, it is not moralizing. It is, rather, anthropology and logic, although formally it will use concepts in the classical fields of social ethics and economics. If there is ethics in it, this only consists in helping society realize what it wants, in showing the solution to one of society's main problems which is consistent with its desires and implied by them. So finding the answer about what society should do in society itself and only there (without any input of an externally given rule), is "endogenous social choice." This approach is, in fact, practically a necessity.

Indeed, a unanimous opinion is an epistemic necessity because no alternative opinion exists and can be sincerely expressed. In particular, you and I, as members of the society, share this opinion by hypothesis. This necessity also requires, however, that people, in holding this opinion, are sufficiently relevantly informed and reflexive, and abide by the general rules of rationality and logic. Rationality implies, in particular, that the terms are given their intrinsic meaning (for instance, an opinion about justice has to be impartial from the very concept of justice, and

---

[6] The adjective "global" means here "overall," in any given society. It does not refer to its recent use as meaning extending to the whole world (the present text was written before this latter sense became used, or at least widespread).

[7] In addition, various kinds of mutual consideration, information and interaction, and the cultural dimension, will intervene in the ways of determining the degree of redistribution.

hence, the relevant opinions about justice have to be impartial – as an actual or a notionally constructed property).[8]

Moreover, if a society not encompassing everyone possible is considered, a unanimous opinion of its members may not be shared by some external observer. However, for issues specific to this society – such as distribution within it – such external observers are a priori unconcerned and may not care. If they happen to care, the way of dealing with such a situation can be the object of a broader rule considered by the larger society. However, a condition of rationality may be that such external views are irrelevant (given that the society members' considered view is by assumption sufficiently informed, reflective, and rational). If this does not suffice, one can add, as a primary moral stance, that such external views should be discarded, because they are irrelevant, nosy, and intrusive, and, if taking them into account would oppose a unanimous desire of the society members, because this would violate the autonomy, self-rule, and freedom of the society, the freedom of its members and their dignity as responsible agents, and democracy within this society. We will shortly see, in fact, that freedom and unanimity imply one another, and hence jointly constitute the basis of the social ethical construct. Note that unanimity precludes that some members of the society (possibly a minority) be harmed or exploited by others – and thus would need protection.

Now, it will turn out that implementing unanimous views of society members suffices for solving the problem considered. After the distinction of "macrojustice" about the general rules of society and global (overall) distributive justice from the multifarious cases of "microjustice" (and "mesojustice"), the problem of determining global distributive justice is solved in two steps by the principle of unanimity. Straightforward unanimous views imply that the global distribution has a particular structure, "equal labour income equalization" (this will be shown in Parts I and II of this study). However, this structure includes a parameter, the degree of equalization, solidarity, community, and reciprocity, which can a priori differ across societies. This parameter is then determined from consensus again, but in assuming, when necessary, sufficient information and impartiality – the latter an intrinsic property of the concept of justice. This information and impartiality can be actual or notional or a mix of both. This constitutes the topic of Part IV of this study. Parts III and V are devoted to comparing the present analysis and results with other practical redistributive schemes and philosophical analyses, and with social ethics developed in economics.

The obtained distributive structure will result both directly from the condition that there should be no unanimously preferred alternative ("Pareto efficiency") and from the general rule of society, which will turn out to be social freedom. Social freedom means freedom from others' forceful interference, and hence an absence of imposed domination and of the use of force and violence in social relations. One way of expressing it is constituted by the classical basic

---

[8] Part IV of this study develops and uses this remark.

rights – which are the basis of our Constitutions. Social freedom for all derives from unanimity which desires it either directly, or, more precisely, through a reasoning which also implies impartiality (an intrinsic property of a conception of justice) because each individual has to want social freedom for her own actions and, hence, has to want it for all individuals. This derivation also requires discarding possible negative effects of social freedom, as shown in Chapter 4 (with regard to basic rights). Conversely, a measure about a society that opposes the unanimous desires of its members violates the social freedom of each of them. Thus, unanimity or consensus, and social freedom, can be said to constitute the joint basis of the derived solution.

However, the solution will also rest on other properties, impartiality and equality, on the one hand, and information, on the other hand. Equality is required by impartiality and rationality.[9] Applied as required, it will be essential for leading to the obtained distributive structure (in Part II). Impartiality and information will have a basic role for determining the degree of equalization, solidarity, community, and reciprocity (in Part IV).

3.2. Impartiality and equalities

An opinion about justice has to present a property inherent to the concept of justice: impartiality. A judgment is impartial when no final reason for it refers to a particular relation to the person who so judges, such as her interest or the interests or judgments of persons in a particular relation to her or whom she favours for a reason irrelevant to the nature of the considered judgment. It should be noted that judgments of individuals about a distribution among them can be unanimous only if they are impartial with respect to interests. Indeed, these individuals' interests are opposed in a distribution, by nature and definition. Hence, these individuals' judgments cannot coincide if they are biased by their own interests or by those of people in a particular relation with them or whom they particularly like (self-centeredness), and *a fortiori* if these judgments only reflect these interests. Thus, unanimity in judgments about distribution requires impartiality. The converse, however, is not true: there can be various different impartial judgments, and in particular various views about justice. These views will nevertheless be closer to one another than pure interests are, in some sense.[10] However, full consensus requires further conditions, such as sufficient mutual information or convincing, or recursively taking impartial views of impartial views.[11]

---

[9] This requirement is, more precisely, that of "*prima facie* identical treatment of identicals in the relevant characteristics." See Chapter 23 and, for a complete analysis, Kolm, *Justice and Equity* (1971; English translation 1998), Foreword, Section 5.

[10] The minimal property of convergence of individuals' views is the following: for preferences between two states, unanimity in self-interested preferences will imply unanimity in the considered impartial and notably moral preferences, but the converse does not hold and there will generally be cases of impartial unanimity for favoring an individual's interest at the cost of another's (see Chapters 20 and 21).

[11] This is the topic of Part IV of this study.

These impartial views often exist in individuals, along with their partial self-interest and self-centeredness. In his *Theory of Moral Sentiments*, Adam Smith calls each individual's moral conscience the "impartial spectator" within her. We will then have to find devices for having these views influence the outcome or be known to a policy maker. However, an individual's impartial view can also be notionally constructed from her self-centered or self-interested preferences (a notional "impartialization" of her judgment).[12]

Impartiality in particular logically implies that justice is ideally constituted of the relevant structures of equality of something (this was well seen by Aristotle who states, in *Nicomachean Ethics*: "Justice is equality, as everyone thinks it is, quite apart from any other consideration"). This equality is ideal in the sense that it is *prima facie*, that is, in the absence of overpowering reasons. These reasons can include impossibility, and relevance of other principles (which can be ideal equalities in other items).[13]

However, impartiality and equality are structures which can apply to varied contents, and this can lead to varied and even opposed conceptions of justice. They are, for instance, satisfied by distributive principles such as an ideal of equal income, to each according to her work or to her needs, equally full right to the product of one's capacities and the outcome of free exchanges, and so on. Thus, the proper application has to be determined (possibly a compromise among such possibilities).

3.3. Information

Justice cannot be based on ignorance, mistaken beliefs, confusion, or misunderstandings. This is a requirement of rationality. Hence, individuals' appropriate views are those that have the relevant information, possibly as a notional property. This includes sufficient information about others, including about the reasons and causes of their moral views ("formative information"), and information about how it feels to have such opinions ("empathetic information"). Note that it is not impossible that impartiality itself would result from knowing others as well as one knows oneself (a notional conception, of course), and hence that partiality is but the fruit of ignorance. This mutual information is promoted by discussion and dialog.[14]

3.4. The basic philosophical position

Defining justice as what society thinks it is rejects the a priori endorsement of a particular conception of justice. Such an endorsement would violate impartiality, objectivity, fairness, and justice among views of justice, and hence its rejection can be seen as a requirement of consistency. It would also a priori be arbitrary: why

[12] See Part IV.
[13] See note 9.
[14] See Chapters 15 and 17.

would my view of justice be better than yours? Asserting that such a revealed truth is a priori preferable to alternatives can only be arrogant. It would also be paternalistic toward the considered society and its members and would a priori not respect their preferences and choices as concerns values, and hence their moral autonomy. Such particular views probably are what Rawls rejects as "intuitionism."[15] Then, where else can principles of justice be found except in society itself?

However, defining justice as what society thinks it is can be said to derive ought from is. Philosophically, it is naturalistic (although not guilty of a "naturalistic fallacy") and pragmatic. The described exercise is also partially transcendental in the sense that some of its results rest on inherent properties of the concept of justice, the specific property of impartiality to which can be added the general one of rationality, including information and reflection.

4. THE STRUCTURE: MACROJUSTICE AND ELIE

4.1. Macrojustice, microjustice, global or overall distribution

People see issues of justice and fairness in numerous aspects of society. This is in fact a priori a thoroughly pervasive issue: for any advantage for a person on inconvenience for her, any possession, asset, right, capacity, duty, liability on handicap, one can ask: "Why is it not allocated to someone else through transfer or the adequate compensation?" However, these aspects are very strongly differentiated and hierarchized in scope and importance. *Macrojustice* is the concern of justice largest in scope.[16] It includes two things: the general basic rules of society, and global distributive justice which derives from them principles for allocating the benefits from the main resources of society. An example of basic rules is provided by the classical basic rights, and we will see that they in fact should be these rules. Since these rights include that of free exchange, global (overall) distributive justice will be concerned with the distribution of income. With people spending their income, this distribution will determine the bulk of the distribution of goods in society. Practically, the structure of the general income tax and the main redistributive transfers aim at implementing global distributive justice (however, respecting rights to free exchange in the strict sense would imply basing distributive taxes not on earnings but on capacities to earn or wage rates,[17] a property which, for given capacities, implies an absence of wasteful disincentives or incentives). Global

---

[15] Rawls' own basic reference consists of "considered judgments" in "reflective equilibrium." This constitutes sane advice, but is not very explicit and precise. However, one thing he sees that should be considered is the possibility of deriving the solution from a social contract in an "original position." Now, both social contracts and original positions are concepts belonging to the family of endogenous social choice. We shall see, however, that Rawls' theory of the original position has general and specific problems of justification (Chapter 21), and that endogenous social choice offers other methods (Part IV in general).

[16] See *Modern Theories of Justice* (1996a), Chapter 1.

[17] See Kolm 1974. We will see that information about wage rates is, on the whole, more available than that concerning incomes (Chapter 10).

distributive justice is the concern of this study. Besides macrojustice, society displays multifarious issues of *microjustice*, dealing with particular, specific, or local questions, with all kinds of issues, size, scope, importance, and criteria. Some can be very important (particular lives may be at stake), while others are trivia. It also is fruitful to consider a field of "mesojustice," concerned with questions that are particular and specific, and yet importantly concern everyone, such as with education and health.

4.2. Equal labour income equalization

The result of the derivation of global distributive justice will turn out to have a very simple and remarkable structure. It says that the individuals' product of the same notional labour should be equally shared. This is the principle of *equal labour income equalization* or ELIE. This notional labour is the "equalization labour." This principle is redistributive if the equalization labour is not zero, because the individuals have different productive capacities, and hence, different wage rates. ELIE erases these differences for the equalization labour, but not for the rest. For example, the (re)distributive transfers would amount to equally sharing individuals' earnings during one day and a half per week. This duration can be different, and the volume of present-day actual national redistributions would be achieved by such a scheme with durations between one and two days per week (from the United States to Scandinavian countries). Moreover, the equalization labour should also specify characteristics other than duration, notably education and training, and intensity of labour (all this will be made precise in later chapters). ELIE amounts to a balanced set of transfers where each individual receives or pays the same multiple of the excess of the average wage rate over her wage rate (a tax for individuals more productive than average, a subsidy for individuals less productive than average); the factor of proportionality is the equalization labour. An individual with a lower productivity than another receives an income transfer higher in this proportion. The information necessary for the implementation of this distributive policy consists of the wage rates, which are globally easier to know than most items on which present actual taxes are based.[18]

These ELIE transfers are based on individuals' *given* capacities, once the equalization labour is chosen. Hence, they produce no wasteful disincentives or incentives, they induce no Pareto inefficiency (their base is "inelastic" in economists' terms – that is, it is not affected by individuals' choices and actions). Pareto efficiency means that no other possible state is preferred by everyone (with possible indifference for some). The principle of unanimity implies and requires that the best possible state be Pareto efficient (this will provide the shortest derivation of ELIE from the principle of unanimity).

---

[18] Chapter 10 will show how the present subculture of academic economists attaches a biased, mistaken, and excessive importance to this issue of information.

The set of ELIE transfers is also equivalent to each individual yielding to each other the product of an equal labour (a fraction of the equalization labour). This is a general balanced labour reciprocity.

4.3. The equalization labour

The equalization labour represents a degree of redistribution, equalization, solidarity, reciprocity, and economic community in the considered society. It measures the degree of equal sharing of the income values of individuals' productive capacities, or the degree of individuals' mutual rights in these values of others' capacities. It also turns out to be the minimum disposable income as a fraction of the average productivity, for individuals who are not responsible for their low earnings (individuals who can earn nothing[19] receive this amount, and others have more than it if they work more than the equalization labour). This coefficient also is the proportion in which a deficit in given productivity is compensated by an extra income transfer.

Individuals' self-interest favours high equalization labour for people less productive than average and low equalization labour for people more productive than average. However, the relevant view of individuals for determining this parameter is their conception of what is appropriate for society and just, rather than their self-interest. The determination of these conceptions and the resulting derivation of justice in society constitute the topic of the theory of endogenous social choice. Part IV of this study will present this theory and its application to the determination of the degree of redistribution, using methods that will be briefly outlined in Section 7 of this chapter.

4.4. Relations with the main distributive theories

Global distributive justice, and notably this structure, will logically result from the facts of social freedom and consensus (each turns out to imply the other, as it will be shown[20]). It is closely related to the main distributive concepts, principles, and theories, most of which have a place in the derivation. This will be the case for the classical basic rights – which are one presentation of social freedom – ; for the classical process-liberal theory of "full process-freedom" which derives the other legitimate rights from free action, exchange, or agreement; for lowering income inequalities; and for social efficiency in Pareto's sense (derived from the criterion of unanimity). Basic needs can intervene in the choice of the equalization labour. The equalization of the products of the equalization labour is an allocation according to desert, as opposed to according to merit. The choice of the equalization labour, derived in Part IV by endogenous social choice, will meet a number

---

[19] Because of lack of marketable capacities or of standard unemployment (see Chapter 13).
[20] In Chapters 2 and 4.

of subtheories of the latter, among which various theories of consensualization by information, dialog, or notional constructs, such as theories in the family of the "original position"[21] and related ones, and the theory of the distributive or moral surplus.[22]

The ELIE structure turns out to be the application of Plato's and Aristotle's theory of justice to labour and individuals' productive capacities.[23] This theory consists of the two following principles: each individual merits the product of her actions, and what is given to society should be equally shared. The first part implies that each individual is entitled to the "full product of her labour." The second, however, implies that the a priori advantage provided by the availability of the given productive capacities is equally shared. The outcome depends on whether these capacities are measured in output or in time of use (whose units can be equated across individuals as a basic moral stance), and the general case will turn out to be the ELIE distribution, where the products of a notional "equalization labour" are equally shared – which amounts to given transfers from the more productive to the less productive individuals (see Section 5.5 below and Chapter 9).

The obtained distribution and distributive scheme will be compared with the various distributive modes, structures, principles, and methods actually applied or proposed by philosophers or economists, according to their various aspects, in Parts III and V of this study. Such comparisons will also be met all along the presentation, when opportunity makes them relevant.

5. THE REASON: RESOURCES, RIGHTS, AND FREEDOMS

5.1. Bases

5.1.1. The structure of implications

Unanimity leads to the solution through a sequence of implications (which are summarized in Figure 1–1 in Section 6). It first leads to the ELIE structure, and then to the full solution through the determination of the equalization labour. The next chapters of the present part of this study show the reasons that lead to the ELIE structure derived in Part II. These reasons are and articulate as follows. The social or ethical reasons will be based on unanimity, although the direct valuation of basic rights can play a role. These reasons lead to this structure through the requirement that the measures of the distributive policy be based on valuable

---

[21] Which have to differ from Rawls' or Harsanyi's presentations, though.

[22] See *The Optimal Production of Social Justice* (Kolm, 1966a).

[23] See Plato's *The Laws* and Aristotle's *Nicomachean Ethics* and *Eudemian Ethics*. The exact way in which ELIE distributive schemes apply these ideas, and in particular their *diorthic justice*, is presented in Chapter 16.

inelastic items. A base of a measure is elastic when agents can modify it and inelastic otherwise. The elasticity matters when the agents want to modify the base as a result of the measure. Valuable inelastic bases are given resources (the classical "natural resources"). Unanimity will imply inelastic bases directly through Pareto efficiency and, more interestingly, through its requiring social freedom which implies such bases for distributive policies (as we will see). In the given natural resources, only the value of given productive capacities will remain for distribution because the other aspects of these resources turn out to be discarded *for the purpose of macrojustice*[24]: nonhuman natural resources are discarded for reasons of relative importance, localness, and impracticability; eudemonistic capacities (capacities for deriving satisfaction) are by consensus (for this purpose); and rights to use capacities and benefit from this use are discarded because of social freedom. Then, the question of the measure of productive capacities will lead to the ELIE structure. The specification of these various implications and of their reason are developed in Chapters 2, 3, and 4 for the issue of social freedom and in Chapters 5 as concerns resources and 6 as concerns capacities. The main points are summarized in the rest of this section.

5.1.2. Unanimity efficiency

The principle of unanimity implies that a state should not be chosen if another one is unanimously found better (with the possibility of some indifferences). Hence, the chosen state should not have this property; that is, it should be "Pareto efficient." Pareto efficiency is usually considered for individuals' evaluations of their own self-interest. Then, measures of a distributive policy based on elastic items create effects of disincentive or incentive of the kind that, *prima facie*, jeopardizes Pareto efficiency. This is one of the most classical results and topics of economics.

One can, moreover, consider the social and moral judgments of the members of society, which are either actual judgments of theirs or notional judgments constructed from their actual views, as will be explained in Part IV of this study. Such judgments evaluating the distribution normally favour each individual's interest when the others' interests are given. This can result from impartiality since the individual normally favours her own interest. Hence, each individual morally favours that some interests are better satisfied while no interest is less satisfied. Moreover, a state chosen by endogenous social choice certainly is such that no other possible state is morally found better by all individuals. Hence, this state should be such that no other possible state favours some individuals' interest without impairing any other's. That is, it should be Pareto-efficient with regard to interests. Therefore, a policy based on elastic items also *prima facie* jeopardizes Pareto efficiency for the social-ethical individual evaluations: from the situation

---

[24] The question of information about the distributive basis is the topic of Chapter 10.

it yields, it is possible to improve all interests (with some possible indifferences), and hence also to improve all social-ethical evaluations.[25]

5.2. Social freedom

5.2.1. The forms of social freedom: Basic rights and process-freedom

However, this conclusion about the policy base also results from the consideration of social freedom. This consideration is, furthermore, interesting in itself because it provides the general rule of macrojustice in the form of the classical basic rights, as well as the basic theory of full process-freedom (see Chapter 3). We will see that with the proper conceptions, these rights result from unanimity. However, they can also be endorsed for mere direct ethical or social reasons, as they usually are.

In fact, social freedom, that is, individuals' freedom from forceful interference, is classically considered under two alternative forms, which differ in emphasis, style, and use. One form consists of the classical basic rights or freedoms (or just "basic rights" or "freedoms"), which specify various topics and fields of their application,[26] emphasize their own moral value in asserting themselves as imperatives, and are incorporated in legal processes and constitutions, and enshrined in historical declarations. The other form is process-freedom, that is, freedom to act, and to benefit from the intended consequences of one's acts, without forceful interference. This presentation is more theoretical and hence simpler than the statement of basic rights. It emphasizes the noninterference with the consequences of acts, which is more implicit in the classical statements of basic rights, where it appears, in particular, in the respect of property or of properties when property rights have been obtained from free exchange or other free action (free exchange implies mutual interference, but not forceful one). Process-freedom is, indeed, mostly applied to the economic aspect of life in society. Full process-freedom, that is, the assumption that process-freedom prevails throughout society and extending in time, develops into an elaborate theory, including that of free exchange and of the legitimacy of rights resulting from it. This theory, morally endorsed by "process liberalism,"[27] constitutes the central social-ethical theory of the modern world, by its endorsement and also by its being the focus of the criticism addressed to it. However, we shall see that the main moral defects of this system, such as the possible poverty, inefficiencies, destructions, selfishness, or hostilities that can result from markets, are not, in fact, necessary consequences of the principle of process-freedom, but

---

[25] Such individual social-ethical evaluations, impartial and increasing with all interests, will be considered, defined and used in Part IV. However, individuals' social ethical evaluations can also have other structures. For instance, the case where individuals have preferences for equalities in the allocation of specific goods will be considered in Chapter 16 (the necessary structure of such preferences is presented in Kolm 1977a).

[26] Such as rights to move, communicate, worship, participate in political decisions, apply to positions, hold property; freedom from arbitrary arrest; and rights to security and to due process of law.

[27] In non-English European languages, this is just "liberalism" with an emphasis on "economic liberalism" (see note 31).

result from particular applications of it. In particular, process-freedom does not imply an absence of distributive policy – as held by classical process liberalism. Indeed, the policy measures do not interfere with acts or their intended consequences if they are based on inelastic items.[28] They can notably redistribute the rent of individuals' given productive capacities (that is, the value of their availability for use). This can provide income to individuals who can obtain only too little or nothing from the market.

The classical basic rights or freedoms (or basic rights or freedoms) are the object of official definitions with very numerous cases of application. They are, indeed, the basis of our constitutions, and hence the framework and source of law. They are enshrined in historical declarations.[29] They essentially protect the individual. Individuals, they say, have the right to safety for themselves and their property (property is legitimate possession). They have the right to do anything that does not infringe upon others' basic rights. They, in particular, have the right to express their views, move around, and so on (but they may not be a priori entitled to other means to use these rights). They have the right to benefit from due process of law. They also have the right to be a candidate for positions. And they have the political right to participate in collective or public decisions (that concern them). The structure of taxation (according to means) and minimal subsistence are sometimes added. However, these rights essentially amount to an absence of forceful interference from other agents, including the government (except for protecting such rights).[30]

Full process-freedom means that process-freedom prevails throughout society, and its moral endorsement is "process liberalism."[31] It is analyzed by an elaborate theory, emphasizing free exchange and the time dimension, and developed by a long tradition involving law, economics, and philosophy.[32] This is the theory of

---

[28] They can only indirectly affect the acts, for instance through "income effects."

[29] The 1789 Declaration of the Rights of Man and of the Citizen intended to be more philosophical and universal than the American texts (the previous Declaration and the simultaneous Bill of Rights). It has to be accompanied by the 140 pages of records of the debates of the National Assembly, which explain their meaning, intent, and reason (these debates may constitute the foremost historical text in political philosophy). The first draft was written by Jefferson, Condorcet, and Lafayette and presented at the National Assembly on July 11, 1789. More details and references will shortly be proposed.

[30] Further discussion will be provided in Chapter 4 (see also Kolm 1989a/1991, and 1993a).

[31] This is just called "liberalism," notably "economic liberalism," in pre-twentieth-century English and in the other European languages. However, present-day English uses "liberalism" in another sense, implying public transfers and interventions. Hence the expression "process liberalism." The irony, however, is that, in the end, process liberalism does imply public transfers and interventions, as we will see, although specific ones derived from the concept of process-freedom.

[32] A full integrated and deductive presentation of this theory can be found in *The Liberal Social Contract* (*Le Contrat social libéral*, 1985a). John Locke (1690) is the early landmark author. In recent times, Robert Nozick (1974) emphasized the time regress structure of this theory, but omitted the two reasons for a role of the public sector much larger than the right-protecting "minimal state": the correction of market and exchange "failures" by "liberal social contracts" (see Chapter 3 and Kolm 1985a and 1996a, Chapter 5), and the distribution based on capacities described here. Note that the theory for which Murray Rothbart (1973) used the term "libertarianism" is a fundamentally different one. Indeed, for process liberalism, the limit to an individual's freedom is others' liberal rights (that is, basic rights or rights created by the liberal process). By contrast, for these "libertarians," the limits to an individual's freedom is others' force.

the legitimacy of rights and property resulting from free action including free exchange. This constitutes the central social ethics of modernity, whether it is supported or criticized (as by the variety of classical socialist ideas). From the definition of process-freedom, full process-freedom entails that distributive policies should not interfere with agents' acts or with the intended consequences of their action. This implies that distributive policies should be based on other items, that is, on inelastic ones, which finally means on given or "natural" resources (since these items should also be valuable for making sense for distribution). These resources include given human capacities to produce or to enjoy. Hence, full process-freedom does not preclude distributive policies; it only requires them to have a specific form. In fact, two main criticisms are standardly addressed to the classical process-liberal praise of the market, in addition to the psychosocial considerations alluded to such as encouraging selfishness: the poverty of individuals who can earn only little (or nothing) from the labour market; and the other incapacities or diseases of the market system, which can make it inefficient. However, this classical process liberalism omits two aspects of the full theory of process-freedom: process-freedom can strictly be seen as not implying self-ownership (each individual's full ownership of herself),[33] and as implying the adequate corrections of "market failures."

First, individuals who can earn only little from the market can receive transfers based on their given capacities to earn. These transfers can notably come from individuals who are relatively well-endowed with such capacities. These transfers will thus be based on given capacities, which are inelastic items and human natural resources. Not being based on individuals' acts or their intended consequences, they respect process-freedom (and do not create incentives or disincentives of the type that impairs Pareto efficiency). These transfers can be justified by the fact that individuals are not considered to be a priori entitled to the full value of their given productive capacities (we will see that, then, the required transfers will depend on the morally relevant measure of these capacities, which can be measured by the output they can produce, the input they can use, or a mix of both). Then, these transfers amount to a distribution of the rent of productive capacities, which does not abide by full self-ownership (the assumption that individuals own all the rights concerning themselves). The rent of an asset, in particular of a capacity, is the a priori value of the availability of this asset, irrespective of its use. Of course, the right to use a capacity and to benefit from this use belongs to the holder of this asset as a direct application of the definition of process-freedom, since acting is using one's capacities. And yet, this individual may have

James Buchanan's "public choice" is libertarian in this respect (see Kolm 1996a, Chapters 12 and 13). Hence, a present tendency to apply the term "libertarian" to process liberalism entails much confusion. In addition, Rothbart "borrowed" this term, which used to apply to left anarchism, a position equally critical of government but otherwise diametrically opposed and related to the "general reciprocity" noted earlier. Chapter 22 will compare these theories in more detail.

[33] The question of rights in human beings is fully discussed in Chapter 5.

to pay a rent for this possibility, and also may receive similar rents from others. We will moreover see that, for the purpose of macrojustice, a consensual view holds that individuals are entitled to, or accountable for, all that concerns their capacities to enjoy income or consumption.[34] We will also note that the income from nonhuman natural resources is but a small fraction of labour income, and hence *a fortiori* of the rent of productive capacities. Moreover, the present owners of most nonhuman natural resources have bought them, and hence a rationale for a redistribution of these resources could not practically be realized. In addition, many of these resources are seen as appropriate for distribution in the framework of microjustice.[35] Therefore, global distributive justice focuses on the allocation of the rent of productive capacities.

Second, markets are inefficient when they meet "market failures" due to questions of information or costs of exclusion and contracting, in situations of nonexcludable public goods, externalities, price rigidities, and so on. Achieving, as much as possible, notably through public actions, what free exchanges would have led to in the absence of the causes of these failures, can be seen as implementing agents' free choices impaired by these impediments, and hence as realizing their process-freedom. This public realization of agents' implicit agreements is in the nature of a social contract and is a "liberal social contract."[36]

5.2.2. Reasons for social freedom: Unanimities, basic rights, and costlessness

The most common evaluation of social freedom bears on its presentation as the classical basic rights. These rights are legal in "democratic" countries where they are, indeed, constitutional and the very basis of constitutions. Hence, the structure of distribution and taxes they imply are the constitutional ones. One may also just take these rights for granted because their respect is compulsory. However, there also are direct and important reasons for these rights. The essence of these rights is that they forbid forceful interference and violence, harm, and robbery. They are necessary for the possibility of enjoying other goods. And they are also seen as having a deeper value because they mean not being submitted to the unilateral decision of another will; thus, they are particularly necessary for the existence of agency, they are a condition for dignity, and respecting them is respecting mankind and taking others "also as ends" (I. Kant).

For all these reasons, basic rights are also demanded by endogenous social choice and unanimity, in two possible ways. Indeed, practically everyone wants these rights for all in present-day modern societies (possibly everyone who sufficiently thinks about it). At any rate, each individual wants these rights for herself. This generally is a matter of fact. Moreover, the very definition of an action implies

---

[34] See Chapter 6.
[35] See Chapter 5.
[36] Chapter 4 presents a very brief summary of this theory. See Kolm 1985a, 1987a, 1987b, 1996a, Chapter 5, and many applications.

that the agent wants it and its intended consequences. Hence this agent has to want an absence of forceful interference with the corresponding acts and consequences. That is, she necessarily wants process-freedom and basic rights for herself. Then, the individual's judgment concerning justice, being impartial by definition, should equally want these rights for everyone (whether this view is actually held by the individual or is a notional construct).[37]

However, these various reasons for favouring basic rights can lead to their adoption only if this is possible and if this does not entail costs of any nature that could reverse the final conclusion. Now, such obstacles are commonly pointed out. The idea that it is not possible that all individuals have all these rights – that they are not copossible – is implied by the long tradition that holds that these rights should have priority and yet should be "equal for all and maximal" (Rousseau, Condorcet, the 1789 Declaration, John Stuart Mill, Rawls, and so on). The classical basic rights have also been reproached for their individualism (by Robespierre and Marx, for instance), and for their providing only "formal freedom" rather than "real freedom" (Marx's terms, and an idea developed by a long line of critiques emphasizing the fact that these rights do not guarantee the other means of action, and hence, the actual possibility of the actions they permit). Moreover, the market system permitted by full process-freedom and property rights is often criticized on three types of grounds: the market system may produce inefficiencies and insufficient output because of its well-known microeconomic or macroeconomic imperfections or failures; it may lead to unjust distribution, notably for people who have nothing to sell but their labour force which is poorly paid or rejected; and the market system may entail labour alienation, domination in the wage relationship, selfishness, which it rewards and encourages, and hostile competitive social relations.[38]

However, all these defects depend on particular interpretations and applications of basic rights and full process-freedom, rather than on necessary ones (and, one may add, rather than the most rational ones). This will be shown in Chapters 2 through 4, but the reasons can be summarized in the present outline. To begin with, full process-freedom is better seen as implying both a correction of the "market failures" and a redistribution that prevents poverty and distributive injustice, although its principle will impose specific types of measures for both these policies. Indeed, full process-freedom corrected for "market failures" according to "liberal social contracts" is by construction immune from inefficiencies in Pareto's sense that could be introduced by these shortcomings of the market system. It entails, on the contrary, the well-known virtues of efficiency of the market due to motivations and a decentralized use of information. Moreover, people who can earn only little – or nothing – from the labour market can receive, without interfering with

---

[37] See Chapter 21.

[38] A general analysis of the possible defects of process liberalism is presented in *Modern Liberalism* (*Le Libéralisme moderne*, 1984b), and also in *The Good Economy, General Reciprocity*, op. cit.

process-freedom, income from (given) natural resources, and notably some of the rent of others' given capacities.

These distributive possibilities have an important consequence as regards the definition of the basic rights or freedoms. Any use of such a right uses other means. Thus, there are two options for defining these rights. Either they include nothing of these other means: they then are the pure, strict, bare, naked, or "formal" rights or freedoms. Then, it often happens that someone cannot actually use such a right or benefit from it because she has none of these other means necessary for the use. Or someone can have only little of these other means, and hence can benefit only little from this freedom. There can, in particular, be large inequalities in these benefits across individuals. Then, it is commonly suggested that these bare rights be complemented by the allocation, to each individual, of some of these other means, which enable her to use the freedom and benefit from it. In Marx's terms, the "formal freedom" becomes "real freedom." One has, however, to determine the amounts of these other means for the various rights or uses. They are generally not determined by technical necessities and considerations alone. The various rights can thus be more or less favoured (this more or less favours the various individuals, who can also receive different amounts of these means). However, when there is a policy distributing or redistributing income among the individuals, with a concern about justice, the choice of the other means for using basic rights can be left to the individuals using and spending their income. One can then otherwise guarantee only the "formal" freedoms, and therefore define, as basic rights, only the bare, minimal, and formal rights. The resulting allocation of these other means then respects consumers' preferences, which is a condition for Pareto efficiency. In contrast, so respecting consumers' preferences with allocation of specific means for the use of the various rights – which requires different means for the various individuals because their preferences differ – demands an enormous and *de facto* unattainable amount of information about individuals' specific tastes.

Then, this definition of basic rights as bare rights or formal freedoms, stating the formal possibility without also providing any other means, permits the full copossibility of these rights: all individuals can have all these rights in full. Restrictions in the uses of these rights will result from the other means used. Indeed, when several uses of basic rights conflict with each other, this conflict can always be attributed to an allocation of particular other means (such as occupation of a specific space or medium at a specific date). Sufficient specification of the allocation of rights in these other means make this conflict disappear. This specification can result from individuals' buying these means with their income, or from allocations in the field of microjustice.[39]

Moreover, most of the various possible psychosocial defects of basic rights or of markets are not imposed by them but result from their chosen applications. They

---

[39] For a single individual, her uses of her various (bare) basic rights limit each other through her allocation of other resources among these various uses.

are their individualism, the selfish and possibly hostile relations, attitudes, and sentiments fostered by the market system, and so on. Process-freedom, however, permits gift-giving, reciprocity, cooperation, and cooperatives. Basic rights permit traditions and communities that do not violate them.

In the end, the various classical shortcomings or vices of basic rights and process-freedom are not necessary and intrinsic to them. They do not arise or they vanish with proper understanding and applications of these rights and freedoms. Therefore, basic rights and process-freedom can be desired for their intrinsic value, or be required by unanimity or by unanimity of people's conception of justice.

5.3. Capacities

5.3.1. The focus of macrojustice on productive capacities

A tax based on acts directly, or through their effects, violates process-freedom, and so does any balanced set of transfers based on the same such items for all individuals.[40] At any rate, any transfers based on elastic items impair Pareto efficiency. For both reasons, unanimity (and, possibly, direct appreciation of basic freedoms) require that distributive policy consists of allocating given valuables, that is, "natural resources." Note that capital has been produced by past acts, by definition, and the relevant view is intertemporal. Thus, the scheme is: allocate rights in given (natural) resources, and let full process-freedom in action, interaction, exchanges, or agreements – with protection, if necessary, against aggression or "failures" of the free process. However, the issue of macrojustice leads to a narrower specification of the relevant substance of the distributive policy. Natural resources are either human, and they are the given capacities, or nonhuman. Capacities include productive capacities, which can be used for production and notably for providing an income, and capacities to derive satisfaction or happiness from a given consumption or situation, the eudemonistic capacities.[41]

There is a de facto consensus, in the population, for thinking that someone should not pay a higher income tax than someone else for the sole reason that she is able to derive more pleasure from given income (and hence, from each level of posttax income) or, on the contrary, that she enjoys extra income less than the other does (and hence suffers less from its loss), if one can make such comparisons. That is, eudemonistic capacities are unanimously deemed irrelevant for the just overall distribution of income. For the purpose of macrojustice, the individuals are deemed accountable for their own eudemonistic capacities, or entitled to

---

[40] In a strict sense, lump-sum taxes redistributed by subsidies based on (depending on) acts or their consequences imply no direct forceful interference with acts or their consequences (since the recipient can refuse the subsidy).

[41] The nature of capacities will be considered more closely in Chapter 6, and is analyzed in detail in Kolm 1996a, Chapter 6.

them. For this purpose, these capacities are considered private items, irrelevant for public redistribution. It is thus consensually thought that they should not directly influence the corresponding distribution. Of course, individual differences in capacities to enjoy or in sensitivity to pain can be relevant for particular questions outside macrojustice. For instance, people suffering from deep depression should be helped, but this pertains to medical microjustice rather than to macrojustice. Thus, eudemonistic capacities do not directly appear in the ELIE principle (although they indirectly influence prices and wages through demands and markets).

Moreover, labour income is very much larger than income derived from nonhuman natural resources in social income, and productive capacities would produce still more with more labour; most nonhuman natural resources have been bought by their present owners, and hence a principle of justice for allocating them is hardly applicable; and many are seen as properly allocated by considerations of local justice or microjustice.[42] Hence, macrojustice can focus on the allocation of rights in productive capacities.[43] However, process-freedom requires that each individual has the right to use her capacities and to fully benefit from this use. Hence, the distribution only bears on the value of the a priori availability of these capacities, that is, their rent.[44]

5.3.2. Sharing the value of productive capacities

A productive capacity permits transforming labour into output – say, into income or consumption one can buy with it. Equivalently, the productive capacity permits obtaining leisure for each amount of foregone earned income. The markets compare the products of various labours in income units, which can also buy consumption. On moral grounds, however, it is also relevant to equate the values of units of time of life of individuals (a labour value, or leisure or life value). The amount of an individual's productive capacity available can be measured by the total product it can provide (with no leisure in a relevant sense), or by the total labour it can use, which is also the total leisure it can permit (with no output). These are its rent in income value and in leisure-labour-life value, respectively. In the general case, this rent is measured partly in input for some amount of leisure-labour, and partly in output, for the rest. Then the equal sharing yields an equal sharing of the output of the later part. That is, an equal redistribution of the individuals' incomes produced by the same labour (but with their different respective productivities).[45] The choice of this "equalization labour" reflects the moral weight attributed to output and consumption relative to time of life (leisure or

---

[42] See Chapter 5.

[43] The allocation of nonhuman natural resources is analyzed in full in the book *The Liberal Social Contract* (*Le Contrat social libéral*, 1985a). The main issues and solutions will be noted in Chapter 5.

[44] The various types of rights in an asset, for application to capacities, are considered in Chapter 6.

[45] A detailed derivation of this solution is presented in Chapters 9 and 12.

labour). It is also the degree of redistribution (of output) in the society, and hence, a degree of solidarity, community, and – we will see – reciprocity. The equalization of incomes producible by this equal labour defines the distributive transfers. Given these transfers, the individuals, in addition, freely chose their actual labour and receive the corresponding market earnings. This result can equivalently be presented as the individuals receiving the same income for the same "equalization" labour (the average of their corresponding outputs), and receiving their market earnings for the *extra* labour they choose to provide (they could also choose to work less with the corresponding loss, but this will not be the normal case). The obtained distributive scheme is "equal labour income equalization" or ELIE.

The case where the equalization labour is zero corresponds to an absence of transfers and is full self-ownership. Then, the individuals equally fully own themselves. In the opposite limiting case, the equalization labour is the highest possible labour – a case considered (but not endorsed) by Ronald Dworkin (1981). With full self-ownership, individuals who can earn only little from the market consume only little. Correspondingly, with maximal income equalization, individuals who can earn much from the market have to work very much to pay their high redistributive tax (Dworkin's "slavery of the talented").[46] In general, an individual more productive than another is freer than her in the former case and less free in the second, in the sense that, for each labour, her disposable income is higher than the other's in the former case and lower in the second; or, equivalently, for each disposable income, she has to work less than the other in the former case and more in the second. The other cases do not present this kind of domination (the domains of choice intersect).

The classical leftist ideal of equal income, however, a priori means equal actual disposable income. Yet, taking all aspects of this classical position into account will show that it is realized by an ELIE with an equalization labour in the neighbourhood of the lowest normal labour.[47] However, in a large society such as a nation, the equalization labour will turn out to be much lower, in between the cases of this equal income and of full self-ownership.

5.3.3. Meaning and history

In fact, the classical historical formulations of basic rights, or the applications that followed them, introduced public aid to individuals who can earn only little (or nothing) from the labour market. They also stated a financing by taxes according to means. However, for earned income, taxing according to "ability to pay" means according to ability to earn, that is, to earning or productive capacities. Hence, the outcome finally consists of transfers according to productive capacities. This precisely is the result obtained in the present analysis.

[46] See Chapters 7, 9, and 12.
[47] See Chapter 11.

Process-freedom amounts to the right to use one's capacities and to receive all the benefits from this use. This right has a price, which is the rent of the capacity. Classical process liberalism equates process-freedom with self-ownership. Self-ownership of a capacity implies the right to use it and to benefit from this use, that is, the corresponding process-freedom. However, the converse does not hold. A capacity is an asset. The right to use an asset and to benefit from this use has a price, the rent of this asset. Yet, someone who has the right to use an asset and to benefit from this use can be either the owner of this asset or its tenant. The difference is that the owner owns the rent and hence does not pay it, whereas the tenant pays the rent. In particular, with process-freedom, an individual may own the rent of a capacity of hers, and this is self-ownership, or she may have to pay this rent to someone else, and this is self-tenancy. Process-freedom implies self-ownership or self-tenancy. This contrasts with the classical process-liberal implicit belief that process-freedom implies self-ownership. Moreover, an individual may have to pay the rent for only part of her capacities (she may be owner for a part and tenant for the rest). She may also jointly pay a rent for a capacity of hers and receive rents for others' capacities. This can more or less equalize the distribution of the income values of productive capacities without interfering with process-freedom. In particular, ELIE distributions amount to each individual receiving the money rent of the same fraction of each other's given productive capacities, or of the same productive capacities measured by the labour that can use them.[48]

The basic value can be taken to be process-freedom or self-ownership. From a notion of natural right, John Locke (1690) derives not only the right to safety, but also full self-ownership, although he also emphasizes ownership from labour rather than from first occupation (which may justify self-ownership if applied to capacities), and he states a right to means of subsistence. However, from the eighteenth century on, process liberalism doubtlessly intended its basic value to be process-freedom. This is clear in the statements of basic rights, as well as in innumerable commentaries at all levels of sophistication. However, this theory actually endorsed full self-ownership, from the unwarranted belief that process-freedom implies it.

5.4. Summary: Unanimity, efficiency, and basic rights

The implication leading from unanimity to a policy sharing natural resources involves the concepts of basic rights and process-freedom, and Pareto efficiency. These concepts are interlocked by a network of implications. Unanimity directly implies Pareto efficiency. We also have seen that it implies basic rights, either directly or through the fact that each person desires them for herself (she has to) while impartiality then requires that she wants them for the others as well

---

[48] Chapters 9 and 11 more precisely show this property.

(given that the conceivable impossibility and detrimental allocative and distributive effects are avoided by the proper conceptions of these rights as nonrival and of process-freedom as implying the liberal correction of market failures and not implying full self-ownership).

However, the classical basic rights include political rights of participation to political or collective decisions. This will implement any unanimous desire. Hence, basic rights imply the principle of unanimity.

Moreover, the classical basic rights also include the right to be a candidate for positions. Now, if a state is not Pareto-efficient, by definition there exists another state preferred by everybody (with the possibility of indifference for some people). Then, any person can propose, as a political program, the implementation of this other state. Given the general right of political participation, she will win with the unanimity of votes. Or, if several such programs are proposed, at any rate there will be no voice for the Pareto-dominated state. This holds with any voting rule or weighted voting. Therefore, the classical basic rights imply Pareto efficiency in this way. Hence, Pareto inefficiency implies that there is some violation of the classical basic rights. As a consequence, it is unconstitutional in countries with a constitution based on these rights. Issues of information and the constraints they may create can easily be introduced in this reasoning.

Basic rights and process-freedom – we have seen – are essentially two ways of looking at the same thing, the former both empirical and moral, the latter theoretical and developing into the elaborate theory of full process-freedom. Moreover, basing measures of distributive policy on inelastic items is necessary and sufficient for their respecting Pareto efficiency, and for their respecting full process-freedom in a strict sense. Process-freedom entails the well-known efficiency of market systems due to interested incentives and a decentralized use of the relevant information; furthermore, it is conceived as including the correction of inefficiency-generating "market failures" according to "liberal social contracts" which implement the hypothetically process-free outcomes.[49] This latter task is the role of the allocation function of the process-liberal public sector. It complements the distribution function which allocates the given (or natural) resources, and notably the value of human capacities.[50] These two reasons lead to a public sector much more important than the "minimal state" restricted to the policing of rights, but whose allocative and distributive task is well-defined from these applications of basic freedoms and unanimity.

6. A SUMMARY OF ISSUES, REASONS, AND RELATIONS

A network of implications thus leads from endogenous social choice implying the endorsement of unanimity to the ELIE structure of overall distribution and the

[49] See Chapter 3.
[50] Richard Musgrave (1959) appropriately calls these functions the allocation and the distribution "branches" of the public sector.

determination of the degree of redistribution and community (the equalization labour). This network is represented in Figure 1–1. The nodes are unanimity, classical basic rights, full process-freedom, Pareto efficiency, the sharing of natural resources, the restriction to productive resources, the restriction to productive capacities, the ELIE structure, and the determination of the equalization labour. Arrows indicate implications (the reason is sometimes indicated).

7. THE THEORY OF ENDOGENOUS SOCIAL CHOICE AND THE DETERMINATION OF THE DEGREE OF REDISTRIBUTION: A SHORT OUTLINE

The derivation of the ELIE structure of global distributive justice has used the rule of unanimity solely for choosing basic rights and Pareto efficiency, and for discarding a direct relevance of eudemonistic capacities for macrojustice redistribution. By contrast, the determination of the degree of equalization (the equalization labour) can use most aspects of endogenous social choice applied to the problem of distribution. The point is to show how all individuals deeply agree about the solution, in spite of the opposition of their interests. The concepts and methods of endogenous social choice, and this application, are presented in Part IV of this study. The following remarks aim only at providing a glimpse of the problems met and of the methods used.

Determining distribution from unanimity a priori constitutes a challenge, since individuals' interests are by definition and nature opposed to one another in a problem of distribution. The degree of distribution (the equalization labour) of an ELIE scheme precisely epitomizes this opposition, since an individual's interests are favoured by its being either the highest or the lowest possible, depending on whether an individual's productivity falls short of the average or exceeds it. However, the relevant evaluations of the individuals for solving this problem is not their interest but their *social and ethical* judgment, and notably their view about justice, which by nature should be impartial toward all individuals' interests. This raises a number of problems, though: individuals may not have such views (which should then be notionally built from their other preferences); these views may differ across individuals; and these views should be made to properly influence the outcome, possibly in being known to a policy maker, while individuals also have self-interested or self-centered preferences.[51] Endogenous social choice consists of providing solutions to these questions.

These relevant social and moral views of the society or of its members can concern general sentiments of community, solidarity, or reciprocity, or judgments about just distribution (both can lead to the degree of redistribution). Although expressed by individuals, such views are more part of the culture than intrinsically

---

[51] Self-centeredness includes favouring certain other people because of their particular relations with oneself, or because of a particular liking irrelevant to issues of justice.

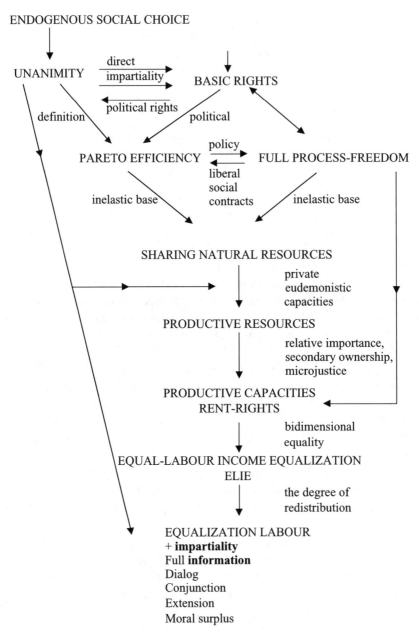

ENDOGENOUS SOCIAL CHOICE

UNANIMITY

direct
impartiality

BASIC RIGHTS

political rights

definition

political

PARETO EFFICIENCY

policy

liberal
social
contracts

FULL PROCESS-FREEDOM

inelastic base

inelastic base

SHARING NATURAL RESOURCES

private
eudemonistic
capacities

PRODUCTIVE RESOURCES

relative importance,
secondary ownership,
microjustice

PRODUCTIVE CAPACITIES
RENT-RIGHTS

bidimensional
equality

EQUAL-LABOUR INCOME EQUALIZATION
ELIE

the degree of
redistribution

EQUALIZATION LABOUR
+ **impartiality**
Full **information**
Dialog
Conjunction
Extension
Moral surplus

Figure 1–1. The logical structure of macrojustice.

individual. They are more norms than ordinary tastes. They can thus be estimated from an overall sociological and cultural analysis, or from a specific analysis of individuals' social-ethical preferences. The latter will be emphasized in the present work. However, a common culture in itself tends to make these views of individuals more or less proximate to one another, either in the society as a whole or in subgroups within it.

The considered convergence of these views of individuals can be actual, notional (theoretical), or a mix of both. It will result from properties which are inherent to the nature and definition of these social-ethical conceptions, and from relations of various types among individuals' views. These properties and relations can also be actual, notional, or a mix of both. These properties are impartiality, information, and general properties of rationality. *Impartiality* is an a priori property of the concept of justice. It is only a structural property which can have various applications. And yet, impartiality of some sort is a necessary structure and property of all conceptions of justice. Full relevant *information* is also a necessity, since ethics cannot rest on ignorance, confusion, mistaken beliefs, and misunderstandings. This is one aspect of rationality, and an ethical view should also abide by the other general aspects of rationality. The relevant impartiality and information of individuals will be about the same overall items: the interests or the social-ethical judgments of all individuals. Hence, these properties in themselves constitute a type of relation among the individuals' views they characterize. More important, they provide an important progress in the direction of consensus. Indeed, impartiality among individuals' interests erases the opposition due to interests, which is the hallmark of problems of distribution.[52] And properly informed and rational views cannot differ because of divergent beliefs or irrationalities. Furthermore, we will see that full consensus finally results from extensive conceptions of information about, or impartiality among, individuals' social-ethical views.[53]

Concern and information about others and their views are closely related. Concern requires some information, and sufficiently extended and deep information about others entails concern. Indeed, knowing others' sentiments and emotions in the deep sense of feeling how they feel certainly entails this concern (*empathetic information*). The same result obtains from sufficiently knowing the reasons of others' evaluations, and the causes of their relevant preferences due to influences or life experiences, with the same experiencing knowledge of the sentiments elicited by these facts (*formative information*). Then, with everyone's perfect and full information about others, including these types of information, individuals' preferences about the situation cannot but coincide. This state, however, will often have to be only notional and, then, it should be theoretically modelled.[54]

[52] See Section 3.2 of this chapter and Chapters 20 and 21.
[53] See Chapters 19 and 21, respectively.
[54] See Chapter 19.

Information about others is mutual and often comes in the form of a *dialog*. Information about facts, reasons, judgments, and sentiments can be transmitted in this process. This improves information about others and also, possibly, concern for them and impartiality. It may also make views converge, possibly to a consensus with full relevant information. However, these transmissions can also meet a number of difficulties. One can then consider a notional dialog in building a theory of this process of information and influence. The considered dialog can also stop short of full consensus and be completed by any method of social choice such as vote, exchange agreement with mutually conditional concessions, a notional such exchange which is by definition a social contract, or any other method of endogenous social choice. Inequalities in means and capacities to communicate and persuade can be compensated or checked by rules (such as the Athenian *isēgoria*, equal time of public expression).[55]

A more specific theory of individuals' impartial concern can assume that each individual considers that her relevant items are replaced by those of all individuals successively in time (*moral time-sharing*), as uncertain possibilities (*moral risk*), or as various aspects of a *multiple-self* personality. These items can be the interests relevant in the considered distribution (income or welfare, for instance), or individuals' social-ethical views. These individuals' evaluations are impartial (with equal duration or probability). They are closer to one another than the initial individual evaluations each of them synthesizes. However, they still differ across individuals. Yet, consistency suggests treating this new difference as the initial one has been, in assuming that each individual holds each of the new views successively, as uncertain possibilities, or in a multiple-self fashion. The new individual views are still more similar, and yet still different, and the same operation can be repeated. This *moral regress* tends to consensual preferences, and in beginning the process by individuals' relevant interests, a unanimous evaluation of them is obtained.[56]

Another way of solution starts from the fact that individuals actually care for others' allocations in a way that depends on these others' particular relations with them – such as being their neighbours, children, or brothers, or belonging to the same group or category of any kind, and so on. An individual's impartial evaluation of a distribution can be obtained from her actual evaluation in assuming she considers all allocations of society members as being those of individuals *in the same relation* with herself (including her own allocation).[57] These impartial evaluations are closer to one another than are the initial self-centered views. Remaining differences can be reduced by an iterative process taking these individuals' new views as the object of each individual evaluation.

---

[55] The theory of dialog is presented in Chapter 20.

[56] This theory is presented in Chapter 21. It includes, in particular, the rational theory of the "original position," which is a type of moral risk.

[57] The theory of this impartialization of individuals' judgments is proposed in Chapter 21.

Individuals generally have both self-interested or self-centered concerns, and the noted social-ethical views (they sometimes give priority to the former in a structure of "lexical self-interest"). However, endogenous social choice should directly rest on the latter views, and therefore should discard self-interested concerns from individuals' overall evaluations. This can be done at the individual or at the social level.

For instance, if an individual action or expression does not affect this individual's interest, no interested reason induces her not to reveal or manifest her ethical view. This happens when the individual is "small in a large number" (a "mass effect"). It also happens when the issue does not affect the interest of this particular individual, and then her ethical and all-encompassing views coincide if nothing else intervenes[58] (they are *interest-neutral* judgments). In particular, for an ELIE, individuals whose productivity is average neither receive a subsidy nor pay a tax. Their interest is not (directly) affected by the equalization labour or degree of redistribution, and hence their view about it a priori reflects their social-ethical opinion only. Moreover, since such opinions of the individuals have no reason to be correlated with their productivity, these average-productivity judgments provide an unbiased sample of interest-neutral opinions in the whole society.

Self-interests are also erased, but at the global level rather than at that of individuals, by the method of the *moral surplus*. An initial remark can be that simple majority voting equally weights the votes of individuals who are deeply concerned by the choice and the votes of people who are almost indifferent about it. Hence, votes should be weighted by a measure of concern. However, we have seen that, for transfers implementing global distributive justice, the relevant measure of the relative concern of individuals excludes their eudemonistic capacities. Hence, this measure boils down to income or money equivalent, or willingness to pay (either positive or, for a loss, negative). The algebraic sum of individuals' money or income equivalent of a choice, or willingnesses to pay for it, is the classical "surplus."[59] Preferring an alternative to another when this replacement yields a positive surplus – the method of the surplus – is the standard principle in benefit-cost analysis. The theory of the moral or distributive surplus applies this principle to the distribution among individuals.[60] An individual has two types of reasons to be concerned with this distribution: her self-interest, and other reasons and notably concern about ethics and justice. An individual's willingness to pay for a distribution of income (or income value of it) for a reason of self-interest precisely is the amount she receives (or yields, then with a negative sign). In a pure redistribution, these

---

[58] Such as envy, jealousy, malevolence, unfair favouritism, and so on.

[59] The general and complete theory of the surplus is presented in Chapter 26. There, the difference between money or income equivalent and willingness to pay is made precise, and it is shown that the classical difficulty with the method of the surplus it underlines (pointed out by T. Scitousky in 1941) is in fact an asset of this theory (see Kolm 1966a).

[60] The full presentation and analysis of the theory of the moral or distributive surplus constitute the first parts of the essay *The Optimal Production of Social Justice* (Kolm 1966a).

transfers balance, and hence the (algebraic) sum of these amounts is zero. There-fore, in the surplus of a redistribution, the values corresponding to these self-interests cancel out, and the effect of this motive vanishes. Hence, there only remains the balance of individuals' income equivalents or willingnesses to pay for other reasons, here their moral judgments about the distribution. Therefore, a distribution from which all changes yield a negative surplus is selected by these moral judgments only (this method will be precisely analyzed).[61] This method also amounts to the moral "compensation principle" (that is, individuals who like a change can compensate those who dislike it), or to the highest social income including moral external effects.

Both these methods of interest-neutral (in particular average-productivity) judgments and the moral surplus work even when the individuals give priority to their self-interest (lexical self-interest or selfishness).

The methods of endogenous social choice show, in general, how individuals deeply agree about the just distribution or about ways of determining it. This consensus can be overt, or hidden but real, or also conceptual in deriving logical consequences from actual views. Endogenous social choice solves the problem of social choice in considering both the psychological and the social dimensions of individuals. The classical failures of standard social choice theory are due to its considering only maimed, truncated, and rigid individual preferences, devoid of their relevant psychological structures and social interactions, and hence, un-realistic in precisely the required dimensions. Individuals have a sense of justice, either explicit, or implicit but logically necessary. Their corresponding sentiments are transformed by sufficiently knowing about one another or interacting among themselves. And these structures and phenomena have specific properties which can provide the solution. Individuals' social-ethical views are, in fact, much more social items than intrinsically individual ones. Social choice or justice is a so-cial problem, to be solved by the social and cultural dimension of individuals, as concerns both interpersonal relations and the corresponding dimensions of individuals' information and sentiments.

8. PRESENTATION OF THE BOOK

Macrojustice desired by society is but poorly hidden by individuals' ignorance and selfishness. Unveiling it is the subject of this study. This is done in three stages respectively showing the bases of the solution, its structure, and the degree of solidarity, in Parts I, II, and IV respectively. Parts III and V compare this finding with existing or proposed distributive policies, with political philosophies, and with the general social ethics of economics.

The bases consist of freedoms and resources (Part I). Freedom (Part I.2) is ba-sically social freedom, that is, an absence of forceful domination (Chapter 2). This

---

[61] In Chapter 19. The reference in note 60 also considers cases where individuals care for others' welfare or happiness, the interested valuations of indirect effects of the distribution, and other issues.

is classically manifested as the process-freedom of process liberalism (Chapter 3), and as the classical basic rights (Chapter 4). Resources (Part I.3) are nonhuman natural resources (Chapter 5) and capacities (Chapter 6). The outcome is that desired macrojustice has social freedom as basic rule, and then has to share the value of the given productive capacities.

This sharing leads to the distributive structure of equal labour income equalization analyzed in Part II. This derivation and the main properties of the result are presented in Chapter 9, which is, in a sense, the central chapter. The rest of Part II prepares or complements this chapter. Chapter 7 presents a general nonformal overview of the issues. Chapter 8 considers the technical structure of individual production and the resulting models. The general derivation of equal labour income equalization is the topic of Chapter 12 (Chapter 9 focuses, for simplicity, on the case of equal duration income equalization). Chapter 13 considers specifically the treatment of involuntary unemployment. Chapter 10 focuses on the issue of the information necessary for the distributive policy, and shows that it is at least as available as for other policies. Finally, Chapter 11 considers "income justice," that is, evaluations and policies based on incomes, and shows, in particular, that income egalitarians' complete view is best realized by a particular ELIE scheme. The classical "principles of public finances" of "ability to pay" and "benefit taxation" are also considered.

This result is compared with other policies and philosophies in Part III. The terms of the comparison are set out in Chapter 14. Chapter 15 focuses on the actual or proposed schemes of transfers and aid, such as support of low incomes, negative income tax (income tax credit), universal basic income, or the welfarist "optimum taxation." Chapter 16 considers political philosophies, including Plato's and Aristotle's theory of distributive justice, the full self-ownership of classical process liberalism, and landmark "historical" egalitarian proposals of the last few decades such as those of Rawls, Dworkin, and Walzer.

Part IV shows the general methods of endogenous social choice for determining the degree of community, reciprocity, solidarity, or equalization. Chapter 17 shows the dual nature – both individual and social – of social-ethical views and of their implementation, the aspects of minimum income and of degree of redistribution of the coefficient, and properties of the way of determining it. The three basic properties of impartiality, consensus, and information (notably, "empathetic" and "formative" information) are considered in Chapter 18. Chapter 19 shows how to erase the self-interested bias in individuals' views, either at the individual level with interest-neutral judgments, or at the social level with the method of the surplus evaluating redistributions. The ethics of communication and dialog, and its theory, are the topic of Chapter 20. Finally, Chapter 21 analyzes the methods of impartialization toward consensus. This includes the impartialization by the notional extension of individuals' evaluation of the situations of individuals in a given social relation with them. It also includes the impartializations by conjunction in considering that each individual can have the relevant situations of all individuals successively in time, as uncertain possibilities (moral time-sharing and moral risk), or as the dimensions of a multiple self, and in reaching unanimity through repetition of the operation (moral regress) – an alternative being a convenient aggregation.

Finally, Part V compares the obtained result for justice in society with the social ethics that have been proposed or can be proposed in the framework of economics. For this purpose, it presents a broad overview of economics' social ethics, in emphasizing the issue of the meaning of concepts, principles, and criteria, that is, the aspect that is often not the strongest point of these theories. This overall presentation may have an interest in itself. Its bulkiness and specificity lead to presenting as a separate last part, rather than along with the other comparisons – with policies and philosophies. Were it presented in comparative Part III, this analysis would have delayed too long the study of the degree of redistribution, presented in Part IV, which completes the presentation of the obtained result. Yet, the comparisons with policies and philosophies probably help situate the obtained result, and hence, are at their place in Part III. In fact, Part V was absent from a first version of this study, but economist readers almost all demanded further comparisons with normative ideas emanating from economics (this comparison already existed with theories for which it was the most necessary). And it seemed that this could not be done in a way shorter than the present Part V.

In this part, Chapter 22 presents economic analyses that are cases of the obtained structure of macrojustice or closely related to them, such as classical liberalism and other liberty-based views of Marx, constitutional public choice, Hayek, or libertarians; income egalitarianisms; and the possible solutions to the problem of defining a proper social ordering. The basic form of distributive principles, which associates a substance of direct concern and a structure of interpersonal comparison, is presented in Chapter 23, which shows, in particular, the rational necessity of the *prima facie* properties of permutability (symmetry) and equality, and the possible meanings of the extraordinary concept of utility. Then, Chapter 24 focuses on the two polar types of substance of direct concerns, happiness and freedom, and on the issue of the various comparisons concerning them. Various issues concerning responsibility, desert or deservingness, merit, equality of opportunity, basic needs and the formation of capacities, "fundamental insurance" and "fundamental reciprocity," and others are presented and analyzed in Chapter 25. Finally, Chapter 26 presents the general theory of equivalence, which considers properties in various situations that all individuals find as good as each other, and its relation with efficiency.

9. SUGGESTIONS FOR THE READER

As shown by the simplicity of the result – ELIE distribution and basic rights – the whole topic is very simple. However, it uses two kinds of styles, each in a moderate and easy form, which could be labelled the philosophical and the economic (with simple formal models). It is probably the case that most readers prefer to enter into the topic with one or the other of these languages. This is quite possible. Then, "economists" may prefer beginning with Chapter 9, for grasping the core of the structure and meanings of the ELIE distributive schemes. Chapters 8, 12, and 13 then justify and complete the formal model. And Chapter 10 deals with the issue of information (which tends to particularly worry economists). However, the justification of this distributive structure cannot avoid considering the (easy) philosophy of social freedom and its forms (Chapters 2, 3, and 4), and of the relevance of resources and capacities (Chapters 5 and 6). In an alternative strategy, the mathematical models can be skipped (although each time something is lost), but it is necessary to have a grasp of their conclusion and its meanings; for this purpose, these results and their meanings and conditions are always repeated or announced "in words." The same holds for the methods of endogenous social choice presented in Part IV. Moreover, a number of readers familiar with the literature may want to read the comparisons of Part III at a rather early stage. And the overview of economics' social ethics with an emphasis on meanings, presented in Part V, although it is set up for the purpose of comparison with the obtained result, can also be read for itself.

10. A NOTE ABOUT FORM

The subtitle of this volume, *The Political Economy of Fairness*, was suggested by the publisher. The title, *Macrojustice*, describes the basic intent and the heart of this work, but this name is not common and may a priori seem a little odd. "Fairness" sounds smoother – and possibly more subtle – than justice (and it can be used as John Rawls did). "Economy" can indicate that the topic and intent belong to economics – the allocation of resources and fiscal policy – as well as the formal models used. But "political economy," with the adjective, may suggest that economics is closely integrated with political philosophy and social philosophy – notably as concerns freedom in the first part and, in the fourth part, community, the psychosociology of value, and a few methods such as dialog, original positions, and so on (this is much deeper than just voting – a recent use of the term "political economy"). This may also suggest the importance attached to the issue of meaning in the comparison with economics' social ethics in Part V.[62]

Let us also note that references will be either by authors' name and date, as is usual, or by the full title of the work when this is fitting in the discussion. The precise referencing is gathered at the end of the volume.[63]

---

[62] Hence, "philosophical economics" might have been a better expression than "political economy," but it is not common (yet).

[63] Finally, it may be pointed out that references to other works of the author are exclusively due to the fact that a person's mind and reflection has a unity, while repeating these ideas would be both impossible because of place and unnecessary when they are available.

2

Social freedom

1. PRESENTATION

The rest of Part I of this study completes the reasons and presents the sequence of implications that lead to the structure of global or overall distribution analyzed in Part II. There will be two kinds of items: social freedom and resources.

Social freedom means that there is no relation of force among individuals, including when they act in groups or in institutions. This indeed amounts to each individual being free from any other individual's forceful interference. This freedom is thus defined by (or as) a type of social relation, rather than a priori by a domain of possible choice or action – hence the adjective "social." Social freedom also means that all individuals agree about what is done, although an individual may have to buy others' acts or others' agreements to her acts, in exchange for something. The respect of others includes that of the intended consequences of their acts, and hence of rights obtained in previous free actions or exchanges. Social freedom is commonly considered under two forms: the classical "basic rights" or "basic freedoms" (which are the basis of "democratic" constitutions), and the theory of free exchanges and the resulting property (notably through markets) approved of by "process liberalism." We will see that social freedom can notably be justified as unanimously desired, given the relevant desires and possible uses of this liberty (this chapter and, particularly, Chapter 4). Social freedom – along with Pareto efficiency directly required by the principle of unanimity – will provide the moral base of the derivation of the structure of the distribution or redistribution.

Indeed, social freedom or efficiency will imply that what is to be distributed are given resources. The resources to be distributed in macrojustice will then be shown to reduce to the value of productive capacities by considerations about facts, consensus, and social freedom (and efficiency). Indeed, issues of relative importance, practicability, and allocations in microjustice, will show that global distributive justice in macrojustice should restrict its concern to human resources (Chapter 5); consensus then discards eudemonistic capacities as concern for policy in macrojustice (Chapter 6); and social freedom amounts to individuals having the full right to use their capacities and benefit from the consequences – but not necessarily the full right in the rent of these capacities (the value of their availability) (Chapter 6). Finally, the proper measure of this value for equal sharing provides the result (Chapter 9).

Chapters 2, 3, and 4 consider social freedom, and Chapters 5 and 6 are about resources – nonhuman ones in Chapter 5 and capacities in Chapter 6. Chapters 2, 3, and 4 concern, respectively, social freedom in general and the two aspects under which it is usually considered, process-freedom and the classical basic rights. The present Chapter 2 presents a short summary of the properties of social freedom and reasons for it, which will be considered in more detail in Chapters 3 and 4. Section 1 presents the definition of social freedom and its main features. Section 2 focuses on its main distributional consequence: the individuals should be the tenants of themselves, but are not necessarily entitled to the a priori value or rent of their given capacities (this contrasts with self-ownership). Section 3 points out the two classical forms of social freedom, process-freedom considered by process liberalism, and basic rights. Section 4 shows the logic of the reasons for social freedom. These reasons will be analyzed in more detail about basic rights in Chapter 4 because this moral discussion usually concerns these rights – and the full justification requires the consideration of the theory of full process-freedom outlined in Chapter 3.

2. SOCIAL FREEDOM: DEFINITION

Social freedom prevails in a society when no individual is forced by others as individuals, groups, or institutions, except, if necessary, for preventing her from forcing others. Each individual in this society is said to be socially free. This freedom is defined by an absence of others' forceful interference with her, and by this condition only. But others' social freedom implies that she does not use force against them either. This individual is "free from" forceful interference, and also "free to" do anything that does not forcefully interfere with others. Indeed, society cannot further restrict her freedom, since this would be forceful interference. Although the logically and morally basic concept is freedom from forceful interference, the expression of social freedom commonly focusses on the dual aspect, the limits to action. For instance, the 1789 Declaration of the Rights of Man and of the Citizen defines freedom as the right to do anything that does not harm others (article IV).[1] Of course, an influential threat of harming is considered a use of force.

---

[1] The classical expression "negative freedom" has been used in various different senses. For Isaiah Berlin (1958), who also calls it "political freedom," it denotes, indeed, a limit to others' interference with an agent. However, it requires a few precisions and it is not only the complete ban of force that is denoted here by "social freedom" (it admits of degrees). Moreover, Kant and J. S. Mill, for instance, have "negative freedom" refer to all the kinds of "external" possibilities of the agents, adding capacities, means, properties, and so on, to the limitation of being forced by others (see the Appendix). Berlin also emphasized the distinction between freedom "from" and freedom "to," in restricting the former to

Social freedom thus is defined by and as a type of social relation, rather than by a domain of choice given a priori (as would be Robinson Crusoe's freedom).[2] It is social by the nature of its definition and of the constraints that define it, which concern first others' acts affecting the free person, and second this person's acts affecting others. In addition, of course, an individual's acts and choices are limited by the availability of her other means and possibilities of all types. Moreover, the respect of others' social freedom, the absence of forceful interference, may have to be enforced, and this is the only possible legitimate use of force permitted by social freedom: individuals can only be forced not to force.

Social freedom, or nonforceful social relations, also amounts to an absence of domination. It constitutes a relational equality (and ideal equality of something is a requirement of impartiality and rationality).[3] There can, of course, be unequal free exchanges and the corresponding de facto domination (an extreme case is exploitation as conceived by Marx). However, we will see that, contrary to a classical belief, social freedom need not be conceived as banning distributive transfers – but only as requiring a particular base and structure for these transfers.

The ban of force makes social freedom be the exact opposite of another kind of freedom whose form in social relations is also considered: the freedom conceived by the school of thought that Murray Rothbart (1973) labelled "libertarians" (thus hijacking a name long and classically used for a very different philosophy, that of the classical left anarchists). Indeed, in this "neolibertarian" conception, there is no a priori limit to individuals' freedoms. Hence, in social relations, the only limit is the other's force. Slavery is consistent with this freedom. The same view is implicit in James Buchanan's (1975) conception of "public choice" and a "constitution," although the balance of forces and the terms of the truce may explicitly or implicitly imply social freedom. The point here is that a present fashion that joins, under the label of "libertarianism," both these schools and social freedom, constitutes a confusion that prevents understanding the most basic issues.[4]

Since social relations in social freedom ban force, they are with unanimous agreement of the concerned persons. These agreements can include free exchanges of any type. However, individuals enter these interactions using their assets, which take the form of various rights. These rights can themselves just manifest social freedom, and hence be implied, entailed, and defined by it. In fact, social freedom itself takes the form of rights (it amounts to the classical basic rights). However, the basic point here concerns the effect of time. Indeed, freedom from forceful interference applies to the actions of the individuals. An action is a set of acts with an aim, an intention. Forceful interference with an action can directly affect either

negative freedom in his sense (social freedom does not a priori include concepts such as "freedom from need" and the like).

[2] As Marx would put it, characterizing freedom as a set of possible choices is like "characterizing a negro slave as a man of the black race."

[3] See Chapter 23 and *Justice and Equity* (Kolm 1971, English translation 1998), Foreword, Section 5.

[4] See Kolm, 1996a, Chapters 12 and 13.

the acts or their intended consequences. Its required absence takes the form of rights and obligations. Yet, the consequences can occur at dates later than those of the acts. Then, at a moment of time, there can be pending rights and obligations or liabilities that manifest the social freedom of actions whose acts occurred in the past. These rights constitute individuals' assets and means of action at this later date. They can be of all types, such as protection, claims from promises, or rights about what one can do with existing things, in the category of property rights. The acts that created these rights can in particular be agreements accepted by all parties, including free exchanges and sales and buying. Moreover, other individuals can always propose to buy these rights or agreements about the way they are used.

Institutions can secure the prevention of individuals' use of force against others and their legitimate rights. They can also result from the working of social freedom, as the result of free agreements of various types (possibly including implicit agreements – see Chapter 3, Section 6).

With social freedom, the incompatible desires of several persons entail peaceful actions and a result, using two kinds of items: rights and voluntary agreements, the latter using rights. These rights are of three kinds. First, there are the basic rights or freedoms, which are but social freedom itself and state important domains of its application. The second category consists of the derived rights created by the working of social freedom. They result from past free acts, including transforming and producing, giving, and the collective free acts of agreeing, contracting, or exchanging. When social freedom prevails throughout society and time, the rights about all that has been freely created, transformed, transferred, exchanged, or given are well defined. The only rights that are not so defined are the initial or primary rights in given resources – the classical "natural" resources. This constitutes the third category of rights. Such an initial or primary right in a given resource can possibly be transferred, for instance sold, or rented out. Natural resources include given human resources or capacities.

One can try to have social freedom also allocate given (natural) resources. A classical and widespread proposal is first occupancy. Applied to capacities, this yields self-ownership since an individual can doubtlessly be considered the first occupant of herself. However, the moral value of the role of time, the legitimacy of being the first in time, as general and unique principle, certainly begs justification (yet, this principle is commonly unanimously accepted for various cases of allocation in microjustice).

Another way of allocating given resources by social freedom, which is more germane to this principle, consists in a general, unanimous agreement about this allocation. Compensatory transfers can freely be used among the individuals for obtaining another's agreement, and this would define and justify such transfers. The agreement can be about specific principles to be used, and about delegating choices to particular societies or processes. The agreement, or part of it, will have to be notional, because of practical impossibilities due to large numbers of participants (and also the consideration of participants belonging to different generations) – it would then be a "liberal social contract" (see Chapter 3, Section 6).

In fact, the present study shows how the principle of unanimity of preferences (rather than that resulting from an agreement) solves a large part of the problem: the allocation of human natural resources. It rests, however, on the fact that the relevant preferences of the individuals are their moral preferences as concerns distributive justice, rather than their self-interested preferences. These moral preferences can be actual or inferred (as shown in Chapter 21). Then, unanimity will first justify social freedom itself, thus providing the dual, joint justification by these two principles noted in Chapter 1. It will also distinguish macrojustice and global distributive justice from microjustice. It will then allocate eudemonistic capacities to their holder for macrojustice (see Chapter 6), while social freedom implies the same conclusion for the right to use one's capacities of any kind and benefit from this use (see next section). This will lead to ELIE schemes whose degree of redistribution will also be so determined (see Part IV of this study). The result finally differs from the most famous derivation of an allocation of natural resources from social freedom: the unthoughtful assumption of classical "process liberalism" that social freedom implies full self-ownership.

3. FREEDOM AS SELF-TENANCY, AND RENT-RIGHTS IN CAPACITIES

Given resources prominently include given human resources or capacities. However, acting or resting is using one's capacities, and hence social freedom implies that the holder of a capacity has the right to decide about its *use* – that does not violate others' such freedom – to use it, and to benefit from this use and its consequences.[5] Now, a person's right to choose the use of an asset, to use it, and to benefit from this use implies that she is the owner, the tenant, or the usufructuary of this asset (she may have different such rights about various parts of the asset). The difference between an owner and a tenant relevant for our present purpose is that a tenant has to pay a rent for benefiting from the availability of this asset, whereas this is not the case for the owner.[6] That is, the owner has, and the tenant does not have, the rent-right concerning this asset. Social freedom thus implies that individuals are the owners or the tenants of themselves, that is, self-ownership or self-tenancy – or a mix of both. If they are only tenants, or in the measure in which this is the case, they have to pay a rent, which is the value of the availability of the asset, to holders of the corresponding rent-rights. These holders are other individuals, and these payments are transfers which can be made through the intermediary of a

---

[5] The issue of their being intended consequences, and the related question of responsibility, will be noted in Chapter 3 and is discussed in Kolm 2001a.

[6] For our purpose, a usufructuary is like an owner: she can either use the asset and benefit from the use, or receive the rent from a tenant. The issues of selling or destroying the asset are not raised here, and the transmission of the right after death is irrelevant.

public distributive agency. Therefore, social freedom does not preclude distributive or redistributive transfers. These transfers are banned only in the case of full self-ownership, which is only one particular possible case. We will in fact find that, for the purpose of macrojustice, individuals should have self-ownership of their eudemonistic capacities (from consensus, see Chapter 6), but not necessarily of their given productive capacities. In the measure in which they are tenants and not owners of their given productive capacity, they pay a corresponding rent-right to other individuals. These are distributive transfers, which distribute a given natural resource.

4. THE RESULTING DISTRIBUTIVE STRUCTURE

The rent of an asset is a priori independent from the choice of the specific use of this asset by the tenant (if there is no effect of this particular action on the market value of the rent through the price system). The considered transfers should be based on the rent itself and not, notably, on the use of the asset, for two reasons. A tax based on the use or its consequences (such as a resulting income) would constitute a forceful interference with this act and hence violate social freedom.[7] Moreover, a tax or subsidy with such a base would induce disincentive effects of the type that jeopardizes Pareto efficiency (a classical remark of elementary economics), and the principle of unanimity requires Pareto efficiency.[8] More generally, this efficiency, and hence the principle of unanimity, require that transfers are essentially based on "inelastic" items (i.e., items that do not depend on actors' acts), and social freedom bans taxes on the other, "elastic" items (see Chapter 4). Moreover, for distributive transfers, these inelastic or given items should have an economic value: they should thus be the given resources, classically called the "natural" resources. These resources are nonhuman or human (capacities). The economic value of the availability of a durable resource is its rent.

  This holds in particular for productive capacities – capacities that can be used for producing and notably for earning. Part of these capacities are actually used in labour. This produces a very much larger share of the economic value of the social output than do the nonhuman given resources (see Chapter 5).[9] Moreover, educated or trained labour also (indirectly) uses given capacities and labour that have been used in learning or training. In addition, many nonhuman natural resources are specific and local and allocated by rules of microjustice, often by consensus. And, for many others, their initial allocation has been made to past owners different from the present ones, and this cannot practically be reversed (Chapter 5).

---

[7] Such a tax base can be justified for implementing social freedom impaired by various phenomena – for instance an "external effect" or a lack of information: see Chapter 3, Section 6.
[8] Chapter 10 shows that taking income as tax base because it would be an observable proxy for unobservable capacities is not a justification to be retained – although it has been famous in economics. The actual reasons for basing taxes (and subsidies) on incomes are analyzed in Chapter 11.
[9] Although social accounting includes the rent of nonhuman natural resources directly consumed – such as residential land – while it only includes the product of capacities used in labour.

Furthermore, we will see that, for the purpose of macrojustice, consensus endorses full self-ownership of one's capacities to be satisfied or happy – or eudemonistic capacities – (Chapter 6). Hence, the rent of productive capacities remains the only distribuand available for global distributive justice in macrojustice.

Finally, social freedom permits a redistributive policy, contrary to the belief of classical process liberalism that equates it with full self-ownership (see Chapter 3). For macrojustice, however, it restricts this policy to the allocation of the rent-rights in individuals' given productive capacities. The result of an equal sharing will depend on the measure of these capacities. These capacities, indeed, can equivalently be seen as producing output, income, or consumption for given labour time or effort, or leisure or time of life for required levels of income or consumption. Full self-ownership is a kind of equality: each individual owns one producer (herself); or they all own the same number of hours of human life per day or year (say), and one may morally equally value the same time of life of various persons. This, however, discards inequalities in possible output, which can also be valued. Then, in the general case where capacities are measured partly by the labour that uses them and partly by the output they produce, the result of an equal sharing of individuals' productive capacities consists of an equal sharing of the proceeds of the same labour (with the different individual productivities), that is, "equal labour income equalization" (this derivation is fully presented and discussed in Chapter 9).

5. THE TWO FORMS OF SOCIAL FREEDOM: PROCESS-FREEDOM AND BASIC RIGHTS

Social freedom is classically presented under two different forms: the classical basic rights which constitute the basis of our constitutions, and process-freedom, which underlies the theory of full process-freedom, whose moral endorsement is process liberalism.[10] These are the two classical avatars of the same principle, social freedom. Precision and specification are required by both, though, especially by the second. The classical basic rights or freedoms (or basic rights or freedoms) are short moral and legal statements describing main general aspects and applications. By contrast, full process-freedom is an elaborate theory developed mainly over the last two centuries by contributions of philosophy, economics, and law, and emphasizing market exchanges and property rights. Chapters 3 and 4 summarize the main issues about process-freedom and basic rights, respectively.[11]

Freedom to act and to benefit from the intended consequences of one's acts without forceful interference constitutes process-freedom. Full process-freedom

---

[10] The question of the uses of the terms liberal and liberalism will be noted in Chapter 3.

[11] I. Berlin's concept of "negative freedom," which should emphasize the use of force in the restricted interferences, and is not necessarily full and complete, also lacks being explicit about rights and notably property rights resulting from past freedom and notably free exchange. By contrast, both the classical basic rights and the theory of full process-freedom are explicit about this issue.

is the situation where this is the general rule of society, for acts respecting others' process-freedom and extending over time. Respect of consequences of past acts includes that of rights and property acquired through free exchanges. However, classical process liberalism values an interpretation of this theory tainted by two problems. First, free markets present a number of "market failures" (analyzed by public economics) that jeopardize Pareto efficiency. This includes issues of nonexcludable public goods, "external effects," or price rigidities causing macroeconomic disorders. Second, this interpretation endorses full self-ownership with the possible resulting poverty of people who receive only low wages from the labour market (or cannot find employment). However, these interpretations of the theory of full process-freedom are not the only options. On the allocative grounds, process-freedom can be seen as requiring the implementation of what it (and notably free exchanges) would have led to in the absence of the causes of the "failures" such as lack of information, transaction costs, or difficulties of excluding from the benefits of goods. These putative free choices or agreements are "liberal social contracts" (see Section 6 of Chapter 3).[12] On the distributive grounds, process-freedom can at least as rationally be understood as not implying individuals' a priori full ownership of the value of their own given productive capacities (see Chapters 3 and 6). This leads to a distributive structure with various possible levels of redistribution from full self-ownership.

The specification required by the basic rights approach is different. These rights state the individuals' possibility to do a number of things. This possibility, however, depends on both the bare right to do it and (other) means available for this action. The stated rights can be restricted to the former bare rights. They have often been interpreted in this way. This has indeed been the source of innumerable cases of criticism addressed to them. For this reason, Marx accused these rights of being only "formal freedom," whereas "real freedom" requires some (other) means in addition. Adding some (other) means constitutes an aspect of the distribution of resources. These means have to be found somewhere. However, if the individuals have sufficient incomes, they can buy these other means when they want to use these rights. But with the classical assimilation of process-freedom with full self-ownership, the individuals who can receive only little or nothing from the labour market may not have sufficient income. Then, the only possible way that poor people can benefit from basic rights is that these rights are understood as implying some (other) means. However, we have seen that another interpretation of full process-freedom – arguably a stricter and sounder one – implies the possibility of other distributions, notably excluding poverty (for societies with sufficient overall productivity). Then, the definition of basic rights need not a priori include these (other) means. They indeed have better not so as to respect consumers' sovereignty in their choice of acting, consuming, and spending their income in using these rights (other means given for free constitute subsidized consumption). This is

---

[12] And a full develoment in Kolm 1985a.

also a necessary condition for the Pareto efficiency of the allocation of these other means (this efficiency is notably violated by equal other means for individuals with different tastes). Then, basic rights will be the bare and strict rights only.

This has the further important consequence of making basic rights nonrival and copossible. Indeed, when various acts using basic rights (of any nature and any holder) cannot jointly exist, this impossibility can be attributed to issues about the allocation of means used along with these rights, which may have to be sufficiently specified (they may, for instance, be rights to do such thing at such place and time). With such specifications, basic rights can all exist jointly without limitation. They will always be used at satiety. Acts will be limited by desires, costs, and complementary (other) means and their costs, but not by basic freedoms. One consequence is that the classical and age-old statement that basic freedoms should be "equal for all and maximal" while having priority over other considerations is hardly meaningful (the bare rights can be full for all, and then they are trivially both equal and maximal).

6. WHY SOCIAL FREEDOM?

The requirement of social freedom can be justified either directly or indirectly from its requirement by unanimity properly defined or from the institutional status of basic rights.

One may directly appreciate that social freedom means that no individual is forcefully submitted to the will of others as individuals or through institutions. This is a most common position nowadays, and it has clear reasons. Free exchanges respect social freedom and constitute important manifestations of it; they constitute a mutual interference but not a forceful one, since they have to be freely accepted by all participants. With social freedom, individuals' rights that may limit or constrain others' actions are personal protection or result from past free and freedom-respecting actions or agreements (the theory of full process-freedom investigates this notion – see Chapter 3).[13] Social freedom thus bans domination in interpersonal relations. This constitutes a relational equality. There can of course be free exchanges with much de facto inequality in means of exchange and in the result. However, low incomes that can result from such situations can be corrected by the distributive transfers whose possibility has been noted, which allocate rent-rights in given capacities. Not being forcefully submitted to the will of someone else is often a matter of dignity and self-respect. And not so bullying other persons is a respect for them as persons and for mankind in them.

Indirect justifications of social freedom rest on unanimity or institutions. They can refer to full process-freedom with emphasis on the market system, or to basic rights. For instance, full process-freedom developing in a free market with corrections of "market failures" de facto is the only way of guaranteeing Pareto efficiency in a complex economy; and the principle of unanimity requires Pareto efficiency.

---

[13] And Kolm 1985a.

As for the classical basic rights, their rule seems to be unanimously desired in present-day modern societies (they may be desired by everyone who sufficiently considers the issue). At any rate, each individual wants to be able to act and to reap the intended benefits from her action without other people's or institutions' forceful interference. This even is an intrinsic necessity from the fact that she wants to perform her chosen action aiming at these effects. Then, this individual's judgment about justice, which has to be impartial by definition, wants this process-freedom (or basic rights) for everyone, whether this judgment is actually held or is notionally built up from the individual's other views (as presented in Chapter 21). In any event, the individuals want general social freedom if this situation does not bring in other shortcomings. These vices cannot be inefficiencies with the noted corrections of "market failures." Possible distributive injustice and notably poverty can be avoided by the noted possible distributions. Basic rights have also been reproached by their individualism, and market societies, in addition, can rely on and foster selfishness, insincerity, hostile competitive relations, or labour alienation. These aspects, however, are not implied by social freedom but only permitted by it, and their seriousness can be very diverse: they only depend on the chosen application. Process-freedom, indeed, permits gift-giving, free cooperatives, and communities and cultures that respect individuals' basic freedoms. However, the efficiency of markets basically rests on self-interested behaviour. This can constitute an important social dilemma leading to various arrangements for activities of different types.[14] Yet, both alternatives – selfish exchange and altruistic giving – are ways of using process-freedom, and this issue is not about the existence of this liberty, but only about the choice of actions and relations that use it.

Finally, basic rights are the basis of the constitutions of "democratic" countries. Whether or not this suffices to make them moral, it makes them compulsory. Moreover, the distribution and taxes that they imply thus are the constitutional ones. Hence, their mere derivation constitutes an important exercise.

7. OUTLINE

The liberal theory and process-freedom on the one hand, and classical basic rights, on the other hand – basically the two faces of the same coin – are considered in Chapters 3 and 4, respectively. In Chapter 3, the process-liberal ethics, the concept of process-freedom, the theory of full process-freedom, and the corrective "liberal social contracts" are presented in short reminders (Sections 1, 2, 5, and 6). The way in which process-freedom permits redistributing the rent of given capacities, and thus differs from full self-ownership, is discussed in Section 3. And its restricting distributive policy to the allocation of the given resources, as does Pareto-efficiency, is the topic of Section 4.

The nature of classical basic rights, their relation with process-freedom, and their importance and history are outlined in Section 1 of Chapter 4. Section 2

---

[14] This constitutes a main topic of *The Good Economy, General Reciprocity* (Kolm 1984a).

focuses on the reasons for endorsing these rights. Social freedom is usually, and historically, defended or argued for under its form of the classical basis rights. They are, indeed, specifically presented as moral stances, and more developed defenses have followed this way. It thus is adequate that full justifications also focus on this form. The analysis will specify and elaborate the general structure of the reasons for social freedom.

In brief, basic rights are the basis of "democratic" constitutions, and hence, they are legal and their respect is compulsory. They can be seen as self-evident because they mean nonviolence and are needed for benefiting from the other goods. They mean nondomination and are required for dignity. They are a condition for "the pursuit of happiness," self-realization, and the existence of agency. Respecting them is treating others "also as ends" (Kant). Most people want these rights in modern societies. At least, each wants them for herself, and has to because this means wanting to be able to do what one wants. Then, this individual's actual or notional conception of justice, being impartial by nature, should equally want them for everyone. However, these rights have also been criticized. They may not be copossible. Applied in the free market, they may lead to unjust distribution and poverty, to inefficiencies of various types, and to selfishness and hostile relations. And they in general are individualistic. However, these rights are copossible if they are conceived as "formal freedoms," otherwise accompanied by other means (possibly bought with incomes). With the proper conception of process-freedom, they permit distribution or redistribution of a certain type and hence the relief of poverty, and the correction of inefficiencies. And they do not preclude giving, altruism, and communities that respect them (adjustments between these attitudes and market efficiency only constitute choices within the scope of basic rights).

Finally, the political, fiscal, and distributive requirements of classical basic rights are considered in Section 3 of Chapter 4. The original historical texts imply both benefit taxation for the financing of public goods – which is in line with "liberal social contracts" – and redistribution according to capacity to earn of the type obtained here.

Appendix A. A NOTE ON OTHER CONCEPTS OF FREEDOM: NEGATIVE, POSITIVE, AND MENTAL FREEDOMS

The concept and term of "negative freedom" has often been used (e.g., by Hobbes, Rousseau, Kant, Bentham, Constant, John Stuart Mill, Isaiah Berlin), but in different senses. For Berlin, it is freedom from others' interference. This becomes the notion of social freedom used here if it is specified that this interference uses force – and not only, say, proposals of exchange –, that this applies to interference with intended consequences of actions (hence the theory of derived legitimate rights) – Berlin may accept these specifications – , and if this freedom is conceived of as fully satisfied in the absence of further qualification. However, negative freedom is more often given a more extensive meaning, adding the various possibilities and means of action (that is, means-freedom – see Chapter 3). All these authors, moreover, consider negative freedom because they want to oppose it to another kind of freedom that they label "positive." By this adjective, they never mean the other means of action, including income, goods, or capacities, as some economists have believed. In general, and precisely for Kant (and Rousseau), positive freedom is the possibility of the will ruled by reason to have its way. Obstacles to this possibility are of two kinds. One is made of the constraints in the large sense, certainly including others' interferences and limits or scarcities of means of all kinds, external as well as capacities. The corresponding possibilities constitute "negative freedom" in the extensive sense. However, the most interesting (for Kant) obstacle to willful reason is the individuals' "inclinations" – say their tastes and desires. Overcoming these latter obstacles constitutes "autonomy." Hence, Kantian "positive freedom" is extended "negative freedom" and "autonomy." John Stuart Mill is not far from that, but he emphasizes that this positive freedom permits the will to choose a personality and the corresponding lifestyle. Hence, for these authors, negative freedom is a condition of positive freedom – and negative freedom is understood extensively. Berlin acknowledges this classical meaning of positive freedom, but he is particularly concerned with transformations of this notion into justifications for violating individuals' negative freedom in his restricted sense, and hence social freedom, in the name of a "superior freedom," be it the usual arguments of totalitarian ideologies or other reasons such as a reference to a social contract (a putative, imaginary free agreement – Berlin did not know about the "liberal social contracts" noted in Chapter 3).

Finally, the mental freedom of transforming one's own mind is not necessarily the painful war on desires envisioned by the pietist Kant. Controlling one's desires can take many forms, including the careful control of their birth taught by advanced Buddhism. Moreover, mental freedom can also form desires, aspirations, or preferences in such a way that they do not seek or prefer the impossible. Then, constraints become nonbinding and negative freedom in any sense becomes irrelevant (although one may still fight oppression as a defense of dignity). This is a central idea and ideal of various "wisdoms," of Oriental philosophy, of Hellenistic philosophies (notably stoicism), and of religions in their recommendation of accepting or willing what is ("willing God's will"). Philosophical Buddhism offers the most advanced psychological theory and mental technique of this approach.[15]

These various conceptions of positive and mental freedom will not be relevant for determining the structure of global distributive justice (Parts I to III). However, they have a relevance for the topic of Part IV. Indeed, the determination of the degree of redistribution by the methods of endogenous social choice will require considering individuals' impartial conceptions of justice. This is Kantian in various ways. First, these individuals' views can certainly be seen as a requirement of reason. Moreover, the solution results from an intrinsic property of the concept of justice, impartiality, which is a necessary, a priori, and analytic property of the concept. In fact, impartiality and the "impartialization" of individuals' judgments, on the one hand, and Kant's own universalization in his "categorical imperative," on the other hand, are concepts with some similarity. Moreover, these individuals' views of justice are a priori in conflict with their own self-interests (as rational autonomous judgments conflict

---

[15] See Kolm 1982a.

with "inclinations"). However, individuals may not actually have such views of justice. These evaluations may then have to be notionally constructed, and the result may have to be more or less imposed to the actual individuals or to some of them. This then belongs to Berlin's conception of imposed positive freedom. However, the evaluation is derived from individuals' own views: this would be endogenous social positive freedom (social contracts – which will also find a role – also are in a sense, but less so because of the "exogenous" choice of the "state of nature" and rule of agreement).

3

The liberal theory

1. PROCESS LIBERALISM

"This is mine because I made it or bought it with well-earned money": This view expresses the common sentiment about distributive justice that underlies and founds the moral theory of process liberalism. There, legitimate ownership results from action, basically from free action.[1] The "well-earned" qualificative indicates the time-regressive structure of the theory. Note, however, that people have neither made nor bought their own given capacities with which they produce or earn.

Process liberalism is a moral theory in social ethics, which is the moral valuation or hypostasis (or moral secular enshrinement) of process-freedom; that is, it consists of holding that individuals should be free to act and benefit from the consequences of their acts without forceful interference. Process liberalism has an important place in almost all societies because it defends a basic freedom and right. Moreover, process liberalism is the basic and central social-ethical theory of the modern world, a place and role it has been holding for the last couple of centuries. It is demanded by the classical "basic rights", notably under the form of the respect of property. The full process-freedom it wants amounts to social freedom, although in focussing on some aspects and some applications, notably in the field of the economy. It will shortly be reminded that a consequence of process-freedom is the legitimacy of property rights acquired according to its rule, and of the corresponding free exchanges and free markets.

In European languages other than present-day English, and in the English anterior to the twentieth century, process liberalism is just called "liberalism," implying, notably, economic liberalism. However, present-day English has given another sense to the terms "liberal" and "liberalism," one implying notable

---

[1] In a strict and classical sense of the term, action implies freedom. Someone forced to do something valuable may also be entitled to this product because of her effort, possibly more or less as a compensation for its painfulness, or for the use of time or of energy, but this is another question.

equalizing redistributions and roles for government intervention. Whence the use of the qualified term "process liberalism" for denoting the "liberalism of the ancients" or of other European languages. This linguistic history is quite ironic, though, since we will see that the classical liberal theory's belief that process-freedom implies an absence of redistribution and a minimal state restricted to the direct protection of the corresponding rights is unwarranted (this theory, somehow the descent of John Locke's, has been developed by a long tradition of philosophers, economists, lawyers, and legal processes). We will see that, rather, full process-freedom can rationally be understood as permitting distributive policies and requiring much larger roles for the public sector, although with quite specific structures and principles. Hence, in the end, the logically most defensible conception of the liberal theory in the non-modern-English (former English and non-English) sense turns out to be a form of liberalism in the sense of present-day English, although a very specific form.

The topic of this part of this study concerns the distributive implications of full process-freedom and its relation with basic rights and social efficiency. It does not include the repetition of this classical theory, although the shortest possible reminder is proposed. I have developed the full logic of this theory in another work,[2] with discussions, comparisons, and applications. Basically and generally, however, the theory of full process-freedom results from the long tradition analyzing it over a couple of centuries, in the abundant "liberal literature," in philosophy, economics, theoretical legal studies, and applied law. This includes the theory of property rights and of the legitimacy of free exchange. Each piece of this literature analyzes a more or less extended or restricted aspect of this theory or of its application.[3]

Section 2 presents the nature and situation of process-freedom: its definition, its relation with the points of view of social freedom and of basic rights, the place of exchange and of liberal rights, the relation with various historical conceptions, and the relation with allocation from responsibility and merit. The essential points of the classical theory of full process-freedom are summarized in Section 3. Section 4 shows that process-freedom implies particular rights in capacities. It implies that individuals are the owners or the tenants of themselves (self-ownership or self-tenancy). Self-tenancy implies that other agents can have rights in the rent of the capacity – i.e., the value of its availability. Process-freedom does not imply full self-ownership as classical process liberalism has it. Then, equal sharing of the value of capacities with the proper measures yields the solution. Section 5

---

[2] *The Liberal Social Contract* (*Theory and Practice of Liberalism*), 1985a.

[3] Apart from the noted book, a very brief summary can be found in my *Modern Theories of Justice* (1996a, Chapter 6). In the recent literature in English, Nozick (1974) emphasizes the time-regress structure of process-free legitimate ownership, but he notably bypasses liberal social contracts (see Section 6) and the distributional issue considered here, which constitute the two bases of the process-liberal public sector and public finances.

shows that the same conclusion obtains in considering the policy: either process-freedom or Pareto efficiency (and hence, unanimity) requires it to be restricted to the allocation of given resources. Finally, Section 6 summarizes the principle of the "liberal social contract," which proposes extending the principle of process-freedom to the enforcement of what its outcome would have been in the absence of the various obstacles it meets in the classical situations of "failures" of markets or agreements.

2. PROCESS-FREEDOM

The social ethics of freedom crucially rests on distinctions about the nature, impact, and origin of constraints. The basic conceptual distinction necessary for understanding both the question of basic rights and the ethics of distribution is the following, whose specific application will constitute most of the present topic. An agent's *action* is a set of *acts* using *means* for an *aim* (or for joint aims).[4] This structure entails the basic threefold distinction of freedoms. (1) *Means-freedom* is the availability of means. (2) *Act-freedom* is reduced by forceful interference with acts, which use otherwise given means. (3) For a given act with given means, *aim-freedom* is reduced by forceful interference with the intended aim, an interference that could be imposed at any point of the causal chain relating the act to the aim (including directly on the intended aim). For instance, I may freely work (act) with my tools and capacities (means) in order to earn an income (or to obtain consumption or satisfaction from it). Then, discriminating limitation of my right to work would restrict my act-freedom, an income tax limits my aim-freedom, and my properties and capacities determine my means-freedom. The domain of possibilities relevant to the agent results from freedoms of all three types.[5] *Process-freedom* is defined as act-freedom plus aim-freedom. The considered interferences can be produced by individuals or institutions. Note that the understanding of "means" is restricted here so as not to include act-freedom (and aim-freedom) or the rights that secure them.

The difference between this presentation and that of social freedom or of basic rights is a matter of emphasis due to the use of the concepts. Act-freedom is clearly present in all three cases. Aim-freedom, by contrast, is emphasized in process-freedom because one wants to emphasize the issue of entitlement from (free) action. By contrast, it is more implicit in the classical formulations of basic rights. However, it exists in the respect of property that can be obtained by action (respecting others' rights) and notably exchange. As another instance, freedom

---

[4] The theory of action is a classical and main topic of psychological philosophy. It is essential for the theory of justice and is briefly summarized in Kolm 1996a, Chapter 1 (an extensive analyzis is provided in Kolm 1982a [1994]).

[5] An important part of the theory of rights results from the discussion of the nature of means and of their relation with act-freedom (see Kolm 1985a, 1996a Chapter 4).

of expression would not exist if one can speak or write but in such a way that the audience cannot hear or does not receive the writings. The emphasis on consequences (aim-freedom) will also permit the explicit building of the theory of secondary rights (not basic ones or the initial distribution of given resources) legitimized by their resulting from past process-freedom in individual action of free exchanges or agreements. Pointing out means is also necessary for considering the roles of acquired or received rights and of capacities, and for distinguishing them from act-freedom (a basic right). By contrast, the protective or defensive right to security for oneself and one's (legitimate) properties is not explicitly emphasized in the formulation of process-freedom. It is implicitly present, however: it suffices to consider that a particular act can be that of living safely, quietly, and undisturbed using one's legitimate rights. And a legitimate right resulting from past free action (individual or in free exchange or agreement) is protected by aim-freedom applied to this action.

When individuals' acts or their consequences can limit those of others one way or the other, the question is solved in using two types of items: mutual agreements and the respect of rights – most of which are consequences of past acts or agreements. Agents can obtain others' agreements in exchange for some other acts, which can include transfers of rights (including property rights). Hence, process-freedom in interaction means respecting the pending, relevant rights, and free, unanimous agreements, possibly through exchanges.

Such free and voluntary exchanges or agreements constitute a mutual interference, but not a forceful one, since one is not forced to buy, sell, or agree. Hence, they are admitted (and are of prime importance). In fact, offering someone the terms of an exchange that respects her rights and freedoms (hence not including a threat of violating them) augments her domain of free choice rather than restricts it. For each participant, the result of the agreement or exchange constitutes the intended consequence of her action of agreeing or exchanging, and others' interference is not forceful since the agent can refuse. Giving is also a nonforceful interference and thus is admitted; it also extends the receiver's domain of free choice (possible social pressure for giving constitutes another topic).

For developing into a full theory, process-freedom should be completed by a theory of the legitimacy of the agents' means. The consideration of time permits the derivation of part of the solution from process-freedom itself. Indeed, some means at a given time can be the intended consequences of acts in process-freedom at previous dates, either individual acts or agreements, and notably exchanges. These means appear as secondary or derived rights. However, there will remain to define rights in a priori given resources (considered in Chapter 5). If the set of existing rights is "complete," then agents' acts respecting these rights cannot forcefully interfere. These rights then constitute the basis of free agreements about using or changing them, in providing, for such agreements, individuals' means and states of reference or of threat (that is, the existing state if no agreement is reached).

The distinction of act, means, and aim has various echoes in a number of classical views. Aim-freedom is probably a case of Aristotle's and Plato's *commutative justice*, which rewards people's "voluntary" acts "in proportion" to "merit" ("geometric equality"), and is in particular to be applied in the sphere of exchange (see Plato's *The Laws* and Aristotle's *Nicomachean* and *Eudemian Ethics*). The various classical basic rights state act-freedoms, but imply aim-freedom, as we have noticed (in particular, in the explicit right to property when property results from exchange). Classical basic rights were criticized by Robespierre, Marx, and others for not guaranteeing sufficient means and for being individualistic. Marx accused them of being "formal" freedom, and he called "real freedom" process-freedom – and to begin with act-freedom – along with sufficient means (or means-freedom). Process liberalism justifies the ownership of acquired means by their resulting from past process-freedom in producing, exchanging, or receiving as a gift (legitimacy from process-free acquisition). The issue of distinguishing a right to freely act from (other) means is a crucial one in the theory of rights.[6] Isaiah Berlin's (1958, 1969) "negative freedom" is described as protection from forceful interference. It certainly is act-freedom in general. However, Berlin also adds, at a point, that his negative freedom includes "classical economic rights." This suggests that he probably more generally means process-freedom.[7]

The ethics of process liberalism rests on entitlement from action. In its standard conception, an action is a set of acts with an aim or several joint aims; it is, for the agent, intentional, free, voluntary, willful (and meaningful). Allocation justified by freedom (rather than by general causality) should more specifically entitle the agent to the *intended* consequences of her action. The discussions that this qualification can raise – notably concerning issues of by-products, responsibility, and information – are not needed for the present topic of macrojustice.

Process-freedom relates to the other allocative concepts based on freedom. Aim-freedom could be derived from the notion of *responsibility* since the agent may be held responsible for intended consequences of her acts and may be entitled to what she is responsible for.[8] However, the notion of responsibility can also be used for deriving a different and opposite conclusion: since the agent cannot be held responsible for her given capacities, she may not be fully responsible for the consequences of her acts, which depend on these capacities. The point is that responsibility is not a fully defined criterion, but only a class of judgments assigning according to action (including the absence of a required act). It needs other considerations or principles to be made precise. Aim-freedom is one of

---

[6] See Kolm 1996a, Chapter 4. See also the discussion of the nonrivalry among basic rights – and hence of the logical possibility of full process-freedom – with a sufficient definition of the allocation of means in Chapter 4.

[7] A right such as free expression remains unspecified in Berlin's description, although Berlin doubtlessly endorses it.

[8] See the discussion in Kolm 2001a.

them. Justifying assignment by responsibility is in part a tautology, because the concept of responsibility is then chosen for this use, and the problem is to specify it. However, the point is then to direct attention to a type of justification, relating the assignment to the agent's actions. This justification relates, in the end, to some aspects of the direct justifications for basic rights discussed in Chapter 4, notably those using concepts of the self, of the existence of agency, and of dignity (the main justification of basic rights, however, will rest on their proposed actual or necessary consensual endorsement).

If the action is somewhat painful, aim-freedom is a concept of *immanent merit.* "Immanent" means that the benefit is the result of the action rather than being some specifically chosen reward. The reference is to merit, rather than to desert, because process-freedom entitles the individual to the effects of her capacities used by the action, as is shortly pointed out.[9]

3. FULL PROCESS-FREEDOM

Full process-freedom consists of the general absence of restriction of process-freedom in a society. More generally, the adjective "full" will mean that a principle is completely applied throughout society. Full process-freedom thus implies that people do not violate others' process-freedom, that is, do not forcefully interfere with the acts of others, or with the intended consequences of their acts – notably of past acts – when these acts themselves abide by this rule.[10] In this sense, "your freedom ends where the others' begins." If necessary, this obligation should be enforced as the protection of the corresponding rights of the people who would directly be affected. Among these consequences of past acts are the rights established by various past agreements (note that a property right, in particular, is a bundle of rights concerning an object). The time dimension of society thus is very important for process liberalism – the social ethics valuing process-freedom. Act-freedom includes safety (the particular "act" to exist unmolested), and full process-freedom implies all classical basic rights, including rights to hold property resulting from

---

[9] For this classical distinction, see for instance Vlastos (1962), Lucas (1993), and Pojman and McLeod (1999). For example, the notion of "meritocracy" emphasizes the rulers' abilities. See Kolm 2001a.

[10] The moral constraint of respecting the process-freedom of others constitutes the difference between process-liberalism and theories such as James Buchanan's "public choice" and Murray Rothbart's "libertarianism." For these other theories, the social constraints on an individual's acts are not others' process-freedom but others' force. The freedom they consider is "natural freedom" in the sense of classical theories of the social contract (although not in the sense, also sometimes used, of "natural rights" whose respect implies full process-freedom). For Buchanan, this cannot be otherwise because people, including those in the public and political sector, are not sufficiently moral for a moral rule to be implemented. His theory thus is not a moral theory in the ordinary sense of the term (he would deem such theories to be unapplicable), but a descriptive and explanatory principle and theory. There, the respect of basic rights can only be the terms of a truce – called the "constitution." Putting all these theories in the same bag labelled "libertarianism" misses the most essential distinctions and issues in social ethics. On these questions, see Kolm 1996a, Chapter 13.

full process-freedom, and right to exchange – indeed, the basic intent of these rights is that they constitute full process-freedom (see the discussion in Chapter 4). Expectations of (forceful) restrictions of process-freedom – for instance credible threats of such acts – that influence actual acts are also forbidden by the rule of full process-freedom. So is fraud and deceit in exchange or agreement (they amount to theft). Process-free legitimate rights are the rights that result from anterior full process-freedom.[11] Process-liberal rights are the rights defined by full process-freedom (hence, at a moment of time, they consist of process-free legitimate rights plus complete process-freedom for present acts respecting the rule).

However, valued items do not all result from human action. The others are given resources, classically called "natural" resources. The principle of full process-freedom per se does not allocate the initial rights in these resources (although we will see that it implies some rights in human resources). When these initial rights are defined, process-freedom can define derived or secondary rights in these resources if they are transformed or transferred by exchange, sale, or giving. Hence, a process-liberal ethical theory values full process-freedom and defines initial rights in given resources. Some principles for the allocation of these initial rights make a partial use of process-freedom. This is, for instance, the case of first occupancy and of general agreement about the allocation. Yet, process-freedom per se does not suffice. For instance, the two principles just noted are different ones. And others are possible, such as equal sharing, giving to the needy, and so on. A reminder of the essence of this general issue is proposed in Chapter 5.

Then, a process-liberal moral theory associates full process-liberalism with an allocation of the given resources (of the initial rights in them). At each moment of time, individuals' means result from past process-freedom and past allocation of given resources, and from the present allocation of new given resources; and individuals' rights consist of these means and process-freedom.

If time is kept implicit, the scheme is that of an allocation of given ("natural") resources, over which free action and interaction respecting social freedom develop, including free exchange (a way of seeing things classical in economists' "general equilibrium" theory). The allocation of resources is, more specifically, that of the rights of various types concerning the given resources. Indeed, these rights are varied, and the differences in their allocation will have a decisive importance as concerns the central case of the human resources. Actually, a number of rules for allocating given resources depend on individuals' actions and on society's past life (see Chapter 5) – contrary to the classical and standard presentation of economic theory. This, however, will not intervene in the basic scheme for macrojustice, although the prices of the resources, which depend on all the economic life, will determine the corresponding transfers (the relevant prices will be wage rates).

---

[11] In full process-freedom, past violations require rectification (or a statute of limitation whose choice, however, has to be defined). The logic of this paragraph is developed in detail in Kolm 1985a.

4. RIGHTS IN CAPACITIES IMPLIED BY PROCESS-FREEDOM

4.1. Self-tenancy

The allocation of given resources raises a particular problem when applied to human resources or capacities. This issue turns out to be crucial for three reasons already alluded to and fully explained in Chapter 5. First, these capacities produce most of the economic value and, notably, vastly more than the other natural resources. Second, the allocation of many other natural resources is considered as issues in local justice or microjustice. Finally, the initial allocation of most of these other resources were made in the past, and their present correction is largely an impracticable policy. Given capacities are of various types, including productive capacities, capacities to enjoy, and capacities to learn in education or training (see Chapter 5).[12]

Capacities are particular resources as concerns freedom. Acting is a case of using one's capacities. Act-freedom amounts to the right to use one's capacities without forceful interference. Aim-freedom is entitlement to the consequence or product of this use. It thus entitles the agent to the effect or product of the services of these capacities used by the agent's act or mobilized by it. Hence, these services are fully available to this individual, who is entitled to what she chooses to do with them.

Consider, however, any asset that is a means of action for some agent. This agent chooses to use it and benefits from this use. Two alternative kinds of rights permit this situation: ownership and tenancy. Either the agent owns the asset or she hires it. In the latter case, she pays a *rent* for the availability of this asset for her to use and benefit from this use. By this hiring and paying this rent, she acquires the *use-right* and *benefit-right* of this asset. The receiver of the rent has the corresponding *rent-right*.[13] In a large market with many assets of this kind, this rent depends on the quality of the asset but not on the specific use by the user.

The agent who receives the rent is usually the owner of this asset. However, in many societies and laws, particular assets that have a particular, specific, and large importance for certain users are submitted to some right of the latter to be the tenant of this asset. This agent is thus entitled to this tenancy; in other words, she has a tenancy-right in this asset. This correspondingly restricts the right of the owner who, however, receives the rent, that is, who keeps the rent-right. For instance, housing or farming land and building are often submitted to tenant's

---

[12] And, more completely, Kolm 1996a, Chapter 6.

[13] The right to use and benefit from use without paying a rent is also a possible use of a right of usufruct. However, a usufruct right can also be used only in receiving the rent. Hence, the concept of usufruct per se does not produce the cut that is relevant for the present purpose. Rights in assets and their application to human assets will be considered more closely in Chapter 6.

rights of this kind. These rights can be more or less extensive, such as limitations of dismissal, long duration of hiring contracts, or obligation to rent out to former users or to neighbours. Such rights to hire tend of course to be the larger, the more important (or vital) the asset is for the tenant. In the limiting case, the tenant has in full a right to be tenant, a right of tenancy. Then, the other agent can hardly be called owner in the full sense of the term. She merely has the right to receive the rent; that is, she has this rent-right. Moreover, the rent-right in an asset can be shared among several right holders (they can have shares in this asset's rent). Full ownership of the asset amounts to jointly having tenancy-right and rent-right (plus rights to sell, give away, alienate, dismember, and destroy). An agent can also be the tenant and have part of the rent-right: she then is owner for a part and tenant for the rest.

An individuals' capacities are assets that are particularly important for her. This constitutes a limiting and extreme case of the situation just described. More specifically, we have noticed that process-freedom amounts to having the use-rights and benefit-rights in one's capacities. Yet, it does not imply also having the corresponding rent-rights. Therefore, process-freedom (hence, basic rights or social freedom) amounts to individuals being at least the tenants of themselves, to their having the right of tenancy – the tenancy-right – in themselves, that is, to their having a right of self-tenancy. However, it does not imply that they are the full owners of themselves; that is, it does not imply complete self-ownership. In fact, there can be self-ownership for some capacities but not for others, or for only part of a capacity. Then, for the rest, there is only self-tenancy and the individual pays the corresponding rent to holders of the corresponding rent-rights, which are "external rent-rights."

4.2. Rent-rights in capacities

Process-freedom thus determines the allocation of use-rights and benefit-rights in capacities, but not that of the rent-rights. The rent depends on the quality of the capacity (such as its productivity for a productive capacity), but it generally does not depend on the specific use of the capacity chosen by the individual – at least, for productive capacities, when there is a corresponding large labour market. The benefit an individual can derive from using a capacity of hers depends on the quality of this capacity. Hence, as a result of process-freedom, which implies individuals' use-rights and benefit-rights in their capacities, individuals are more or less favoured by nature (and family influence) according to the quality of their capacities. However, these inequalities and handicaps can be compensated, without impairing process-freedom, by a different allocation of rent-rights. For instance, the less endowed can have external rent-rights in others' capacities.

We will see that, as concerns macrojustice, individuals should have complete self-ownership of their capacities to enjoy (eudemonistic capacities) and of a notable part of their productive capacities (i.e., capacities that can be used for production), from a principle of unanimity in judgment (in Chapter 5 for eudemonistic capacities and in Part IV for productive capacities).[14] Of course, capacities created by the individual herself in education, learning, or training are fully her own from aim-freedom and only given capacities can be the object of others' rights (but learning capacities are largely given, and various circumstances of education have other origins). For the rest of given productive capacities, there can be external rent-rights held by others, possibly through distributive or redistributive institutions.

The process-free individual, being the tenant of herself, has to pay the corresponding rent to these right holders. Conversely, however, she may herself hold some external rent-right in others' productive capacities, directly or through the intermediary of institutions who receive the rent-rights and redistribute them. The balance will be positive for some individuals, and negative for others. In fact, the scheme that will be obtained amounts to each individual owning the output of the same given amount of labour of each other – a set of mutual rent-rights which constitutes a kind of general labour reciprocity. In the global result, the less productive individuals receive and the more productive ones pay. The means of paying can be obtained in any manner, such as from receipts of such transfers or from lower expenditures of consumption, including lower leisure, that is, higher labour (using productive capacities). The net payers will be the more productive individuals, hence those who need the least labour for earning each amount of income. There will thus be some transfer of income from individuals who can earn it easily to those who can only earn it with much labour. On the whole, moreover, the labour necessary for paying this net transfer will be a fraction of the labour chosen by the individuals, for all paying individuals. These receipts or payments are based on individuals' given productive capacities, and hence are lump-sum (i.e., they do not depend on individuals' actions, although these actions globally determine the prices of these capacities, which are the wage rates). These receipts permit the individual to buy consumption, or leisure through lower labour. They are means to these ends. When negative (as payments), they have the same nature in manifesting given liabilities.

An individual who is free to work more or less can choose between income and consumption, on the one hand, and labour or leisure (the complement of labour), on the other hand. The domain of possible choice of these two items can be said to describe "output-freedom." It depends on the individuals' wage rate and productivity, and also on the total net transfer received by the individual or yielded by her (precisely, output-freedom is a means-freedom for the choice of consumption or leisure, but not one for production as such as productive capacities taken by themselves are). In the foregoing distributive scheme, individuals

---

[14] The relation of this result with equal sharing of capacities and its dependency on the measuring rod chosen for measuring capacities are shortly discussed.

receive the more transfer, or yield the less, the less productive they are. Hence, these transfers provide a compensation for differences in productivity. This tends to "balance" the output-freedoms (although the domains of choice cannot coincide when productivities differ). Chapters 8 and 12 will precisely show this issue.

4.3. Classical process liberalism and full self-ownership

We have seen that, when individual capacities are seen as assets means of action, process-freedom amounts to self-tenancy or self-ownership, or a mix of both. This differs from full self-ownership, for the present purpose, by the fact that there can be external rent-rights. Now, classical process liberalism equates process-freedom with full self-ownership. This is in fact a particular case of the preceding description: that where external rent-rights and the corresponding transfers are zero. More productive individuals then have more output-freedom than when this is not the case, in the sense that they can have more consumption for the same labour or more leisure for the same consumption. Correspondingly, the less productive individuals have less output-freedom than in the other cases, in the sense that they can only have a lower consumption for the same labour or less leisure for the same consumption. This allocation of all the rent of her capacities to each individual constitutes a particular ethical stance. Whether it should hold or not is a consequence of the analyses of Part IV about the "degree of redistribution" (from full self-ownership). The answer may depend on the considered society, but it is not an analytic truth resulting from full process-freedom, as classical process liberalism sees it.

Actually, the classical process-liberal thought just equates self-ownership and full process-freedom without analysis or discussion, although process-freedom, on the one hand, and rent-rights, on the other hand, are a priori quite different things. The implicit crucial conception seems to be that process-freedom would imply freedom from having to pay an external rent-right. However, this also forbids receiving such rent payment. Moreover, this payment is given a priori in the sense that it does not depend on the individual's actions (or their consequences). It belongs to the allocation of given (natural) resources. Requiring this payment is more logically seen as the application of a right that belongs to the realm of means and means-freedom rather than as a forceful interference of the kind that restricts process-freedom. Now, full self-ownership generally implies unambiguous inequality in output-freedom, in the sense that, without the considered transfers (from external rent-rights), an individual more productive than another can have more disposable income or consumption for the same labour, whatever its amount, or needs to work less for obtaining the same disposable income or consumption, whatever its level (these comparisons can theoretically depend on the levels of labour or of income, but this is not the common case). Correspondingly, with full self-ownership, individuals whose capacities are little valued by the

market have low income and consumption; they can starve with hard labour or
with unemployment.

4.4. Sharing the value of capacities

However, full self-ownership is also a kind of equality in means: with this rule, each
individual owns one individual, herself. She also owns the same number of hours
of human life per day or year – if one can say. Hence, the requirement of equality –
a *prima facie* requirement of impartial rationality[15] – can lead to very different results, depending on the unit of measurement of the items to be distributed. It is not
meaningless to morally equate one hour of life (or one life) of various individuals.
It can even have rather deep justifications. It only is one-sided because it bypasses
and neglects the value of the outputs each individual can produce. These outputs
depend on individuals' capacities and can vary much from one individual to the
other. A capacity is a possibility of transforming one of these valued items into the
other: more labour or less leisure into more output, or more leisure at the cost of
less output. Using both these measuring rods for defining an equalization of the
value of individuals' capacities leads to considering some equal amount of leisure
for all, and to equally sharing the outputs of the equal complementary labour.[16]
This is equal labour income equalization. It defines the redistributive transfers,
but the individuals are otherwise free to work and benefit from their earnings,
from process-freedom. The "equalization labour" is only notional. The individuals can choose this labour, and then they have the same disposable income.
However, process-freedom with different productivities forbids that they could
have the same disposable income for the same labour for all amounts of labour.
Full self-ownership is the particular case where the equalization labour vanishes.

4.5. The rationale of process liberalism: Ownership or liberty?

Self-ownership implies process-freedom since it implies freedom to use one's
capacities and to benefit from the use, that is, act-freedom and aim-freedom.
But the converse does not hold without a particular interpretation of process-
freedom as implying freedom from having to pay a rent on oneself, while this is
more rationally seen as a particular solution to the question of the allocation of
means, specifically of the given ("natural") resources.

The classical process-liberal discourse implicitly and awkwardly equates self-
ownership and process-freedom, as if this identity goes without saying, while
these two concepts refer to two different entities: freedom and the allocation of
resources. Since this identity rests on an unwarranted and not the most rational
conception, a question is which of these two concepts constitutes the basis of the

---

[15] See notably Chapter 23 and Kolm 1971 (1998), foreword, Section 5.
[16] Chapter 9 includes a more precise and developed presentation.

process-liberal stance. John Locke only sees, as natural, a right to safety and a right to the product of one's labour, hence act-freedom and aim-freedom, and thus process-freedom (he adds a right to minimal subsistence). One could try to apply, to the ownership of capacities, his theory of the ownership of land: this is right from use (a variant of the principle of first occupancy), "provided there remains enough and as good for others." The result is ambivalent. Ownership from use, with the right to self-use of process-freedom, gives self-ownership. However, the proviso that there "remains as much and as good for others" can be satisfied with self-ownership only if the differences in productivities are not considered. Now, equal labour income equalization allocates productive capacities in giving to each individual "as much" in output terms for the equalization labour and in time of life for the rest. These two parts also allocate to each individual "as good" items, if "goodness" is measured in consumption for the first part and in leisure or time of life for the second. Let us note, finally, that Locke's main concern is social freedom rather than wealth, since the basic aim of his theory is to oppose absolute monarchy – and hence, general people's unfreedom – in proposing another basis of social legitimacy.

Although a number of process liberals doubtlessly have seen self-ownership as the basic value, this may not be the case of the most subtle ones, and, essentially, process-freedom doubtlessly generally became the most basic value starting during the eighteenth century (the founding Declarations of Rights of the late eighteenth century considered freedom rather than self-ownership, and even at a point rejected the latter, as the next chapter will point out). The assimilation with full self-ownership, however, endorsed the inequalities and poverties produced by the markets in the industrial revolution. This led to political reactions either destroying process-freedom and basic rights in all domains, or more moderately affecting process-freedom in the economic field through particular redistributive policies. Both these radical and moderate limitations of process-freedom correspondingly impaired economic efficiency. The initial conceptual confusion should now be corrected in decoupling process-freedom from self-ownership, which can result from the proposed thinner distinctions in rights of and in humans.

5. THE BASE OF TRANSFERS, PROCESS-FREEDOM, AND EFFICIENCY

The previous derivation of the overall distribution has led from process-freedom to the conclusion that the distribuand should be given resources, then successively restricted to capacities, to their rent (for process-freedom), and to that of productive capacities (from a consensus about macrojustice).[17]

This result also obtains from the direct consideration of policy measures that have to respect, protect, or implement process-freedom or Pareto efficiency. Endowed with the dominating coercive power, the government is indeed a main agent

[17] See Chapter 5.

that could violate process-freedom – and preventing this is indeed a main concern of classical process liberalism and of historical statements and declarations of basic rights. Pareto efficiency is a direct requirement of the principle of unanimity. Two types of policy objectives have to be considered. One is the realization of process-freedom and of Pareto-efficiency in the presence of various impediments such as lack of information or of possibilities of agreeing, contracting, and so on, in the various "failures" of free action and notably agreements and markets, such as those elicited by nonexcludable public goods or externalities. This "allocative function" will be the object of the next section. The other public objective consists of the distributive policy considered here.

The issue concerns the base of the transfers, that is, the individual-related items of which they are a function. Two types of such items are considered. "Elastic" items are those that are purposefully influenced by agents' choices and actions.[18] The other items are "inelastic." A transfer based on an inelastic item is "lump-sum." Transfers (taxes or subsidies) based on elastic items induce disincentive or incentive effects that generate Pareto inefficiency.[19] This is one of the most standard results of elementary economic analysis. Hence, Pareto efficiency requires transfers based on inelastic items, or lump-sum.[20]

Moreover, distributive transfers should be justified; they should have a reason. Hence the intended base should have a value. An inelastic item with a value is a given resource (a "natural" resource). The base considered here is the normatively "first best" base. It is not a "proxy" used for instance because it is difficult to know the "first-best" base. The issue of information is to be treated fully in itself as an estimation of the intended base. And it will be shown, in Chapter 10, that, for the application that will be developed, the first-best base is, on average, more readily known than the alternative bases usually considered (they will be wage rates and incomes, respectively).

A tax based on acts or their (intended) consequences constitutes a forceful interference with them. It thus violates process-freedom.[21] Hence, taxes that respect process-freedom should be based on given resources. More precisely, they should be based neither on the use of these resources – which is an act – nor on the resulting benefit, but, therefore, on their a priori availability whose value is their rent. Taxing more individuals better endowed with a resource of a given

---

[18] An agent may aim at influencing some item only because it is the base of some tax or subsidy for her (she otherwise may not care for it or would not influence it).

[19] This includes, of course, indirect bases, such as with a guaranteed income that complements earned income and induces not working. Inefficiency is reduced, but remains, if this is replaced by a negative income tax or an income tax credit.

[20] This does not concern, of course, taxes or subsidies correcting "failures" of action, exchanges, or agreement, such as those "internalizing externalities" or financing nonexcludable public goods whose benefit is related to some choices of the agents. These transfers, indeed, aim notably at correcting inefficiencies, and also at implementing process-freedom through "liberal social contracts" (see Section 6). These issues belong to the allocative function of public intervention.

[21] With the qualification noted in the preceding note and in Section 6.

type amounts to an equalizing redistribution of the value of this resource. Then, consistency a priori demands that individuals who have little of this resource should be correspondingly subsidized, and there will thus be a balanced set of transfers achieving some kind of equalization in the distribution of the value of this resource. The result is to be taken as the basic allocation of resources from which process-free actions and interactions can develop (the lump-sum tax paid by the better endowed is a part of this basic allocation and is to be considered and treated as noted in the discussion of the previous section). This consistency justifies that subsidies are also lump-sum, as also required by Pareto efficiency (whereas subsidies based on elastic items, taken by themselves, do not constitute forceful interference and hence do not violate process-freedom).

These given resources, which are the base of the distributive policy, are then restricted, for process-free macrojustice, and for reasons already alluded to and more fully analyzed in Chapter 5, to the rent-rights of productive capacities, whose equal sharing with the proper measuring rods leads to the described solution.

6. LIBERAL SOCIAL CONTRACTS

A free agreement, exchange, or individual action, which would respect all process-liberal rights, may be prevented or impaired by costs or impossibilities in the domains of information, excluding from benefit, establishing constraints, "transaction," contracting, monitoring, and so on, possibly interferring with strategic interdependence and behaviours. For example, an agreement, among the beneficiaries of a public good, for producing and financing this good may be impossible to implement if excluding someone from the benefits of this good is impossible or too costly. Or this agreement may be impossible to reach because the large number of beneficiaries entails excessive costs of information or transaction. An agreement about external effects – which would "internalize" them – may not be implementable because of costs or impossibility of excluding from the benefit of receiving a positive externality or of having the possibility to create a negative one. It may also not be reached because of various transaction costs. And so on. All the situations labelled "market failures" belong here. Assume now, in addition, that in a particular situation of this type another organization – such as a public sector – can more or less realize what the outcome of the action, exchange, or agreement would have been in the absence of this impediment. For instance, this new agent could more or less estimate what this outcome would have been, and it would impose the result and, possibly, the corresponding payments. This implementation can be seen as the defense of the freedom of the considered action, exchange, or agreement against the obstacles constituted by the impediment, even if it implies actual constraints. Thus, there is a case for demanding this implementation in the name of the initial freedom considered, and in particular of a corresponding process-freedom. This is a moral demand, whose realization requires the considered added agent endowed with more or less of the necessary possibilities in information and coercion, and with the moral motivation or political incentive to implement this rule.[22]

More generally, a putative, imaginary, hypothetical free agreement whose outcome should morally be implemented because of the moral virtue of the freedom of this choice, even though this agreement is not actual and the actual implementation uses coercion, has been called a "social contract" for the last four centuries. The various social contracts differ by the object and, importantly, by the assumed conditions of the putative free agreement. The case just considered is a particular type of social contract. This contract takes place solely among the persons who would or should take part in the agreement, hence who are rather directly concerned by its failing to exist (other social contracts usually consider a priori given large communities such as nations). These persons are real, living persons (in opposition to the particular "original position" contracts, such as Rawls', or to classical social contracts among hypothetical ancestors). The subject of the contract is limited to a particular item (such as the public good and its financing, or the externality), whereas other social contracts choose global government or general rules. Moreover, the putative freedom considered here is that of full process-freedom (hence, it bans threats of violence). Such a putative agreement is called a *liberal social contract*. The set of all liberal social contracts in society is *the Liberal Social Contract*.[23]

This constitutes the process-liberal solution to the question of "market failures" of all types, and to the question of the allocative role of the public sector.[24] It implies, for example, a financing of public goods by the classical principle of benefit taxation, in making precise each beneficiary's contribution (this is what the person would have handed out in a voluntary agreement to produce and finance the public good – assuming notably that exclusion from its benefits were possible).[25] It also implies replacing the impossible free prices of externalities by equivalent transfers based on these effects. Macroeconomic "stabilization" policies also belong here: inflation and global demand are public goods or bads; moreover, wage rigidities lose their basic reason with the considered distributive policy (see Chapter 7). Note that, practically, all taxes and subsidies affecting an individual can be presented jointly to her, and can be fully or partially aggregated. Incidentally, however, fiscal democracy would be the better, the more people know what they specifically pay for (distributive taxes and subsidies will be the forthcoming topic); moreover, the principle of the "liberal social contract" taxes for financing nonexcludable public goods or "internalizing" externalities favors the decentralization of the public

[22] Evaluations corresponding to this kind of information are common practice in applied public economics.
[23] One can also add the common case of individual actions when this individual lacks relevant information that the better informed agent has but cannot sufficiently transmit: the latter agent can impose to the former the action she would have chosen if she had the information.
[24] See Kolm 1985a, 1987a, 1987b, 1996a (Chapters 5 and 13).
[25] See Kolm 1987e, f, g, h, 1989c.

sector into specific, specialized public organizations which can be autonomously financed by the corresponding taxes.

Our present topic, however, is not this allocative role of the public sector but solely its possible distributive role. Yet, one aspect of this distribution is, more deeply, allocative, and will not explicitly concern us here. This concerns cases of gift giving. Indeed, gift giving redistributes; as a free act respecting others' freedom, it constitutes an application of process-freedom; and it must sometimes be implemented through a liberal social contract. This can happen for a reason of information about people who need the aid. It also happens in the important case of "collective givings," where several people want to give to the same ones for improving their situations which become nonexcludable public goods for the givers (exclusion would mean suppressing the information about the receiver's situation, and this suppresses the actual desire to give).[26]

[26] See the references of the previous note, Kolm 2000a, and also Chapter 11.

4

Free and equal in rights

1. CLASSICAL BASIC RIGHTS AND FULL PROCESS-FREEDOM

"Men are free and equal in rights." The rights in which men are so declared equal are the classical basic rights, or simply basic rights, or basic freedoms. They constitute the legal and social ethical basis of modern democratic societies (although the term "democracy" does not refer to their main part, the "rights of man," but only to their political part, the "rights of the citizen"). They constitute the base, core, and fountainhead of their constitutions – they are commonly presented as their preamble. Hence, they constitute, in these societies, the most basic and general rule of the law, its prime source, and the most basic and general rule of the relations between persons and between them and institutions. This does not prevent a number of violations of these rights, strictly understood, by lawful rules in these societies. We will notably find examples of this fact in fiscal systems, and we will also see that these violations are not necessary for their very purposes – such as realizing a just redistribution. We will also see, moreover, that these violations also reveal an imperfect application of the political basic rights because they induce inefficiencies in Pareto's sense, hence a lack of respect for the principle of unanimity, whereas this principle is implied by the democratic participation required by these rights.

The basic rights are individuals' freedom to act and to benefit from the consequences of their actions, without forceful interference, when their acts respect others' such freedom. "Acting" covers here any activity or "inactivity," and a brief discussion of the role of political rights is shortly proposed. Basic rights thus are a presentation or an avatar of social freedom. Hence, they amount to process-freedom, and their being the general rule amounts to full process-freedom. The difference is essentially a matter of presentation. Process-freedom is a theoretical, abstract, and general concept, and full process-freedom denotes a full-fledged and refined theory in social ethics. By contrast, the classical statements of basic rights both are more concrete and practical, and allude to philosophical, ethical, and political justifications.[1]

These statements guarantee, for each individual, her safety, her property, and her freedom to do all that does not violate the same set of rights of other individuals. They specify act- and process-freedom for domains where they had particularly been violated: public expression and communication, movement, and protection against government coercion not justified by the protection of these rights. The protection of property implies the right to unfettered free exchange. Individuals can participate in the collective and political decisions that concern them or their property. They have an equal right to be candidate to positions. Taxes for the maintenance of the public force that protects rights and for administrative expenditures are according to means. This can mean benefit taxation since the public force protects property (a liberal social contract for financing this public good would propose a specific benefit taxation), or according to ability to pay and hence to ability to earn – as the distributive taxes that are obtained in forthcoming chapters. A right to public aid is also sometimes added in the rights or in the constitution that derives from them.[2] Basic rights in their classical and legal expression, as process-freedom, are implied by full self-ownership, but do not imply it.[3]

Basic freedoms can be seen, and have classically been seen, under two angles. They just protect individuals and constrain them to respect others. In another classical conception, however, basic rights constitute the source of law, the set of basic social-ethical axioms from which the constitution, laws, regulations, and in

---

[1] The American Declaration and Bill of Rights (1776 and 1789), and the 1789 Declaration in Versailles, were written by the same "group-mind" and sometimes actually the same persons. The 1789 Declaration intended to be more universal and philosophical. The first draft was prepared by Jefferson, Lafayette, and Condorcet and presented at the National Assembly on July 11. The adoption was by votes about each of the seventeen articles, in one week ending on August 26. The Declarations and other statements of basic rights more or less intend to become new Tables of the Law, and hence they are short, terse, and often laconic. We are, however, well informed about their intended meaning because they were prepared by intensive written public reflexion and debate. This is, in particular, the case for the summer of 1789 in France. Practically all public characters proposed their own declaration and justified it. This compendium, along with the record of the debates at the National Assembly during the preparation and vote article by article, constitute the most fascinating and richest volume in political philosophy, and undoubtedly one of the deepest. The text of the 1789 Declaration has to be considered accompanied by these hundred and forty pages. The main philosophical inspirers were first John Locke and second Jean-Jacques Rousseau (although mostly the latter for the emotional involvement), for the respective emphases on the individual and on the people. However, both views were specified and applied in avoiding their respective extremisms of Lockean full self-ownership and the social segmentation, injustice, and self-centeredness it implies, and of the dangerous populist fusion of wills often suggested by Rousseau. A full analysis of this text is proposed in *Free and Equal in Rights* (Kolm 1989a/1991 – and a very partial version in 1993a).

[2] This right was omitted in 1789 by accident, but included in the ensuing Constitution and in later statements of these rights.

[3] See Chapters 3 and 6.

the end the life chosen by individuals and society are to be derived in a waterfall of
successive specifications, precisions, deductions, applications, implementations,
and enactments.[4] In this deductive conception, the basic rights are themselves the
first step of the chain, in specifying or applying the unique social principle, freedom
(seen as social freedom, and given that equality itself is in these rights). These
derivations include the distributive and fiscal consequences, considered here.

2. THE REASONS FOR BASIC RIGHTS

2.1. Constitutional rights and other reasons

The reason for adopting basic rights for deriving the structure of distributive justice
can be retained at any of three possible levels. One may directly consider that these
rights should be adopted. One may also start with the fact that people want these
rights one way or the other, and one may then adopt them as an application of
the principle of endogenous social choice and unanimity. Or one may begin with
the fact that institutions have adopted these rights: they are lawful, and indeed the
basis of law. These reasons for basic rights have been summarized in Chapter 1
(and in Chapter 2 for social freedom in general); they are now considered more
in depth.

The institutional aspect of basic rights can induce three possible reasons for
considering these rights and their consequences. People for whom abiding by the
law is a moral duty thus have a moral reason for this consideration. More cynical
people will consider basic rights solely because respecting them is compulsory.
However, the institutional endorsement of basic rights in itself justifies considering
them, since deriving their fiscal or distributional implications is the determination
of the constitutional taxes, subsidies, distributions, or actions of the public sector.
This simple exercise reveals important properties – which are quite different from
common practice. However, one may also want deeper reasons for considering
basic rights – more social or ethical ones. To begin with, this institutionalization
of basic rights itself had reasons.

Two types of justifications can thus be considered. One refers to unanimity,
consensus, and hence endogenous social choice. The other directly values basic freedoms for a number of possible reasons. These reasons are easily found:
basic freedoms can be valued in themselves – as being "self-evident" – because
they mean nonviolence and an absence of direct domination, because they permit self-fulfilment and benefiting from the other goods, and so on (this list is
soon completed and analyzed). However, basic freedoms may also present various shortcomings and defects. To begin with, is it possible that all individuals
fully enjoy all basic rights? This possibility is implied by most official statements

---

[4] This is why the 1789 Declaration preceded the Constitution, which had to be derived from these rights,
rather than followed it as a summary of its essence (the best advocate of the deductive conception was
Mirabeau assisted by his workshop of Genevan lawyers).

of these rights. However, it is doubted or denied by the long line of scholars who hold that these rights should be "equal for all and maximal" while having priority over other considerations (this is for instance stated by Rousseau, Condorcet, the 1789 Declaration, John Stuart Mill, and John Rawls).[5] An answer to this question is shortly presented; it will rest on the conjunction of a strict definition and of the distributional possibilities considered here. Moreover, the basic rights include freedom to exchange and hence imply the legitimacy of markets, whereas market systems have often been criticized on various grounds such as inefficiency, injustice (notably for generating poverty for a number of persons), labour alienation, the selfishness they rest on and reinforce, and the poor social relations they often induce.[6] In fact, the individualism that is the hallmark of basic rights in general has often been objected to. We will see, however, that these shortcomings are only shortcomings in particular conceptions and applications of basic rights, rather than necessary ones. But let us first point out the issue of consensus and unanimity.

2.2. Consensual rights: Basic freedoms from endogenous social choice

The derivation of basic rights from consensus can start with two alternative remarks.

First of all, practically everyone wants the general respect and prevalence of these rights in present-day modern societies. This may be everyone who is sufficiently informed and sufficiently thinks about it.

In any event, each individual wants these rights for herself. This is a logical necessity since individuals want their actions and their intended consequences by definition, which implies that they want their own social freedom. Practically, an individual does not want to be molested or robbed of her property; she wants to be able to freely communicate and move around, and so on. Then, this individual's judgment about justice in the society should want these rights for everyone, because it has to be impartial. Impartiality, indeed, is an a priori and necessary property of a judgment about justice, from the very nature and definition of this concept. This individual's judgment about justice can be actual, or it can be notionally built up from other views of this person (as explained in Chapter 21).

However, these consensuses can justify full basic rights for all only if this situation is possible, and also only if it still is desired when possible shortcomings are taken into account, such as the various noted effects of free markets and individualism. These two conditions are now considered.

---

[5] This statement has also been qualified by the proposals of maximins in these rights (let the individual who has the least of them have the most possible, although one should then deal with the plurality of these rights), and of adjusting individuals' rights to their specific preferences or needs. These questions are analyzed in Kolm 1985a – see also 1996a, Chapter 4.

[6] A complete analysis of the various possible shortcomings of the market system can be found in *Modern Liberalism* (Kolm 1984b), with an analysis of remedies and alternatives in *The Good Economy, General Reciprocity* (1984a).

2.3. The copossibility or nonrivalry of basic rights: Full (formal) freedom for all

It is possible that all agents fully enjoy all basic rights. This results from understanding these rights in the strict sense, in dissociating them from any other means of action with which they are used. That is, these rights, in this conception, are well described by Marx's expression that they only are "formal freedom," as opposed to "real freedom," which needs both these rights and some other means in addition. They are "bare," "naked," or "pure" basic rights, or basic rights strictly (or minimally) understood. These rights are then distinguished from the allocation and distribution of other means. This specification is appropriate here, because the distribution of other means results from the distributional considerations including global distributive justice, which allocates incomes with which other means can be bought (there can also be allocations in the field local justice and microjustice).

With this strict definition of basic rights, when two or more acts using such rights are not jointly possible, this incompatibility can always be attributed to particular other means also used by these acts, and to questions of defining rights in these other means. These other means are often pieces of space at definite times, or access to some media, or they can be incomes in competitive buying implementing rights to exchange, and so on. This copossibility also holds for the use of several rights by the same agent who has to allocate her various means or resources (capacities or property or other rights) to these different uses. Hence, with this conception of basic rights taken in their pure, bare, and minimal understanding, these rights, in themselves, are always nonrival and copossible, whatever the specific nature and holder of each. Any rivalry in their use is due to other means and their distribution.[7] With this conception, therefore, all agents can have all basic rights in full. Basic rights are always used at satiety. These freedoms are then both equal for all and maximal, and the corresponding noted classical specification is pointless.

2.4. Possible shortcomings of basic rights and their proper conception

Classical defects attributed to basic rights depend in fact on particular conceptions, applications, and uses of these rights. Most of these shortcomings or vices concern free markets. Free markets are, indeed, permitted by freedom of exchange and other actions, and they constitute the central topic of the theory of full process-freedom. The defects of markets commonly pointed out refer to inefficiencies of various types, injustices and notably poverty of people who can obtain only low incomes or no income at all, and various psychosocial effects such as fostering individualism, selfishness, hostile relationships, or alienation. Individualism and

---

[7] See Kolm 1996a, Chapter 4.

its consequences as regards social relations and attitudes are, more generally, a common reproach addressed to basic rights. However, close consideration indeed shows that these defects and vices only apply to particular conceptions – or misconceptions – of basic rights and process-freedom, and to particular choices of ways of using them, rather than being necessary and inherent to them.

The inefficiencies of markets notably refer to macroeconomic diseases (such as large unemployment) and crises and to various microeconomic "failures." They are common arguments for advocating government interventions or the replacement of markets or of part of them by planning of some sort. However, one should know which intervention or plan to choose. Now, a conception of process-freedom implying the correction of market failures by indications given by liberal social contracts (see Section 6 of Chapter 3) avoids inefficiencies as much as possible. This holds both for microeconomic "market failures" to be found with nonexcludable public goods or externalities, for instance, and for causes of macroeconomic diseases, such as problems of information or price rigidities (which are banned by process-freedom and often made less necessary by the appropriate distribution – as with the case of wage floors). The efficiency of markets so corrected, due to motivations and the decentralized use of information, is about the best-known result of economic analysis.

A most common criticism of market systems, and reason for interfering with their working, concerns possible resulting distributive injustice and, notably, poverty for part of the population. However, individuals who receive only little or nothing from the market are not poor if they receive a sufficient transfer. And transfers based on inelastic items do not interfere with process-freedom, as we have seen, and do not produce inefficiency-generating disincentives. In particular, the dissociation of process-freedom from self-ownership permits endowing individuals who can earn only little with some rent of the capacities of the more productive ones.[8] The market can develop from a distribution of given resources, which include the value of given capacities.

Basic rights have also been criticized for their individualism (for instance by Robespierre and Marx). Relatedly, the market system is based on self-interest, possibly on selfishness, which it rewards and hence encourages and reinforces. It fosters rather hostile or hypocritical social relations in exchanges where interests are in part opposed and in competition. The division of labour it implies is a source of the alienation of labour (the product of labour becomes foreign to the labourer). The wage relationship often is more a relation of dependency and domination than one of simple exchange. However, these aspects are often not necessary. The individuals protected by basic rights can form communities. Process-freedom permits not only market exchanges, but also gift-giving and reciprocity.[9] One

---

[8] Issues of information about the base do not affect these remarks (see Chapter 10).

[9] However, expanding the scope of reciprocity and giving in a society dominated by selfishness and self-interested relations raises important sui generis issues of coordination (since, by nature, gift giving cannot be the object of an agreement). This question is analyzed in Kolm 1984a, 2001a.

can try to earn in order to give (this is much emphasized by the clergyman and economist Wicksteed (1888, 1933) who sees, in this "non-tuism," the way of reconciling his two professions). The "declarers" saw no contradiction in adding fraternity to liberty and equality (in rights) in the motto they soon adopted. If workers who have to earn a living at low wage rates have to work much and at the employer's conditions, this no longer holds with the proper distribution and transfers. And one should certainly prefer communities that carry their essential values of culture, solidarity, and social sentiments without violating individuals' basic freedoms.

Yet, there remains the dilemma that selfish behaviour in a setting of free market exchanges has well-known virtues of economic efficiency, while selfish motivations and attitudes certainly do not make the best kinds of social relations and persons. Now, the efficient working of the economy of a large modern society cannot dispense with a large market sector. However, the alternative is between motivations and behaviour all within social freedom. Constraints on free exchanges are a priori no way to make motivations more other-regarding. Hence, this important question of societies does not hinge on the present issue of the respect of basic rights.

In conclusion, full basic rights for all is possible if these rights are properly understood – as pure, "formal" freedoms. Basic rights do not induce inefficiency through free exchange and markets if process-freedom is understood as including the implementation of "liberal social contacts." They do not imply the poverty that can result from markets, notably if full process-freedom is not mistaken for full self-ownership. Although they permit the various shortcomings of excessive individualism, they do not imply them. Then, the full respect of these rights for all is desired by all individuals (in present-day modern societies), or required by their conception of justice.

2.5. Direct reasons for basic rights

The ethical and political evaluation of social freedom generally concentrates on its presentation as basic rights. These freedoms can be directly appraised from an ethical point of view. This should explain why most people support them as the general rule of society (in present-day modern societies), and this clearly was an important reason for their acquiring their central institutional place (the ethical judgments are relevant because these rights do not necessarily serve everyone's interests, and, when they are agreed upon, because agreements commonly refer to some ethical properties of the chosen solution).

Social freedom, which the classical basic rights manifest, says that no individual should be submitted to a relation of force by another agent (individual or institution). The exception can only be forceful prevention of this individual's use of force against another agent. There can also be apparent use of force that in fact only implements a free choice of the constrained agent, notably one of a previous agreement (the cases of hypothetical such agreements, that is, social contracts, and of democratic political systems, could be further discussed).[10] The use of force can affect the individuals directly or through their rights acquired by processes respecting social freedom and in particular by free exchanges (notably property rights); these rights are those described by the theory of full process-freedom.

Hence, social freedom and notably basic rights mean peace, nonviolence, non-domination. Their violation is aggression, injuring, enslaving, robbery, spoliation, gagging, and so on. Their violation by a political power is in the vein of fascism. It should be noted that material inequality and poverty resulting from nominally free but very unequal exchanges (as with market "exploitation") are not sufficient reasons for moral infringements of basic rights because redistribution consistent with process-freedom is possible – notably because process-freedom can be understood as not implying full self-ownership. Moreover, basic rights are necessary for consuming other goods, for living one's own life, for self-fulfillment, for "the pursuit of happiness" (1776), and for "the happiness of all" (1789). Hence, the sound position may just be that basic rights are "clear and self-evident" (1776), and any further discussion may be rather insane ratiocination.

However, basic rights involve more than issues of pain and happiness. They also involve more than the general other values of freedom such as exercising one's capacities (Aristotle), permitting the existence of agency, being responsible for some part of the world, and so on.[11] This relates to the two particular features they have as freedoms, concerning respectively their structure and especially the nature of the constraints that limit them. Although basic rights can be more or less violated, their respect can be full, and hence one can say that they are either respected or not, without considering a matter of degree (degrees can then appear in the other means associated to their use). Moreover, when they are violated, the trespassing consists of an agent's will dominating another's. The respect of basic rights is nondomination of individuals by others and thus constitutes a kind of relational equality. Now, questions of domination go deeper than issues of satisfaction and affect domains of selfhood and agency, in relation to questions of self-respect, dignity, possibly honour. In Kant's distinction between things that have a price and things that have dignity, basic freedoms largely extend in the latter domain. The existential and ontological value of freedom – namely, its being a condition for the existence of agency – is particularly acute when the limit consists of the effects of other wills, because the issue then is the existence of social agency in the setting of social relations. Hence, the Declarations hold their rights to be "inalienable and sacred" (a point which aroused Jeremy Bentham's ire: "rights, nonsense, inalienable rights, nonsense upon stilts"). Only for this kind of freedom, valued for this kind of reason, could Alexis de Tocqueville assert that "he

---

[10] With the proposed acceptance of liberal social contracts for correcting market and other "failures" (Section 6 of Chapter 3), and a possible use of concepts of social contracts for determining the general degree of redistribution (see Chapter 21).

[11] The various values of freedom are analyzed in Kolm 1996a, Chapter 2.

who values freedom for anything but itself does not deserve it and will soon loose it," or can the revolutionists set for themselves the choice of "freedom or death."

Moreover, an individual's action constrained by the respect of another's basic right *ipso facto* incorporates this other's will among its determinants. If this constraint is a moral one, respecting this right is a duty for the actor. If the actor endorses and internalizes this duty, she includes the other's will among the aims of her action. Others' aims and wills are thus included "in the kingdom of ends" of individual actors, in line with Kant's injunction. Hence, basic freedoms constitute the form of this Kantian morality, and the way to it through the internalization of the duty to respect these rights.

A main possible violator of these rights is the holder of legal violence, the state or the government. Historically, these rights were established primarily as protection of the individual against government interference. Hence, basic freedoms have foremost a political role, meaning, and importance. Their respect defines a type of political and social system. This effect is through both protective rights and political rights of participation to public decisions. The protective rights define the private sphere against political action, even that resulting from democratic political choices. Basic rights define the individualistic basis of the life of society.

Individualism is indeed the source of the most common and age-old criticism addressed to basic rights. Emphasizing these rights may elicit selfishness. This individualism would oppose altruism and mutual aid, traditions and cultures, and solidarities which can result from either of these. Basic rights, indeed, are silent about such facts. But they do not preclude them. The central issue is that the dividing line drawn by basic rights is between coercion and freedom, and not, per se, between the individual and the community or the others. Basic rights preclude force used, against the individuals, by others, by the government or the state, and also by communities and traditions. But they permit free associations, noncoercive communities and traditions, and givings of all kinds. Fraternity did not oppose liberty and equality in rights. And when Edmund Burke, for criticizing the Declaration of 1789, opposed to it the rights he thought could be derived from tradition, he came out with a similar list.[12]

However, for efficiently managing a large and complex economy, there is no alternative to markets implementing process-freedom and properly corrected for their various "failures." This correction can follow putative process-freedom with "liberal social contracts." Poverty and distributive injustices can be remedied by the appropriate efficiency-respecting transfers if full self-ownership is not endorsed. And the possible shortcomings of the psychosocial effects of markets are amenable to the same answer as that proposed for the individualism of basic rights in general and to more specific ones already noted. It was indeed pointed out that the market system rests on and, hence, more or less rewards, selfishness, insincerity, hostile relations due to opposed interests in exchange and competition,

---

[12] See E. Burke (1790), *Reflexions on the Revolution in France.*

greediness and materialism, labour alienation, and so on. This issue, we remarked, does not concern the existence of basic rights but, rather, two types of ways of using them in social relations (epitomized by the relations of exchanging and of giving). The solution consists of trying to keep the market mentality, behaviour, and *ethos* in their proper sphere, for having a sufficiently efficient market economy in a sufficiently nonmercantile society. The ways to this end are often in the fields of education and culture. Finding and keeping this balance is a main question of societies importantly involved in the market system – most of them presently.

Finally, the large consensus about basic freedoms, and their being a condition for individuals' activity and enjoyment, make these rights amenable to most kinds of general justifications in social ethics, and many of them have indeed been proposed. This justification can be, for instance, a democratic political choice, tradition, a social contract (a hypothetical unanimous agreement), utilitarianism or the relief of the deepest misery (through basic rights' contribution to happiness or to social efficiency),[13] the promotion of social income or of the lowest incomes, social efficiency per se through decentralized choices (with possible liberal social contracts for remedying "failures"), and so on.

3. POLITICAL RIGHTS, TAXATION, DISTRIBUTION

Besides the protective individual basic freedoms, the overall basic rights also include the political basic rights, the "rights of the citizen" as opposed to the "rights of man." This basically is the right to participate in political decisions (a right to be a candidate to public offices is sometimes explicitly added to it). This right of participation only implies that there is some sort of democratic system whose precise form is left to the specification presented by the rest of the constitution. It can safely be considered that this minimal requirement of democracy implies that unanimity in the relevant decisions should be endorsed. Then, in particular, these political decisions cannot lead to a violation of the protective basic rights if all citizens want them to prevail. These political rights were of course essential in the birthplaces of these rights, whether the British constitutional monarchy, the American "no taxation without representation," the French destruction of absolute monarchy, or the (German and others) local city democracies.[14]

However, the logic of the general issue of the basic freedoms questions the necessity of considering political rights apart from others, as it questions the vagueness of their definition. The intention clearly is that individuals participate in political decisions that concern them, and hence control the corresponding

---

[13] The respect of basic rights can be a condition for a maximin in individuals' welfare ("practical eudemonistic justice," Kolm 1971, and 1985a for the effect of basic rights). In contrast, Rawls (1971) sees basic freedoms as a constraint on and limitation of his maximin in "primary goods." He gives priority to these rights. However, his presentation of the reason for replacing equality by a maximin implies that distribution has "disincentive effects" in being in fact based on earned incomes, a violation of process-freedom.

[14] See G. Jellineck (1895), *Die Erklärung der Menschen und Bürgerrechte.*

official acts. If a choice concerns only one person, the others have no reason to interfere with this choice. However, political decisions are usually political because they jointly concern several persons. Yet, participation can be of many kinds, and the right should be more precise. In particular, people are often concerned in different degrees. If being concerned or not makes a difference, the differences in degrees of concern should also make one. Now, it turns out that the application of the general principle of basic freedoms provides an answer to this question. Indeed, if a choice concerns several individuals, the general ban on the use of force implies that the outcome results from a free agreement among these persons. If this agreement fails to exist as a result of any cause of failure (such as with nonexcludable public goods, external effects, insufficient information, costs of transaction or contracting possibly particularly important because of a large number of concerned persons, and so on), then a liberal social contract indicates what should be done, possibly through the action of a public sector. The influence of individuals' desires on the public action is thus specified, as well as the role of a public administration, and no particular political rights need be considered. The latter can only be useful in situations of institutional second best, as protection against abuse by existing political institutions. They then complement the directly protective rights and aid their being respected and enforced by the dominating public force.

One standard role of political choices and institutions concerns the distribution of goods, wealth, or incomes. Concerns about distribution are usually absent from statements of basic rights, apart from possible implications of the respect of property and of free exchange, and of political decisions and participations. Concerns about basic needs, poverty, and distributive justice are nowadays often consigned into "social rights," which do not have the primacy of basic rights (they are, for instance, rights stated in the 1948 Universal Declaration of Human Rights). However, public assistance to individuals who do not have enough and cannot earn sufficiently was almost included in the 1789 Declaration (it was not almost by chance, because of the necessity to end the debates and produce the text); it was included at the onset of the constitution seen as specifying these basic rights; and it was included in the later statement of basic rights (Condorcet was particularly influencial in this respect).[15] Now, the tax principle retained in this Declaration is according to means, or ability to pay, which, with free exchange, basically means ability to earn. Hence, the actual distributive scheme basically consists of transfers according to earning capacities, for both yielders and receivers. This happens to be the kind of distributive structure that will be derived from the only consideration of the process-freedom aspect of basic rights (or of efficiency).

It is particularly noteworthy that the 1789 "constituents" explicitly rejected two extreme interpretations or specifications of basic rights, respectively stating full

---

[15] It should be added that assisting the poor was a traditional role of the church whose extended property was being confiscated.

self-ownership and the sufficiency and primacy of the political; and respectively inspired by the two intellectual masters of this movement, John Locke and Jean-Jacques Rousseau. The proposal of Abbey Sieyès (the second most philosophical participant after Condorcet) of declaring full self-ownership, inspired by Locke's ideas, was indeed defeated. And Rousseau clearly suggests that, with sufficiently direct, permanent, and integrating democratic political participation, implementing the "social contract" and manifesting the "general will," political power need not and cannot be checked by individualistic protective rights, since it only is the people acting on itself. This idea and its possible (worrisome) consequences were also explicitly discarded.

Moreover, the distributional outlook of the 1789 Declaration is strongly meritarian. The equal right to compete for positions was essential for the able and educated young bourgeois whose ambitions were blocked by the birthrights of the nobility. The "career open to talents" was one of their main claims. The Declaration even goes beyond a strictly individualistic justification in its second sentence, "Inequalities can only be justified by social utility," which qualifies its magnificent opening assertion that "Men are born and remain free and equal in rights."[16] This freedom in the use of talent and in receiving the corresponding rewards, associated to the rejection of full self-ownership, leads to a distributive structure of the type that is obtained here.

Finally, this text considers, as public service and expenditure, the public force for protecting rights and notably property, and a corresponding public administration. It states that the financing should be by a tax "according to means." Apart from a possible reason of ability to pay (which should then largely be ability to earn, and hence, according to productive capacities), this principle can be justified as benefit taxation, since the basic object of the expenditure is the protection of properties which constitute these means. This financing can thus be seen as an application of a "liberal social contract" for realizing the public good constituted by the proper "law and order." It thus is consistent with this theoretical completion of full process-freedom.

It is thus noteworthy that a number of implications of basic rights presented in this most classical founding Declaration rejoin the conclusions derived from an elaborate analysis.

---

[16] The intention of the verb "remains" is to state that the wage relationship does not impair the freedom of the wage earner and the basic equality. The criticism of this view is the basis of Marx's work.

5

Resources

1. THE GENERAL PROBLEM

Resources are to be distributed (acquiescing to particular "natural" or "spontaneous" allocations is to be seen as particular possible solutions). From the general
principle or method of endogenous social choice, this distribution will have to
follow unanimous informed and reflective opinions intervening directly or indirectly (reasons for respecting basic freedoms can also be directly valued). The
distribution concerning macrojustice is considered here. Hence, as we have seen, it
will have to respect basic rights and process-freedom, Pareto efficiency, and other
applications of the principle of unanimity. These criteria will turn out to allocate
a number of rights in resources to particular individuals and to discard others
from the concern of macrojustice. In the end, there will remain the rent-rights
in productive capacities, which will be allocated according to the appropriate
equality.[1]

This outcome will result from a selection in each of four dichotomies. (1) Resources can be *produced* or *given* (nonproduced or "natural"). (2) They can be
nonhuman or human, that is, *capacities*. (3) Capacities can be (roughly) *eudemonistic* (and consumptive) or *productive* (usable in production). (4) Rights in a
resource can be rights to *use and benefit from the use,* or rights to the value of its a
priori availability or *rent.*

The reason for the selection will be process-freedom for dichotomies (1) and
(4). It will be the fact that the topic is macrojustice for dichotomies (2) and (3),
but for different specific reasons: the large relative importance of capacities and
specificities of the allocation of nonhuman natural resources for choice (2), and
the consensual irrelevance of eudemonistic (and properly consumptive) capacities
for choice (3).

---

[1] This equalization, shown in Chapter 9, depends on the relevant measure of the value of capacities, a
choice that amounts to that of the degree of redistribution analyzed in Part IV.

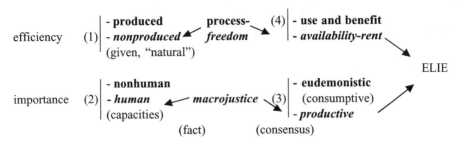

Figure 5–1. The four dichotomies of resources.

This quadruple of dichotomies and their reasons will be closely considered in this chapter and the next. They are summarized by Figure 5–1. (chosen items are italicized).

The choice (1) of focusing on the allocation of given resources results from process-freedom whose aim-freedom part allocates the primary ownership of produced resources to the producer. Basing distributive policy on inelastic given resources also is a requirement of Pareto efficiency (and hence of the principle of unanimity) since basing a policy on an elastic product creates disincentive or incentive effects of the kind that entails Pareto inefficiencies.

This focus on given resources applies to both nonhuman and human resources. For the latter, produced resources consist of improvements in capacities created by training, education, learning, or formation. A person choosing such actions is entitled to the improvement and to its effects from the aim-freedom part of process-freedom. Yet, these actions and their result also rest on capacities for learning or improving, which are largely given.

Process-freedom entails the choice (4) applied to capacities. Indeed, it entitles each agent to the right to use her capacities and to benefit from the result. Hence, only the rent-right remains available for another allocation. This has been noted in Chapter 3 and is further discussed in Chapter 6.

The fact that the issue is macrojustice will turn out to have two consequences. First, the rent of nonhuman natural resources is a very small fraction of the remuneration of labour using productive capacities (see Section 2.2), and productive capacities would produce more with more labour (capital is a produced means of production, and its value can be allocated to the given resources); moreover, many nonhuman natural resources are allocated by considerations of micro-justice (Section 2.3); for these reasons, in particular, global distributive justice focuses on capacities. Second, the consideration of common opinion shows it holds that global distributive policy implementing macrojustice should not be concerned with capacities to be satisfied or happy (for instance, as concerns the income tax). Hence, the proper concern of global distributive policy is the rent of given productive capacities. The place and allocation of nonhuman natural resources is considered in Section 2, and the moral and allocative consequences of the differences between capacities of different types constitutes the topic of Section 2 of Chapter 6.

2. NONHUMAN NATURAL RESOURCES

2.1. Summary

Social freedom, efficiency, and unanimity, which implies both (see Chapter 4), lead the policy of distributive justice to focus on the allocation of the value of given resources. Three properties will be pointed out as concerns nonhuman given (natural) resources. First, their contribution to social output and their value is a very small fraction of those of productive capacities (used directly or in learning). Second, a large part of nonhuman natural resources is considered as relevantly allocated by specific or local considerations in microjustice. Third, a large part of these resources has been long owned by successive owners and cannot practically be the object of a specific distributive policy. These aspects lead to discarding them as issues for global distributive justice in macrojustice, which will therefore focus on capacities. The various criteria for allocating these resources are briefly summarized.

2.2. Global relative importances

As an order of magnitude, the shares of incomes from labor, capital, and nonhuman natural resources in a modern economy can be seen as 80, 18, and 2, respectively. Capital, however, is produced. Then, with uniform and constant proportions of factors of production, the value of capital contains a value due to past uses of nonhuman natural resources equal to $18 \times \frac{2}{80+2}$ percent of national income, that is, less than 0.5%. Hence, present and past labor accounts for more than 97.5% of national income. Different realistic figures, or a different assumption about the history of technology, do not affect the qualitative aspect of the conclusion.[2]

The remaining share of the contribution of nonhuman natural resources (the 2.5% in the foregoing example) is to be contrasted with the fact that the interpersonal redistribution achieved by governments in modern societies can be in the order of magnitude of ten times as large.[3]

John Locke clearly saw the relative contributions of resources, notwithstanding the celebrity of his brief discussion of the allocation of land (italics are his):

---

[2] For more detailed discussions, see Kolm 1985a.
[3] This interpersonal redistributive effect does not include the function of solely producing public goods of taxes and expenditures (but it can include the redistributive effects of these operations, along with direct transfers) – a precise computation is not our present concern.

Labour makes the far greater part of the value. I think it will be but a very modest Computation to say, that of the *Products* of the Earth useful to the Life of Man 9/10 are the *effects of labour*: nay, if we will rightly estimate things as they come to our use, and cast up the several Expenses about them, what in them is purely owing to *Nature*, and what to *labour*, we shall find, that in most of them 99/100 are wholly to be put on the account of labour.... *Labour makes the far greatest part of the value* of things, we enjoy in this World: and the ground ... at most, a very small part of it.... 'Tis *Labour* then which *puts the greatest part of Value upon Land*, without which it would scarcely be worth any thing: 'tis to that we owe the greatest part of its useful Products. (*Second Treatise of Government*, 1689, Chapter 5)[4]

The overall conclusion remains when one considers the relevant modern facts and data for the nature of scarce natural resources, production, and the computation of the rent. Note that given capacities are used in labour not only directly, but also indirectly through their use in learning, training, and education for improving or creating capacities. Moreover, productive capacities are, by definition, capacities that can be used for producing, and notably for obtaining an income, and not only those that are actually so used by labour. There are productive capacities that are not actually so used. They then are at rest or used in some kind of activity of consumption or in leisure, or their production is directly consumed. The value of the services that these capacities provide, or could provide in production, or the value of the availability of these capacities, is not reckoned in the value of the social product, for instance in social accounting. Social accounts only measure the product of actual labour, usually that obtained as income (there are occasional minor exceptions for product directly consumed). But the rent of these productive capacities is a priori to be included in the value that is to be distributed (independently of the chosen use). By contrast, the measures of the rent of nonhuman natural resources in these accounts include all uses of these resources, including directly for consumption, such as with residential land, the measure being at market value. In addition, the value of capacities not usable in production, such as, for the most part, capacities to enjoy or endure (eudemonistic capacities) is also a priori to be allocated to someone (if necessary, adjustments in this respect might be performed indirectly through compensatory transfers and differentials in income or consumption based on these capacities).

Furthermore, the principles of allocation of nonhuman natural resources often refer directly or indirectly to capacities or to means obtained with them, through various principles such as general agreement (which depends on bargaining skills and information), first occupancy, allocation according to capacities or means for using the resource, or according to need or to preference (which are structures of capacities for being satisfied), and so on.

---

[4] The order of magnitude of the relative importance labour and "land" had in the value of the social product was clear to a number of classical economists. Marx is a case in point. Statistics exhibit, in fact, a "97.5% labour theory of value."

The values of natural resources that have been considered are not, of course, their total "use values," which are infinite and irrelevant: a person is willing to pay the same amount for having some air to breathe and a body to live, namely, anything she can give, although she usually receives both for free. Moreover, present-day nonhuman natural resources are quite varied and heterogenous, and are very variously related to societies. They include, for instance, land apart from its equipment or improvement, scarce locations, underground resources, clean air and water, the herzian spectrum, or natural landscapes.

This relative global importance of the various given resources would suffice for global distributive justice in macrojustice to focus on the question of human resources. Two other reasons, not considered, reinforce this conclusion and in the end practically impose it. They respectively refer to the past allocation of most nonhuman natural resources, and to most of them being considered as appropriately allocated by considerations pertaining to the field of microjustice – even though they can be very important for specific persons or in the absolute amount of their value. Indeed, a large number of principles are used and can be used for allocating these resources. The general analysis of this question is presented elsewhere.[5] It lies beyond our present topic, and the next section only proposes a very brief reminder of the possibilities.

2.3. The logic of solutions

The rational requirement of *prima facie* identical treatment of identicals in the relevant characteristics will apply here.[6] But it can have varied applications. The equal sharing of a given resource has always been one of the most common practices and proposals. For instance, this is Aristotle's "arithmetic equality" in "distributive justice," also noted by Plato.[7] However, the equality can also be relative to some item, or, more generally, it can consist of the application of a rule or principle.

Deciding by unanimous agreement is much in line with process-freedom. The threat point, implemented in the absence of agreement, can naturally be the nonallocation of the resource. The natural resource is, then, like the surplus in an exchange, and the agreement chooses the sharing (the surplus is a kind of a priori undistributed resource created by demands and supplies, desires and resources, and the heterogeneity and complementarity of peoples' desires in an exchange). But agents can also decide by unanimous agreement to adopt another rule or principle of allocation. The agreement may entail side payments among the agents, and these transfers constitute compensations which are determined in this

---

[5] Kolm 1985a, Chapter 10 (and 1986b).
[6] The full derivation of this principle from the requirement of providing a reason can be found in Kolm 1971 (1998), new foreword, Section 5 (see also Chapter 23).
[7] See *Nicomachean* and *Eudemian Ethics*, and *The Laws*, respectively.

manner. These payments will be financed with the legitimately owned resources or incomes. It can also be noted that unanimous agreement amounts to applying a principle "to each according to her bargaining or convincing capacities." These talents are human resources which are then implicitly attributed to their holder (they are natural resources, apart from possible improvements by training and education).

Moreover, the agreement can be preceded by an exchange of information which can carry not only threats (possibly just threats of nonagreement, and social freedom bans threats of violence that can influence actions), proposals or demands of compensations, and various possible factual information and strategic influences, but also moral arguments about the allocation. There may even be solely moral arguments. These arguments may influence the listeners and more or less convince them (this general issue is analyzed in Chapter 20 about the allocation of the value of productive capacities).

Finally, practical difficulties of general bargaining and agreement (notably due to various aspects of information) can lead to its remaining hypothetical or putative, that is, to its being a liberal social contract whose result can be implemented by a policy. The allocation is then determined by application of the relevant bargaining theory.

Another most usual and widespread solution for allocating natural resources consists of the right of first occupancy. It also applies process-freedom, with agents using their capacities and legitimate means for occupying the resources, possibly in a peaceful race among themselves. The "occupation" sometimes has to be defined (enclosure, use, and so on). Patents constitute an important present-day application of a principle of first occupancy.

A number of criteria for allocating natural resources, which are used or have been or could be proposed, relate the resource to characteristics of the beneficiary or of its situation. The logic of their ethic leads to the classification of these criteria into two categories, depending on whether they care for individual agents with more or less egalitarian implications, or whether their argument rests on some overall achievement of society. The former rules allocate the resource to individuals who are the poorest overall or in resources of the same nature, or the most miserable. The latter allocate it to agents who can make the best of it because of their means for exploiting it, or their specific tastes or capacities for satisfaction. This latter category includes, for instance, utilitarian-like views; the objective of maximizing social income or wealth; many reasons for allocating various sites in land, mining, and others to agents who have means of exploiting them; for instance, Locke's condition of allocating land to individuals who can till it; the antiquity's (for instance, Plato's) criterion of "giving the flute to the flute player;" Bertold Brecht's dictum that "each thing should be given to he who makes it better"; and so on. Allocation "according to need" can refer to either of these categories: "serve the needy first" belongs to the former category, but the reference to specific needs usually belongs to the latter view.

Several allocative principles can be used jointly. For instance, it is common that a principle is used for allocation among groups or societies and another for allocation among individuals within each group. The former is notably often locational occupancy. In many cases, the allocative rule is generally accepted, and hence should be retained from the principle of consensus. In the end, allocating given (nonhuman) resources of various types is very often an issue for specific and more or less local justice. This adds to the relative importance of human and nonhuman natural resources noted earlier for entailing that global or overall distributive justice resulting from basic rights is basically concerned with the allocation of rights in given capacities.

2.4. An impracticable solution

A long-standing proposal has been to associate full self-ownership with some specific distribution of nonhuman natural resources.[8] This is in particular a natural consequence of identifying self-ownership with process-freedom. The criterion of distribution of the value of these resources can be equal sharing, according to need, compensating the unequal distribution of earning capacities, nationalization for financing public expenditures, and so on. Three reasons make such proposals inadequate for global distributive justice in macrojustice. The first is the small *relative overall* importance of the proceeds from these resources in the income and value to be distributed. The figures noted above can, for instance, be compared with the fact that the redistributed income in modern societies is often about one-third of global income. The second reason is that the various types of nonhuman natural resources are often specifically related to society (location provides an example – a resource is often attributed to people who are in the same area), and these resources' allocation is often considered an issue in the field of local and specific justice or microjustice. One will often meet unanimous opinions that this is the case, and also, not uncommonly, consensus about the relevant criteria. The third reason is that most nonhuman natural resources are already owned, have been for a long time, and are owned by persons who are not the first owners: this makes their overall redistribution according to some criterion of justice fully impracticable.

Indeed, most present ownership of nonhuman natural resources is not first ownership. And owning a resource implies owning the flow of the services or proceeds it yields for the duration of ownership. Almost all present owners of land, stocks in mining companies, and so on, have bought them from previous owners. For them, there was no relevant difference between buying these assets or property in produced goods. Someone may prefer a small house in a large garden, and someone else a large house in a small garden. Indeed, all produced goods include material or services due to nonhuman natural resources used directly and

---

[8] The instances of such proposals are numerous (take, for instance, economist Leon Walras in the nineteenth century).

indirectly in their production. Owning a metallic object is benefitting from the services of the metal coming from the ore (and from the energy that transformed it). Hence, one would not achieve the proper distribution by taxing the present owners for taking the value of the resource and redistributing it, or by confiscating the resources for redistributing them or the proceeds of their sale or of their renting out. Moreover, considering a "rectification" of past allocation from the initial appropriation is just unthinkable for a large part of these resources. For instance, the most valuable land has often been owned by someone for centuries or millenia. One can use the considered allocation for newborn resources, that is, when a new technology makes a useless item become a useful and valued resource, or when increased demand makes a good that was overabundant become scarce and hence valued by users and markets. However, this will amount to a minute part of the existing value of nonhuman natural resources. One can also, in general, tax appreciations of existing resources, but this can be done for produced goods as well. Therefore, a general specific allocation of all nonhuman natural resources, or of most of them, cannot be the solution of a global distributive justice that would endorse self-ownership as regards human resources. By contrast, the distributive scheme that will be obtained here as concerns capacities is in itself very simple and practical.

*

In the end, the allocation of nonhuman natural resources raises multifarious local and specific issues. These issues are often important for some persons. Some are in absolute amount. More or less general criteria of distributive justice are sometimes used or can be used for the allocation of newborn resources (as noted above), or of royalties from oil or mining fields, or in land reforms or "nationalizations" of resources by expropriations. However, ancient and secondary ownership of most nonhuman natural resources; local and specific concern for many of these resources; and the relatively low importance of the value of the proceeds of these resources by comparison to that of labour and of capacities and to the present levels of redistribution; all preclude not only restricting distributive justice to the distribution of nonhuman natural resources, but also their being a concern of global distributive justice in macrojustice, except in particular countries and societies. By contrast, a notable part of the questions of microjustice is related to allocations of such resources of various kinds.

Finally, global distributive justice in macrojustice will be concerned with the allocation of given capacities. However, further specifications are required. This is the topic of the next chapter.

6

Capacities

1. SUMMARY

The foregoing has led to the conclusion that global distributive justice should focus on the allocation of rights in capacities. The present chapter will conclude that two types of rights in capacities should be self-owned – owned by their holder, or "naturally" allocated. They are the rights to use and benefit from the use because of process-freedom, and all the rights in eudemonistic and consumptive capacities for the specific issue of global distributive justice in macrojustice. These are the respective topics of Sections 2 and 3. The distribuand will then be restricted to the rent of productive capacities, whose allocation is considered in Parts II and IV of this study.

2. RIGHTS IN CAPACITIES

2.1. Types of rights in assets

The analysis of process-freedom has shown that it has specific implications as concerns the allocation of rights in capacities. The consideration of possible rights in capacities to begin with rejoins this conclusion.

A person's capacity is a set of characteristics of this person. It has the nature of an asset. Rights concerning an asset can be divided into several categories defined by the permitted use of the asset or by advantages derived from it. The relevant distinction considers four types of rights in an asset: the right to destroy; rights to use (without destroying) or *use-rights*; rights to receive the benefits from this use or *benefit-rights*; and rights to the value of the availability of the services this asset can provide or *rent-rights*. *Ownership* will denote here the conflation of all these rights in an asset; it corresponds to *usus et abusus* in Roman Law. Benefits, of any nature, are specific and depend on specific use, whereas rent corresponds to availability and hence is a priori independent of the chosen use;[1] the distinction is important for the issue of freedom (notably process-freedom, as we will see). In Roman Law, *jus abutendi* is the right to destroy, dismember, or alienate; *jus utendi* the right to use; and *jus frutendi* encompasses benefit-rights and rent-rights. *Usufruct* denotes rights to use and benefit, or to receive the rent. *Bare ownership* is ownership without usufruct. Each right holder has a right of veto with respect to destruction since it does away with her right. In addition, there can be restrictions in the holdings of these rights. The most common concern alienability in exchange or giving (for instance, for capacities, a free individual is not free to fully alienate use-rights in capacities of hers).[2]

A right in a person's capacity can be held by this person – this is a *self-right* – or by another person, a group, or an institution – this is an *external right* in this capacity. Self-ownership, bare self-ownership, self-usufruct, self-use, self-benefit, and self-rent refer to the corresponding self-rights. All self-rights are a priori possible, but social freedom entails limitations of the external rights in capacities.

2.2. Capacity-rights compatible with social freedom

Which rights in capacities are consistent with process-freedom and possible with full process-freedom? We have seen that process-freedom is act-freedom plus

---

[1] Effects of use on the value of availability can occur through price formation, but they will not be actual if the used resource is relatively small in a large market.

[2] The question of the alienability of rights in persons raises classical and important issues which, however, are beyond our present scope. The questions are whether self-rights (rights in oneself) are inalienable or are given a priori and then can be sold or given away to someone else by the right holder. Classical process liberalism, considering as it does all these rights jointly, poses the issue in terms of the right to sell (or give) oneself into slavery. The modern answer doubtlessly is that one has no right to own a slave (this opposes the answer of the seventeenth century such as Locke's for whom a legitimate slave is a prisoner in a just war who freely chooses slavery over death because she does not commit suicide). More interestingly, there is a long tradition of discussing the wage relationship as an alienation of act-freedom and of drawing ensuing judgments or political consequences. There are two aspects to it. One is whether the worker sells the services of her labor or the availability of her capacities or labor power and their use-rights (and hence she loses her act-freedom). The other is whether the worker can choose to escape this relation. This is, for instance, why long-term labor contracts are usually forbidden in modern law. But the worker may have no other actual choice to earn a living. She may have nothing else to sell. The analogy between wage labor and slavery was classical in the eighteenth century and part of the nineteenth century. Adam Smith notes that Philadelphia entrepreneurs prefer to have workers rather than slaves because they can dismiss them in business downturns and do not have to maintain the capital. Rousseau holds that each person should have enough money so as not to have to work for a wage, and yet sufficiently little so as not to be able to hire a worker. The 1789 "declarers," holding that "men are born and remain free and equal in rights," debated whether a wage earner can be considered as remaining free. Wage earners were denied the right to vote in the early nineteenth century because they were considered unfree. Marx is particularly adamant that the wage earner alienates her act-freedom – and has no other choice – and he sees this as a main dimension of the alienation of wage labor (another dimension relates to indirect production and consists in not seeing the final use of one's labour).

aim-freedom (for acts respecting process-liberal rights, in full process-freedom), and we also noticed that this act-freedom is seen as implying the protective right not to be harmed (the corresponding "act" consists of being undisturbed and safe). Destroying a capacity harms its bearer – it may kill her. Hence, act-freedom precludes external ownership of a capacity. There remains the possibility of external usufruct. However, the use of a capacity means choosing the bearer's acts that use it. Hence, act-freedom also precludes external use-rights in capacities. Moreover, the aim of the act of using is to obtain the corresponding benefit, of any nature (such as income, enjoyment, etc.). Therefore, aim-freedom precludes external benefit-rights in capacities. In the end, the only remaining possible type of external rights in capacities are rent-rights.

With process-freedom, in application of this principle the bearer of a capacity freely uses it and is entitled to the resulting benefits (act-freedom and aim-freedom): the use of a capacity is a legitimate means of the bearer. If this person is also entitled to the rent of this capacity, nothing else happens – then, this capacity is self-owned. But if another agent has a rent-right in this capacity, the bearer has to pay the corresponding rent. This can be seen as a price paid for the availability of the corresponding services that this capacity can provide. This availability enables the bearer to freely use this capacity and reap the ensuing benefits of any nature. The bearer so buys a right to use her capacity and to benefit from this use. To the extent of this external rent-right, she is only a tenant of herself. This is a price she pays for the possibility of fully exercising her process-freedom. And the requirement of process-freedom entails that she has to pay this rent. The receiver uses this transfer as she wants, and the payer finds the means to pay as she wants, from any source of income such as the receipt of transfers, earnings, or lower expenditures. The amount paid need not be obtained by a mercantile use of this specific capacity when this is possible. This is just an application of the general case: someone who has to pay a rent for an asset she uses can find the means to pay in any way, and not necessarily through some income-earning use of the asset; such a use may not even be possible, when the asset can only be used for direct enjoyment and consumption. However, it is not impossible that, for facing the payment, one would choose or need to earn some income from using the asset when this is feasible. In any event, the rent, which is the value of the availability of the asset's services, is independent of the specific use chosen.[3] This holds for an external rent-right in a capacity as for the rental of a house, which does not depend on whether the tenant uses it for dwelling or for a professional purpose, or leaves it empty. One characteristic of capacities as assets, however, is that, with process-freedom, the bearer has to have the availability of the use of her capacities, and therefore she has to pay the corresponding value – a rent – to any holder of an external rent-right in capacities of hers. A free individual cannot but hire the capacities of hers that

[3]   Again, this will be the case for global distributive justice in large societies where each particular individual is a relatively small economic agent.

she does not own. Necessary hiring is not specific to capacities. There are other assets an individual needs to hire if she does not own them, such as a house and a number of other necessities depending on needs, culture, profession, and so on. More generally, an individual has to obtain minimal consumption for living.

In the end, global distributive justice with process-freedom consists of the allocation of rent-rights in given capacities, and the payments of these rents constitute the corresponding set of transfers. Then, self-rent implies self-usufruct and amounts to self-ownership. But full self-ownership is not required. However, we will see that, conversely, external rent-rights in capacities will be limited both in the nature of capacities and in amount.

Expressed in transferable money value, a partial rent-right in a capacity is the value of the availability of the services that this capacity would provide in a certain given *notional* use that can define the right. This includes a duration of use, but it can also include other specifications: this will be discussed for labor using productive capacities in Chapters 9 and 12. If this is an external rent-right, the bearer of the capacity pays this rent, but with process-freedom she is free to choose the actual use, which can be different from the use defining the right. Moreover, formally, a capacity is a relation between its use and the outcome, and it will turn out to be important, for global distributive justice, that this function can be seen both ways: as the outcome for a given use or as the necessary use for obtaining a given outcome (the difference will come from the fact that equally sharing capacities will depend on the unit used for measuring them, such as units of output or input, and mixed measures can be retained).[4]

The holder of an external rent-right can be an individual or a group, for instance society as a whole, or an institution. Yet, in the latter cases, one may have to specify the final allocation of the benefit to individuals, who may be said to be the actual right holders (for instance, these holders may have an equal share in the right). This remark will have an important application in coming chapters.

The result that will be obtained consists of an equal sharing of the external money rent-rights of all individuals' given productive capacities for the same labour (or equivalently, each individual pays each other the money rent-right of her productive capacities for the same labour). Individuals with low productive capacities then receive a net transfer that compensates this handicap. Conversely, individuals with high productive capacities have to pay a net transfer. Their productivity enables them to earn this amount with less labour than others. And the labour corresponding to this a priori liability will only be a limited share of the labour they choose to perform. This liability is the intrinsic consequence of their natural luck in their endowment of given productivity.

The assignment of a right in a capacity to the bearer of this capacity will be called its "natural" allocation: choosing this allocation will be referred to as endorsing the capacity's natural allocation. This terminology is itself natural in the tradition

[4] See Chapter 9.

of "natural rights" and of most classical theories of the social contract. However, it implies here no a priori value in itself and any such allocation has to be justified, as others. We have obtained that process-freedom implies endorsing the natural allocation of all capacity rights but rent-rights.

3. TYPES OF CAPACITIES, AND THE IRRELEVANCE OF EUDEMONISTIC CAPACITIES FOR MACROJUSTICE

3.1. Relevant types of capacities

An individual's capacities constitute a set of characteristics of hers that determine what she can do, know, feel, and so on. Their consideration is a limitlessly rich and complex issue. These capacities are often not even properly individual, as with capacities for producing items demanded by others and for the various types of social relations – for speaking a language, for instance. However, the issue of macrojustice crucially rests on questions of capacities, but it does not need a refined analysis of the various types of capacities and of their way of intervening. It needs to first consider productive capacities, that is, capacities that can be used for production, notably for earning a wage income and for production for sale. Production of products directly consumed is classically added, but will not be an issue for macrojustice in modern societies; and this problem need not consider the issue of services directly provided to oneself and to family either (although the latter otherwise raises important questions of justice). Activities other than production use many kinds of capacities, a number of which can also be used in production. For example, a number of physical and mental capacities, such as various skills, strength, stamina, intelligence, memory, relational abilities, etc., are used in both productive activities and in entertainment, culture, sports, socialization, play, and so on. Moreover, it sometimes is relevant to consider activity and rest, and the intensity of energy used in an activity or its low level, as alternative uses of capacities.

However, a particular type of capacities needs to be considered here, notably because of its use in eudemonistic or hedonistic concepts of social ethics. This consists of the capacities to derive satisfaction or happiness from a given situation or consumption, or "eudemonistic capacities." They are the propensities to appreciate, enjoy, like or dislike, or endure or suffer. These capacities are essentially independent from production and productive capacities. There are exceptions since eudemonistic or – more often – hedonistic capacities are used in production by particular professions such as artists of various kinds, cooks, stylists, and certain experts. Moreover, happy individuals may be more productive (or less so). However, the independence from production or productive capacities is doubtlessly the relevant view for macrojustice. These capacities are represented by the classical philosophical and economic concept of a "utility" function, when the corresponding "utility" is taken as having the tangible psychological meaning of some level of happiness or satisfaction.[5] Eudemonistic capacities also include capacities to stand and endure. They are essentially psychological properties, but they can mobilize characteristics of various natures, including properties of the senses and epistemic capacities – capacities for knowing. Moreover, they can and will be added capacities to perform various acts necessary or useful in actions of consuming, experiences of enjoying, or protection from suffering. One can thus more generally consider capacities for consuming, or consumptive capacities, or for making the best of life in general (apart from earning).

Finally, the issue here is the allocation of rights in capacities that are *given* to the person. People also form or improve certain capacities of theirs through training, education, or otherwise. This formation is an act and the created capacities are its consequence (either they are the sole intended consequences, or they arrive in addition to some other output in the case of experience and on-the-job training – which commonly are consciously valued). Hence, process-freedom implies self-ownership in these self-created capacities or improvements. But, of course, the given learning capacities used for this education or training are reckoned along with other given capacities, and learning or training for improving productive capacities is included within labour (characterized by duration, intensity, and so on – these issues concerning labour and formation are precisely presented in Chapter 8).[6]

3.2. The irrelevance, or natural allocation, of eudemonistic capacities in macrojustice

3.2.1. The setting

Eudemonistic capacities will be understood in the possibly broad sense just noted. Process-freedom in using one's eudemonistic capacities and benefiting from this use is trivial because any interference with an individual's enjoyment or satisfaction can be described as affecting the set of (other) means at the disposition of this individual. However, external rent-rights in these capacities could be considered. A set of such rights would be met by transfers or other allocations which can perform compensations or, more generally, be function of these capacities, be based on them. This first raises informational difficulties and, more deeply, conceptual ones. Happiness will have to be compared for the same individual in different circumstances, and, for social ethics and justice, across individuals. Moreover, what is

---

[5] This level can remain an ordinal concept (that is, a number replaceable by any increasing function of it). There is no implication that it is "measurable" or "cardinal" (see Kolm 1996a, Chapter 12). Of course, another use of "utility" functions sees them as mere representations of preference orderings.

[6] The properties of justice of educational inputs provided by the family (which have an aspect of bequest) and by the rest of society are discussed elsewhere (see Kolm 1985a, 1996a).

to be compared depends on the considered ethics and circumstances (for instance, this can be levels of satisfaction or their differences, for satisfaction discounting certain features or causes, and so on). The required interpersonal comparisons, notably, are not always meaningless and impossible, but they are not always conceptually and practically possible either.[7] However, these problems turn out not to be actually relevant for endogenous global distributive justice in large modern societies. In these societies, indeed, everyone thinks that this policy should not directly depend on these capacities, as it will shortly be pointed out. For the purpose of macrojustice, there is a consensus for self-ownership of eudemonistic capacities, for the endorsement of their "natural" allocation. The reason is a complex of interrelated notions involving privacy and concepts of the self, which make eudemonistic capacities generally different from productive capacities in this respect. Then, endogenous social choice should endorse this unanimous opinion. As a consequence, global distributive justice with process-freedom will only be concerned with the allocation of the rent of productive capacities.

It seems, indeed, that for deciding about the just allocation of incomes or goods in general and at a global level, everyone thinks that it would not be serious to take differences in individuals' capacities to derive pleasure from their consumption into account. Such considerations may be relevant for distribution facing particular and specific issues, such as trying to soothe – and thus compensate – a propensity to deep depression by providing more goods, or for allocating specific goods among people who enjoy them very differently, but this will not concern the overall, global and general question of distributive justice. The basic reason underlying this general view seems to be that the satisfaction people happen or manage to derive from their consumption or income, and their mental or physiological propensities to this personal experience, are intrinsically their own, are no one else's concern (and in particular not that of a policy caring for distributive justice), and that this enjoyment and the underlying capacity allocation are purely private concerns and issues. For instance, a main tool for global distributive justice is the income tax, and no one – it seems – thinks that someone should pay more or less income tax than someone else because she is more or less able to derive pleasure from income or extra income.[8] By contrast, individuals with a very high propensity to suffer should undoubtedly be helped, and this has a high priority and importance, but this is an issue for medical local justice rather than for global distributive justice. More generally, individuals suffering from any handicap that prevents their living a normal life should undoubtedly be helped, but this very important object of microjustice – and compassion – is not in the realm of global distributive justice in macrojustice.

---

[7] See Chapter 24 and Kolm 1971 (1998), 1994b, 2001b.

[8] The references to general opinion considered here concern the serious opinion of individuals, not the proposals an individual can put forward for the fun of it.

3.2.2. Two eudemonistic ethics and their place

Moreover, if global distributive justice wanted to take individual differences in eudemonistic capacities into account, and if it could sufficiently compare and know them, it would not even a priori know which way to use this criterion and could end up with contradictory conclusions. Should we give more to the deeply depressed, or should we avoid so wasting goods she can hardly appreciate, while others could make the best of them? If someone has a higher capacity to enjoy than someone else, should the second receive more to compensate for this handicap, or should we rather give more to the former – a more efficient "pleasure machine" – to maximize "total happiness" (if this expression and concept can be meaningful)?

In fact, both principles actually exist in thoughtful judgments, and hence can be considered rational for this reason. However, they do not occur in considerations of macrojustice, and hence this dilemma does not appear to be one for this policy, which will be concerned with other reasons and distributive bases.

Indeed, compensating individuals with low endowments of the considered capacity aims at correcting an inequality. And *prima facie* equality in the relevant items is a requirement of impartial rationality.[9] Moreover, mental or physical endowments may be a cause of suffering, and, *prima facie*, holding suffering to be bad doubtlessy is sane judgment. However, compensating for melancholy, soothing depression with more goods, at the cost of penalizing high spirits, which might be justified in particular cases, do not seem to be topics for macrojustice. Particular assistance is deserved by, or due to, people particularly prone to deep pain, but these are, again, cases for medical microjustice.

The other view exists too. The fact that it corresponds to scholars' utilitarianism is not sufficient in itself for proving its actual relevance (this theory raises many problems, to begin with serious logical ones as regards the limitations of the possibility of meaningfully adding individuals' utilities).[10] Yet, there exist actual judgments in this spirit. For instance, something is given to someone rather than to someone else because she enjoys it more. Or a chore is performed by someone rather than by someone else because it is less painful for her to do than it is for the other. However, such judgments are by nature local because they compare differences rather than the overall individual situations which they take for granted (although these situations can influence the specific pleasures or pains considered). They generally concern only specific goods or acts. They happen in local occurrences which are rather occasional. Most of the time, they also concern issues of minor importance. When they concern behaviour within families or other closely knit groups where people can have intense concerns for others, the importance for the individuals can be larger, but the issue remains local and

---

[9] See Chapter 23 and Kolm 1971 [1998], foreword, Section 5.
[10] A full analysis of the various aspects of utilitarianism is proposed in Kolm 1996a, Chapter 14.

takes place in the private sphere. These are questions of microjustice, not of global distributive justice in macrojustice.

The same conclusion is reached in considering global distributive policies, their bases and the reasons for them. These policies are realized by main taxes such as the income tax, and main transfers supporting low incomes (or wage policies). Actual judgments and debates about these policy instruments fully discard eudemonistic capacities. Indeed, should someone with a joyful character pay a higher income tax for compensating or equalizing, or because she is less depressed than others by a lower disposable income? Or should gourmets pay lower income taxes because they can derive "more happiness" from the gain in income? These hardly seem serious questions. By contrast, actually contending judgments are of two kinds, none considering such differences, and the actual political outcome is a compromise between both. One view holds that earnings are deserved. It will justify this position by the reward of effort, or by process-freedom, but it mostly relies on a concept of self-ownership (of productive capacities). The other view focuses on incomes valued for their use. It appraises income distribution, and notably income inequality and low incomes. It expresses a preference for income equality (a rational position given this choice of relevant item) and an aversion for income inequality. It considers that the limit to this ideal rests in disincentive effects of the tax (and possibly of subsidies) based on income.[11] The actual political choice generally is a compromise (self-ownership is sometimes less loudly voiced, but it remains influential). Interpersonal differences in endowments of eudemonistic or other consumptive capacities are absent from the debate and from the final decision.[12]

3.2.3. Vox populi

This shows that, although people actually manifest different opinions about global distributive policies, they basically agree as concerns the irrelevance of the individuals' differential endowments in eudemonistic (or consumptive) capacities for this issue. An individual's happiness or satisfaction can be seen as resulting from her appraisal of the situation (or consumption) she evaluates with her capacities for being happy or satisfied. These capacities are certain properties of the senses, the body, and the mind. The notion that happiness (or satisfaction, possibly represented by utility levels) is the relevant item for direct justice evaluation amounts to the idea that the pool of the causes of the situation (or consumption) and of eudemonistic capacities constitutes what should be distributed, possibly using compensations, with some ideal of reducing discrepancies in the resulting satisfactions. For a utilitarian ethos, the variations of the corresponding satisfactions

---

[11] This "income justice" is analyzed in Chapter 11.

[12] However, "decreasing marginal utility of income" for each individual often appears in discussions of income inequalities (see Kolm 1966a).

are the items to be directly compared.[13] But we have noticed that people actually do not think that an individual should pay more or less income tax than another just because she seems able to derive more or less satisfaction or happiness than the other from a given income or extra income. This is because they deem eudemonistic capacities and the satisfaction they provide for a given situation or consumption to be private concerns, which should not even be explicitly considered by public global distributive justice and, therefore, should not influence the corresponding distributive transfers (a priori, these transfers could try to compensate for some given differences in these capacities, or to use these capacities for maximizing some "global welfare," depending on people's satisfactions). It does not seem that the income tax schedule should depend on whether the taxpayer is a *bon vivant*, a sybarite, or an atrabilious or depressed person. It does not seem justified to tax propensity to happiness or high mood, nor, a priori, to subsidize – or compensate for – intrinsic sadness, gloom, and discontent. And it does not seem justified either – with respect to the utilitarian ethos – to tax someone highly because she cannot derive much pleasure from extra income (this could be a reason to help her, on the contrary), or to reinforce a fortunate disposition to derive pleasure from extra income with a related tax rebate or subsidy.

This latter discarded view, and the utilitarianism which corresponds to it, are discarded on several related grounds as regards global distributive justice. Views of this type can be found, and doubtlessly can be valid, but in cases of local justice rather than for global justice, as we have noticed. Indeed, they judge variations and usually specific goods, rather than the global situation. Relatedly, they cannot meaningfully be expressed as the maximization of a sum of utilities, except for marginal variations in utilities.[14] The considered policy would accentuate unjust inequalities in the natural endowment of eudemonistic capacities. However, it focuses on happiness and on capacities to experience it, which seem to be private issues rather than concerns relevant to public global distributive justice.

In contrast, production for an income is what one gives to society and receives from it. Hence, it is public by nature, in a sense in which consumption and satisfaction are not (even if it occurs in a private relation). This gives it one possible reason – which satisfaction lacks – for being a possible direct concern for global distributive policy.

In all cases, of course, the considered issue of relevance or irrelevance of eudemonistic capacities for distribution policy implementing global distributive justice solely concerns their direct consideration and, more specifically, the interpersonally comparative intensity of the resulting happiness or satisfaction. Indeed, eudemonistic capacities for each individual separately are related to individuals'

---

[13] For a more explicit and precise presentation, see Kolm 1996a, Chapter 14.

[14] The required cardinal utilities have no rational or psychological meaning beyond small variations (see Kolm 1996a, Chapters 12 and 14).

preferences and choices (they may determine their preference orderings).[15] And these preferences and choices determine supplies and demands and hence prices, and notably incomes and the money value of the rents of all resources.

3.2.4. The scope of public concern with happiness and suffering

Of course, discarding eudemonistic capacities from the direct concern of *global* redistribution does not imply finding happiness unimportant! Happiness, quite the contrary, can be thought to be very important, or, possibly, the only important thing; notably because people care much for it or, possibly, care only for it (this issue is partly a question of definition of terms). The point is that global distributive justice is a public issue concerned with (overall) distribution. If the happiness that an individual derives from a given allocation of goods or a given situation, and her dispositions and propensities in this respect, are private concerns of hers, this benefit from her eudemonistic capacities, and these capacities, are irrelevant to global distributive justice. This does not preclude that these capacities and the happiness they produce can be very important in an overall evaluation of societies. This direct irrelevance of eudemonistic capacities to public global justice solely means that the corresponding criteria of this justice will exclude consideration of these capacities and of their direct effects on individuals' happiness. These criteria will therefore be based on the other causes of individuals' satisfaction (for an individualistic conception of justice),[16] that is, notably, consumption or income (and labor provided or leisure) or the ways and means of their acquisition. For instance, the optimum may have to be Pareto-efficient with utilities representing levels of happiness, and yet its choice among the Pareto-efficient states may have to be determined by criteria that do not refer to these utility levels, but, rather, refer to the distribution of consumption or incomes or to ways, processes, or means through which they are obtained.[17] These incomes or consumption are, then, enjoyed by individuals "with" their eudemonistic capacities.

In particular, the existence of deep unhappiness and insatisfaction, and of misery, are certainly of prime concern for evaluating society, and they are issues for individualistic justice. However, the main reason for misery at a global level is dire poverty preventing the satisfaction of basic needs. And poverty is an issue about the distribution of resources other than eudemonistic capacities (but including

[15] We will see in Chapter 11 that individuals' indifference plays a role in the most common income-egalitarian ethics, for the cases of incomes of individuals who provide different labours.

[16] A conception of justice is individualistic when end values are aspects of the individuals' (but not necessarily their happiness) and for their sake. In other cases, the situations of individuals are by-products or means of other social-ethical aims (see Kolm 1996a, Chapter 1).

[17] There are a priori many such possible criteria. The solution presented in following chapters is one of them. A number of others can be found, notably, in Kolm 1996a, 1996b, 1971, 1993d, 1993e, 1993f, 1999b. A standard method for achieving such a result consists of allocating resources and letting individuals freely interact, notably exchange, in a way that guarantees this efficiency. This allocation can be just and the interaction accepted from social freedom.

productive capacities and rights to their products). The simple distribution of rights to resources derived below will generally suffice for permitting the satisfaction of basic needs (or needed extra assistance will be exceptional and small, and hence again an issue for microjustice, although this policy would be very important in intrinsic value, if not in volume and in number of aided people). People who are miserable because they are deeply depressed, as those who suffer from a severe handicap of any type, should certainly receive a particular aid, but this, again, is an issue in microjustice. Other needs are aspects of the general structure of satisfaction capacities, whether they are assets that permit particular enjoyment or self-realization, or liabilities by the resources demanded by their satisfaction.

3.2.5. Selfhood and incommensurability

In the end, global distributive justice in large, modern societies should undoubtedly endorse the natural allocation of eudemonistic or satisfaction capacities. The basic reason for this allocation has several closely related aspects. One is its noted private character. The satisfaction that a person derives and can derive from her consumption or from life is seen as a private matter for her – or even an intimate concern – and not a proper concern for the redistributive transfers and policy implementing global justice. This allocation also relates to the concept of selfhood and its respect. Satisfaction capacities are seen as belonging to the "core self",[18] because of their relation to feeling, preferences, choice, and action. This is taken as a reason for endorsing their natural allocation. Relatedly, material compensations and transfers are sometimes considered inappropriate by nature for compensating interindividual differences in eudemonistic capacities. Both are bound to be seen as belonging to different and incommensurable "spheres." Furthermore, the very definition of satisfaction or happiness, their sufficient description, and their interpersonal comparison, raise problems which are not only informational, but also, more deeply, conceptual.

3.2.6. Freedom and responsibility?

Other reasons for this endorsement of the natural allocation of eudemonistic capacities have been suggested but are problematic. Rawls argues that individuals' freedom of choice (of their life plans) entails that the relevant end values of justice are their external means of these choices (that is, not their mental or bodily means), namely the act-freedom (and political) parts of the classical basic freedoms on the one hand, and "primary goods" (income, wealth, power, positions, and self-respect

---

[18] The various possible concepts of the self are analyzed in Kolm 1982a, Chapter 19. Only the most straightforward and unsubtle concept is involved here. This does not interfere with the deeper basic philosophy of "selflessness."

or the means for it) on the other hand.[19] However, this view is not sufficient in itself. Indeed, this free choice does not per se rule out the existence, and the possible relevance, of interindividual differences in possible benefits from capacities to be satisfied with each alternative and in particular with the one they choose, and of the capacities which permit or provide this satisfaction.

A more relevant view holds that people are responsible for their tastes, which implies that they are accountable for them.[20] If the considered "tastes" include capacities to derive satisfaction – and not solely causes of preferences and choice – this hypothesis bears on the present issue. However, the term *responsibility* implies that someone can be held responsible for something solely if willfull acts of hers are one of its causes or if she could have prevented it. Any use of this term that violates this condition just is a mistake in the English language (or in any other language that uses this term). The speaker then generally means accountability rather than responsibility. Responsibility is one possible reason for accountability, but there are others, either closely related ones such as aim-freedom, merit, or desert, or possibly more distant ones such as concepts of "natural" rights (or natural entitlement, duty, or liability), privacy, concepts of the self, need, and so on. In fact, with process-freedom, one hardly needs a concept of responsibility, since the individual is entitled to what she has willfully done: this could be her tastes, possibly in choosing them not to be different while this was a possibility. People, however, do not choose their tastes, although they occasionally willfully influence them through purposeful training or habit formation. Therefore, the issue is whether people could change their tastes or could have chosen to have different ones. This question has no easy answer. It involves delicate psychological, social, philosophical, logical, and semantic considerations. And if people could change their tastes or could have chosen to have different ones, this process could hardly provide any desired result instantaneously and without effort. Then, one should distinguish these given constraints, for which the individual is not responsible, from the rest of this choice, for which she can be. This distinction also raises rather subtle logical, semantic, and philosophical issues.

To begin with, responsibility is sometimes simply discarded as irrelevant on the ground that freedom does not exist because of universal causality and determinism, including in the mental causes of action. Even short of this inclusive

[19] Rawls' theory does not include aim-freedom because its ideal of equal incomes, and its objective of maximin in an index of primary goods that include income (the "difference principle"), for incomes essentially including earned incomes, constitute policies based on earned incomes. Adding leisure to the list of primary goods – an addition Rawls has admitted – would face this issue only if the trade-off between leisure and income in the index is specific to each individual and equal to her wage rate. However, equality in these parts of the index would then yield the unacceptable "maximal income equalization" (see Chapter 9) if the unit is income, and full self-ownership – that Rawls does not want – if the unit is time of leisure (or labour). In fact, the ideal of equal disposable income desired by Rawls (and many others) is approximated in respecting process-freedom and Pareto efficiency by the policy presented in Chapter 11.

[20] This was proposed in Kolm (1966a, and its reprints in 1968, p. 154, and 1969, p. 181), discussed by Ronald Dworkin (1981), but also more or less suggested by Saint Augustine and, of course, implied by Jean-Paul Sartre's extensive conception of responsibility.

view, a classical position (generally of the political left) emphasizes the determining influence of the social environment on the individual's formation and thus downgrades her possible responsibility. The intrinsic denial of freedom, however, bypasses the basic definition of this concept, which makes it fully consistent with universal causality: free means caused by the will or, more restrictively, by reason (which needs the will to trigger the free act).[21] Then, however, how does one justify drawing moral consequences from a particular structure of causality? The notion of responsibility may just be unwarranted fetishization (or hypostasis) of the consequentialist reason for punishment (influencing behavior). The answer to this question shifts to the reasons for valuing process-freedom (which includes aim-freedom, entitlement to the consequences of one's action); they have been considered in Chapter 4 with regard to basic rights, notably as concerns the existence and respect of agency. A further crucial problem is, of course, the treatment of joint causes.

The question then becomes the delimitation of the domain of possible choice. This amounts to the specification of the terms "could" or "can" as concerns the creation or prevention of certain aspects of one's tastes, preferences, or eudemonistic capacities. The individual cannot be held responsible for what is given to her about these items or in the process of their change. She could be held responsible for the rest. Tastes are not directly chosen. However, individuals sometimes willfully influence their tastes in playing with habit formation, familiarity, attention, culture, and sometimes reason, often using indirect strategies: they can more or less choose or manage to pay or not pay attention, focus attention, forget about something, get used to, acquire or lose a habit, acquire culture, or try to be influenced by good reasons. There thus are possibilities. However, these formations and transformations are often slow and long, sometimes painful (as with quitting an addiction), and they usually affect only a small part of individuals' tastes. Hence, changing one's tastes does not seem easy, and the concept of responsibility also implies that responsibility is the lower, the more difficult, costly, or painful the missing act is.

Why, however, don't individuals choose their tastes more? They sometimes regret some of their tastes. Different tastes would make them avoid frustrations and dissatisfactions, and permit them to enjoy items that presently leave them indifferent, and they know it. They would probably be happier in liking what their circumstances impose upon them (as hellenistic, buddhist, and some other philosophies advocate – and most religions propose some aspect of acquiescing to what happens to be the case). And all this happens "in the mind" – given the senses. The nature of the limits and possibilities should thus be considered. The most basic issues involve psychology, logic, and "ontology," with questions of self-reference and "weakness of the will" (Aristotle's *akrasia*). People may want to change their tastes, but not at the cost of losing their self, importantly defined by their tastes. People often manifest a "weakness of the will" about changing their tastes: they would like to do it but cannot sufficiently want to do it. This phenomenon has an

---

[21] See Kolm 1982a (1994), 1984b, 1996a (Chapter 1).

ambivalent status as regards freedom (and responsibility): if weakness of the will is considered a property of the will, its existence manifests freedom, whereas if it is seen as imposed on the will as a constraint or an obstacle, it constitutes a lack of freedom. In the former case, the individual is responsible for her tastes. In the latter, she is not. Willfully choosing one's tastes also involves a double personality: the actor who performs the change and the holder of the tastes (either the actor or the resisting holder may be responsible). Moreover, such processes involve a series of self-referential relations, which imply either circularity of infinite regress, such as willing to will, preferring to prefer, desiring to desire, choosing one's principles of choice, or having tastes about tastes.

One conclusion is that the concept of responsibility for one's tastes is not sufficiently well defined and meaningful in itself. Further specification of the meaning of free choice is required. However, accountability for one's tastes can be retained for other reasons. And its being endorsed for the purpose of global distribution of resources (and liabilities) by consensual opinion constitutes a sufficient consideration for the present purpose.

3.3. Differences between productive and eudemonistic capacities

Full self-ownership considers capacities globally. It sees no relevant difference between eudemonistic and productive capacities. We have seen that consensual opinion holds that macrojustice should endorse the natural allocation of eudemonistic capacities. The close analysis of this issue, however, has shown that this view results from quite specific reasons. And these reasons hardly apply to productive capacities.

Eudemonistic capacities are basically capacities to feel and experience emotions, using capacities to evaluate or discriminate, and resting in part on habit, experience, and culture. They can be seen as more intimate, more private, or more constitutive of the individual, than the capacities to act, relate, or even to know (cognitive capacities), which constitute the bulk of productive capacities. The benefit from eudemonistic capacities is direct and inalienable (although possibly compensatable), while that from productive skills is indirect and mediated by society, since it usually passes through labour, income, expenditure, and then consumption. The outcome of eudemonistic capacities – happiness, satisfaction, pleasure, joy, sorrow, pain, anxiety, and so on – is experienced by the capacity holder, whereas the product of productive capacities can be alienated, transferred to others and used or consumed by them, and it normally is with the standard division of labour. As a result, the values of the services provided by productive capacities are objective, clear, well-defined, measurable, directly interpersonally comparable, and in the nature of the income transfers that can redistribute them. In contrast, the values of the services provided by eudemonistic capacities are personal, their interpersonal comparability raises practical and conceptual difficulties, and they are sometimes seen in a sphere too constitutive of the person for it being proper to normally compensate for them by income transfers.

The value of productive capacities in income or consumption they can provide by wage labour or the sale of their product depend on the demand for their services or product. The capacities themselves determine only the type of supply that determines this value. And the demand is external to the worker. Hence, a large part of the income value of the rent of productive capacities originates outside the person. Earned income also depends on demand as well as on the used productive capacities, but process-freedom applied to the free exchange of labour allocates it to the worker, a situation that does not exist for the value of the rent. The satisfaction, happiness, or pleasure that eudemonistic capacities can provide also depend on the adequation between the specific propensities they constitute and the external world. For instance, the relation between tastes and prices – and hence the external supply of goods – influences the satisfaction an individual can derive from a given income (one benefits from preferring cheap goods and is penalized by expensive tastes). This parallels the noted effect about productive capacities. However, individuals usually provide only one type of labour, whereas they consume a large number of types of goods, and many goods are consumed by most people (with similar incomes). Hence, the interindividual differences due to this kind of effects are bound to be much larger for productive capacities than for eudemonistic ones. Moreover, the intensity of satisfaction for given consumption or situation is proper to the person. On the whole, more depends on the individual, and less on the rest of society, in the value of eudemonistic capacities than in that of productive capacities.

On related but more "metaphysical" grounds, self-rights can be justified by a respect of selfhood. An individual would have a "self" including various elements.[22] She would be entitled to these elements or to their integrity, and outside interference with them would be a violation of these intrinsic rights. Then, eudemonistic capacities and the manifestations of the benefits they provide – being happy or satisfied – would undoubtedly all belong to this self. Productive capacities are different for three possible reasons. The first applies a remark just presented. With process-freedom, the distributionally relevant aspect of productive capacities is their rent, the value of the availability of their services. This value in income depends not only on these capacities, but also on the demand for the services or product they enable labour to produce. And this demand has nothing to do with an intrinsic self of the person. It is external to her. In no way can it be seen as "intrinsically belonging" to her. This is to be contrasted with the legitimation of earned income by process-freedom as the result of an act of free exchange yielding the services or product of labour which legitimately uses productive capacities. We have noticed that a corresponding effect of markets on the value of eudemonistic capacities is a priori and on the whole relatively less important. The second difference is that the services from productive capacities can benefit other persons, as opposed to satisfaction or suffering induced by eudemonistic capacities, and hence the former are outside the "self" while the latter are not. Thirdly, even for the capacities

---

[22] As we have noted, we only refer to down-to-earth concepts of the self here. For a full analysis of the various aspects of this issue, see Kolm 1982a, notably Chapter 19.

themselves, eudemonistic capacities can be seen as belonging to a "core self" that experiences feeling and directs action, whereas other capacities would be relegated to an instrumental role of information and action. In particular, for the present topic of social ethics, there are classically two alternative basic views of the human being. In one view, the individual is a sentient being who can incur happiness or suffering through the application or working of her eudemonistic capacities. In the other, the individual is a free chooser and actor, and a classical theory of man sees choice as the effect of preferences derived from the structure of satisfaction capacities (and the will then probably also has to rest in this system). In both cases, the relevant aspect of an individual is her satisfaction capacities as they generate happiness or choice. Productive capacities are, in these respects, more "detachable" and "externalizable," and not so inherent to the relevant core self.

Furthermore, an individual cannot be held responsible for the given productive capacities which we consider here (since, by definition, it is and was not possible for her to influence them), and hence for their productivity for given labour. The analysis of the effects and costs of education and training permits distinguishing the given part of productive capacities (see Chapter 8). Eudemonistic capacities are different. Individuals can more or less influence them by training (getting used to, losing a habit), by education and culture, or by reasoning. However, we have noticed that the question of responsibility in tastes, preferences, or eudemonistic capacities raise deeper issues which blurr the very concept and question. Too much change in these items may produce a different person. This may be a motive for limiting the change. Weakness of the will is a common feature of such changes – and a reason for the common use of indirect strategies constraining one's future choices. And freedom and responsibility are higher if weakness of the will is considered a part of the will rather than an "external" limit to its action. We also noted the various self-referential problems. In the end, both a concept of given tastes for which the individual is not responsible, and that of responsibility in tastes, are not well defined without a much thinner consideration of issues and meanings. However, assigning much responsibility for their tastes to individuals is a logically possible option and, indeed, a position adopted by a number of morals and philosophies.

All these differences have an impact on the possibility of implementing and, more deeply, of defining, the relevant distributive policies. With process-freedom, the benefits from the productive use of productive capacities are essentially earned incomes, and in particular wages. They are relatively well defined, observable, measurable, and interpersonally comparable. In contrast, the benefits from eude-monistic capacities, satisfaction or happiness (or their variations), raise not only difficulties of observation and information, but also intrinsic conceptual problems of meaning, definition and, notably, possibility of interpersonal comparability.[23] Informational issues are no reason for the choice of the distributionally relevant

---

[23] See Kolm 1971 (1998), 1994b, 2001b.

items (the rational determination of proxies for these items, if necessary, is another question). However, the noted difficulties are also conceptual, and they are closely related to the *sui generis* and intrinsically personal aspects of these capacities, and hence to the basic reasons for the actual consensus about the moral irrelevance of these capacities for global distributive policy implementing macrojustice.

*

The conclusion reached so far is that endogenous global distributive justice is only concerned with the allocation of the value of given productive capacities. The resulting structure of the distribution is derived in Part II.

PART TWO

OVERALL DISTRIBUTIVE JUSTICE: ELIE (EQUAL LABOUR INCOME EQUALIZATION)

7

Equal labour income equalization:
General presentation

INTRODUCTION

This chapter outlines the solution of the problem of macrojustice implied by the premises presented in Part I, the essentials of this derivation, and the general properties of this result. Further chapters present this solution, its reason, and its properties with formal models which are increasingly refined, notably as concerns the description of labour and of its yielding product and income. This leads to the successive consideration of constant wage rates, more general individual productivities, explicit modeling of all the characteristics of labour, and total or partial involuntary unemployment. Another chapter discusses the question of information for the implementation of the distributive policy, and Part III compares the obtained scheme with present policies, proposals of assistance schemes, and philosophers' and economists' conceptions.

The present chapter can thus be said to present "the philosophy" of the question – as common language uses this term. It uses no explicit formalization. Readers particularly familiar with formal models may prefer to begin by reading Chapters 9 or 11 (and 13 for the treatment of involuntary unemployment). Chapter 11 presents the most general case, but Chapter 9, which considers labour measurable as a quantity and fixed wage rates, permits an easy discussion of the main issues – actual cases can often be presented in this way for reasons and with adjustments that will be presented in Chapter 8.

The present chapter divides in two parts. Part I presents the solution of the problem of global or overall distributive justice, outlines the reason for its derivation, and points out some of its main properties, notably as concerns low incomes. Part II is more particular since it focuses on the extreme, limiting cases of incomes, labour, and of the degree of equalization. Hence, it is possible to skip Part II at first reading and to pass from the "philosophical" general presentation of Part I to its presentation with a simple formal model in Chapter 9 (the simplicity rests in taking labour as a quantity with constant wage rates, a case explained and justified in Chapter 8, whereas Chapter 12 considers the most general case). However,

Part II presents notable issues, cases, and properties, such as the surprising effects of a "workfare ethics" (no aid without labour) and of a "right to idleness" (possibility of abstaining from work), and the cases of an absence of equalization (self-ownership) and of very high equalization.

The solution shown in Section I-1 is "equal labour income equalization" or, for short, ELIE. Section I-2 notes the various general ethical aspects and meanings of this scheme. Section I-3 then remarks that ELIE de facto and approximately implies a minimum income; more precisely, however, it implies a minimum income in the exact measure in which the individuals are not responsible for their low earnings. The effects of ELIE as alleviating poverty is the topic of Section I-4. This shows the various properties of this aspect of ELIE, the comparisons with other actual or proposed modes of relieving poverty, and illustrative numerical examples. Section II-1 then focuses on the cases of the lowest and highest possible labours and incomes for the individuals. The issues are notably unemployment incomes and "workfare" judgments, minimal necessary labours and a "right to idleness," and a possible right to average maximal labour. Finally, Section II-2 considers the two limiting cases of ELIE, full self-ownership and maximal income equalization, and it notably shows the defects of these extreme solutions, with conclusions as regards the appropriate degree of income value equalization.

I. THE SOLUTION AND ITS REASON, MEANINGS, AND BASIC PROPERTIES

I.1. THE SOLUTION AND ITS REASONS AND PROPERTIES

We seek to determine overall or global distributive justice in macrojustice implied by the closely related principles of unanimity or consensus, and general social freedom (See Chapter 1), and, hence, the constitutional basic rights and process-freedom (Chapters 2, 3, and 4), and Pareto efficiency. We have seen that the issue to be determined is the allocation of the rent-rights in given productive capacities. Indeed, efficiency and process-freedom de facto imply that the issue is the distribution of the (given) natural resources (Chapter 1), and that all rights in given (human) capacities but rent-rights should be allocated to their bearer (Chapter 6). Moreover, by consensual opinion as concerns global (overall) distributive policies, all rights in eudemonistic capacities should be self-owned for macrojustice (Chapter 6). Furthermore, the value produced by nonhuman natural resources is a minute fraction of that produced (and, still more, produceable) by productive capacities, many of these resources concern microjustice, and anterior allocation of such resources can hardly be disentangled (Chapter 5).

However, people are directly concerned not with capacities, but with two kinds of goods. One kind can be considered as constituted by the pair of complementary items leisure and labour. The other good is consumption, bought by disposable income. Note that labour is a priori multidimensional: it is defined by a set of characteristics such as duration, speed, intensity, attention, previous formation in training or schooling, and so on.[1] Leisure is the complement of labour in all these dimensions, and it thus includes leisure time, more leisurely work, and so on. We will see, however, that duration, or a duration adjusted for taking differences in the other characteristics into account, is often particularly important (Chapter 8). As concerns the other good, process-freedom implies free selling of services and output of labour and buying of goods, and hence it enables one to conflate, for the present purpose, output and earnings on the one hand, and disposable income and consumption on the other hand.

A capacity is not in itself a final desired or disliked good or bad: it is a means that permits one to relate two such finally desired or disliked items. Productive capacities, notably, provide output-income-consumption for given labour and leisure. Equivalently and symmetrically, a capacity can be seen as providing, for a given output, the leisure that remains after labour has produced it. This relation is the individual productivity or production function.

The foregoing shows that macrojustice implies a sharing of the value of individuals' productive capacities, with no other relevant differences among the individuals. Hence, rationality requires a *prima facie* objective of identical treatment.[2] However, there are two goods: income-consumption, and leisure (or labour). The leisure (or labour) of different individuals has no reason to be differentiated for its direct effects on the individuals (that is, irrespective of differences in productivities). These two goods are the items in which the distribution a priori takes place. Moreover, they constitute inputs and outputs of the productive capacities, and hence, provide two measures of their amounts, which yield different results in the equalization but can a priori be combined. These views lead to two different but equivalent ways of obtaining the result. These derivations will be precisely shown in Chapter 9, but their essence can be outlined.

The allocation of the value (the rent) of productive capacities is a priori done in the two goods that concern the individuals: income-consumption and leisure. Being a priori allocated some leisure means owing the complementary labour, or the output one can produce with it. These pairs are the individuals' allocations relevant for the considered distribution and its distributive justice. Nothing else can relevantly differentiate the individuals here (their eudemonistic capacities are irrelevant for macrojustice, so are any particular associated needs, and they are free to use their productive capacities and earn and merit or deserve the product). Then, the rationality of justice requires the identity of these initially allocated bundles. Equal owed labours are transferred in the form of the value of their outputs, and these values are equally shared for providing the equal individual incomes.[3]

---

[1] "Effort" consists of intensity with difficulty or painfulness: it is not a pure labour input concept.

[2] See Chapter 23, and a more detailed analysis in Kolm 1971 (English translation 1998), foreword, Section 5.

[3] Chapters 9 and 12 show with pecision the question of the equal sharing of the relevant values of individuals' productive capacities.

This allocation is superimposed on full process-freedom where the individuals freely work and earn without impediment, tax, or subsidy. This association can equivalently be seen as individuals freely deviating from a benchmark constituted by the allocated leisure or labour and income, in working more or less and keeping the corresponding earnings or incurring the corresponding loss in foregone earnings. In fact, however, this distributive "benchmark" will turn out to be such that most individuals will choose to work more.

The result is *equal labour income equalization*, ELIE for short. Each individual yields her product of the same labour and receives an equal share of the sum, that is, the average. This labour is the "equalization labour." Since these individuals generally have different productive capacities and productivities, the amounts paid by each a priori differ, and so do the net results of the transfers for each. More productive individuals pay more and, in the end, the more productive pay and the less productive receive since the overall set of transfers is balanced. The equalization labour, a notional benchmark, generally differs from the actual labours chosen by the individuals.

This result also constitutes a possible equal allocation of the rent-rights of productive capacities. Indeed, it means that the individuals equally share the income values of the capacities used by the same equalization labour for all; and keep for themselves the value of the availability of the rest of their own productive capacities, which corresponds to the equal notional complementary leisure. This result equivalently refers to the two possible ways of comparing or measuring capacities and productivities for implementing the equal sharing of their whole value. Productivities, indeed, relate labour and leisure on the one hand and income or consumption on the other. Then, the given allocation is, for a part, equal leisure, and for the other equal income resulting from the complementary (equalization) labour. From this benchmark, the process-free individuals choose to work more or less in keeping the corresponding earnings (or losses).

Full self-ownership is the particular case where each individual owns all the rent of her own productive capacities; that is, the reference (benchmark) labour and the transfers vanish. This is a particular equal allocation, obtained when individuals' productive capacities are measured by the labour that could use them. This limiting case a priori just constitutes one possibility among many others.

An individual's earnings for the equalization labour is her "equalization income," and the average of these is the "average equalization income." ELIE amounts to each individual yielding her equalization income and receiving the average equalization income. Hence, the net result is that individuals whose equalization income falls short of average receive and those whose equalization income exceeds average yield. The equalization labour and incomes vanish with full self-ownership.

For instance, the incomes that the individuals could earn during one day and a half a week would be equally redistributed, and the individuals are otherwise free to work as much as they want for an untaxed and unsubsidized income. In fact, the volume of actual redistributions at national levels are those of ELIE with equalization labours from one to two days a week (from the United States to Scandinavian countries) – but the structures of these actual present-day redistributions are not those of ELIE. The other dimensions of labour will also have to be made precise (intensity, speed, attention, previous training or education, etc.) – see Chapter 8.

Practical realization can take various forms, depending on the institutional setting, but the common case will be a realization by a balanced set of contributions or taxes and subsidies (which will constitute most of the operations of the "distribution function" of a public sector). An individual less productive than average for the equalization labour will receive a subsidy equal to the excess of the average equalization income over her own, and an individual more productive than average for the equalization labour will pay a distribution tax equal to the excess of her equalization income over the average.

ELIE also amounts to a set of bilateral transfers where each individual pays $1/n$ – where n is the number of individuals – of her equalization income to each other. This shows how the ELIE set of transfers can equivalently be seen as a set of bilateral transfers or as a set of balanced transfers to and from a redistributive center (the fiscal administration).

The information necessary for the realization of this distribution consists of the individual productions for the equalization labour, or the competitive wage rates. These wages are the basic data exhibited by the labour market, and nine-tenths of labour is wage labour in industrial countries. On the whole and on the average, this information is more readily available than that required for implementing the bulk of present-day tax or subsidy rules. Facing the problems of information raised by various particular cases by recoupment, comparison, estimates, proxies, and so on are the usual routine of fiscal administrations. This question will be considered in detail in Chapter 10.

There are two particular borderline cases. In one, the equalization labour vanishes: this is full self-ownership. In the other, the equalization labour is one that produces the highest possible income: this is maximal income equalization. They would be the solution if, respectively, only leisure or only income mattered for the choice of justice and hence had to be equalized. We will see, however, that maximal income equalization is utterly unrealistic at national levels and is also ethically defective (Section 7), and hence the equalization labour should be far from maximal (this borderline case will nevertheless be considered for the information it brings about the logic of ELIE). In fact, we will see that the equalization labour will have to be lower, even substantially so, than most actual labours. It should be pointed out that the classical ideal of equal disposable incomes, a standard leftist position, is not the considered maximal income equalization. Maximal income equalization, indeed, implies that there are transfers from individuals with high productive capacities to individuals with low productive capacities that do not correspond to actual labour and production, but to potential ones during the actual leisure of the individuals. Taxing income one *could* have produced during leisure is generally not found ethically adequate. The exact and complete position of present-day income egalitarians will be considered in Chapter 11. It turns out to be best realized by an ELIE with an equalization labour in the neighbourhood of the lowest normal standard full labours.

I.2. ETHICAL MEANINGS OF ELIE

ELIE has a number of characteristic (necessary and sufficient) properties which present ethical meaningfulness in themselves. Although they are logically equivalent, they show different meaningful moral aspects of this scheme.

The very way in which ELIE has been arrived at shows a number of these aspects. ELIE adds a number of other equalities to full process-freedom. One is *equal given allocation of income and leisure*. This is a type of *equality of opportunity* from which the individuals are free to deviate in working more (or less) and in receiving the corresponding extra earnings (or incurring the loss of foregone income). ELIE is an *equal sharing of the value or rent of the given productive capacities*, with, in the general case, one part measured in income or consumption and the other measured in labour or leisure value. These two parts can be considered in themselves. Hence, ELIE can be seen as *equal self-ownership* – but not necessarily full self-ownership. The complement is the equalization labour and the equalization of its products is a rational necessity. From a complementary point of view, ELIE also is *equal common ownership* of the income values of individuals' capacities that can be used by the equalization labour, a community that is translated as equal sharing. It consists of erasing the effects of differences in individuals' productivities on individuals' incomes and consumptions for this equalization labour. For this equalization labour, it is *equal pay for equal work* (a principle applied here for erasing the effects of differences in productivities rather than solely for banning various discriminations as in its usual applications – basic rights guarantee against discriminations); *equality of opportunity* in this sense; *from each equally in labour, to each equally in money*; or, in money, *from each according to her capacities, to each equally* (while "to each according to her capacities" holds for the rest of labour). Note that ELIE is equality of opportunity in two opposite understandings of the concept: equal freedom to use one's particular capacities for deviating from the equal given allocation of income and leisure, and equal pay for equal work for the equalization labour.

The ELIE distribution thus provides a certain compensation of the advantage of having a higher productivity and of the relative handicap of having a lower one. The equalization labour is an index of solidarity, compensation, redistribution, or equalization. We will see, however, that when it is excessive, the relative advantage and disadvantage of having a high or low productivity are not only erased but, in fact, reversed in a symmetrical way: the distribution can become exploitative of the ablest who lose freedom and welfare because of the high tax they have to pay. However, we will also see that the equalization labour should not exceed the normal full labour (note that it does not seem appropriate that people pay taxes for productive capacities not used for earning).

ELIE also amounts to each individual yielding to each other the same fraction $1/n$ of her equalization income, where n is the number of individuals, and receiving a corresponding amount from each other. With constant wage rates, ELIE amounts to *each individual yielding to and receiving from each other the product of the same labour.* Hence, *macrojustice is justice as balanced labour reciprocity* in this sense. The equalization labour is also an index of this reciprocity or mutuality.

ELIE also implies that a lower productivity or wage rate is compensated by an extra income transfer (or lower tax) proportional to this gap.

ELIE also means that productive capacities are pooled for the equalization labour, with an equal distribution of the proceeds, while they are self-owned otherwise. In this sense, the equalization labour constitutes an *index of economic productive or patrimonial communitarianism* of society, and the complementary leisure is, correspondingly, an index of economic productive or patrimonial individualism of society. This is more communitarian than the relation in a simple community of exchanges – which also exists here – although this differs from cultural communitarianism. This aspect is an important issue for the determination of the equalization labour discussed in Part IV.

I.3. MINIMUM INCOME

In a large community such as present-day national communities, which are the communities within which most of the redistribution achieved by public finances takes place, the equalization labours that can realistically be considered will be below most freely chosen actual labours. This is in tune with the size of actual redistributions since, as noted above, redistributions of similar volumes would be reached by ELIE with an equalization labour of one to two days a week. This also relates to the basic moral reason of not redistributing incomes that are only potential (see Sections 3 and 7). Precisions about characteristics of labour other than duration (intensity, previous education and training, etc.) would not affect this remark. Now, an individual who works more than the equalization labour has a final disposable income higher than the average equalization income (since her income is the average equalization income plus the earnings provided by the extra work). An individual who can obtain no earnings from the market (and hence who usually does not work) receives the average equalization income from ELIE. An individual with a very low wage practically receives the average equalization income (her equalization income which she yields is very low). The (other) cases of involuntary unemployment, including those of people in partial quantitative or qualitative involuntary unemployment,[4] are dealt with in Chapter 13, where it is shown that these people finally dispose of the average equalization income

---

[4] Qualitative involuntary unemployment includes jobs not using the worker's level of qualification.

if they work no more than the equalization labour (in particular, with complete involuntary unemployment), and have a higher disposable income otherwise.

Hence, the average equalization income appears de facto as about a lower bound of incomes. The only possible exceptions are those of rare individuals who freely choose to work very little while they could easily obtain an income higher than this level: they may be neglected when considering global distributive justice in macro-justice and, moreover, they are definitely and unambiguously responsible for their low income (more precisely, the lower the individual's productivity, the closer her income is to the average equalization income, and the higher her productivity, the easier it is for her to obtain a higher income – and hence the more responsible she is if she does not).[5] Hence, given average productivity, a sufficient equalization labour permits one to provide a sufficient level for this minimum income.

I.4. THE EFFICIENT AND FINANCED RELIEF OF POVERTY: PROPERTIES, COMPARISONS, AND A NUMERICAL EXAMPLE

I.4.1. The ELIE relief of poverty

Involuntary poverty results from people not being able to earn sufficient income. ELIE subsidizes people who can only earn less than average for the equalization labour. It thus alleviates poverty. It can do it sufficiently if average productivity and the equalization labour are not too low. Its realization of this result has the following characteristics:

1) The *rationale* of ELIE is that it is the structure of the *just allocation of resources resulting from social freedom or basic rights*. These classical basic rights are the protective rights (Berlin's "negative freedom" – see Chapter 2), and they include no right to the relief of poverty or to income transfers per se. ELIE's alleviation of poverty is not its *direct* aim; it solely is a consequence of its more general logic. This basic rationale of ELIE entails all its other characteristics.
2) ELIE is a *Pareto-efficient* scheme, since its transfers are based on the market value of the availability of inelastic given productive capacities. That is, it induces *no social waste*. Indeed, this property entails that the global distributive policy is an ELIE. And Pareto efficiency is required by the condition of unanimity (see Chapter 1).
3) ELIE is a *financially balanced* scheme. It jointly defines the subsidies and their financing by its taxes.
4) The beneficiaries of ELIE subsidies are the legitimate owners of the rents on productive capacities that generate these transfers. ELIE is *not an assistance scheme*. It is an implementation of property *rights*. These are rights in others'

---

[5] In fact, the actual social unit will be the household rather than the individual in a strict sense, and hence people who work only part time for bringing an income complement to the family do not raise a problem here.

capacities, but, as previously noted, there is a basic reciprocity. These aspects are bound to have favourable influences on social attitudes and the receiver's dignity.

5) ELIE subsidies are not provided under a *condition of resources* or income, but they are under a *condition of capacities* for earning income. These are the given capacities for which the individual is not responsible, whereas, given these capacities, individuals are responsible for their labour, earnings, and the resulting income.

I.4.2. Comparison with other schemes

In all these respects, ELIE widely differs from classical actual or proposed assistance schemes such as specific aids in kind, guaranteed income, negative income tax or income tax credit, universal basic income, or welfarist "optimum income tax." These comparisons will be developed in Chapter 15.

In brief, guaranteed income, negative income tax, and welfarist "optimum" income taxation induce *wasteful disincentives*. Wasteful disincentives are also induced by the financing of the subsidies of universal basic income, guaranteed income, negative income tax, and aid in kind if they are financed by the usual, wasteful, taxes. Aid in kind is also Pareto inefficient if it induces people to consume more of the goods given to them than they would have bought had they received the same value in money income. That is, practically, in all these cases there are other solutions that are preferred to these schemes by everyone.

Universal basic income, by definition, provides an equal lump-sum amount to everyone without condition, including to rich people (who, on the contrary, pay with ELIE). As a result, if this income is sufficient to alleviate poverty, the total amount is extraordinarily high and practically cannot be raised. And if the total amount can actually be raised, the basic income is insufficient for alleviating poverty. Is it a good idea to insist on handing out 500 dollars a month to the wealthiest individuals? Is it necessary for guaranteeing their freedom? Aren't there better uses of this money, people who need it more?

The scholarly studies of welfarist "optimum taxation" will be closely considered in further chapters, notably in Chapter 10 about the issue of information because it justifies basing transfers on earned incomes by their being a proxy for unobservable capacities. This reason is problematic and, as we will see, these studies optimize the schedule of the tax but not its base. Moreover, they consider people's eudemonistic capacities, which are unanimously considered irrelevant for macrojustice (Chapter 6). And they use a given "social welfare function," while social-ethical principles are not a priori given in this form.[6]

---

[6] By contrast, this kind of "optimum" taxation has a domain of validity in certain cases of microjustice, notably with a utilitarian form, as with the determination of nonlinear public tarifs in Kolm (1969b, 1970b), where individuals' utility functions are different and uncertain – in opposition to the assumptions of the "optimum income tax" models.

Aid in kind is particular only if the resulting structure of consumption differs from that which the aided people would have chosen with an equivalent aid in income. Then, it is paternalistic, it violates "consumer's sovereignty," it assumes that the aided people are unable to see their "true needs" even when they are provided the appropriate information, it is bound to raise in the most acute ways the problems of dependency, assistance, lack of dignity, and cultural interference or disruption, and it is Pareto inefficient. It should thus be justified by specific reasons which will generally put it outside the field of global distributive justice in macrojustice.

I.4.3. A numerical illustrative example

A numerical example can illustrate the working of ELIE as a support to low incomes. In the following numerical examples, labour is measured by duration and individuals' production functions are assumed to be linear (constant wage rates). This structure and the way in which it can take other characteristics of labour into account will be discussed in Chapter 8. The figures and situations considered here are for the case of France in 1995,[7] but the discussion can easily be adjusted to other economic, social, and institutional frameworks. Average income is 10,500 francs per month. Take as equalization labour duration one third of standard working time. Average equalization income is 3,500 francs per month.

Someone earning 6,000 francs per month yields her equalization income of $6,000/3 = 2,000$ francs, but receives the average 3,500 francs and hence receives a net subsidy of $3,500 - 2,000 = 1,500$ francs, and ends up with a disposable income of $6,000 + 1,500 = 7,500$ francs per month. A wage earner at the official minimum wage of 5,400 francs per month has an equalization income of 1,800 francs, receives a net subsidy of $3,500 - 1,800 = 1,700$ francs, and ends up with a disposable income of $5,400 + 1,700 = 7,100$ francs. Someone who could find employment at half the official minimum wage, that is, a low 16 francs per hour, would end up with an income about equal to the official minimum wage ($2,700 + 3,500 - 900 = 5,300$). However, this minimum is an official constraint on paid wages, and hence this person is not employed under present law (firms freely hire under this constraint on wages).

With this scheme, someone unemployed receives the 3,500 francs per month of the average equalization income (this holds if this person's productivity is zero, and also, as it will be shown in Chapter 13, if this person cannot find employment or is partially unemployed in being hired for no more than the equalization duration – one third of the time here). This amount becomes 3,800 francs – the official "poverty line" – if the equalization duration is increased from 1/3 to the neighboring 36% of official standard working time, and 4,400 francs if the equalization

---

[7] They are taken from a proposal presented to the French General Planning Commission.

duration is augmented by one fourth. Moreover, unemployment insurance, the decrease in involuntary unemployment due to competitive process-freedom and to the possible substitution of an ELIE distribution to the reason for labour-market and policy-induced wage rigidities (minimum wage laws and taxes on wage bills), and good macroeconomic, labour-market, and education policies, may reduce the remaining poverty due to unemployment to exceptional cases, which can be the object of a specific extra aid to needs. Furthermore, it suffices that one earns 1,500 francs per month for obtaining a disposable income of $1,500 + 3,500 - 500 = 4,500$ francs. Hence, with free hiring for employers, the suppression of the minimum wage law makes everyone better off. Indeed, practically an appropriate ELIE scheme can replace at once low-income and unemployment subsidies and minimum wage laws, in making everyone better off. Finally, someone who can obtain 6,000 francs per month can secure 4,500 francs in working only half-time ($3,000 + 3,500 - 2,000$). Anyone who, from any situation, chooses to work less or more, loses or gains exactly the corresponding variation in her output (hence, everyone's free choice is efficient).

The ELIE transfers received are the lower, the more productive the receiver (but they do not otherwise depend on her income). Individuals whose productivity exceeds the average for the equalization labour, for instance whose given wage rate exceeds the average, yield transfers equal to the difference (proportional to the excess of wage rates above average in the case of given wage rates). These resources pay for the subsidies: ELIE defines and includes both the aids and their financing – contrary to other assistance schemes. Contrary to other realizations and proposals, also, these transfers or taxes do not induce the payers to work less. On the contrary. These transfers, based on given productivity and not on output, earnings or labour, have no disincentive price effects. In fact, they have a positive incentive income effect in inducing the payers to work more in order to more or less compensate for the loss (since leisure is usually not an "inferior good"), and pay the tax. Hence, ELIE induces more productive people to work more. These payments are low for people only slightly more productive than average. For high productivities, for given wage rates these payments tend to the fraction of earned income equal to the duration of the equalization labour as a fraction of the working time of the person. This working time is generally high for such productive individuals – this often goes with interest in the job and responsibility, but it also is induced by the high wage rates and the income effects of transfers, while the lump-sum ELIE transfers induce no opposite disincentive price effect. On the whole, for the figures of the previous paragraphs, this distributive tax is not likely to exceed one fourth of earnings (and it does not depend on labour).

This balanced set of transfers should constitute the bulk of the distributive structure of public finances. The public sector must, in addition, finance other publicly provided goods and services. The provision and financing of these goods and services will a priori be chosen without consideration of global distributive justice and macrojustice, since this issue is taken care of by the considered distributive scheme. That is to say, financing should be according to users' benefits, notably through "benefit taxation." More precisely, this classical principle of public finances finds a specific application in the theory of the "liberal social contract," which applies the theory of full process-freedom to the cases of failures of market and free exchange.[8] The actual flows of public finances are the sum of these components, which result from different rationales – democracy, however, would benefit from tax payers being informed of the justification of the amounts demanded from them.[9]

The presentation of the general theory of global distributive justice in macrojustice continues in the next chapters with complete general models (with the central analysis in Chapter 9). However, even very simple straightforward properties of the result have noteworthy particular consequences, notably as concerns the limiting cases of labour, income and redistribution, and moral judgments about them. Part II of this chapter presents these issues which, though not as central as the rest, shed light on important properties of the obtained solution and on its relation with common moral judgments.

II. THE LOGIC AND ETHICS OF EXTREMES: LOWEST AND HIGHEST LABOURS, INCOMES, AND EQUALIZATIONS

II.1. LOWEST AND HIGHEST LABOURS AND INCOMES

Lowest incomes raise particular issues, as can lowest labours and, in particular, unemployment and minimal labours necessary for paying required transfers. By contrast, the symmetrical highest possible incomes and labours present no actual and practical interest, but have some purely theoretical interest for the analysis of the general logic and meanings of ELIE schemes. Let us consider these two limiting cases. For the lowest labours and incomes, we begin with the case of general transfers, of which ELIE is a particular case.

II.1.1. The ethics of labour and leisure and their implications

The fact of working or not raises widespread specific moral judgments which can have drastic effects on distributive schemes. Choosing not to work may be a right, but someone who (freely) makes such a choice is often denied a right to public aid. These two views are common. The right to choose not to work is seen as a rather basic freedom because forced labour is a step in the direction of slavery (although

---

[8] Chapter 3 proposed a short reminder of this issue.

[9] Specific issues of microjustice or mesojustice not solved by process-freedom and free exchange can in addition be dealt with by public actions and finances, but they require specific justifications. The latter can refer to particular handicaps, external effects of parents on children, culture, and so on, and may notably affect domains such as education, health, housing, or culture.

the required labour may be limited and the requirement indirect – as with having to earn in order to pay a tax, without direct interference with the acts of labour). This right to idleness is improperly but suggestively called "right to laziness" in Paul Lafargue's famous pamphlet with this title. One has to eat, though, and another widespread moral judgment is that individuals who freely choose not to work while they could, in receiving a remuneration, should not receive public support. There should be no subsidy or compensation for voluntary unemployment. This can be called the "workfare rule," and it is commonly applied to aid to low-income earners (the case of involuntary unemployment is often distinguished in subjecting aid to the condition of actively seeking employment). These common moral views can have very important consequences when they are associated to Pareto efficiency (hence, to the principle of unanimity) or to social freedom, notably in banning a distributive policy and requiring full self-ownership, through a sequence of logical implications.

This results from the interference between these views and taxes or subsidies that are lump-sum, that is, independent from the person's actions and their intended consequences. Indeed, someone entitled to a lump-sum subsidy receives it when she chooses not to work even if she could obtain some earnings. And someone who has to pay a lump-sum tax has to work at least for paying this tax (if she has no other income). Hence, a general workfare rule, applied to the possible choices of individuals, forbids lump-sum subsidies. And a general right to idleness forbids lump-sum taxes. Both conditions jointly forbid any kind of lump-sum transfers. Finally, if one considers a balanced set of lump-sum transfers, there is at least one tax and one subsidy, and either of the two conditions – the workfare rule or the right to idleness – suffices to forbid the set of transfers.

Now, transfers that are not lump-sum have incentive or disincentive effects of the kind that jeopardizes Pareto efficiency. And Pareto efficiency is a direct requirement from the principle of unanimity. Moreover, taxes that are not lump-sum forcefully interfere with the taxpayers' acts or their intended consequences, and hence violate process-freedom. Hence, Pareto efficiency requires that taxes and subsidies are lump-sum, and process-freedom requires that taxes are lump-sum. That is, process-freedom or Pareto efficiency requires that taxes are lump-sum, and Pareto efficiency also requires that subsidies are lump-sum.

Therefore, a right to idleness bans lump-sum taxes, whereas Pareto efficiency or process-freedom require taxes to be lump-sum. Hence, a right to idleness plus either Pareto efficiency or process-freedom imply that there are no taxes. Moreover, a workfare rule bans lump-sum subsidies, whereas Pareto efficiency requires subsidies to be lump-sum. Hence, a workfare rule and Pareto efficiency imply that there are no subsidies. In addition, distributive transfers constitute a balanced set. Hence, if there are such transfers, there are both taxes and subsidies (at least one in each category).

Now, in the framework considered, an absence of the transfers constitutes full self-ownership. Therefore, for a balanced set of transfers, full self-ownership is implied by Pareto efficiency plus either a workfare rule or a right to idleness; by full process-freedom and a right to idleness; and hence, from a right to idleness plus either Pareto efficiency or full process-freedom.

However, the individuals may not actually prefer and choose not to work or to work as little as possible. Then, the considered efficient and process-freedom respecting lump-sum transfers are possible in respecting the workfare rule or the right to idleness. Moreover, the ethical judgments about unemployment incomes and necessary labours are bound to depend on their levels.

At any rate, these moral judgments about the fact of working or not and its relation to income are widespread and hence should a priori be considered by endogenous social choice. Forced labour violates a basic right. Having to work in order to pay a due is not exactly forced labour, and yet this creates, de facto, a constraint on the choice of labour and leisure. This obligation, however, may be more or less stringent. Such a minimal necessary labour hampers a possible right to abstain from working. Such a right has, for instance, been eloquently defended by Paul Lafargue (Marx's son-in-law) as the "right to laziness." On the contrary, the "work ethic" wants people to work. It may be good for them (and their family) and save them from idleness, "the mother of all vices." The "dangerous classes" would be less dangerous if occupied at the workshop (and the more so if they are occupied to exhaustion). In more modern views, work may be favorable to social integration. Moreover, work will make people contribute to society. It may be particularly offensive that people could have an income without working when they can work. They would be social parasites. "He who does not work does not eat," says Saint Paul of Tarse, echoed by the former Soviet constitution. "No work, no meal." Aid may have to be restricted to the deserving working poor. The poor may have to work in "national workshops" as in France in 1848. Present-day schemes of "negative income tax" or "income tax credit" are justified as an improvement over guaranteed minimal income, which can induce aided persons to abstain from any work, not so much because they reduce the inefficiency (this was the main initial reason for proposing this policy), but for the intrinsic moral value of working or of contributing, or for the effects of labour on the person, her family, or her social integration. Most unemployment compensations and minimum incomes are granted under the condition of actively seeking employment.

These judgments about working or not, and about aid, are moral ones, more or less supported by the consideration of sociological and psychological effects for "workfare." They can forbid distributive policies respecting efficiency and social freedom, and hence jeopardize these properties or ban redistribution from self-ownership. However, these judgments essentially only concern the limiting-case issue of working or not. Hence, they hardly belong to the realm of considerations of macrojustice. These views, when they have to be taken into account, should thus only lead to local modifications of the general distributive rules. If they are widely shared, or sociologically and psychologically justified, the ensuing infringement of economic efficiency, hence of the principle of unanimity as concerns economic variables only (which leads to the lump-sum policy bases), is justified by consensus as concerns a larger set of issues.

II.1.2. Lowest labours and incomes with ELIE

II.1.2.1. The general case

The general results about the interference between efficient and process-free distributions on the one hand, and the moral and social values concerning labour and its absence on the other hand, apply in particular to ELIE distributions. However, the fact that these schemes' base consists of the causes of labour incomes for which the individuals are not responsible (given productive capacities) introduces a qualification of aids and liabilities according to individuals' responsibility.

In ELIE distributions, the set of transfers is balanced. Individuals receive the excess of the average equalization income over their own equalization income or pay the reverse excess. Individuals no more productive than average for the equalization labour can choose not to work. Then, if they are less productive than average, they receive a transfer while they do not work. This transfer does not exceed the average equalization income. This limit is reached for individuals who can obtain no income from the market. However, these individuals' labour is not demanded, and they are also involuntarily unemployed. The subsidy they receive – the average equalization income – is the corresponding unemployment aid. Individuals who are little productive receive a little less as transfer, in particular if they choose not to work. This transfer is the lower, the more productive the individual is (for the equalization labour). The implicit moral reason is that individuals are induced to work less when their productivity is lower, and the considered productivity is given to them; hence, they are less responsible for choosing not to work when their productivity is lower, and as a consequence the unemployment compensation they receive is higher; conversely, the higher the productivity, the higher the responsibility for choosing not to work (say the "laziness"), and the lower the subsidy. As a consequence, the scheme is continuous, from the individuals with no productivity to others. In contrast, a workfare rule would demand individuals with low, or very low, productivity and wage to provide some labour, thus introducing a discontinuity. Moreover, the more productive the individual, the higher the incentive to work is for her, both because her wage is higher and the transfer she receives is lower. Finally, the considered possible voluntary unemployment respects both the individuals' free choice and Pareto efficiency. They would be violated, by contrast, by some particular "workfare" requirement or successful inducement to work.

Individuals more productive than average for the equalization labour have to pay the difference. They have to work at least to pay this liability (if they have no other income). This payment is the higher, the more productive the individual is (for the equalization labour). But the more productive the individual, a priori the less labour she needs for producing a given amount. In fact, however, the minimal labour induced by this necessary payment depends on the structure of the individual's production function (output or earnings as a function of labour). The minimal labour that this required payment induces for the payer is the labour that produces this amount. But for comparing this minimal labour across individuals, with different payments and productivities, one has to compare with the equalization labour since all individuals have the same disposable income for this labour (this is the average equalization income). Now, when individuals work more or less, their disposable income varies as their earnings (since the distributive transfers are lump-sum). Hence, someone can work less than the equalization labour as long as the corresponding loss in earnings does not exceed the average equalization income (if she has no other source of income). Therefore, she can withdraw less from the equalization labour in working when she is more productive, in the sense of using less labour for producing the average equalization income before reaching the equalization labour.[10] Hence, individuals more productive in this sense have a higher minimal necessary labour. This minimal labour can go from zero (for individuals with an equalization income equal to average) to becoming close to the equalization labour (or any other combination of labour characteristics that produces as much) for very productive people. When labours are measured by quantities (such as durations – see Chapter 8) with constant wage rates, the considered productivities are proportional to the wage rates, and hence the higher the wage rate, the higher the minimal required labour.

The two foregoing paragraphs describe, respectively, the *unemployment income of the less able* and the *minimal necessary labour of the more able* (where ability is for the equalization labour). This advantage and this requirement are aspects of the compensations for differences in personal productive capacities provided by ELIE distributions.

Both unemployment incomes and minimal necessary labours vanish in the case of full self-ownership. They become the highest for very high equalization labour. Consider, however, plausible levels. The examples will be with constant given wage rates per unit of labour duration.

An equalization labour of one and a half day a week provides a volume of redistribution of the order of magnitude of that of present-day redistributions at national levels. Then, an individual three times more productive than average needs to work only one day to pay her due. Indeed, this person pays her income of 1.5 days and receives average income for 1.5 days; but the latter amounts to her income of 0.5 days, and hence, the person finally pays her income of one day. And extremely productive individuals have to work at least almost one day and a half. In fact, practically all of them work much more.

An individual's minimal necessary labour is the higher, the more productive she is in the required sense. However, the higher the individual's productivity, the higher the price incentive to work more is, the easier it is to earn given extra

---

[10] The very simple algebra or geometry of these situations will be explicit in Chapters 9 and 11.

income, the more costly leisure is in terms of foregone income, and the higher the income incentive to work more is because the tax the person has to pay is higher. And the minimal labour corresponds to an absence of income. Hence, the constraint of minimal labour, which exists only for individuals more productive than average, will not normally be effective for realistic equalization labours. The exceptions could only concern productive people with a very strong preference for leisure, even at very low income and consumption. These exceptional characters can probably be discarded from considerations about macrojustice. In fact, individuals more productive than average will generally work more than the equalization labour for the likely values of the latter (as will most individuals except the involuntarily unemployed or those with very low productivity). This implies that their labour neatly exceeds the minimum.

The highest unemployment income is the average equalization income. For example, it is about one third of average income if the equalization labour is about one third of a standard duration of labour.

A "workfare rule" forbidding that people could receive a subsidy when they choose not to work, requiring some labour for any income, would force an ELIE scheme to vanish into full self-ownership. However, it would not be in tune with the basic rationale of ELIE, which is a right in society's productive capacities. Moreover, voluntary unemployment may actually be chosen by no one or by only very few people. And if some specific aid to low incomes were added to a general ELIE distribution, some requirement of providing some work (or actively seeking employment) for obtaining this extra aid can be added to it, notably if this is deemed favorable to social integration or to family or mental balance. However, this would again be beyond the realm of global distributive justice in macrojustice.

II.1.2.2. Involuntary unemployment

Voluntary unemployment entails, per se, no inefficiency. Individuals who can offer or produce nothing normally valued by the market are unemployed for this specific reason which, again, entails no inefficiency. Yet, there can be other, standard cases of involuntary unemployment, with downward wage rigidity. This situation will be particularly studied in Chapter 13. This involuntary unemployment will be reduced by general process-freedom favoring the free working of labour markets; by the ELIE distribution policy, which can reduce the reasons for wage rigidities in labour markets and in policies of wage floors; and by measures favouring employment in labour market, education, and macroeconomic policies; while unemployment insurance reduces the effects of unemployment on incomes. These aspects do not belong to the domain of overall distributive justice. However, the ELIE concept also includes a solution for the incomes of the involuntarily unemployed individuals. This unemployment of an individual may be total or partial, and partial unemployment may consist of limits on duration or on other characteristics of labour (such as underqualified employment not making proper use of the individual's skills).

The constraint that imposes total or partial involuntary unemployment is given to the individual. The construction of ELIE schemes describes what is given to the individual in the form of her production function. This function, however, is defined for all labours that the individual can a priori perform. Yet, an individual working to earn income will not choose to work more if she cannot earn more as a result. Hence, for this individual, given her behaviour, not being able to work more is formally equivalent to not being able to earn more by working more. This remark permits one to describe the constraint of total or partial involuntary unemployment as included within the structure of the individual's production function. It suffices to replace the technical "real production function" by the "actual production function" that describes the individual's possibilities to earn as a function of the labour she *offers* even if part or all of this labour is not actually employed and earning income. The latter production function is the mathematical "truncation" of the former at maximal labour earnings. It is identically zero for full involuntary unemployment, which thus formally amounts to not being able to produce anything valued by the market. More generally, this device transforms actual partial or total involuntary unemployment into a notional voluntary choice, but with the handicap of the actual, truncated, production function. Then the general ELIE theory applies with these actual production functions.

In particular, fully unemployed individuals are treated as individuals who can supply nothing with market value, and they therefore receive the average equalization income. Partially unemployed individuals end up also receiving this income if their work does not exceed the equalization labour. If they choose to work less than what they are offered, however, they lose the corresponding loss in output, and hence their choice entails no inefficiency.

II.1.3. Maximal labours

In the situation opposite to those where labour is the lowest, an individual works and earns as much as she can. The precise definition of maximal work need not retain us here, because the following reasonings using these maximal labours correspond to ELIE schemes that are in fact rejected by consensual moral views, and only aim at exhibiting the general structural properties of this distributive rule.[11] The highest social income (sum of individual incomes) is generally obtained with the highest individual incomes. An individual's maximal income is the total rent, measured in income, of her productive capacities. The sum of these rents is society's income rent of its productive capacities.

---

[11] Maximal work in a period may not be sustainable, and we may want maximal sustainable income. High work can affect health and life duration. We certainly will not want to define highest income with life duration being an endogenous variable.

An individual who works maximally earns the total income rent of her productive capacities.[12] This amount generally differs across individuals. These differences may a priori be the focus of an assessment concerning justice. It might be deemed just that the income an individual can obtain in working maximally be the same for all. As previously shown, full process-freedom or Pareto efficiency require that this be realized through a set of lump-sum transfers. This set will also have to be balanced. Then, considering the particular situation of labours where each individual works maximally, it appears that these transfers should amount to an equalization of the individuals' maximal incomes. That is, each individual is demanded her maximal income and is handed out the average maximal income. This is *maximal income equalization*. Of course, since each individual receives, in exchange for her maximal income, the average maximal income, she can choose to work less than maximally, provided her foregone earnings do not exceed the average maximal earnings. More productive individuals are at a disadvantage for this purpose since relatively low leisure (decrease in labour from maximal labour) suffices for making them lose this amount, whereas less productive individuals can take more leisure before losing this amount. Maximal income equalization equally shares the total income rent (income producible by labour). We will see, however, that the choice of this limiting case as the actual solution is rejected for several reasons which are consensual views (one of them will be that this solution implies an equal sharing of some incomes that are only potential, rather than actually earned).

II.2. FULL SELF-OWNERSHIP AND MAXIMAL INCOME EQUALIZATION: THE LIMITING CASES

II.2.1. The two pure concepts of equal allocation of rents of productive capacities

Let us now focus on and compare the two borderline cases. Maximal labour for an individual can always be taken with productive characteristics (duration, intensity, previous training and education, etc.) larger than what they are with her actual maximal labour in assuming that the difference is unproductive (produces no extra income). Therefore, maximal labour can be taken to be the same for all individuals (with productive characteristics not lower than what they actually are for all individuals). Then, maximal income equalization is ELIE with the maximal labour as equalization labour. In contrast, full self-ownership is ELIE with a nonexistent equalization labour.

Both maximal labour equalization and full self-ownership are equal allocations of the rents of productive capacities. The difference comes from the good used as measure. Maximal income equalization is equal sharing of the full income value of

---

[12] The production function can be taken as a nondecreasing function of the parameters that describe the productive characteristics of labour: See Chapter 8.

the rent. Full self-ownership is an equal distribution when capacities are defined by the largest labour they can transform into output or income (or leisure they can free in not working). In other words, these two distributions are equal allocations of the rent of productive capacities when this rent is measured, respectively, in income value and in labour value (when labour is measurable by a quantity – see Chapter 8). They thus also achieve equal allocation when either income or labour and leisure are respectively taken as the "measuring rod" of values. The actual difference between these two allocations results from the fact that individual productivities differ, and these productivities are the rates of substitution between these two "numéraires." Other ELIE schemes are intermediate cases, with equal distribution of the rent defined or measured by income for the equalization labour and by labour or leisure for the rest.

II.2.2. Rights to idleness and to average maximal income, and the workfare rule

Both full self-ownership and maximal income equalization can be characterized by conditions bearing on individuals' possibilities in the limiting conditions of labour. These conditions apply to a balanced set of lump-sum transfers, this latter property being required, as noted, by full process-freedom or efficiency. The three separately necessary and sufficient conditions are:

For full self-ownership:
- The *right to idleness*: Each individual has the possibility of not working.
- The *workfare rule*: No individual can have an income if she chooses not to work (no income for voluntary unemployment).

For maximal income equalization:
- The *right to average maximal income*: Each individual should be able to obtain average maximal income.

The set of transfers is a priori balanced as a financial condition. However, we have seen that full self-ownership obtains without this condition, for lump-sum transfers, if the right to idleness and the workfare rule are jointly required.

   With maximal income equalization, each individual obtains the average maximal income as disposable income when she works maximally. The possibility, for each individual, to choose a labour that secures a disposable income not lower than the average maximal income whatever the others do is a priori a more general property, and yet it requires maximal income equalization. Assume, indeed, that given a balanced set of lump-sum transfers, each individual can otherwise freely choose her labour and her corresponding earnings.[13] Assume, moreover, that each individual can obtain a disposable income not lower than the average maximal income with a possible choice of her labour and whatever the others do. Then,

---

[13] Assuming each individual's earnings to be independent from others' labours, which is relevant for relatively "small" agents in a large society and independent individuals' choices of labour (see Chapter 8).

if each individual chooses this labour of hers, the sum of individuals' disposable incomes is not lower than maximal social income, and is in fact maximal social income since it cannot be larger. Then, each individual's disposable income is average maximal income. And maximal social income is also the sum of individuals' earnings since the set of transfers is balanced. This implies that each individual's earnings are maximal. Then, the transfer faced by each individual amounts to the replacement of her maximal earnings by the average maximal income and earnings. This is maximal income equalization.

II.2.3. Unequal outcome-freedoms

Outcome-freedom is freedom of the choice of outcomes, which are here pairs of income or consumption and of leisure (complementary to labour). It is described by the domains of possibility of such choices. It results from the conditions of the choice: process-freedom, capacities as means of labour, and the given allocation of goods and leisure implemented by the ELIE transfers. An outcome-freedom is larger than another if it permits obtaining more income for each labour and more leisure for each income (further discussion of this domination by inclusion of the possibility sets has no relevance here). Both full self-ownership and maximal income equalization will tend to produce unequal outcome-freedoms, but with a reverse effect of the influence of productivities.

Indeed, with full self-ownership, an individual more productive than another in the sense that she can earn more for all labours is freer in this sense.

In contrast, with maximal income equalization, an individual who can earn more extra income than another in passing from any nonmaximal labour to maximal labour is less free in this sense. Indeed, with maximal income equalization, an individual obtains the average maximal income when she works maximally. She can also work less than maximal labour, at the cost of losing the corresponding foregone earnings. She then has a disposable income lower than average maximal income by these foregone earnings. Therefore, if an individual is more productive than another in the sense that she obtains larger extra earnings in passing from any labour to maximal labour, her foregone earnings are higher when she withdraws from maximal labour to a given labour, and hence her disposable income remaining from the average maximal income is lower.

Hence, both full self-ownership and maximal income equalization tend to produce unequal output-freedoms. These inequalities depend on individuals' productivities, although with a reverse effect: more productive individuals tend to be outcome-freer with full self-ownership and outcome less free with maximal income equalization.

II.2.4. Unemployment incomes and minimal necessary labour

In particular, with maximal income equalization, the individuals whose maximal earnings are below average can abstain from working and will receive an unemployment income equal to the average maximal income minus their maximal earnings. This income is the higher the lower the individual's maximal earnings. Individuals who can earn nothing receive the average maximal income.

Again, with maximal income equalization, individuals whose maximal earnings exceed average face a minimal necessary labour. This is the labour with which they can earn the net transfer demanded from them, their maximal earnings minus the average maximal income. People who need very little extra work in order to earn this last earnings in amount equal to the average maximal income, before reaching maximal earnings, have a very high minimal necessary labour. This is the case that Dworkin's (1981) striking image of the "slavery of the talented" intends to describe. This "talent" is that of earning, and these individuals are formally free though they have to work very much for paying their due.[14] However, it should be noted that the high productivity required for this result is that for extra production just before maximal labour and earnings, which is at odds with the common structure of decreasing returns in production.

By contrast, full self-ownership entails no unemployment income and no required labour, and is indeed characterized by these properties among ELIE schemes (and other sets of lump-sum transfers).

II.2.5. Ill treatment of people with very low or very high productivities

A notable point is that both full self-ownership and maximal income equalization treat particularly badly one category of persons: those with very low and very high earning capacities, respectively. References will be to "ability" or "talent" for earning income. With full self-ownership, people with very low productivity will have very low income and consumption (starvation of the unable), they may have to work much for earning more (exhaustion of the unable and de facto "slavery" of the unable), and they have little output-freedom (unfreedom of the unable). With maximal income equalization, people who are extremely productive when they work very much (see above) have to work very much (exhaustion of the talented and de facto "slavery" of the talented), they may have to accept low disposable income and consumption in order to obtain some rest (starvation of the talented), and they have little output-freedom (unfreedom of the talented). In both cases, these individuals have high work, low rest, low income and consumption, and low output-freedom. This may violate possible human rights to minima in income, consumption, rest, or freedom.

However, these extreme cases of productivity may not exist. Or they may be sufficiently rare to be discarded from concerns for macrojustice and treated in an ad hoc manner.

---

[14] Before Dworkin, Pazner (1977) had the intuition of this property. In the case of constant wage rates, maximal income equalization has indeed been suggested by Pazner and Schmeidler (1972), and discussed by Varian (1974, 1975), Pazner (1977), and Dworkin (1981).

The effects of full self-ownership are straightforwardly seen. For maximal income equalization, an example may be enlightening. As a matter of illustration, let us measure labour by its duration and assume wages to be proportional to it. Assume also maximal sustainable work to be 16 hours per day almost every day. Then, an individual who can obtain a wage rate equal to four times the average has to work 12 hours a day for the sole purpose of paying her due (this is her income for 16 hours less one fourth of it which she receives as the average production during this time). For obtaining a standard of living costing the average earnings for 8 hours a day, she has to work two hours more, say 14 hours almost everyday. Such labour durations exist in a number of well-paid or interesting professions. Practically, the question of the nature of the work will be essential, but this is not the present topic. The issue of information about capacities will be considered in Chapter 10. Rather, let us remark here that a person who can earn the average wage is not taxed and can secure the same income in working 8 hours a day. And someone who can earn nothing enjoys both twice this consumption and full leisure. This illustrates the reverse inequality.

II.2.6. Consequences for the choice of ELIE

Hence, people with very low productivity in the case of full self-ownership, and with very high productivity in the case of maximal income equalization, will have very low output-freedom, consumption, and rest. And output-freedom will tend to be unequal (by relevant inclusion of the domains of choice) in both cases, although with a reverse effect of productivities. Hence, full self-ownership is to be discarded if there are people with very low productivity, maximal income equalization is if there are people with very high productivity, and both might be objected to because of the inequality in output-freedom they generally entail. This leads to choosing ELIE distributions intermediate between these two extreme cases.

Moreover, the maximal income equalization solution would lead to extraordinarily high amounts of transfers. If, as an order of magnitude, maximal labour is five times the present actual labour (for instance, working about 16 hours a day every day throughout life without vacation or retirement), the required transfers would be five times the transfers necessary to fully equalize present earned incomes.

In addition, maximal income equalization amounts to equalizing productivites for each "bracket" of labour (for example, if labour is unidimensional, the productivities of the hth hour of labour, for each h; and multidimensional brackets can also be defined). However, actual labours will be short of maximal ones. And the meaningfulness, as regards justice, of equalizing productivities of "brackets" that are not filled with actual labour, and hence, that are occupied by leisure, is problematic. As we have already noticed, such an equalization is in fact rejected by people, even by the most "income-egalitarian" ones. They see no moral justification and no distributive justice in taxing productive people for what they could have earned during their leisure time,[15] or in the symmetrical subsidies. In fact, we have seen that the likely equalization labour in a large society will be short of most actually chosen labours, thus avoiding equalization of productivities for nonworked "brackets." Moreover, an important ethical view sees the equalization of earned incomes as ideal (this is a common position of the rather far left,[16] and also, for instance, an ideal for philosophers such as John Rawls and Michael Walzer – income is one of Rawls' "primary goods").[17] However, we will see that when this ethic is considered in full, the scheme that implements its intention is an ELIE with an equalization labour around the lowest normal full labour (Chapter 11).[18] In the end, the equalization labour will be between zero (full self-ownership) and this lower normal full labour. In fact, half normal full labour will appear as a maximum representing a very "redistributive" (from full self-ownership) and "leftist" policy, in a large and diverse society. Part IV of this study will discuss the issues and methods of the determination of the equalization labour.

[15] The aim of such a tax could be to induce these productive people to work more, which they may have to do for paying the tax. However, this is an objective different from distributive justice. And it has to be justified.

[16] A more radical and genuine "leftist" position, however, emphasizes not equality and income, but, rather, mutual gift giving and reciprocities (see Kolm 1984a).

[17] See the discussions in Chapter 16 below and in Kolm 1996a, Chapter 8.

[18] "Normal full labour" intends to exclude part-time labours providing complementary incomes to the household, the cases of total and partial unemployment, and exceptionally low labour supplies in general. This can be the official labour duration in countries where there is one – that is, the earnings of overtime work will not be taxed or subsidized.

8

Models of labour and productivity

1. MODELING LABOUR

1.1. Characteristics and capacities

Equal labour income equalization can be presented with more or less complex (and complete) or simple models of the economy. Simple models may provide good descriptions, or sufficient approximations, in a number of cases. They can also be useful for focusing the presentation and discussion on crucial properties, or for didactic or illustrative purposes. The crucial issues will be the description of labour, the structure of individuals' production function showing earnings as a function of labour, and the situation of the labour market (notably, the absence or presence of involuntary unemployment). The present chapter focuses on the question of the description of labour and of the structure of the production function. It thus constitutes *a preliminary for the following chapters that use its conclusions. It contains no ethical consideration* – and hence, can possibly be skipped at first reading. However, its considerations are necessary for justifying formulations of labour that are usual, or that are used in the following chapters. For instance, can one speak of a "quantity of labour" or an "amount of labour"? What does this mean? What does an expression such as "she works twice as much" mean? If labour is measured by its duration, these expressions can make sense. One can then easily introduce the consideration of the speed of labour, all the rest remaining the same (if that is possible). However, what about the other characteristics of labour, such as intensity of attention (which can result in speed, but also in the quality of output), intensity of physical force, or the effects of previous education or training? There is also the issue of distinguishing labour from its painfulness (or the opposite), on the one hand, and from its productivity, on the other hand. Again, *one can begin by reading the uses of the results in the following chapters,* but the possible meaning of the formulations used are proposed here.

The present section provides a general discussion of the issues, which the next two sections translate into specific modelling. The distinction of labour

135

characteristics from given capacities is followed by the analysis of the presentation of labour as unidimensional (Section 1.2), and of the representation of involuntary unemployment (Section 1.3). The formalization is general in Section 2 and shows, in Section 3, how labour can often be sufficiently represented by its duration, possibly notionally adjusted for the effects of the other characteristics of labour.

The relevant characteristics of labour are those that can influence the product and pay or earnings. There are a number of them such as duration, speed, fraction of actual work in a given period, intensity, attention, concentration, physical force, steadiness or regularity, flexibility and adaptability, reliability, previous experience or training, previous formation and specialized or general education, and so on. These characteristics are related. Some can be conflated into others, such as the fraction of time of actual labour in a period with speed, and both with duration. Others may be rival: this can, for instance, happen for speed and attention or reliability. Our present purpose requires a distinction between these characteristics of labour and individuals' particular given capacities used in the performance of this labour. The relevant effect of these capacities will be described by the "production function" giving earnings as a function of labour. We have noted that earnings constitute the relevant variable here, rather than, say, physical output (or consumption that these earnings can buy), because of the basic assumption of full process-freedom (which implies unfettered selling, buying, and exchanges). An aspect or a parameter of the activity of labour describes given capacities if no individual can choose or change it as concerns her own labour. Otherwise, it will be described by characteristics of labour. Hence, the capacities considered here are *given* capacities. Other capacities (or aspects of capacities), which are created by the individual, are in fact intermediate outputs of her productive activity, and the acts of their creation are in fact dimensions of labour. Previous formation chosen by the individual constitute the outstanding example. We thus have labour, with characteristics that can be changed by the individuals who work (for at least one of them), and (given) capacities, with characteristics that cannot be changed by these individuals and which determine the individuals' production functions relating labour provided to earnings.

1.2. Unidimensional labour

One often considers that someone works more or less, or, even, more or less than someone else. This implies that the considered labour has ordered manifestations, and, in fact, an ordinal unidimensional representation. This can describe a given situation or constitute a notional construct. More specifically, quantities of labour are often considered.

Labour may relevantly have only one dimension. This dimension then is often its duration. Then, labour may, furthermore, have the structure of a quantity. Such cases may occur in specific situations, sometimes important ones. Or they may suffice as an approximation for given situations and problems. Or, again, their consideration may be useful for expository, didactic, illustrative, experimental, investigatory, mind-focusing, or other cognitive purposes.

More important, perhaps, is the fact that labour can very often be considered unidimensional, and indeed a quantity, in being measured by duration adjusted for the other relevant characteristics. This results from the consideration of *steady* work. When work is steady in a given period, this means that the relevant process is the same in each (small) unit of time in this period. If this relevant process is production, this means that the relevant characteristics of labour other than duration, the characteristics of productivity (capacities), and the output, remain the same in each (small) unit of time. This implies that output is proportional to the duration of the period. The coefficient of proportionality will depend on the other characteristics of labour and on the characteristics of productive capacities. All these characteristics thus affect production through one or several multiplicative factors affecting duration. Then, if the effects of the nonduration characteristics of labour on the one hand, and of the given capacities that differ across individuals on the other hand, can be described as affecting different multiplicative factors, one can, for all relevant purposes, measure labour by its "adjusted duration" defined as its duration multiplied by the multiplicative factors influenced by the nonduration characteristics of labour. A precise model and examples will shortly be provided. Note that this jointly justifies models of unidimensional labour and linear production functions – that is, output (income) is proportional to the "quantity" of labour measured as (adjusted) duration, and the coefficient of proportionality is a constant given wage rate depending on given productive capacities. Note also that one can consider periods as short as one wants, and hence, very often, consider that production is in steady state in each of these periods.

Unidimensional labour with nonlinear individual production functions can be found in a number of particular situations. They are also to be considered because the treatment of involuntary unemployment with unidimensional labour will use such a case of nonlinear production function, as is shortly explained. The foregoing justification of considering unidimensional labour with duration adjusted for other characteristics of labour will be less frequently valid for nonlinear production functions than for linear ones, but it may be relevant. This will happen when the nonduration characteristics of labour enter the production function through multiplicative factor(s) multiplying duration and not depending on the characteristics of given capacities that differ across individuals. These latter characteristics intervene otherwise, and they can be described as transforming an "adjusted" duration of labour into output (income), where this duration is actual duration multiplied by the noted multiplicative factors. Such a production function can display varying returns of the adjusted duration.[1] That is, there is, in the considered

---

[1] For instance, getting tired can create classical decreasing returns, on-the-job training can create increasing returns.

period, steady state for the effects of nonduration labour characteristics, but not for those of the characteristics of given capacities.

1.3. Involuntary unemployment

An important issue is the consideration of involuntary unemployment. Let us first note that three facts and policies, different from global distributive justice considered here, but that are included in the overall policy and interfere with the issue of involuntary unemployment, should be considered or implemented. First, involuntary unemployment has microeconomic causes in the working of markets that, most often, violate process-freedom for reasons related to distribution. Now, process-freedom requires the microeconomic policy to suppress these causes, and distribution is taken care of by the policy presently considered. These microeconomic causes of involuntary unemployment include collective market behavior introducing price and wage rigidities, and policies such as wage regulations or various taxes on employment or on the wage bill. Second, the correct macroeconomic policy should also aim at suppressing involuntary unemployment. Third, unemployment insurance, which can be a private scheme but is usually supported by the public sector, suppresses or attenuates the detrimental consequences of involuntary unemployment, notably as regards earned income. If there remains involuntary unemployment, or at least uninsured one, the proportion of people in this situation may be sufficiently limited for this issue to be considered outside the question of global distributive justice in macrojustice.

However, involuntary unemployment can also be treated within the distributive justice realized by ELIE schemes. Individual production functions describe the income the individual can obtain for each labour she decides to perform. ELIE schemes are concerned with the question of justice raised by the nonidentity of these functions. Involuntary unemployment brings in a limitation to individuals' earning possibilities, which can be treated along with all possible causes of such limitations. We now distinguish two production functions for each individual. The *technical production function* gives the income the individual can earn as a function of each *labour actually performed*. The *real production function* gives the income the individual can obtain from her labour for each labour *she proposes*. If, for each labour she proposes, she can actually work, then these two production functions coincide. However, it may be that, for some proposed labour, employers can use or want to use only part of it. Then, only this part is actual work, and the income earned for this proposed labour is the income earned for this accepted, taken, and actual labour. These two production functions then differ (if the earnings of the accepted and actual labour fall short of the earnings for the proposed labour if this proposed labour were fully accepted). If the accepted labour vanishes (its duration is zero), there is *full involuntary unemployment* for this person. If some labour is accepted, although this falls short of the proposed labour, then there is *partial involuntary unemployment* for this person. In the case of full involuntary unemployment, the real production function is identically zero. As a consequence, an individual who cannot sell her services for an income will be equally treated whatever the reason for this, whether no one values her services or whether no one can make use of them because of quantitative constraints.

A few remarks should be added:

1. The limitations of partial involuntary unemployment can bear not only on labour duration, but also on other characteristics of labour. For instance, the individual may not find a job corresponding to her level of education or using other skills of hers as much as she wants. That is, the situations of underqualification of labour are particular cases of partial involuntary unemployment.
2. Moreover, the various types of unemployment can occur for independent workers who sell their products on the market, through constraints on the quantity or quality of the products they can sell.
3. Involuntary unemployment has been defined with respect to potential supply of labour. It can also be considered only for the specific labour the individual would have chosen if solely faced with her technical production function.[2]

Finally, an individual's output and income a priori depends not only on this individual's labour, but also on others'. However, for macrojustice in a sufficiently large society with independent individual decisions and full process-freedom, this externality can be discarded for the same reason as with the classical competitive model (each individual takes the rest of the economy as given).

2. FORMALIZATION

We consider n individuals indexed by i.

If x denotes a generic variable, x_i denotes a specification of it corresponding to individual i. Then, if x is a quantity, $\bar{x} = (1/n)\Sigma x_i$ denotes the average of the x_i.

An individual's labour can be described as a set of different relevant characteristics such that there may be more or less of each, and each can be represented by a real number larger when there is more of it. The relevance of a characteristic means, here, that it has an effect on the individual's output. These characteristics are defined in such a way that more of one augments output or leaves it unchanged. These characteristics are called *productive characteristics*, and the numbers are their levels. Duration, speed, or years of schooling can be such numbers. Intensity of attention can be described by a number of psychometric measures, but it can also be described by proxies depending on the particular job, such as, for example, the proportion of nonfaulty outputs. If we need to consider different types of training or education, each is described by a different characteristic. Each relevant aspect of labour can similarly be considered. These characteristics are a priori ordinal concepts, but they can often be represented by meaningful specific numbers.

[2] Note that if, for an individual, this specific labour supply is zero while any labour supply would not be employed at any rate, her unemployment can be said to be both voluntary and involuntary.

Index j denotes a characteristic, and ℓ^j denotes the corresponding real number, its level, for an individual. An individual's labour can thus be described by the vector $\ell = \{\ell^j\}$. By convention, the absence of labour is denoted as $\ell = 0$ (labour duration, which is one of the characteristics, has level zero, and the other characteristics are in fact undefined). The highest possible level of ℓ^j is denoted as $\widehat{\ell^j}$, and $\widehat{\ell} = \{\widehat{\ell^j}\}$ denotes their vector.

Leisure corresponding to labour ℓ is $\lambda = \widehat{\ell} - \ell$. According to the nature of characteristic j, $\lambda^j = \widehat{\ell^j} - \ell^j$ can be leisure time, more leisurely work, lower training or education, and so on.

The constraint on labour that can create involuntary unemployment is denoted as $\ell \leq \widetilde{\ell}$ (that is, $\ell^j \leq \widetilde{\ell^j}$ for all characteristics j) if ℓ denotes actual labour; or, if ℓ denotes the labour proposed by the individual, by the fact that if $\ell^j > \widetilde{\ell^j}$, then the extra level of characteristic j, $\ell^j - \widetilde{\ell^j}$, cannot contribute to the production of extra output or income. This involuntary unemployment is full, rather than partial, if $\widetilde{\ell} = 0$.

Individual i's labour will be $\ell_i = \{\ell_i^j\}_j$. The set of these labours for all individuals is described by the matrix $L = \{\ell_i\}$. The considered highest level of each characteristic will be taken to be the same for all individuals and not lower than the actually highest level for any of them. Hence, $\lambda_i^j = \widehat{\ell^j} - \ell_i^j \geq 0$. The exact value of the $\widehat{\ell^j}$ will not matter.

A production function gives the income an individual can earn in working ℓ. A technical production function results from the individual's given productive capacities (and the market value of the labour services or output). The differences between these functions for the different individuals constitute our main concern. Real production functions add concern for involuntary unemployment. We have noted that the individual's output can be measured in earned income because of the assumption and moral endorsement of process-freedom. Let p_i denote this income.

A priori, individual i's production function writes $p_i(L)$, meaning that individual i's earned income a priori depends not only on her labour ℓ_i, but also on others' actual labours. For both individual i's technical and real production functions, the $\ell_{i'}$, for $i' \neq i$ in L are the actual labours (and not the proposed labours when there is involuntary unemployment). We have $p_i(L) = 0$ if $\ell_i = 0$.

However, the most relevant case, for our purpose, is that where, in the relevant domain, $p_i(L)$ depends only on ℓ_i and not on $\ell_{i'}$ for $i' \neq i$, for all i. This will indeed be the relevant case for a relatively large society where each individual's labour and production are small compared with all labour and production, and the ℓ_i are chosen individually. This independence of the individual production functions is in particular the case if the economy is perfectly competitive. At any rate, this will suffice for the purpose of considering global distributive justice in macrojustice in a relatively large society. Then the production functions write $p_i(\ell_i)$.

3. LABOUR AS DURATION

In some cases, the only characteristic of labour that the individuals can choose is its duration. In others, the consideration that this is the case constitutes a sufficient approximation. In still other cases, it is possible to reduce reality to such a case in considering a (fictive) labour duration adjusted for taking account of the effects on output of the other characteristics the individuals can choose. For instance, one hour (week, month) of labour with a given speed, intensity, or previous training, formation, or education would be equivalent, for production, to another duration with reference levels of these variables. Or, possibly, assuming such a structure would constitute a sufficient approximation.

For a given labour $\ell_i = \{\ell_i^j\}_j$, where j denotes the characteristics, denote as $j = 1$ the characteristic of duration, and write $\theta_i = \ell_i^1$ and $\ell_i' = \{\ell_i^j\}_{j \neq 1}$. The following properties are assumed to hold either exactly, or as a satisfactory approximation for the purpose at hand, which is the determination of global distributive justice in macrojustice.

Assume the considered labour is in steady state. That is, in each (small) unit of the duration θ_i, the production process (including the value of its output) is identical. Then it follows that the output of labour ℓ_i is proportional to the duration θ_i and, hence, the technical production function can be written as

$$p_i(\ell_i) = \theta_i \cdot f_i(\ell_i').$$

Note that duration θ_i can be taken as being as short as one wants and that nonsteady labour can be described as a succession of periods of steady labour. Function $f_i(\ell_i')$ is individual i's output per unit of time. This will be assumed to hold for each individual.

Assume, moreover, that the personal, specific productivity of each individual influences output in a way called "product augmenting" in the theory of productivity, that is, in multiplying the output. Formally, this writes $f_i(\ell_i') = a_i \cdot f(\ell_i')$ and $p_i(\ell_i) = a_i \cdot \theta_i \cdot f(\ell_i')$ where a_i is a constant depending on individual i, and the function f does not depend on the individual. This means that the rates of transformation between the various input parameters (ℓ_i^j) for $j \neq 1$ do not depend on the specific individual i for given ℓ_i'; that is, they are technical "objective" data.

In particular, one can have, for some characteristics j, $f(\ell_i') = \varphi^j(\ell_i^j) \cdot \psi^j$, where ψ^j can depend on the $\ell_i^{j'}$ for $j' \neq 1$ and $j' \neq j$, but not for $j = 1$ and $j' = j$. Then, characteristic j influences output as if it influenced the speed of labour. In particular, such a j can precisely be labour speed, or the fraction of time of actual labour, and if ℓ_i^j is their measure, $\varphi^j(\ell_i^j) = \ell_i^j$. Intensity of labour, for instance attention, also often intervenes through a specific multiplicative factor $\varphi^j(\ell_i^j)$. This function φ^j can a priori have any form, but it again is the unit function $\varphi^j(\ell_i^j) = \ell_i^j$ if one takes for ℓ_i^j, as a proxy for attention, the fraction of nondefault outputs (and defaulted items are discarded). It may then be that all the other characteristics ℓ^j concern training, formation, and education, which, therefore, necessarily also intervene globally through a specific "objective" multiplicative factor. We can thus have

$$p_i(\ell_i) = a_i \cdot \theta_i \cdot s_i \cdot \tau_i \cdot g(\alpha_i) \cdot h(e_i),$$

where s_i is speed, τ_i the fraction of time of actual labour in formal working time (s_i and τ_i can be conflated into a single variable $\sigma_i = s_i \tau_i$), α_i intensity of labour or attention (with $g(\alpha_i) = \alpha_i$ if α_i is the fraction of nonfaulty outputs taken as a proxy for attention), and e_i is a set of parameters describing training, formation, or education (the most summary description could be the number of years of schooling).

Another natural way of introducing training, formation, or education in the considered structure consists of adding the corresponding time to the duration of labour *stricto sensu*. That is, these learning activities constitute indirect labour whose duration is added to that of direct labour. If a given formation is used in the labour of various periods considered (hence, each is short of lifetime labour), assigning this time in proportion to labour duration may be an acceptable approximation. Appropriate discounting may also take care of time preference, obsolescence of knowledge or, on the contrary, its valorization through experience. These additions assume that other factors of productivity intervene similarly in education or training and in "direct" labour. If it clearly is not the case, this may be taken care of by an appropriate weighting (for someone who is better or more active at working than at learning, or the converse).

In the end, we obtain individual production functions of the form

$$p_i(\ell_i) = a_i \cdot \theta_i \cdot f(\ell_i').$$

Then, one can define the *adjusted labour duration* for individual i as $\theta_i' = \theta_i \cdot f(\ell_i')$. This is the duration of labour adjusted for the effects of the other characteristics chosen by individuals. One then has $p_i(\ell_i) = a_i \theta_i'$. Then, coefficient a_i amounts to a wage rate of individual i corresponding to the adjusted labour duration. Formally, this case reduces to the *unidimensional linear* case

$$p_i(\ell_i) = w_i \ell_i$$

where ℓ_i is a unidimensional measure of labour expressed in units of equivalent time, and w_i is the corresponding given unit productivity or competitive wage rate.

This unidimensional linear case is, formally, a particular case of the more general unidimensional individual production function $p_i(\ell_i)$, where ℓ_i is unidimensional and the function p_i need not be linear. The labour variable ℓ_i may, in particular, be labour duration (θ_i), or an adjusted labour duration as just defined ($\theta_i' = \theta_i \cdot f(\ell_i')$). However, the use of adjusted labour duration for nonlinear p_i cannot be justified as straightforwardly and generally as with the linear form.

Very largely, when characteristics of labour other than duration are chosen, unidimensionality and linearity are justified jointly. However, it will be useful to consider a nonlinear *real* production function in order to study the ELIE treatment of involuntary unemployment, because the relevant real production function will be a truncation of the technical one at the maximum income obtainable by the partially or totally involuntary unemployed individuals (see Chapter 13).

Following chapters consider the ELIE distribution with successive cases of the individual production functions:

- A general function $p_i(\ell_i)$ with a priori multidimensional labour represented by the vector of characteristics ℓ_i. (Chapter 12).
- The unidimensional case where ℓ_i has only one dimension, which generally is duration or equivalent adjusted duration. We will in fact generally use for ℓ_i the fraction of working time in total time. This total time can be total adjusted time $\widehat{\theta'} = \widehat{\theta} \cdot f(\widehat{\ell'})$ where $\widehat{\theta}$ is total time and $\widehat{\ell'} = \{\widehat{\ell^j}\}_{j \neq 1}$. Then, $0 \leq \ell_i \leq 1$, and $\lambda_i = 1 - \ell_i$ is leisure similarly measured. (Chapter 12).
- The linear unidimensional case $p_i(\ell_i) = w_i \ell_i$, which is formally particular but has in fact a large relevance (notably with adjusted duration). (Chapter 9). Number ℓ_i will then be taken as the worked fraction of total time, for convienience in presentation. Total time then is taken as unit for measuring wage rates. If it is in fact adjusted total time $\widehat{\theta'} = \widehat{\theta} \cdot f(\widehat{\ell'})$, then individual i's wage rate w_i is $w_i = a_i \widehat{\theta'}$. Then, indeed, $p_i(\ell_i) = a_i \theta'_i = a_i \widehat{\theta'} \cdot (\theta'_i / \widehat{\theta'}) = w_i \ell_i$ with $\ell_i = \theta'_i / \widehat{\theta'}$.
- The explicit consideration of involuntary unemployment. (Chapter 13).

Chapter 10 considers the question of the information necessary for the implementation of ELIE schemes. The conclusion is that this information is globally easier to obtain or to approximate than is the case with most general tax or subsidy policies. Chapters 14, 15, and 16 then compare ELIE with the other distributive policies, proposals, or philosophies.

9

Equal duration income equalization

1. PRESENTATION AND BASIS

1.1. Presentation

This chapter derives the structure of global (overall) distributive justice in macro-justice implied by endogenous social choice, equal labour income equalization (ELIE), and shows its various properties and meanings, in the standard case (linear production functions, Section 1.2). In Section 2, the ELIE structure is derived from the duality of goods and measures (consumption-income and labour-leisure), process-freedom, and the required equality. Then, the various aspects or meanings of this result are pointed out, such as equal sharing of an equal share of the income value of productive capacities, partial equal pay for equal work, from each equally in labour (or according to her capacities) and to each equally, remuneration according to desert for one part and merit for the other part, general balanced labour reciprocity, or partial proportional compensation of productivity differentials. Section 3 focuses on the logic of ELIE. It considers the limiting cases of unemployment income of the less able, labour duty of the ablest, and highest incomes and labours. Section 4 displays the geometry of ELIE. It shows that freedom, and hence equal freedom, can be considered in two ways, directly as process-freedom or in the space of the result, and it characterizes ELIE in these two cases. The consequences of particular rights and rules, such as a workfare rule or a right to idleness, are pointed out in Section 5. Section 6 gathers the various meanings or meaningful properties of ELIE, and the meanings of the crucial coefficient k. Finally, two appendices develop respectively the consequences of measuring values in labour-leisure-life value (Appendix A), and the characterization of ELIE as equal linear output-freedom (Appendix B).

1.2. Linear production functions

The simplest and most standard form of labour production, to which actual production can be reduced often exactly and most often as a sufficient approximation, provides a clear, simple, and sufficient structure for discussing the logical and moral reasons, requirements, meanings, and properties of ELIE distributions. This is the topic of this chapter. Chapter 12 explicitly considers more complete and complex structures, and Chapter 13 completes this presentation by focusing on the explicit introduction of involuntary unemployment. The issue of information is the topic of Chapter 10.

The common simple case of individuals' production function is a linear function of labour duration, $p_i(\ell_i) = w_i \ell_i$, where ℓ_i is individual i's actual or adjusted labour duration, and w_i is her corresponding given unit productivity or competitive wage rate. Labour duration ℓ_i may be actual duration or equivalent duration adjusted for the levels of the other characteristics of labour as shown in Chapter 8. It was shown that this structure with adjusted duration is common, at least as a sufficient approximation, for periods of steady labour. And labour can practically always be considered steady in periods taken as sufficiently short. When duration adjusted for the other characteristics of labour is considered, this adjustment should be done for all the considered labours and durations: labour of each individual, maximal labour, leisure of all individuals, and the equalization labour. Aspects or features of the activity of labour that are given to the individuals – and which can a priori differ across them – are reckoned as given parameters of individuals' capacities, and hence as determinants of the w_i (it may alternatively be possible to integrate them in an adjusted duration).

Moreover, we choose maximal labour duration as unit of time and of labour. Then, $0 \leq \ell_i \leq 1$. Individual i's leisure is $\lambda_i = 1 - \ell_i$, with $0 \leq \lambda_i \leq 1$. As a consequence, w_i is also individual i's maximal earnings, and the value of the rent of her productive capacities measured in income units.

2. THE ASPECTS OF THE REASON FOR ELIE

2.1. The two goods and units

An individual is concerned, here, with two goods: her income y_i, which buys consumption, and her leisure λ_i, which also represents its complement, labour $\ell_i = 1 - \lambda_i$.

Income units are earned and spent in market exchanges. They are markets' common measuring rod of production, goods, and consumption. Income units are also transferable across individuals. By contrast, units of leisure are not directly transferable across individuals. However, in a society where "man is the measure of all things," units of leisure, that is, of free time, of different individuals, have a priori no reason to be considered differently on moral grounds. The fact that the corresponding labours have different productivities is not relevant for this moral consideration. Productivity solely is a matter of fact rather than of justice, that is, rather than a *prima facie* moral concern for a priori and intrinsic ethical judgments. It refers to the mercantile side of society, not to its humanistic moral dimension.

More productive individuals are more useful workers, but not a priori morally worthier persons. Moreover, we have noticed, in Chapter 6, that individuals' eudemonistic capacities are irrelevant – by their direct consideration – for the issue of macrojustice and global distributive justice (from consensus), and hence they cannot make a difference for the social ethical value of different individuals' time of life and leisure. Just as "a dollar is a dollar" in markets, one man's time of life and notably free time is *prima facie* worth that of another for this basic moral evaluation. This is a characteristic of a society of individuals equal in dignity and equally worthy of consideration.[1]

There thus are two possible measures of values, measuring rods, or numéraires: income units (say dollars); and leisure, labour, or lifetime units, which measure leisure value, labour value, or lifetime value. Both have meaning. We will see that their chosen relative importance coincides with the basic choice of the degree of income equalization.

2.2. Process-freedom and the resulting allocation of resources

Full process-freedom implies that the individuals are free to use their labour ℓ_i (act-freedom) for earning $w_i \ell_i$ (aim-freedom), given the basic allocation distributing given resources. Full process-freedom also implies that the individuals have the use-rights of their capacities or own the use of their productivity. However, they do not a priori own the rent of their productive capacities and have the corresponding rent-rights (see Chapters 3 and 6). The basic allocation of resources is, for global distributive justice, the allocation of these rent-rights.

The general form of the lump-sum allocation of society's resources is, for each individual, a vector of the two goods, income η_i and leisure μ_i. Being granted leisure μ_i practically means being demanded the complementary labour $k_i = 1 - \mu_i$, which amounts to being liable of the product of this labour, $k_i w_i$. The rational necessity of identical treatment of identicals in the relevant characteristics[2] implies the identity of these vectors for all individuals: $\eta_i = \eta$, $\mu_i = \mu$, and $k_i = k = 1 - \mu$ for all i. From process-freedom, individual i freely deviates from this allocation in choosing labour ℓ_i and disposable income y_i, such that $y_i - \eta = w_i \cdot (\ell_i - k)$. Equivalently, she chooses to work ℓ_i for the earnings $w_i \ell_i$, while she receives η and pays $w_i k$ for the labour liability k, and her disposable income is $y_i = w_i \ell_i + \eta - w_i k$. However, total consumption equals total production: $\Sigma y_i = \Sigma w_i \ell_i$. Hence, $n\eta = k \Sigma w_i$, or $\eta = k \overline{w}$ (where $\overline{w} = (1/n) \Sigma w_i$ is average wage and productivity). Individual i receiving basic leisure $\mu = 1 - k$ means that she yields labour k, that is, its output $k w_i$. Hence, in income value, individual i

yields the value kw_i and receives the value $k\overline{w}$. The global result is that she receives the net transfer $t_i = k\cdot(\overline{w} - w_i)$, a subsidy if $t_i > 0$ and a tax of $-t_i$ if $t_i < 0$. Of course, $\Sigma t_i = 0$.

2.3. Capacity rent sharing

This result directly constitutes a distribution of the rents of society's capacities. From each individual i is taken away the same fraction k of the rent of her own productive capacities, as a transfer of the income value kw_i, and the proceeds are equally redistributed, each individual then receiving an equal share of the total, $(1/n)\Sigma(kw_i) = k\overline{w}$. Moreover, each individual just keeps for herself the remaining fraction $1 - k$ of the rent of her productive capacities (as she keeps for herself all benefits from her other capacities – see Chapter 6).

Equivalently, each individual receives the same fraction k/n of each other's productive rent, since, in income values,

$$t_i = k\cdot(\overline{w} - w_i) = (k/n)[\Sigma_{j\neq i}w_j - (n-1)w_i].$$

2.4. Equal duration income equalization

This result amounts to each individual yielding her earnings during labour duration k, w_ik, for individual i, and receiving an equal share of the total, $k\overline{w}$, or an equal share of each of these individuals' earnings, kw_j/n. This is *equal labour duration income equalization*, the form of ELIE for labour measured by its duration. Labour or duration k is the *equalization labour* or *duration*. The amount kw_i is individual i's *equalization income*, and $k\overline{w}$ is the *average equalization income*, equal to the income earned for labour k at the average wage rate $\overline{w}$.

2.5. The borderline cases

Coefficient or duration k has two limiting values, 0 and 1. For $k = 0$, $t_i = 0$ for all i and each individual receives all the rent of her productive capacities: this is full self-ownership. For $k = 1$, $t_i = \overline{w} - w_i$ for all i and all the income rents of productive capacities are equally shared.

2.6. The choice of the equalization measure

The question of the choice of unit of measure of value shows another meaningful aspect of the solution. In Part I, we have obtained that the problem of global distributive justice in macrojustice respecting social freedom and notably constitutional basic rights and process-freedom consists of the allocation of the rent of productive capacities. We also know that impartial rationality implies an equal sharing of this rent between the individuals (individual preferences have been

found irrelevant for macrojustice – Chapter 6). However, this rent has to be measured in order to define equal shares. Now, the rent of an asset is, by definition,
the value of its availability. Availability is possibility of using. Hence, the rent is
the value of full use. However, a person's life can be used at labour or at leisure. If
person i only works, she produces income w_i, which is, therefore, the rent of her
productive capacities measured in income. But if a person only rests, she enjoys
full-time leisure, a benefit of value 1 measured in leisure or lifetime value. Hence,
the labour or leisure value of a person's productive capacities is 1.

This duality comes from the fact that productive capacities are relevant because
they determine productivities, and productivity is not a quantity but a function
relating two directly relevant quantities: labour and income. Productivity is both
output and income per labour, and leisure available when labour produces a given
income. Hence, a piece of productive capacities can be defined by the labour that
uses them or by the income they produce. The total available for individual i's
productive capacities thus is 1 in labour value and w_i in income value. These
measures are the rent values of the individual's productive capacities.

Therefore, the total productive rent for the n individuals of society is Σw_i in
income value and n in labour, leisure, or lifetime value. Hence, equal sharing
allocates to each individual $\overline{w}$ if the measure is in income and 1 if the measure is
in leisure, labour, or lifetime.

The latter solution is realized by full self-ownership where each individual keeps
the rent of her own capacities. The income value of each individual's productive
capacities is not relevant for this solution. Note that the leisure an individual
can enjoy is only her own. The former solution can be reached from full self-
ownership by taking the income value w_i from each individual i and replacing it
by the average $\overline{w}$. This is maximal income equalization. These two solutions differ
if the w_i are not all the same, and they are in general very different.

Individuals are concerned with both income and leisure. Life requires both.
With full self-ownership, individual i's share of productive rent is 1 in leisure
value and w_i in income value. The income evaluations are unequal and harsh
for unproductive individuals. With maximal income equalization, individual i's
share of productive rent is $\overline{w}$ in income value and $\overline{w}/w_i$ in leisure value (the labour
time she needs for producing $\overline{w}$). The leisure or labour evaluations are unequal
and harsh for productive individuals.

A compromise consists in measuring part of the rent in one value and the rest in
the other, and in equally sharing each. The fraction k of the total rent has the income
value $k\Sigma w_i$. Its equal sharing attributes $k\overline{w}$ income units to each individual. The
remaining fraction has the leisure or labour value $(1-k)n$. Its equal sharing
attributes $1-k$ units of time to each individual. The latter allocation has the
income value $(1-k)w_i$ for individual i. Hence, each individual i finally receives
the resource $v_i = (1-k)w_i + k\overline{w} = w_i + k\cdot(\overline{w} - w_i) = w_i + t_i$ in income units
(and $1 - k + k\overline{w}/w_i$ in units of time). From the reference of full self-ownership,
she receives the net transfer t_i in income value. This amounts to equal labour

income equalization. However, number k acquires a different meaning: it is the fraction of the social productive rent that is reckoned in income units, while the rest is reckoned in units of leisure, labour, or time of life.

2.7. Equal partial self-ownership. Equal sharing of an equal share

The result can be seen under many meaningful angles.

The form $t_i = k \cdot (\overline{w} - w_i)$ of the net transfers directly shows that they achieve *from or to each according to the excess or deficiency of her productivity to average*, where "according to" is given its usual meaning of "in proportion to," with the number k as common coefficient of proportionality.

The result constitutes *equal partial self-ownership* for time $1 - k$, given that the income value of the rest is equally shared.

In income value, the result constitutes an *equal sharing of an equal share* of each individual's rent of her productive capacities. The fraction k is this equally shared equal share. Each individual keeps the same fraction $1 - k$ of the rent of her productive capacities for herself. The equal sharing is in transferable income value. In the end, each individual receives the net transfer $t_i = k \cdot (\overline{w} - w_i)$ and owns $v_i = (1 - k)w_i + k\overline{w} = w_i + t_i$ in income value.

2.8. Equal pay for equal work

Equal pay for equal work is a classical claim of fairness in remunerations. The obtained result amounts to each individual i receiving, for the same work k, the same pay $k\overline{w}$ rather than her product $w_i k$. Equivalently, for labour k, each individual i is paid the same average wage rate $\overline{w}$ rather than her unit productivity w_i. Individuals are otherwise free to work more at their own wage rate w_i or less at the cost of foregone earnings at this rate w_i. The scheme erases the effects, on incomes, of the differences in productive capacities, for labour k. Note that traditional uses of the principle "equal pay for equal work" refer, rather, to various discriminations that are usually banned by basic rights.

2.9. From each equally in labour, to each equally in money

The obtained scheme amounts to each individual yielding the income value of the same labour k, that is kw_i for individual i, and receiving the same amount $k\overline{w}$.

2.10. From each according to her capacities, to each equally

The result is also equivalent to each individual yielding according to her capacities and receiving the same resulting amount. "According to" is given here its usual sense of "in proportion to." The coefficient of proportionality is the number k, and individual i yields kw_i and receives $k\overline{w}$, the same for all.

2.11. Desert and merit

The semantic distinction between the concepts of *desert* and *merit* brings another light on the meaning of ELIE schemes. The difference is that in allocation "according to action" (or labour, or effort), the effect of the actor's capacities is endorsed with "merit" and is not with "desert."[3] Merit entitles the individuals with the effects of their capacities and the corresponding benefits. This is not the case for what an individual can deserve because of her action, labour, or effort. In these uses of these terms, an individual merits the product of her labour or effort. Hence, individuals providing the same labour or effort, but with different capacities leading to different outputs, receive these different outputs. By contrast, two individuals providing the same labour or effort deserve the same reward for this action, irrespective of their actual output due to different capacities. These meanings indeed correspond to usual expression. "Meritocracy" is the allocation of social power according to capacities. "The career open to talent" is a concept of merit (this was a main motive for the historical Declarations of rights). Aim-freedom in process-freedom is a concept of merit. However, an ELIE distributive scheme amounts to giving each individual the same reward $k\overline{w}$ for the same labour k, proportional to this labour, for this equalization labour: this applies a concept of desert.

In fact, the whole scheme conflates process-freedom with this distribution. Consider, then, an ELIE distribution with equalization labour duration k. Individual i freely chooses to work for duration ℓ_i. With the realistic values of k, generally $\ell_i > k$. Then, individual i's reward taking the ELIE transfers into account can be presented as follows. For labour k, individuals receive income $\overline{w}k$, proportional to k and the same for all, independent of their specific productivity w_i, and hence paid at the average wage rate $\overline{w}$: this is remuneration according to desert. However, for the rest of labour, $\ell_i - k$, individual i receives income $w_i \cdot (\ell_i - k)$, her actual product, depending on her specific productivity w_i, and hence different for individuals with different productivities: this is remuneration according to merit.

Hence an ELIE distribution in social freedom also amounts to: *to each as she deserves for the equalization labour and as she merits for the rest.*

2.12. Macrojustice as general balanced labour reciprocity

Reciprocity between two individuals is a relationship in which each yields something to the other, with a relation between both transferred items that attributes to this relationship some aspect of balance, fairness, or equality. In the framework presently considered, there are only two measuring rods for establishing a comparison between such transfers: income and labour. Transfers equal in income value would cancel out.[4] Hence, the equality has to be in labour value: each transfers to

---

[3] See, notably, Vlastos (1962), Lucas (1993), and Pojman and McLeod (1999).

[4] In a large society, the considered reciprocities will not be face-to-face reciprocities in which people can transfer both ways materially identical things, because of the intrinsic value of the relationship, or of the

each other the product of the same quantity of labour. This will be called balanced labour reciprocity. On balance, there is an income transfer from the more productive individual to the other, proportional to the difference in their productivity in earning, where the coefficient of proportionality is the amount of labour used for producing the transfers.

The term reciprocity has been used in many senses, including that of the noted related bilateral transfers showing some sort of balance. However, the most common and interesting use also refers to the conditions and motivations of the transfers that have to be more or less voluntary. These modalities are not our current concern, but one may hope that the aspect of justice of such labour-balanced reciprocities may be a factor that can favor the acceptance and more or less the voluntariness of these transfers.[5]

In *general balanced labour reciprocity*, each individual yields to each other the product of the same labour. Thus, there is also pairwise reciprocity between each pair of individuals, with the same labour values mutually transferred. Globally, each individual yields to society and receives from it the same labour value. Note that an amount of labour of an individual also measures a fraction of the rent of her productive capacities.

Hence, one can call *general balanced labour reciprocity* the redistribution where *each individual yields to each other the product of the same labour,* or the distribution where *each individual owns the same share of each other's productive rent,* or, equivalently, *owes the product of the same labour to each other.*

In this case, if α is this labour (or rent share), individual i receives the net transfer

$$t_i = \alpha \cdot [\Sigma_{j \neq i} w_j - (n-1)w_i] = \alpha \cdot (\Sigma w_j - n w_i) = k \cdot (\overline{w} - w_i)$$

where $k = n\alpha$. Hence, a general balanced labour reciprocity of labour α creates an ELIE distribution with equalization labour $k = n\alpha$. Conversely, an ELIE distribution with equalization labour k can result from a general balanced labour reciprocity of labour $\alpha = k/n$.

Therefore, considering the results only, *ELIE and general labour reciprocity amount to the same.*

This shows that *process-free or efficient macrojustice is justice as reciprocity.* ELIE can thus also be described as:

– *From each, to each other, the product of the same labour,* or
– *From each, to each other, according to her capacities,* where "according to" means "in proportion to" (the same proportion for all).

One consequence is that, in ELIE, each individual can be seen as yielding to the rest of society and receiving from it the product of the same amount of labour.

---

symbolic value of the transfer, and in conceptually earmarking each transfer by the identities of the giver and the receiver (consider, for instance, mutual transfers of wedding rings, or of drinks and meals).
[5] See Kolm 1984a, 2000a, 2000b, 2004b.

2.13. Partial compensation of productivity differentials

An ELIE redistribution also amounts to a *proportional partial bridging of the gaps between the individuals' resources* w_i. This property has two aspects.

First, in the set of equivalent pairwise reciprocities just described, the pair of transfers between individuals i and j, with $w_i > w_j$, amounts to a single *transfer of* $(k/n)(w_i - w_j)$ *from the more productive individual i to the less productive j*: this transfer is *the fraction* (k/n) *of the gap between their productivities or productive rents* in income value.

The global result, however, is the conflation of all these transfers, for each individual. Yet, an ELIE redistribution also amounts to a similar property at this level. The value of an individual i's consumption and leisure can be called her wealth or total (disposable) income.[6] In income (money) value, individual i's given wealth is w_i, and the net transfer t_i transforms it into $v_i = w_i + t_i$. For two individuals i and j with $w_i > w_j$, we have $t_j - t_i = k \cdot (w_i - w_j)$ and

$$v_i - v_j = w_i - w_j - (t_j - t_i) = (1 - k)(w_i - w_j).$$

Hence, ELIE *diminishes the wealth gaps all in the same proportion* $1 - k$. This can go from nothing in full self-ownership ($k = 0$) to complete equalization with maximal income equalization ($k = 1$).

These properties characterize ELIE schemes, that is, they are necessary and sufficient. This is obvious for the pairwise transfers of $\alpha \cdot (w_i - w_j)$ between all pairs of individuals i and j with $w_i > w_j$, since this amounts to the reciprocal transfers of αw_i and αw_j both ways, and we have seen that this set of transfers amounts to ELIE with equalization labour duration $k = n\alpha$.

With respect to the global result, assume the individuals receive net transfers, T_i for individual i, whose overall effect is to diminish all pairwise gaps in individuals' wealth in the same proportion: $(w_i + T_i) - (w_j + T_j) = \beta \cdot (w_i - w_j)$ for all i, j with $0 \le \beta \le 1$. Then, $T_i - T_j = (\beta - 1)(w_i - w_j)$ for all i, j. This implies that there is some number c independent of i such that $T_i = (\beta - 1)w_i + c$ for all i. If the set of these transfers balances, $\Sigma T_i = 0$, and hence $nc = (1 - \beta)\Sigma w_i$ or $c = (1 - \beta)\overline{w}$, and $T_i = (1 - \beta)(\overline{w} - w_i)$ for all i, that is, denoting $k = 1 - \beta$, $T_i = k \cdot (\overline{w} - w_i) = t_i$, for all i.

2.14. Concentrating the distribution

An ELIE transforms the "natural" allocation of the rents of productive capacities where each individual i receives w_i into the allocation where each individual i receives her total income or value

$$v_i = w_i + t_i = (1 - k)w_i + k\overline{w}$$

---

[6] This wealth is for the considered period (the stock-flow distinction is not relevant here).

with $0 \leq k \leq 1$. Each v_i is a weighted average between w_i and the average $\overline{w}$ of the w_j, with the same weight. We have $v_i = w_i$ if $k = 0$ and $v_i = \overline{w}$ if $k = 1$. Formally, this constitutes a *uniform linear concentration* of the distribution of the w_i, or, for short, a *concentration* of this distribution, with degree k (see Kolm 1966b).

Other properties and characteristic properties of ELIE are considered in forthcoming sections.

3. THE LOGIC OF ELIE

3.1. The framework

With ELIE, each individual i receives the net transfer $t_i = k \cdot (\overline{w} - w_i)$, a subsidy if $t_i > 0$ and a tax of $-t_i$ if $t_i < 0$. If $k > 0$, $t_i \gtrless 0$ as $w_i \lessgtr \overline{w}$. Individual i is thus endowed with the total income

$$v_i = w_i + t_i = (1 - k)w_i + k\overline{w}.$$

Then, she freely chooses her actual labour ℓ_i with $0 \leq \ell_i \leq 1$, she freely earns the corresponding earnings $w_i \ell_i$, and she ends up with the disposable income, used for consumption,

$$y_i = w_i \ell_i + t_i = w_i \cdot (\ell_i - k) + \overline{w}k.$$

This shows the substitution of $\overline{w}k$ for $w_i k$.

Individual i's leisure is $\lambda_i = 1 - \ell_i$. Its income value is $w_i \lambda_i$, and we naturally have

$$y_i + w_i \lambda_i = (1 - k)w_i + k\overline{w} = w_i + t_i = v_i.$$

The whole problem can be given a particularly enlightening geometrical presentation shown in the next section.[7] However, let us first note the particular properties that will appear with this figure. They concern the equalization labour (k) and average income ($k\overline{w}$), and the limiting cases of income and labour, notably unemployment compensations and labour duty.

3.2. Equalization labour and income

If individual i chooses to work $\ell_i = k$, she receives the disposable income $y_i = k\overline{w}$, the same for all individuals. This manifests "equal pay for equal work." We have $y_i > k\overline{w}$ if $\ell_i > k$ and $y_i < k\overline{w}$ if $\ell_i < k$.

We have noted that present-day national redistributions have a volume similar to that of an ELIE with an equalization labour duration of one to two days a week. Most people work much more than that, notably if we except total or partial involuntary unemployment (which will be the topic of Chapter 13 and is not

---

[7] See Kolm 1996b.

presently considered), and complementary incomes in households. At any rate, we have seen and will point out again that ELIE is the globally just distribution only if $\ell_i \geq k$ for most individuals working full-time and as much as they want. Hence, generally $\ell_i > k$ and, therefore, $y_i > k\overline{w}$. In fact, the average equalization income $k\overline{w}$ appears as a de facto minimum income for macrojustice. In particular, people with higher w_i earn much more in working more than k. People with lower w_i also generally choose to work more, and hence earn more. However, the lower w_i, the lower the gain from extra work and the loss from lower work. Yet, if individual i chooses to work $\ell_i < k$, then the lower w_i, the lower the income loss from $k\overline{w}$, $w_i \cdot (k - \ell_i)$. If individual i with $w_i < \overline{w}$ chooses not to work, $\ell_i = 0$, she nevertheless receives disposable income $t_i = k \cdot (\overline{w} - w_i) > 0$. At any rate, $y_i > k \cdot (\overline{w} - w_i) > 0$ for $w_i < \overline{w}$. Individuals who can earn nothing in the labour market, hence with $w_i = 0$, have an income equal to the average equalization income $k\overline{w}$. In the other cases, the minimum income $k \cdot (\overline{w} - w_i)$ is the higher and the closer to $k\overline{w}$, the lower w_i. Individuals with $w_i = 0$, who have the disposable income $k\overline{w}$, constitute a particular case of involuntary unemployment that is also, in a sense, voluntary, since labour with a productivity and wage rate of zero is neither demanded for production nor supplied for an income. However, we will see in Chapter 13 that, in the ELIE treatment of involuntary unemployment, all totally or partially involuntarily unemployed individuals have a disposable income of at least $k\overline{w}$. In the end, the average equalization income $k\overline{w}$ appears roughly and de facto as a minimum income. Exception can doubtlessly be discarded for concerns about macrojustice. More precisely, however, the lower w_i, the closer y_i is to $k\overline{w}$ for each level of labour ℓ_i. And y_i can be notably lower than $k\overline{w}$ only for productive individuals (high w_i) who choose to work less than k. Then, more specifically, $k\overline{w}$ is a minimum income in the measure in which the individuals are not responsible for their low income (in being able to earn much but choosing to work little).

This average equalization income $k\overline{w}$ is the earning of the average wage during the equalization duration. When there is a standard duration of labour θ, one can write $k\overline{w} = (k/\theta) \cdot \overline{w}\theta$. Then, $\overline{w}\theta$ is average income. Hence, this de facto minimum income is the fraction of average income equal to the fraction of the equalization duration in the standard labour duration. (The examples presented in Chapter 7 correspond to such a ratio of 1/3.)

3.3. Extremal values: Less able's unemployment income, ablest's labour duty, and average maximal income

3.3.1. Limiting situations

The lowest and highest levels of income and leisure individuals can obtain with an ELIE distribution are particularly interesting for actual social reasons or for what they reveal about the logic of this distribution. They correspond to income in case of unemployment, minimal labour necessary for paying, and maximal obtainable income – compared, notably, with average maximal income. The result is that people less productive than average obtain an income when they do not work (for $k > 0$), but cannot obtain average maximal income (for $k < 1$). And people more productive than average have to provide some minimal labour for paying (for $k > 0$), but can obtain the average maximal income (and more if $k < 1$). The unemployment compensation of the less able and the labour duty of the ablest merely result from the fact that the transfer received by the former ($t_i > 0$) and yielded by the latter ($t_i < 0$) do not depend on their labours or earnings – this practically is a necessary and sufficient condition for full process-freedom and for Pareto efficiency. The unemployment compensation, $t_i = k \cdot (\overline{w} - w_i)$ for $w_i < \overline{w}$, increases when w_i decreases and k increases. It is the highest for individuals who can earn no income, and it is then the average equalization income $k\overline{w}$. The minimal necessary labour, noted below, increases with w_i and k. It is the highest for the most productive individuals, and it tends to the equalization labour k for individuals much more productive than average.

These advantages of the less productive and duties of the more productive are aspects of the compensations for "natural" handicaps and advantages in earning capacities realized by ELIE. They may face objections concerning "workfare ethics" for unemployment income and a "right to idleness" concerning minimal necessary labour (see the discussions in Chapter 7). Note, however, that the unemployment considered here does not impair Pareto efficiency. It is voluntary (for $w_i = 0$, it can be seen as both voluntary and involuntary in the senses previously noted). Moreover, de facto, for the actually possible levels of k, practically all individuals (or, rather, households) submitted to a minimal necessary labour will choose to work much more. In fact, we noted that most productive people will work more than the equalization duration k, and the minimal necessary labour is lower than k. Moreover, this concerns productive people who can earn much with moderate extra work – the more so the higher the minimal necessary labour is for them. And minimal labour would correspond to zero income and consumption. Exceptions can only be very rare and can certainly be left out of the concern of macrojustice.

3.3.2. The less able's unemployment income

Precisely, if individual i chooses not to work, $\ell_i = 0$ and $y_i = t_i$: she receives an unemployment income $y_i = y_i^o = t_i$ if $t_i > 0$, that is, if $w_i > \overline{w}$ when $k > 0$. Then, y_i^o is higher when w_i is lower, from 0 for $w_i = \overline{w}$ to $k\overline{w}$ for $w_i = 0$. It increases with k, from 0 for $k = 0$ to $\overline{w} - w_i$ for $k = 1$.

3.3.3. The ablest's labour duty

If individual i has no other source of income but labour (in addition to the considered transfers), one should have $y_i \geq 0$, or $w_i \ell_i + t_i \geq 0$, that is,

$$\ell_i \geq \ell_i^o = -t_i/w_i = k \cdot [1 - (\overline{w}/w_i)].$$

This is guaranteed by $\ell_i \geq 0$ if $\ell_i^o \leq 0$, that is, either $k = 0$ (full self-ownership) or $w_i \leq \overline{w}$. If $k > 0$ and $w_i > \overline{w}$, $\ell_i^o > 0$ constitutes a minimal necessary labour. It is necessary for paying the tax $-t_i$. It is the higher, the higher $w_i/\overline{w}$, from 0 if $w_i = \overline{w}$ to k when $w_i/\overline{w}$ becomes very high. For given w_i, it increases with k, from 0 for $k = 0$ to $1 - \overline{w}/w_i$ for $k = 1$.

3.3.4. Highest incomes and labours

Individuals obtain their highest disposable income in working maximally (for $w_i > 0$), and this income then is total income: $\ell_i = 1$ entails $y_i = w_i + t_i = v_i$. We have

$$v_i - \overline{w} = t_i + w_i - \overline{w} = (1 - k)(w_i - \overline{w}).$$

Hence, $v_i = \overline{w}$ if $w_i = \overline{w}$ (then, $t_i = 0$) or $k = 1$. If $k < 1$, $v_i \gtrless \overline{w}$ according as $w_i \gtrless \overline{w}$, and v_i increases with w_i from the average equalization income $k\overline{w}$ when $w_i = 0$ to $(1 - k)w_i$ if $w_i/\overline{w}$ becomes very high. Individual i's highest or total income v_i is a decreasing or increasing function of k according as $w_i \gtrless \overline{w}$, from $v_i = w_i$ for $k = 0$ to $v_i = \overline{w}$ for $k = 1$.

3.4. Limiting cases

With *full self-ownership*, $k = 0$, $v_i = w_i$, and $t_i = y_i^o = \ell_i^o = 0$ for all i.

With *maximal income equalization*, $k = 1$; $v_i = \overline{w}$ for all i; $t_i = \overline{w} - w_i$; $y_i^o = \overline{w} - w_i$ for $w_i \leq \overline{w}$; and, for $w_i \geq \overline{w}$, $\ell_i^o = 1 - \overline{w}/w_i$, which corresponds to the leisure $\lambda_i^o = 1 - \ell_i^o = \overline{w}/w_i$ equal to the labour with which the individual i can earn the average income $\overline{w}$. We have $y_i^o = \overline{w}$ when $w_i = 0$, and ℓ_i^o becomes high when w_i is high (the situation of Dworkin's "slavery of the talented").

4. THE GEOMETRY OF ELIE

4.1. The figure

The geometry of the question is particularly enlightening. Figure 9–1 shows it.[8] The two axes bear quantities of the two goods. Leisure λ is measured on the horizontal axis from point 0. Hence, labour $\ell = 1 - \lambda$ is measured on this axis from point L such that $0L = 1$ and toward the left. Income (and consumption) y are measured on the vertical axis. The domain of possible bundles is defined by $0 \leq \lambda \leq 1$ or $0 \leq \ell \leq 1$, and $y > 0$.

The budget line of individual i has equation

$$y_i = w_i \ell_i + t_i = w_i \cdot (\ell_i - k) + \overline{w} k$$

---

[8] See Kolm 1996a.

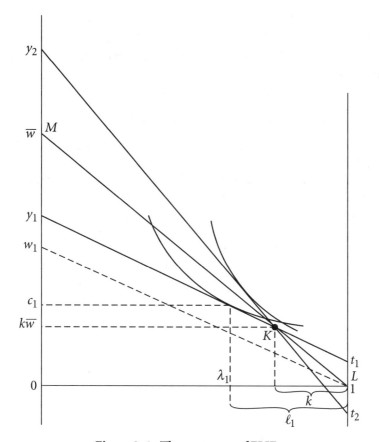

Figure 9–1. The geometry of ELIE.

or

$$y_i + w_i\lambda_i = v_i = w_i + t_i = (1 - k)w_i + k\overline{w}.$$

Its slope is $-w_i$.

It intersects the vertical line $\ell = 0$ at $y_i = t_i$, which is $y_i = y_i^o \geq 0$ if $t_i \geq 0$ (hence, when $w_i \geq \overline{w}$ if $k > 0$).

It intersects the axis of incomes at income $y_i = v_i = w_i + t_i$.

It intersects the axis of leisure and labour at labour $\ell_i^o = k \cdot [1 - (\overline{w}/w_i)]$ if $w_i \geq \overline{w}$.

It passes through point k of coordinates $\ell_i = k$ (hence, $\lambda_i = 1 - k$) and $y_i = k\overline{w}$. These coordinates do not depend on individual i. Therefore, all budget lines pass through point k. Hence, individual i's budget line is the line passing through point k with slope $-w_i$.

An individual with a lower productivity and slope in absolute value w_i is compensated by a larger transfer and ordinate of the intersect with the line $\ell = 0$, t_i, in such a way that her budget line continues to pass through point k.

When k varies from 0 to 1, point k varies on the line ($\ell = k$, $y = k\overline{w}$), from point L with $\ell = y = 0$ for $k = 0$ representing full self-ownership, to point M with $\ell = 1$ and $y = \overline{w}$ for $k = 1$ representing maximal income equalization. This line has slope $-\overline{w}$.

4.2. The moral geometry of freedoms and equalities

"Justice is equality," as Aristotle puts it and as is confirmed by the analysis of impartial rationality.[9] The equalizands can be varied, however. They often are freedoms of some sort ("Men are free and equal in rights"). This freedom can be the free use of some items, themselves equal or not. When they are not, the reason can again be a kind of equality, such as equal endorsement of an unequal "natural" allocation. Moreover, freedom a priori refers to action in circumstances, but it has consequences and can also be represented by a domain of possible choice in the space of consequences. The choice of the place where the liberty is considered matters for interpersonal comparisons. In the question considered here, the basis is social freedom. In the form of full process-freedom, it entails equal complete process-freedom for all individuals. This implies specific equalities concerning capacities. Full process-freedom first amounts to equal rights to use one's capacities and benefit from the use. However, it also implies the (equal) endorsement of the "natural" allocation of the corresponding benefits of productivities which are generally unequal. The consequence of an individual's choice is an allocation of income or consumption on the one hand, and leisure (or labour) on the other hand. The domain of an individual's possible choice of this pair of items can be said to describe her "outcome-freedom." These are the "budget sets" in the foregoing description (see Figure 9–1). These domains cannot coincide for individuals with different productivities (the slopes of the budget lines are $-w_i$). Identity of these domains and full process-freedom (or Pareto efficiency) are exclusive of each other when productivities differ. However, the equal sharing of the rent values of productive capacities, in the two-dimensional space of outcomes or with the relevant measures (Sections 2.2 and 2.6), leads all individual budget lines to pass through the same point K. This is the geometric manifestation of this equality. This can be seen as all individuals being a priori endowed with the vector of income k and leisure $1 - k$, which corresponds to point K, and being free to work more or less than labour k in benefiting from the extra earnings or incurring the loss of foregone income. Indeed, the budget condition $y_i = \ell_i w_i + t_i$ can be written as

$$y_i - k = w_i \cdot (\ell_i - k).$$

This freedom from an equal allocation is similar to the classical principle for allocating a bundle of goods of "free exchange from equal sharing." A notable

---

[9] See Chapter 23 and Kolm 1971 [1998], Foreword, Section 5.

point, however, is that, in the case of the present scheme, the "terms of trade" or "rates of transformation" facing the individuals are generally different from one to the other since they are the individual productivities w_i. This is due to process-freedom which allocates, to each individual, the use of her capacities and the corresponding benefits.

Domains of free choice in the space of outcomes – the budget sets – coincide with ELIE if and only if the productivities w_i are equal (the slope of the budget lines are $-w_i$). However, they are related by inclusion in the two limiting cases, full self-ownership with $k = 0$, and maximal income equalization with $k = 1$, where point K becomes point L and point M, respectively. In each case, indeed, for any two domains, one always is a subset of the other (or they coincide in cases of equal w_i). Then, one can compare individuals' outcome-freedoms represented by domains of possible choices in the space of outcomes (income and leisure). Indeed, when an individual's domain strictly includes that of another, the former can have more income and consumption than the latter for any leisure and labour (except for $\ell_i = 0$ for $k = 0$, where all $y_i = 0$, and for $\ell_i = 1$ for $k = 1$, where all $y_i = \overline{w}$), and more leisure for any income and consumption (except for $y_i = 0$ for $k = 0$, where all $\lambda_i = 1$, and for $y_i = \overline{w}$ for $k = 1$, where all $\lambda_i = 0$). She can thus be said to be "outcome-freer" than the latter who then is "outcome less free" than her. However, the effect of productivity on this ranking is reversed in these two cases: a higher w_i makes the possibility set expand when $k = 0$ and shrink when $k = 1$, and hence an individual with a higher productivity than another is outcome-freer than her with full self-ownership ($k = 0$), and outcome less free than her with maximal income equalization ($k = 1$). These inequalities in outcome-freedom can be objected to. This will be manifested by the choice of an equalization labour k that is neither 0 nor 1, hence $0 < k < 1$.

Moreover, apart from comparisons among individuals, the absolute situation of the individuals in the domain of outcomes matters. With full self-ownership ($k = 0$), individuals with low productivity w_i can have only low income and consumption, even if they work much. With maximal income equalization ($k = 1$), individuals with high productivity w_i have to work much to pay their taxes, even if they accept to consume only little. These situations can respectively be starvation and possible exhaustion of the less able, and exhaustion and possible starvation of the ablest – this "ability" being according to the labour market's judgment. Avoiding these situations is among the reasons for the choice of coefficient k.

With $0 < k < 1$, individuals' outcome-freedoms cannot be compared by inclusion of the possibility sets in the space of outcomes. An individual more productive than another can choose more disposable income and consumption for each labour $\ell > k$ and less for each $\ell < k$, and more leisure for each consumption $y > k\overline{w}$ and less for each $y < k\overline{w}$. She is freer for $\ell > k$ and $y > k\overline{w}$, and less free for $\ell < k$ and $y < k\overline{w}$. Indeed, in these two domains of the space of outcomes, the individuals' possibility sets are ranked by inclusion. The comparison of these outcome-freedoms among individuals can be one aspect of the choice of the equalization labour k.

4.3. Equal linear output freedom

Finally, one can a priori order the freedom offered by domains of choice by "more," "less," or "as much," often by the *ordinal* freedom index of a *freedom function*, depending on this domain or its characteristics. This function increases in particular when the domain relevantly expands in gaining new possibilities and losing none, but it permits, in addition, the comparison of the freedom offered by intersecting domains of free choice. In particular, equal freedom, at various levels, is so defined. For the present problem, the parameters can be the transfer t, intercept of the budget line with zero labour $\ell = 0$, and the slope w. The freedom function increases with both of them. For each level of freedom, the freedom function implies a t as function of w. For all the individuals i with given w_i, equal freedom and the condition $\Sigma t_i = 0$ determine a level of freedom. Then, one can show (see Appendix B) that ELIE is the case of equal freedom when the freedom function can be taken as *linear* in the two variables. This means that, with a lower w, freedom can be maintained by a proportionately higher transfer t (possibly a lower tax). The coefficient of proportionality, independent of levels and individuals, is the equalization labour k. The property of ELIE as *equal linear outcome-freedom* is remarkable. However, the justification of ELIE comes, rather, from social freedom plus the appropriate equal sharing of the value of given capacities.

5. PARTICULAR RIGHTS AND RULES

As any actual and balanced set of transfers that guarantees process-freedom or efficiency, ELIE that is not full self-ownership attributes income to the unemployed, including the voluntarily unemployed. Income for people who do not work is sometimes praised in the name of real freedom, and sometimes condemned from a judgment of "workfare." In the same conditions, individuals more productive than average have, on the contrary, to provide some contribution which requires some work. They are the people who can the most easily earn a given amount thanks to their given endowment of high productive capacities. However, this ingrained duty is sometimes objected to, although such a constraint will not normally be actually binding.

A "workfare rule" banning unemployment income means $y_i^o = 0$ for all i. It implies $k = 0$ if the w_i are not all equal.

A "right to idleness" means $\ell_i^o \leq 0$ for all i. It implies $k = 0$ if the w_i are not all equal.

Moreover, a general "right to average maximal income" implies $v_i \geq \overline{w}$ for all i since v_i is the highest possible earnings individual i can choose and obtain.

However, $v_i = w_i + t_i$, and hence, $\Sigma v_i = n\overline{w}$. Thus, we must have $v_i = \overline{w}$ for all i, and therefore $t_i = \overline{w} - w_i$ for all i, which implies $k = 1$ if the w_i are not all equal.

Hence, with ELIE[10], if the w_i are not all equal, the workfare rule, the right to idleness, and full self-ownership imply one another, and the right to average maximal income holds if and only if there is maximal income equalization. We have noticed, however, that the likely values of k will be far from the latter case and will imply only limited necessary labour from the ablest.

6. THE MEANINGS OF ELIE AND OF ITS DEGREE

6.1. Maxims of ELIE

As a conclusion, let us gather and summarize the various social-ethical and log-ical meanings of the ELIE distribution and of its coefficient k, which have been met. ELIE and coefficient k can be seen in a number of ways, showing different characteristic (necessary and sufficient) properties which have different and no-table ethical and logical meanings. These properties are logically equivalent and each can be taken as defining ELIE. However, only one property constitutes the basic justification and is self-sufficient for this purpose, because social ethics is a basically deductive construct or endeavour. This consists of the reasoning that led to the ELIE structure from social freedom (notably justified by the properly con-ceived consensus) and the rationality of equality, implying full process-freedom and the proper equal sharing of the rent of productive capacities in macrojustice. Yet, the other properties show other important meanings worthy of consideration.

Application of the general principle of social freedom, for instance of the con-stitutional basic rights, or of Pareto efficiency, to global distributive justice in macrojustice, shows that the solution is full process-freedom with the distribu-tion of the rent-rights of productive capacities. This distribution provides indi-viduals with a basic allocation, which can a priori only consist of quantities of the two goods present here, income (or consumption) and leisure – allocated in demanding the product of the corresponding labour. Equality of these bundles give process-free budget lines passing through the same point K with labour k in Figure 9–1, and the income dimension of K has to be $k\overline{w}$ from the balance of products or transfers.

We have noticed that ELIE also consists of *equally sharing all the rents of produc-tive capacities in measuring the fraction k in income and the rest in labour, leisure, or life time*. It is also defined as *equal sharing of an equal share* of each person's income productive rent. Given that what is not self-owned is equally shared in transferable income, ELIE is also defined as *equal self-ownership in labour value* (a generally partial ownership) or, correspondingly, *equal liability in labour*.

---

[10] And more generally with Pareto-efficiency or full process-freedom and the corresponding balanced transfers.

This ELIE thus satisfies principles applied for this equalization labour k: *Equal pay for equal work; From each equally in labour, to each equally in money; Same average wage for the same labour.* It also satisfies: *From each according to her capacities, to each equally* (in money terms, and k becomes a coefficient of proportionality). And ELIE is also: *To each as she deserves for the same labour and as she merits for the rest.*

Considering now direct interindividual transfers, we have seen that ELIE is *general labour reciprocity* defined as: *From each equally in labour to each other;* or, in money, *from each according to her capacities to each other.* This also implies: *From each, to each less productive, according to their productivity differential.*

We have also obtained that ELIE is *equal proportional narrowing of all gaps in total incomes from full self-ownership.*

Finally, we have seen that ELIE also amounts to an *equal proportional narrowing of the distance of each individual's total income to the average* (a concentration).[11]

These latter properties just result from the fact that ELIE *soothes productivity differential with some proportional compensation in transfer,* and is financially balanced.

6.2. Meanings of coefficient k

These properties of an ELIE distribution scheme and possible reasons for it all imply corresponding properties and meanings of coefficient k. This number measures the equalization labour, in duration possibly adjusted for other characteristics of labour (see Chapter 8), as a fraction of maximal labour similarly defined. The ELIE distribution amounts to equally sharing individuals' possible product of this labour. We have $0 \leq k \leq 1$, and $k = 0$ corresponds to full self-ownership. Coefficient k thus is a degree of equalization and equal distribution of the possible product. It represents a degree of patrimonial communitarianism or resource

---

[11] ELIE can also be characterized by a set of three structural properties. Call $t = \{t_i\}$ and $w = \{w_i\}$ the vectors of the t_i and w_i, respectively. Transfers t are a function of w: $t(w)$. If π denotes a permutation of the i and $x = \{x_i\}$ a set of n x_i, denote $\pi x = \{x_{\pi(i)}\}$. The three properties characteristic of ELIE are, then:

(1) Linearity, which is equivalent to the two properties: for all w and w', $t(w + w') = t(w) + t(w')$, and $t(\mu w) = \mu \cdot t(w)$, where μ is any positive scalar.
(2) Permutability: $t(\pi w) = \pi \cdot t(w)$.

The third property can be any of the three following:

(3) $\Sigma t_i = 0$.
(3') If all w_i are equal, $t(w) = 0$.
(3'') If all w_i are added the same number, $t(w)$ does not change.

Indeed, properties (1) and (2) imply that, for all i, $t_i = a w_i + b \overline{w}$ with two constants a and b, and any of the third properties then imply $b = -a$ and hence the ELIE form.

These results imply in particular the two following properties. If all w_i are added the same number, the transfers t_i do not vary. If all w_i are multiplied by the same scalar, so are the t_i and the $v_i = w_i + t_i$, and $\tau_i = t_i/w_i$ and $v_i/w_i = 1 + \tau_i$ do not change (this can in particular result from a change in units).

Other axioms characterizing the final allocation that would be chosen by the individuals after an ELIE distribution have been proposed by François Maniquet (1998a, 1998b) in an approach that differs from the present one and its earlier presentations (see Chapter 24) by its not considering social freedom.

commonalism, where community leads to equal sharing. It is also a degree of solidarity for facing the given inequalities in individuals' earning capacities (hence, in productive capacities and in the market demand for them). Number $1 - k$, a degree of self-ownership, also represents a corresponding degree of individualism of the society. Number k also measures the amount of labour equally paid, or remunerated according to desert rather than to merit. It is also a degree of general balanced labour reciprocity between the individuals; of the reduction of the gaps of individuals' total incomes from the situation of full self-ownership; of compensation for the differences in given productivities; and of concentration of individuals' total incomes toward the mean. However, coefficients k and $1 - k$ are also, perhaps more deeply, the degrees of relevance of income-consumption value, and of labour-leisure value, respectively, in the measure and definition of the equalizand for sharing the rent of individual productivities. The determination of coefficient k from endogenous social choice, hence of its level "desired" by a society and the social and moral views of its members, is the topic of Part IV of this study.

Finally, an individual can jointly belong to several redistributive communities, with a priori different degrees of community of resources or redistribution k. For instance, beyond the family (which is the usual social unit for income), there is the nation whose taxes and policy usually perform most of the redistribution, and there can be some lower regional or local level, a community of nations, and even the whole world (for a de facto low possible k). Then, the taxes or subsidies corresponding to these various levels add up (algebraically) for each individual. For instance, if index j denotes such a community to which individual i belongs, with k^j, $\overline{w}^j$ and t_i^j being the corresponding coefficient, average wage rate and subsidy or tax for individual i, with $t_i^j = k^j \cdot (\overline{w}^j - w_i)$, individial i's overall subsidy or tax becomes $t_i = \Sigma_j t_i^j = \Sigma k^j \overline{w}^j - w_i \Sigma k^j$.

Appendix A. LABOUR-LEISURE-LIFE VALUE

An individual i's leisure λ_i can be measured by the income it could produce if used as labour, $w_i \lambda_i$, and symmetrically this individual's consumption or income y_i can be measured by the labour with which this individual can produce it, y_i / w_i. Hence, individual i's total income can be measured in income or money value, $v_i = y_i + w_i \lambda_i$, or in labour-leisure-time value $v_i / w_i = y_i / w_i + \lambda_i$. Transfers of income among individuals do not change the social total income Σv_i or the average $\overline{v} = (1/n) \Sigma v_i$. However, a transfer of income from a more productive individual to a less productive one saves labour – discarding further adjustments – or saves labour-leisure value: with $w_i > w_j$, transferring one dollar from individual i to individual j saves $(1/w_j) - (1/w_i)$ units of labour time. Equating labour units of different individuals is standardly done in measures of social productivity. Moreover, labour is foregone leisure and leisure is "free time" and is therefore a measure of freedom; this gives to this measure of value a strong normative meaning (for instance, exploitation in Marx's view is seen as a theft of freedom thanks to the labour theory of value).[12] Hence, the sum of individuals' wealth or total income (leisure included) measured in labour, leisure, or life time of the holder is a meaningful and interesting index of social wealth, which is in fact properly considered a measure of social freedom. This is $\Sigma(v_i/w_i)$ or the average $L = (1/n)\Sigma(v_i/w_i)$.

Without transfers, hence with full self-ownership, $v_i = w_i$ for all i, and hence, $L = 1$. With income transfers such that individual i receives t_i (or yields $-t_i$ if $t_i < 0$), $v_i = w_i + t_i$, and, if $\tau_i = t_i/w_i$ denotes individual i's net transfer in labour-leisure-time value, $L = (1/n)\Sigma(1 + \tau_i) = 1 + \overline{\tau}$ where $\overline{\tau} = (1/n)\Sigma\tau_i$ is the average of the τ_i. The net gain is $\overline{\tau}$. With a set of balanced transfers, that is, with $\Sigma t_i = 0, \overline{\tau} > 0$ means that transfers have, on average, been from more productive individuals to less productive ones.

With an ELIE set of transfers, $t_i = k \cdot (\overline{w} - w_i)$ for all i, $t_i/w_i = k \cdot [(\overline{w}/w_i) - 1]$, and

$$\overline{\tau} = k \cdot [\overline{w} \cdot (1/n)\Sigma(1/w_i) - 1].$$

Now, $\widetilde{w}$ such that $(1/\widetilde{w}) = (1/n)\Sigma(1/w_i)$ is the *harmonic mean* of the w_i. Then,

$$\overline{\tau} = k \cdot [\overline{w}/\widetilde{w}) - 1].$$

If the w_i are not all equal, $\overline{w} > \widetilde{w}$ and $\overline{\tau} > 0$.

The average gain in time $\overline{\tau}$ is the largest, the largest the equalization labour k. However, for individual i, both $v_i = w_i + t_i = k\overline{w} + (1 - k)w_i$ and $v_i/w_i = 1 - k + k\overline{w}/w_i$ decrease when k increases when $w_i > \overline{w}$. The ratio $\overline{w}/w_i$ is individual i's labour time necessary for producing the average $\overline{w}$. When $k = 1$ and w_i is large, individual i's remaining time value $1 - (\overline{w}/w_i)$ can be low (a "slavery of the talented"). Individuals' wealth (total income) are equal in income value (the v_i) when $k = 1$, and in labour-leisure-life value (the v_i/w_i) when $k = 0$ (full self-ownership). The choice of coefficient k thus is a compromise between the inequality of the v_i and the inequality of the v_i/w_i. For unit-comparability, the inequalities will be in the

$$v_i/\overline{w} = k + (1 - k)(w_i/\overline{w})$$

and the

$$v_i/w_i = 1 - k + k \cdot (\overline{w}/w_i).$$

One can choose a measure of inequality such that, for variables x_i with average $\overline{x} = (1/n)\Sigma x_i$, and denoting $x = \{x_i\}$, the absolute measure $I(x)$ is invariant under an equal variation of all x_i, and the relative measure $I(x)/\overline{x}$ is invariant under a proportional variation of all x_i. Such a function is of the form $I(x) = f(\{x_i - \overline{x}\})$ where function f is linearly homogenous. For instance, the standard deviation and

---

[12] See Adam Smith in *The Wealth of Nations* (Chapter V): "Equal quantities of labour, at all times and places, may be said to be of equal value to the labourer. In his ordinary state of health, strength and spirits; in the ordinary degree of his skill and dexterity, he must always lay down the same portion of his ease, his liberty, and his happiness. The price which he pays must always be the same, whatever may be the quantity of goods which he receives in return for it. . . . Labour alone, therefore, never varying in its own value, is alone the ultimate and real standard by which the value of all commodities can at all times and places be estimated and compared. It is their real price; money is their nominal price only."

the Gini coefficient are such measures of inequality. Then, α and β being constants, $I(\{\alpha + \beta x_i\}) = \beta \cdot I(x)$. Therefore,

$$I(\{v_i/\overline{w}\}) = (1 - k) \cdot I(\{w_i/\overline{w}\})$$

and

$$I(\{v_i/w_i\}) = k \cdot I(\{\overline{w}/w_i\}).$$

These inequalities respectively decrease and increase when k increases. A balanced solution can take them to be equal, which gives a coefficient k

$$k = I(\{w_i/\overline{w}\})/[I(\{w_i/\overline{w}\}) + I(\{\overline{w}/w_i\})].$$

The general discussion of the choice of coefficient k is the topic of Part IV.

Appendix B. ELIE AS EQUAL LINEAR OUTPUT-FREEDOM

The basis of the theory is (full) social freedom from an equal allocation (sharing the value of given resources). However, liberty can also be considered in the field of results that are income or consumption y and leisure λ, that is, as output-freedom. The generic variables are considered without individual indexes i and are later specified by these indexes. The individual provides labour ℓ, has wage rate w, earns $w\ell$, enjoys leisure $\lambda = 1 - \ell$, receives the lump-sum subsidy or tax t (a subsidy if $t > 0$ and a tax of $-t$ if $t < 0$), and has disposable income $y = w\ell + t$. This equation for given w and t defines, in the space of y and ℓ (or λ), the individual's budget line, which delineates her budget possibility set. She chooses ℓ (and λ) and hence y in this budget set, in fact on this line because she likes income (consumption) and leisure, by assumption. This possibility set is the individual's domain of free choice, and it fully characterizes her outcome freedom. This freedom increases when this set expands in including the former set, notably in permitting higher income for each given labour or higher leisure for each given income. This set, delineated by the budget line, is characterized by it, hence by two parameters, notably transfer t and wage rate w (they could also for instance be t and the "total income" $t + w$, or $t + w$ and w). From the noted comparison by inclusion, this freedom increases when t increases for given w, and when w increases for given t (only for $\ell = 0$, a higher w does not permit a higher y). Since this freedom is compared by "larger than," one can consider an ordinal index of this freedom, depending on the possibility set, hence on the two parameters t and w, say the real number $f = F(t, w)$, where function F is increasing in t and in w. This can also be written as $t = \varphi(w, f)$, where φ is a function decreasing in w and increasing in f. All budget sets that have the same freedom f are characterized by the fact that their budget line is tangent to a concave decreasing (nonincreasing) curve in the plane (λ, y), which is their envelop defined by $t = \varphi(w, f)$ for given f. This envelop curve shifts toward higher y or λ when parameter f increases.

This liberty is equal for all individuals i when $t_i = \varphi(w_i, f)$, with the same f, for all i. If the t_i are balanced transfers, $\Sigma t_i = 0$. Then, the condition $\Sigma \varphi(w_i, f) = 0$ gives the possible level of equal freedom f, which determines the corresponding envelop curve.

ELIE schemes correspond to the case where the output-freedom function F can have a *linear* form (this would also be the case if the variables were t and $t + w$, or $t + w$ and w). Indeed, this function can then be written, with some positive number k, as $f = t + kw$. Hence, function φ becomes $t = f - kw$. If the t_i are balanced transfers, $\Sigma t_i = 0$, and hence, with equal freedom f for all i, $f = k\overline{w}$ where $\overline{w}$ is the average $\overline{w} = (1/n)\Sigma w_i$. Therefore, $t_i = k \cdot (\overline{w} - w_i)$ which characterizes ELIE schemes ($k < 1$ is required for the possibility that an increase in one variable t or w compensates a decrease in the other for maintaining the same output-freedom). The envelop then restricts to point $K(\ell = k, y = k\overline{w})$. This linearity means that a lower individual productivity can be compensated by a proportionately higher transfer (or lower tax) for maintaining output-freedom, the coefficient of proportionality being the same for all levels and individuals and equal to the equalization labour k. These considerations will be generalized for other structures of freedom functions F (and any number of goods) in the application of the general theory of freedom orderings to budget sets, in Chapter 24.

10

Information

1. REALIZATION, IMPLEMENTATION, INFORMATION

The realization of the required distribution or policy depends on the information, motivation, and power of the appropriate agents. This chapter considers the question of the realization and implementation of ELIE schemes, and in particular that of information. The basic issues are presented in Sections 2 and 3 and the various aspects are more fully developed in Section 5, whereas Section 4 shows the problems of an alternative conception influential in economics. Section 2 notes the required information, the fact that ELIE can be achieved by purely interindividual rights, the various moral aspects of this distribution, the various ways in which people's motives associate self-interest and social and ethical views, and the consequences for implementation and information about individual capacities. Section 3 discusses the question of obtaining the required information, which concerns wage rates for given capacities, in observing labour markets, paysheets, and the characteristics of labour, as concerns, notably, the questions of education and training and the intensity of labour (effort). The conclusion is that this information is, on the whole, more easily obtained than that needed for other taxes or aids. The economic literature about "optimum income taxation" puts forward the issue of information, but raises a number of logical and conceptual problems that are noted in Section 4. Finally, an Appendix considers more in depth the issue of obtaining the information about the value of given capacities. It shows how the nature of ELIE favours individuals' participation in this respect. It also points out that information and implementation in fact take place in a "fiscal game" between the people and the administration. It relates the fiscal policy choice to the basic values of social freedom and efficiency. It finally considers second-best ELIE policies determined by the maximization of the relevant inequality-averse maximand.

2. MODES AND MOTIVATIONS OF IMPLEMENTATION

2.1. Situation of the problem

The implementation of the transfers t_i requires knowing what they should be. The implementer will commonly be a fiscal authority, although in some cases there can be other types of realizations (such as interpersonal rights, or voluntary reciprocities). The needed information is that of the transfers t_i for the various individuals i. They will be subsidies of amount t_i if $t_i > 0$ and taxes of amount $-t_i$ if $t_i < 0$. Chapter 9 has shown that an ELIE distribution with a unidimensional linear production function consists of transfers $t_i = k \cdot (\overline{w} - w_i)$, where w_i is individual i's unit productivity and competitive wage rate for given capacities, and k is the equalization labour duration. The considered durations can be adjusted for taking the effects of the other chosen characteristics of labour into account. Chapters 7 and 8 discussed the more general case where labour can be explicitly multidimensional, and the production functions giving earned income (equivalent to output because of full process-freedom) can a priori have any form. Chapters 12 and 13 will analyze this case more precisely. Individual i's labour is then generally a multidimensional set of characteristics ℓ_i, where the characteristics can be, notably, duration, speed, attention, previous education and training, etc., as discussed in Chapter 8. Then, individual i's earned income is $p_i(\ell_i)$. The obtained ELIE solution will be the complete equalization of the incomes that the individuals can produce with the same "equalization labour" k (now in general multidimensional). That is, $p_i(k)$ is individual i's "equalization income," $\overline{p}(k) = (1/n) \Sigma p_i(k)$ is the "average equalization income," and the net transfer for individual i is $t_i = \overline{p}(k) - p_i(k)$, a subsidy if $t_i > 0$ and a tax of $-t_i$ if $t_i < 0$. We henceforth call ELIE this general case, and when necessary specify as EDIE, for "equal duration income equalization," the particular case, studied in Chapter 9, of unidimensional labour measured by its duration (possibly adjusted for differences in the other chosen characteristics) with linear production functions $p_i(\ell_i) = w_i \ell_i$. With EDIE, k is the equalization duration and $t_i = k \cdot (\overline{w} - w_i)$ (we have noted that ELIE can very often be reduced to EDIE, possibly with appropriately adjusted durations, and either exactly or as a sufficient approximation).

The needed information thus is that of the $t_i = \overline{p}(k) - p_i(k)$ for ELIE, and in particular $k \cdot (\overline{w} - w_i)$ for EDIE. Knowing k is a matter of social ethics, politics, and sociology: this is the topic of Part IV of this study. There remains to know the p_i for labour k or the w_i ($\overline{p}$ and $\overline{w}$ are the averages).

This chapter presents an outline of the ways and means of obtaining this information and of how to deal with its imperfections. A general conclusion will be that, *on the whole and on average, obtaining this information is no more difficult, and is often easier, than the similar information gathering needed by other large-scale redistributive schemes of taxes and subsidies,* assuming the same self-interested motivations of the tax payers in all cases. In particular, the view, familiar among academic economists, that the reason for basing taxes on income – notably earned income – is that capacities are unobserved, misses the ethics of macrojustice, the possibilities of obtaining the required information (the value of these capacities), and the actual reasons for basing taxes on incomes (these reasons will be discussed in Chapter 11, and it will turn out that the underlying ethics is actually realized by a particular ELIE scheme).

In addition, we recall in this first section that the ELIE structure has a number of meanings that can more or less influence the possibilities of realization with regard to both information and constraint on people. Indeed, ELIE can be seen as resulting from interindividual rights, it has a number of different, although equivalent, aspects of fairness and equal reciprocity, it largely results from unanimous opinions, and it will be lawful. There tends to result a number of possible mental structures of the citizens, associating self-interested and moral motives, that influence the possibilities of realization and implementation.

2.2. Interindividual rights

ELIE amounts to each individual having the right to an equal share of each other's equalization income since

$$t_i = \overline{p}(k) - p_i(k) = (1/n)\Sigma_{j \neq i}\, p_j(k) - (n-1)(1/n)\, p_i(k).$$

In particular, EDIE amounts to each individual owning a rent-right of the same duration in each other's earning capacities. Hence, the realization of the transfers can be left to the private enforcement of these rights between persons. The issue of fiscal information and enforcement no longer exists. It has been decentralized into interpersonal monitoring.

However, although such a realization is possible if the society within which this distribution occurs is small, a larger size of this society raises problems for it. Each individual transfer $(1/n)\, p_i(k)$, and the duration of each rent-right for EDIE, k/n, will be very small in any large society, and each person will have such a right in each other. The external right holders in any person's capacity rent, that is, all the others, will need the same information ($p_i(k)$ or w_i) and will need securing this person's payment to them. And each individual needs this information and implementation concerning all others.

Hence, people have an advantage in grouping their gathering of this information and enforcement of their rights and in entrusting these jobs to single agents. Information about each individual is a public good for the others, and most means of enforcement also present this kind of property. Centralization of the transfers leads to n relations and n transfers (between each individual and the central redistributive agent), whereas relations between each pair of individuals are $n \cdot (n-1)$ in number and the number of transfers is either this number or half of it if only the net result is transferred in each pair. The central agents will de facto be public administrations that establish and raise the tax or distribute the subsidies. However, the very fact that these transfers implement interpersonal rights, rather than being Leviathan's share or beneficience, may be favorable to people more or less accepting the tax and being less eager to cheat about its base. All the more so if these rights and transfers are seen as having some rationality, legitimacy, goodness, or fairness. Now, these rights are such that each individual owns the product of the same labour of each other and owes her this product of her labour (with EDIE). And the whole set of transfers has several equivalent properties endowed with a strong appeal of fairness.

2.3. Judging ELIE

Indeed, ELIE is "from each her production by an equal labour and to each equally." EDIE is "from each according to her capacities, to each equally" or "to or from each according to the gap between her productivity and the average," where "according" means "in proportion." Furthermore, it is universal balanced or equal reciprocity where each yields to each other the product of the same labour, or according to her productivity. It is also filling the same fraction of the gaps between each pair of total incomes.

These principles seem particularly appropriate for conveying a sense of fairness, justice, or reciprocity. In fact, this set of transfers results from unanimous opinions and impartiality, strictly so for the ELIE structure, but also, though in different ways, for the determination of coefficient k (see Part IV). All that, again, may make people less reluctant to yield information (about their capacities) and money. Moreover, these transfers will be lawful, and misreporting information about one's productive capacities will then amount to evasion rather than just avoidance.

2.4. Types and degrees of voluntary contributions

If a person i is sufficiently motivated by these moral or social sentiments, she will want to yield the amount $p_i(k)$ to the collectivity (then, an equal redistribution of these contributions realizes ELIE). A priori, this person knows her productivity function $p_i()$, and all the information she needs to receive is the equalization labour k, the same for everyone, which will be publicly announced. This person may also directly yield $p_i(k)/n$ to each other, if this is practicable. She may also yield $p_i(k) - \overline{p}(k)$ without receiving anything if this is positive, and then she needs to receive, as information from the outside, k and $\overline{p}(k)$. Note that $\overline{p}(k)$, or $\overline{w}$ in the case of EDIE, can be estimated statistically, in knowing the distribution of the p_i or of the w_i without knowing specifically each individual's productivity.

However, people may have no such moral or social sentiments. More realistically, they may have such feelings, but this has no effect or only moderate effect on their actual individual behavior as payers or truth-tellers for several possible reasons.

First, people commonly "are of two minds," with social morality dwelling in one mind and self-interest occupying the other. The latter may prevail in the considered behaviour. It is not uncommon, then, that people feel more or less grateful for being forced to contribute, that is, to behave as the moral persons they know they should be. In a Rousseauan-Kantian view, these persons are spontaneously "unfree" because their strict self-interest (and hence, their "inclinations") prevail over their moral duty as they clearly conceive it. Then, the external coercion to contribute is in fact a liberation (from their nonmoral self-interest). These persons are "forced to be free" in this sense. Such a coercion could then be justified as realizing a type of liberal social contract.

Second, people may both agree with the overall distributive scheme and be self-interested, prefer that the whole scheme is enforced, and yet unambiguously prefer that they do not pay themselves if this does not influence others' contributions. In other words, the overall distributive scheme is a public good for them, but they tend to be free riders of this good when they can. For the net positive contributors, the public good can also be the situation of the less endowed people who receive net transfers. Then, people would vote for the scheme and want it be implemented, even using coercion, and yet they may evade, avoid, or cheat in their own private fiscal behavior.

In a third type of situation, people may desire to voluntarily contribute or demand their true due, or yield information about themselves, if they know the others do the same. They may, for instance, voluntarily contribute their fair share if the others contribute as they should – a common social and moral sentiment. Then, coercion is needed in order that each individual be sure that the others contribute. These constraints, however, are not effective, they are not binding, since each individual, knowing that the others contribute, voluntarily contributes herself. They are nonetheless necessary. This somewhat paradoxical situation of "free coercion" is rather common. The establishment of a coercive power is certainly made easier by the fact that the coercive measures are not actually implemented. However, this kind of behaviour a priori does not help much for obtaining the information for setting the right constraints, since one cannot impose the revelation of an information that one does not know. Yet, the positive effect reappears when one considers that more information can be obtained by particular fiscal investigations that are costly and hence solely occasional. People, indeed, may cheat and hide less if they know that others (and not only themselves) can be investigated, because they may be less reluctant to do their share in "revelation" when this information will be obtained about some others.

However, let us consider now the practical issue of information in the worst possible case, that where individuals' behaviors are purely and strictly self-interested.

3. OUTLINE OF THE PRACTICAL SOURCES AND METHODS
OF INFORMATION

The required information consists of the productivities p_i (for labour k) or w_i. The w_i are also the competitive wage rates. Knowing or estimating them raises issues and can use methods that are met in the application of any rule for policy, tax, or subsidy. In fact, this information and estimation is easier to obtain than in most other cases, both for gathering information and for facing the issue of evasion or unjustified claims. This comparison holds in particular for the classical alternative of taxes based on incomes – notably earned incomes – and the various kinds of subsidies.

The w_i are wage rates. Wage rates are market prices for the various types of labour. Markets – particularly, competitive markets – standardly exhibit their prices. Prices constitute their public information and are common knowledge in competitive markets. Quantities exchanged, by contrast, are usually known only by the buyer and the seller, and hence this also is the case for their value. Here, the prices are the w_i, the quantities the ℓ_i, and the values earned incomes $w_i\ell_i$. Hence, a large part of the required information will come from the observation of the labour market.

The largest part of labour incomes in developed countries are wages (for instance, this is over 85% in the Western European country with the largest agricultural sector). Many other jobs can more or less closely be compared with wage-earning jobs.

The standard paysheet bears total amount paid, wage rate, number of hours of labour, type and category of work, and sometimes seniority and bonuses. When wage rate is not directly present, it just is total pay divided by labour duration. The type and category of work reveal many different things. They often imply requirements about intensity or attention and speed. But they mainly indicate skills. And they very often closely depend on previous formation, general and specialized education, and also on seniority and the experience that goes with it.

Moreover, paysheets also sometimes distinguish pay for overwork beyond a certain duration of labour; bonuses for particular intensity, effort, painfulness, or for quality resulting from attention, intensity, or effort; and bonuses for particular previous educational level, training, and experience. Just discarding these extra pays provides the information needed $p_i(k^o)$ with an equalization labour k^o that does not include these particular extra intensity, effort, education or training, or duration (it will, in general, just have to be adjusted for a still lower duration, for which a proportional decrease will often suffice exactly or with a sufficient approximation).

The various characteristics of labour are often publicly or easily known. They are often more or less implied by the mention of the type of job, which can be more or less precise. Labour contracts, or the labour market, more or less specify these characteristics, or requirements that imply them. Moreover, wage differentials observed on the labour market provides the market value of these characteristics. All this holds for characteristics (in addition to duration) such as previous education, formation, training or experience; speed; intensity of attention (which can be revealed by speed, the quality of output, the proportion of faultless pieces, costs or inputs saved, etc.); steadiness; adaptability; flexibility; capacity of initiative; and so on.

The information about wage rate, labour provided, and earned income often come jointly. Information about two of them permits the derivation of the third. Information about the wage rate is often primary. This is, however, not the case for some types of work. Then, productivity and the equivalent wage rate can easily be obtained from total earned income and labour provided. Information about labour can be demanded along with an income report. It can also be estimated from the technique of the work in question, and from the standards of the profession or of comparable labours. This later information can also be used to check reporting about labour. Moreover, the implicit wage rate can often be obtained by the observation of unit wages paid for comparable labour. Fiscal rules and administrations routinely practice many estimations of this kind.

Three main characteristics of labour are duration, intensity, and previous training or education. They are not a priori and intrinsically separated as concepts. Speed and fraction of time of actual work in a unit of working time can be reduced to duration or considered as dimensions or factors of intensity. Education, formation, training, and experience have duration and intensity. Piece rate wages depend on intensity, speed, and training. Intensity will often be of attention. The conceptual and practical problems will very much depend on the case. Duration is often rather easily considered (although issues are raised for a number of intellectual activities). Intensity can be considered through a number of proxies, which can be speed or quality of output (for instance, fraction of faultless products, and so on). Intensity of labour is a priori chosen, but there can also be a given capacity for it, which is an aspect of given productive capacities.

Education is sanctioned by diplomas whose role is to inform about labour capacities. This indication, however, works in several ways. Diplomas intend to testify about knowledge, know-how, or skill, in various possible degrees. All three mix – also in various degrees – acquired elements and given capacities (for knowledge, these capacities are memory, learning capacity, capacity of concentration and work, etc.). The information about given capacities is the one sought after here. It has been found that the role of education and diplomas as screening devices in order to provide information about given capacities is much more important and basic than it seems. Thus, diploma inform about given capacities, and the corresponding productive value is well displayed in the labour market. However, acquired knowledge and skills cannot be discarded as one of the values of education, and still more so for specific formation and training. These acquired elements depend themselves on given capacities for learning and on learning work in all its dimensions of duration, speed, intensity, attention, and so on. The distinction between given capacities and the rest of labour is also required at this level. Global duration of education, formation, or training is usually known. It can be added to the duration of the work whose qualification it augments (with adjustment for intensity for people who did not learn with the same intensity they use in working). If several of these works benefiting from the same formation are considered, the duration of this formation can be allocated to these labours in proportion to their duration and added to these durations (one can also use time discounting for taking account of various effects such as time preference, the obsolescence of education, or on the contrary its valorization by experience). Diploma importantly inform about capacities for learning, for given learning work, and the labour market shows their productive value.

The selfish, uncivic, and unreciprocal interest of an individual i consists of making believe that her $p_i(k)$ or w_i is lower than it is. If earned income is observed, she will generally want to make believe that her labour is higher than it is. This can be made with any of the labour characteristics. If reports are demanded about p_i, w_i, or ℓ_i, this will require false reporting. If ELIE (or EDIE) is an official scheme, such reports, or the corresponding behaviours, constitute tax evasion rather than tax avoidance. There will thus be legal, official, and moral obstacles to such cheating. Moreover, we have noted that duration of labour can often be clearly checked. Labour intensity is often implied by the specification of a job, with no or little possibility of variation, while this specification and its requirements can be observed. And we just noted the facets of the question of education with respect to information about capacities and work. In all these respects, there will exist some particularly difficult cases where uncertain estimates and sometimes proxies will have to be used, but they will not constitute a large fraction of the whole – and all tax or subsidy schemes have such cases.

Finally and on the whole, an ELIE or EDIE tax-subsidy scheme does not seem to be more difficult to establish than any large-scale existing one. It is simpler in conception, definition, and application, and in many respects it is simpler with respect to information needed. This seems clear both on the subsidy side, as compared with many schemes of support of income or needs, and for taxes. For instance, the wage rate for "normal" labour is as easily and often more easily observed or estimated than total earnings (the basis of standard income taxes). One just has to think of all the ways of evasion and avoidance with presently existing tax schemes, or of all the ad hoc and more or less arbitrary rules for defining what should be the basis of an income tax or of indirect taxes.

One can do more conceptual thinking for determining formulas and rules that establish the p_i and w_i in the various cases. Application will then be made by the tax administration, which will have, as usual, to determine rules of thumb or proxies for application in particular cases. These procedures involve nothing really new.

Main issues about implementation will however be considered more in depth in Section 4, but it may be useful to first present a few remarks about an influential trend of thought in economics in this respect.

4. "MISPLACED EMPHASIS"

For the social philosopher or scholar, it suffices that the implementation of the distributive scheme is normally possible. The rest is an issue for tax administrations, who are good at that when they are given clear basic principles. And the ELIE principle is about the clearest and most general possible: it is the contrary of an accumulation of recipes mixing practicalities and a variety of ad hoc ideas of microjustice for facing each particular case. Scholars who let their thinking be directed by casual superficial remarks about difficulties of implementation and in particular information are bound to run in the wrong direction. The problem of information has no chance to be dealt with correctly if one does not know what we need to be informed about in the first place. Therefore, one should first present the theory of the just and optimum distribution without thinking of issues of information. Only when this is done can one look for the needed information, imagine ways of obtaining it, and, when uncertainty remains, compute best estimates, select best proxies, and apply to this issue the general theory of choice under imperfect information. (Note that unfortunate confusion is added by the common misuse of the word "information" in the field of "social choice," when it is taken to mean the moral choice of the ethically relevant variables.)

Unfortunately, one of the few sentences ingrained in the collective mind of a number of academic economists is "earned income is taken as tax base as a proxy for unobservable individual productive capacities." First of all, we do not know why tax capacities (note that the underlying theory is not ELIE), except perhaps because given capacities constitute an inelastic tax base (and hence one that does not introduce Pareto inefficiency). Second, ELIE is not concerned with capacities themselves but solely with their *market values*, that is, wage rates (explicit or implicit ones), and we have noted that this information is globally at least as easy to obtain as earned income. The market value of capacities is the required information because of the basic hypothesis of the respect of process-freedom and, hence, of free exchange. In fact, it is not impossible that the noted sentence means that wage rate is the proxy for capacities. This would be fine for the present purpose, although for ELIE wage rates are not proxies for the right base but constitute this right and first-best base. However, choosing earned income or wage rate as base makes a very large difference, and income is the standard actual tax base and the base used in studies that begin with using the noted sentence. These studies seek to optimize the tax schedule but seem to forget to optimize the tax base.

It is ironical that this subculture has adopted the noted sentence probably after James Mirrlees' very famous paper on "Optimum income taxation" (1971) because this paper ends with the appropriate remark that the amount of labour is as observable as earned income, and when we know both, we know the wage rate – the market value of capacities. Partha Dasgupta and Peter Hammond (1980) redressed the situation in replacing, as the variable chosen by the worker but unobserved by the tax authority, labour duration by "effort."[1] However, the proper domain of application of this remarkable study is probably not macrojustice either because the remark presented by Mirrlees about his own work still largely holds with this new variable. We have noted, indeed, that various relevant dimensions of "effort" are often more or less observable. Effort – to be precise – is a mixed concept that means intensity and the resulting painfulness. Information about it is provided by the requirements of the specific job and tasks, the observation of their performance – notably in speed, steadiness, or reactivity – and of its result in quantity and quality of output or in costs or inputs saved. These facts are often explicit determinants of the pay. The wage differentials observed in the labour market give the market value of the various characteristics of labour, and, along with the worker's choice, indicate both the value of her effort and its painfulness (in money equivalent).

More precisely, intensity, in effort, is of physical force or attention, and more often of the latter in modern production. It often is a given characteristic of a job, implied by its specification. This is very frequent for physical force and common for attention. Intensity can also often be directly observed by watching the labour activity. The relevant corresponding parameters of the performance can be specified. They can be objects of reports, checkings, monitoring, and so on. Intensity of labour, and notably of attention, can also often be estimated by speed, regularity, steadiness, or fraction of time of actual work per unit of labour time. It can also often be estimated by some measure of the quality of output. These measures can be of various kinds, according to the case. They can be customers' satisfaction, fraction of nonfaulty produced items, or any other. Intensity can also often be estimated by inputs or costs saved. The specificities of the observability of intensity of labour – when it can be freely chosen – depend on the type of job, but on the whole there is a wealth of ways of obtaining this information more or less precisely, often exactly, and often sufficiently for providing a satisfactory estimate. And these characteristics correspond to specific wage differentials observed in the labour market and sometimes indicated on the paysheet in the form of job specification, bonuses, or penalties. In the latter cases, the tax base can discard differentials in effort just in discarding these bonuses or penalties.

Moreover, the noted studies use, as principles of optimality, the maximization of a "social welfare function" function of individuals' "utilities," with the borderline cases of utilitarianism and of maximin in comparable utilities (that is, "practical justice" in Kolm 1971 – which uses the more general leximin). Hence, these studies' stand about information is properly extraordinary: they deeply worry about information concerning wage rates and productivities, but they accept offhand, without discussion, that one should have full information first about all

---

[1] The case of educational choices has been considered by Sheshinski (1971). The issue of information in this respect has been considered above and in Chapter 8.

individuals' utility functions, tastes, and preferences; second, about their comparisons across individuals, which do not always make sense; third – and still more extraordinary – about properties of these utilities that do not even actually exist, such as the structure that permits their addition for utilitarianism or that required by other types of aggregation (in other words, they know angels' sex); and fourth, about the "social welfare function." Indeed, while they worry so much about information which is often public and is largely documented or implied by people's paysheet (provided by employers), these studies solve all these other problems by the stroke of a magic wand: in assuming that all individuals have the same utility functions, tastes, and preferences (!), in assuming a specific form for this function (why not, then?), and in doing the same for the "social welfare function." Mirrlees justified the identity of individuals' utilities by suggesting that the effect of their differences is another question, and he considered all the spectrum of values of the substitution parameter of the social welfare function. This position has been accepted in such academic studies, but would be of little use for actual applications. Fortunately, however, this problem does not arise for the specific question of general income taxation if one obeys the de facto consensual common-sense view of the irrelevance of individuals' eudemonistic capacities for this issue (these scholars are late victims of Jeremy Bentham's insincerity when he brandished utilitarianism as a political weapon against revolutionary rights, while not thinking it actually makes sense).[2]

This shows the reason for proposing that the reason for basing redistributive taxation on earned income is that it is a second-best policy due to lack of information: it simply is a lack of seeing that the actual reason for choosing this base is a moral one. Redistribution is indeed the issue considered in these studies since taxes and subsidies balance and there is no net receipt (and when one was introduced in later studies, it usually was an exogenous amount and the focus and interest was in the sharing of this burden). However, the actual judgments of people and policy makers about the overall distribution implemented by the income tax *directly* focus on the distribution of incomes (rather than being basically concerned with the effect of this distribution on individuals' "utilities").[3] This was bypassed by these pieces of scolarship because their authors believed that social ethics could exclusively be thought of in terms of such a "social welfare function." In fact, however, the factually intrepid device of considering that all utility functions are identical (and that the social welfare function is symmetrical in them) could in part lead to the assimilation of this evaluation with that of income inequality.[4] Of course, the qualifications of income egalitarianism that will be presented in Chapter 11 and lead to an ELIE structure were still further away from the considerations of these studies.

---

[2] See Kolm 1996a, Chapter 14.

[3] Utility, with a eudemonistic meaning, would be relevant for the relief of people handicapped by a particularly high propensity to suffering, depression, or the like. This is not an issue for macrojustice or the income tax.

[4] As in Kolm (1966a), Atkinson (1970), and an extensive further literature.

Now, the assumption of identical individual utility functions eventually justifies the assertion that individuals' productive capacities constitute the first-best basis of taxation. The reason is not a directly ethical one (as with ELIE). It is, rather, that productive capacities then are the only remaining inelastic characteristics that differ across individuals in the model, and, hence, Pareto-efficient distributive taxes and subsidies cannot but be based on them.[5] Productive capacities intervene only, in this model, because they provide individuals' trade-off between their labour and their income. The most important point, however, is that the ethical theory used – the maximization of this social function, depending on individuals' utilities – is not relevant for macrojustice, while income taxation is a (or the) main tool for macrojustice.[6]

The basis of this irrelevance is the very reliance on eudemonistic capacities, which are consensually discarded by thoughtful judgment for global distributive justice (see Chapter 6). This shortcoming is somewhat attenuated by the assumption that individuals' utility functions are identical functions of income and labour, but not fully so because there remains the effects of this function for different incomes and labours (hence, for people with different productivities); we noted, furthermore, that this assumption and the choice of this utility function – the same for all individuals – are in need of justification. At any rate, these "social welfare functions" imply some comparison of individuals' utilities, and particular structures of them for this purpose. The question of the meaningfulness or meaninglessness of such structure is considered in Chapter 24. If ordinal comparability suffices for "practical justice" (leximin or maximin in ordinally comparable utilities), more demanding structures are required for the other cases. Moreover, the ethics of these "social welfare functions" should be justified. For instance, the maximization of a sum (utilitarianism) requires these functions to be cardinal (defined up to an increasing affine function). Now, this structure generally has no tangible or actual meaning – as distinct from mathematical meaning.[7] It can be given a tangible meaning "in the small," that is, in the neighbourhood of indifference for each agent (ibid.), but this is inappropriate for macrojustice and income taxation (however, local criteria can provide necessary conditions). Moreover, on an ethical ground, a utilitarian intention may be valid as representation of criteria of the type: "give this to him rather than to her because he likes it more than she does," or "let him do it rather than her because it is less painful for him to do than it is for her" (ibid.). Yet, such criteria are found relevant only in occasional cases of microjustice (see Chapter 6). As for the maximin (or leximin) of "practical justice," it certainly is valid in some cases (first take care of the most miserable),

---

[5] Individuals also differ by the local structure of their common utility function at their actual different consumption and labour, but these structures depend on these consumptions and labour (and on productivities), and hence, are elastic items.

[6] Given the ELIE structure, the determination of the degree of distribution (coefficient k) may be led to using maximands of this kind, but these functions will be specifically determined, and they apply to the obtained structure (see Part IV).

[7] See Chapter 4 and Kolm 1996a, Chapter 12.

but not for being the sole determinant of overall distributive justice in normal situations.[8]

These remarks also show that theories of this kind may be relevant, but for cases of microjustice, notably with a utilitarian formulation. And indeed, the same theory had been previously used for determining optimum schedules of public tarifs (generally nonlinear ones) – for public services, firms, or utilities – with, in addition, individuals with generally different preferences which are generally uncertain for the policy maker who chooses the tarif schedule in uncertainty.[9]

Finally, it may be that certain sources of information used as indirect information for estimating the w_i or the functions p_i are elastic (influenced by individuals' choices), with the possibility that this induces inefficient disincentives or incentives. But this is limited by people's uncertainty about the way the tax or subsidy is computed in this case. For instance, education obtained long in advance (and which provides not only income but also status and other things) is bound not to be very sensitive to tax computations performed much later. On the whole, such issues can exist, but they constitute a very secondary point, and it doubtlessly is mistaken to see such questions as the problem of optimum taxation. Optimum taxation first has to determine what the optimum taxes and subsidies should be in terms of base and schedule or rates. The problem of gathering the needed information can only be second. And possible effects of a forecast of this use of this information on behaviour influencing the observed variables can only be a third-rate concerns. Considering such effects as "the problem" of optimum taxation does not seem to make sense. It is, at best, misplaced emphasis (an apt expression of Leif Johansen [1981]). One will not study the right information problem and its consequences if one does not first know which information is needed.

Appendix. MORE ON ESTIMATION, BEHAVIOUR, AND EFFICIENCY

A.1. Estimations

Let us now consider more in depth the issue of the implementation of ELIE distributive schemes as concerns estimation, individuals' behaviour, efficiency, and second-best policy.

The ELIE policy provides or demands subsidies or taxes $t_i = \overline{p}(k) - p_i(k)$ or, in the simplified form (explained in Chapter 8), $t_i = k \cdot (w_i - \overline{w})$. Sign k represents the multidimensional or unidimensional chosen "equalization labour," and function $p_i(\ell)$ and w_i individual i's given earning capacity for labour ℓ or per unit (wage rate), that is, the corresponding prices of labour. Now, unit prices, or prices as function of quantities, for goods with their various characteristics, precisely constitute the public information in functioning markets. This holds for types of labour with its duration and various characteristics which can be or imply required levels of education or

[8] This is in line with the presentation in Kolm 1971 (see the discussion at the end of this reference).
[9] Kolm 1969b, 1970b.

training, and which can more or less imply degrees of intensity of work (attention, strength, and so on). In contrast with prices or price functions, the values and quantities exchanged between transactors are a priori known to these agents only. In particular, in the labour market, this is the case of earned incomes and of the labour provided. Practically, as concerns the base of the tax or subsidy, and by comparison with the income tax, ELIE schemes can just be seen as disregarding the income from overtime work, and bonuses for particular intensity or training or education (with the adequate adjustment of the rates). These are common information on paysheets.

For the effect of education itself, however, the detailed, practical application of the principle has theoretically to distinguish the effects of duration and effort – which are labour – and costs in expenses and foregone earnings for the individual, from talent (innate or acquired in the family) and external aid (notably public or from the family). The specific detailed analysis of the issue is easy to elaborate. Some possible methodological schemes have been pointed out in Chapter 8. Practically, rules of thumb will be used, as with all tax rules. Note that, as regards disincentives and inelasticities, in many respects and in most cultures educational choices are little affected by taxes on earnings to be paid decades later in unknown situations, and with unknown bases and rates, and depend much on the interest in the future job and in the specific subject and studies, on the corresponding expected social status, and so on.

In the end, the needed information can be gathered by the various methods usually used for taxes: demands of reporting, administrative checking, penalties, approximate estimations, proxies, rules of thumb, and so on. One should not forget the situation and practice of present actual taxation and the estimations, errors, imprecisions, approximations, omissions, evasion, avoidance, unreporting, underreporting, and the like as concerns, for instance, the income of many professions (professionals, farmers, various services, small firms and large ones for different reasons, and so on), payments of extra labour, transactions of many types, assets and their value and its variation, various benefits, income received from abroad and wealth held abroad, gifts and transmission, the value of real estate and properties of various types, and so on. The situation and result depend very much on specific taxes and countries. For large taxes, it is not uncommon that one third of the value of the base evades the tax.[10] Due to underreporting and underestimation of the base, the *product* of the income tax in the United States is at least 15% lower than it should be.[11]

Hence, on average, the difficulties in estimating the desired base is not easier for most taxes or subsidies than they are for ELIE schemes. Indeed, a number of aspects make this estimation definitely easier for ELIE policies: the base consists of prices or price functions, paysheets are contractual and official documents with much of the relevant information (such as salary for given duration, given training or education, and given type of job, which often implies intensity – and education, formation, or experience), the taxes and subsidies have a single focus, their role in achieving basic and general distributive justice and the way in which they do this is clear and unambiguous and can and should be well explained, and the implied degree of distribution should

---

[10] This magnitude of error is not out of line with that in other aspects of society, even as concerns physics: civil engineers very carefully compute the characteristics of bridges for facing any possible kinds of risk, and in the end add up 30% in strength for security.

[11] See Slemrod (2002). The rest of this work and the references it mentions are very informative and relevant concerning actual taxation.

be the object of a large social debate (as explained in Part IV of this study). These later properties are bound to make these taxes more readily accepted than many others with diffused, unclear, or dubious objectives, chosen through very indirect and imperfect representation – if there is any. This may help diminishing evasion or false reporting.

If now the comparison as concerns information is no longer with actual tax or subsidy policies but with those proposed by economic theoreticians, the discrepancy becomes very large indeed. Some of these theories require the knowledge of demand and supply functions of all individual agents, consumers, and firms: all elasticities and cross elasticities at the individual level and in a sufficient domain. The most charitable way of treating a comparative discussion of this informational requirement is not to start it at all. Other theories need similarly to know indifference loci, hence ordinal utility functions of the individual: this is, for instance, the case of policies based on the "theory of equivalence," which are discussed in Chapter 26. Other theories want still more: they need to know utility functions of the individuals that have structures of cardinality and of interpersonal comparability. They thus go beyond the issue of information to the question of meaningfulness or meaninglessness (this is discussed in Chapter 23) – and this happens to be the case of the discussed "welfarist" "optimum income tax" studies. Compared with these "informational" requirements, only asking for a kind of wage rate seems to be very modest. It should also be noted that, although Pareto efficiency depends on individuals' preferences, they need not be known by a policy favouring this efficiency when it lets it result from individuals' interactions in social freedom from a distribution of given resources (as with the obtained solution for macrojustice).

A.2. Democracy, participation, functional finance, community

Coming back to actual fiscal policies, it is noteworthy that false reporting and evasion depend very much on the type of taxpayer, on her attitude toward the considered tax or subsidy, and, on average, on the general ethos of society in this respect. Although economics tends to favour a description of a purely self-interested taxpayer, this forgets a dimension of duty and honesty, and of sense of citizenship, community, and participation which is sometimes notable and can become more important according to the type of tax or contribution. Fiscal cheating, false reporting, and tax evasion are sometimes acts of resistance to oppression or arbitrariness. In more normal situations, the simple moral requirement of honesty and indictment of cheating on legality through false reporting or evasion have more or less influence, depending on people, societies, and circumstances. Honesty often provides a leverage which multiplies the efficiency of the threat of penalties (in fact, pure voluntariness is probably favoured by an a priori absence of penalties). However, one may have not to expect too much in willful compliance, sincere reporting, and voluntary contribution for taxes whose specific uses are unclear to the taxpayer, are blurred and confused, include obvious wastes and mistaken spendings, aim at least in part at supporting the power of politicians (and more or less their wealth), and which are chosen by a dubious political system with important lobbying influencing a problematic representation. A priori allegiance to the political system sufficient for full voluntary compliance to official fiscal demands is a particular case. In particular, the standard view of democracy excludes such blind obedience, since the control of public finances is one of the classical basic rights. Willful compliance to demands of contribution and the corresponding sincere reporting thus often depend on the adhesion of the taxpayer to the collective project implemented by the tax – if any. Short of a blind global faith in the political system, and in particular in a genuine democracy, such adhesion requires a minimum understanding of the project. This is much helped by functional finance, clearly identifying and matching means and objectives. Now, the overall distributive justice implemented by an ELIE scheme is a paragon of functional finance. It has a single objective. This role can be clearly explained and understood. The various possible positions as regards overall distributive justice are particular cases of this scheme. Of course, since the issue is distribution, individuals' interests can be opposed in this respect. However, we have seen that, when things are fully considered, there is unanimity in favour of this structure of distribution. The remaining issue thus is the degree of "redistribution" represented by coefficient k. Now, the discussion in Part IV of this study proposes that, in a given community, there will tend to be a kind of common view about this level. Then, the general understanding of the rationale of these taxes and subsidies, and the relative acceptance of the justness of this level, given that all other people are subject to the same scheme, can certainly limit tendencies to cheating and false reporting. In this respect, honesty tends to be supported by the sense of community. And generally accepted redistribution of one kind or the other is one of the hallmarks of a community.

A.3. Taxpayers' and beneficiaries' behaviour and the fiscal game

Nevertheless, the issues raised by the gathering of the required information can be faced directly. Estimates can be derived in various ways. The classical worry of economists concerns the case where an estimate uses, as information, the observation of an item that the taxpayer or the beneficiary of the subsidy can influence, and this person acts so as to influence this information in order to pay less or receive more. This act can be a genuine act or reporting. Such effects are classically met by fiscal administrations in recouping information from various sources. A model of the behaviour of the taxpayer or of the beneficiary can relate the observed behaviour to the item one needs to know about and establish a more or less precise correlation. This can go from refined studies to rough rules of thumb, such as those that are commonly used for correcting reporting concerning specific classes of agents and items. It should be emphasized that an estimation is not a tax law. The taxpayer or beneficiary has no official guarantee about the relation between the observations and the estimate of the base of the tax or subsidy. Yet, her choice of the considered action is determined by her belief about this relation. But the administration's proper choice takes care of this belief. And the clever taxpayer or beneficiary knows it – which affects her actual belief. The situation then is of the game-theoretic kind. The taxpayer's or beneficiary's "strategies" are her actions and reporting. The administration's "strategies" are the tax, the inquiries of various possible kinds, and possible penalties for false reporting and a method of checking. The solution with a given tax law and a specific base is a Stackelberg domination by the taxpayer, but it is different if the strategy in the previous establishment of the rule is considered. All kinds of situations and solutions are a priori possible. It should be reminded that Cournot-Nash solutions have no particular reason to prevail. It is, however, bound to be important that the game is generally repeated or sequential in time.

A.4. Social freedom and efficiency

However, the first thing is to express the objective of the administration, since this is not an exogenously given agent, and her action is not the simple costless application of known and certain values of taxes and subsidies. The equalization labour or the coefficient k are given (their determination is the topic of Part IV). However, there remains to determine the productivities $p_i(k)$ or the wage rates w_i corresponding to the given capacities. This can entail various administrative costs, the choice of estimating procedures, that of the relevant variables, possibly of proxies, playing the game just described with taxpayers or beneficiaries, checking, choosing penalties, applying them or not, and making most such choices in situations of imperfect information and uncertainty. And the administration also has to consider the effect of all this on taxpayers and beneficiaries, and on the rest of society.

The realization of macrojustice aims at respecting process-freedom and Pareto efficiency, and at relevantly equalizing rent-rights in productive capacities. The strategy for Pareto efficiency consists of having it result from process-freedom, possibly corrected for "failures" in markets, agreements, or agents' information. Practically, this means that taxes or subsidies should be presented to the agents as independent from their actions, as much as possible. The amounts demanded or supplied can be asserted as independent from these actions. This will not happen if they are based on information influenced by such actions or their consequences. And it suffices that agents believe that their future taxes or subsidies be so influenced. In these cases, the elasticities of these taxes or subsidies with regard to the agent's actions should be made as low as possible. One way is the development of direct investigation about productivities. False reporting can be checked with high penalties.[12] The alternative of securing Pareto efficiency by the maximization of a social maximand function of individuals' utility functions is not actually available. This implies, indeed, a series of extraordinary requirements about knowing the tastes and preferences of all individuals. First, this method demands knowing individuals' ordinal utility functions, hence the demands, supplies, direct and cross elasticities, and rates of substitutions, for all individuals, in a sufficient domain. If one finds knowing about wage rates difficult, what should be said about utility functions (indeed, if such functions exist)! Then, for defining the specific social maximand, corresponding utility functions should be defined, should be comparable across individuals, and, in fact, generally should be meaningfully representable as quantities (except for the particular and extreme criteria of maximin or leximin for which interpersonal comparisons by more or less suffice – see Chapter 23). Such issues no longer belong to the field of information but to that of meaningfulness, with the possible disease not only of ignorance but indeed of nonsense, which is of another order of magnitude in seriousness. In fact, the studies about "optimum income taxation" referred to above assume that all individuals have identical utility

---

[12] A vast economic literature about this topic can be used (the normative analysis of the optimum policy in this respect, using a public evaluation function, is very simply presented and was introduced in Kolm 1973b).

functions, hence identical tastes and corresponding demands and supplies, plus an identical practically quantitative structure of the levels of utility! Fortunately, endogenous social choice forbids finding the solution to overall distributive justice along these lines, because of the noted consensus about the irrelevance of eudemonistic capacities for this question (Chapter 6). These problems will be discussed more in detail in Chapters 23 and 24, while Chapter 26 presents and discusses the various solutions based on the theory of "equivalence", that is, having one Pareto-efficient situation that all individuals find as good as another situation that is just but has to be impossible (only ordinal preferences will have to be known, but often in an extended domain, and the logico-ethical validity of the principle is problematic).

A.5. Maximization

The ELIE equalizing redistribution of the values $p_i(k)$ into their average $\overline{p}(k)$ amounts to the equalization of the individuals' "compensated equalization incomes," $x_i = p_i(k) + t_i$ for individual i, by the choice of transfers t_i such that $\Sigma t_i = 0$. This equalization can be achieved by the maximization of a maximand function $M(x)$, where $x = \{x_i\}$ is the set (vector) of the x_i, which is increasing (benevolence), symmetrical (invariant under any permutation of the x_i), and inequality-averse, by the choice of the t_i under the constraint $\Sigma t_i = 0$. Such a function increases when the x_i become more equal in a number of possible specific and precise senses. The question of these functions will be called back to mind in Chapter 23.[13] Maximin and leximin in the x_i are limiting cases. If there are other constraints on the realization of this policy, the maximization of $M(x)$ with all actual constraints permits the definition of a second-best ELIE policy. Then, the outcome may not be the equality of all the x_i. The basic reason is that increasing a lower x_i may imply decreasing by much more one or even many other ones (or it may be impossible). Among these other constraints, some may come from questions of information because the estimates of the $p_i(k)$ rely on the observation of items that are influenced by the policy (by the transfers t_i). These estimates are then moreover bound to be uncertain, and, with a probability estimation, the maximand becomes $EF[M(x)]$, where E denotes the mathematical expectation operator and $F[M(x)]$ a specification of the von Neumann-Morgenstern cardinal specification of ordinal maximand M – along the classical theory of rational choice in uncertainty.

---

[13] The relation between such functions and the measure of unjust inequalities is the topic of Kolm 1966a, Sections 6 and 7 (which also presents the basic properties of these measures). The most complete and up-to-date survey of such properties is probably found in the *Handbook on Income Inequality Measurement*, edited by Jacques Silber (1999). Among other surveys in book form, the most complete is probably that by Peter Lambert (2001). As a beginning of the discussion, one could consider a function M of the form $M(x) = \Sigma(x_i + c)^\alpha$, with two parameters c and α such that $c \geq 0$ and $0 < \alpha < 1$. Parameter c could be about the size of $\overline{p}(k)$. Coefficient α is discussed at length in the literature. This simple structure has a limit in that it makes a change in a subset (e.g., a pair) of the x_i augment or diminish the overall inequality independently of the given values of the other x_i. This can be justified or not. Other and, notably, more complex forms can meet possible objections.

11

Income justice

1. INTRODUCTION AND SUMMARY

Income distribution is one of the most considered issues in judgments about over-all distributive justice. These judgments often complain about income inequality and approve of its reduction. Moreover, a main tool for overall distributive justice, the income tax, is based on actual incomes and its progressivity is commonly justified as a means of reduction of inequalities in disposable incomes. This describes an ideal of equal disposable individual incomes (hence, household incomes are adjusted for family size). This ideal happens to discard a relevance of eudemonistic capacities; this is another manifestation of this general view about macrojustice (see Chapter 6).

This ideal also discards a relevance of differences in individuals' earnings for the distribution of disposable incomes. However, earnings depend on both labour and productivity. Then, these income egalitarians state that individuals' disposable incomes should not differ because of differences in productive capacities. But when it comes to the possible effects of labour, the view of most present-day income egalitarians is that someone who works more than someone else (longer, harder, at more painful or dirtier jobs, etc.) deserves a compensation for this extra work. This compensation is an extra income that compensates the painfulness of this extra labour (including foregone leisure). It a priori refers to a concept of indifference for an individual (but this is not the interindividual comparison of individual satisfactions or of their variations, which are found irrelevant for macrojustice). Moreover, if the individual who provides more work freely chooses her labour, she is responsible for it, and hence it is felt that others do not have to subsidize it, that is, to pay this extra labour more than it is worth for them. Then, when this extra labour is sufficiently limited, these two conditions imply that the compensation is precisely the product or earnings provided by this extra labour (see Section 2.1.4). Hence, the individual receives the product of her extra labour. She receives more if she is more productive. This is self-ownership, but *only* for the differential labour. Now, individuals' labour inputs often differ in duration, intensity or conditions, but, in large societies, a large majority of individuals' labour inputs are rather close to one another.

The described compensation cannot hold for all pairs of different labours. The best possible specification of the described moral view then seems to have it to hold by comparison with the lowest normal full labours. Indeed, the considered policy of macrojustice can abstain from considering the cases of exceptionally low or high labours. Then, all the considered differences in labour provided will be limited. For low labours, the reference to the lowest normal full labours discards voluntary part-time jobs (possibly as second incomes in the household), excentric low labours, and involuntary unemployment, which will be specifically considered in Chapter 13. The result then is an ELIE distribution with an equalization labour in the neighbourhood of these lowest normal labours (see Section 2.1.5). This policy creates no inefficiency-generating disincentives effect (moreover, the more productive individuals are generally induced to work more by the tax they have to pay). If, in addition, some other degree of self-ownership is found relevant, this is manifested by a lower equalization labour.

The present-day redistribution of incomes is in fact limited by the consideration that there is some validity in partial self-ownership. This is, in varying degrees, the view of most people, and it also corresponds to the outcome of political debates and conflicts. The disincentive effect of the tax, although often pointed out, is in fact a secondary reason which is actually superseded by the moral view about self-ownership. Then, ELIE schemes with equalization labours lower than that corresponding to the income egalitarian ideal describe these ethics endorsing some validity for self-ownership – and they induce no inefficiency.

Other reasons are also provided for basing a redistributive tax on income. We have noticed that the view of some scholars that income is taken as base as an observable proxy for unobservable individuals' capacities is not really justified (Chapter 10 and below). In contrast, the classical "principle of public finance" of taxing according to "ability to pay" suggests a reason which may be practical ("take the money where it is") but could also be inspired by the utilitarian-like idea that rich people suffer less from the same loss than do poor people. This principle may diminish inequality in disposable income, but only taxing richer people more does not say much about it. The most important, however, is that, for earned incomes, ability to pay is ability to earn: the tax should be based on earning capacities (as ELIE schemes are). This can be naturally realized by each individual yielding her output for the same labour, which depends on the total required proceeds of the tax (if the individuals equally benefit from the expenditure, the whole operation becomes an ELIE).

The principle of taxing according to "ability to pay" traditionally opposes that of "benefit taxation" (and equal lump-sum per capita contributions). Benefit taxation implies that the public services and their financing be distributionally neutral. The bases of the tax are the individuals' benefits rather than incomes. However, taking public expenditures, services, and infrastructure globally, the benefits received from them roughly increase with income, and in a kind of progressive manner (Section 5.3).

In the end, a classical conception of an ideal income equality limited by the disincentive effects of the distribution misses essential issues, such as the positive incentive effects, the value of leisure, the treatment of different labours, Pareto efficiency, and the common partial valuing of self-ownership. These issues all lead to the relevant ELIE distributive scheme.

The complete common income egalitarian ethics is the topic of Section 2, where it is shown how it is best satisfied by a particular ELIE distributive structure. Section 3 considers the various possible reasons for basing a tax on incomes, and for not redistributing more. The scholars' welfarist "optimum income tax" is the topic of Section 4. Section 5 focuses on the implications of the classical principle of public finance, taxing according to "ability to pay" and "benefit taxation." Finally, Section 6 fully shows the flaws in the common view of incentive-limited income egalitarianism.

2. INCOME EGALITARIANISM

2.1. The income egalitarian ethics

2.1.1. An ideal of income equality

Endogenous social choice derives its conclusions from citizens' opinions about distributive justice, and, being a scientific exercise, it considers closely and fully their meaning, intent, and implications. One of the most common ways of evaluating global distributive justice focuses on income distribution. This is not the only way, however; for instance, full self-ownership only cares that there is no redistributive transfers and treats income distribution with benign neglect. The focus on income rather than on specific consumption goods is natural for macro-justice with process-freedom and the resulting respect of consumers' choices. Moreover, the consideration is often that of disposable incomes rather than only of the transfers (as is the case with an ELIE scheme). Furthermore, such views commonly express worries and negative judgments about increases in income inequalities, and satisfaction about their decrease. Whatever solution is provided for the delicate question of comparing income inequalities, these opinions manifest a *prima facie* ideal of equal disposable incomes. A standard precision consists of taking care of family size for transforming household incomes provided by statistics into the equivalent of individual incomes.

On practical grounds, the income tax, based on actual and notably earned incomes, nowadays constitutes the main tool of global distributive justice. This is notably achieved by its progressivity which tends to reduce income inequalities. And part of the proceeds of this tax is used for providing various aids to people with low incomes. Moreover, much of the other expenditures provide public goods free of charge (while income is required for buying marketed goods). On the whole, the income tax generally intends to have an effect of diminishing income inequalities. It is seen as a tool for this purpose. A common view is that it directly affects, by its base (and that of distributive subsidies), the relevant objective of global distributive justice, income, transformed into more equally distributed disposable income available for consumption. This reveals a *prima facie* ideal of equality in disposable incomes (the reasons for the limitations of this equalization are shortly discussed).

The ideal of income equality implies that other differences across individuals are considered irrelevant for this judgment of justice. In contrast with classical competing views, this irrelevance concerns notably the differences in individuals' eudemonistic capacities and needs on the one hand, and production on the other hand. Individual production results from individual labour and productivity. The irrelevance of eudemonistic capacities and needs, for the purpose of global distributive justice in macrojustice, is in line with the general consensual opinion (see Chapter 6).

2.1.2. Equal income and equal work

However, when the opinion of these income egalitarians is closely considered, it turns out that they unambiguously favour this equality only when individuals provide the same labour. That is, this view holds the traditional principle of "equal pay for equal work." However, this principle is usually applied for banning discrimination according to race, sex, age, family origin, and so on. Such discriminations are in fact banned by the basic rights. Income egalitarians extend this principle for banning dependency of disposable income on productivity and eudemonistic capacities and needs, at least when labours provided are the same.

This view is easily translated as an unqualified ideal of equal incomes (apart from possible qualification for "disincentive effects") because, in most societies, the large majority of people provide rather similar labours (irrespective of their productivities). However, if individuals are free to choose their labours, they generally strictly choose different ones. Moreover, Pareto efficiency also generally implies that individual labours are different, because individuals have different preferences as regards labour and leisure on the one hand, and income or consumption on the other hand. In fact, individuals' free choice of labour implies this efficiency if there is no market distortion.

The principle of "equal pay for equal work" entails equal incomes if equal labour is also required. This joint equality in incomes and labour inputs (notably duration) has been proposed by a number of utopian socialist ideas, and sometimes applied in early times of authoritarian socialist regimes. There are also various legal rules for labour duration, but they generally do not accompany equal incomes and admit overtime work. Of course, imposing equal labour violates process-freedom and basic rights, and is Pareto-inefficient because people have different tastes as concerns leisure and consumption. Equality in both pay and labour also impairs material incentives to efficient labour. However, most present-day income egalitarians accept that people can choose different labours and accept, more generally, an economy largely ruled by markets.

2.1.3. Incomes for different labours

Hence, the basic stance of income egalitarianism is that individuals should have the same income when their work is the same (irrespective of their productivity). However, when one person works more than another, most present-day income egalitarians think she deserves a compensation for this extra labour. This compensation is for the extra painfulness of this labour. When the person who works more freely chooses her labour, the modern income egalitarian thinks, in addition, that this compensation should not exceed the contribution of this extra labour to society's wealth, because the person is responsible for this extra work (hence, others do not have to pay for that). Now, it happens that, with this free choice, and when the two compared labours are not too different, the extra income that compensates this person in the sense that she is nearly indifferent between providing this extra labour for this extra income or not, is about equal to the value of the production of this extra work (see next section). This amount thus defines the extra income.

Since the basic reference is to the painfulness of labour, working more can mean working longer, harder when the intensity is painful, with more effort, time, and foregone earnings in previous education or training, or at labours that are more disagreeable in any way – such as more dangerous, dirtier, and so on – given that these labour conditions permit the corresponding extra output. The compensatory extra income is determined by indifference between pairs of labour and income for the same individual (hence, this differs from interpersonal comparisons of satisfactions or of their variations, which have been found irrelevant for the purpose of macrojustice in Chapter 6).

When there are more than two persons, the comparison can be with the lowest labour provided by these persons, or with some reference labour slightly lower. There can then be equal income for this equal reference labour, but free choice of their actual labour by the individuals who keep their market earnings for this extra work. For instance, when there is an official duration of labour that is used for the definition of wages in labour contracts or agreements, there can be an equal basic income for this labour, whereas bonuses for overtime work or particularly painful jobs are not taxed.

The comparison has been for labours not too different from one another. Now, in most societies the large majority of the population provides labours that are not very different in duration or intensity. Note that part-time jobs that provide complementary income for the household should be discarded, as well as unemployment (see Chapter 13). And abnormal labours, notably abnormally low labours, can be discarded for the purpose of defining macrojustice. Hence, in the end, the considered scheme is an ELIE with an equalization labour in the neighbourhood of the lowest normal full-time labours – say $k = k^e$, where k^e is this "income-egalitarian equalization labour." This seems to be the best specification of the set of moral stands or "intuitions" of present-day income egalitarians.

This solution amounts to self-ownership for productive capacities used above the equalization labour k^e. Self-ownership is precisely what income-egalitarians do not want. However, this is only differential or marginal self-ownership, for the small differences $\ell_i - k^e$, where ℓ_i is individual i's labour. Moreover, this extra income is not justified by self-ownership, but results from the association of compensation for painfulness with the individual's free choice of labour.

This specification of the income egalitarian ideal elicits two remarks. First, the difference between the incomes of two individuals with labour $\ell_i \neq k^e$ and different wage rates does not correspond to a compensation for extra painfulness. However, such an exact compensation for each pair of individuals (when there are more than two of them) is not possible. The compensation is only for each individual and the reference labour k^e or the lowest actual normal full labours. At any rate, all incomes are close to one another and only little above the equalization income $\overline{w}k^e$.

Moreover, the choice of the income-egalitarian equalization labour k^e in the neighbourhood of the the lowest normal full labours (rather than at any other value in the neighbourhood of normal labours) is due to the fact that people (including income egalitarians) do not feel it proper that individuals pay a tax, or receive a subsidy, because they *could* earn much, or little, in labours they do not actually perform. It is not felt proper that leisure be taxed, or subsidized, for the income the individuals could have obtained in working instead. This leads to the choice of a $k^e \leq \ell_i$ for all the considered labours ℓ_i.[1]

2.1.4. The logic of the solution

Consider an individual i with income (or consumption) y_i, labour ℓ_i, and an ordinal utility function $u^i(y_i, \ell_i)$. For simplicity in presentation, consider the case of unidimensional labour ℓ_i and a linear individual production function $w_i \ell_i$ where w_i is individual i's given wage rate or unit productivity (see Chapter 8). The same results would obtain with a more complex description of labour. Then, asuming differentiabilities, denote $u^i_y = \partial u^i / \partial y_i$, $u^i_\ell = \partial u^i / \partial \ell_i$, and $v_i(y_i, \ell_i) = -u^i_\ell / u^i_y$. For any other levels of income y and labour ℓ, if the differences $|y_i - y|$ and $|\ell_i - \ell|$ are sufficiently small, one has

$$u^i(y, \ell) = u^i(y_i, \ell_i) + (y - y_i) \cdot u^i_y(y_i, \ell_i) + (\ell - \ell_i) \cdot u^i_\ell(y_i, \ell_i).$$

If the difference in incomes compensates the painfulness of the difference in labours, one has $u^i(y, \ell) = u^i(y_i, \ell_i)$. Hence, $y - y_i = (\ell - \ell_i) \cdot v^i(y_i, \ell_i)$.

---

[1] See also the corresponding remarks in Chapter 7.

If, moreover, individual i freely chooses her labour and income with a budget constraint of the type $y_i = w_i \ell_i + y_i^o$ where y_i^o is a constant, then $v^i(y_i, \ell_i) = w_i$. This is both a condition of free choice for individual i and of economic efficiency. Then,

$$y_i - y = (\ell_i - \ell)w_i,$$

that is, comparing with the reference labour $\ell < \ell_i$ and income $y < y_i$, individual i's extra income $y_i - y$ is equal to the production of her extra labour $(\ell_i - \ell)w_i$.

In the foregoing discussion, ℓ and y can be the labour and income of another individual, or they can be the equalization labour and the average equalization income k^e and $\overline{w}k^e$.

2.1.5. The income-egalitarian ELIE

Hence, the best specification of the complete common present-day income-egalitarian ethics seems to be an ELIE distribution with an equalization labour $k = k^e$ in the neighbourhood of the lowest normal full labours. The income of an individual i then is

$$y_i = k^e \overline{w} + w_i \cdot (\ell_i - k^e).$$

The part $k^e \overline{w}$ is large and the part $w_i \cdot (\ell_i - k^e)$ is small. The part $k^e \overline{w}$ is equal for all and abides by the principle "to each according to her work," irrespective of individuals' own productivities, or "equal pay for equal work," for the same labour k^e for all. An individual i who works $\ell_i > k^e$ is compensated for this extra labour $\ell_i - k^e$ by the amount $w_i \cdot (\ell_i - k^e)$. This is, for her, an exact compensation for the "disutility" of this extra labour (because $\ell_i - k^e$ is sufficiently small). This is also this individual's extra output, the output she produces by this extra work. Hence, this amount corresponds to a principle of self-ownership. However, this is partial self-ownership, only for this limited extra labour. It is, in this sense, "marginal self-ownership." For all individuals, individual satisfaction is that which corresponds to a labour k^e and a disposable income (consumption) $k^e \overline{w}$.[2]

In large modern societies, the very large majority provides very similar amounts of work. This is normal or standard labour. There often is an official labour duration used for individual labour contracts or for collective agreements about wages. Most of the individuals who voluntarily work notably less provide complementary incomes for the household, and this is not to be considered as full work and income. Involuntary unemployment is reduced by full process-freedom

---

[2] Hence, the solution also looks like an "egalitarian equivalent" criterion of the type used in Kolm (1966a) and Pazner and Schmeidler (1978) – see Chapter 26. The "egalitarian equivalent" to each individual's allocation for this individual would be the pair $(k^e, \overline{w}k^e)$. However, the considered situation differs from the classical one in that the reference is equal labour or leisure for all individuals, while, as concerns production, the labours of individuals with different productivities are different goods (this treatment of labour is also in Kolm, op. cit).

and by the realization of global distributive justice, because they lower the possibility and the necessity of wage rigidities, which is a cause of this unemployment
(downward wage rigidities, implemented one way or the other, aim at protecting
against low wages). Involuntary unemployment is also reduced by the appropriate
macroeconomic, labour, and education policies. It is alleviated by unemployment
insurance. Moreover, Chapter 13 shows its integration into an ELIE scheme, with
the conclusion that unemployed individuals do not receive less than the average
equalization income, and receive this amount if their unemployment is full or
partial at no more than the equalization labour. On the whole, these cases can
be discarded for the present overall consideration. Furthermore, proportionately
rare cases of very high, or otherwise very low, labour are not of primary concern
for macrojustice.

Many societies have an official standard labour duration, but individuals are
free to work overtime. Then, the considered income egalitarian ethics can propose
that everyone receives the same income for the official labour, whereas overtime
labour is remunerated at the competitive wage of the labour market. Then, "equal
pay for equal work" holds for standard labour, and self-ownership is the rule for
overtime labour.

We have noticed that k^e should not be higher than the considered labours ℓ_i.
Precisely, if, for some of these i, we had $\ell_i < k^e$, this individual would have a disposable income $y_i = w_i \ell_i + k^e \cdot (\overline{w} - w_i) = \overline{w} k^e - w_i \cdot (k^e - \ell_i)$, which means
that she pays $w_i \cdot (k^e - \ell_i)$ for her extra leisure $k^e - \ell_i$ – she buys this leisure at its
market price w_i. However, the equal unit income $\overline{w}$ would then be not only for
units of actual labour for all individuals, but also, for individuals with $\ell_i < k^e$,
for some units of time which are used in leisure rather than at work. Now, as has
been pointed out, a general ethical view, notably shared by income egalitarians,
is that it is not proper to tax individuals' leisure in valuing it at the fictive income
it would produce if this time were actually used at work (trying to induce productive people to work more in taxing leisure at this value would be something
else, not based on a distributive reason and needing justification). Conversely,
compensating someone for the low wage she could obtain in labour she does not
perform does not seem appropriate either. This view concerning leisure relates to
the ethics of equally valuing individuals' time on moral grounds (see Chapters 7
and 9).

This leads to the choice of a k^e slightly below the chosen normal ℓ_i, say in
the neighbourhood of the lowest of these labours. There is no need to say that
k^e should be exactly equal to the lowest. This solution, however, is a theoretical
possibility. Yet, if k^e is chosen and adjusted to be equal to the lowest of the freely
chosen normal labours, say ℓ_i, hence $k^e = \ell_i$, the corresponding individual i
has income $y_i = k^e \overline{w} = \ell_i \overline{w}$. This amounts to individual i being remunerated at
the average wage rate $\overline{w}$, rather than at her productivity w_i, without facing any
tax or subsidy. In the general case where $w_i \neq \overline{w}$, this individual's free choice is
inefficient. However, if there are sufficiently many individuals, this inefficiency

for only one of them may not be a serious defect (this individual receives $\overline{w}k^e$ for working k^e, and all the other individuals considered work and receive more – or as much – but are as satisfied as if they had this labour or leisure and this income). Of course, choosing k^e equal to the lowest ℓ_i a priori requires considering the individuals' choices of their labour as a function of the level of k^e, which determines taxes and subsidies. This can be performed by the groping of an iterative adjustment (during which the individual with the lowest of the considered ℓ_i may change).

Practically, however, the choice of an ELIE with an equalization labour around half standard working time would already constitute a substantially income-egalitarian and "leftist" stand in present-day large societies (yet, this would be short of a "utopian" position).

2.2. The income-egalitarian policy

The conclusion is that the standard, common income-egalitarian ethics, with its usual qualifications concerning compensation of labour differentials (and reward for extra work), is best realized by an ELIE distribution with an equalization labour in the neighbourhood of the lowest normal labour (the exact specification is of no importance). Then, for the bulk of labour, equal work entails equal pay. But individuals who work more or whose work is more painful or disagreeable in any way are compensated for the difference. This happens to give them what they contribute to society with this extra work. The equality of these two numbers is a technical result due to the fact that labour is free or efficient (and labours are not too different).

With this scheme, all individuals freely choose their labour. "Equal pay for equal work" is not interpreted as imposing equal work to all (as it is in forms of "authoritarian socialism"). The most common present income egalitarianism accepts or demands freedom, notably of choosing one's labour, and the individual who works more (than k^e) receives the full income value of her extra work.

Relatedly, this scheme is Pareto efficient – as required by the principle of unanimity. This is to be contrasted with the common accusation that income-egalitarian policies induce economic and social waste. This results from the fact that ELIE transfers are lump-sum: they induce no "price effects" generating inefficiency. Yet, they induce "income effects", which may be rather large compared with full self-ownership, as a result of the high level of the equalization labour $k = k^e$. These effects induce no waste (Pareto wise). They induce the individuals who pay the distributive tax to work more for compensating for the loss (if leisure is not an "inferior good" as is usually the case), and, in a sense, for paying for the tax. And these individuals are the more productive ones. The individuals who receive the distributive subsidies may symmetrically work less (but they are the less productive individuals). Moreover, for all, higher or lower work corresponds to lower or higher leisure. In the end, these variations in labour and output can be considered as irrelevant in themselves, notably with the standard economic view holding that all that matters is Pareto efficiency and the distributional selection of a solution among the states that have this property.

However, a widespread idea is that the limit to the equalization of income rests in the disincentive effects. A strict and complete equalization of earned incomes would have to use transfers based on earned income. This leads the considered view to think that progress in this direction has to use transfers based on full earned incomes $w_i \ell_i$ (although this is not necessary: for instance, ELIE transfers of $t_i = k \cdot (\overline{w} - w_i)$ usually induce some equalization). The commonly expressed concern is that the ablest individuals are led to work less (this is the price effect when labour is provided mainly for income – there also are motives of activity, status, interest, power, and so on – and the income effect has the opposite consequence). Both the price and income effects then tend to induce the less productive people to work less, but this is usually more regretted because of the sociological and psychological effects of unemployment (social integration, mental balance, or effect on the family) or form a judgment of the type of the "work ethics." Now, full equalization of full earned incomes leads the individuals in a nonsmall society to provide no work for income at all. This situation is, of course, Pareto inefficient. The large size of the population prevents remedies by direct cooperation or by each working in order that the others continue to work (punishing free riders in such a sequential game fails because the punishment – abstaining from work – cannot affect solely specific others, and because it requires, for being effective, cooperation among many punishers to begin with, which raises the same problem as the one it tries to solve). In the end, there is no actual earned incomes and transfers. The basic flaw of this conception, however, is that the full standard income-egalitarian ethics contains other stances than equalizing earned incomes, as we have seen, and the final result is the obtained income-egalitarian ELIE. Moreover, many ethical stances are not fully income egalitarian and see some validity, at least partial, in self-ownership. And the result of political fighting and interaction leads to some mix of income egalitarianism and self-ownership. This is the main actual reason, by far, for the limitation in equalizing redistributions. Disincentive effects are only secondary, uncertain (because of the reverse income effects on high earners), and, indeed, commonly a pretext for justifying some degree of self-ownership. As an actual reason, they are largely superseded by some defense of self-ownership, an ethical distributive reason.

This ethical consideration also applies to the obtained ELIE scheme. Many people who see some rationale in the income-egalitarian stance do not deny all validity to self-ownership. Since these two views are implemented by ELIE schemes with $k = k^e$ and $k = 0$ respectively, these views are best represented by ELIE schemes with equalization labours k between 0 and k^e. Such distributions respect Pareto efficiency and freedom of the choice of labour.

At any rate, the political conflict, in the society, between income egalitarians and advocates of self-ownership, or between views that tend more toward one side or the other, are best solved by the choice of an ELIE with an intermediate level of k. Both Pareto efficiency and free labour supply are then respected and, indeed, these respects impose a solution of this type (see Chapter 1). However, Part IV will be more specific about the proper ways of determining the level of coefficient k.

3. WHY TAX INCOME?

3.1. The functions of the income tax

The main tool of global (overall) redistribution in present-day societies is the income tax, through its progressivity and uses of its proceeds (along with those of other taxes) for providing subsidies or goods free of charge. A tax is of course taken from income, but the point is that the income tax is based on actual income, it depends on it. In contrast, ELIE taxation is not based on full income and notably full earned income, but only on income earned by a notional labour, the equalization labour – however, it fully equalizes these incomes. This in particular holds for the case just obtained with $k = k^e$, which best implements the views of standard income egalitarians. Yet, the income tax has other functions than redistribution: it finances general public expenditures and can be an instrument of macroeconomic "stabilization" policies. However, the distributionally neutral financing of public expenditures other than distributive transfers is through benefit taxation whose base is benefit from public expenditures and a priori not income. Similarly, distributive public transfers that implement private altruism for reasons shortly to be considered (notably because they constitute "collective gift giving," a kind of contribution to a public good) are not a priori based on incomes. Moreover, macroeconomic stabilization works through income effects and hence the corresponding taxes or subsidies need not be based on actual incomes (a base which induces inefficiency-generating disincentive price effects). Why, then, the income tax – that is, a tax based on actual income? Given the importance of this tool, the answers one can find in the population are likely to provide important information about the existing opinions, notably as concerns distributive justice; and this information is essential for applying endogenous social choice.

It turns out that several different reasons for taxing income and for its distributive role can be observed in the population, in scholars' studies, and in classical principles of public finance. The public sees raising public funds and redistribution. Policies add macroeconomic stabilization. The classical principles of public finance are taxing according to "ability to pay" and "benefit taxation." Finally, classical scholarly studies justify taxing income by a reason of information: income would be a proxy for unobservable capacities. However, raising funds, global stabilization and, *prima facie*, benefit taxation taxing each individual according to the benefit she receives from the corresponding public expenditures, do not justify basing the tax on actual incomes. Distributive income transfers can aim at, and be based on, other items than incomes. They can also be based on incomes, notably for income egalitarians, although we have seen that the full consideration of the usual form of this philosophy leads to another base, namely, given productivities. Ability to pay refers to raising funds with a distributive concern. The possible relation of benefit taxation to income will be noted. And the informational argument (income as proxy), discussed in Chapter 10, will be considered synthetically and comparatively.

3.2. The public's view

The public at large first notes financing public expenditures and notably publicly provided public goods; but this reason is not redistributive, and it does not *prima facie* justify using actual income as base. In contrast, the reason everyone gives for the progressivity of the tax, and for public aids (in cash or in kind), is distribution, with reference to inequality and to the satisfaction of basic needs. This includes income egalitarian views. Indeed, taxes or subsidies based on income constitute the direct tool of income equalization. This view is sometimes associated with the necessity of obtaining a net public revenue with remarks of the type of "taking the money where it is." Indeed, the income egalitarian ideal exists and is politically influential. However, we have seen that the policy that best implements the common and complete form of this ethics is not a tax based on income, but a variety of ELIE. Moreover, why is the income tax not more redistributive and progressive?

3.3. Why is the income tax not more progressive?

Several answers are provided to this question. A secondary one refers to benefit taxation: even the poor benefit from public goods and hence should contribute something to their financing. Two other reasons exist, but the one most voiced and the main one differ. We have noticed that the reason most heard about concerns the disincentive effect. It is mainly presented for high incomes: higher income taxation would induce the payers to work less. This reason is, of course, highly ambiguous, as has been suggested. Through income effects, a higher tax induces payers to work more for compensating the loss (leisure is usually not an "inferior" good) and for paying the tax. However, the disincentive indeed exists through the price effect, and the total consequence is the addition of these two effects. Yet, lower labour is higher leisure, and, as a result of their freedom of choice, people equally value the loss of output and income and the gain in leisure and are indifferent about this variation (at least for variations of limited size). Hence, the concern should probably not be labour and incentives, but, rather, the effect of the tax on Pareto-wise inefficiency. The limiting extreme case of the full equalization of earned incomes is not usually considered. Moreover, we have seen that the best implementation of the standard income-egalitarian philosophy is an ELIE scheme which entails no price effect and therefore neither inducement to lower labour nor inefficiencies. The disincentive effect is also noted for the subsidy side, where recipients may notably be induced to stop working. The worries, however, concern more the effects of not working on the person, her family, her mental balance, and her social integration, and the general ideal of a "work ethics," than the loss of output (which is at any rate low for these low-income earners).

However, we have remarked that the actual main and basic reason for limiting redistribution and progressivity is not disincentive effects, but, rather, a purely ethical reason. It consists of the idea that there is some validity in self-ownership even beyond that of eudemonistic capacities for macrojustice. Most individuals usually see some reason both in limiting income inequalities and relieving poverty and in self-ownership, although they put various weights on these values. Some would ban only extreme inequalities, or only focus on alleviating poverty, and for the rest largely support self-ownership. Others are essentially income egalitarians but concede that gifted people receive some limited degree of advantage from their marketable talents. And the political interaction finally results in a case intermediate between income egalitarianism and the full self-ownership of classical process liberalism. This ethical reason for limiting income equalization very largely supersedes the reason concerning disincentives; it makes it of little importance at a global level.

We have seen, however, that these ethical positions are rationally implemented by ELIE schemes with $k < k^e$ – rather than by income taxation with some degree of progressivity. This solution, moreover, induces no disincentive effects on high productivity payers (it leads them, on the contrary, to work more through income effects and for paying the tax), and no Pareto inefficiency. In the end, the rational implementation of what is desired by the population is **not a partial equalization of all of incomes but a total equalization of part of incomes** – a part expressed as a given notional labour.

4. THE WELFARIST "OPTIMUM INCOME TAX"

We have seen, in previous chapters, that comparing individuals' eudemonistic capacities (utility functions) or their variations is consensually – and understandably – considered irrelevant for the redistribution implementing macrojustice (Chapter 6), and that wage rates are, on average, no more difficult to know than incomes (Chapter 10). Now, economics has developed an exercise, called "the optimum income tax," which is based on the opposite assumptions: the objective is the maximization of a classical "social welfare function" which is a function of individuals' utilities, and the reason for basing the tax on income is that it would be an observable proxy for unobservable capacities (Mirrlees, 1971). Why, however, would capacities be the first best base? The answer is not an ethical one, as with ELIE schemes, since the ethical objective is taken to be the maximization of the social welfare function. The reason doubtlessly is that capacities are assumed to be given and would constitute an inelastic base permitting one to tax individuals without inducing inefficiency-generating disincentives. A priori, however, there are other possible inelastic individual characteristics, such as their tastes (utility functions). However, the model used by these studies does not allow for this possibility because it assumes that all individuals have the same utility function. This assumption is not really justified, but is certainly retained for convenience. This utility, moreover, is assumed to be known by the policy maker. Individuals' productivity is also assumed to be known, but since, with identical utility functions, this productivity is all that differentiates individuals, the only relevant information about these productivities is their distribution in the population. This permits assuming that the specific productivity of each individual is not known, and, hence, that earned income might be taken as an observable proxy for it. This is, in the end, the suggested justification for taking earned income as the tax base. These studies emphasize a different, formal, aspect, namely that the income tax can be nonlinear. Finally, the considered income tax is purely redistributive, without a net public income and other expenditures.

A formally similar model had been used for issues of microjustice, where the "welfarist" ethics based on utility functions is justifiable (Kolm 1969b, 1970b). Moreover, in this study individuals' utility functions are assumed to be a priori different from one another and not known by the policy maker (who thus performs a choice in uncertainty). The model is used for determining the optimum a priori *nonlinear* tarif of public utilities. Another study of optimum taxation used taxes based on wages (Kolm 1974) – then for maximizing the lowest welfare level (this maximin or, more generally, leximin, in interindividually comparable ordinal utility is "practical justice" analyzed in Kolm 1971).

Mirrlees concluded his study in remarking that if one knows both income and labour duration, then one knows the wage rate and the productivity (with a competitive labour market). This remark undermines the very reason proposed for basing the tax on earned incomes – rather than on productivity. However, Partha Dasgupta and Peter Hammond (1976) saved the model in replacing labour duration by effort, which is generally less observable – and measurable. Chapter 10, however, showed various ways of observing or estimating effort. The basic point, yet, is that difficulties of information should be faced fully both in theory and in practice, rather than only in considering the use of one proxy.

5. THE "PRINCIPLES OF PUBLIC FINANCE": ABILITY TO PAY AND BENEFIT TAXATION

5.1. The two classical principles

For distributing the burden of taxes raised for financing public expenditures, traditional public finance classically opposes two principles: "ability to pay" and "benefit taxation." The principle of benefit taxation holds that taxes should reflect the benefits the taxpayers derive from the public expenditure they finance. Consequently, it intends the expenditure and its financing not to be redistributive.

The tax is about just a price paid for the benefit of the expenditure. This is the principle to be retained for the "allocation function" of the public sector, rather than for its "distribution function." This principle does not in general precisely determine the tax by itself because a surplus generally remains to be distributed. Yet, this issue generally is secondary. Moreover, it is faced by the application of the theory of the "liberal social contract" (see Chapter 3).

5.2. Ability to pay and to earn

The principle of taxation according to "ability to pay," in contrast, specifically concerns distribution, and a priori takes income or wealth as base – although this will shortly be questioned. It says that individuals with higher income or wealth should pay a higher tax, even if they receive similar benefits from the corresponding public expenditure – indeed, irrespective of this benefit. This principle opposes both benefit taxation and equal per capita taxes. It is roughly both distributive and merely practical when it is applied as "take the money where it is." It is more precisely ethical if it is justified by the assumption that wealthier people suffer less from losing some income than do poorer people. It then suggests a kind of utilitarianism. Strictly speaking, "ability to pay" only suggests a tax increasing with individuals' income or wealth. This may diminish income inequality, but this result depends on the specific tax schedule and on the chosen measure of inequality. A priori, the only condition of diminishing more higher incomes is in itself a quite weak egalitarian property. It is for instance satisfied by a proportional tax that leaves unchanged "intensive" measures of inequality (measures invariant to scale). An equalizing effect is clearer when the expenditure financed by this principle consists of aid to low-income earners. However, by itself, the principle does not even suggest progressivity ("taking the money where it is" may suggest progressivity). "Ability to pay" is, to begin with, a very imprecise principle that requires much specification.

However, for earned income – by far the main part of primary income on average – ability to pay is ability to earn. And ability to earn consists of earning or productive capacities. Denote as b the level of the public expenditure to be financed by taxation, and as θ_i individual i's contribution, with $\Sigma\theta_i = b$. Use the notations of Chapter 8 for individuals' productivities. With labour ℓ, individual i earns $p_i(\ell)$. The highest labour is $\widehat{\ell}$. Then, "according to ability to earn" can mean $\theta_i = \varphi[p_i(\widehat{\ell})]$ for all i, where φ is an appropriate increasing function. Possibly, $\theta_i = a \cdot p_i(\widehat{\ell})$ with $a = b/\Sigma p_i(\widehat{\ell})$. Or, in the case of unidimensional labour $\ell_i \in [0, 1]$ and linear production functions $w_i\ell_i$, $p_i(\widehat{\ell}) = w_i$, $\theta_i = \varphi(w_i)$, and in particular $\theta_i = aw_i$ with $a = b/n\overline{w}$ where $\overline{w} = (1/n)\Sigma w_i$, and $\theta_i = (b/n)(w_i/\overline{w})$.

However, a favoured interpretation of "according to ability to earn" consists of associating with a level of expenditure b a notional labour L such that $\theta_i = p_i(L)$, with $b = \Sigma p_i(L) = n \cdot \overline{p}(L)$. Labour L is a labour that, equally performed by all individuals, provides the required amount. This contrasts with another equality, equal sharing $\theta_i = b/n$, which is what "ability to pay" intends to reject. In particular, in the unidimensional linear case, $\theta_i = w_i L$ with $0 \leq L \leq 1$. Then, $b = n\overline{w}L$ or $L = b/n\overline{w}$. This is formally identical to the former solution, with $a = L$. But number a has now been given a tangible meaning. Then, again, $\theta_i = (b/n)(w_i/\overline{w})$.

In the case where expenditure b provides equal additive benefits to all individuals, that is, each individual receives value b/n, the whole scheme is redistributive. Specifically, the net benefit of each individual is $b/n - \theta_i = \overline{p}(L) - p_i(L)$, that is, the net transfer t_i of an ELIE with equalization labour $k = L$.

5.3. Benefit taxation, income, and distribution

5.3.1. The principle of benefit taxation

Benefit taxation is a priori neither based on income nor distributive. It is based on individuals' benefits from the public expenditures. If each individual paid the value these services have for her, the expenditures and their financing would be distributionally neutral. There often is, in fact, a surplus to be distributed because the sum of the individuals' willingnesses to pay for the services they receive from these expenditures generally exceeds the cost covered by the taxes. When the goods provided are public goods (collective consumption), this surplus sharing is not a priori defined, but process-freedom suggests solving this question by a "liberal social contract" (the taxes are the putative voluntary contributions in a notional agreement among the directly concerned persons – see Chapter 3). These taxes are to be seen as prices for the public services. They provision the budget of the "allocation branch" of the public sector, while our present concern is the conceptually distinct "distribution branch" (using Richard Musgrave's terms). These taxes, equal or closely related to users' values of the uses of the public services, have a priori no reason to be related to incomes. However, there can be some relation between these values and incomes. Moreover, some expenditures specifically aim at, or consist of, redistribution.

5.3.2. Income-related benefit taxation

Some public expenditures serve more people with low incomes or wealth. When they are tailored for this purpose, they should be considered along with redistributive transfers to be discussed shortly. However, globally and on average, individuals with higher income or wealth tend to benefit more from public services. They have more wealth and activities directly or indirectly taking advantage of these services or equipments. They have more property to protect, more cars or car trips using public roads, more years in higher education for their children, more property in firms benefiting from public research, on average more interest in museums or subsidized art; public amenities are better in rich neighbourhoods than in poor ones; and so on. Hence, globally and on average, benefit taxation tends to be positively related to income or wealth. Therefore, income could be taken, as a rough proxy, as base for benefit taxation. However, this seems to tend to lead to an approximately proportional tax, rather than to a progressive one. Yet, benefit from public services or infrastructures often requires a minimum of complementary private means: at least one car for using roads with private cars, at least a first year in higher education, and so on. Hence, the value of the services provided by a public service to an individual as a function of her income is, roughly, a linear function above an income threshold (which a priori differs across services and can be zero). Adding these values for each level of income for all public services yields the overall tax schedule giving the individual's tax as a function of her income. This addition of these specific schedules which are linear above a threshold gives a total schedule which is a concave and piecemeal linear function of income. That is, this "benefit income tax" is progressive with sorts of income "brackets," having increasing constant rates from one to the next. This somehow resembles actual income tax schedules.[3]

5.3.3. Collective gift-giving

Finally, benefit taxation is distributionally neutral by definition ... except when the expenditure consists of subsidies (or other aid) specifically aiming at a distributive objective. Then, the "benefit," apart from this aid, consists in this aid being desired by a number of people beyond the recipients. The benefit tax is these persons' contribution to the transfer. These persons want these transfers, for reasons of altruism or of a sense of justice, and they pay for them. This could a priori be achieved by private gifts, either direct or through charitable institutions. However, there are two reasons for a realization by the public sector. One is that, commonly, several (possibly many) givers want the situation of the same receivers to improve. This is *collective gift-giving*.[4] Then, the recipients' situation is a public good for the possible givers.[5] It is, more specifically, a nonexcludable public good because excluding could only mean hiding information about the improvement of the receiver's situation. This very particular kind of "exclusion" could not be used for demanding payment since the person wants the aidee to be aided, not just knowing how much she is. Moreover, this ignorance *ipso facto* undercuts the actual concern and motivation to give. And if the corresponding voluntary gift then is forcefully taken from the ignorant giver, this has to be done by a public sector because there is no longer a conditional exchange. With information of the givers and

---

[3] The remarks of this paragraph are developed in Kolm 1985a, Chapter 16.

[4] For a full analysis and applications of collective gift-giving, see Kolm 1984a, 1985a, 1987e,f,g,h, 1989c, 2000a.

[5] The complex of possible motivations in giving and, in particular, in collective giving is analyzed in Kolm 1984a. This includes people particularly valuing their own giving for enhancing or maintaining their self-image in their own eyes, norm following, imitation, and so on.

nonexclusion, the realization of this collective gift-giving again has to be enforced by a public sector for the classical reason of avoiding the free riding of this public good. Spontaneous, private sustainability of such an arrangement extending in time, where each would give in order that the others continue to give – a classical sequential game – is often jeopardized by the large number of participants, which prevents retaliation to be specifically aimed at punishing a particular free rider and requires coordinated punishing. Now, the most common situation is that of individuals relatively selfish where each is ready to give only relatively little for the receiver to receive some amount. This entails that the cogivers should be in relatively large number. This also generally forbids direct agreements leading to private contracts to jointly give to the recipients. Finally, in a large society, the givers often do not know the needy recipients, and this very information would also constitute a public good for the givers. Private charitable organizations can help in this respect, but the optimality of their action is not guaranteed (it depends on their motivations, on the structure of this "industry," and on other factors).

6. THE PROBLEMS WITH INCENTIVE-LIMITED INCOME EGALITARIANISM

Actual income egalitarianism is commonly presented as an ideal of income equality limited by the resulting disincentive effects. This view has been found to raise a number of doubts and questions about its meaning, relevance, application, truthfulness, and necessity. Since it appears to be widespread and central in many conceptions, let us gather, complete, consider more closely, recapitulate, and summarize the questions it raises.

Income egalitarianism is the view that income inequalities are *prima facie* morally unjustified. This is the classical, standard view of the rather far left of the political spectrum.[6] We will note, however, that this view is also often present in many people's minds, although as only part of their overall moral judgment about distributive justice. Income egalitarianism is notably applied to earned income. There, this view basically means that differences in earning capacities do not *prima facie* constitute a good reason for differences in disposable income or consumption. This is, for instance, the view of philosopher John Rawls. The conclusion should be an equalization of incomes. However, if earned incomes are equally redistributed, no labour for earning an income will be individually freely supplied in a nonsmall society. "Individually" means short of a binding agreement among workers, which may be excluded for practical reasons due to lack of means of coercion or to difficulties of collective agreements among numerous agents. Individuals freely working so that others also continue working later – a classical repeated-game logic – is bound to not work either because of the large number

---

[6] A more radical classical position objects to markets and favors reciprocities, giving, or Kropotkin's "taking from the heap" and adding to it, at least for satisfying parts of needs and desires (see the analyses in Kolm 1984a).

of people: punishing individuals who do not work by not working cannot be aimed at these specific "free riders" and would require agreement among many "punishers" (an agreement which raises precisely the same difficulties as those it intends to solve for the initially considered agreement).

A classical answer of the "authoritarian left" has been to impose labour supply. From a requirement of equality, it will be equal labour. There will be equal labour and equal pay (or equally redistributed pay). This situation, however, will generally be Pareto inefficient because people have different preferences with respect to labour, leisure, and consumption. Moreover, free labour supply may also be desired or required for several possible reasons. Free labour supply can be a direct moral requirement, as an application of act-freedom and basic rights. It can also be required for the informational efficiency provided by the decentralized use of information about individuals' productive capacities and preferences as regards labour and leisure. Free labour supply can also use the efficiency of motivation and responsibility which is undercut by the fact that labour is required. Relatedly, required labour cannot be monitored and controlled in detail, notably as concerns intensity, effort, adaptation, initiative, and so on. In fact, it may finally just not be actually possible to impose labour performed, either for practical reasons or as a result of the social or political forces in society.

With free labour supply, a possible solution consists of withdrawing to only partial equalization. The result roughly resembles actual practice. Scholars commonly explain this practice in this way, in holding that equalization is not stronger so as to limit its disincentive effects – this view will shortly be objected to on several grounds. Along this line, Rawls replaces an ideal equality by the inequality of the maximin of his "difference principle" in order to use incentives to produce – which also means reducing disincentives.[7]

These views, however, are problematic for the following reasons:

1) The disincentive effects are not so obvious, as it has already been suggested. The income effect induces the high-income earners, whose income is reduced, to work more, and they roughly are the more productive people. They may even consider working more just for paying the tax. Moreover, price effects can often be more or less manipulated in such a way that they induce higher labour. For instance, if the distribution is polarized into relatively similar high incomes and low incomes, respectively, then the price effect of transfers from high to low incomes boosts the labour supply of the low-income earners when their subsidy is an increasing function of income, and of high-income earners when their tax is a decreasing function of income (for instance, an increasing function of the gap between the income and a higher given level).[8] Note that the classical income tax, an increasing function of each income, has the reverse effect, that

---

[7] Rawls' metric is not income but an index of "primary goods" one of which is income (see a discussion in Chapter 16 and in Kolm 1996a, Chapter 8).
[8] See also Chapter 13.

is, a price effect inducing lower labour. This is also the case for subsidies of "negative income taxes" or "income tax credits," which augment low incomes by a fraction of the gap to a higher level (a minimum guaranteed income is the particular case where this gap is fully filled – thus inducing abstinence from any work that would earn less than this level). However, these effects result from the choice of the specific modalities of taxes based on income. In the end, the only disincentive effect that is always unavoidable is that of the income effect for people who receive subsidies. These generally are the individuals with the lowest productive capacities, and hence the global effect is likely to be low. And even this effect may not be manifested because of social reasons for working, habit, and the organization of employment (which often offers full-time occupations only).

2) Lower labour is higher leisure which people enjoy and choose. And free choice (and Pareto efficiency) implies that people equally value both in the neighbourhood of their choice. Hence, a priori, lower labour cannot be regretted without also rejoicing for higher leisure. Rejecting this view would constitute "work ethics." It might sometimes have some moral, psychological, or sociological reason when applied to aid inducing an absence of labour (social integration and responsibility, effect on the family, etc.). Yet, *prima facie*, it constitutes problematic moralistic paternalism.

3) This shows that the drawback of the considered policies is Pareto inefficiency rather than disincentive per se and the effect on output.

4) Pareto inefficiency is due to price effects. It is absent with lump-sum taxes and subsidies. This is, in particular, the case of taxes and subsidies based on the value of given productive capacities, whose reasons for macrojustice have been shown, while the issue of knowing these values has been discussed in Chapter 10.

5) In particular, since income egalitarians usually also admit that people who work more are entitled to receiving compensation for doing so, the most faithful implementation of their idea is not the equalization of earned incomes, but, rather, ELIE with an equalization labour in the neighbourhood of the lowest normal labour, as has been shown in Section 2. One consequence is that, as all ELIE schemes, this one entails no wasteful and disincentive price effect and no Pareto inefficiency.

6) Moreover, a less extreme and more common opinion feels that income egalitarianism has part of the moral truth, but only part of it. It feels that self-ownership also has some legitimacy. This more "centrist" and widely held view is the first reason for the adoption of only partial income equalization. The desire to limit disincentives (and also Pareto-inefficiency in the measure in which this is understood) is often present, as shown by the discussions about the rates of the highest brackets of the income tax or about the possible labour disincentive effects of subsidies to low-income earners. However, this is a secondary reason compared with the ethical one for restraining redistribution. In addition,

disincentive results from the chosen mode of realization of partial income equalization, which is the partially equalizing redistribution of earned income. This entails a degree of Pareto-inefficiency. That is, other possible solutions can better satisfy everyone. This conclusion may be affected if people's moral views are integrated among their preferences along with their common – and notably self-interested – economic concerns. But this inefficiency in fact disappears when the conclusion noted in the previous paragraph is introduced.

7) Indeed, since the most appropriate conception of full income egalitarianism is ELIE with an equalization labour in the neighbourhood of standard actual labours, and full self-ownership amounts to an ELIE with zero equalization labour, partial income equalitarianism making room for some self-ownership is naturally realized by ELIE with a lower equalization labour. This is the standard ELIE. It happens to create no disincentive and wasteful price effect and no Pareto-inefficiency. It is full equalization of part of earned income, rather than partial equalization of all earned income.

7. CONCLUSION

In the end, income egalitarians want income equality and believe that this ideal has to be limited because of disincentive or incentive effects (with free labour supply). However, most of them are also morally concerned by differences in labour. Then, the best specification of their full ideal is an ELIE distribution with an equalization labour close to the lowest normal full labour (k^e). This scheme entails no inefficiency-generating disincentive effects. At any rate, the actual reason for limiting income equalization is much less disincentive (and inefficiency) than a compromise between the basic ethics of income egalitarianism and of self-ownership. The classical principle of taxation according to "ability to pay," which is ability to earn for earned income, also leads to ELIE-like structures. And the opposite, nonredistributive principle of "benefit taxation" de facto roughly leads to taxation somewhat progressive with respect to income.

This kind of consideration of people's moral views is required by the general principle of endogenous social choice, which derives social-ethical solutions from the opinions of individuals and society. However, this consideration should be full and analytical, because popular views are not uncommonly unaware or mistaken about the implication of their basic moral stance. The issue of income justice has provided instances of this situation.

Since the full view of the most extreme income egalitarianism is best represented by a particular ELIE distribution, more moderate global egalitarianisms naturally correspond to ELIE distributions with lower equalization labours (the issue of specific egalitarianism, demanding equality for several goods, will be discussed in Chapter 16).[9] These positions can correspond to personal opinions or political

[9] See also Kolm 1977a, 1996b.

compromises, or to the social-ethical solutions discussed and derived in Part IV of this study. Actually, an equalization of about half standard labour duration corresponds to a very egalitarian – but realistic – position. The transition from actual fiscal practices to the appropriate ones can be done through reforms of the income tax, of the main subsidies supporting low incomes or earnings, and of the financing of public expenditures in general. In particular, the base of the income tax should shift from earned incomes to incomes that can be earned with a given notional labour, and hence to earning capacities and wage rates properly understood (see Chapter 10). The system of aids and supports should be similarly modified, as described in Chapter 7. Then, when overall distribution is specifically taken care of, particular public expenditures should be more financed through specific benefit taxation, which can be more or less separated from or aggregated to other taxes and subsidies. The strategy of fiscal improvement and reform in the direction of the obtained structure will be precisely discussed in Chapter 27.

12

General equal labour income equalization: The model

1. THE GENERAL CASE

The formalization of labour and productivity set up in Chapter 8 permits the precise presentation of the logic of the properties discussed in Chapter 7, in cases more general than those where labour is representable by a quantity or duration (possibly adjusted for differences in other characteristics) and output is proportional to it, which were the focus of Chapter 9. This is the topic of the present section, whereas Section 2 comes back to the case of unidimensional labour, but with a general production function, a case which will find an application in the treatment of involuntary unemployment in the next chapter.

1.1. The solution

Individuals in number n indexed by i each have a labour denoted as a set ℓ_i of chosen characteristics. Individual i working ℓ_i earns $p_i(\ell_i)$, where $p_i()$ is her production function. We have $p_i(0) = 0$ ($\ell_i = 0$ means that there is no labour: its duration is zero and the other characteristics are undetermined).

The obtained distributive justice consists of the equal sharing of the rent-rights in given productive capacities, that is, of the value of the production functions $p_i()$. The value of these functions consists of the fact that they yield both income for labour and leisure for the labour necessary for obtaining a given output or income. This distributive allocation can only be in terms of the goods considered in the problem: income (or consumption goods) and leisure. Let us call back to mind that income and the consumption bought with it amount to the same because of the assumption of full process-freedom; and that individual leisure is the generally multidimensional vector $\lambda = \widehat{\ell} - \ell$, where ℓ is the vector of parameters of labour characteristics and $\widehat{\ell}$ the vector of their maximal levels, as defined in Chapter 8 (these maximums are the same for all individuals, and if an individual cannot reach the maximum for one characteristic, this is described as her production function not increasing beyond this highest possible individual level: inability to work more is described as inability to earn more by working more; the maximum for each characteristic will be at least as high as it is for each individual, but its exact level will have no consequence). Moreover, individual i receiving an initial allocation of leisure μ_i means that she a priori yields the product of the corresponding labour $\widehat{\ell} - \mu_i$.

Full process-freedom implies that each individual i is free to choose her labour ℓ_i and receives the proceeds $p_i(\ell_i)$, given her initial distributive assets or liabilities. This initial distributive allocation is a priori in the form of income η_i and leisure μ_i for individual i. The rationality principle of identical treatment of identicals in the relevant characteristics[1] yields the identity of the individual bundles (η_i, μ_i), say $\eta_i = \eta$ and $\mu_i = \mu$ for all i. Denote as $k = \widehat{\ell} - \mu$ the labour corresponding to leisure μ. That is, individual i a priori transfers income $p_i(k)$ and receives income η, that is, receives the net transfer $\tau_i = \eta - p_i(k)$, a receipt if $\tau_i > 0$ and a payment of $-\tau_i$ if $\tau_i < 0$.

Given this basis, individual i chooses to work ℓ_i and earns $p_i(\ell_i)$. Her final disposable income is $y_i = p_i(\ell_i) + \tau_i$. Since production has to equal consumption in this closed economy, $\Sigma y_i = \Sigma p_i(\ell_i)$. Therefore, $\Sigma \tau_i = 0$, or $n\eta = \Sigma p_i(k)$, and hence $\eta = (1/n)\Sigma p_i(k) = \overline{p}(k)$, and $\tau_i = t_i$ defined as $t_i = \overline{p}(k) - p_i(k)$. Individual i's disposable income finally is

$$y_i = p_i(\ell_i) + t_i = p_i(\ell_i) - p_i(k) + \overline{p}(k).$$

This constitutes an equal sharing of the possible products of the same labour k, the *equalization labour*. In this general ELIE scheme, individual i yields her *equalization income* $p_i(k)$ and receives the *average equalization income* $\overline{p}(k) = (1/n)\Sigma p_i(k)$, that is, receives the net transfer

$$t_i = \overline{p}(k) - p_i(k),$$

which is, for a public distribution, a subsidy if $t_i > 0$ and a tax of $-t_i$ if $t_i < 0$.

The limiting case where, for all individual i, $k = p_i(k) = \overline{p}(k) = t_i = 0$ and $y_i = p_i(\ell_i)$ is full self-ownership.

We have $\Sigma t_i = 0$, and $t_i \gtrless 0$ according as $p_i(k) \lessgtr \overline{p}(k)$.

1.2. Properties

These transfers are also equivalent to each individual i yielding to each other the fraction $1/n$ of her equalization income, since

$$t_i = \Sigma_{j \neq i}(1/n) \cdot p_j(k) - (n-1) \cdot (1/n) \cdot p_i(k).$$

This is the aspect of *balanced reciprocity* of the distribution.

If $p_i(k) \leq \overline{p}(k)$, $t_i \geq 0$, and, since $p_i(\ell_i) \geq 0$ for all ℓ_i, $y_i \geq 0$ for all l_i, and in particular for $\ell_i = 0$ where $p_i = 0$ and $y_i = y_i^o = t_i$. If $p_i(k) < \overline{p}(k)$, if individual

---

[1] See Kolm 1971 [1998], Foreword, Section 5.

i does not work she receives an unemployment income

$$y_i^o = t_i = \overline{p}(k) - p_i(k) > 0.$$

If $p_i(\ell_i)$ is the technical production function (see Chapter 8 and also Chapter 13), there is no "involuntary unemployment" of individual i (at least if one does not have $p_i(\ell_i) \equiv 0$). Voluntary unemployment entails no Pareto inefficiency. If a *workfare rule* forbids that an individual receive an income when she is voluntarily unemployed, an ELIE scheme obeys this rule only if $p_i(k) < \overline{p}(k)$ for no individual i, hence $p_i(k) \geq \overline{p}(k)$ for all i, and therefore $p_i(k) = \overline{p}(k)$ for all i. This is satisfied by $k = 0$, and in general solely by this solution, which is full self-ownership.

If $p_i(k) > \overline{p}(k)$ and individual i has no other resources, and hence is submitted to the constraint $y_i \geq 0$, she must choose a labour ℓ_i that satisfies

$$p_i(\ell_i) \geq p_i(k) - \overline{p}(k).$$

If each individual i has a *right to idleness*, that is, she should be able to choose $\ell_i = 0$, then $y_i \geq 0$ entails $p_i(k) \leq \overline{p}(k)$ for all i, which implies $p_i(k) = \overline{p}(k)$ for all i. This is satisfied by $k = 0$, and in general only for this case, which is full self-ownership.

Finally, denote $p_i^m = \max_{\ell_i} p_i(\ell_i)$ individual i's maximal earnings, and $\overline{p}^m = (1/n) \Sigma\, p_i^m$ the average maximal earnings, which is also the average maximal income since incomes are earnings plus or minus the transfers of a balanced set. A *right of each individual to be able to have a disposable income of $\overline{p}^m$* implies that there exist possible individual labours ℓ_i^* such that $p_i(\ell_i^*) + t_i \geq \overline{p}^m$ for all i. Since $\Sigma t_i = 0$, this implies $\Sigma\, p_i(\ell_i^*) \geq n\overline{p}^m = \Sigma\, p_i^m$, and hence, $p_i(\ell_i^*) = p_i^m$ for all i, since $p_i(\ell_i^*) \leq p_i^m$ for each i. Then, $t_i = \overline{p}^m - p_i^m$ for each i, since we have both $t_i \geq \overline{p}^m - p_i^m$ and hence $t_i - \overline{p}^m + p_i^m \geq 0$ for all i, and $\Sigma(t_i - \overline{p}^m + p_i^m) = 0$ because $\Sigma t_i = 0$ and $\Sigma(p_i^m - \overline{p}^m) = 0$. This is maximal earnings or income equalization.

With full self-ownership, $k = 0$, individuals with $p_i(\ell_i)$ low for all ℓ_i have a low income; and if, for two individuals i and j, $p_i(\ell) > p_j(\ell)$ for all $\ell \neq 0$, then individual i's domain of choice of income and leisure includes that of individual j, and she is outcome-freer.

Note that the three conditions considered (workfare, idleness, and maximal income) refer to hypothetical choices by the agents whose actual choices may be different.

2. THE UNIDIMENSIONAL CASE

If ℓ_i is unidimensional, $p_i(\ell_i)$ will be nondecreasing (see Chapter 8). The condition $y_i \geq 0$ writes $p_i(\ell_i) \geq p_i(k) - \overline{p}(k)$ and requires $\ell_i \geq \ell_i^o$ defined by the equation

$$p_i(\ell_i^o) = p_i(k) - \overline{p}(k).$$

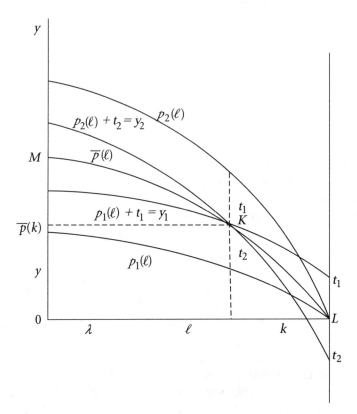

Figure 12–1. The geometry of ELIE: general case.

This will generally determine a single level ℓ_i^o, positive if $p_i(k) > \overline{p}(k)$. Then the condition $y_i \geq 0$ implies $\ell_i \geq \ell_i^o$ with the necessary minimum labour $\ell_i^o > 0$.

A "right to idleness," or a "workfare rule" for voluntary unemployment, generally implies $k = 0$ and full self-ownership, as in the general case just discussed. The effects of full self-ownership on poverty and on inequality in outcome-freedom are also as with the general multidimensional case.

Consider, moreover, that the variable ℓ_i is a duration of labour, possibly adjusted for the other chosen characteristics of labour as described in Chapter 8. Let us choose the maximal labour as unit, and so ℓ_i denotes the laboured fraction of time, with $0 \leq \ell_i \leq 1$. Then, $\lambda_i = 1 - \ell_i$ is the corresponding leisure. If individual i chooses $\ell_i = 1$, she obtains her maximal earnings $p_i^m = p_i(1)$ and her maximal disposable income $v_i = p_i(1) - p_i(k) + \overline{p}(k)$. We have $p_i(1) \geq p_i(k)$ and hence $v_i \geq 0$. Moreover, $\Sigma v_i = \Sigma p_i(1)$, and hence, for the averages, $\overline{v} = (1/n)\Sigma v_i = \overline{p}(1) = \overline{p}^m$, the average maximal income and earnings. Then, $v_i \gtrless \overline{p}(1)$ depending on $p_i(1) - p_i(k) \gtrless \overline{p}(1) - \overline{p}(k)$.

If every individual has the right to be able to obtain average maximal income, $v_i \geq \overline{p}(1)$ for all i. Hence, $v_i = \overline{p}(1)$ for all i since $\overline{v} = \overline{p}(1)$. This implies $\overline{p}(1) - \overline{p}(k) = p_i(1) - p_i(k)$ for all i, which is satisfied for $k = 1$, and in general for this level of k only. This is maximal earnings or income equalization. This is a particular case of the more general one considered earlier (with the multidimensional case, where the individuals explicitly choose the whole set of labour characteristics).

With maximal income equalization and $k = 1$, the minimal necessary labour ℓ_i^o satisfies $p_i(\ell_i^o) = p_i(1) - \overline{p}(1)$. The higher the "final productivity" $p_i(1) - p_i(\ell)$ for given ℓ, the higher ℓ_i^o is for given $\overline{p}(1)$. This corresponds to Dworkin's suggestion of the "slavery of the talented." However, high "final productivity" tends to be at odds with the standard tendency of decreasing returns in the individual's production – described by a concave function $p_i(\ell)$.

Finally, if, for two individuals i and j, one has $p_i(1) - p_i(\ell) > p_j(1) - p_j(\ell)$ for all ℓ such that $1 > \ell > \ell_i^o$, then, with maximal income equalization with $p_i^m > 0$, $y_i < y_j$ for each given $\ell = \ell_i = \ell_j$ such that $y_i > 0$, $\ell_i > \ell_j$ for each given $y = y_i = y_j$, such that $0 \leq y < \overline{p}(1)$, individual i's domain of free choice of income and leisure is included in that of individual j, and she is "outcome less free."

Figure 12–1 shows all these cases. The axes respectively bear leisure λ from 0 to 1, and hence labour ℓ from point L such that $0L = 1$ and to the left, and income (or consumption) y. Various curves representing individual production functions or productivities $p_i(\ell)$, that is, earned incomes as a function of labour, are drawn, as is the average productivity curve representing $\overline{p}(\ell)$. All these curves pass through point L with $\ell = 0$ and $p_i(0) = \overline{p}(0) = 0$. They intersect the income axis for the maximal earned incomes $p_i(1)$ and $\overline{p}(1)$. The point on this axis with income $\overline{p}(1)$ is denoted as M. The average productivity curve $\overline{p}(\ell)$ runs from L to M.

Individual i's income curve, describing her available income as a function of her labour (or leisure) is the vertical translation by t_i of her productivity curve, since $y_i = p_i(\ell) + t_i$. Then, $t_i = y_i^o$ is the ordinate of this curve for $\ell = 0(\lambda = 1)$. The ordinate for $\ell = 1(\lambda = 0)$ is $v_i = p_i(1) + t_i$. This curve intersects the leisure-labour axis for $\ell = \ell_i^o$.

For $\ell = k$, $y_i = \overline{p}(k)$. Hence, all these curves pass through the same point K of coordinates $\ell = k$ and $y = \overline{p}(k)$. This point is on the average productivity curve. For full self-ownership, it is in L ($\ell = 0$, $\lambda = 1$). For maximal income equalization, it is in M ($\ell = 1$, $\lambda = 0$).

All the previous discussions can be presented with Figure 12–1.

13

Involuntary unemployment

1. THE ESSENCE OF THE QUESTION

An individual may face a situation of the labour market where she cannot work more than a certain level. If this level is zero, she is fully involuntarily unemployed. If not, and if she accepts this level and would like to work more, she is in partial involuntary unemployment. This partial unemployment can affect any of the productive characteristics of labour: duration, level of qualification, intensity, etc. This can also be manifested as a limit on the sales of the product of labour (no buyer, or other quantitative or qualitative limits).

The ELIE distribution distributes the value of individuals' earning capacities due to their productive capacities. The noted constraints affect these earnings capacities: if the labour proposed by the worker exceeds the constraint, the earnings are limited to those obtained by the accepted and actually performed labour, defined by the constraint (these labour and earnings may be zero). Hence, earnings as a function of actual labour are not defined for labours beyond the limit, and earnings as a function of proposed labour present this threshold at the earning level of the highest possible labour. This constraint limits the individual's earning capacities, and it is imposed on the individual. Therefore, it should be incorporated in an ELIE distribution. However, the individuals' production functions used in ELIE theory give each individual's earnings as a function of her labour for all labours, and they are nondecreasing functions of the productive characteristics of labour. The solution consists in considering production functions giving the individual's earnings as a function of the labour she proposes ("labour supply") rather than of the labour she actually performs when they differ. This description amounts to assimilating not being able to work more with not being able to earn more by working – which leads an individual working for money not to work more.

One of the results that will be obtained, for labour representable by the adequate unidimensional quantity (see Chapter 8), is that *a person involuntarily unemployed with a labour lower than the equalization labour obtains a disposable income equal*

212

to the average equalization income. This holds in particular if this person is *fully involuntarily unemployed.* Therefore, this complete involuntary unemployment amounts to the case where the person's production function has value zero: there is no difference, in the end, whether the impossibility to obtain an income is due to the productive capacities (as valued by the market) or to the constraint of the market; someone who cannot sell her labour or its product is equally aided, regardless of the reason for this impossibility. Moreover, in the case of partial unemployment, *if the person chooses to work less than the labour available, her income decreases by the amount of the loss of output.* Hence, the ELIE aid induces *no wasteful disincentive.*

However, as Section 2 will remind us, this ELIE treatment will only apply to residual involuntary unemployment, after its reduction by full process-freedom and the overall distributive policy which undercut wage rigidities that cause it, and by macroeconomic and educational policies, and given unemployment insurance. Section 3 then defines the basic concepts of the real and technical individual production functions. The corresponding application of ELIE is presented in Section 4, and Section 5 presents its various properties.

2. INVOLUNTARY UNEMPLOYMENT POLICIES

However, before considering the application of ELIE to involuntary unemployment, one must consider whether this problem will reach the application of this scheme with the correct overall policy. Indeed, other aspects of the optimization tend to restrict involuntary unemployment, its causes, or its effects.

Process-freedom promotes perfect markets, and hence the decrease or disappearance of a number of microeconomic causes of the price or wage rigidities or mark-ups that underlie and cause involuntary unemployment. This refers to both noncompetitive practices in markets and notably labour markets, and to public actions such as minimum wage laws or various taxes based on the wage bill. Market or official downward wage rigidities aim at sustaining wage earners' income. Their intention is distributive, and effects of wage levels can concern overall distribution. Now, ELIE aims at achieving global distributive justice. In particular, it has been shown in Chapter 7 that everyone gains from replacing minimal wage rules or laws by a standard ELIE scheme. Hence, a role of ELIE is to replace such market rigidities or public measures as means of distribution, and this replacement suppresses the induced involuntary unemployment.

Moreover, the effects of involuntary unemployment on individuals can a priori be taken care of by unemployment insurance, a specific remedy.

Finally, it is not superfluous to recall that reducing involuntary unemployment is an aim of a number of policies: macroeconomic policy to begin with, and specific policies concerning the labour market and education.

However, residual involuntary unemployment can be incorporated in the treatment of productive inequalities by ELIE, as indicated in this chapter.

3. REAL AND TECHNICAL PRODUCTION FUNCTIONS

The *real production function* of an individual describes the income this individual can obtain for each of her possible labour proposals. The *technical production function* of the individual is this function when there is no involuntary unemployment for this individual. In the former case, if the individual's labour proposal exceeds the labour demanded by employers or buyers of labour's products, for any productive characteristic of her labour, actual labour is this demand and income is the corresponding pay.

We have noticed that income is the relevant output as a result of process-freedom. Involuntary unemployment can affect any of the productive characteristics of labour (duration, intensity, qualification level). Involuntary unemployment can be complete, and in this case, the individual's real production function consists of a zero income for all labours. When the constraints on labour are those that can create partial involuntary unemployment, the individual can freely choose to work less, and then she is not actually involuntarily unemployed (this can happen with any of the productive characteristics of labour, and the situation can be different for various characteristics).

Formally, let ℓ denote the labour of an individual, and $P(\ell)$ her technical production function.

Consider, first, the case of unidimensional labour (see Chapter 8). A particular possible form of $P(\ell)$ is the linear one: $P(\ell) = w\ell$, and ℓ generally is labour duration. If there can be involuntary unemployment, denote as $\tilde{\ell}$ the highest labour available for the individual. If ℓ denotes the individual's actual labour, $\ell \leq \tilde{\ell}$. If $\tilde{\ell} = 0$, the involuntary unemployment is complete. If $\ell = \tilde{\ell}$ and the individual would like to work $\ell'' > \tilde{\ell}$, there is involuntary unemployment.[1]

The "real production function" then is defined as $p(\ell) = P(\ell)$ for $\ell \leq \tilde{\ell}$ and $p(\ell) = P(\tilde{\ell})$ for $\ell > \tilde{\ell}$. That is, $p(\ell) = \min[P(\ell), P(\tilde{\ell})]$. The real production function is the *truncation* at $\tilde{\ell}$ (and $P(\tilde{\ell})$) of the technical production function. Then, of course, $\ell = \tilde{\ell}$ describes labour *proposed* by the worker. Figure 13–1 shows the technical production function $P(\ell)$, the added unemployment constraint $\ell \leq \tilde{\ell}$, and the resulting real production function $p(\ell)$.

Consider now the case of multidimensional labour, $\ell = \{\ell^j\}$, where j denotes a productive characteristic of labour and ℓ^j its level. The labour constraints are $\ell^j \leq \tilde{\ell}^j$ (this can be assumed for all j, given that this constraint cannot be effective if $\tilde{\ell}^j \geq \hat{\ell}^j$ — the maximum, see Chapter 8), denoted as $\ell \leq \tilde{\ell}$ if $\tilde{\ell} = \{\tilde{\ell}^j\}$. Then, denote $\ell^{j\prime} = \ell^j$ if $\ell^j \leq \tilde{\ell}^j$ and $\ell^{j\prime} = \tilde{\ell}^j$ if $\ell^j > \tilde{\ell}^j$, that is, $\ell^{j\prime} = \min(\ell^j, \tilde{\ell}^j)$ and

---

[1] We assume here individuals working for income. Hence, an individual would not want to work more if this does not give her higher earnings.

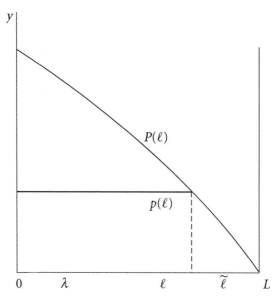

Figure 13–1. The two production functions.

$\ell' = \{\ell^{j'}\}$. If $P(\ell)$ again denotes the technical production function, the real production function is $p(\ell) = P(\ell')$. Then, if $\ell^j > \tilde{\ell}^j$, the proposed level ℓ^j is not used and actual labour only has the level $\tilde{\ell}^j$ of this characteristic.[2]

For complete involuntary unemployment, $\tilde{\ell} = 0$ (that is, the corresponding labour duration is zero), and hence, for all ℓ, $\ell' = 0$ and $p(\ell) = 0$.

4. ELIE

Then, ELIE applies with the individual i's real production functions $p_i(\ell_i)$. If k denotes the equalization labour and $\overline{p}(k) = (1/n)\Sigma p_i(k)$, individual i receives the net transfer $t_i = \overline{p}(k) - p_i(k)$, a subsidy if $t_i > 0$ and a tax of $-t_i$ if $t_i < 0$, and her disposable income becomes

$$y_i = p_i(\ell_i) - p_i(k) + \overline{p}(k).$$

If there is complete involuntary unemployment for individual i, $p_i(\ell_i) = p_i(k) = 0$ and $y_i = \overline{p}(k)$.

First, consider the case of unidimensional labour. The constraint on labour is $\ell_i \leq \tilde{\ell}_i$. If $k \geq \tilde{\ell}_i$, $p_i(k) = p_i(\tilde{\ell}_i)$ from the definition of p_i. If there is involuntary unemployment (partial if $\tilde{\ell}_i > 0$), then $\ell_i = \tilde{\ell}_i$. Then, $p_i(\ell_i) = p_i(\tilde{\ell}_i)$, and therefore, $y_i = \overline{p}(k)$, the announced result.

---

[2] Constraints on labour associating several productive characteristics of labour with possible substitutions (or complementarities) can be found, but they do not seem to constitute a sufficiently widespread phenomenon to deserve explicit consideration here (where the topic is macrojustice).

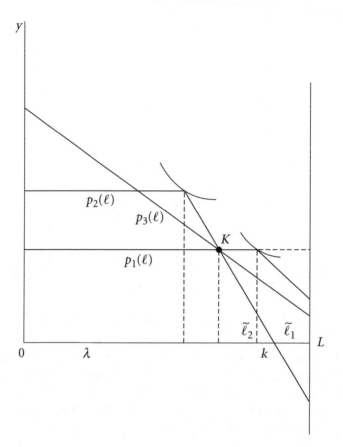

Figure 13–2. Unemployment ELIE.

If, moreover, the individual chooses to work $\ell_i < \widetilde{\ell}_i \leq k$, then $y_i = p_i(\ell_i) - p_i(\widetilde{\ell}_i) + \overline{p}(k)$. Hence, her income diminishes by $p_i(\widetilde{\ell}_i) - p_i(\ell_i)$ from the case where she works $\widetilde{\ell}_i$, which is the loss in output. Therefore, this application of ELIE entails no waste-generating disincentive.

Figure 13–2 represents various possibilities.

Consider now the case of multidimensional labour. A productive characteristic is denoted as j, and the ℓ_i, $\widetilde{\ell}_i$ and k are now vectors of their levels: $\ell_i = \{\ell_i^j\}_j$, $\widetilde{\ell}_i = \{\widetilde{\ell}_i^j\}_j$, and $k = \{k^j\}$. For actual labour, $\ell_i^j \leq \widetilde{\ell}_i^j$. If $\widetilde{\ell}_i^j \leq k^j$ for all j, $p_i(k) = p_i(\widetilde{\ell}_i)$ from the definition of the real production function p_i. If, then, individual i is involuntarily unemployed with regard to all productive characteristics, $\ell_i = \widetilde{\ell}_i$, and $p_i(\ell_i) = p_i(\widetilde{\ell}_i)$. In this situation, $p_i(\ell_i) = p_i(k)$ and $y_i = \overline{p}(k)$: the individual's disposable income is the average equalization income. If individual i chooses to work $\ell_i^j < \widetilde{\ell}_i^j$ for some productive characteristics j, her income loses the full output lost from the previous case. Hence, this subsidy entails no waste-generating disincentive.

5. PROPERTIES

The properties of ELIE shown with general production functions in Chapter 12 apply with the real production functions. They thus need not be repeated here. The only particularities come from the constant-income parts of the real production functions, for labours higher than the constraints leading to involuntary unemployment (in any productive characteristics of labour). For example, talented people whose employment is sufficiently restricted face no necessary labour and in particular, in the theoretical case of very high equalization labour k, no "slavery" and exhaustion or starvation.

The only new parameter added consists of the labour constraint $\ell_i \leq \widetilde{\ell}_i$ (possibly multidimensional). For the sake of simplicity, let us only discuss the unidimensional case (similar phenomena will occur in the multidimensional case). The properties that are shown can fruitfully be considered geometrically in Figure 13–2.

When $\widetilde{\ell}_i \geq k$, then $p_i(k) = P_i(k)$ and $\widetilde{\ell}_i$ affects neither $\overline{p}(k)$ nor, for any individual, i', $t_{i'} = \overline{p}(k) - p_{i'}(k)$, and this holds, in particular, for t_i.

When $\widetilde{\ell}_i < k$, then $p_i(k) = P_i(\widetilde{\ell}_i)$ and $p_i(k)$, $\overline{p}(k)$ and $t_{i'}$ for all i' depend on $\widetilde{\ell}_i$. In particular,

$$t_i = (1/n)\Sigma_{i' \neq i}\, p_{i'}(k) - [1 - (1/n)]\, p_i(k).$$

Hence, for a given increasing technical production function $P_i(\ell_i)$, $p_i(k) = P_i(\widetilde{\ell}_i)$ varies as $\widetilde{\ell}_i$, and therefore t_i increases when $\widetilde{\ell}_i$ decreases. With regard to justice, this constitutes a compensation for the loss in possibilities entailed by the decrease of $\widetilde{\ell}_i$. The result, however, is that y_i for each given $\ell_i < \widetilde{\ell}_i$ increases when $\widetilde{\ell}_i$ decreases, and this holds in particular for $y_i = t_i$ for $\ell_i = 0$. Similarly, $y_i \geq 0$ or $p_i(\ell_i) + t_i \geq 0$ writes $\ell_i \geq \ell_i^o$ if $p_i(\ell_i^o) + t_i = 0$. We have $\ell_i^o < \widetilde{\ell}_i$, and when $\ell_i^o > 0$, ℓ_i^o varies as $\widetilde{\ell}_i$ does: a lower $\widetilde{\ell}_i$ entails a lower minimal necessary labour. In particular, when $\widetilde{\ell}_i$ decreases, an individual can pass from the necessity of a minimal labour ($\ell_i^o > 0$) to the possibility of choosing voluntary unemployment with an income ($t_i > 0$). An individual submitted to a labour constraint who chooses to work less benefits from this constraint becoming more stringent (the transfer compensates for restrictions in possibilities independently of the individual's choice).

*

In the end, involuntary unemployment should be treated by a number of measures some of which are implied by process-freedom, but the residual can be included within the ELIE policy with the defined real production functions of labour. There results that involuntarily unemployed individuals have a disposable income equal to the average equalization income if their unemployment is complete or, if it is partial, when it does not exceed the equalization labour.

PART THREE

COMPARISONS WITH POLICIES
AND PHILOSOPHIES

14

Comparison: General issues

1. INTRODUCTION

The obtained result – namely, the distinction of macrojustice, social freedom, the ELIE distributive scheme and, in the next part, the degree of redistribution – is derived from endogenous social choice and unanimity, along with facts and basic rationality. This result is thus obtained deductively rather than comparatively. It does not see itself as some "preferred solution." It derives from the observation of people's well-considered preferences, rather than from some moral preference of some exogenous "ethical observer" (except if she chooses to respectfully rely on people's own appropriate preferences). In particular, the ELIE distributive scheme so results from unanimity and the corresponding efficiency, and from social freedom and the classical basic rights which, at any rate, constitute the basis of modern constitutions and – one can say – modern social ethics. This constitutes its reason and justification. However, and as a consequence, it presents a number of specific (and remarkable) properties which have, in themselves, ethical meaningfulness or practical value. Yet, a number of other distributive schemes are applied or proposed by scholars or policy makers. Some are relevant for issues in microjustice or mesojustice, rather than in the field of macrojustice. However, others are applied or proposed definitely for the question of macrojustice or for occupying its field. It is probably interesting to compare these solutions and schemes to the obtained one, both for enlightening the logic of the question in providing comparisons, frame, and possibly alternatives, and for choosing actual policies.

These comparisons are performed at three levels in this volume. First, the most closely relevant comparisons are proposed alongside the discussions of the result. For instance, income taxation has been considered with income egalitarianism in Chapter 11, and with the welfarist "optimum income taxation" theory in Chapter 10 *a propos* of the issue of information. Classical liberalisms and other liberty-based ethics have been considered with social freedom and basic rights in Chapters 3 and 4. Proposals for sharing nonhuman natural resources have been discussed (Chapter 5). Second, the present Part III proposes the general relevant terms of comparisons, and specific comparisons with various schemes of aid to the poorest and with main specific egalitarian philosophies (such as those of John Rawls, Ronald Dworkin, and Michael Walzer). Finally, Part V of this study includes comparisons of the obtained results with the various social ethics that have been and can be proposed within the view of society developed by economics. This is done within an overall presentation of the essence of economics' social ethics, which may have an interest in itself and, although it is as short as possible, is nevertheless somewhat bulky. For these reasons, this presentation has been relegated in a separate and last part, after Part IV, which discusses the choice of the degree of redistribution that completes the presentation of the result.[1] In contrast, the presentation of the general practical terms of the comparisons, and of the comparisons with distributive schemes and philosophies, are shorter and show properties, illustrations, and issues of application which probably helpfully complement and enlighten the previous theoretical derivation and discussion. The present Part III thus proposes, in three chapters, the practical properties relevant for the comparison (Chapter 14), the comparison with practical redistributive schemes (Chapter 15), and the comparison with main modern egalitarian philosophies (Chapter 16).

The main issues of the comparisons are set out in this chapter. First, the main features of ELIE schemes are noted in Section 2. They include rationality, ethical meaningfulness with varied meanings, efficiency, clarity, financial balance, simplicity, availability of information, and rights to resources. The types of redistributive schemes available for comparison will then be pointed out in Section 3. They are the actual tax systems, reform proposals, welfarist optimum taxation, philosophers' proposals, and schemes of social transfers. Finally, the main terms of the comparisons are presented in Section 4, including rationale and objective, base of tax or subsidy, financial balance and comprehensiveness, incentives and disincentives, efficiency and inefficiency, availability of the required information, practical realizability, understandability, acceptability, and "psychosocial" effects.

2. PROPERTIES OF ELIE

Let us first call to mind the essential properties of ELIE, which are explicitly or implicitly presented in the foregoing chapters.

2.1. Rationality

ELIE has been derived by deduction from endogenous social choice and unanimity applied to the issue of macrojustice, which first leads to social freedom and the

---

[1] The comparison with various proposals emanating from economics was demanded by practically all the economist readers of a first version, which did not include Part V.

constitutional basic rights. It is not the offspring of intuition discovering optimality out of thin air. It is not proposed for its intrinsic properties. These properties happen to be the consequence of the deductive exercise. In particular, ELIE is not proposed for a couple of properties in forgetting about other aspects, as is the case of many reformers' proposals. Finally, ELIE is not the battered result of the cumulative historical hazards of the life of a country – as actual public finance schemes are. The resulting properties of ELIE, however, can also be appreciated in themselves. This, at least, would satisfy a most common metaethical view that says that both basic principles and consequences have to be directly and jointly considered in judging a recommendation.[2]

2.2. Ethical meaningfulness

ELIE has a number of remarkable ethical meanings, which are different although logically equivalent. The deepest probably is its resulting from consensus applied to macrojustice and hence from social freedom and basic rights. Yet, its direct ethical meanings are no less interesting. They relate to global fairness and to reciprocity and have been presented and discussed in Chapters 7, 9, and 12: *equal process-freedom and equal basic allocation; from each according to her capacities and to each equally; equal (partial) self-ownership; equal sharing of an equal share of productive capacity rents; reward according to desert for an equal labour and to merit for the rest;* for the equalization labour, *equal pay for equal work, equal average wage,* or *from each equally in labour and to each equally in money; from or to each according to the gap between her capacities and the average; general bilateral balanced labour reciprocity; from each, to each other, the product of the same labour,* or *according to her capacities; and from each, to each less productive other, according to their productivity gap; compensating lower productivity by a proportionately higher transfer.*

Moreover, ELIE implements fundamental rights: not only the classical basic rights but, more directly, rights in the given resources of society. Therefore, even though it turns out to help people with low earning capacities, its basic rationale is not assistance, charity, or grants. It thus does not have the common corresponding effects on the receiver's dignity and dependency (or at least sentiments of it). ELIE does not even result from rights to assistance, welfare, or the satisfaction of needs, which can in part also entail such negative effects. Rather, ELIE's moral references are justice, equality, equal labour reciprocity, freedom, and rights to given resources.

The actual or notional convergence of the views of the members of a society about the degree of distribution (the equalization labour) will be the topic of Part IV.

---

[2] Interactive adjustment between a principle and its consequences is the topic of Plato's "dialectics" in *The Republic.* When the consequences are specific examples of application – rather than general properties, as is the case here –, this becomes Rawls' "reflective equilibrium."

2.3. Clarity

ELIE schemes are particularly clear not only in meanings and form (see the former and following paragraphs), but also in intention and function. In this sense, it has both "intrinsic" – formal and semantic – and "extrinsic" clarity. ELIE constitutes a distributive scheme, often for application by public finances and budgets. Then, it is distinguished from the functions of the budget other than distribution, essentially its "allocative" function for financing public or publicly produced goods, optimizing externalities, and so on (there also is a macroeconomic "stabilization" function, but this can also be related to "allocation" because it constitutes indirect means for dealing with the "market failures" that cause the macroeconomic problems). That is, ELIE is the main rule for what Richard Musgrave (1959) calls the "distributive branch" of public finances. ELIE has only one objective: global (overall) distributive justice. It does not try to realize several things at once, as do present-day taxes or subsidies which mix rationales of macro and micro distributive justice, economic allocation, efficiency, stabilization, and so on, with much confusion, double counting, omissions, and ad hoc arguments, and, as a consequence, an impossibility of serious optimization. In the end, of course, ELIE has to be superimposed with the realizations of the other functions of the budget – allocation and the financing of public or publicly produced goods, and stabilization. In this synthesis, taxes and subsidies can be algebraically added and solely the result be presented to each individual, or the taxes and subsidies realizing various functions can be separated, or the payments can be global with the indication of how it results from the various functions. Clarity, honesty, and democracy require that the citizens know the reasons for their taxes and hence are shown the separation and the various reasons as precisely as possible. Yet, as a relatively secondary point, simplicity in realization leads one to favor having to write or receiving a single paycheck in the end.

2.4. Financial balance

ELIE schemes are financially balanced. Receipts equal expenditures. This is necessary for the distributive objective not to interfere with other considerations – which would have been introduced by the financing of a deficit or the use of a surplus. This balance makes a difference with distributive schemes that consider solely the structure of taxes – notably the income tax – or solely subsidies without considering their financing – notably for aids to low-income earners (or proposal to grant the same "universal basic income" to everyone).

2.5. Simplicity

The structure of ELIE, and still more of the particular case EDIE, are particularly simple. Indeed, one probably cannot find a simpler distributive scheme (full self-ownership and maximal income equalization are particular cases). A "universal basic income" is simpler in itself, but not if one considers the financing of the scheme. Equalization of a given fraction of actual incomes would not be simpler and would raise other problems such as inefficiency. This simplicity is a notable virtue for the understanding of the rule by the general citizenry – a condition for democracy, honesty, and acceptance by the people. It also is an important advantage for implementation (if we neglect lower employment for tax officials and fiscal experts and lawyers!).

2.6. Efficiency

ELIE schemes are Pareto efficient because they are based on inelastic items: individual's given productivities. In Chapter 10, we saw that elasticities that might be introduced through the estimation of the base can, in most cases, raise only minor and secondary issues (which are present with all non- per capita taxes or grants, not to mention the effects of elastic bases).

2.7. Information

The issue of information has been the specific topic of Chapter 10.[3]

3. THE VARIOUS DISTRIBUTIVE SCHEMES

The distributive schemes that have to be considered for comparison have the various following natures:

1. *Actual taxes and aids*, notably those used with an intent of global redistribution, such as the income tax and similar taxes, which can be more or less progressive.
2. *Reform proposals* that propose moderate changes in the actual tax schemes – rather than drastically different alternatives.
3. *The welfarist "optimum taxation"* proposed by economists, either based on payment or income (Kolm 1969b, 1970b, for microjustice; Mirrlees 1971, for the income tax) or based on wage rates and the value of productivities (with "practical justice" – maximin or leximin in interpersonally comparable "fundamental utility" – in Kolm 1974).
4. *Philosophers' proposals*, notably those of income egalitarians such as Rawls, Dworkin, or Walzer, or classical process liberalism represented by Nozick (see also Kolm 1985a, with, notably, "liberal social contracts" and the theory

---

[3] Moreover, a number of formal properties of ELIE schemes have been pointed out and studied in the various early analyses from 1966 to 1996 and 1997 (see Appendix A of Chapter 25). See also note 11 of Chapter 9. François Maniquet (1998a, 1998b) pointed out a set of formal properties that imply the allocation resulting from individuals' choices under an EDIE distribution. These properties can thus constitute "axioms" for this distribution. But this is not the social freedom considered here.

of liberal public economics). Facing these two polar types of "nonwelfarist" individualistic social ethics are the "welfarist" ones, used by both philosophers and economists, including "practical justice" (with ordinal preferences), the variety of utilitarianisms,[4] and the general maximization of so-called "social welfare."

5. Particular proposals or realizations for *social transfers*, notably for alleviating poverty, such as various schemes of aid, the negative income tax or "income tax credit," or the "universal basic income" (give the same amount to everyone without condition). These schemes have a particular focus and style of their own, although a "negative income tax" can result from optimum income taxation and the universal basic income has sometimes been defended on philosophical grounds (for instance, by Philippe van Parijs 1990, 1995).

6. Finally, the obtained result can more generally be systematically compared on any ground with all distributive proposals, as is shown in Part V of this study. Some principles are particular cases of the obtained result, such as classical process liberalism and full self-ownership (including Marx's theory of exploitation), income egalitarianisms, and the determination of social maximands proposed in Part IV. Liberalism can be compared with other liberty-based visions, such as Hayek's spontaneous order, Buchanan's constitutional public choice, or Rothbart's libertarianism. The obtained result can be situated within the general theory of distributive criteria, which apply an interpersonally comparative structure on the relevant "substance," such as freedom, means, income, goods, preference, and happiness or satisfaction. This issue leads notably to the comparisons of freedoms, which are either social freedom or freedom a priori defined by domains of choice, and of happiness or preferences. Freedom-based principles can take the form of equality of opportunity, and allocation according to desert, merit, or responsibility. The satisfaction of basic needs and the formation of capacities can be essential policies, in the fields of microjustice and mesojustice, which may however be superseded by the proper overall distributive justice securing incomes that informed individuals are free to spend for satisfying their needs as they see them. Finally, possible incompatibilities of valuable properties lead to theories of second-best optimality and justice. This can in particular happen, for various reasons, as concerns relevant equalities and Pareto efficiency. Among the methods of solution is the theory of "equivalence" presented at the end of Part V.

4. ISSUES: THE TERMS OF THE COMPARISON

The relevant topics for the comparisons belong to a number of different categories.

---

[4] Including "metaphorical utilitarianisms" or "utilitaromorphism" (see Kolm 1996a, Chapter 15).

4.1. General structure

A practical policy, notably a distributive policy, is a set of four elements: a *tool*, which is a function of a *base* through a *rule*, for implementing some *objective*. The tool can, in particular, consist of transfers of incomes, or goods or services taken or handed out. The best tool, base, and rule are in principle determined by the objective, given the possibilities as concerns practicalities, information, and social and political life. There may be a unique objective, or several ones, or a main one with secondary concerns. The four elements of the policy conflate in "direct" policies, such as transfers to alleviate poverty, provide a basic income, or diminish some income inequality.

4.2. Rationale and objective

A distributive scheme may have various rationales and objectives. For instance, it may aim at:

– Respecting rights, notably basic rights.
– Alleviating poverty.
– Satisfying basic needs.
– Achieving equality in something, notably in resource allocation, incomes, amounts of more or less specific goods or services, satisfaction, the satisfaction of basic needs, basic or other rights, process- and means-freedoms, or freedom of choice.
– Maximizing "social welfare."
– Maximizing social income (an objective related to classical principles of compensation or of the "surplus").
– Securing or maximizing freedom.
– Securing or maximizing social efficiency.

These various objectives sometimes only constitute different perspectives or specifications (for instance, the satisfaction of basic needs may specify the alleviation of poverty or be included in extended basic rights, and there are several possible types of freedoms). They have basic common points, such as the existence of an explicit or implicit ideal equality or their individualism (with a possible qualification for "social welfare"). They also sometimes have crucial basic differences, such as an emphasis on, or an ultimate reference to, general happiness or welfare, types of freedom, or various means or types of consumption (the difference between conceptions of "direct" justice will be revealed by the items that should ideally be equalized).[5] Moreover, a measure or principle can have jointly several objectives which can be related in various ways. This includes the various aims usually considered

---

[5] Direct justice is opposed to indirect or derived justice that is implied by another objective such as direct justice about other items or some properly social or collective aim (see Kolm 1996a, Chapter 1).

for actual fiscal measures and the various qualities of a policy or principle. Finally, these rationales or objectives often raise theoretical and practical issues of definition, comparison, often the definition of a metric, or actual measurement – such as for welfare, freedom, need, and so on.

4.3. The base of the policy, notably of taxes and subsidies

This base can, for instance, be income (notably earned income), capacities or their market values (wage rates), specific consumption, or needs (for subsidies). The distributive base can be the item whose ideal equality is sought after (that is, the equalizand, and the scheme then is a "directly" equalizing redistribution). This can, for example, occur for income or for the part of rent-rights in capacities that is measured in income (see Chapter 9). The distribution may, however, not be fully equalizing, because this would excessively violate some other relevant criterion, such as Pareto efficiency or when striking a balance between equalization of earnings and self-ownership. In other cases, the base of the measure is not the final objective (for instance, the objective may refer to welfare or needs and the base to income). This includes cases of "indirect" or "derived" justice. The rule has to be determined accordingly, and this optimization should also include the choice of the base. Issues of "second-best justice" are then often raised.

4.4. Financial balance and comprehensiveness

A distributive scheme may or may not be financially balanced. When it is not, it generally considers solely (or mostly) receipts or expenditures. For instance, consideration of tax progressivity considers solely fiscal receipts. On the contrary, assistance schemes consider only subsidy transfers, which are part of public expenditures. Schemes of "negative income taxes" or "income tax credit" focus on subsidies, but they relate to the resource side in presenting themselves as an extension of (positive) income taxation. ELIE schemes are financially balanced. The welfarist "optimum income taxation" of some models also are, but there is a major difference. These latter models consider the assumption of balance to be an imperfection of the model, retained for the purpose of simplification. Indeed, they have no other theory of how to (optimally) finance general public services, goods, and expenditures. By contrast, the balance of ELIE schemes is an actual virtue because their only objective is distribution: they leave the financing of other expenditures to the computation of the "allocation branch," *prima facie* according to benefit taxation (more precisely, the theory of the liberal social contract). The issue of financing is sometimes crucial. For instance, as direct computation shows, schemes of universal basic incomes are unbearably costly if they want this income to be sufficient for the poorest, and they let the poor starve if the overall cost is an actual possibility.

4.5. Incentives and disincentives

The disincentive effects of distributive schemes constitute one of their most discussed properties. They can occur both for taxes and for subsidies. The most commonly considered are the disincentive effects on labour. It is very widely expressed that the main drawback of distributive or redistributive schemes are their disincentive effects leading to lower labour and output. As a scholarly example, the reason for Rawls' "difference principle" is the disincentive effect of distribution, notably on high-income earners. This view, however, has to be strongly qualified and the question should be closely considered. The obvious image is that no labour for an income will be freely provided if earnings are equally redistributed among a nonsmall number of persons. However, even this view should be made precise, as it has already been alluded to. In the stated conditions, people have an interest in agreeing among themselves so as to provide some work and generate some income. Yet, this agreement may be prevented by transaction costs if the number of people who should agree is too high. If the agreement is made, it may have to be binding. And institutions or practical means for this coercion may not be available. However, in an ongoing process, voluntary labour can be provided by the fear that others stop working if one does. Yet, the large number of participants can make this "repeated game" solution unavailable. Indeed, a free-riding individual may not even be noticed and hence may not elicit others' retaliation; retaliation affects all others and not a specific free rider; and a single individual's retaliation may have no actual effect, and so efficient retaliation itself requires coordination among rather numerous individuals, which raises the initial difficulty. However, Chapter 11 showed that the common conception of income egalitarians is in fact richer than just income equality and that, as a result, it leads to a very different solution with almost equality in incomes and social efficiency in the relevant ELIE scheme.

Moreover, lower labour is higher leisure, which the individuals commonly appreciate and which they freely choose when they choose to work less. This free choice implies that they prefer this extra leisure to the output that this foregone labour would produce. Hence, what is relevant is a priori more Pareto inefficiency than lower output. However, since labour and output are often considered, let us focus on them. We consider, as usual, the case where there is free labour supply (this is shortly discussed). The traditional distinction between the price effect and the income effect of a tax or a subsidy is relevant here. Price effects exist only when the base is elastic. Price effects, and not income effects, are responsible for Pareto inefficiency. ELIE schemes, based on a notional given income and on the values of given productive capacities, induce no price effect and only have income effects. Therefore, they induce no Pareto inefficiency.

Through income effects, taxes induce a higher labour supply if leisure is a "normal" good and a lower one otherwise, and subsidies have the reverse effect. In the common case, leisure is a normal good. Then, through income effects, taxes tend to augment labour and output (people work more in order to compensate, at least in part, the income loss due to the tax, and perhaps to pay the tax). And the income effects of a redistribution from more productive people to less productive ones induce more of the highly valued labour of the more productive and less of the less valued labour of the less productive. These are all the effects of ELIE schemes.

The price effect of taxes and subsidies on labour and output depend on the specific modalities. Through this effect, a tax will induce higher labour and output if it is a decreasing function of these variables, for instance an increasing function of their gap to a given higher level. And a subsidy will have the same effect if it is an increasing function of labour or income. Hence, as already noted, if the income distribution is polarized with high and low levels, a redistribution from high to low can be performed in this way in increasing everybody's labour and earned income, and hence social output, through this price effect. Then, the only remaining disincentive effect of a redistribution is the income effect on the subsidy side, and it only affects the poorer people. However, if the income distribution is more continuous, a problem is raised by the link between the noted tax and subsidy schemes, with, necessarily, disincentive price effects somewhere in between. Of course, taxes increasing with income and subsidies decreasing when income increase have a disincentive price effect which can be more or less intense. For a subsidy, the worse is a guaranteed income, and schemes of "negative income tax" or "income tax credit" aim at limiting the discontinuity and the intensity of this effect.

These effects assume a free labour supply. This freedom can be a direct moral requirement, as an application of act-freedom. Free labour supply may also be a requirement for the efficient decentralization of the use of information about people's productive capacities and preferences between labour, leisure, and income. This informational advantage of free labour supply is reinforced by its permitting motivations of responsibility or favouring innovation. It may also just not be actually possible to impose labour performed, either for practical reasons or as a result of the social or political forces in society. It should also be added that the poorest's labour may be desired, as a matter of policy, for reasons such as social integration or participation, mental balance, family stability, and so on.[6]

4.6. Efficiency, inefficiency

We just recalled that the price effect of taxes or subsidies with elastic bases create Pareto inefficiencies. ELIE schemes introduce no Pareto inefficiency since their base is inelastic. Pareto inefficiency means that there exist other possible social states preferred by everyone (with the possible indifference of some). It thus violates the basic principle of unanimity (see the discussion in Chapter 1). However,

---

[6] "Work ethics" and "workfare" have been discussed in Chapter 7.

implementing these other states may raise problems, notably of information (the discussion of Chapter 10, however, tends to conclude that such informational issues should be specifically considered rather than asserted off-hand).

4.7. Information gathering

Each distributive scheme requires its proper information. The base has to be estimated, whereas the rates, rules, or schedules result from the definition of the policy. Chapter 10 has discussed the question of gathering the required information about the base in the case of the value of productive capacities. Along the way, it has presented a number of remarks valid for other bases. A large part of the information-gathering issue belongs to the routine of tax administrations.

More precisely, the various difficulties, costs, and limits of obtaining the necessary information should be integrated within the optimization problem. This may affect the choice of the best proxies or simplifications, and the actual working of tax administrations. The outcome may be a balance between these aspects and accepting some implementation of the scheme that is short of the first-best optimum. Yet, this issue should result from the considered complete optimization. At the very least, it cannot be decided off-hand, on the face of a simple elementary, partial and possibly mistaken remark, without considering the actual informational situation.[7]

4.8. Practical realization

The practical realizability of a distributive scheme depends notably on its simplicity, on the needed information, on its acceptance by the public, on administrative means and on the political outlook. Complexity raises administrative and private costs, multiplies difficulties of information, and may lead to the use of simplifying proxies and hence to the corresponding imperfect implementation of the scheme and its rationale. The simplest measure is the uniform per capita and lump-sum universal basic income; however, it ceases to be so when the financing of these subsidies is considered, as it has to. ELIE is among the simplest schemes. Its rationale is particularly meaningful. Its various ethical aspects also have meaning and understandability. Part IV will show how individual opinions about the degree of redistribution (the equalization labour) can converge when individuals take an impartial social-ethical view, possibly as a consequence of dialog or information about others.

4.9. Understandability and acceptability

People may understand and accept the distributive scheme in various possible degrees. Understandability is favored by simplicity. Acceptability means that people

---

[7] See, for instance, the discussion in Chapter 10.

find some justice in the scheme independently of their own situation with regard to it. It first requires that the scheme be based on items that people consider relevant. For instance, we have seen that individuals' satisfactions are generally considered irrelevant for macrojustice (but not for some assistance schemes). The perception of a lack of relevance can lead to a sentiment of arbitrariness and, hence, of injustice. Acceptability also depends on the measure in which tax and subsidy rates are perceived as fair. This will be discussed in detail in Part IV for ELIE's equalization labour. People's moral acceptance of the scheme may favor its realization, but this is not guaranteed for the various possible reasons discussed at the onset of Chapter 10.

4.10. Psychosocial effects

A distributive scheme can implement justice and receivers' rights, or assistance and charity, or again a kind of reciprocity, and rights can be in freedoms or resources, or in welfare or need satisfaction. This objective can make a large difference as regards the status, responsibility, and dignity of the individuals involved.

5. CONCLUSION

This chapter has shown the various specific properties of ELIE schemes, the various distributive schemes with which it can be compared (actual policies, proposals for assistance, philosophers' and economists' studies), and the various important issues of the comparison. The income tax, income egalitarianism, and welfarist "optimum income taxation" have already been considered (Chapters 10 and 11). Assistance schemes and philosophies will be the respective topics of Chapters 15 and 16.

15

Comparison with distributive schemes

1. INTRODUCTION

ELIE results from a philosophy but ends up with a specific practical and simple distributive scheme. It can thus be compared not only with philosophies of social ethics and justice, but also with the specific distributive schemes that are applied or proposed. Chapter 14 noted these schemes, the relevant issues of the comparison, and the corresponding properties of ELIE. Taxation based on income has been considered in Chapter 11, and in Chapter 10 for the theory of the "welfarist optimum income taxation" because of its particular stand concerning information. The focus will now be on schemes of assistance, guaranteed minimum income, "negative income tax" or "income tax credit," and "universal allocation" or "basic income," along with ELIE. These schemes are first introduced in considering the rationales that led to them (Section 2). We then consider and compare the issues of financing, efficiency and incentives, freedom and dignity, information and realization, and comprehensiveness (Sections 3 to 7). The structural properties of the schemes will then be shown and compared (Section 8). Finally, the various relevant aspects of each scheme will be summarized (Section 9). ELIE will sometimes be considered for the case of unidimensional labour and proportional earnings (fixed wage rates), where it becomes EDIE (equal duration income equalization – see Chapters 8 and 9).

2. RATIONALES

ELIE, whose structure results from consensus and social and basic freedoms, manifests rights in society's resources (more specifically, its human resources). Its direct rationale is not the satisfaction of needs. But, of course, individuals use their resources for satisfying their needs as they see them, and they can satisfy their most urgent needs if they have enough resources. The degree to which the least endowed people can satisfy their needs – notably their basic needs – will depend on the equalization labour and on the level of coefficient k, for given average

233

productivity in society. A sufficient level will permit the satisfaction of basic needs (this may be one reason intervening in the choice of this level).

This contrasts with the other realized or proposed practical and specific distributive schemes, such as specific aid, income support, "negative income tax" or "income tax credit," or "universal allocation" of a "basic income." These schemes more directly aim at the satisfaction of the needs of the poorest people, whether the aid is for specific consumption or through support of income. Their rationales generally *prima facie* endorse self-ownership, and object to it solely when it elicits inadmissible poverty (and also an obligation to work as concerns the rationale for a "basic income"): these schemes are proposed as cauteries on self-ownership. Whereas ELIE is basically about intrinsic and direct rights to resources, the schemes for supporting low incomes or consumption are directly concerned with the use and utility of the incomes or other aids – and they sometimes consider only this – ; they are consequentialist.

The focus on needs is the purest for the direct provision of specific consumption, or for its subsidy. Aid in income leaves the choice of the needs to satisfy to the receiver. Satisfying basic needs in this manner is the aim of schemes that complement too low incomes so as to reach the required given level. This, of course, tends to induce people with low earning capacities not to work at all. This entails both social waste (Pareto inefficiency) and the various social effects and moral judgments attached to receiving subsidies without working. These social effects can include the role of labour for social integration and for family and personal balance of the worker, and the possible effects of a culture of dependency on autonomy and dignity. Well-known moral judgments object to subsidizing people who do not work (the "work ethics" of "workfare") and who do not merit or deserve it (as with the classical restriction of aid to the "deserving poor"), and unemployment compensations are commonly restricted to people actively seeking employment.

Schemes of "negative income tax" aim at attenuating these effects in subsidizing only a fraction of the gap between a reference income and lower earned incomes, at a rate equal to the lowest income tax rate which applies to the bracket immediately above this reference level (see Section 8 and Figure 4). The main initiator of this proposal, economist Milton Friedman, intended to reduce inefficiency and dependency. The large-scale application with the "earned income tax credit" in the United States is more motivated by the work ethic and the desire to avoid pure dependency. This scheme affected 20 million American households in 1998 (one out of four, and 29% of the households with children). Other countries have adopted a similar policy. In these schemes, the resulting disposable incomes of the aided people depend not only on the subsidy rate, but also on their earnings, and hence on their wage rate and on their work. It is not solely determined by the needs it can satisfy. The income provided for zero labour and earnings, which does not depend on earning capacities, may not suffice for the satisfaction of basic needs; and people who can solely obtain very low wages from the market cannot have much more (this amount is, in the American scheme, a yearly 2,040 dollars for a family with one child and 3,033 dollars for a larger family).

In contrast, the schemes of "basic income" or "universal allocation" aim at permitting the satisfaction of these needs, even for people who choose not to work. They just provide the same lump-sum amount to everyone without condition. These proposals emphasize the freedom this allocation provides to the individuals. However, they also state that this allocation constitutes an equal claim everyone has on society's resources. Yet, they generally do not specify which resources this would be, or which resources could provide the required amount. The proposals think of nonhuman natural resources (none has proposed using the rent of productive capacities by taxes based on given wage rates).[1] Yet, we saw in Chapter 6 that most nonhuman natural resources are a priori allocated, and taxing them would thus be arbitrary; many of them are consensually allocated by considerations of microjustice; and their overall value is but a small fraction of that of human productive resources. In fact, the main practical drawback of these schemes is that, because this basic allocation is equally given to everyone, either it is sufficient for satisfying the basic needs of people who have no other income, and then the whole scheme is unbearably costly, or this overall cost is within actual possibilities and the basic allocation is too low to permit the satisfaction of basic needs of the poorest people (these schemes are proposed for replacing all other aids or transfers).

ELIE is the solution for global distributive justice in macrojustice resulting from consensus and, in particular, social freedom and the classical basic rights (see Part I). It does not necessarily include all transfers for justice in society: it solely suggests that the other transfers are normally better considered as issues in microjustice. In particular, if the chosen equalization labour and coefficient k are not sufficient for permitting the satisfaction of basic needs, notably for the people whose labour is little remunerated by the market, then ELIE can be complemented by the necessary aid or income support. However, the latter transfers are likely to amount to a relatively low total volume. The philosophy is: First give people the share of resources they are entitled to, and then, if these resources plus their earnings do not suffice for catering for their basic needs, provide specific aid or extra income support for this particular purpose.

All these types of transfers can be presented as rights and as required by justice, and all manifest some kind of social solidarity. However, they are quite different in these respects. ELIE transfers realize a priori rights in resources (without reference to the use of the corresponding incomes), whereas the other transfers can be seen as rights to assistance, although universal allocations also are sometimes presented as rights to general resources. ELIE manifests primary distributive justice leading to an equal distribution of certain resources – namely, the potential product of everyone's equalization labour, plus self-ownership for the rest. Assistance schemes can also be seen as realizing distributive justice, but they can also be

---

[1] As in Kolm 1974, for achieving "practical justice," that is, maximin or leximin in comparable utility.

motivated by benevolence, compassion – possibly charity. However, the solidarity resulting from a concept of degree of community constitutes the basic rationale for the choice of the equalization labour and coefficient k, and assistance schemes can also manifest solidarity and, possibly, community.

3. FINANCING

ELIE is a financially balanced distributive scheme (or redistributive scheme from the benchmark of earnings). From its very logic, transfers received (subsidies) are exactly balanced by transfers yielded (taxes). ELIE schemes can even be described as sets of transfers each from one individual to the other: if individual i can produce the value $p_i(k)$ with the equalization labour $k(kw_i$ for EDIE), each individual i transfers the amount $\alpha_i = p_i(k)/n$ to each other, or each individual i transfers $(\alpha_i - \alpha_j)$ to each other individual j such that $\alpha_j < \alpha_i$.

Financing is by usual income tax in the theory of welfarist "optimum income taxation,"[2] and this probably is also the theoretical view for the "negative income tax" schemes. This induces inefficiencies and disincentives. The other schemes solely describe expenditures. Hence, their cost and financing always constitute major questions. The financing that is presently used, or explicitly or implicitly considered, for them, notably the general actual tax resources, always induces inefficiencies and disincentives.

We have in particular noted that the major drawback of proposals of basic income or universal allocation is their cost. This leads to questioning the schemes' basic proposals. There seems to be a problem in these schemes' insistence to hand out 500 dollars each month to Mr. Bill Gates and other rich people because this guarantees their freedom (for the case their stocks crash down to zero and they choose not to work). It seems that this money would be better used if granted to poor and poorly paid people, or just saved to make the total cost of the scheme manageable. In contrast, ELIE restricts its aid to people who cannot obtain much from the labour market, and it allocates it in proportion of this handicap (for EDIE). Symmetrically, it finances its transfers by taxing people who can receive a good income from the labour market, in proportion of this advantage (for EDIE).

4. EFFICIENCY AND INCENTIVES

ELIE is a Pareto-efficient redistributive system because its transfers are based on inelastic parameters (that is, parameters independent of people's choice and action), the market value of given productive capacities. Elasticities that might be introduced by the process of gathering information about these values are secondary and doubtlessly minor (see Chapter 10). ELIE transfers are

---

[2] See Chapter 10.

"lump-sum" in the sense that they are based on inelastic parameters, but they are not identical for all people.

The issue of disincentives introduced by assistance schemes, notably with regard to labour supply, constitutes one of the main concerns expressed in the discussion of these schemes: aid may induce people to work less, or not at all. This is seen as inducing waste. Indeed, this effect may reduce national income as commonly measured, although it commonly will not be by much because the reduced work generally has low wages, and other effects of the aid may augment national income (such as consumption by the poor receivers with high propensity to consume, in the adequate macroeconomic situation). However, on the other hand, foregone work is replaced by leisure that the concerned people find more valuable (at the new prices) since they choose it and hence prefer it. This leads to the concept of waste rather convincingly promoted by economic theory: lack of Pareto efficiency.[3] The only things that could be added to it are vicarious biases in favor of work ("vicarious" means here in views other than the worker's own judgment). As we have noticed, these views can, for instance, hold work to be beneficial for social integration (if the alternative is no work at all or solely spurious jobs), for the person's family, for the concerned person herself despite her own view, or they may favour it for a purely moralistic reason (work ethics).

Although it is Pareto efficient, ELIE can affect labour supply by "income effects" (rather than "price effects," which generate inefficiencies and labour disincentives). The lower-wage people receive income, and this may induce them to work less (and, possibly, not at all).[4] However, the higher-wage people have to yield income, and this may induce them (and even, possibly, force them) to work more. These labour services that increase are more valued by society's demand than those that decrease.

Subsidies of "basic incomes" or "universal allocations" are also inelastic and lump-sum, and so they produce no Pareto inefficiency per se. However, because they are universal, their total amount will have to be quite high if they can cover basic needs. Hence, if this scheme is financed by standard taxes, which induce inefficiencies, the total resulting inefficiency is likely to be large.

The negative income tax was initially proposed in order to reduce the disincentive effect of schemes of guaranteed income that complement low incomes to a given level. It has the further effect of generally reducing the Pareto inefficiency entailed by these policies. However, it still induces such inefficiency, and it has a disincentive effect on work through both a price effect and an income effect. Moreover, these subsidies have to be financed.

As a general rule, the financing of any set of transfers through standard taxes induces Pareto inefficiencies. This also generally reduces the supply of factors

---

[3] The justification of Pareto efficiency can rest on unanimous choice and collective freedom rather than on "welfare," utility, or happiness (see Chapter 1 and Kolm 1996a).

[4] Leisure being a "normal good."

(such as labour) through price effects, although it tends to augment it through income effects.

5. FREEDOM AND DIGNITY

ELIE fully respects social freedom. This property has even been the source of its derivation. This also holds for lump-sum gifts, such as "basic incomes." However, in contrast with ELIE, all other schemes can induce violations of process-freedom by their financing, for instance, if it comes from present general taxation. This effect will be the strongest, the largest the amount obtained; for instance, it would be very large for the provision of a sufficient universal basic income.

Moreover, ELIE and the provision of basic incomes differ by their provision of available means, and hence, of means-freedom, to the individuals. Individuals have means from wealth, transfers, and earnings thanks to earning capacities. Basic income gives the same subsidy to everyone. In this respect, this is equal treatment of unequals. ELIE constitutes a compensation for inequalities in capacities (see Chapter 9) in transferring from individuals with high earning capacities to individuals with low ones (however, the comparison could only be complete in introducing the effects of the financing of the basic income).

The realization of assistance schemes often has a detrimental effect as concerns the essential issue of the dignity of the aided people, in their own eyes or in others'. Receivers in ELIE solely receive their due share of the value of natural resources. This rationale is not assistance, neither for consumption nor for the relief of low earning capacities. It should not give rise to questions concerning the dignity or the self-respect of the receiver. Seeing it as reciprocity emphasizes this aspect. With general ELIE, each person yields to each other the same share of the product of the same work. With EDIE, in particular, each person yields to each other the product of the same work. Hence, between each two persons, there is mutual transfer of the money value of the same amount of the basic human value: human time and effort. This can be seen as constituting the deepest mutual equality. Among other schemes, basic incomes equally received by everyone seem a priori the more prone to avoiding issues of dignity and self-respect. However, the financing of the scheme should also be considered. If people equally contributed to it, the scheme would have no actual effect (all the incidence of this taxation should be included, and inefficiency-inducing taxes lead to a global loss in the end). In the other cases – the general situation – there is an actual redistribution, and hence, there still are people who, on the whole, receive from others (nonhuman natural resources mostly are already allocated and others would not suffice; indirect effects also a priori induce redistribution).

6. INFORMATION AND REALIZATION

The implementation of all redistributive principles and schemes raise the issue of the estimation of their base and of information about it. This issue concerns not only the expenditures of the scheme, but also the receipts for its financing. For instance, the provision of a universal basic income seems to raise this issue solely minimally (it suffices to ascertain that each individual receives the lump-sum amount), but this is not the case if one considers the raising of the necessary funds (which will be very high for a sufficient basic income). The information needed for the transfers are, according to the type of scheme, individuals' or households' given earning capacities and wage rates, total actual income or wealth, actual consumption, or needs and their various reasons. There is not one such information that is easier to obtain than another in all cases; each is more easily obtained than the others in certain cases. The labour market displays wage rates which are the value of productivity for various types of work and capacities. The general issues are those that are standard in the actual application of tax rules. One point is that it is very important to distinguish the theoretical objective, derived from ethical considerations, from practical problems of information and estimation: the estimation question has no chance to be correctly dealt with if one does not know what should be estimated to begin with. This question of information has been fully discussed in Chapter 10, for ELIE and with comparison with other schemes.

7. COMPREHENSIVE VIEWS

Most of the questions and problems raised by principles and schemes of transfers stem from two overall issues. One is quasi technical: it consists of considering all the financial effects, and in particular not forgetting the financing of transfers. The other is conceptual and philosophical: it consists of seeing clearly the basic overall rationale of the scheme, which is often only implicit. ELIE is quite clear about these two issues.

In issues of social policy, seeing expenditures independently of their financing can lead to conceptual mistakes. Even when several ways of distributing the same amount are compared, the overall ethical picture in each case depends on the distribution of the burden of the cost. And, often, schemes with different total volumes, and hence different costs, are to be compared. Let us add here that the various indirect effects have to be considered solely in the measure in which they should not be discarded for the present judgment because of an ethic of process-freedom. In particular, the consideration of ELIE schemes justified by process-freedom has a priori no basic reason to be concerned with their indirect effects.

The proposals of universal basic incomes raise the issue of the effects of the financing in a particularly acute way. They are proposed for replacing all other transfers, but their cost will have to be higher than that of these transfers because everyone equally receives, if this basic income is to be sufficient for people's "existence," which is the rationale of the proposal. Most of the virtues of various types of these schemes come from the equal distribution to everyone. This holds for issues of information, dignity, simplicity, and understandability, and this equality implies the inelasticity and hence the Pareto efficiency of these allocations. However, this distribution to everyone also accounts for the high cost. If such a scheme is compared with an alternative (the status quo or any other), the cost appears as burdens on specific individuals. If these burdens are also equal, then they compensate the allocations and the whole scheme actually vanishes (except for the waste induced by inefficient taxation and, possibly, monitoring). Hence, the scheme has a reality only if these burdens are unequal. Then, it has a redistributive effect, but this effect all passes through the receipt side. The proposed schemes, however, are usually not explicit about this question. The distributive effects of these schemes are, therefore, not presented. Nothing a priori suggests they will be just, or will not augment unjust inequalities. If these schemes imply the recourse to usual general taxation, their redistributive effects are the corresponding ones (including those of progressive income taxes, and others). This shortcoming of not sufficiently considering the financing and receipt side, that is dramatic for such expensive schemes, also exists for less expensive ones that omit this issue.

8. COMPARATIVE STRUCTURES

A principle or scheme of social transfers determines a curve of disposable income as a function of earned income or of labour for each individual. This function encompasses the main structural features of the scheme. Hence, the comparison of the structure of these functions provides the basic structural comparisons of the schemes. Figure 15–1 shows, in this respect, disposable income as a function of labour for four schemes: a guaranteed minimal income (a), a negative income tax (b), a universal basic income (c), and EDIE (d). The bold lines represent these functions. For illustration, all functions from which these are built are assumed to be linear as a result of constant rates and fixed unit wages, because this is a common case and, at least, a simplification for presentation. Quantity of labour, wage rate, and disposable income for individual i are denoted by letters ℓ_i, w_i, and y_i, respectively. The focus is on the lowest incomes, and only these parts of the curves are represented. The effect of an income tax is represented for the negative income tax scheme (scheme b) because it is an intrinsic part of this scheme's idea. For comparison with this case, an income tax could have been represented above guaranteed incomes (scheme a). An issue is the lowest income level submitted to the income tax. There is no transfer that is a function of earned income with EDIE (scheme d). No income tax is specified for basic income schemes (scheme b), and hence none is represented.

Earned income is $w_i\ell_i$. Guaranteed income consists in replacing $w_i\ell_i$ by y^m whenever $w_i\ell_i < y^m$ (scheme a). The disincentive effect created by the kink in the curve of disposable income at $w_i\ell_i = y^m$ led to proposals of negative income tax represented in scheme b. With a negative income tax with a constant rate of tax and subsidy, at least in the zone considered, as it was proposed, earned incomes lower than the given level y^c are complemented by a subsidy equal to a given

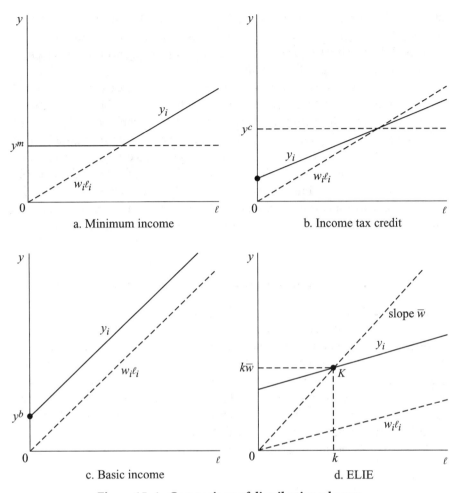

Figure 15–1. Comparison of distributive schemes.

fraction α of the gap:

$$y = w_i\ell_i + \alpha \cdot (y^c - w_i\ell_i) = \alpha y^c + (1-\alpha)\, w_i\ell_i.$$

Hence, $\ell_i = 0$ implies $y = \alpha y^c = y^0$, the same for all individuals. Therefore, the curves of disposable income are straight lines issued from the same point of the income axis with income y^0, and passing through the intersection of the lines of earned income $y = w_i\ell_i$ with the constant-income line $y = y^c$. Universal basic income schemes amount to translating all lines of earned income up by the same amount y^b (scheme c). These lines are therefore also all issued from the same point of the income axis (their slopes are the w_i if there is no income tax, and less if there is such a tax). For EDIE (scheme d), the curves of disposable incomes are straight lines with slopes w_i passing through the same point K with $\ell_i = k$

and $y_i = \overline{w}k$, where $\overline{w}$ is the average of the w_i. This is but another representation of Figure 9–1. Efficiency results from the slopes remaining w_i. In all cases, each individual chooses her labour ℓ_i, and hence, her disposable income in choosing a point of her line of disposable income.

For each of the three schemes EDIE, negative income tax (with the assumed linearity) and universal basic income, the individuals' disposable income curves representing disposable incomes as a function of labour constitute a "pencil" of straight lines, all passing through the same point. These points are on the income axis ($\ell_i = 0$) for universal basic income and negative income tax, whereas this is not the case for EDIE (point K). For each individual, the line of disposable income is parallel to the line of earned income (slope w_i) for EDIE and for the universal basic income, whereas this is not the case for negative income taxation, where the lines of earned and disposable incomes intersect on the same line at given $y = y^m$.

9. SUMMARY OF PROPERTIES OF MODES OF DISTRIBUTION

ELIE is justified by consensus, social freedom, and basic rights. Its other properties, which result from this derivation, are just side bonuses rather than justifications in themselves. These properties have just been noted with the comparisons, and they are gathered in Chapter 14. For the purpose of comparison, let us similarly gather, as briefly as possible, the problems raised by each of the other modes of distribution. Waste (social waste) will refer to inducing Pareto ineffiency. "Disincentives" will not be noted in themselves because leisure is often valuable (hence possible intrinsic values of labour such as its role in social integration or for the worker's family or personal balance are not noted).

Minimum income

- Wasteful.
- The origin of resources should be made precise (possibly a wasteful tax).

Negative income tax or income tax credit

- Still wasteful, although less so.
- Resources may implicitly be drawn from the positive side of the income tax, and then they are wasteful.

Universal allocation, basic income

- Why insist on giving 500 dollars per month to the wealthiest people? Some people may need them more than they do.
- As a result, the tax is gigantic if the poorest are sufficiently aided, and this aid is far too low if the resources can actually be raised.
- This tax for financing creates the actual distributive effect, and it will probably be wasteful.

"Welfarist optimum income taxation" (see Chapter 10).

- It optimizes tax rates and schedules, not the tax base.
- Individual utilities are probably irrelevant for macrojustice, and the income tax is a main tool of macrojustice. People do not think that the income tax should depend on individuals' capacities for enjoyment. Moreover, how does one pass from individuals' utility functions to the unique individual utility function of the model?
- Requirements of social ethics and justice are a priori not manifested by a social maximand or a "social welfare function."
- Observable wages and wage differentials provide information about labour productivities. Earned incomes are by no means the only observed item. There may be some cases of estimates using more or less elastic parameters, but this is a secondary problem, and by no means "the theory of optimum taxation." The various ways of estimating the values of tax bases are the routine work of tax administrations.
- Welfarist criteria have domains of relevance in microjustice. This holds for the utilitarian ethos: see the similar model applied to the determination of optimum nonlinear public tarifs with different and uncertain individual utilities (Kolm 1969b, 1970b). This also holds for "practical justice" (maximin or leximin in interpersonally comparable "fundamental" preferences or utilities, Kolm 1971 [1998]),[5] used for optimum taxation based on wages (Kolm 1974).

Income tax

Taxation is not based on income for a reason of information but because of moral ideas. The rational application of these ideas, however, lead, rather, to ELIE. See Chapter 11.

---

[5] Note that the maximin in Rawls' "difference principle" proposed at the same time is not in terms of utilities – which Rawls rejects – but of an index of "primary goods" whose weights and measures are to be determined (some are position, power, and self-respect); moreover, the reason for replacing equality by a maximin consists of "disincentive effects" whose relevance, and origin in the distributive system, require closer consideration (see Chapter 16).

16

Comparisons with philosophies

1. INTRODUCTION

The principle of ELIE compares with a number of well-known positions in social ethics and theories in political philosophy.

The life of modern societies for the last two centuries is shaped by the fight between two universalist distributive principles[1]: self-ownership in process-freedom and the lowering of income inequalities. Now, both full self-ownership and the proper implementation of the standard philosophy of income egalitarians are particular ELIE schemes (see Chapter 11 for income equality). Indeed, ELIE turns out to be the simplest more general principle that encompasses these two opposing principles. Note that it has been derived from applications of the principle of unanimity and consensual opinions about global distributive justice. ELIE therefore constitutes both the common ground for the rational comparison of these two classical contenders, and the field of solutions intermediate between them (including these two cases). Most ELIE solutions will be intermediate between these two polar positions: ELIE is income equalization for the equalization labour and self-ownership for the rest.

The crucial parameter of ELIE is, indeed, the equalization labour. Its vanishing yields full self-ownership. When it is around lower standard working time, ELIE constitutes the possible first-best implementation of the most usual ideal of income egalitarians (see Chapter 11). We have noted that higher equalization labours, and notably the borderline maximal income equalization, are not to be retained (Chapter 7).

In fact, it can be claimed that the principle of ELIE in full process-freedom realizes these two classical ideals better than the specific views of their proponents. For income egalitarianism, it takes into account the common additional sentiment

---

[1] "Universalist" stands here in opposition to claims based on birth (except for property inheritance), social "order" or ascribed status.

244

that people who work more (longer, harder, with more training work) deserve an income compensation for the extra pain and, possibly, for the extra contribution. Moreover, a notable consequence of the ELIE income equality is that it does not induce the wasteful disincentives which constitute the practical shortcoming of the ideal of equalizing earned incomes and forces it to retreat to distant second bests. For the classical process liberalism supporting both full process-freedom and full self-ownership, the application of full process-freedom in liberal social contracts provides the process-liberal solution of the various cases of market failures (this also holds for the other cases of full process-freedom).

However, ELIE has not been obtained for the purpose of presenting the synthesis of – or the compromise between – the two great ethics of distribution of the modern world, or for comparing or improving them. Rather, it results from basic and practically necessary structures: social freedom applied as process-freedom and entailing aim-freedom, and impartial rationality entailing a certain equality.[2] Now, this association of entitlement from free action and of equality for the rest takes us much beyond, deeper, and before, the idiosyncratic conceptions of justice of modernity. It takes us into the *philosophia perennis* of justice, in the general conceptualization and systematization of basic conceptions of mankind. Then, the natural place to turn to is, of course, the work of thinkers such as Plato and Aristotle. Indeed, *The Laws* for the former, and *Nicomachean Ethics* and *Eudemian Ethics* for the latter, contain the theory of justice resulting from equality and freedom. They contain it to a point that is deeply embarrassing for the discipline of social ethics or political philosophy, because it turns out that the deepest and most important, basic, and relevant ideas about distributive justice in a broad sense are the ideas presented in these writings of twenty-four or twenty-five centuries ago. Now, it turns out that ELIE is a direct application of Plato's and Aristotle's theory of distributive justice, with an important further specification as concerns capacities, which are both given and a determinant of the result of action (and hence should both be equally shared and benefit their holder). This will therefore be our first topic (Section 2). One can also consider that this close relation between these two theories is not surprising, because they derive from neighbouring epistemic positions: the obtained result derives from endogenous social choice, whereas Aristotle and Plato state that they only describe people's common view of justice.

More generally, full – and hence equal – social freedom for all, and ELIE distributive schemes, are particular forms of the general necessary structure of justice combining equalities in freedoms and allocations. The result is in particular a form of free exchange from an equal allocation, although the labour or leisure of different individuals have a priori different market prices (Section 3). Conversely,

[2] See Part I for freedom and Kolm 1971 (1998), foreword, Section 5, for the rational necessity of equality (see also Chapter 23).

three important theories of global distributive justice are three particular cases of the ELIE structure: full self-ownership, "total income" equalization, and income egalitarianism. Full self-ownership, the basic theory of modernity for the last two centuries, is considered in Section 4, with its relation with full process-freedom and neighbouring theories that do not a priori rest on process-freedom (such as neo-"libertarianism" and the original "public choice"). The opposite limiting case of ELIE, maximal income equalization, appears in Section 5. For the case of constant wage rates, it was proposed as a particular scheme by Pazner and Schmeidler (1972), and it turned out as the result of Ronald Dworkin's (1981) income-egalitarian proposal to apply the principle of free exchange from equal sharing to all given resources, except eudemonistic capacities, but including productive capacities valued for the income they can yield. Although Pareto-efficient, this solution is factually irrealistic, morally illogical, as unegalitarian as full self-ownership, and against a consensual moral view (following Pazner's [1977] intuition, Dworkin noted one of its shortcomings, the so-called "slavery of the talented," and for this reason resorted instead to an application of the theory of "fundamental insurance"[3]). Yet, one preliminary argument of Dworkin, his discarding eudemonistic capacities in the equalizand for the problematic reason that "one is responsible for one's tastes," elicited recent discussions about the scope of the equalizand, in the direction of Plato's and Aristotle's classical and elaborate analysis (Section 6). More standard conceptions of income equality underlie the theories of John Rawls and Michael Walzer, discussed in Section 7. Yet, both theories differ from the comparable income-egalitarian ELIE (Chapter 11) which follows the most common view of income egalitarians. Both are more or less Pareto inefficient and have a problem with the treatment of leisure, but also insert an income-egalitarian ideal in a broader and structured conception of justice: the priority of basic rights and the "difference principle" for Rawls, and the segmentation in separately egalitarian "spheres of justice" for Walzer. These general structures are compared with the hierarchized distinction of macrojustice and microjustice (and mesojustice), the respect of the nonrival classical basic rights, and the resulting ELIE distribution. An important issue concerns the proper scope of allocation through the market system in a society. Rawls, moreover, presents a justification of his conclusions, which is compared with the necessary reasons leading to the macrojustice solution. Finally, the whole set of principles and criteria of justice is considered, in relation with the corresponding types of social relations and societies, and the various different but related threefold taxonomies (Section 9). The obtained ELIE will thus have been compared with the other ideas, in particular those that propose a solution for global distributive justice (comparisons with a number of other ideas and authors are presented in Chapters 9, 10, 11, 14, and 15, and in Part V).

---

[3] See Chapter 25.

2. PLATO'S AND ARISTOTLE'S THEORY OF DISTRIBUTIVE JUSTICE: ITS APPLICATION, AND RELEVANT CONTINUATION

2.1. Commutative justice and process-freedom

Plato and Aristotle purport to describe what people think justice is, rather than a theory of their own. For allocating items to people, they hold that the key distinction is between items that are influenced by the individuals' will and those that are not. The just allocation of the former constitutes the domain of *commutative justice*. This includes, notably, the field of economic exchanges. For this justice, the principle of justice is "geometric equality," which means "in proportion to," and has in fact to be read as "as the relevant increasing function of." What is allocated is the effect or result of voluntary action. And what it depends on is individuals' "merit" (*axia*). This is also called "retributive justice." Merit, these authors explain, can have several meanings. They distinguish two issues: the assignment of something to an individual, and what is assigned. The criterion of assignment can have three successive levels. (1) The individual can be the cause of what is allocated. (2) He can voluntarily be this cause; then, merit is *responsibility* (inaction is a particular action when other relevant actions could have been chosen). (3) The individual can, in addition, incur a pain or cost of any kind necessary for or from an action that yields a valued result; the criterion then is *effort*, manifesting the agent's *virtue* (and this is "aristocratic" justice); symmetrically, the action can have a negative effect but entail some advantage for the agent (and this can be vice). The second issue is what is assigned. Both Plato and Aristotle quote the Pythagorean saying: "If one receives or incurs what one does, this would be right justice." They make it precise that in interpersonal interactions (called "exchange" in a broad sense), the relevant effect of merit is measured by the need satisfaction of the beneficiary or, for a negative effect, by the resulting tort. This implies that the actor is entitled to the effects of other possible causes of this final effect than her decision or effort, such as used services or capacities of hers. Hence, for production for exchange, commutative justice is aim-freedom and "to each her product" or its market value. With the foregoing models and notations, individual i choosing to provide work ℓ_i receives merited commutative income $p_i(\ell_i)$.[4]

The second domain of justice is that of *distributive justice*. It applies to the distribution of items that do not depend on individuals' will, and the principle is "arithmetic equality," that is, strict equality and in particular equal sharing.

Distributive justice is of two kinds. Distributive justice in the strict sense applies to items that are not a priori attached to the individuals. Then, if their total value is

---

[4] "Merited" is here rather than "deserved" because the reward includes the value of the use of the individual's productivity function $p_i()$. This is an application of a common and classical distinction (see common uses of the term "merit" – such as in "meritocracy" –, its analysis by Vlastos [1962], or the comparisons of the terms by Lucas [1993] or Pojman and McLeod [1999]). See also Chapter 9.

E and there are n individuals, each receives $e = (1/n)E$. In particular, this applies to given nonhuman natural resources.

2.2. ELIE as diorthic or rectificative justice

Items that are a priori allocated to the individuals but do not result from their will and free acts are the object of *rectificative* or *diorthic* justice. This is a part of distributive justice but can also be considered a category of justice of its own. When the individuals are unequally endowed with these items, there should be rectificative or compensatory interindividual transfers that restore the corresponding equality. Indeed, if individual i is endowed with such items of value d_i, distributive justice should affect $(1/n)d_i$ of this value to each individual in taking it from individual i. Hence, each individual i should, in the end, loose value d_i but receive value $(1/n)\Sigma d_i = \overline{d}$, the average of the d_i. That is, she receives $\overline{d} - d_i$ if $d_i < \overline{d}$ and yields $d_i - \overline{d}$ if $d_i > \overline{d}$. As Aristotle writes: "One should add to he who has less than average the amount by which she has less, and withdraw from he who has more than average the amount by which he has more."

Individual i's just income finally is the sum of her commutative, distributive, and rectificative or diorthic incomes:

$$y_i = p_i(\ell_i) + e + \overline{d} - d_i.$$

Let us apply this theory to the problem of global distributive justice in macrojustice. Commutative justice attributes to each individual i the fruit of her labour, $p_i(\ell_i)$. We have also seen that the given nonhuman natural resources are discarded (Chapter 6). They correspond to the given E, and hence, term e disappears. Rectificative or diorthic justice applies to the rent of individuals' given productive capacities. Productive capacities usable by labour k are measured in income value, which is $p_i(k)$ for individual i, and the rest is valued as labour or leisure, and hence, is intrinsically equally distributed. For the former, the rectification consists in equalizing the values, that is, demanding income $p_i(k)$ from individual i and giving her the average $\overline{p}(k) = (1/n)\Sigma p_i(k)$. In the end, individual i's income is

$$y_i = p_i(\ell_i) - p_i(k) + \overline{p}(k) = p_i(\ell_i) + t_i$$

with $t_i = \overline{p}(k) - p_i(k)$.

Equivalently, one can say that the equal given allocation is in terms of the two goods of the problem, leisure $\widehat{\ell} - k$ (or $1 - k$ for EDIE), and a given income η, and that individuals are free to deviate from this allocation in choosing their labour ℓ_i (and hence, leisure $\widehat{\ell} - \ell_i$) and in receiving the corresponding extra income or incurring the variational loss of foregone earnings. Individual i's receiving leisure $\widehat{\ell} - k$ means, in income terms, her yielding the product of the corresponding labour $p_i(k)$. Then, individual i, choosing to work ℓ_i, finally has the disposable income $y_i = p_i(\ell_i) - p_i(k) + \eta$. However, total consumption equals total production, $\Sigma y_i = \Sigma p_i(\ell_i)$, and hence, $\eta = \overline{p}(k)$, and therefore, $y_i = p_i(\ell_i) + t_i$ with $t_i = \overline{p}(k) - p_i(k)$.

The Plato-Aristotle solution of letting individuals entitled to or accountable for the result of their actions, and of equalizing among them the resources they do not create voluntarily, is in fact very widely held at all places and times. Plato and Aristotle assert that they are merely reporting, possibly putting in form, common ideas of their society. This principle is in fact equality (whose rational necessity is generally felt, if not precisely proven), plus the concepts of aim-freedom, immanent merit or desert (where "immanent" means reward according to effects of choice or action), and responsibility. However, these principles can be variously applied to the same issue, because of the possible choice of what intrinsically constitutes the choosing agent rather than being resources or means amenable to equalization, as concerns items such as her tastes, capacities of various types, various properties or aspects of her social situation, and so on, or because of possible specifications in the definition of equality.

In particular, the obtained general theoretical result of ELIE admits a number of specifications according to the value of the equalization labour k. Among them are three polar cases:

- For $k = 0$, full self-ownership.
- For $k = \widehat{\ell}$, or $k = 1$ in the case of EDIE, maximal income equalization (see Chapters 7, 9, and 12).
- For $k = k^e$ in the neighbourhood of the lowest normal full labour, the solution is the realization of the classical ideal of income egalitarians (see Chapter 11).

Full self-ownership and income egalitarianism are the two classical polar contenders for global distributive justice. Sections 4 and 7 will particularly consider them. The final solution for large societies will be with k between their two values. The third polar position, maximal income equalization, which was considered in Chapters 7, 9, and 12 for its purely theoretical interest, is again presented here (in Section 5). However, we first see, in Section 3, how macrojustice and ELIE schemes in general are particular cases of general structures of justice.

3. FREEDOMS AND EQUALITIES

Concepts of justice (among equals in the relevant characteristics) are combinations of ideal equalities in freedoms and allocations. In this respect, ELIE can be seen as equal full process-freedom, equal sharing of the rents of productive capacities properly measured, and equal self-ownership of eudemonistic capacities (and of use-rights and benefit-rights of all capacities, an implication of process-freedom). Alternatively, it can be seen as full process-freedom for deviations from the equal allocation represented by income $\overline{p}(k)$ and leisure $\widehat{\ell} - k$ (hence labour k), represented by point K in the figures of Chapters 9 and 12 (taking $\widehat{\ell} = 1$ for unidimensional labour), and equal self-ownership in eudemonistic capacities.

This shows that ELIE belongs to the family of concepts of free action or exchange from an equal sharing or allocation.[5] However, the individuals' opportunity sets in the domain of income and leisure or labour generally differ across individuals because they depend on individuals' productivities (as a result of aim-freedom, which entitles the individual with the output of her action performed using her capacities). This differs from, for example, free exchange from an equal sharing of goods where all the individuals face the same market prices of these goods. The difference comes from the fact that individuals' labours are not the same goods as concerns production because they can produce different incomes – while they can be equated, for the same characteristics (notably duration), on moral grounds.

4. FULL SELF-OWNERSHIP

Full self-ownership with full process-freedom is the theory of classical process liberalism. This has been the central social-ethical theory of modernity. Valuing self-ownership and process-freedom is more or less found at most times and places, but the claim to their universality in large societies, and the important realization of this principle, is the mark of the formation of modernity during the last two centuries or so. The various other social-ethical views in these societies (socialisms, social protection, income egalitarianism, and so on) were and still are defined in opposition to this ethic and its various aspects and consequences. Full self-ownership with process-freedom has been defended by innumerable positions and publications. Its elaborate study includes John Locke's *Second Treatise*, most legal theory, a long tradition of economists (for whom this ethics was often implicit) in the nineteenth and twentieth centuries, Marx's theory of exploitation, and a number of more recent scholars (shortly to be noted).

A basic point, however, is the justification of this theory, and notably the relation between its two parts, self-ownership and process-freedom. With the standard conception of ownership, full self-ownership implies full process-freedom. This implication is implicit for John Locke who derives full self-ownership – and simultaneously full process-freedom – from a concept of natural rights. Locke's basic aim was to find a legitimacy that could be opposed to absolute political power and have an individualistic base. This is the role of his theory of property. However, the enlightenment, for the similar purpose of fighting arbitrary power and the resulting injustice, directly emphasized individuals' freedoms and rights. Then, from the late eighteenth century on, the standard justification was reversed and tended to derive self-ownership from process-freedom. We have seen in the first two parts of this study that this derivation fails with a strict conception of process-freedom that does not implicitly assume self-ownership in the first place. Yet, this derivation has been and is one of the most frequent positions in social ethics. It is assumed, implicit, suggested, or asserted in innumerable

---

[5] See Kolm 1971, Part II.

political and economic debates, and is sometimes a little more elaborate in various ways.

A number of freedom-based concepts have been used to defend self-ownership, using a confusion and lack of distinction between the various rights in human assets (Chapter 6). In particular, notions of equality of opportunity have often been mobilized. For instance, the historically powerful slogan "the career open to talents" defends nondiscrimination, but, as it was used, also self-ownership, since the talented seize an opportunity if they can reap the benefits from the use of their talents, and no redistribution of the rent of these capacities was considered. The classical apologetic description of the USA as the "land of opportunity" is along the same line. Entitlement from aim-freedom, immanent merit or desert, and responsibility were also often used to justify full self-ownership. Such arguments were in particular often used for opposing public interventions and policies, and notably, of course, redistributions (from the outcome of full self-ownership and process-freedom). For instance, the concept of entitlement was used to oppose fiscal redistribution, and that of responsibility for opposing the construction of social security systems.

In a number of conceptions, the concept of a person or an individual includes basic means of subsistence. This is general in oriental philosophy and was common in European thought a few centuries ago. For John Locke, for instance, the right to safety includes that of basic subsistence. However, with the refinement of basic rights as bare rights, the pure rights of the person – including the right to hold legitimately acquired property – tended to exclude an a priori basic right to have some goods. The 1789 encoding of basic rights met this dilemma head on. One of the most interesting debates in social ethics in modern times concerned the crucial issue of the consistency between basic rights and tranfers, and occurred on August 26, 1789, at the French National Assembly. This was the day of the final adoption of the Declaration of Rights. The adoption, during one week, had been of one article at a time, at unanimity after debate (a hectic public debate among over 500 persons, out of which miraculously came the few short, terse, and marvelously coined sentences of the articles – a clear instance of the general will at work). The basic rights agreed upon implied full process-freedom. There remained to adopt the last article, the seventeenth. Some wanted it to state a right for the poorest to receive public assistance, thinking that, with proper implementation, this was not inconsistent with full process-freedom.[6] Antoine de Condorcet was a leading supporter of this right. Others thought that the implied transfers would violate process-freedom and the implied right to property. Since time was getting short, they settled for the awkward solution to reject this proposal – and the adopted seventeenth article seems to repeat the right to property stated in Article 2 –, but to include the right to public assistance at the beginning of the ensuing Constitution

[6] One aspect is that assistance to the poor was one of the roles of the church and a common justification for its vast properties (which were soon to be confiscated for backing the new money – the "assignats" – issued for financing the war launched by European kings against the Republic).

which was supposed to be "deduced" from the rights of the Declaration (and this right was introduced in the later revolutionary declarations of rights).

Full self-ownership is usually considered the opposite of "egalitarianism." This is why its proponents often like to present it as (a kind of) equality of opportunity, which would oppose equality in results or outcomes in "end-state." Its derivation from full process-freedom would derive it from the basic equality of equal full process-freedom and basic rights for all ("Men are free and equal in rights"), but this rather yields the more general ELIE. However, full self-ownership can be derived (and tentatively justified) as an equality of resources. It suffices to choose the appropriate measure of human resources. This can be done in two ways. In one, a unit of human resources is taken to be those of an individual. Then, with full self-ownership, each individual owns one such unit: herself.[7] The second approach is more refined and refers to the considerations of Chapters 9 and 12. The measuring rod for productive capacities is taken to be individual time in labour using this capacity or in leisure these capacities permit their holders to enjoy for a given earned income. This constitutes and provides a measure of the quantity of the capacity. It also constitutes and provides a measure of its value in labour or leisure value or time of life. Then, this measure of the total capacity of a person in a given period is the same for all.

In recent times, an axiomatics of the theory of full process-freedom, the theory of the liberal social contract, and a discussion of the ownership in capacities and of the corresponding distributional issues are included in *The Liberal Social Contract – Theory and Practice of Liberalism*.[8] The classical liberal theory associating full process-freedom and full self-ownership is presented by Robert Nozick (1974), who emphasizes the time-regress structure of process-free self-ownership, but considers neither actual market failures (he discusses a public good, but one with possibility of exclusion) nor the possibility of redistributing in respecting full process-freedom. Others want, on the contrary, short statutes of limitation (very short for Milton Friedman).[9] James Buchanan's "constitutional Public Choice" and the neo-"libertarians" (Murray Rothbart, David Friedman, etc.) do not a priori present full process-freedom because the freedom they consider is limited by relations of force rather than by the morally justified respect of others' process-freedom – the neo-"libertarian" ethic in fact restricts to the indictment of anything done by a government. Then, however, a collective agreement, which has the nature of a truce, can decide to respect basic rights and process-freedom. This is a possibility for J. Buchanan, and this is doubtlessly part of the implicit collective agreement considered by David Gauthier (1986) (who mentions "usual rights" in passing). All these studies treat market failures very differently. We noted that Nozick discards them. Neo-"libertarians" think the public sector is always

---

[7] This aspect is fully discussed in Kolm 1985a.

[8] Kolm 1985a. This work also includes other related issues such as the general theories of social contracts and of the allocation of nonhuman natural resources.

[9] Personal communication.

worse. F. Hayek and M. Friedman see market failures as minor and think they should be dealt with using considerations of welfare (Friedman also considers the relief of poverty with a negative income tax, which has been compared with ELIE in Chapter 15, and a public financing of education – through the distribution of "vouchers" to families). Buchanan and the school of Public Choice see market failures as very important, and as the object of constitutional agreements and of the "political market." Gauthier proposes for them a specific theory which, however, requires a cardinal utility whose meaning is question-begging.[10,11]

5. MAXIMAL INCOME EQUALIZATION, AND DWORKIN

The limiting case of ELIE opposite to full self-ownership is maximal income equalization. A general principle for allocating given resources is free exchange from equal sharing, and in particular, perfectly competitive exchange from equal sharing (Kolm 1971, Part 2). Ronald Dworkin (1981) proposed to use this principle for allocating all the resources of society, hence for global distributive justice, except eudemonistic capacities (with reference to "tastes"), but including productive capacities measured by the income they could produce. The result for these capacities is maximal income equalization (see Chapters 7, 9, and 12), considered for constant wage rates. This treatment of productive capacities had been suggested, also in the case of constant wage rates, by a scheme proposed by Pazner and Schmeidler (1972) and mentioned by Varian (1975, 1976) and Pazner (1977). This result is not the general ELIE because of the choice to measure productive capacities by the income they can yield, rather than by the labour that can use them and hence by the complementary leisure (this would de facto give the other limiting case, full self-ownership), or by some combination of both numéraires (which gives the general ELIE solution).[12] The issues raised by Dworkin's theory can be classified into: a number of specific problems either noted and faced or not; the morals and logic of the obtained solution; the special reason for discarding "tastes," namely the individuals' "responsibility" for them (also used in Kolm 1966a and critically discussed in Chapter 6), which launched a particular use of this concept (often using this name for accountability); and finally Dworkin's

---

[10] This is the bargaining solution proposed by Raiffa, Kalai, and Smorodinski.

[11] The basic features of all these proposals and others are analyzed in detail in Kolm 1996a, Chapters 12 and 13.

[12] ELIE has been obtained in distinguishing, in the rights concerning individuals' productive capacities, the use-rights and benefit-rights, attributed to the holder of the capacity for respecting social freedom as full process-freedom, from the rights to the value of the rent, which can be measured in output-income or in labour-leisure. In contrast, the noted proposals leading to maximal income equalization more or less directly consider that each of the n individuals owns $1/n$th of each individual productive capacities (in fact, as a kind of mutual slavery). Then, since leisure or time of life is not transferable in itself from an individual to the other, the only way an individual has to benefit from her share in another is to demand the transfer of the corresponding product or income, hence possibly to ask her to work for producing this output – as with slavery. As a result, the overall final equality can only be that of income values, that is, maximal income equalization. Hence, the different initial viewpoints lead to different results in the end.

retreat from this solution to a version of "fundamental insurance," which will be considered in Chapter 25.

This scheme raises a few particular issues. Dworkin proposes solutions and criteria for the allocation of indivisible commodities. A notable point is that this scheme, in endorsing the outcome of exchange, endorses the "natural" allocation of individuals' capacities for exchanging, bargaining and dealing in markets. It thus allocates these capacities as it does eudemonistic capacities, while they are not of this kind, but rather belong to the category of productive capacities in exchange and market economies. This constitutes a contradiction that cannot be escaped.[13] The same issue is raised for other exchanges, for instance for spending incomes (which may be equal), but it is the most acute when the exchange starts from the allocation of given resources. Another issue is that Dworkin seems to include capital in the equally shared resources. Yet, capital is produced resources and not given ones, with an intertemporal view. However, such a view would raise the problem of the allocation of bequest, which is a use of one's wealth for the giver and a given resource for the receiver.

Market exchange from equal sharing results in all individuals having the same incomes at market prices. Hence, this scheme is a case of equal incomes. For given resources and a Pareto-efficient market (such as a perfectly competitive market), the outcome is Pareto efficient.

The productive capacities of individuals create their productivities, that is, their earned income as a function of their labour or, equivalently, their trade-off between leisure and income or consumption. Dworkin measures these capacities as the income producible by maximal labour. With different individual (total) productivities, equal sharing gives rise to transfers from the more productive to the less productive individuals. If, however, capacities are measured by the labour-leisure dimension of productivities, the total amount is the same for each individual, and equal sharing of the whole requires no transfer and is satisfied by full self-ownership. Using a combination of both measures yields general ELIE schemes. The former case is maximal income equalization. We have seen its various moral shortcomings in Chapters 7, 9, and 12. Dworkin saw one – already more or less suggested by the noted previous works also for constant wage rates – for which he coined the striking image of the "slavery of the talented." The ablest individuals are in fact nominally free, but they have to work much to pay their high distributive tax (in spite of their high productivity). Equivalently, "buying back" leisure from the benchmark of maximal work and equal income, at the cost of foregone earnings, is very costly for them, and is the more costly the more productive the individual (for high levels of labour). Yet, the standard structure of decreasing returns to scale, applied to labour, is bound to attenuate this effect because it will make extra labour less productive at high levels (but this does not show with the assumed constant wage rates). Moreover, if the most productive

---

[13] See the discussion in Kolm 1996a, Chapter 9.

individuals accept low incomes in order to gain rest, there may also be "starvation of the talented." In addition, we have seen that maximal income equalization often leads to output-freedoms (that is, freedoms for the choice of income and leisure) that are unequal in the unambiguous sense of an inclusion of domains which implies having more income for each labour (except zero labour) and more leisure for each income (except average maximal income), the ablest being less free.

This solution is the equalization of the income value of all resources except eudemonistic capacities. Dworkin presents it as the equalization of all the individuals are not responsible for (all "resources"), followed by free exchange. From the foregoing remarks, this solution appears as philosophically self-contradictory in the sense that it begins with an egalitarian intent and ends up very inegalitarian (with talented individuals as losers). The resulting situation is symmetric to self-ownership with inversion of the relation between advantage (and outcome-freedom) and capacities.[14] This should be a "repugnant conclusion" for an egalitarian promoter of the principle. Hence, judging a principle also by the consequences of its application (Plato's dialectics, Rawls' "reflexive equilibrium") requires dropping the principle. This is precisely what Dworkin did in the end, retreating, for allocating productive capacities, to an application of the method of "fundamental insurance" – that is, the compensations are the transfers that would have resulted from a hypothetical insurance about having the considered characteristic (see Chapter 25, and an application in Chapter 21).[15] However, first, this solution rests on individuals' tastes for safety and other things, while Dworkin has assumed tastes to be irrelevant for the allocation of resources.[16] And second, the assimilation of a choice of justice to individuals' choices in uncertainty is a priori unwarranted.[17] In addition, Dworkin requires what he calls the "envy test," that is, no individual prefers another's allocation to her own, which is extensively studied as "equity" in Kolm (1971) – and only depends on individuals' tastes.[18] Maximal income equalization generally does not satisfy this criterion (this results from the inclusion of individuals' domains of free choice noted in Chapters 7, 9, and 12).

We also noticed that maximal income equalization would require transfers several times higher than those that would be necessary to fully equalize present incomes: this is not realistic. Moreover, this maximal income equalization includes

[14] See Chapters 7, 9, and 12.

[15] See also Kolm 1966b, 1970c, 1985a, 1987b, 1996a, 1998, 2001b.

[16] This is the relevant initial allocation, the equal sharing, which does not depend on differences in individuals' tastes, preferences, or eudemonistic capacities. Of course, the final allocation, resulting from the markets, will depend on supplies and demands, and hence, on individuals' preferences and tastes.

[17] This shortcoming is faced, in the theory of fundamental insurance in the noted references, in accepting this putative insurance only when public opinion endorses it. This will be further discussed in Chapter 25, Section 5. The most elaborate discussion of the shortcoming is in Kolm 2001b.

[18] Early proponents of this idea in economics have been Jan Tinbergen (1946) and Duncan Foley (1967). Note that this criterion does not properly deal with the sentiment of envy in which people care *jointly* for their and others' situations (the proper theory is developed in Kolm 1995a).

equalizing the value of the potential product of productive capacities that are not used for producing (but are at rest or used in "leisure"). This is morally objectionable, even though these capacities are given to the individuals who may be responsible for their choice of labour, and therefore, for using or not using these capacities at work. This moral view is in fact very widespread: people do not think that a productive individual should pay a tax on the income she could have earned during her leisure time or part of it, or that individuals with a low wage rate should be compensated for the poor earnings they would have received during part or all of their actual leisure time had they used it for working.[19] There is a sense in which the moral value of a person's leisure is not higher than that of another for the mere reason that her wage is higher. This points to the solution of the question within its own logic.

The solution, indeed, consists of acknowledging that productive capacities do not only provide income for given labour, but also, equivalently, leisure for given earned income, and in morally valuing leisure per se. Leisure is free time of life, freedom from labour (a generally constrained and often alienating activity). Its moral evaluation should a priori be independent of its market value as foregone earnings, and hence, of the individual's productivity. Moreover, the irrelevance of eudemonistic capacities for our present purpose (see Chapter 6) implies that they are not relevant for distinguishing the value of leisure of different individuals, that is, an individual's leisure will not be valued more than that of another person because she is assumed to enjoy it more (or to be more able to enjoy it). This leads to a priori equally valuing the same time (and other characteristics) of leisure of different individuals, and hence the same labour as foregone leisure (and to measuring an individual's tax or subsidy by the labour or foregone leisure of this individual that could produce it). Productive capacities are then measured by their use and their amount by their possible use. Then, full self-ownership is an equal allocation of productive capacities, and the leisure an individual can enjoy is only the nonuse for production of her own productive capacities. Yet, full self-ownership is precisely that which income egalitarians oppose (and Dworkin is a priori even a "total income" egalitarian). However, one can and generally should a priori directly morally value both income-consumption, and leisure and free time (given the irrelevance of eudemonistic capacities). Then, both units for measuring the amounts of capacities to be shared can or should be used, which leads to a composite measure and to an ELIE distribution (Chapter 9).

6. RESPONSIBILITY

However, recent discussions have been inspired by another aspect of Dworkin's presentation, his use of the concept of responsibility for discarding "tastes," which in fact is problematic – but is not necessary. Dworkin presents the foregoing scheme

---

[19] Inducing individuals whose labour is particularly useful to society not to take too much leisure is better done in letting their wage reflect this value of their labour (and an ELIE redistribution can equalize part of the rents of capacities).

as "equality of resources" opposed to "equality of welfare."[20] His "resources" do not include eudemonistic capacities. Discarding the latter for the relevant equalization (which could be made through compensations), or endorsing their "natural" allocation, is done by Dworkin in discarding "tastes." If "tastes" include a consideration of more or less intense satisfaction, then the result is indeed obtained. The reason Dworkin proposes for discarding tastes is that individuals are responsible for their own tastes.[21] This question has been discussed in Chapter 6, and we have seen that it cannot be answered without further specification of the concept of freedom of choice. We also noted that the common view of discarding eudemonistic capacities (and tastes) for issues of macrojustice rather rests on notions of privacy and respect of the self. In fact, the question of responsibility may intervene at another point in Dworkin's scheme, although he does not mention it in this respect: in justifying that individuals are entitled to the outcome of their free and voluntary exchanges (from given resources) – although aim-freedom can also be used in this respect.

The general principle that individuals are accountable for or entitled to the items they are responsible for, and of equally sharing the rest among them, is a classical widespread and ancient view. It is a theory of justice presented by Plato and Aristotle (Section 2). This basic principle has also been used in benefit-cost analysis for leaving to users the advantages or costs for which they are responsible, rather than including them in the public objective.[22] Yet, Dworkin, rather than these references, probably inspired recent discussions and application of this principle by Cohen (1989) and Arneson (1989, 1990), who in turn inspired a number of economic studies by Roemer, Fleurbaey, Maniquet, Bossert, Van de gaer, Schokkaert, Vandermeule, and probably others.[23] Some of them will be considered in Chapters 25 and 26.

7. INCOME EGALITARIANS

7.1. Varieties of income egalitarianisms

As we have noted, income equality is the classical ideal of the left, more exactly of the leftist view that is rather extreme, and yet focuses on distribution (rather than on deeper changes in social relations and ethos).[24] The basic view of income egalitarianism is that individuals' consumption has no valid reason to depend on their given capacities or social circumstances. This ideal equality logically results from discarding relevance of both productive and consumptive (or eudemonistic) capacities. However, we also noted, in Chapter 11, that these views also generally

---

[20] Analyzed as eudemonistic "Justice" in Kolm 1971 (Part III), along with other equalities, in freedoms and in allocations.

[21] The question of individuals' responsibility for their tastes is presented in Kolm 1966a in the discussion of the reasons for taking income as the direct concern of justice.

[22] See Kolm 1970d, 1976c.

[23] This topic is analyzed in Kolm 2001a.

[24] Such as "general reciprocity" in Kolm 1984a.

admit that people who work more deserve higher income corresponding to this extra work. In looking for the reasons of this extra income for extra labour, two of them appear: the main one is compensation for the extra pain, but merit for producing more for society is also sometimes acknowledged. They apply to differences in labour, on the top of a more basic general principle of equal income for equal labour, which is the central concept with priority, while neither merit endorsing differences in productivity nor differences in preferences about leisure and labour (or any other preferences) intervene in the remuneration of this basic equal labour. The presence of such variational or differential parts of justice applied to deviations from a basic reference state considered as just constitutes a quite frequent structure of conceptions of justice which cannot a priori be accused of irrationality.[25] Then, we saw that, given that a sufficient proportion of the freely chosen full-time labours are not too dispersed, this ideal for global distributive justice in macrojustice is best realized by an ELIE distribution with an equalization labour around the lowest normal full labour. This solution, with free choice of labour, is Pareto efficient and creates no wasteful disincentives, as all ELIE schemes.

A number of present-day philosophers would probably endorse an ideal of income equality. All present important conceptual general discussions, but three of them particularly focus on this issue in presenting it within very specific and relatively elaborate systems. None, though, has reached the simple conclusion just recalled. They are John Rawls (1971), Ronald Dworkin (1981), and Michael Walzer (1983). Before considering various aspects of their proposals, let us note a point that is at the center of our present topic. Dworkin's general device is an equal sharing of all resources followed by competitive exchange (Section 6 provided precisions). Since these resources include all productive capacities valued and measured by their possible output, this implies the equalization of "total incomes," including the value of all leisure counted at the unit value of the wage rate (the $v_i = y_i + \lambda_i w_i$ of Chapter 9), although Dworkin does not explicitly consider leisure (as he does not explicitly consider any "other" consumption goods). By contrast, Rawls and Walzer see income as the value of (nonleisure) consumption, as does standard income egalitarianism. Hence, only they belong, in fact, to the present section. The difference between these two incomes is very large. One consequence of Dworkin's view consists of the extraordinary features of maximal income equalization, which, we also noted, is ethically nonreceivable for several reasons. Another, however, is that this solution is Pareto efficient (with perfect markets),[26] while Rawls' and Walzer's are not. They are not so efficient for various reasons that will be noted, but one of them is their omission of leisure.

---

[25] See, for instance, the discussion of the comparisons of variations in satisfaction presented in Chapter 6, which constitute the valid ethical basis of judgments of the utilitarian type (see Kolm 1996a, Chapter 14).

[26] The various devices that Dworkin proposes as second-best resource equalization when equal sharing is not possible (cases of indivisibility) should avoid introducing Pareto inefficiencies and have to be considered more precisely in this respect.

7.2. Leisure and efficiency

In particular, Rawls wants to ideally equalize the distribution of "primary goods," one of which is income (and wealth) while the others are "power, (social) position and self-respect" – or the means to it. He considers that from such an equal allocation, it is possible that all individuals have more of these goods at the cost of losing equality, because of incentive effects. Then, he proposes to replace the ideal of equality by a maximin in an index of primary goods. Rawls is not precise about the policy tools for implementing this policy. However, as regards income, the implicit assumption in this respect has to amount to income taken away from, or not paid to, the most productive individuals as an increasing function of their received (notably earned) income.[27] This relates to the ideal of equalizing disposable incomes, and it results from the fact that the assumed incentive effect requires a "price effect" (income effects – the only ones for lump-sum taxes – generally induce people who have to yield or pay more to produce or work more rather than less).[28] Then, since this primary income is essentially earned income, and leisure is absent, the distribution or redistribution destroys Pareto efficiency. Hence, there are policies other than the chosen ones that are preferred by everybody (with possibly some indifferences).

Later, Rawls has admitted that leisure should be considered, and he suggested it should be one of the primary goods.[29] The result remains Pareto inefficient for the same reason if the same tools are used for the redistribution. This inefficiency also holds if income transfers are based on the index of primary goods with leisure as one of these goods, since the rate of substitution between income and leisure (their relative weights in the index) cannot be equal to the competitive wage rate (the "efficiency price") for all individuals as their productivities differ. And if the competitive wage rate were taken as the rate of substitution in the index for each individual – these rates and the corresponding weights in the index would thus differ across individuals – the result would be maximal income equalization (as concerns income and labour), which is Pareto efficient but has all the shortcomings noted earlier (injustice toward the "talented," unequal outcome-freedoms, shocking equalization of the values of leisure measured at the individuals' wage rates, gigantic transfers, and so on).

More generally, Rawls wants a solution that is not dominated by another possible one better for all individuals for all the goods he considers or for their index. This, however, is not Pareto efficient because these goods are not "satisfaction" (and an index that would be a linear approximation of individual preferences would not be the same for all individuals).[30] Yet, neither would this solution a

---

[27] The following remarks are an application of standard elementary economic analysis.

[28] This occurs when leisure is not an "inferior good," which is the normal case.

[29] My reference is to a private discussion in 1986 in Paris.

[30] We just saw this property for the case where leisure is one of the primary goods. This also holds for the other primary goods because power, position, and self-respect are not marketed goods (if buying and selling them were possible, which can in part be conceived, and if these exchanges were morally accepted,

priori violate Pareto efficiency if these goods were all intermediate goods rather than final consumption goods (the efficiency or lack of it would depend on individuals' relations in the uses of the goods they receive). In this respect, however, goods such as leisure or, probably, dignity (or even social status derived from "positions") have to be considered as "final." In fact, Rawls discards the directly ethical consideration of individual preferences as irrelevant for justice because of individuals' freedom of choice – of their life plans. Yet, for various reasons it is difficult to discard the issue of Pareto efficiency and the questions of unanimity and social waste it represents.

First, as Rawls emphasizes, distributive justice concerns only a part of the quality of society. There remains "the good," as different from "the right" or "the just." Although goodness is not the topic of Rawls' study, he does admit its importance. And happiness, or something like this, would doubtlessly have a place in the good society. This does not imply a kind of utilitarianism maximizing a "sum of utility." But it probably favours Pareto efficiency. Second, Rawls advocates classical basic rights, with priority. And we saw in Chapter 1 that these rights practically imply Pareto efficiency. Indeed, they imply the political right to vote, and the nondiscrimination right to be candidate for positions. Now, if a policy led to a Pareto-inefficient state, this would imply, by definition, that there exists another possible state preferred by all individuals (with possible indifference for some, but not all). Then, a political candidate proposing another policy leading to this unanimously preferred possible state would win by the unanimity of the votes, and anyone could be this candidate. And the inefficient policy would not be chosen either if there were several unanimously preferred proposed programs. Hence, practically, the classical basic rights entail Pareto efficiency. They are bound to be violated somewhere if it fails to exist. Therefore, the difficulties of Rawls' distributive scheme with Pareto efficiency are in the nature of a contradiction. In addition, if an existing state is not Pareto efficient, the existence of another possible state that everyone prefers (with the possible indifference of some) manifests a constraint that can be seen as a restriction of collective or social freedom – whatever the nature of this constraint.

The answer consists of acknowledging the noted income-egalitarian ELIE as the solution. This, however, results from endorsing the view, commonly added to income-egalitarian positions, that people who work more deserve higher income, and this ELIE has been obtained when these differences are relatively marginal for the bulk of people. Yet, Rawls explicitly expresses the view that a higher effort should not be a reason for a higher disposable income, basically because the capacity for effort has been induced by family environment given to the individual. He does not mention painfulness or disagreeableness of labour, which may be related to his discarding eudemonistic capacities as concerns justice. Or, possibly,

these goods would not differ from those bought with income, and there would be no point in the ideal equality in each of them).

the given environment also provides capacities to withstand pain or unpleasant-ness. In contrast, most income egalitarians also think extra effort merits extra income, or they approve of compensation for its painfulness, which leads to the income-egalitarian ELIE presented in Chapter 11.

Following Max Weber's remark that people desire equality for each of a number of goods, Walzer thinks justice to be equality in each of a number of "spheres." One of them is consumption in a restricted sense, represented by the corresponding "income." Others tend to be important services, such as access to health care, education, postal services, and so on. Such a society will or may fail to be Pareto efficient for several possible reasons. One is equality in various goods or groups of goods (some of which are final) among people with different tastes or capacities. Walzer, however, notes favorably that in fact people's actions would reintroduce inequalities favoring individuals who particularly enjoy specific goods, which tends to alleviate this inefficiency. Yet, this theory says nothing about issues such as leisure, efficiency, incentives, and the choice of the size of spheres and notably of income.

In the end, Rawls (initially) and Walzer bypass leisure, while Dworkin implicitly fully values it at the price of the wage rate. In contrast, the standard income-egalitarian outlook takes leisure (in all its dimensions) into account when it holds that individuals working more deserve extra income.[31] And it does not imply that the value of all leisure measured at the value of labour be included in an equalized "total income." The income-egalitarian ELIE mirors this popular view. It induces no Pareto inefficiency. If, moreover, an income egalitarian is only a moderate one and does not thoroughly reject the idea that there may be some reason in self-ownership, this is expressed by lower levels of coefficient k than k^e. Still lower levels represent more balanced positions, as well as the corresponding ethical, social, or political compromises.

7.3. The general structure of justice

Any theory of overall distributive justice has to face the problem of the relation between justice, with its requirements of equality,[32] and the plurality of goods and situations. The solution described here consists of acknowledging the hierar-chy of justice as conceived by people, with the multifarious cases of microjustice amenable to a variety of criteria, and macrojustice consisting of the general rules of society and the global distributive justice they imply. Macrojustice is then spec-ified as social freedom and the classical and constitutional basic rights and their implication in the domain of global distributive justice: incomes determined by

---

[31] Larger work can refer to duration, intensity, training, education, or to painfulness for any reason (dirt-iness, tediousness, absence of interest, and so on), and leisure can consist of a decrease in any of these dimensions.

[32] Including the particular equality of ideal marginal or variational equalities for ethical criteria maximizing sums (of incomes or income equivalents, of welfares or happiness in the domains of meaningfulness of the concepts, etc.).

free earnings and the ELIE transfers. Income egalitarians (in the broad sense) such as Dworkin, Rawls, and Walzer also face this problem. All the proposed solutions differ widely. There are ideally equalized goods, and possibly something else for solving problems raised by this equality. These goods are (given) resources for Dworkin, "primary goods" for Rawls, and goods in "spheres of justice" for Walzer. Dworkin then lets the market reallocate the equally distributed resources (and before all, one should add, transform resources into consumers' goods since most of them are not), after proposing solutions for impediments to equal sharing such as indivisibilities. Rawls is worried by "incentives" that permit unequal situations providing more primary goods for all than situations with equality. He proposes to solve the problem by a maximin.[33] However, the operations max and min are a priori solely defined for unidimensional variables.[34] After mentioning that, actually, the same individuals have the lowest endowments in all primary goods (this is not exact in all societies), Rawls resorts to an index of primary goods for performing the remaining operation of maximization. Walzer stays with equality in each of his "spheres." However, he notes that actual social life – possibly militancy – will bring inequalities in each sphere in favoring the people who like more the corresponding good, and he approves of this outcome where each individual receives somewhat more of what she prefers (this is a step toward Pareto efficiency).

There results the various positions with regard to the segmentation of justice and equalizands. In the end, Dworkin sees only one general "sphere" of justice. Rawls also arrives at an overall index for the maximin, although he also considers the classical priority of basic rights. Walzer stays with his spheres of relatively similar importance, although he acknowledges a little porosity among them under the pressure of life.

7.4. The place of the market

The allocation of anything to any individual or other agent can be questioned on grounds of justice, and of distributive justice since any other agent could receive the benefit or bear the cost, by transfers of the item or by compensations. One particular mode of allocation is selling, buying, and the market. This can be applied to many items. Then, given process-freedom, the corresponding issue of justice vanishes into the broader issue of income distribution and global distributive justice. Market solutions have many possible forms. They are not restricted to classical perfect competition. They include, for instance, allocating rare goods by auction, and markets, sales or buying organized by non-market institutions. With an efficient market, these solutions have the virtue of securing Pareto efficiency as concerns the allocation they achieve. This property can be a reason for favouring this solution. However, there can be practical or moral reasons for not leaving a

[33] For maximin in income, see Kolm 1966a.
[34] On the definition and properties of multidimensional maximins, see Kolm 1996b.

particular allocation to the market sphere. The practical reasons can consist of any of the causes of "market failures," including external effects, nonexcludable public goods, or problems of information or transaction costs. This notably jeopardizes efficiency. Some of these practical reasons can be faced by a duplication of the market solution by a public sector applying benefit-cost analysis, the theory of the liberal social contract, and benefit taxation (Chapter 3). This keeps the issue within the market sphere as concerns distributive justice and Pareto efficiency. Moral objections can aim at the fact of market exchange or also extend to these putative exchanges. They may be associated with factual difficulties, or not.

There are three kinds of possible moral reasons for not leaving an allocation to the sphere of market exchanges and of general income distribution. The market may not properly convey the values relevant for the allocation; and the attitudes, motivations, and type of interpersonal relations entailed by market exchange may have general shortcomings and, more particularly, be improper in the specific considered situation. The former case occurs when income distribution and individuals' preferences (or tastes) and information – which are the elements determining market allocations – do not suffice or are not combined as required. For instance, even with a policy of public information, they may fail to secure basic health or education, the protection and thriving of cultures, the protection of historical and natural heritage, or pure research. The second issue refers to the various psychosocial effects or requirements of the market concerning individuals' mentalities, attitudes, motivations, and relations, which have been considered in Chapter 4. The related third category rejects market exchange, because of this type of effect, for specific goods or in specific situations. For instance, this concerns goods that are morally inalienable (such as basic rights), or that it would be improper to obtain for money. Indeed, some goods can properly only be given or received for free; or as a gift or return gift in a relation of reciprocity; or they can only be exchanged with goods of a certain class, possibly of the same type as they are; or they can only be "bought" with particular goods or services (a case akin to the anthropologists' "special purpose money"); or they could not or should not even be attributed a money value (Kant opposes goods that have a price to goods that have a dignity). In addition to the noted fields, interpersonal relations or services provide many instances of these cases.[35] All allocations that are not made through the market system (or its public imitation) raise particular issues of justice for which specific criteria have to be proposed. These are the fields of microjustice or mesojustice.

7.5. Types and degrees of the segmentation of justice

Overall justice, therefore, is segmented. So is Walzer's system of "spheres." However, the structures are quite different. The various domains of specific justice are on the whole very numerous, they are strongly hierarchized in scope and

[35] These issues are analyzed in Kolm 1983a, 1984a, 2000a, 2000b, 2000d.

importance, with macrojustice and global distributive justice having a particularly broad scope. These domains and the principles of fairness they use are
determined by the reasoned consideration of people's moral views of various
kinds, of the alternatives, and of the various effects and consequences. In contrast,
Walzer's "spheres" seem to be in relatively small number, of roughly similar orders
of magnitude, and solely determined by a priori sentiments of sectorial equality.
Rawls also has several "primary goods": "income and wealth, power, position, and
self-respect." Yet, they do not define a segmented justice since they are aggregated
into an index – which implies in particular a very un-Kantian substitutability between income and wealth on the one hand and the dignity of "self-respect" on the
other hand. The segmentation in Rawls' theory occurs with the classical priority
of basic liberties and nondiscrimination (also a classical basic right). Dworkin
does not consider such issues.

The criteria of justice for the various separated issues can be of various kinds,
depending on the specifics of the questions, although the logical requirement of
prima facie impartiality and of some sort of ideal identical treatment of identicals
in the relevant characteristics will be present. The Pareto inefficiency that can
result from separate criteria and multidimensional equality in "final" consumption goods when preferences differ may not appear because the appropriateness
of considering the issues separately may be included in people's all-encompassing
preferences. When this is the case, people endorse the responsibility of losses in
welfare for securing some fairness as they see it. Moreover, there can also be adjustments of various types and degrees between the allocations in *prima facie* separate
domains, for more or less remedying inefficiencies defined with nonethical (purely
self-interested) preferences.

Equal allocation in specific consumption goods is a common and justified
solution for goods that both satisfy basic needs and are particularly scarce in the
society (equality among people with similar basic needs for the considered goods).
However, it has been demanded more extensively (for instance, surprisingly, by
economist James Tobin [1970], apart from the case of Walzer already discussed).
Prima facie equality can indeed demand it, but the differences in individuals'
preferences entail that other distributions are usually preferred by all to such
"pluriequal" allocations – they are not Pareto efficient. A number of solutions have
been proposed for facing this dilemma. One consists of free exchange from such a
pluriequal allocation. All individuals prefer the outcome to this allocation (with
the possibility of indifference). The efficiency depends on the exchange. ELIE is in
fact a solution of this type (with the characteristic that one good is leisure or labour
with prices a priori specific to the individuals – the wage rates or productivities).
Another solution consists of extending the equal allocation of several goods into
identical domains of individual free choices, or, equivalently, into the fact that no
individual prefers any other's allocation to her own ("equity," see Chapter 24).
The former case with the same prices for all individuals is a particular instance of
identical domains. Still another solution considers allocations that all individuals

find as good as the same equal one ("egalitarian equivalence," whose history, logic, and validity will be considered in Chapter 26). The issue of the consistency of the two foregoing solutions with Pareto efficiency has been closely analyzed. One more interesting solution consists of considering overall allocations such that all more equal ones are preferred by no individual and found worse by at least one.[36] This definition depends on that of the comparison "more equal" for multidimensional allocations. For instance, with one such definition, the criterion becomes that no individual prefers any weighted mean of all individual allocations to her own (this mean is a "linear convex combination" of these allocations, a vector in their "convex hull").[37] Pareto efficiency implies prices for these goods (their "efficiency prices"), and, with these prices, the obtained criterion turns out to imply that each individual could buy, with her income so computed, any other's bundle of the goods they both consume (one kind of goods that are consumed each by only one individual is leisure, since, for the purpose of efficiency, individual leisures are different goods with different market prices – the wage rates).

Classical basic rights (or freedoms) must have priority, as they have in democratic constitutions (see Chapter 4). Rawls acknowledges this fact and structure, but bypasses two basic points in this respect: the structure of the relations between these rights, and the distributive consequences of these rights. These rights include nondiscrimination (which Rawls sees as a separate principle). An essential point is that they are nonrival, whatever their nature and their holder, when they are defined strictly (without specific attached means) and the distribution of means among the individuals is sufficiently specified. Then, indeed, any conflict in the use of these rights can be attributed to the allocation of these means, or, for rights of the same agent, to the scarcity of this agent's resources.[38] In contrast, Rawls takes the classical position stating that these rights should be "equal for all and maximal" (expressed for instance by Rousseau, the 1789 Declaration, and John Stuart Mill). This statement would be trivial if these rights were given their strictest definition (without accompanying means) since, then, they can be full for all. If some "real" means are associated with these rights, then the condition of maximality does not really fit because there is no a priori limit to these means for most of these rights (means of expression, movement, protection, and so on), and the chosen means have to be specified and justified. Finally, the strict respect of basic rights implies full process-freedom and the structure of distribution presented in previous chapters (and hence, for income egalitarianism, the corresponding ELIE).

7.6. Why equality?

In all these theories, and others, the basic formal concept of justice is equality as fact or as ideal. The various theories differ by the items to which they apply this

---

[36] See Kolm 1977a, 1996b.

[37] This property was labelled *superequity* (Kolm 1973a).

[38] See Section 3.2 and Kolm 1996a, Chapter 4.

structure, and also, possibly, by the reason for which they endorse it. Most people and scholars do not give a reason and, following Aristotle, take it for granted that "justice is equality" ("justice is equality, as everybody thinks it is, quite apart from any other consideration," in *Nicomachean Ethics* and *Eudemian Ethics*). In contrast, equality is a consequence of the fact that rationality in the broadest sense of "for a reason" implies *prima facie* identical treatment of identicals in the relevant characteristics. *Prima facie* means in the absence of an overpowering reason, which can be impossibility or interference with another criterion (which can be ideal equality in other items). Moreover, the property of impartiality that all conceptions of justice have by nature indicates the relevant characteristics. This question will be presented in Chapter 23.[39]

7.7. Justification

Rawls insists on the justification of the principles he proposes, in a presentation that constitutes a large part of his contribution. This justification is his concept of "reflective equilibrium," which consists of iterative consideration of principles and their consequences (similar to Plato's "dialectic" in *The Republic*). This seems to leave much room to "intuition" (that Rawls rejects), even though it is elaborate intuition. Rawls also introduces, among things to be considered for this choice, his theory of the "original position." Individuals are "in the original position," "behind the veil of ignorance," when they do not know the individuals they will actually be and are also very uncertain about other things. In this situation, the individuals choose the rules of society. Their not knowing who they will be is supposed to guarantee the impartiality of their choice. This result is in fact not a priori guaranteed because individuals can have different preferences about becoming various individuals, and as concerns uncertainty. This possible shortcoming is not actualized in Rawls' conception, however, because Rawls assumes that the possibility of very bad risks and the individuals' risk aversion are such that all the individuals in the original position choose the same maximally cautious rules: the respect of basic rights with priority, and the highest possible level of the index of primary goods for the individual who has the lowest level of all (the "difference principle").[40] Rawls is satisfied with the fact that there exists a possible set of uncertain prospects in the original position that gives this result. He thinks

---

[39] The full presentation can be found in Kolm 1971 [English translation 1998], Foreword, Section 5.

[40] Rawls also considers a principle of nondiscrimination, which is classified second in his order of priority of principles, after basic freedoms and before the "difference principle." As a general principle, it cannot be justified by maximal self-interested cautiousness in the original position, however. Only particular instances or applications could be so justified. In particular, efficiency may require unfair discrimination and may require it strongly. Accepting it may be a matter of life and death, possibly for everybody. Hence, there is a need for considering the various possible types of discrimination, their moral unfairness and its intensity, the cases and types of discrimination that are banned with priority, and a corresponding theory of second-best fairness for other cases and types.

that this supports his "reflective equilibrium" leading to the principle he states. These principles are not deduced from a theory of the uncertain events and of the individuals' choices facing them. Moreover, equating a choice of justice with an individual choice in uncertainty is problematic (see Chapter 21, and Kolm 1996a, Chapter 8).

The justification proposed here, applying endogenous social choice, rests on the principle of unanimity. Unanimity is also the case in Rawls' concept of the original position, among the individuals in this situation. However, macrojustice as basic rights and the ELIE structure of global distributive justice only considers the views of actual individuals. The determination of the degree of redistribution (coefficient k), in Part IV, will use a number of possible methods, most of them again using the views of actual individuals, but some considering judgments of individuals who are transformed in order to improve their impartiality. Among these latter concepts and methods, presented in Chapter 21, the idea of the original position has a place, and we will see how some of the shortcomings of this theory can be remedied.

7.8. Private happiness

Income egalitarians of any type should first of all explain why they deem individuals' happiness, satisfaction, preferences, tastes, and eudemonistic capacities to be irrelevant for the direct consideration of justice, and why they differ, in this respect, from individuals' income or consumption. We have seen and discussed the fact that Rawls' argument is based on freedom of choice (of life plans using primary goods and basic rights) and Dworkin's essentially on responsibility, while the common view of this aspect basically rests on issues of privacy and of the self (Chapter 6).

8. HAPPINESS

All the theories that have been considered contrast notably with those that do not a priori endorse the "natural" allocation of eudemonistic capacities. These include in particular "practical justice," the leximin in interpersonally comparable ordinal "fundamental" preferences or utilities, taken as efficient second-best eudemonistic egalitarianism (Kolm 1971, Part III). These theories also include the variety of theories of the family of utilitarianism, with their specific forms and scopes of validity (the justification of a strictly utilitarian judgment, and the scope of such views, have been noted in Chapter 6).[41] For all these conceptions, basic issues are those of the scopes of their logical meaningfulness and moral relevance. These issues will be further discussed in Chapter 24.

---

[41] The presentation and discussion of the various concepts of the utilitarian family can be found in Kolm 1996a, Chapter 14. See also Chapter 24.

9. JUSTICE IN SOCIETY

9.1. Variety and structure

Macrojustice is embedded in two ways, factually and conceptually, in the general question of justice in society. It is a part of this question, characterized by the fundamental and general character of basic rights and by the large volume of distribution it determines. Yet, the few principles of its solution belong to the general set of concepts and principles of justice. A short overview of this general question may help situate these specific concepts and provides some indication about the rest.

The issue of justice is pervasive. It just results from the plurality of social entities with actually or potentially opposed interests. It exists even when it is not debated or fought for. In particular, everything can a priori be distributed in many ways, through allocation or compensation.

There exists a variety of principles of justice. They seem a priori to be quite numerous, although we will see that they can be organized and classified in a small number of deeply meaningful categories related to the degree and type of integration of the individuals in the society. However, some scholars hold a monovalued conception. They are, for instance, "utilitarians," (process-)liberals, or "egalitarians," implying that a single principle is the good one in all applications. Now, for each principle, one can easily find cases of application where it is not the appropriate one, and cases where the relevant principles are different, these judgments being held at unanimity (including the opinion of the noted scholars when they are shown the cases). Hence, at least from endogenous social choice and the principle of unanimity, the world of justice is plurivalued, multiprincipled, a domain for moral polyarchy. Yet, this set of principles is not an amorphous heap or a collection of specimens. It is strongly structured and notably hierarchized in scope and importance of application of the principles. In particular, macrojustice and its very simple solution take a large place and perform a large share of the overall volume of the allocation.

9.2. Dimensions, types, and degrees of integration or individuation

Justice can be concerned with the situation of any social entity, in particular individuals; it is then individualistic justice, the case considered here. Distributive justice is a judgment about the place of the interface between opposite desires, conflicting interests, and interferring existences of these entities and notably individuals. A principle of justice characterizes and justifies this place. It thus also characterizes a type of social relations, and a type of society organized by such relations. The various principles thus correspond to more or less closely integrated or, on the contrary, individualistic societies, in various ways. This shows in particular in the tripartition of the principles of justice according to the assignment of the benefits from individuals' capacities either to their holder (the "natural" entitlement) or to the concern of the policy of distributive justice, into the purely individualistic full self-ownership (which implies social freedom), principles directly concerned with incomes, notably earned with productive capacities (and notably with some income-egalitarian ideal), and principles directly concerned with individuals' happiness, satisfaction, or the corresponding needs (including utilitarian views or egalitarian ones in eudemonistic "practical justice"). The policy then is directly concerned with, respectively, no capacities, productive capacities alone, or both productive and eudemonistic capacities.[42] Relatedly, the classical revolutionary triple motto "liberty, equality, fraternity" intended to epitomize a triple level of relations and sociality and their principles: individualism in liberty, republican citizenship in equality, and community in fraternity.[43] These categories, in fact, encompass families of specific principles. Thus, liberty also stands for entitlement from action, free exchange, or agreement; for responsibility; and for reward for desert and merit from action. Fraternity implies caring for others' misfortune, pain, need, or happiness, and hence, taking such issues as measuring rods for the distribution. These two types of issues disappear in an equal distribution of goods or income. And in free exchange, each un-Kantianly considers others only as means, although she also *ipso facto* offers herself as a means for them.

There are many aspects and dimensions in the degree of individualism or communitarianism of a principle of distributive justice. Such a principle has both a substance (a material) that denotes the nature of what it is basically concerned with, and an interpersonal structure that determines the allocation – these questions will be considered in more detail in Chapter 23. A principle is more integrative when it redistributes more and in view of such "substances" that are more "intimate" to the individuals, such as, in decreasing order, happiness and pain, needs, productive capacities, incomes, and nonhuman resources.

However, the structure also has such a consequence. In the social objective, the individuals may be absent, present but only in an amorphous aggregate, very present as units but undifferentiated in unqualified equality, or fully individualized in their specificities, with intermediate cases of various types. In the first two cases, the objective is social as such. The second kind of objective can be an aggregate or some kind of quantity of the "substance" in society. For instance, this can be social income, a utilitarian sum, or more specific global objectives such as overall health or education. Objectives of the first kind are still more intrinsically social, such as national power or glory or the promotion or defense of culture per se (they may be promoted by the former, aggregate objectives, and they may be public goods). All these objectives are not individualistic. However, maximizing a sum of individual items implies allocating to individuals in comparing the variation

---

[42] For this tripartition, see Kolm 1971 and a complete analysis in 1996a, 1996b.
[43] This remark is extended and analyzed in Kolm 1989 [1991].

of the individuals' items (such as income or satisfaction). Such views exist for satisfaction (see Chapter 6), and they emphasize interindividual comparisons (the question of the logic of comparisons of variations is considered in Chapter 24). For income, this view relates the principles of "compensation" to that of the "surplus" (see Chapters 19 and 26).

By comparison, however, the two other types of structure take the situations of individuals as objectives. Interindividual equality, at least as an ideal, is both strongly individualistic in that it emphasizes individuals as units, and strongly social by the demanding comparison. However, it makes a large difference, both for individuals and for the nature of society, whether this equality is qualified ("to or from each according to her. . .") or unqualified, and, in the former case, according to the nature and scope of the qualifications. Unqualified equality emphasizes the existence of the individual as a society member as its sole characteristic. It corresponds to a political ethos of republican citizenship ("one man, one vote," equal basic rights or provision for basic needs, equal contribution to collective defense, equal sharing of very scarce and needed goods, or a more extended equal sharing in "stoic" Republics). In contrast, qualified individual treatment takes care not only of separate individual existences, but also of interindividual differences. This is shown by principles in the form of "to or from each according to her. . . ." With such qualifications, justice goes beyond mere existential individuation, into differential individuation. The individual is more fully considered than in un-qualified equality. By the same token, however, society applying such principles may be more or less intrusive into an individual's situation or life, except when the principle describes a freedom, on the contrary ("according as she chooses").

In fact, there are three great types of such references. In one, the individuals are instrumental for a global social aim. This is from or to each according to her possible contribution to some higher good. This good can be of varied type, such as intrinsic value with Bertold Brecht's "each thing should be given to he who makes it better," value appreciated by people (and possibly gods) with the antiquity's "give the flute to the flute player," the good of some social entity as with John Kennedy's "do not ask what your country can do for you but ask what you can do for your country," possible contribution to some overall aim as with "from each according to her capacities," or such an objective aggregating individuals' goods as with utilitarian giving to the sybarite who can derive more pleasure than others. The reason of the allocation then is synergy of the items allocated with some individual characteristics such as skill, means for using, need, or productive or enjoying capacities, or an incentive effect such as income inducing production.

This kind of reference takes the individual as means, for best or worst – even though the overall good may be a public good or may be redistributed. In con-trast, the second type of reference directly aims at the individuals – though obeying some rule may also be a transcendent aim. These references are about individuals' rights or goods. The right aspect includes concepts of natural rights, allocating, for instance, according to locational proximity, first occupancy, or self-ownership in capacities (in a sense a case of proximity and occupancy). The other type of individual references, according to the good of the individual, may be as she sees this good or otherwise. This concern is characteristic of community solidarity – as expressed, in its strong form, by expressions such as "fraternity" or "paternalism." This relation is more or less strong according to three dimensions: the scope of individuals' aspects for which this concern exists; the intimacy or superficiality of these aspects for the individual; and the intensity of the concern. The intimacy-superficiality refers to differences, in this respect, between items such as suffering, happiness, satisfaction, need, dignity, capacities for social life, productive capacities, income, and other means of action.

Finally, the third type of reference specifies the direct concern about the individuals and their specificities in emphasizing their aspect of agency. The individuals become grown-up. The issue is respect for their choice and the other face of it, responsibility. This also comes in degrees. The lowest level is judging individuals' own good as they themselves do, notably through the classical "respect of consumers' preferences." The upper level consists of respecting individuals' choices in decision, action or effort, of allocating according to desert, merit, responsibility, or process-freedom, and in the end simply of not interferring and respecting social freedom and the corresponding liberal and property rights. Distributive justice then becomes what has sometimes been presented as the opposite of "social justice" (Hayek).

9.3. Overall multiprincipled justice

The problem thus a priori consists of determining a principle for each specific question of justice, that is, of distributing principles over such questions in society. Now, we have noticed that these questions are a priori pervasive; for instance almost everything can be distributed differently among individuals, or redistributed among them, by transfers or compensations. Each principle has properties, in particular for specific applications. The logical relations among these properties, and the social meanings of these properties, often are not obvious and require logical (often mathematical) and philosophical analyses. Since questions are interrelated, so is the application of principles, which thus interfere. Moreover, a question may have to be faced with several principles jointly. These principles may then be consistent and complementary. However, this sometimes is not the case. Such situations are amenable to solutions with several possible structures, notably compromises, priorities, or application of a principle from the outcome of another ("superimposition," e.g., free exchange from an equal allocation).[44] All these relations between properties and principles raise questions of logic (and mathematics) that can be more or less complex. A pervasive and major issue is that this analysis requires specifications of properties and concepts that should

---

[44] The association of principles is analyzed in Kolm 1990a.

be actually meaningful ("actual" is opposed here to purely formal). For instance, the issues of cardinal utility, interpersonal comparisons, or the comparison of inequalities are well known, and Chapters 23 and 24 will further discuss these topics. It is by now absolutely uncontroversial that the general analysis of principles of justice has to jointly mobilize thinking from philosophy, economics, logic and mathematics, sociology, and history (there are now much too many studies that are brilliant from one point of view, but in the end are also more or less naïve, inapplicable, sterile, or mistaken because they forgot notions that are obvious in other disciplines or can be reached with a little more thinking of one type or the other). Part V of this study, concerned with comparisons with economics' social ethics, will show examples of all these issues.

Many scholars have emphasized the necessity of moral polyarchy in justice, notably when they based their reflexion on empirical observation or enquiries, be it in social psychology for Leventhal, Mikula, or Weinberg; in economics for Bar-Hillel and Yaari, and Young; in sociology for Elster; or in law for Zajac. A number of philosophers defended this view, emphasizing the relation between principles or the method of their choice (this includes Edel, Brandt, Weinberger, Rois, Gallie, Delaney, Hampshire, Daniels, English, Kamenka, Waltzer, and Berlin). In a recent study, David Miller (1999) suggests that principles of justice only belong to three categories, which either distribute some good equally or allocate according to need or to desert, respectively corresponding to the social relations of citizenship, community, and instrumental relations (exchange is supposed to implement desert although it rather rewards merit), and paradigmatically represented by the institutions of politics, the family, and the market. More specifically, Miller considers the two tendencies for allocating individual outputs, equally (in "solidarity") or according to labour, and presents and discusses the results of a number of enquiries and questionnaires about individuals' opinions in this respect. This is the very problem of overall distributive justice and of the choice of the degree of redistribution (coefficient k).

However, macrojustice has special characteristics. The direct relevance of eudemonistic capacities and happiness have been discarded for this issue (Chapter 6). This is also the case for needs if the degree of redistribution and social productivity permit the satisfaction of basic needs. And social freedom as process-freedom permits free exchange. Moreover, the allocated resource, although large in volume of value, is particular in nature. Indeed, individuals' given productive capacities are given to society, but each is intimately associated with its individual holder – as are all capacities. This makes the degree of equalization of the income value of these capacities more a question of degree of sense of community than a question of political equal sharing. For instance, voting about the level of coefficient k with "one person, one vote" will not be an appropriate solution for determining this level. Deeper considerations of the degrees of community and of individuation of society are needed. This is a main concern for the next part, where the solution of this problem is considered.

9.4. The trinities of justice

There has for long been attempts to classify the various principles of justice. This is, indeed, a natural exercise: all science begins with taxonomy, which is just making ideas and concepts clearer in pointing out the most relevant distinctions. Considering and comparing these classifications can thus provide an adequate recapitulative summary of the issues. Moreover, this comparison is very enlightening. These classifications are both similar in providing corresponding trichotomies of the principles, and yet more or less different in details in ways that reveal more or less crucial questions. The principles considered here concern direct individualistic justice. That is, the "justiciables" are individuals, and the principles concern their directly morally relevant properties (according to the principle).[45] Moreover, the principles considered do not refer to a priori given social positions but to "individuals per se". The three categories present concepts that are the basic (or direct) concerns, or the "substance" of justice.

The most integrated presentation of this categorization is derived from the assignment of the two types (for short) of individuals' capacities, the eudemonistic and the productive capacities. Self-ownership makes individuals entitled to all their capacities, and hence also accountable for their possible relative shortcomings in providing them income or satisfaction. If individuals are entitled to their eudemonistic or consumptive capacities (and hence accountable for their shortcomings) but not to their productive capacities or at least to the value they can produce, the substance or basic (or direct) concern of distributive justice consists of incomes or goods. Finally, if justice is concerned with the joint effects of all capacities and resources, its substance or basic concern becomes satisfaction, happiness or "utility" resulting from both goods and capacities to enjoy them. These substances are then integrated into various possible structures, such as an ideal of equality in income or in satisfaction, or the social criterion of the highest sum of incomes (social income) or utilities (utilitarianism). These are polar cases. Principles can also be intermediate (ELIE is generally intermediate between self-ownership and an ideal of equal incomes, inequality-averse maximands are intermediate between ideal equality and the highest sum). Moreover, a defined society for some defined problem can use a mix of criteria. One can thus situate the justice so used with respect to substances by a point in an isosceles triangle having the three polar types at its summit, the amount of each substance being proportional to the distance of the representative point to the opposite side. Although precise measures raise various problems, this representation is often qualitatively enlightening for comparing societies or sectors, and for considering evolutions.

The various trichotomies use items in each category that are varied, different, yet related.

---

[45] See Kolm 1996a, Chapter 1.

In the first category, they are, notably, self-ownership, process-freedom, exchange, the market, according to labour or merit, and responsibility.

The second category encompasses income or goods.

The third category includes "utility," satisfaction, happiness and needs.

However, a number of distinctions should be made clear. "Need" implies some claim to a right that it be satisfied, possibly by others' resources (in contrast with "desire," which evokes the opposite implication). However, the issue of need is a vast one, with many relevant distinctions.[46] In particular, some needs are for items that are final consumption and others for means of action. Allocation aiming at satisfaction, need satisfaction, or directly at the individual's happiness, is often considered the one normal for the life of communities, families for instance. However, the spirit of community is also manifested in other ways, such as structures of highest sum (of incomes, specific goods, or utilities), or sharing the values of individual capacities.

The issues of labour, productive capacities, merit and desert are essential here. Merit refers here to immanent merit, as a claim to the result of one's actions. As we have already seen, merit differs from desert in that it entitles to the effect of capacities used in the action while this is not the case for desert. Allocation "according to labour" can a priori mean one or the other.

A number of classifications of principles of distributive justice follow such a trinitarian scheme. The noted allocation of capacities is one. When the basic (direct) concern – or substance of justice – is made of goods or income, the structure considered is often equality. The triple motto "liberty, equality, fraternity" can be seen as following this scheme if equality is applied to goods or incomes (and not only to basic rights). Plato and Aristotle note allocation according to merit for the result of one's actions, and equal sharing of given goods. They do not seem to consider the third pole, and yet they go near to a concept of instrumental need (and collective benefit) when they advocate allocating items to people who are able to make the best of them ("give the flute to the flute player" was the standard example). Auguste Blanqui (and after him Karl Marx) also considers a threefold distinction of allocative principles with his three "historical stages" of "capitalism," "socialism," and "communism." Naturally, capitalism is related to the market and process-freedom, whereas communism implies "to each according to her needs." For the intermediate case, however, they avoid "petit-bourgeois egalitarianism" and allocate "according to labour." This was classically understood as merit, allocating "the full product of one's labour" – and so eliminating "exploitation." However, it would be more in tune with the corresponding political ethos to understand "according to labour" in a desert sense, discounting the effect of different capacities provided by nature or the family. Since the principles also add "from each according to her capacities," the resulting distribution

---

[46] See an analysis and references in Kolm 1996a, Chapter 11.

would be one closely considered here (for the equalization labour). Finally, we have noted David Miller's recent distinction of references to desert (rather, merit), equal sharing (of goods), and needs, which would interestingly correspond to the market, politics, and the family. Yet, one may want to keep the normative intent, and hence favour conditions extending the scope of transfers motivated by the principle "from each, voluntarily, according to others' needs."

PART FOUR

THE DEGREE OF COMMUNITY, EQUALITY, RECIPROCITY, AND SOLIDARITY

17

The degree of redistribution, solidarity, community, and reciprocity

1. IMPORTANCE AND METHOD

1.1. Place and general method

In the foregoing analysis, the distinction of issues and remarks about their relative importance, associated with principles of unanimity and impartiality (and hence, of the relevant equality), have led to the conclusion that global distribution should have a structure of equal labour income equalization (ELIE). Individuals should equally share their product of the same "equalization labour" k – obtained with their different given capacities. The corresponding distributive transfers should amount to the implementation of this principle. This equalization labour or coefficient k is rich in very important meanings: it turns out to be, for the considered society, a degree of redistribution (from full self-ownership); of income equalization; of solidarity for facing the unequal natural distribution of capacities; of community in rights to resources; of labour reciprocity (the redistribution amounts to each individual yielding to each other the product of the same labour, or to each owning this product of each other); of income compensation for lower productivity; and of decrease in disparities in individuals' total incomes.[1] Coefficient k will also turn out to be the minimum guaranteed income for individuals not responsible for their low income, as a fraction of the average wage.

The determination of this coefficient k is shown in the present part of this study. This will complete the determination of the required global distribution, and hence also, in adding the other applications of basic rights, of macrojustice in society. Macrojustice is a very important part of the social optimum, the main one as concerns the problems raised by opposed interests, notably for allocating society's scarce resources.

Moreover, the determination of this coefficient k will apply the general method for determining the social optimum. Hence, it also has the interest of showing this general method. However, this application concerns a structurally and formally

---

[1] For the EDIE form for the last two properties.

quite specific issue – although it is basic and very important for society. This particularity will entail particularly interesting and meaningful possibilities for determining and implementing the result. It is due to the two specifications that reduce the problem to the choice of coefficient k: the question is one of distribution and, more specifically, of finding the parameter of an ELIE (or EDIE) structure. At each step of the solution, we will see the general method, or the method general for a distribution, and the application to coefficient k of an ELIE.

This structure has itself been derived, in Part I, from the basic structural requirements of unanimity and impartiality – the latter required for issues concerning justice. Indeed, unanimity led to social freedom (the classical basic rights and process-freedom) and to the natural allocation of eudemonistic capacities. And impartiality was used for social freedom (and basic rights) and for the rationality of the relevant equality. Now, unanimity, impartiality for justice, plus, when necessary, the relevant information will constitute the three basic structures that will entail the solution of the rest of the problem (determining coefficient k). The use of unanimity entails that the method belongs to endogenous social choice. Of course, the point – the challenge – is to derive, from a criterion of unanimity, the solution to a problem of distribution where, by definition, individuals' interests are directly opposed.

The present chapter shows the general nature of the determination of the social optimum and of this application. Chapter 18 discusses the three basic properties of the general solution, impartiality, consensus, and mutual information, and their relations. Chapter 19 focuses on individuals' disinterested distributional preferences and on the methods of discarding self-interests from the evaluation: the consideration of interest-neutral judgments and the distributional surplus. The theory of consensualization through dialog is the object of Chapter 20. Finally, Chapter 21, the last of this part, shows how consensus can be derived from various types of impartialization of judgments.

In the present chapter, the rest of this section emphasizes the dual nature of social-ethical views, which are both views of individuals and of society, and points out their required properties. The various aspects of coefficient k are then recalled, with its relation with minimum income and total redistribution (Section 2). Section 3 notes the complementarity of the holistic and individualistic approaches. It analyzes individuals' opinions, the relations between their impartial views and their self-interest, and individuals' reasons for desiring to be coerced. Section 4 shows that the result cannot be obtained by self-interested voting, and it points out the possible relevance of several distributive communities.

1.2. Society and its individual members: Two faces of the same coin

Endogenous social choice proposes that what is good for society is what informed and reflecting society thinks is good for it. In particular, we will look for the coefficient k that society thinks is appropriate. Classical methodological individualism would object to the concept that society can think, reflect, know, prefer, or have an opinion, on the grounds that only individuals could have such activities or characteristics. However, first, this turns out to be a mistaken dispute when the nature of society, individuals, and their relations is properly and fully taken into account. Second, the societal or holistic and individualistic viewpoints should be reconciled or jointly defined, and this will straightforwardly result, here, from the reference to the proper consensus or unanimity (which in particular can prevent "society's will" from exploiting some society members).

The point is a dual tautology. Society is made of its members who are made by society. Individuals constitute society, which creates and shapes them. Whether or not society is "but" the set of its members, it creates them physically, genetically, and educationally by their parents, and educationally and otherwise by other social interaction. They are taught or inculcated language, thinking, and behaviour (children raised by animals cannot even walk). Society is no less within the individuals than the converse. It seems sounder to see an individual as a piece of society than society as "only" a collection of individuals (although some particular problems elicit the latter view). Even societies constituted by more superficial encounters have to develop common rules of communication, understanding, and behaviour. And the individuals of a constituted society are in a state of constant influence, intercourse, and interaction among themselves. Many social phenomena can indeed be analyzed as individuals' actions or interactions, or as their result. However, these individuals' motives, means, information, preferences, and worldviews, which determine their behaviour, in fact mostly result from previous interactions. Persons make persons, and hence, society has a high degree of self-creation. Moreover, this individualistic approach is not the fruitful first approach for some of the most important social facts. Language is the paradigmatic example, and it closely relates to the others. Although language is communication, the study of chatting behaviour will not be the first and deepest approach to it. And language implies or manifests concepts and thinking. Among these concepts are those that concern society, its proper organization, and justice. More generally, most of culture is better understood per se, globally, or historically, rather than as an outcome of individual interactions, although these may have some place in the explanation. This holds, in particular, for society's conception of itself, in particular for the degree in which it (its members) see(s) this society as a community for the different relevant issues (culture, politics, economic relations, resource ownership, mutual aid, and so on). And both the social and the individualistic approaches have a role to play in the understanding and explanation of norms and institutions. At any rate, most properly social facts are ceaselessly made alive, used, validated, sustained, and submitted to evolution, through interindividual interactions of various types.

All this holds, in particular, for the views, conceptions, opinions, and sentiments that underlie the meanings of coefficient k: the degrees of community or individualism, of solidarity and of reciprocity, and their practical consequences in the degree of redistribution or in the support of needs or low incomes. These views provide a main core of political opinions. Public debate about them constitutes a crucial part of democracy. They make up an important part of opinions about social ethics and justice, and all such opinions are elaborated socially. They result from the debates and fights of social and political life and history. Individuals usually adopt some existing political outlook under various influences. These views are best conceived as reflecting group-minds before being individual preferences. They are cultural products, although democracy filters their influence through individuals' responsibility.

Individuals, indeed, do not generally build their own political opinions but, rather, adopt one of the "political kits" available in the ideological marketplace of their society. This adoption is rarely carefully thought out and the result of individual reason. People often adopt the view of their parents, or of their friends (and when they endorse the opposite one for seeking distinction or manifesting autonomy, this is no more the outcome of autonomous reason). Views about morals, social ethics, and justice are thus primarily pieces of society's culture. Those of each individual are basically part of what Sigmund Freud calls her *kultur überich*, her "cultural superego."

Relatedly, individuals commonly see their moral positions as duties required from them rather than as tastes and related preferences. They see their moral stance as transcending their personal desires, which they often constrain. Its common relation to religion, interpreted in Durkheimian fashion, shows its basically social nature.

Expressed moral views are also often disguises for self-interest. This "pharisianism" (Max Scheler) is often pointed out by economists. This, of course, does not prove that only self-interest exists but, rather, shows the opposite. Why, indeed, would such arguments be used if only self-interest mattered? This homage vice pays to virtue can only be explained because the person who presents this moral argument thinks others are bound to be influenced by it, or because she likes to be seen as a moral person (a preference that is beyond self-interest proper and can induce moral behaviour). Actually, it often happens that individuals who present moral views for supporting their interest (or those of people they like) are not clear in their own mind whether they themselves believe in these moral arguments or not. In other cases, the objective is only to counterbalance other partial arguments with opposite conclusions.

Summing up, if uttering lips and writing hands are individuals', the view that "society speaks through" individuals has something to it, especially concerning topics such as the present one. "Group-minds" and common sentiments are meaningful concepts. Yet, society also "amounts to its members," and its views are meaningless if they are not views of its members or somehow derived from them. The conciliation of these social and individualistic aspects will result from the more or less explicit consideration of two closely related issues. One consists of the multiplicity of individuals' psychological dimensions, to begin with the co-existence of self-interest and of sentiments and views concerning others, society and moral, and of the relations between these two sources of judgments and conducts – possibly these two parts of a "self." Adam Smith could wholeheartedly praise the virtue of egoism for promoting efficiency in *The Wealth of Nations* only because he had emphasized the moral role of the "impartial spectator" within each individual's breast in his *Theory of Moral Sentiments*: justice, notably among interests, belongs to the judgments of impartial spectators. The other issue consists of the interactions among individuals' views, which shape these views. The noted double inclusion results: individuals are within society and society is within individuals, and the former entails the latter.

In particular, the views of individuals about social ethics, notably concerning distribution, their sense of justice, their sense of community, their ideas about social solidarity, and so on, generally reflect views more or less shared by the members of the considered society or by a fraction of them. They have been formed by influence, and they influence the views of others. Even though they are held by individuals, they are properly individual neither as concerns their subject nor by their origin. They thus differ from consumers' tastes about consumption (finding analogies would have to emphasize the role of education, fashion, and advertisement in consumers' tastes). A consequence is that the determination of the appropriate coefficient k, which has to depend on individuals' views for reasons of implementation, democracy, and ethical theory, cannot be a "purely ethical" endeavour, possibly relying on purely psychological traits such as given preferences. It necessarily depends as much on sociology and political life as on ethics "proper." In fact, the three cannot be separated. This is reminiscent of Rousseau's assertion: "morals and politics cannot be separated, and he who wants to study them separately is bound to misunderstand both."

1.3. Individuals' moral views

Finally, reasons of endogeneity, information, and respect for individuals lead one to derive the solution from the views of the members of society, as discussed in Chapter 1, but these views may have to be cleansed for a number of possible features. To begin with, ethics cannot be based on false presentation of facts, ignorance, confusion, mistaken beliefs, and misunderstanding, and hence the relevant views of individuals should be immune from these imperfections. This applies, in particular, to ignorance about other persons and to the obstacles to information and communication that entail it. Moreover, expressed moral views have to be discounted for biases, untruthfulness, omissions, lies, and hypocrisies – for instance those that aim at defending particular interests (pharisianism) or conceptions.

Furthermore, a view of a particular nature has to abide by properties that are intrinsic to this nature. Notably, a view about justice has to be impartial, from the very notion, concept, and definition of justice (although impartiality can have various focuses and structures). That is, this view should not be biased in favour of the interests or other desires of its holder, or of people she particularly likes, just because they are their interests or desires. Hence, if actual or expressed judgments present such biases, as they commonly do, these particular distortions should be erased for obtaining individuals' impartial judgments, or, as a limiting case, these impartial views have to be derived from purely self-interested or self-centered ones. We will analyze various methods for achieving such laundering away of partiality, self-interest or self-centeredness. One, for judging redistributions, achieves this cleansing at the aggregate level (this is the method of the moral or distributive surplus discussed in Chapter 19). Another, also for redistributions, focuses on the views of individuals whose interests are not affected (Chapter 19). Other methods obtain the result, and in particular its property of impartiality, from individuals' full information about others' reasons and sentiments (Chapter 18), which can result from communication and dialog (Chapter 20). This information and dialog can be actual, notional, or a mix of both. Still other methods notionally derive individual's impartial views from their self-interested opinions or from their views about distribution in particular actual groups (Chapter 21). Each solution will either make individuals' views closer to one another (for instance in erasing the oppositions due to self-interest) or it will aggregate them in some sense.

Such transformations of individuals' views can be notional or hypothetical, but they can also be actual through information or suasion, or they can consist of selecting the relevant aspects of individuals' views by the appropriate observation of behaviour or questions. They can consist of a mix of these methods.

The rest of this chapter makes precise a few issues about ELIE that are important for individual or social views about the proper coefficient k. It also makes precise some relevant aspects of individuals' views. The following chapters present the philosophy and techniques of the solution.

2. VARIOUS ASPECTS OF THE DEGREE OF REDISTRIBUTION

2.1. ELIE and coefficient k: Structure and meanings

Although they are logically equivalent, the various possible meanings of the ELIE distributive scheme are important for individuals' or society's opinions about the equalization labour or coefficient k. ELIE is, or amounts to, an equal sharing of the individuals' proceeds of the equalization labour. Each receives an equal share of this output in return for this equal labour. This amounts to a common ownership of the rent of the productive capacities used by these equal labours, interpreted as equal sharing of their money or income measure. This also amounts to each individual owning the product of the same labour of each other, and owing to each other the product of an equal labour of hers (with EDIE); hence to each individual equally working for each other (yielding her the product of the same labor). Consequently, this amounts to each pair of individuals mutually transferring to each other the product of the same labour – this is general equal labour reciprocity.

For simplicity in presentation, the discussion will be carried out for the case where the equalization labor k is unidimensional, in fact a quantity that is a duration (possibly adjusted for other characteristics of labor such as intensity or formation) as explained in Chapter 8. Everything that will be said for this case can equivalently be said for multidimensional labour and for the various dimensions of labour (duration, intensity, formation and education, and so on). Each individual i with productivity (competitive wage rate) w_i receives the net transfer $t_i = k \cdot (\overline{w} - w_i)$ where $\overline{w}$ is the average of the w_i, a subsidy of t_i if $w_i < \overline{w}$ and a tax of $-t_i$ if $w_i > \overline{w}$. This ELIE then is an EDIE (equal duration income equalization). The equalization labour or duration k, measured in such a way that $0 \leq k \leq 1$, constitutes a coefficient or degree of community or equalization of capacities or resources, of equal labour reciprocity, and of solidarity. Its complement $1 - k$ correspondingly constitutes a coefficient or degree of self-ownership, and of the individualism of society as concerns resources. Coefficient k also measures the relative social or moral value attached to product or consumption as compared with leisure and labor in the measure of the rent of productivities relevant for the equalization (Chapter 9). Very generally, this coefficient epitomizes and focuses the opposition, in society, between individualism and communality, self-centeredness and solidarity, and self-ownership and economic and patrimonial community. The discussion of its level is in fact mainly a discussion of this more general issue, which is a fundamental question about societies. Coefficient k provides a convenient, simple, and meaningful parameter for analyzing this issue. Correspondingly, and still more deeply, the level of coefficient k can be seen as manifesting the divide between the two viewpoints about society that exist within each normal individual, self-centeredness and impartiality[2]: the allocation of productive human resources is "self-centered" for the fraction $1 - k$ and "impartial" in this sense for the fraction k (however, this is impartiality restricted to output or consumption only, and the determination of coefficient k will result from broader uses of the concept).

The notable particular solutions are the two limiting cases of full self-ownership with $k = 0$ and maximal income equalization with $k = 1$, and the income equalization ELIE with a $k = k^e$ approximately equal to the "lowest normal full labours" (Chapter 11). The actual cases will be between full self-ownership and income equalization, with $0 \leq k \leq k^e$.

2.2. Minimum income

Individual i, working ℓ_i, has the disposable income

$$y_i = w_i \ell_i + k \cdot (\overline{w} - w_i) = k\overline{w} + w_i \cdot (\ell_i - k).$$

An individual with no marketable productivity, $w_i = 0$, has an income of $k\overline{w}$. We have seen, in introducing involuntary unemployment in Chapter 13, that an

---

[2] This obvious psychological duality is classically noted. The nonselfish self is, for instance, Adam Smith's "impartial spectator" within each individual. It takes what Thomas Nagel (1986, 1991) calls the "view from nowhere," although we will see that it is more moral if it is a "view from everywhere," and that it can also be a "view from before" (in theories of the "original position") or a "view from everywhen" (in theories of "moral time-sharing" – see Chapter 21).

individual with $w_i > 0$ who is involuntarily unemployed also has an income of $k\overline{w}$ if she is fully unemployed or if she is partially unemployed at a labour not higher than the equalization labour k, and she has a higher income in the other cases of partial unemployment. An individual with a very low w_i has an income close to $k\overline{w}$. In working $\ell_i = k$, any individual has the income $k\overline{w}$. Any individual with $w_i > 0$ can have an income $y_i > k\overline{w}$ in working $\ell_i > k$. An individual i has an income $y_i < k\overline{w}$ only if $w_i > 0$ and she works $\ell_i < k$. If $k \leq k^e$, this implies that she works $\ell_i < k^e$. That is, she could have an income $y_i \geq k\overline{w}$ in working normal labour, but she chooses to work less: she has a strong taste for leisure, and she "buys" much of it at the cost of having an income lower than $k\overline{w}$. Therefore, she probably should be held *responsible* for this low income. Moreover, such cases are rare, exceptional (and thus not a concern for macrojustice). Hence, a policy concerned with low incomes should focus on the level $k\overline{w}$, which is to be taken as the minimum income for practical purposes. Therefore, given the average wage $\overline{w}$, coefficient k and minimum income imply each other. Approximately, the equalization labor as a fraction of standard labour is like the minimum income as a fraction of average labour income.

Societies often define a minimum income for their members. Then, this consideration alone suffices for determining the level of coefficient k. Minimum incomes are determined by moral considerations and, often, political action, and they depend on the degree of solidarity – and hence the sense of community – in the considered society. Given these facts, they tend to increase with society's productivity and wealth, but $\overline{w}$ also does, and hence this may not influence their ratio k. The minimum income should in particular permit the satisfaction of basic needs, about which there is often a large consensus in a given society (these needs include physiological and cultural needs, means of securing self-respect, others' respect and dignity, means of social life and participation, and so on, and hence they largely depend on various aspects of the society).[3]

The basic point is that coefficient k and minimum income are determined jointly. However, it is also possible to dissociate the global distribution, defined by coefficient k, from the guarantee and provision of a minimum income, which would be considered an issue in microjustice, notably if k and $\overline{w}$ are sufficient for there to remain only relatively few people requiring this specific policy.

2.3. Total redistribution

In a society with a system of redistributive transfers, denote as τ_i the net transfer faced by individual i in this system – that is, the sum of her receipts minus the sum of what she yields – from the benchmark of full self-ownership. In the present practice of redistribution, these receipts should include the use value of freely provided public services or goods (which, in the presented structure of public finance,

---

[3] The definition and determination of basic needs are analyzed in Kolm 1959, 1977b, 1996a.

should be financed by benefit taxation in addition to the distributive ELIE scheme). The τ_i can be of either sign (or zero), and $\Sigma \tau_i = 0$ since they constitute a redistribution. The global amount redistributed is $T = (1/2)\Sigma|\tau_i|$. The distribution $\tau = \{\tau_i\}$, and the distribution $t = \{t_i\}$ of an EDIE, can be compared through the distribution of their difference $\tau - t = \{\tau_i - t_i\}$. In particular, there is a level of coefficient k that gives an EDIE with the same global redistributed amount as redistribution τ. This amount is $(1/2)\Sigma|t_i| = (k/2)\cdot\Sigma|w_i - \overline{w}|$, and this k is $k(\tau) = 2T/\Sigma|w_i - \overline{w}| = \Sigma|\tau_i|/\Sigma|w_i - \overline{w}|$. This is the *corresponding equalization labor* for redistribution τ. The global level of redistribution in a society can be discussed in terms of this $k(\tau)$. One can, for example, say that social income produced during duration k is redistributed – a rather meaningful concept or presentation. However, of course, the specific structure of the redistribution matters much (it may in particular amount to a set of transfers from individuals with higher w_i to individuals with lower w_i – EDIE is a particular redistribution of this type, it is a "concentration" of the w_i).[4] A rough estimate of $k(\tau)$ for present-day national redistributions has given values from one to two days per week, depending on countries.

3. DETERMINATION AND IMPLEMENTATION

3.1. The holistic approach

Reflexion and research about what the level of coefficient k should be in a given society can approach the problem in two ways: it can take a holistic and macrosociological view, and it can rest on a more individualistic conception and be more technically analytical.

The holistic approach estimates the level of coefficient k desired by the society from the consideration of collective and social conceptions and practices, such as the level of global redistribution, the support of (involuntarily) low incomes, or the underlying general degree of solidarity and of sense of community. The fact that individuals' interests can be strongly opposed about the distribution does not prevent the frequent existence of an approximate consensus about these facts in a given society, when the question is posed at a social and moral level (even if the defense or expression of interests often more or less obliterates the expression of this moral and social view). The ELIE framework bans certain aspects of the redistribution that influence judgments about it, such as the disincentive effects and inefficiencies created by other modes of redistribution (for instance the taxes and transfers based on incomes presently used). This elimination of the disincentive effects and of the related inefficiencies will tend to augment the degree of redistribution that seems appropriate. The holistic investigation permits obtaining estimates of coefficient k, using various considerations such as general cultural analysis; notably, the study of the ethos and self-view of the society as regards

---

[4] See Kolm 1966b.

integration and solidarity; the social view and preferences concerning equality and inequality; specific data such as the support of low incomes and the actual global level of redistribution; relevant parameters such as the actual disincentive effects; comparison with other societies; and historical evolution. This approach is complementary to the other one, which is explicitly individualistic, microeconomic, and more technically analytical. Both describe the same phenomenon but see it from different angles and focus on different pieces of information (somehow as microeconomics and macroeconomics do).

3.2. Individuals' opinions

3.2.1. Individuals' impartial views

The second approach starts from the views of the individual members of the society. Endogenous social choice precludes that other people's views be relevant, except in case of external effects or for providing information (or advice). This is a condition of autonomy, freedom, self-rule, democracy, and respect for this society and its members. The problem is one of distribution, and ELIE schemes – based on inelastic items – respect Pareto efficiency as concerns interests: some individuals have to lose when some gain. Specifically, coefficient k epitomizes, focuses, and polarizes the oppositions of individuals' interests in the distribution, and its level directly raises such oppositions (individual i benefits or loses from a higher k depending on $w_i \lessgtr \overline{w}$). However, the relevant views for determining coefficient k concern justice, and hence that of an individual differs from her own interests. Notably, these views have a property and a structure of impartiality. That is, each individual's relevant view is that of the "impartial spectator" within herself, sometimes conveniently described as the view of her corresponding moral and social "self." Individuals often have such views, in addition to their self-interests and to their partial (biased) preferences for favouring specific others (family, friends, and so on). The problem then consists of having these views relevantly influence the distribution, possibly in being known to a policy maker, while they are often hidden by individuals' interests in acts or in expression. These questions of implementation are shortly considered.

It is not uncommon that individuals act essentially according to their self-interest, but express and manifest their moral views about society in collective decisions at "constitutional times or moments" (that is, when basic structures of society are decided for a long time ahead), especially given that an individual's expression may have no actual effect in a collective choice by a large number of people. Now, a rule of resource ownership (or a degree of redistribution) can certainly be considered as such a basic structure, along with basic rights and, indeed, as part of them.

However, individuals may also be simultaneously motivated by their interest and by social moral views. In a frequent limiting case, they give priority to their interests. Then, however, they often still have moral and social judgments, but these views are not manifested in acts or expressions whose consequences can be at odds with the individual's interest. This is the structure of "lexical self-interest." With joint motives in general, and in particular with lexical self-interest, an individual can reveal her moral and social opinions by actions or expressions that do not affect her own interest, that is, that are "interest-neutral." This is the case, notably, in collective actions or choices where the individual is "small in a large number" (a "mass effect"). Moreover, for particular distributional choices, there can be specific individuals whose interest is not at stake, and hence who have no self-interested reason to hide their moral view or lie about it. Indeed, some distributional choices concern the interests of a limited number of people only. Even when the choice concerns most interests, these may be individuals whose interest is not affected and whose moral view can constitute a representative sample. In particular, the choice of coefficient k of an ELIE does not affect the interests of the individuals i with an average productivity $w_i = \overline{w}$, since this entails $t_i = 0$ for all k. Moreover, indivduals' interests can also be erased at a social level for the choice of a distribution. In particular, they cancel out in the computation of a "distributive or moral surplus," as is shortly explained.[5]

Finally, if individuals are fully deprived of this impartial viewpoint, it can be notionally built from their actual preferences by methods that are analyzed in Chapter 21. These methods are "extension" or "conjunction." With "extension," each individual evaluates the distribution as if it were attributed to individuals in the same social relation with her (a notional relation for most of them, for instance as if all individuals – herself included – were her brothers, children, cousins, or neighbours, or if they were common members of society). This extends, to the whole distribution, the individual's actual judgments for sharing among people she equally cares for (but this judgment a priori depends on the chosen social relation). With "conjunction," each individual notionally considers that she could be each actual individual as uncertain events (theories in the family of the "original position"), successively in time (method of "moral time-sharing"), or as various aspects of a multiple personality.

3.2.2. The convergence of impartial views

In the choice of a distribution, individuals' interests are in direct opposition in the whole domain of choice: in the choice between any two distributions, some individual interests are at odds. This will a priori not be the case for individuals' impartial moral and social views, which are bound to have a domain of "overlapping consensus."[6] However, these views need not a priori be identical either. Choices or

---

[5] For a complete presentation of the theory of the distributive or moral surplus, see Kolm 1966a.

[6] This is Rawls' expression, but we apply it here not to specific topics, as he does, but to the fact that some distributions may be unanimously preferred to others by individuals' moral views, although some individual interests are opposed in the comparison.

preferences for which they coincide – that is, the domain of consensus or unanimity – are *ipso facto* endorsed by endogenous social choice (see Chapter 1), provided the individuals are relevantly informed and reflective. This may provide the solution, for instance if the individuals sufficiently share a common view of the nature of the society and of justice within it. Such a situation may result from a common culture or from sufficient dialog or argumentation. Of course, arguments that have a moral form but are solely presented for supporting particular interests (pharisianism) are to be discarded or balanced against one another.

There can also be moral disagreements, however. They can be faced with a variety of complementary methods that lead to or stem from consensus at a deeper level. These methods, which will be fully presented, belong notably to the following categories. (1) Moral disagreements can be narrowed down or suppressed by the same reasons and methods used for self-interest (this includes the methods of "extension," "original positions," "moral time-sharing," social contracts, and aggregation). (2) The consensual discarding of eudemonistic capacities for macrojustice (see Chapter 6) leads to comparing two distributions by the sum of individuals' willingnesses to pay for the difference or income equivalents of it, and this evaluation turns out to rest only on individuals' moral preferences because the self-interested values cancel out in the addition (this will be the method of the "distributive or moral surplus"). (3) Individuals' moral judgments can be homogenized by sufficient mutual information about the reasons, causes, and experience of others' moral sentiments ("formative" and "empathetic" information); this information can be notional or more or less actual and promoted by dialog.

3.2.3. Different spheres

However, most people mostly act selfishly outside their family. In particular, their behaviour does not seem guided or influenced by considerations of overall distributive justice. Does not this prove that they have no preferences concerning this topic? Some economists, in particular, would classically endorse this conclusion (they are led to it by the conjunction of their methodological individualism and of their behaviourism). This, however, would be wholly mistaken. Actions of everyday life and global (overall) distribution constitute different spheres for both conception and implementation. The latter field is global, collective, public, political, moral, social, and foundational. The former is private and current, with interactions largely constituted by exchanges. These differences entail a number of structural differences as concerns conception, choice, decision, responsibility, implementation, and the role of coercion (as we will shortly see). Technically, global distributive justice is a collective concern, a nonexcludable public good, for individuals concerned by it who are on the whole very numerous, and this by itself provides reasons for its realization by the public sector.[7] More broadly,

---

[7] Considering distributive justice as a public good, and the working out of the consequences of this view, constitute the main topic of my 1966 study *The Optimal Production of Social Justice*.

people usually consider such moral social issues to be a task for the political and public sector. Basing the transfers of global redistribution on inelastic items (items independent of people's actions), as ELIE does, reinforces the division between these two fields. This division is in fact ingrained in the theory of macrojustice. Indeed, social freedom (process-freedom) or Pareto efficiency entail that the proper global distribution solely allocates given resources (see Chapter 1). It is chosen irrespective of individuals' private acts when they consume, produce, or exchange, as respect of this individual freedom. And these acts take this distribution as given. In any event, individuals, in their private actions, do not have the information about people's situations (e.g., their wealth) that they can directly or indirectly influence, and about the state of the global distribution, that would enable them to have a purposeful effect on this distribution through these acts (they can only affect issues of microjustice). Finally, as market selfishness goes along with altruism within the family (Wicksteed's *non-tuism*), it can also go along with a sense of justice for larger, political communities, to be implemented by political and public means. Then, in a sense, the field of market and exchange allocations is, in scope, between two non-market distributions, the family at the microlevel and the public-political distribution at the macrolevel. The objects and principles of these distributions are specialized, moreover: while the family lovingly distributes final, consumption goods, public macrojustice should justly distribute given resources.

Yet, people often also vote in accordance with their self-interest. However, they do this even when they are "small in a large number," for instance in large elections, where they know that their own vote can practically have no effect. One reason for such votes is that people think that so "revealing" their interest is what is demanded from them, as in a kind of poll, or for the purpose of synthesizing these interests in an aggregation. The main point, however, is that the choice of the degree of redistribution and of the rule of resource ownership is to be seen as a choice at the most basic political level only, the constitutional level, along with basic rights (which entail the ELIE structure as noted in Chapter 1). People's revelation of their corresponding preferences is to be considered in this context where their view commonly puts more weight on general principles than it does in their everyday life.

3.2.4. Interest-neutral individual judgments

Moreover, people whose interest is not affected by a distributional choice have no self-interested motive not to reveal their social and moral views in expressions, answers, votes, or other acts. For the choice of the coefficient k of an ELIE, this is the case of individuals with average productivity $w_i = \overline{w}$, since, then, the tax or subsidy transfer that concerns them is $t_i = k \cdot (\overline{w} - w_i) = 0$ for all values of k. Since the moral preferences of individuals have no reason to be correlated with their productivity, the social or moral views of these average-productivity individuals a priori provide a normal sample of these views in the population. More precisely, average-productivity individuals express their moral views under a few additional assumptions: the possible effect of the considered distributional choice on these individual's economic interest through changes in supplies and demands should be sufficiently limited or is not known to them; these individuals should have no immoral preferences about others' incomes (such as with envy, jealousy, or malevolence); and their moral view is that of justice if it has the required impartiality rather than favouring people closer to oneself or that one prefers for a reason irrelevant to the considered issue of justice. However, quite often these obstacles to truthful revelation by these people are not actual; or the effects are about compensated for such an observing individual (for the material effects or for sentiments about others' situations); or they can be discarded in neglecting some of the considered individuals – for whom they matter; or again they do not appear at the statistical level because opposite deviations for different individuals make up for one another; and finally these issues can also be discarded by adequate analysis.

Similarly, in a collective decision or gathering of information in a large society – such as a vote, a poll, or a "moral surplus" soon presented – an individual "small" participant has no relevant chance of influencing the outcome. Hence, there is no reason why, if asked her moral view, her answer or vote would be biased in favour of her interest. As we noted, one reason why, most of the time, these people vote or answer according to their interest, is that they think this to be what they are asked to do, for the purpose of providing the corresponding aggregation of interests or the information about them (in addition, they often lack a clear view about their chances to make a difference in the result, and interest may be more easily perceived than morals and justice).

3.3. Desired coercion

Society has not only to determine the appropriate distribution and, in particular, the level of coefficient k; it also has to implement this policy. The same individuals whose views lead to this choice will incur the implementation and also, in a democracy, realize it in some way. Distribution allocates constraints on interests, and hence its realization constrains and limits interested behaviour. Individuals' appropriate self-restraint and voluntary transfers would probably be the best way of realization. However, this behaviour commonly is too demanding on moral grounds.[8] Implementation then should use coercion. But the individuals' social and moral views, which have to want this necessary means, should in the end desire this coercion of all individuals – themselves included. It should also be noted that the distributional constraints of global distributive justice do not differ from the constraints that protect basic rights, since the latter include legitimate

---

[8] In addition, the measures that concern one individual depend on characteristics of the others that she would have to know. However, this information could be provided to individuals without coercion (for ELIE, an individual, knowing her w_i, need only know k and $\overline{w}$ for knowing her transfer t_i).

property rights, and one aspect of an ELIE scheme is that it constitutes rent-rights in productive capacities.

The duality of possible viewpoints – holistic and individualistic – also appears here. People can see – and often see – coercion as legitimate because it stems from accepted political institutions or processes, even if this constrains their desires and notably their interests. However, the same effect can result from, or be explained by, several individualistic mechanisms such as the following ones – and all reasons can intervene jointly.

(1) As the result of a rather common sense of fairness, people may agree to do their proper share (in yielding taxes or in not receiving larger subsidies) if they know the others do theirs. They have the guarantee that the others do their share if these others are forced to do so. Then, everyone is coerced, and yet, as a consequence, de facto everyone freely contributes.

(2) The realization of justice, or the aid to individuals who benefit from the transfers, can be jointly desired by individuals, and hence be public goods in this classical sense. Then, payers may want to avoid paying individually, while they nevertheless prefer the case where all pay to the case where no one pays. They tend to be free-riders. Coercion is then used for checking free riding (as with the classical conception of public goods).[9] This case differs from the former one in that people will want and try to free-ride even if they know the others contribute.

(3) Individuals may be clearly conscious of the duality of their interests and of their moral views. Yet, they may be unable to have their moral will sufficiently check their self-interest in their choices or acts, because of a rather common kind of weakness of their moral will, a moral *akrasia*. Then, they may welcome a coercion that forces them to behave morally – to be as moral in act as they are in desire – although they may more or less try to avoid it under the influence of their interests. The policy then amounts to a kind of Ulysses' bonds, preventing the individual from following the sirens' call of selfishness.

These three effects can be mixed in various degrees, and are bound to be associated with other relevant phenomena, such as the individuals caring about others' judgments concerning the moral quality of their behaviour,[10] and more holistic conceptions. However, the quality of society is probably improved when justice is more freely implemented. This was implied by the ancient meaning of

---

[9] Since the situation extends in time, voluntary contribution could result from the individuals' desire that the situation continues, but this is practically excluded for macrojustice as a result of the large number of participants. Indeed, this number prevents efficient retaliation for two reasons. First, retaliation cannot hurt only specific individuals. Second, since the punishers are small, effective punishing requires cooperation among a number of them to begin with – and this cooperation faces the very difficulties it intends to solve (the large number also prevents the possibility of the required information).

[10] This very important phenomenon is analyzed in Kolm 1996a, Chapter 13.

the term "justice" as the individual virtue of having the right attitude toward others (this is, for instance, its meaning for Aristotle and for Adam Smith). The particular feature of ELIE that it is a formal general labour reciprocity (each yields to each other the product of the same labour), seems very favourable to this free implementation, which then becomes a social system of behavioural reciprocity.

All the remarks about implementation are valid for basic rights and for the structure of ELIE, in addition to the level of coefficient k, and hence for the whole of macrojustice. They explain how this implementation is consistent with the respect of the political part of basic rights, which demand that the individuals participate in political choices.[11]

However, in the measure in which the determination of coefficient k presented in forthcoming chapters uses individuals' views only notionally corrected for possible actual lack of information or impartiality, there may be no conscious full endorsement of the solution by some people – those whose view is so notionally corrected – who can be more or less numerous. Then, a political moral implementation may be constrained by actual social and political life, in particular as a consequence of the respect of the political basic rights for a moral reason or as a social and political necessity (these rights traditionally focus on the issue of taxation). There can thus be a problem of second-best. Technically, this will be facilitated by the fact that the methods for determining the appropriate coefficient k will provide functions to be maximized, which can be under constraints of any type, including political ones. Moreover, actual progress in the relevant information and impartiality, or simply in people's desire of seeing their deficiencies notionally corrected, make these social and political constraints actually lead to the first-best solution.

4. SELF-INTEREST AND SOCIAL VALUE

4.1. From majority voting to the moral surplus

The effect of coefficient k on individuals' self-interest represented by their income, and hence their preference about k in this respect, is quite clear. Individual i pays $-t_i = k \cdot (w_i - \overline{w})$ if $w_i > \overline{w}$, and receives $t_i = k \cdot (\overline{w} - w_i)$ if $w_i < \overline{w}$. Hence, individual i prefers a lower k if $w_i > \overline{w}$ and a higher k if $w_i < \overline{w}$, as regards

---

[11] This kind of analysis should, of course, replace the classical conception of the implementation of social ethics by a "benevolent dictator" who has the will and the power of implementing the ethical solution with only, possibly, some difficulty for gathering the relevant information. Such an entity hardly exists. Dictators rarely are benevolent, or, at least, have the required benevolence. A priori, the very existence of a dictator violates political basic rights. In fact, information is not the only problem: motivation and power are no less important, and all three issues are closely interrelated. In any event, the optimum always depends on the possibility of implementation, which provides constraints. And in democracies, both the values of the optimality and the possibilities of implementation depend on individuals' views. Hence, the relevant analysis should first and foremost rest on a realistic psychology, properly including the place of moral and social views and the effects of information and of social interaction.

her self-interest. Therefore, with respect to the level of k, concerned individuals divide into two groups with diametrically opposed interests. We have seen the importance of the third, limiting case, where $w_i = \overline{w}$ and $t_i = 0$ for all k, for revealing moral views about the level of k (interest-neutrality). Indirect effects of the distributional choice on interests through variations in supplies and demands are bound to be limited and can be discarded here (or introduced as a qualification and refinement).

Therefore, simple majority voting solely motivated by self-interest would choose the highest or the lowest of two k's, or a very high or very low k in a choice among all values of k, according as the median w_i falls short of $\overline{w}$ or exceeds it.

However, simple majority voting is probably not a relevant criterion for this question, for two reasons. First, self-interested simple majority voting is not in general and a priori morally appropriate for pure distributional choices because it tends to lead to a situation where a small majority imposes very large transfers to a large minority. This can be avoided thanks to a number of facts such as the following ones, which can intervene more or less jointly. For legal, social, political, informational, or practical reasons, the choice may have to be that of a non-lump-sum tax inducing disincentive effects which limit its possible yield and may affect other people than the payers in restricting production, demand, or employment. The choice may be restricted by a priori basic rights such as property rights, previously incorporated in a constitution chosen for a long time ahead, for future generations, by a large required majority, and possibly influenced by moral considerations. The vote may have to be about several issues at the same time as with usual political elections. Some moral – non-purely self-interested – considerations may influence the vote. And there can be the game-theoretic effects of political competition. In the present case, the ELIE structure constitutes a constraint on the possible distributions, yet not a sufficient one in itself for avoiding having either full self-ownership with $k = 0$ or the "slavery of the talented" with $k = 1$.

The second shortcoming of simple majority voting is more general: this method equally counts the votes of individuals who are almost indifferent between the options and those of individuals who have strong preferences between them; of those who gain or lose almost nothing in the choice and of those to whom it imposes large losses or provides vast gains. Hence, simple majority voting is relevant only when intensities of individuals' preferences have a number of possible alternative properties such as being similar, irrelevant, not measurable, not interpersonally comparable, not revealed, or symmetrically distributed. Note, however, that in the choice of a pure distribution, it is impossible that a small majority of *weakly concerned* people defeats a large minority of *strongly concerned* ones since, in choosing one distribution rather than the other, the sum of individuals' losses or gains balance. With an ELIE, in particular, in the choice of $k = k^1$ rather than $k = k^2$, the variation of individual i's tax-subsidy t_i is $\Delta t_i = (k^1 - k^2)(\overline{w} - w_i)$, and $\Sigma \Delta t_i = 0$. Moreover, one can correct the defect of simple majority voting by replacing it with *weighted voting*. Then, however, if the weights are the gains and losses, votes about a purely distributional choice always give a tie, and this is in particular the case for the choice of the k of an ELIE, as just noted. Yet, such weights describe material *self-interest* only, whereas individuals also have other motivations, notably social-ethical ones about the distribution and transfers of incomes. Indeed, individuals very frequently express opinions about distributive justice, poverty, equality, or the legitimacy of self-ownership. These are basic issues of the programs of political parties who organize the vote. Then, if the weights can also include, in addition, individuals' willingness to pay for the implementation of their *moral views* (or the money value this implementation has for them), these views will *determine the outcome* because the parts of the weights that represent *self-interested benefits or losses from the transfers cancel out* in the addition. This happens even if all people were ready to actually pay *only very little* for the real-ization of their social or moral views – the case of lexical self-interest. This will constitute the method of the "moral surplus," which is analyzed in Chapter 19.[12] Weights that would measure not only willingness to pay of the individuals, but also the effects of their capacities to be satisfied (such as classical "utilities"), would not be relevant for macrojustice (see Chapter 6) – and they raise logical problems of definition and comparison.

If the individuals have the same moral rankings of the possible distributions (independently of any intensity of preferences), the method of the moral surplus will yield the distribution they deem to be the best one on moral grounds. In the other cases, the moral surplus arbitrates among individuals' different moral views and aggregates these ethical opinions. It yields a solution even in case of general lexical self-interest (that is, when individuals actually give an absolute priority to their interest). This method of arbitrage may be accepted by consensus at a deeper level. And indeed, for macrojustice, the consensus about the irrelevance of individuals' capacities for happiness leads to taking willingnesses to pay or income equivalents as a measuring rod for distributional choices. Moreover, the individuals' preferences used for the moral surplus can be actual preferences or preferences notionally corrected for the effects of deficiencies in information, moral concern, or impartiality.

The surplus method, in general, is the basic principle for choices of benefit-cost analysis in scientific public finance, although its usual applications add individu-als' money equivalents, or willingnesses to pay, concerning individuals' interests only. It is equivalent to the classical principle that "the beneficiaries can compen-sate the losers" (including the tax payers). It also amounts to choosing the highest aggregate social income, an income that, for the moral surplus, should include in-dividuals' money measure of their moral satisfaction (only comparisons between states matter for this measure). Hence, this criterion is in fact very much an aggre-gate and social principle. It nevertheless "respects individuals' preferences," while discarding happiness or satisfaction, which can be influenced by eudemonistic

---

[12] See Kolm 1966a.

capacities. Finally, measuring ethical preferences by individuals' willingness to pay for distributional changes constitutes a "bridge" between the a priori heterogeneous spheres of interest and of moral and social judgments that may raise questions. However, for strongly self-interested individuals (as economists are used to present them, for instance), the possibility of lexical self-interest constitutes an incommensurability between interest and moral values at a structural level.[13]

4.2. Levels of community and distribution

The appropriate level of coefficient k will a priori depend on the considered society, since it depends on society members' sentiments of community, solidarity, and reciprocity. These sentiments, indeed, jointly determine the values and the implementation of the redistribution. Families usually pool all their earnings, and they also share most of their nonworking time and activities. An ELIE at world level cannot expect to redistribute more than a small percentage of incomes (the formation of capacities and education for the poorest will become the issue).[14] The present redistribution in nations has been noted, with corresponding equalization labours of one to two days per week. An individual can thus be involved in several redistributive communities, with generally a different coefficient k for each. These communities can in particular correspond to successively larger populations, such as the family, the nation, the world, with possibly also a regional or local level, or some supranational community of nations.

[13] Classical technical problems raised by the method of the surplus are dealt with in Chapter 19.
[14] Our present topic does not include questions of culture and of the formation of desires. Modern lifestyle and education are sometimes fully detrimental.

18

Impartiality, consensus, and information

1. THE VARIOUS ANGLES OF APPROACH

We have seen that the facts about macrojustice, the relevant unanimous views, and the structure of impartiality required by conceptions of justice, entail that distributive justice in macrojustice has a structure of equal labour income equalization (ELIE). There remains to determine and realize the degree of community, redistribution, solidarity, or reciprocity: coefficient k. Chapter 17 has shown various basic aspects of this number and of the realization of the corresponding distribution. We now turn to the philosophy and the techniques of its determination. Endogenous social choice requires that the solution be derived from the views of society and of its members. The approaches to this determination are amenable to a dual division concerning, respectively, "who" evaluates and what is primarily evaluated. On the one hand, the evaluation can be seen as collective, cultural, sociological, and the result of the public ethos and debates; or it can be seen as made by the individual members of society. On the other hand, coefficient k can directly result from the view about global aspects of the society such as its degree of community or solidarity, or of individualism; or it can result from judgments about the interpersonal distribution of income or welfare, given that this distribution has the structure of an ELIE for the indicated reasons. These approaches, however, join one another when they are sufficiently deeply worked out. We now focus on the approach by individuals' judgments, in considering their views about the distribution (and sometimes directly coefficient k). The present chapter outlines the basic general concepts, and the following ones of this part present the specific methods.

The explicit emphasis on individuals' evaluations, even if these views are social facts and are cultural, collective, shared, and influenced, is an ethical standpoint required by basic rights and democracy. These principles require, indeed, that views, evaluations, and judgments be taken into account through individuals, even if they are also, or more, social and collective phenomena. Whether they are individuals' own or not, the views have to be endorsed by individuals who take responsibility for them – the notion of responsibility is attached to individuals. The social and moral views are taken into account through this "individualistic filter." This is an "individualism of responsibility," different from the classical ethical individualism which refers to the fact that the objects that are ultimately valued by the judgment refer to individuals (such as their happiness, freedom, welfare, rights, income, and so on). This latter aspect refers to the second noted dichotomy, between evaluating individual items or inherently collective or social facts (as with nationalism, for instance). Most of the forthcoming analyses follow the former approach in ultimately valuing individuals' items directly or indirectly. They thus are individualistic on both grounds: they are individuals' evaluations of individuals' interests or values. However, the individuals' evaluations will be their views about justice, which intrinsically consider the values for other individuals, and are basically concerned with the bundle of individual items, with its structure, and with comparisons among these items. Moreover, the interrelations and influences among these individual views will be emphasized in various ways.

The three bases of the individualistic way of solution, consensus, impartiality, and information, are noted in Section 2, which discusses the former two. Section 3 then focuses on information, notably on the two particular types of information that may lead to consensus, empathetic information and formative information, and on the role of dialog. Finally, Section 4 points out that the whole of the solution rests on the same property of impartial, informed consensus, and that impartiality itself may, in theory, result from the noted exhaustive information.

2. OUTLINE OF THE INDIVIDUALISTIC WAY OF SOLUTION

2.1. The three bases. Consensus

In the end, three phenomena will provide the solution: unanimity or consensus, impartiality, and information. Each can be applied about various issues, however, with the effect that there are various possible techniques, methods, and specific theories, which will turn out to be complementary. Consensus makes the solution belong to endogenous social choice. It also provides the relation between individuals' judgments and the holistic, cultural, or sociological evaluation. Of course, since the issue is distribution (with a Pareto-efficient mechanism), some people lose when others gain and individuals' interests are opposed. Therefore, consensus does not refer to interests. It refers to individuals' conceptions of justice concerning the distribution. It may be about the solution or about aspects of evaluations that entail it.

2.2. Defining and using individuals' conceptions of justice

A priori, an individual may or may not have a sufficient conception of justice. When she has a judgment in this respect, it may influence her actions, or she may tell this opinion, or this may not be the case or she may do that in various possible degrees, notably because this may interfere with her interest. Solutions to these various problems will have to be found, notably for finding the notional conception of justice of people who actually lack one, and for all people's conceptions of justice to properly influence the outcome, possibly in being known and used by a policy maker.

2.3. Impartiality

A characteristic structure of a conception of justice is its impartiality. An impartial judgment is about items as to which individuals' preferences of any nature are opposed. It entails a solution to this opposition and to the problem of distribution it constitutes. It can notably apply to the distribution of tangible items, which raises opposition among individuals' interests. However, impartiality can apply in a variety of ways, depending on the items it is applied to, on individuals' characteristics it may refer to, and on the structure of the judgment of which it is a feature. For instance, impartiality among interests can a priori be among individuals' income, consumption, welfare, various need satisfactions, freedoms, rights, or powers. It can refer to individuals' needs, to eudemonistic capacities, or to various possible aspects of individuals' situations. It can also be about variations or about absolute levels. This possible variety implies that individuals' impartial judgments about individuals' interests need not coincide. Impartiality in itself is far from implying consensus (as many scholars tend to believe),[1] although it makes a crucial step in this direction. Moreover, there can also be impartiality among individuals' social or moral judgments, notably among their conceptions of justice (which are each impartial among individuals' interests). All these remarks will be used in the solution. Individuals' relevant impartial judgments will have to be found in their actual views, elicited from them, or notionally built up from them (the various methods will be considered).

2.4. Homogenizing moral views

Possible differences in individuals' impartial views describing their relevant conception of justice are differences about social-ethical judgments. They can be resolved in various ways which will be presented and analyzed in detail. One way consists in making second-degree evaluations of these views, in treating them as they themselves treat differences in self-interests, and in continuing in a converging recurrence (Chapter 21). Aggregations of moral views and contractual agreements among them also provide meaningful and convenient possibilities

---

[1] Adam Smith's theory of the "impartial spectator" in his *Theory of Moral Sentiments* seems to be a case in point.

(Chapters 19 and 21). However, particularly noteworthy solutions rest on the issue of information.

3. INFORMATION

3.1. Moral importance and types

The individuals' relevant conceptions are the informed ones, since ethics and in particular justice cannot rest on ignorance, mistaken beliefs, confusion, or misunderstandings. Hence, the conceptions of justice to be considered are with full relevant information. This is, indeed, a condition of rationality. This information may have to be notional, at least in part. Information, however, can apply to a number of items and, in addition to usual items, the present consideration of individuals' views concerning justice introduces two particular types of information of individuals about one another, the "formative" and the "empathetic" information. Both induce a narrowing down of differences in individuals' views, a homogenization of these views, with in the end an identity.

3.2. Formative information

An individual's conception of justice, and more generally her social sentiments (which constitute one source of the notional, constructed conceptions of justice),[2] largely result from information about values and facts that she has been submitted to in her family and other social environments, and possibly from life experiences that affect later conceptions through the information about these experiences (including recollection about them). This is the "formative information." Conceptions of justice of two persons who received the same formative information can only result from differences in their relevant sensitivities. However, the acquired causes of these sensitivities can be seen as resulting from formative information. Hence, the only possible remaining source of differences in these individuals' views are the effects of genetic differences on sensitivities. Moreover, the presently relevant differences do not consist of being more or less sensitive to injustice (since only conceptions of justice are considered here, and not trade-off between desires for justice and self-interests). Rather, the relevant differences are those that could lead to different conceptions of justice, such as relative sensitivities to various types of need satisfaction or freedoms. One can surmise that, in a given society, acquired differences are much more important than those of genetic origin, in particular for the issue of macrojustice considered here. Hence, with (notional) full information, individuals have identical formative information, and, for this reason, their relevant conceptions of justice will tend to be quite similar. This is a

---

[2] As shown in Chapter 21.

case of "causal laundering," which erases differences in conceptions in laundering away differences in their causes (this laundering can be notional or can be more or less actually achieved through providing information).

3.3. Empathetic information

Moreover, information includes individuals' knowledge of the others' conceptions of justice. However, knowing such a conception is not only knowing that it exists, and possibly the reasons that underlie it. It also includes knowing what it is and notably how it feels to have such a sentiment. This latter knowledge is "empathetic information." Full empathetic information implies duplicating others' corresponding feelings with the same intensity and duration, that is, sharing these sentiments. Hence, full information of all society members makes them share the same sentiments and judgments about justice.[3] This consideration constitutes the most basic and justified homogenization and, hence, consensualization, of individuals' social-ethical judgments. Practically, mutual information about individuals' opinions can go some way in this direction (for instance, in a dialog). However, it will often fall short of reaching this exhaustive information. The rest should then be considered through theory. However, limited knowledge about psychology can make this difficult. But this ideal can then be approached by a few more specific technical methods which will be presented, such as the theories of dialog (Chapter 20), "moral risk" or the relevant "original position," "moral time-sharing," and the "multiple self" (see Chapter 21). Other methods can also implement this consensus ("interest-neutral evaluations," the "moral surplus" – see Chapter 18).

3.4. Dialog

Information about the causes of others' judgments and the sentiments that underlie them can be provided by communication and dialog, which transmit factual information, reasons, and affects. A process of dialog also informs people about the ways in which others accommodate the various causes and sentiments corresponding to various judgments. Such a process can be actual, notional, or both in various possible associations. This process reaches a steady state when the relevant information and the judgments of the individuals are the same. Consensus, however, is morally acceptable only if individuals are informed of all relevant facts

---

[3] Full information can also result in each individual knowing the view and feeling the sentiments of each individual in a separate manner, as possible alternative considerations, rather than in a synthetic and integrated way. However, when a choice has to be made, and information about all cases is equally full, this choice will result from a synthesized view. Then, this synthesis may depend on the synthesizing individuals' characteristics other than information in the considered extended sense. These differences can then only be the genetic ones alluded to above, with the same likely limited consequence for issues of macrojustice.

and reasons and are sufficiently reflective (yet, consensus per se guarantees that no individual is clearly hurt by others).

Moreover, information uses means which can be more or less scarce, such as material and physical means, and psychological means for expression, attention, reflexion, memory, and so on. Information is limited by these scarcities. The information and opinions resulting from a dialog may be more or less close to an individual's initial information and opinion, depending on the relative importance of the means the individuals use in trying to convince others by information about their initial judgment, its causes and reasons, and the sentiments that underlie it. However, differences in the availability of means of information and in their uses across individuals may not be morally justified. In this case, impartiality requires equalities in these means or the appropriate compensations. This underlies the frequent rules aiming at such impartiality or equality in means of presenting one's views (such as the Athenian *isēgoria*, equal time of public expression).[4]

4. STRUCTURAL REMARKS

The bases of the determination of coefficient k, namely, consensus, impartiality, and information, are the same that led to the other aspects of the solution of the question of macrojustice, that is social freedom (basic rights and process-freedom) and the ELIE structure for global or overall distributive justice. Indeed, social freedom or basic rights were shown in Part I to result from consensus and impartiality. Pareto efficiency directly results from the unanimity principle. Either of these two properties entails restricting distribution to that of given natural resources. The endorsement of the natural allocation of eudemonistic capacities for global distributive justice resulted from a consensual view. And the equal sharing of resources, which, relevantly applied, led to ELIE, was an application of impartiality. Even information intervened in the remark that the wage rates w_i are more readily known than other possible bases of a distributive policy.

Finally, formative and empathetic information constitute a thorough and complete application of the issue of information. Pushing this concept to its notional limit leads one to consider individuals who know others as they know themselves, including feeling how they feel for empathetic information. Such an individual may, as a consequence, have to be impartial in some way in judging the overall situation. Then, full information in this extensive sense would imply impartiality. The bases of the solution would thus be reduced to two: information and consensus. It would even be reduced to one, information, if empathetic information leads to a uniformization of individuals' moral views. However, apart from a possible conceptual satisfaction about the resulting generality and the reduction of the number of bases, in practice properties of impartiality and consensus have to be explicitly considered for the solutions.

---

[4] The theory of the moral determination of the solution by dialog will be presented in Chapter 19.

19

Disinterested judgments and the moral surplus

1. ERASING SELF-INTEREST FROM JUDGMENTS ABOUT DISTRIBUTIONS: THE METHODS

The just, global distribution determined by endogenous social choice derives from individuals' conceptions of justice, and only from this part of their overall judgments. Hence, it should not be directly influenced by individuals' special relation to their own interest. Individuals' self-interested judgments should therefore be banned from the individuals' evaluations on which the global evaluation is based: the individuals' overall judgments used should be laundered for their self-interest, or individuals' non-self-interested evaluations should be singled out from their overall judgment for use in the global evaluation. Not uncommonly, individuals have a dual standard, one self-interested and the other moral and impartial, which they express in different occasions. However, individuals also often have an integrated view resting on both motives, and the relative importance they attach to them can be very varied. Individuals also have preferences favouring the situation of particular others for reasons irrelevant to impartial justice, notably the closeness of the social relation with them. This extends self-interest into self-centeredness. No practical effect results if this concerns family altruism because an individual's income is in fact her household's. Self-centeredness is more generally considered in Section 4.4, and in Chapter 21 where it will be the basis of one method of solution.

Erasing the self-interested motive in the individuals' evaluations can be done in various ways. One can analyze the structure of the overall preferences of each individual and try to discriminate among the effects of various motives for banning those of self-interest. One can also restrict consideration to the preferences of individuals whose interest is not affected by the considered distribution (interest-neutral evaluations). A neighbouring method consists of asking their relevant moral or social evaluation to individuals whose expression has no actual influence, possibly because they are "small in a large number" (a "mass effect"), and hence who have no self-interest in lying. These methods may provide sufficient samples of the impartial opinions of the population (and they provide the solution when the individuals' relevant impartial social-ethical preference orderings coincide).

However, the erasement of self-interested judgments can also, for a distribution, be performed at the aggregate level, in comparing distributions by the sum of individuals' willingnesses to pay for them or money value of them.[1] Indeed, an individual's willingness to pay for a reason of self-interest, for an amount of money she receives (or yields), precisely is this amount (counted negatively for a loss or a tax). Hence, for a pure redistribution, the sum of these amounts is zero. Then, in the sum of individuals' willingnesses to pay for the redistribution, only their willingness to pay for disinterested reasons remains (this is shortly the object of a detailed analysis). Evaluating by the sum of individuals' willingnesses to pay is the classical method of the surplus (which, however, is usually not applied to the choice of distributions).[2] This method basically assumes that the intensity of satisfaction an individual derives from units of income is irrelevant for the considered social-ethical choice. Now, this irrelevance of capacities for being satisfied or happy is precisely a consensual view for the question of overall or global distributive justice in macrojustice (see Chapter 6).

All these methods apply in particular when individuals give priority to their own interest (lexical self-interest).

The present chapter therefore focuses on the three methods that erase the self-interested motives from individuals' evaluations of a distribution: the analysis of the structure of individuals' jointly self-interested and disinterested preferences about a distribution; the consideration of evaluations of individuals whose interest is not affected by a redistribution or by consequences of their expression; and the method and principle of the surplus. These methods are closely related: the structure of individuals' preferences is useful for the other two; and the self-interest-neutral individual evaluations or expressions, on the one hand, and the surplus principle, on the other hand, are complementary in that they erase the self-interested judgments about a distribution at the individual and aggregate levels, respectively. In all three theories, we will see both the general case and the application to global distributive justice (that is, the determination of coefficient k of an ELIE scheme). Disinterested judgments and their "revelation" are considered in Section 2. Section 3 outlines the general theory of the distributive or moral surplus. Section 4 then considers the structure of individuals' overall preferences, with both a self-interested and a disinterested motive, about a distribution that has the structure of an ELIE. Then, Section 5 analyzes the global distributive surplus, that is, the application of the theory of the moral or distributive surplus to the determination of coefficient k of an ELIE.

---

[1] The question of the difference between willingness to pay and money or income value or equivalent appears in the theory of the surplus and will be considered in Section 3 and in Chapter 26.

[2] The theory of the moral or distributive surplus is presented and analyzed in full in the essay *The Optimal Production of Social Justice* (Kolm, 1966a).

For considering these methods, individuals' judgments about a distribution to individuals are considered. For a simple focus on social-ethical judgments, let us discard here individuals' interested concerns for others' incomes due to these incomes' effects on demands and supplies of goods. For transfers among individuals, these effects can only be due to differences about the types of goods they consume. One may also discard individuals who are particularly sensitive to such effects. Moreover, all the forthcoming discussions can be introduced in a model taking these effects explicitly into account (one conclusion is that, in the method of the "marginal surplus," these effects of the distribution, which affect prices, vanish with competitive markets).[3]

2. DISINTERESTED OR SELF-INTEREST-NEUTRAL JUDGMENTS

An individual's judgment comparing distributions is not influenced by her self-interest when her own income remains the same. This is a disinterested judgment. Thus, the income of a single individual, or a transfer between two individuals, can be judged disinterestedly by the other members of society, that is, by almost everybody. For redistributions with a specific structure, there is generally a subset of individuals whose income is not affected, and hence whose overall and disinterested judgments coincide.

For instance, with an ELIE, each individual i receives (or yields) transfer $t_i = k \cdot (\overline{w} - w_i)$, and individuals with average productivity (or wage rate) $w_i = \overline{w}$ face a transfer $t_i = 0$, whatever the chosen level of coefficient k. Their income and their self-interest are not affected by this choice, and they are the only individuals in this situation. Hence, their preferences about the distribution, the set of transfers t_i, and coefficient k, are their disinterested preferences.

Moreover, even when an individual's income and self-interest are affected by a distributional choice, if the outcome is not affected by her expression of her judgment, she has no self-interested motive not to present her impartial moral judgment when she is asked about it. Even if the individuals' expressed judgments influence the outcome (such as in a vote or as a less formal influence of opinion), it often happens that a single individual's view has no actual influence because she is "small in a large number" (this constitutes a "mass effect").

Either of these two reasons can apply to a number of the individuals, and hence provide a smaller or larger sample of the disinterested judgments of the population. This sample is a priori representative and unbiased for the considered issue, because the noted reasons for selection bear a priori no relation to individuals' disinterested judgments. For example, in the case of an ELIE, these judgments have a priori no reason to be correlated with the individuals' productivities. A sufficient sample of the disinterested views of society members can thus be obtained. Moreover, the individuals in an interest-neutral situation a priori

---

[3] See the previous reference.

desire their disinterested judgment to be implemented, and hence they tend to express it.

In particular, the individuals' disinterested preference orderings of the relevant distributions may coincide, as a result of a common culture and rationality, of sufficient formative or empathetic information (Chapter 18), of a sufficient dialog (Chapter 20), or of a sufficiently convincing theory of the required moral judgment (Chapter 21). Then, the noted interest-neutral judgments provide the unanimous disinterested preference orderings. This consensus can be accompanied with any variety in individuals' relative preferences and intensity of concern between their self-interest and their social-ethical values (some may be keen on these values and others almost indifferent about them). In other cases, when individuals' social-ethical preference ordering differ, the individuals whose interest is not at stake may try to favour the realization of their disinterested view in distorting their expression, taking others' expressions into account, in the end in a game-theoretic interaction. However, the individuals whose expression has no actual influence, notably because they are "small in a large number" without cooperation, are not induced to play such a game. Moreover, sincere expression may be a moral requirement for moral views, and it entails no cost in self-interest for the considered individuals.

We noticed that an individual has no interest in hiding or distorting her disinterested judgment for favouring her interest when her voice has no practical effect because she is "small in a large number" (a "mass effect"). She should, in addition, not think her view is used as representative in a very small influential sample. However, people commonly vote in the sense of their interest in large elections where this situation is the case. There are several possible reasons for that. They may not be fully conscious of the negligible probability that their own vote makes a difference (that it is "pivotal"). Their interest may be clearer to them than the moral stance they should hold. This moral stance may be biased toward their interest in a rather sincere pharisianism. Then, they may feel a duty to express their interest as an implicit cooperation with others with similar interests. A widespread reason for voting according to interest, however, is that the individuals think that revealing their interest is what is demanded from them for making a synthesis or an aggregation. Indeed, when people are explicitly asked their moral view and know the answer will have no actual influence whatsoever, several of these reasons for favouring their interest disappear and they are much more likely to actually reveal their moral view.

Disinterested evaluations of distributional choices can also be made by large proportions of individuals without interfering with their self-interest if each choice concerns few individuals' incomes. The income of one individual can be disinterestedly evaluated by the $n - 1$ others. A transfer between two individuals can be disinterestedly evaluated by the $n - 2$ other individuals. Hence, such distributional choices can be disinterestedly evaluated by almost all members of the society. In the case of a transfer between two individuals, if all the others want this transfer, possibly accompanied by compensations among themselves,[4] then $n - 1$ individuals choose this transfer in the standard case where the individual who receives likes it and the individual who yields does not. And there can be a series of choices of this kind. This permits considering a number of principles of partial or overall distributional choices. For instance, the noted quasi-unanimous desire for a transfer possibly accompanied by compensations among the individuals whose income is not at stake, applied to transfers between all pairs of individuals, practically amounts to the method of the surplus discussed shortly.[5] However, these variations of only one or two incomes may be prevented by a priori structures of the distribution (as with an ELIE form).

3. THE GENERAL DISTRIBUTIVE SURPLUS

3.1. Reasons, properties, and form of the distributive surplus

3.1.1. The distributive surplus

We have seen in Chapter 6 that differences in individuals' capacities for deriving satisfaction, pleasure, or happiness are consensually considered irrelevant for policies implementing global (overall) distributive justice. That is to say, individuals are seen as entitled to or accountable for these capacities of theirs, or it is held that the "natural" allocation of these capacities should be endorsed, for the purpose of global distributive justice. Endogenous social choice leads to endorsing this unanimous view. Consequently, the relevant evaluation of an individual is not in terms of her happiness, pleasure, satisfaction, "utility," etc., but in terms of goods or, synthetically, money or income equivalent for this individual. Then, happiness, satisfaction, or pleasure result from the individual's appreciation of goods, incomes, or anything she is concerned about, "with" her eudemonistic capacities.

Hence, the relevant measuring rod of individuals' values consists of goods or incomes enjoyed by the individuals. In a market economy with free buying justified by process-freedom, this measuring rod is income. Therefore, the relevant social-ethical value of an individual's preference for a state over another is her *money or income equivalent of this replacement*, or her *"willingness to pay" for it*. The difference between these two measures will be emphasized. Such an amount is positive if this replacement is desired and negative when it is not: in this latter case, the absolute value of the willingness to pay is a required compensation. The structure of individuals' preferences thus is a priori relevant; only individuals' capacities for enjoying are not and are seen as purely private matters for the considered issue. This relates to the fact that, in individuals' evaluations, only the ordinal structure of their preferences is related to their actions (it determines them in the classical theory of choice), and these actions materially concern other

---

[4] Individuals who are thus led to accept the transfer have a mixed motive, both disinterested and interested.
[5] See Kolm 1966a.

people, whereas intensities (and natures) of satisfaction can be seen as purely private concerns for their holders.

A value for an individual, or her willingness to pay, can a priori be for any reason. The value of a redistribution of incomes for an individual, or her willingness to pay for it, includes, first of all, the value or the willingness to pay for a reason of self-interest, her self-interested willingness to pay or value. In money equivalent or in willingness to pay, this is exactly the amount she receives or yields (then measured negatively) in the redistribution. Hence, since in a redistribution the sum of the amounts received and yielded by the individuals balance (by definition of a redistribution), the sum (algebraic sum) of the individuals' self-interested money values or willingnesses to pay for a redistribution is zero. Therefore, in the sum of the individuals' money values or willingnesses to pay for a redistribution, there only remains values or willingnesses to pay for non-self-interested reasons, their disinterested values or willingnesses to pay. The individuals' interested money values or willingnesses to pay cancel out in the sum. Now, we precisely want the choice of a distribution (an ELIE is one) to be determined by the individuals' disinterested evaluations. Hence, an evaluation by the sum of individuals' money values or willingness to pay provides a solution to this problem. Conversely, the sum of these money or income values or willingnesses to pay is the only aggregation of these evaluations that has this property of erasing self-interests about a redistribution, and hence only leaving the disinterested evaluations of it.

Now, evaluating by the sum of individuals' willingness to pay or income or money equivalent happens to be the most common criterion in applied welfare, normative, and public economics. This sum is called the "surplus," and this method is variously called (as is shortly called back to mind) the method of the surplus, the compensation principle (choose a change if the beneficiaries could compensate the losers), the highest social income, or just benefit-cost analysis.

The standard applications of this method, however, consider purely self-interested individuals and do not apply it to the distribution of income or wealth. The application to distribution with non-purely self-interested individuals is fully analyzed in the essay *The Optimal Production of Social Justice.*[6] The standard applications sometimes justify the comparison and addition of money values for different individuals by the remark that income distribution is assumed to be optimal or to be taken care of by other policies. Now, the use of the method for determining the distribution will rest on the condition that any deviation from the chosen distribution produces a negative surplus (at least not a positive one). Hence, the considered willingnesses to pay will basically be for the incomes and their distribution chosen by this method.

Moreover, the canceling out of individuals' self-interested money values or willingnesses to pay entails that the surplus can have a positive or negative sign, even when individuals' willingnesses to pay for disinterested reasons are small or very small, that is, when lexical self-interest prevails. Then, self-interested and

---

[6] Kolm 1966a.

disinterested views are incommensurable in the usual sense of the term. They belong to different "spheres," which are distinguished, for the present purpose, by the orders of magnitude of money equivalents (although money measures are used for expressing, comparing, and aggregating individuals' disinterested values).

In the essay *The Optimal Production of Social Justice*, the concept of the surplus is presented first in its rational form of the "relative dual (and marginal) surplus," and, second, for application to the question of the choice of a distribution by endogenous social choice. These two aspects are briefly called back to mind and discussed here, and then applied to the specific problem considered. Moreover, the surplus principle yields a Pareto efficient outcome, as will be shown in Chapter 26.

3.1.2. The relative dual and marginal surplus

The principle of the surplus used here[7] differs from the usual applications not only by its field of application (distribution), but also by the criterion itself. Two money or income evaluations between two states have to be distinguished. Consider two states A and B, and individuals in state A who consider its replacement by state B. The noted values can be positive or negative. Individual i's money or income equivalent or value of having state B rather than state A is the amount of income or money $M_i(A, B)$ that, given to her when in state A, makes a situation (a third state) she finds as good as being in state B. In contrast, individual i's willingness to pay for having B rather than A is the amount of money or income $W_i(A, B)$ that she is ready to pay for having in addition B replace A; that is, she is indifferent between state A and state B minus the amount of money or income $W_i(A, B)$. These two numbers have the same sign, positive if individual i prefers B to A and negative if she prefers A to B. However, they are generally different.[8] Their relation is that $M_i(B, A) = -W_i(A, B)$ and $W_i(B, A) = -M_i(A, B)$. The social surplus of replacing A by B is either $S^m(A, B) = \Sigma_i M_i(A, B)$ or $S^w(A, B) = \Sigma_i W_i(A, B)$. We then have $S^m(A, B) = -S^w(B, A)$ and $S^w(A, B) = -S^m(B, A)$. The applications of the principle of the surplus often take a state of reference A (such as the present state) and advocate the realization of a state B, which maximizes the surplus over possible states. However, this maximand, and hence the advocated state B, depend in general on the reference state A. In particular, the principle implies preferring state B over state A when the surplus for having B rather than A is positive and the reverse when it is negative (since $S^m(A, A) = S^w(A, A) = 0$). However, $S^m(A, B)$ and $S^w(A, B)$ can be of different signs when there are several individuals with different preferences between A and B. Then, $S^m(A, B)$ and $S^m(B, A)$ are of the same sign, as are

---

[7] And in the noted essay of 1966a.

[8] They are equal when the individual's utility function has a specification that is quasi linear in money, a property also called "constant marginal utility of money."

$S^w(A, B)$ and $S^w(B, A)$.[9] In this case, whether one takes equivalents or willingnesses to pay as criterion, the principle advocates both staying in A when in A and in B when in B, or both going to B when in A and to A when in B (depending on whether these signs are negative or positive). This possibility is usually considered the main drawback of the surplus principle. However, this need not be so. One can take, as principle for preferring state B to state A, the condition that *both* $S^m(A, B) > 0$ and $S^w(A, B) > 0$. This is equivalent to other meaningful pairs of relations: $S^m(B, A) < 0$ and $S^w(B, A) < 0$; $S^m(A, B) > 0$ and $S^m(B, A) < 0$; and $S^w(A, B) > 0$ and $S^w(B, A) < 0$. Then, the principle will advocate choosing, among the possible states, a state A such that, *for all possible states B*, there holds a pair of relations which can be expressed in any of the four following meaningful forms:

$$S^m(A, B) \leq 0 \quad \text{and} \quad S^m(B, A) \geq 0,$$
$$S^m(A, B) \leq 0 \quad \text{and} \quad S^w(A, B) \leq 0,$$
$$S^w(A, B) \leq 0 \quad \text{and} \quad S^w(B, A) \geq 0,$$
$$S^m(B, A) \geq 0 \quad \text{and} \quad S^w(B, A) \geq 0.$$

Then, for a given set of possible states, one can investigate the existence and the uniqueness of such solutions. It turns out that this duality of conditions plays the role of conditions of concavity, or of second-order local conditions in standard maximizations (as shortly appears). This application of the concept of the surplus is the *relative dual surplus principle*.

Finally, the problem is the determination of a unique solution for implementation. Its solution, and in particular the uniqueness, result from sufficient consideration of individuals' views, reasons, judgments, and distinctions. If the solution is unique, local conditions suffice. The method then is that of the marginal surplus.

We will see the general classical uses and meanings of the principle, and the precise logic of its application to distributions (the marginal distributive surplus). Section 5 then shows the application to the determination of coefficient k of an ELIE.

3.2. A convergence of principles and its reason

The principle that something should be done if it pays more than it costs, or of seeking the highest benefit, seems to be basic economic wisdom. It is, of course,

---

[9] The possible reversal is due to the "income effects" between the two states A and B, which a priori differ across individuals. This property was first noted by Tibor Scitovsky in 1941. He pointed out that, if A and B are two different alternative quantities of a good held by an individual, $M_i(B, A)$ and $M_i(A, B)$ for this individual differ in the general case where the classical "constant marginal utility of money" does not hold. Then, if the cost of the quantity $B - A$ is between these two values, the surplus principle gives different conclusions whether considered in the states with quantities A or B (either do not move to the other, or move to the other, in both cases).

standard for the choice of a single agent, but it has also been applied for long to the case where the various benefits or costs do not accrue to the same agent, and this is still the basic principle of public finance for the scientific choice of public projects. This implies a global conception of society, in the sense that units of value, in money terms, are not distinguished with respect to the specific individuals (or households) who benefit from them or incur the cost. It is sometimes explicitly assumed that interpersonal distribution is taken care of by another policy. However, the particular application of the distributive surplus will in fact determine the distribution. Of course, costs and benefits may not necessarily actually be received or paid in money, and, when they are not, they are replaced by the monetary equivalents for the concerned individuals or by their willingness to pay (or required compensation). This expression in money terms permits a straightforward comparison of benefits or costs accruing to different persons (in an exchange economy – justified by process-freedom – taking money as the standard of the comparison basically means that the standard consists in amounts of goods rather than, for instance, some bizarre "units" of happiness or pain). This principle has actually been presented in five forms.

(1) Its direct statement is the principle of the *surplus*, inaugurated by Jules Dupuit (1844), which is the common and general criterion in benefit-cost analysis in public finance for the choice of public projects. The surplus is the algebraic sum of individuals' money equivalents or "willingnesses to pay" (sum of the positive ones minus sum of the lowest required compensations for having the project accepted by those who suffer from it, including the benefits or costs that actually are in money, one of these costs consisting of public funds paid by the taxpayers). The principle says that the project should be implemented if its surplus is positive.

(2) Another form is the celebrated *compensation principle*, which says that a project should be realized if "the beneficiaries can compensate the losers" – this amounts to a positive sum of the initial willingnesses to pay. The crucial point here is that the compensation may be only fictive, hypothetical ("can compensate"), as emphasized notably by Hicks and Kaldor (1939), and supported by Coase (1960) – during a famous and intense debate. If the compensation is effective, the principle just boils down to Pareto-efficiency or mutually beneficial exchange. If it is not, the principle has in itself a specific distributive effect.

(3) A third form is the principle of *maximizing social income* – the sum of individuals' incomes – when income is measured extensively in counting nonmonetary advantages or costs by their money equivalents for the individuals (or their willingnesses to pay or lowest required compensations). Maximizing social income or its growth rate is de facto a very widespread objective of public policies. Economist and judge Richard Posner (1977, 1981) advocates maximizing social income as the principle for all judicial decisions. Adding or

subtracting the money equivalent of nonmonetary advantages or costs (such as "social costs") to a national or other global income whose maximum is desired is a standard proposal.

(4) Fourth, this principle also amounts to *value-weighted majority voting*, with votes weighted, for taking account of the intensity of voters' preferences, by the value of the proposal for the individuals measured by their money equivalent or willingness to pay (or required compensation), or by weights proportional to these values; the intensity of voters' preferences is thus compared with an interpersonally comparable standard (see Chapter 17).

(5) Finally, these principles also amount to *Bentham's* (1973) *utilitarianism* since this author states that individuals' utilities whose sum should be maximized should be measured in money terms "for lack of a better measure."

This impressive convergence of proposals and common practices suggests making precise the rationale for this principle. A distributive principle is generally implied. Since justice is, by logical necessity, *prima facie* equality in the relevant items, the nature of a principle is revealed by what it implies should be equal.[10] For the foregoing criteria, this is the unit value of the amounts of commodities or services (measured in money), whoever receives or loses them, or, equivalently, the social value of the unit money values for the different individuals. This leads to the explicit or implicit addition, subtraction, or compensation of these values, or to their being the standard of comparison. The structure is the same as that of utilitarianism, with the replacement of "happiness" by goods or money, or its measure by these units – as proposed by Bentham.

Individual levels of happiness or satisfaction, or their variations, are absent from the foregoing criteria (while they would be the material of the formally comparable utilitarianism). However, if individuals care about others' happiness or satisfaction, this will notably affect individuals' willingnesses to pay for others' income. Hence, individuals' happiness or satisfaction can be taken into account in the criterion, but they are through individuals' judgments in this respect.[11] In contrast, individuals' preference orderings directly appear because they determine individuals' willingnesses to pay or money equivalents.

As we have seen in Chapter 17, the surplus method improves on majority voting in that it takes the intensity of individuals' preferences into account (through willingnesses to pay). This principle, in discarding the direct ethical relevance of eudemonistic capacities, avoids the logical problems that plague the very concept of utilitarianism.[12] And, applied to distributions, it is the only principle that discards the direct effect of individuals' self-interests, and hence directly rests on individuals' social-ethical values (which makes it applicable to cases of lexical self-interest).

[10] See Kolm 1971 and Chapter 2.
[11] The full logic of this issue is worked out in the noted essay (Kolm, 1966a).
[12] See Kolm 1996a, Chapter 14.

3.3. General theory of the marginal distributive surplus

Precisely, denote as y_i the income of individual i and as dy_i a small variation of y_i. Individual i's self-interested money (income) equivalent of dy_i and willingness to pay for it is dy_i. This individual, however, can also have other reasons for evaluating the y_j for any individual j and their distribution. Denote as $v_j^i \cdot dy_j$ individual i's own money income equivalent of dy_j for these reasons.[13] The number v_j^i for $j \neq i$ is individual i's marginal money income equivalent of individual j's income y_j. Then, individual i's money income equivalent of the transformation of y_j into $y_j + dy_j$ for all j is $\sigma_i = dy_i + \Sigma_j v_j^i \cdot dy_j$. The surplus of this transformation is

$$\sigma = \Sigma \sigma_i = \Sigma dy_i + \Sigma_{i,j} v_j^i \cdot dy_j.$$

If this transformation is a redistribution, $\Sigma dy_i = 0$, and hence,

$$\sigma = \Sigma_{i,j} v_j^i \cdot dy_j = \Sigma_j (\Sigma_i v_j^i) \cdot dy_j = \Sigma v_j \cdot dy_j$$

with $v_j = \Sigma_i v_j^i$. The self-interested values cancel out. Thus, the surplus σ has a sign even if the $|v_j^i|$, and possibly also the $|v_i|$, are very small (lexical self-interest).[14]

The v_j^i a priori depend on the distribution $y = \{y_k\}$, and hence the surplus σ depends on y and on its vector variation $dy = \{dy_k\}$: $\sigma = \sigma(y, dy)$ (σ is a differential directional surplus). A distribution selected by the surplus principle is a possible y such that, for no possible distribution $y + dy$, one has $\sigma(y, dy) > 0$.

Moreover, a stability condition is that, for all possible distribution $y + dy$, the surplus of going from this distribution to distribution y is positive (or zero): $\sigma(y + dy, -dy) \geq 0$ (this condition plays, for surplus theory, a role similar to second-order conditions for maximizations). Note that $\sigma(y + dy, -dy)$ is the sum of individuals' willingnesses to pay in y, for the variation dy.

These conditions generally determine a solution. Binding constraints both provide conditions for y and correspondingly reduce the set of conditions provided by the obtained surplus criterion in limiting the possible $y + dy$. The solution depends on the functions v_j^i of y and on these constraints. If transfers are free both ways between two individuals i and j, the corresponding condition is $v_i = v_j$ (because the surplus condition gives $v_j - v_i \leq 0$ for a small transfer from i to j and $v_i - v_j \leq 0$ for a small transfer from j to i). If the only constraint is $\Sigma y_i =$ constant, then the surplus conditions are that numbers v_i are the same for all i (this constitutes $n - 1$ generally independent conditions, and hence, with the constraint, n conditions for determining the n incomes y_i). If all individuals are purely self-interested, $v_j^i = 0$ for all i, j and y, hence $\sigma \equiv 0$, and the solution is fully indeterminate. However, self-interest is generally better described by lexical self-interest (very small v_j^i), at least for some individuals, and this generally suffices

[13] If individual i is concerned with her own income y_i only for a strictly self-interested reason, $v_i^i = 0$. However, other cases, with $v_i^i \neq 0$, can occur, for instance for comparing incomes for a reason of comparative justice.
[14] If the individuals are numerous, the $|v_j^i|$ can be small while the $|v_j|$ are not, and the $|v_j|$ can be small while σ is only of the first degree of smallness.

for determining the solution. The study *The optimal production of social justice*[15] provides a full discussion of the distributive surplus solution, notably as concerns existence, uniqueness, stability, the case of two individuals, limitative constraints (such as nonnegative incomes or other minimal incomes), individuals' evaluations of others' moral evaluations, total amount depending on the distribution, several goods, price effects, and so on. However, our concern here is the application to the determination of coefficient k of an ELIE, that is, the case where the dy_i are of the form $dy_i = dt_i = (\overline{w} - w_i) \cdot dk$ (which entails $\Sigma dy_i = 0$). This is the topic of forthcoming Section 5.

3.4. Two important particular cases: Same disinterested preferences and degrees of altruism or communitarianism

3.4.1. Same disinterested preferences

A common culture, full formative or empathetic information, or a sufficiently convincing dialog – and this information or dialog can be more or less notional – can lead to the case where the individuals have the same disinterested preferences about the distribution. Same disinterested preference orderings means that the ratios v_j^i/v_ℓ^i are the same for all i, j, and ℓ (for each y). That is, there exists $2n$ numbers a^i and b_i such that $v_j^i = a^i b_j$ for all i and j. Then, individual i's money income equivalent of the transformation of distribution y into distribution $y + dy$ is $dy_i + a^i \Sigma b_j \cdot dy_j$ and the surplus of this transformation is $\sigma = a \Sigma b_j \cdot dy_j$ where $a = \Sigma a^i$. If there is no malevolence, $v_j^i = a^i b_j \geq 0$ for all i, j, and if there is some disinterested concern, $v_j^i = a^i b_j > 0$ for at least one i and one $j \neq i$. Hence, one can take $a^i \geq 0$ for all i, $b_i \geq 0$ for all i, and we have $a^i > 0$ for at least one i. Therefore, $a = \Sigma a^i > 0$. Hence, the surplus principle chooses a y such that for no possible $y + dy$ one has $\Sigma b_j \cdot dy_j > 0$. Then, for each individual who has a disinterested judgment, hence with $a^i > 0$, at such a y there is no possible $y + dy$ such that $a^i \Sigma b_j \cdot dy_j > 0$, that is, that she disinterestedly prefers to y. The surplus principle implements the common disinterested preferences of the individuals.[16] This is, indeed, a necessary property of any principle of endogenous social choice: it should yield the consensual social-ethical solution when all individuals agree on this ground. This property holds even if the a^i are very different, possibly not of the same order of magnitude. That is, it does not depend on individuals' relative degrees of self-interestedness and disinterestedness (there can, in particular, be lexical self-interest).

3.4.2. Degrees of altruism and communitarianism

An opposite polar case focuses, on the contrary, on individuals' comparisons between their interest and others' interest. In this simple polar case, they only

---

[15] Op. cit.
[16] For a more complete presentation, see Kolm 1966a. See also Section 4.

discriminate between dollars for themselves and for others, without discriminating in any respect among the others who receive (or yield) these dollars. They see others as some kind of G. H. Mead's "generalized other." Then, let v^i denote individual i's willingness to pay for one dollar being received by someone else. That is, $v^i_j = v^i$ for all $j \neq i$. If individual i is purely self-interested, $v^i = 0$. If $v^i = 1$, individual i considers dollars for herself and dollars for others on an equal footing, in a kind of complete economic communitarianism. The figure v^i, with normally $0 \leq v^i \leq 1$, thus constitutes an index of individual i's altruism or sense of community.[17] Individual i's money income equivalent of replacing distribution y by distribution $y + dy$ is $\sigma_i = dy_i + v^i \Sigma_{j \neq i} dy_j = (1 - v^i) dy_i$ for a redistribution with $\Sigma dy_i = 0$. The surplus of this transformation then is $\sigma = \Sigma \sigma_i = -\Sigma v^i \cdot dy_i$, and the surplus condition is $\Sigma v^i \cdot dy_i \geq 0$ for all possible and admissible $y + dy$. If, for instance, small transfers both ways between individuals i and j are free, the condition implies $v^i = v^j$. If all such transfers are possible and the only requirement is $\Sigma dy_i = 0$, v^i should be the same for all i. All the conditions have the same form as in the general case in replacing v_i by v^i and in changing signs (v^i a priori depends on y).

4. DISTRIBUTIONAL PREFERENCES AND GLOBAL DISTRIBUTIVE JUSTICE

4.1. The relevant items: Freedom of choice and transfers

Individuals derive personal satisfaction from the set of their own consumption c_i and labour ℓ_i or leisure $\lambda_i = 1 - \ell_i$. With process-freedom, individual i freely chooses her c_i and ℓ_i in her budget possibility set, on the border $c_i = w_i \ell_i + t_i$ where t_i is the net transfer she receives ($t_i > 0$) or yields ($t_i < 0$). This possibility set is the individual's domain of freedom. It is defined by the pair of numbers (w_i, t_i), the slope w_i of the budget line and its intercept t_i with the leisure line $\ell_i = 0$. Hence, the relevant distribution is that of the t_i or, equivalently, of the individuals' freedoms of choice defined by the pairs (w_i, t_i) since the w_i are given. Since the w_i are the only relevant parameters that differentiate the individuals, any impartial, non-self-centered evaluation of the distribution should be symmetrical in the pairs (w_i, t_i).

Denote $t = \{t_i\}$ the set (vector) of the t_i, and $f(t)$ some ordinal evaluation function of t: a higher level of f is preferred. With an ELIE (EDIE) distribution, $t_i = k \cdot (\overline{w} - w_i)$, with $0 \leq k \leq 1$. Call, then, $\varphi(k) = f(t)$. The preferred level of coefficient k gives the highest level to function $\varphi(k)$. With the required differentiabilities, this implies either $\varphi' = 0$ and $\varphi'' \leq 0$, or $k = 1$ and $\varphi' \geq 0$, or $k = 0$ and $\varphi' \leq 0$. Now, denoting $s_i = \overline{w} - w_i$ from which $t_i = k s_i$, $\varphi' = \Sigma s_i f'_i$ and $\varphi'' = \Sigma_{i,j} s_i s_j f''_{ij}$.

---

[17] $v^i < 0$ denotes malevolence. With $v^i > 1$, individual i freely gives to others. v^i a priori depends on y and in particular on y_i.

4.2. Individuals' distributional preferences

Consider now, for individual i, an ordinal utility function $u^i(t_i, t)$. The first argument, t_i, denotes individual i's self-interest. Given t_i and w_i, individual i freely chooses consumption c_i and labour ℓ_i or leisure $\lambda_i = 1 - \ell_i$ that satisfies $c_i = w_i \ell_i + t_i$. The second argument of function u^i, vector t, denotes individual i's concern about the distribution for reasons other than her self-interest (the t_i component of vector t is absent if individual i cares about her own income only for a self-interested reason, and it is present otherwise, for instance when individual i morally evaluates the whole distribution, including her share in it). Then, assuming the required differentiability, denote $u^i_o = \partial u^i / \partial t_i$, $u^i_j = \partial u^i / \partial t_j$, and $v^i_j = u^i_j / u^i_o$ which is individual i's marginal willingness to pay for t_j, that is, for individual j's income.

An individual i has three kinds of preferred levels of coefficient k: an overall preferred level k_i; a self-interested preferred level k^s_i which maximizes u^i with respect to the first argument t_i only; and a disinterested preferred level k^d_i which maximizes u^i with respect to the vector-argument t. A priori, k^s_i depends on a fixed value of the vector-argument t, and k^d_i depends on a fixed value of the first argument t_i. However, $du^i / dk^s_i = u^i_o s_i = u^i_o \cdot (\overline{w} - w_i)$, and hence, with the usual $u^i_o > 0$, $k^s_i = 1$ if $w_i < \overline{w}$, $k^s_i = 0$ if $w_i > \overline{w}$, and k^s_i is indeterminate if $w_i = \overline{w}$. Hence, k^s_i does not depend on the given vector t. Moreover, an individual's disinterested judgment certainly should not depend on the satisfaction of her self-interest. Motivations that might lead to such a relation, such as more or less sincere or unsincere pharisianism (defending one's interests with moral arguments) or a sense of guilt about one's fortune, should probably be discarded from valid causes of objectively moral judgments.[18] Then, k^d_i does not depend on the level of the first argument t_i. More generally, function u^i can be written as $u^i(t_i, t) = \tilde{u}^i[t_i, f^i(t)]$, where f^i is a function of t ordinally describing individual i's disinterested evaluation of the distribution. Then, k^d_i is the level of k that maximizes f^i.[19]

Level k_i generally is between k^s_i and k^d_i. Denoting as $S_i = (1/u^i_o)(du^i/dk)$ individual i's marginal willingness to pay for coefficient k, and $r_i = \Sigma_j v^i_j s_j$ (with $s_i = \overline{w} - w_i$ and $t_i = k s_i$), one has $S_i = s_i + r_i$. Then, the levels k_i, k^s_i, and k^d_i respectively each satisfy one of three possible conditions: $0 < k_i < 1$ and $S_i = 0$, $k_i = 0$ and $S_i \leq 0$, or $k_i = 1$ and $S_i \geq 0$; $k^s_i = 0$ and $s_i \leq 0$, $k^s_i = 1$ and $s_i \geq 0$,

---

[18] We also of course do not consider here comparative externalities of envy, jealousy, sentiments of superiority or inferiority, or desires for conformity or distinction. The technical way of discarding such effects is presented in Kolm 1995a.

[19] The symmetry in the pairs (w_j, t_j) of an impartial preference ordering represented by function $f^i(t)$ means that this function can be written as $f^i(t) = \varphi^i(\{w_j, t_j\})$ where function φ^i is symmetrical in the pairs (w_j, t_j). If, moreover, the ordering represented by function φ^i of the sets of pairs (w_j, t_j) for any subset of the j does not depend on the pairs for the remaining individuals, then function φ^i is additively separable, that is, there are functions γ^i increasing and g^i such that $\varphi^i = \gamma^i [\Sigma_j g^i(w_j, t_j)]$. Then, one can in fact take, as function φ^i or f^i, $\Sigma_j g^i(w_j, t_j)$, and $f^i_j = \partial g^i(w_j, t_j)/\partial t_j$. The same remark holds when functions f^i can be taken as the same for all individuals i.

or $0 < k_i^s < 1$ and $s_i = 0$; $0 < k_i^d < 1$ and $r_i = 0$, $k_i^d = 0$ and $r_i \leq 0$, or $k_i^d = 1$ and $r_i \geq 0$. Number s_i is a constant, whereas numbers r_i and S_i a priori depend on the level of coefficient k. We have $S_i \gtrless r_i$ depending on $s_i \gtrless 0$. Hence, when $w_i = \overline{w}$ or $s_i = 0$, $S_i = r_i$ and $k_i = k_i^d$. Moreover, the foregoing implies, when $w_i < \overline{w}$, or $s_i > 0$, $k_i = k_i^s = 1$ if $k_i^d > 0$, and $k_i < k_i^s = 1$ only if $k_i^d = 0$ (indeed, $r_i \geq 0$ entails $S_i > 0$). Similarly, when $w_i > \overline{w}$, or $s_i < 0$, $k_i = k_i^s = 0$ if $k_i^d < 1$, and $k_i > k_i^s = 0$ only if $k_i^d = 1$ (indeed, $r_i \leq 0$ entails $S_i < 0$).

If the individuals share the same disinterested preference ordering of the distributions, one can take $f^i = f$, the same for all i, and $k_i^d = k^d$, the same for all i. This can result from a common, shared view of global distributive justice, possibly resulting from a common culture, from sufficiently convincing dialog, or from full formative or empathetic information (these dialog and information can be more or less notional). However, the intensity of the respective concerns for this justice and for self-interest may differ across individuals.

When individuals care for others' incomes only globally, this can be described with the foregoing formulation in taking $f^i(t) = \Sigma_{j \neq i} t_j = -t_i$ for a redistribution with $\Sigma t_i = 0$. Hence, $k_i^s = 1$ and $k_i^d = 0$ if $w^i < \overline{w}$; $k_i^s = 0$ and $k_i^d = 1$ if $w^i > \overline{w}$; and k_i^d and k_i^s are indeterminate when $w^i = \overline{w}$. Individual i's overall preferred level of k, k_i, can have an intermediate value.

The determination of the k_i, k_i^s, and k_i^d provides possible solutions in taking, as level of coefficient k, an average across individuals. The most natural is the average of the k_i^d, $k^d = (1/n)\Sigma k_i^d$. However, one can also consider averages of k_i, $\overline{k} = (1/n)\Sigma k_i$, or of k_i^s, $k^s = (1/n)\Sigma k_i^s$ which is $k^s = m/n$ where m is the number of individuals with $w_i < \overline{w}$ if $w_i = \overline{w}$ for only few i. If individuals are solely self-centered, the k_i^d are not defined, and $k_i = k_i^s$ for all i, and hence $\overline{k} = k^s$. However, these solutions probably require more justification (k^s is much higher than $1/2$ in large societies where m is usually much larger than $n/2$, but the actual meaning depends on the definition of maximal labour $k = 1$). The level $k = k^d$ is nevertheless probably an adequate solution when the k_i^d are not too different.

4.3. Distributional surplus and interest-neutral evaluations

The two methods for discarding self-interest, the individual one with interest-neutral evaluations and the collective one with the surplus, can be presented with this explicit consideration of individuals' preferences.

If $w_i = \overline{w}$ for some individual i, function u_i, in its general form, does not depend on her first argument $t_i = 0$ for all levels of k. Therefore, $k_i^d = k_i$: individual i's preferred level of k is her disinterested preferred level of k. If, in particular, k_i^d is the same for all i (notably when one can take $u^i = \widetilde{u}^i(t_i, f)$ for all i), then the k_i for average-productivity individuals provides the solution.

For the surplus, the marginal social surplus of coefficient k is $s = \Sigma S_i = \Sigma r_i = \Sigma_{i,j} v_j^i s_j$, since $\Sigma s_i = 0$: only the disinterested individual money values v_j^i intervene. The chosen k satisfies $s \cdot dk \leq 0$ for all possible deviations dk. Thus, it satisfies $0 < k < 1$ and $s = 0$, $k = 0$ and $s \leq 0$, or $k = 1$ and $s \geq 0$. In the first case, the stability condition is $\Sigma_{i,j,\ell} v^i_{j\ell} s_j s_\ell \leq 0$, with $v^i_{j\ell} = \partial v^i_j / \partial t_\ell$. This solution will shortly be discussed. If $u^i = \tilde{u}^i [t_i, f^i(t)]$, $v^i_j = v^i_f f^i_j$ with $v^i_f = (1/u^i_o) \cdot \partial u^i / \partial f^i$ and $f^i_j = \partial f^i / \partial t_j$. If, moreover, all individuals share the same disinterested preferences for the noted possible reasons, one can take $f^i(t) = f(t)$, the same for all i, and hence $f^i_j = f'_j$ for all i. Then, $s = v_f \Sigma f'_j s_j$ where $v_f = \Sigma v^i_f$. With $v^i_f > 0$ for at least one i expressing one moral concern (which can be small), and $v^i_f \geq 0$ for all i expressing an absence of malevolence, and hence $v_f > 0$, the condition becomes $\Sigma f'_j s_j \cdot dk \leq 0$ for possible variations dk, which is a condition for the maximization of function $f(t)$. The solution does not depend on individuals' relative intensities of their interested and disinterested concerns, that is, on functions $u^i(t_i, f)$ and on v^i_f.

Hence, when the individuals have the same disinterested preference ordering of the distribution, the surplus gives the same solution. But the surplus also gives a solution when these disinterested orderings differ. It constitutes an aggregation of the individuals' evaluation of the distribution, both of their overall and of their disinterested evaluations. It rests on the discarding of eudemonistic capacities, a unanimous view for macrojustice. A unanimous disinterested ordering of the distribution can result from a common culture. It can also result from sufficient formative or empathetic information, and from discussion and dialog, which can be actual, notional, or a mix of both. Moreover, we will see in Chapter 21 how impartial individual evaluations of the distribution can be notionally built from individuals' self-interested or self-centered evaluations, and how these orderings can be justifiably led to be identical.

4.4. Self-centered judgments

An individual usually particularly favours not only her interest, but also the interest of other individuals who are in a more or less close social relation with her, or who have characteristics she particularly likes (and that could not justify favourable treatment for a reason of justice). For instance, she commonly favours members of her family, friends, neighbours, or people who have similarities with herself or belong to the same groups or categories (nation, residence, profession, class, language, religion, club, and so on). This constitutes self-centeredness, including self-interest. For members of the household, this is not really distinguishable from self-interest for the present purpose since an individual's income is, rather, her household's. Supporting one's family, and particularly helping one's friends, neighbours, fellow-citizens, and so on, is usually seen as moral behaviour and a moral duty. More generally, altruism is seen as the paragon of moral behaviour. However, altruism can be unfairly selective. In fact, self-centeredness is exactly the opposite of impartiality, the basic property of justice. One should help one's nephew, but nepotism is the symbol of unfairness. And macrojustice is concerned with justice.

Hence, in the motives of individuals' evaluation of the distribution, one should distinguish self-centered motives (including self-interest), on the one hand, from sense of justice, on the other hand. Then, an individual's ordinal evaluation function of the distribution can be written as $u^i(t, t)$, where the two vector-arguments t stand, respectively, for these two motives. An individual's true sense of justice should probably not depend on the satisfaction of her self-centered views – as we saw for self-interest. Then, u^i can be written as $u^i = \widetilde{u}^i[t, f^i(t)]$, where the ordinal function f^i denotes individual i's preference ordering of the distribution t for a motive of justice (more precisely, global distributive justice). Functions u^i and f^i are maximized by the levels k_i and $\widetilde{k}_i$ of coefficient k, respectively. One possible solution is the average $k = (1/n)\Sigma\widetilde{k}_i$. The justice orderings defined by functions f^i may be the same, and hence the $\widetilde{k}_i$ are the same, for several or all individuals i. This, again, can result from a common culture, from actual or notional (or a mix of both) formative or empathetic information or dialog concerning this issue, or from the specific methods developed in forthcoming chapters.

An individual's self-centeredness may reduce or be practically reduceable to her self-interest. In particular, this individual's income can be her household's, and she may particularly favour no other member of the considered society (but she might estimate differently the interest of people outside this society). Then, disinterested judgments and views of justice coincide, and $\widetilde{k}_i = k_i^d$.

5. THE GLOBAL DISTRIBUTIVE SURPLUS

5.1. The general case

The theory of the distributive surplus presented in Section 3 is now applied to an ELIE distributive structure, for determining coefficient k. Marginal money income equivalent and marginal surplus are money income equivalent and surplus per unit of a small increase. Using notations of Sections 3, 4.1, 4.2, and 4.3, v_j^i denotes individual i's marginal money income equivalent of individual j's income or lump-sum transfer. With an ELIE, individual i receives (or yields) transfer $t_i = ks_i$ with $s_i = \overline{w} - w_i$.[20] Individual i's marginal money income equivalent of coefficient k is

$$S_i = s_i + \Sigma_j v_j^i s_j.$$

Thus, the marginal surplus for k is

$$s = \Sigma S_i = \Sigma_{i,j} v_j^i s_j = \Sigma v_j s_j$$

---

[20] It is possible to select individuals' motives for valuing incomes. This will show through the v_j^i used. For instance, one may launder individuals' valuations for unethical sentiments such as malevolence, envy or jealousy, or, more generally, only consider v_j^i motivated by considerations of justice – and more precisely, of global distributive justice.

since $\Sigma s_i = 0$ and denoting $v_j = \Sigma_i v_j^i$. The sign of s is determined even if the $|v_j^i|$, the $|v_j|$, or $|s|$ are small (small $|v_j^i|$ denote lexical self-interest).[21]

The surplus criterion implies that no small change from the chosen k yields a positive surplus. Hence, the chosen k with $0 \le k \le 1$ satisfies $s = 0$, or $k = 0$ and $s \le 0$, or $k = 1$ and $s \ge 0$.

Number $v_j = \Sigma_i v_j^i$ is overall marginal money income equivalent of individual j's income for disinterested reasons. It measures a kind of social benevolence toward individual i (discarding v_i^i if it is not zero) – which could a priori be negative. The obtained marginal surplus s is the correlation between the v_i and the s_i. Indeed, denoting $\bar{v} = (1/n)\Sigma v_i$, and since $s_i = \bar{w} - w_i$ and hence $\Sigma s_i = 0$ and $\bar{s} = (1/n)\Sigma s_i = 0$,

$$s = \Sigma(v_i - \bar{v})(s_i - \bar{s}) = -\Sigma(v_i - \bar{v})(w_i - \bar{w}).$$

The stability of the chosen k for $0 < k < 1$ requires that the surplus of going from $k + dk$ to k not be negative, that is, $s(k + dk) \cdot (-dk) \ge 0$, or $s(k + dk) \cdot dk \le 0$, or, since $s(k) = 0$, $(ds/dk) \cdot (dk)^2 \le 0$ or $ds/dk \le 0$. That is, $\Sigma_{j,\ell} v_{j\ell} s_j s_\ell = \Sigma_{i,j,\ell} v_{j\ell}^i s_j s_\ell \le 0$, where $v_{j\ell}^i = \partial v_j^i/\partial t_\ell$ and $v_{j\ell} = \partial v_j/\partial t_\ell = \Sigma_i v_{j\ell}^i$.[22]

If v_i increases, s increases or decreases depending on $w_i \lessgtr \bar{w}$, and this tends to augment or diminish, respectively, the k for which $s = 0$. Hence, higher (vs. lower) social benevolence toward an individual tends to push the chosen k in the direction favourable to this individual's interest (vs. in the opposite one), as it should be.

The principle of the distributive surplus acquires a particular meaning in the present application. Since $s = -\Sigma(v_i - \bar{v}) \cdot (w_i - \bar{w})$, $s = 0$ means that the "social benevolences" v_i are uncorrelated with the productivities (wage rates) w_i. If $s > 0$, the correlation is negative, that is, on average, v_i is larger for individuals with smaller w_i, and hence k should be augmented for increasing $t_i = k \cdot (\bar{w} - w_i)$ for individuals with $w_i < \bar{w}$. The opposite holds when $s < 0$, and then k should be diminished. These reasons for changing k vanish when $s = 0$. That is, the degree of redistribution is such that the relative social preferences for increasing the various incomes do not depend, in a statistical sense, on individuals' productivities, wage rates or "total incomes."[23]

The condition $s = 0$ also writes $\Sigma(w_i - \bar{w})v_i = 0$ or $\Sigma(v_i - \bar{v})w_i = 0$: the vector of benevolences v_i should be orthogonal to the vector of deviations of productivities from their mean $w_i - \bar{w}$, and the vector of deviations of benevolences

---

[21] If individuals are sufficiently numerous, the $|v_j^i|$ can be small while the $|v_j|$ are not, and the $|v_j|$ can be small while s is not.

[22] The $v_{j\ell}^i$ and $v_{j\ell}$ are not second derivatives since $v_j^i = u_j^i/u_o^i$, except when u_o^i can be taken as constant (the case where one specification of ordinal function u^i has "constant marginal utility of money," that is, is "quasi linear" in individual i's money or income).

[23] This property holds more generally whatever the social values of individuals' incomes. If, for instance, there is a social maximand $M(t)$, with $t = \{t_i\}$ and $t_i = ks_i$, such as $f(t)$ previously considered or the maximands obtained in later chapters, then, denoting $M_i = \partial M/\partial t_i$, the first order condition for the choice of k if $0 < k < 1$ is $\Sigma M_i s_i = 0$, which gives similar results.

from their mean $v_i - \bar{v}$ should be orthogonal to the vector of productivities w_i. The condition also writes $\Sigma v_i w_i = n\bar{v}\,\bar{w}$, or, denoting $\alpha_i = v_i/\Sigma v_j$, $\bar{w} = \Sigma \alpha_i w_i$ or $\Sigma[\alpha_i - (1/n)]w_i = 0$.

5.2. Important particular cases: Same disinterested orderings and degrees of altruism or community

Two remarkable particular cases have been pointed out. A common culture or actual or notional full information and dialog can provide cases where all individuals share the same disinterested preference ordering. Then, we have seen that the surplus principle is satisfied by the common, disinterestedly best distribution. The solution does not depend on individuals' relative balance between their self-interest and their disinterested views. On the contrary, these individuals' balances become the sole relevant consideration when the individuals consider others' incomes globally, and they represent degrees of altruism or of sense of community. These properties should now be considered with the particular distributive structures of an ELIE.

Using the foregoing notations, when individuals share the same disinterested preference ordering, one can take $f^i(t) = f(t)$ for all i, with $\tilde{u}^i[t_i, f(t)]$, and write $v^i_j = a^i b_j$ with $a^i = v^i_i = \tilde{u}^i_f/\tilde{u}^i_o$ and $b_j = f'_j$. Then, $v_j = \Sigma_i v^i_j = ab_j = af'_j$ with $a = \Sigma a^i = \Sigma v^i_i$, and the marginal surplus of coefficient k is $s = \Sigma v_i s_i = a\Sigma s_i f'_i$, which has the sign of $\Sigma s_i f'_i = -\Sigma(w_i - \bar{w}) f'_i$ since $a > 0$ (because $a_i \geq 0$ for all i from the definition of f^i and $a_i > 0$ for at least one i if there exists some relevant disinterested sentiment).

The solution then is $0 < k < 1$ and $s = 0$, or $k = 0$ and $s \leq 0$, or $k = 1$ and $s \geq 0$. It is the k that maximizes $f(t)$. The condition $s = 0$ says that the vector of deviations of productivities from their mean is tangent to a variety $f =$ constant in the n-dimensional vector space of t (this is the outcome of the maximization for k of $f(t)$ with $t_i = (\bar{w} - w_i)k$ for all i, hence with a t on the line so defined when parameter k varies).

In the case of degrees of pure altruism or sense of community, $v^i_j = v^i$ for all $j \neq i$ and $v^i_i = 0$ for all i, and $f^i(t) = \Sigma_{j \neq i} t_j = -t_i$. Then, $v_j = \Sigma_i v^i_j = \Sigma_{i \neq j} v^i = \Sigma v^i - v^j$, and the marginal surplus of coefficient k is

$$s = \Sigma s_i v_i = -\Sigma s_i v^i = \Sigma(w_i - \bar{w})v^i$$
$$= \Sigma(w_i - \bar{w})(v^i - \tilde{v}) = -\Sigma(s_i - \bar{s})(v^i - \tilde{v}) = \Sigma(v^i - \tilde{v})w_i$$

in denoting $\tilde{v} = (1/n)\Sigma v^i$ (and $\bar{s} = 0$). The marginal surplus s is the correlation between individuals' altruism and productivity.

The surplus solution is k with $0 < k < 1$ and $s = 0$, or $k = 0$ and $s \leq 0$, or $k = 1$ and $s \geq 0$. An increase in an individual's altruism or communitarianism (v^i) augments or diminishes s depending on $w^i \gtrless \bar{w}$, and hence tends to augment or diminish the chosen k depending on $w^i \gtrless \bar{w}$, which in both cases reduces transfer

$t_i = (\overline{w} - w_i)k$, as it should. The condition $s = 0$ is $\Sigma s_i v^i = 0$, or $\Sigma w_i v^i = n\overline{w}\,\widetilde{v}$, or, denoting $\beta_i = v^i/\Sigma v_i$, $\overline{w} = \Sigma \beta_i w_i$ or $\Sigma [\beta_i - (1/n)] w_i = 0$. It says that productivities w_i and altruisms v^i are uncorrelated, and that the vectors of deviations from the mean of the w_i or v^i are perpendicular to the vector of the other magnitudes or of their deviations from the mean.[24]

5.3. Comparison with neighbouring methods

Heuristically, the (marginal) surplus method leads one to give coefficient k a (small) increase when $s > 0$ and a (small) decrease when $s < 0$, and to stop when $s = 0$. Pairwise social choice is often realized by majority voting. This would amount to replacing each individual marginal surplus S_i by its sign, $\text{sgn } S_i$, and to make k vary as noted depending on the sign of $m = \Sigma \text{sgn } S_i$. The result, however, is often bound to be very different, notably with more or less lexical self-interest such that the $|\Sigma_j v^i_j s_j|$ are small. Indeed if S_i is close to $s_i = \overline{w} - w_i$, the result will tend to be $k = 0$ or 1 depending on whether the median w_i exceeds $\overline{w}$ or falls short of it. There may then be misery for individuals with low w_i or "slavery of the talented" for individuals with high w^i. The majority rule presents the intrinsic drawback of giving the same weight to people much concerned and almost indifferent. Weighting votes by interests, hence here by $s_i = \overline{w} - w_i$, provides no solution for a redistribution, here because $\Sigma s_i = 0$. The surplus $s = \Sigma v_i s_i$ amounts to weighting votes by individuals' interests themselves weighted by social disinterested willingness to pay for them.

Another solution would be to use, as weights, individuals' "additional pleasure." If individual i's marginal utility of money is u^i_m, the criterion would be $\Sigma u^i_m s_i \gtrless 0$. However, there is no actually meaningful concept of u^i_m that can be added in this way,[25] and, at any rate, such eudemonistic capacities are unanimously considered not relevant for defining the transfers of global distributive justice (Chapter 6).

---

[24] Each v^i a priori depends on t_i (self-interest) and on $-t_i$ (net transfers received by others, for altruism). The stability condition writes $\Sigma s_i^2 \cdot (dv^i/dt_i) \geq 0$.

[25] See Kolm 1996a, Chapter 12.

20

Communication and dialog

1. DIALOGICAL ETHICS

1.1. Consensus, information, communication, dialog

Endogenous social choice endorses the views common to the members of the considered society provided they are sufficiently informed and reflective (and other people's rights are respected). When these people disagree, they usually begin by discussing, trying to convince one another in exchanging information about facts, reasons, and values. This sometimes suffices to produce a consensus; at least, it often makes views and preferences closer to one another. Moreover, full relevant information is necessary for an ethical view which cannot rest on ignorance, mistaken beliefs, confusion, and misunderstanding. And, for social and notably distributive issues, full relevant information of an individual implies information about others that a priori only these others have. This may include knowing others' interests and situations, but it also includes information about others' views: formative information is about the reasons and other causes of others' social and ethical preferences, and empathetic information is about knowing others' corresponding feelings including feeling how they feel (Chapter 18). This essential information about others generally has to come directly or indirectly from them. Hence, communication involving society members has a basic role.

Therefore, the information transmitted is about facts, reasons, and also sentiments and feelings. The communication has to be mutual and reciprocal. It also generally takes an iterative form. Indeed, the information individuals want to transmit to others depends on what they know about others' information and judgments, as well as on their own information and judgments. But these transfers of information generally modify the receiver's information, and also possibly her judgment. This induces this latter person to send new information, and so on. Hence, an important part of this mutual information will take the form of dialog, discussion, or debate.

The analysis of communication and dialog about the considered issue provides the link between the two noted approaches as concerns the nature of the relevant opinions: these views about the nature of society, social ethics, and justice are held by individuals, and yet they also are collective, social, and cultural facts. The analysis of these relations and interactions among individuals shows the mechanism that generates these individual and social views.

The rest of Section 1 analyzes the various aspects of such social-ethical use of communication and dialog, while Section 2 considers the formal theory of the formation of consensus in such processes. Section 1 thus considers the normative use of such actual or notional processes (1.2), their relation with rationality and their intrinsic social effect (1.3), the relation between individuals' values and interests (1.4), the limits and means of communication and the question of inequalities in this respect (1.5), and the philosophies of an ethics of communication (1.6). The theory of consensualization processes is presented for the choice of a coefficient (k in ELIE theory) in Section 2.1, and for general preferences orderings in Section 2.2.

1.2. Modalities

Communication and dialog provide the solution if they lead to sufficient consensus with full relevant information of all concerned individuals. However, they meet difficulties and entail costs in transferring, formulating, decoding, interpreting, and understanding messages. Information can even be refused by people who like to keep prejudices, a priori judgments, or entrenched positions that it would shake. These difficulties can be faced in two ways, which can be associated: the consideration of notional or hypothetical information, communication, and dialog, and the use of other ways of solution. Notional information and communication can more or less complement actual ones. They require, of course, a sufficient theory of the relevant psychological structures.

However, communication and dialog (actual, notional, or both) may provide only a part or an aspect of the solution, or a domain of possibilities for it, and the full solution is then reached by the application of another of the methods considered. Such methods should have a moral reason, but they can also be favoured because of difficulties in communication and information, and in their theoretical representation for notional constructs (notably as concerns formative and empathetic information). It is, indeed, very usual that information, communication, and dialog, failing to provide full consensus by themselves, are associated with another means of solution such as votation, agreement of the exchange type (mutually conditional concessions), arbitrage, judicial decision, etc., and, possibly, a social contract, the surplus principle, and so on. Information and dialog will generally make individuals' views beyond their pure self-interest, about a distribution, closer to one another — although the converse effect can result from unveiling, revealing or polarizing oppositions.

Communication can transmit information about facts and about reasons (arguments), and it can also importantly transmit affects, emotions, and sentiments. The latter influence causes of judgments that are in the nature of tastes. Communication can take many forms. It can be formal or informal, elaborate or casual, private or public, one way or multilateral, with or without rules, and one-shot, recurrent, or permanent. It includes education and example. Dialog, discussions, and debates are processes involving multilateral communication. They induce the transmission of the relevant information. But they also entail a change in the nature and dimension of communication, in opening the possibility of going a shorter or longer way in the direction of a merging of individuals' reasons and sentiments – of their "minds and hearts."

1.3. Roles of communication and dialog

Consensus with full relevant information provides the solution for endogenous social choice, and, in fact, full information in an exhaustive sense (including full formative and empathetic information about others) entails consensus. Consensus by itself, however, which can be with insufficient information, cannot thus claim optimality. Indeed, consensus can result from shared but mistaken beliefs, and it is often due to different beliefs or to different understandings of the meaning of terms. Moreover, the moral value of consensus is derived from the value of individuals' freedom of choice, and this freedom should define free as caused by reason.[1] Hence, morally relevant individual judgments have to follow the norms of rationality of the various kinds. In particular, opinions have to result from autonomous choice (in the sense of Rousseau and Kant) and be selected by reason as much as possible, or at least screened by it.

In fact, communication and dialog should be seen as means of rationality, which is the ultimate criterion, with its various forms and aspects.[2] Consensus beyond self-interest will largely result from the fact that rationality is objective in the sense that it transcends individual specificities. The role of communication and dialog for favouring rationality has various aspects. First of all, a rational judgment should be based on, and use, all the relevant information, and communication and dialog usually crucially contribute to this dimension. Moreover, communicating, debating, arguing, and convincing force one to mobilize objective public language and the various aspects of rationality. As a general rule, rationality is better promoted by a collective effort, and motivation for it and for its quest is spurred by debating opposite views, criticizing, answering, and arguing. In this process, relevant information and reasons are sought for, put to light, and

---

[1] Freedom is a structure of causality. An individual's action, choice, or opinion is freer when more causal chains that lead to it pass through the sets of elements and processes that constitute this individual's will or reason. The focus is on reason here. Then, for opinions, judgments, or preferences, freedom amounts to autonomy in the sense of Kant: chosen by the application of reason. For a full presentation and application of this theory of freedom, see Kolm 1982a, 1984b, 1993d, 1996a, 1996g, 1999b.

[2] Endogeneity of social choice is to be seen as one aspect of rationality.

transmitted; they are checked by criticism; errors, ignorance, inconsistencies, and contradictions are exposed; the meaning of concepts is checked, elaborated, and refined; arguments are verified and weighed; and different tastes, preferences, sentiments, and emotions are shown and confronted: individuals can take others' into account, and are led to question their own, which can be influenced and modified. Individuals will generally be the more motivated to engage in such a process the more they think the issue is important and the more they care for it. Global distributive justice undoubtedly is one of the most important issues that can be so considered.

Moreover, communication and dialog can matter not only for their outcome, but also intrinsically, because they are social facts. Their very existence is constitutive of a society, and a major dimension of this constitution – possibly the most important one. Now, the issue considered here precisely amounts to determining the degree to which the considered group constitutes a community. Then, the communication and dialog that can be means of this research influence the answer and are part of it. Communication and rights to resources are, of course, different aspects of society. However, communicative interaction is bound to favour a general sense of community, increase the degree of mutual empathy and altruism as concerns the considered distributive issue, and increase information about others required for the mutual trust that can sustain some enduring labour reciprocity.

1.4. Values and interests

However, the issue concerns individuals' and society's social, ethical, and impartial views, and individuals a priori also seek their personal interest and favour that of particular others. Hence, individuals' expressed preferences may be influenced by these particular interests, or may only defend these interests. This objective may be explicit, or it may be hidden behind particular moral arguments (pharisianism). In the latter case, the arguments will have to look objective and impartial. It suffices, for that, that they advocate favourable treatment for people having characteristics possessed by the individuals they want to favour, and which are not their relation to the person presenting the argument (including being this person). It is generally possible to find such characteristics (for instance, with an ELIE, all levels of coefficient k can be presented as an impartial solution, and individuals with a high, or low, productivity w_i can argue for a low, or a high, level of k on moral grounds). With positions so influenced by particular interests, no consensus is possible for choosing a distribution since, by definition, self-interests are opposed in this choice.

The outcome of the dialog and debate should thus result from social-ethical views only. It can be among individuals in their impartial moments and moods. These may predominate in historical times when political constitutions are chosen. Moreover, individuals who are "small in a large number" may have no noticeable individual influence on the process, and hence, they have no actual incentive to particularly defend their own interest and that of people they favour (a minute moral motivation favouring truth-telling, or the simple avoidance of the small effort of inventing a lie, should suffice for them to present their genuinely moral views). The most remarkable fact, however, is that the process of discussion in itself may lead participants to more objective and impartial views.

Indeed, the simple awareness of others' interests, and their concrete expression, may erode purely self-centered views. A longer and steadier dialog is bound to reinforce this effect. An individual may be induced to consider others' interests by seeing others do that, through imitation, and by seeing them consider her own interest, in a kind of reciprocity. The process may lead toward individuals taking an impartial view of all interests, including their own. And since the discussion will also be about the type of impartial view, the reasons for it, and the moral or social sentiments and emotions that accompany it, the same process is bound to produce similar such moral and social views. Participants would thus be impartial but not foreign, and therefore they will know and manifest their society's sense of community, solidarity, and justice.

1.5. Communicative imperfections and *isēgoria*

Communication – as Aesop told us about its basic means, the tongue – can be the best and the worst of things. It can transmit mistakes and confusion. Lies require it. It can induce irrational collective enthusiasm. Dialog reduces these possibilities. It can, however, just be a more subtle and efficient way of inducing others to adopt one's view (for truth and the good – as with Socrates – or for other purposes). Dialog can make views more apart, rather than more similar, in revealing, polarizing, and exacerbating oppositions. People may react to others' views or arguments in making their own more entrenched or further apart, as an assertion of their identity. However, besides these pathologies of dialog, the most common problem is that of the variety of individuals' endowments in means of communicating and convincing.

The consideration of full information discards this issue. However, in most actual dialogs about broad topics, this full information is bound to remain a more or less distant ideal (and this will particularly tend to be the case with the exhaustive understanding of full information that guarantees a consensus about broad ethical views). Then, the states of views actually reached will depend on individuals' endowments in means of communicating and convincing. Now, individuals' means of convincing others are generally different, sometimes widely so. Then, the better endowed in this respect will push the outcome toward their own a priori preferences, whether self-interested or moral ones. Some of these means can be resources and possibilities for acquiring information, and for formulating and presenting one's arguments and having them efficiently reach and move other people. Others can be personal skills, such as capacities to present, express, dissimulate, move, convince, reply, and so on.

A priori, this may be legitimate use of legitimate means. However, differences in these endowments and in their effects on the outcome may also have no ethical relevance and legitimacy for a number of issues. This is likely to include most of the uses presently considered. This leads to requiring equality, or lower inequality, in these means of convincing. When people are or become impartial, they may apply this impartiality to these means, and then refrain from using their own corresponding advantages, listen carefully to others and seek out and closely consider their views, and give them appropriate means to form, express, present, and defend these views. Short of this, a priori equality in these means or in some of them can be a rule of the game, through distribution of material means, education to expression, or various compensations. Such equalities are indeed commonly set up. In Athenian democracy, *isēgoria*, the right to equal time of public expression, was one of the four basic equalities (along with equality in abiding by the law or *isonomia*, equality in choosing the law by voting, and, ideally, equality in access to public positions by rotation or lottery). Modern democracies often impose some equality in access to media during electoral campaigns, but this is for constituted political parties. They are, in fact, extremely unequal in this respect, with almost all people having no possibility of public expression (which is through the mass media), while this privilege is restricted to politicians, journalists, and – indirectly – the media owners.

1.6. History

Discussion, dialog, or debate are basic methods for trying to find answers to various questions, notably moral ones. This is to be found at all times and places, in a large variety of forms, including private discussions, dialogs in groups of more or less equal persons, public and political debates (notably among public figures for convincing voters), the process of justice and law, and scholarly debates. Dialog can also be philosophically self-conscious, a philosophical method, and, in the end, the very basis of a philosophy. Socrates' maieutics is more a method for convincing than for discovering the solution (which is a priori known to the philosopher). The organized debates in scholastic *disputatio* or found in the buddhist *madyamika* are models of carefully structured dialogical argumentation.

Finally, a few modern philosophers have held that interpersonal communication implies the solution to the moral problem of justice. As far as convincing uses rationality, this may not differ from an ethics based on rationality. However, part of the sources of moral judgments are in the nature of tastes and moral or social sentiments. Consensus can result from convincing. Now, in matters of truth, an argument's capacity to convince a rational mind is an increasing function and a test of its truth content. This suggests extending the property of convincingness as a criterion for other values, notably ethical ones. This can be related to the ethics of consensus. This conception could underlie attempts of finding answers to moral questions in the analysis of rhetoric and argumentation, as that of Chaim Perelman.

Bruce Ackerman focuses on dialog. Moreover, communication and language are the two faces of the same coin. And a moral application of the "linguistic turn" in philosophy would try to find the answer in the meaning of terms. It would recast the question "What is it, which is just?" into "What does the term 'just' mean?", or, rather, "What is meant by the term 'just'?", in the considered framework.

Seeing meaning as a precondition of communication, a necessary requirement of its possibility, Jürgen Habermas relates this view to Kantian "transcendence" (however, communication is possible, to an extent, with less than precise meaning). Moreover, since discussion can be a practical device for obtaining an answer, he relates his "Communicative Ethics" proposal of finding ethical answers in the outcome of discussions to the "pragmatic" philosophy of Dewey, Pierce, and James. However, classical pragmatism is concerned with truth rather than with ethics, and its criterion that "it works," which is valuable for factual knowledge, may lead, when applied to distributive justice, to some *realpolitik* endorsing peace or consensus resulting from unequal powers to threaten or to speak, which is the opposite of fairness and morals. These inequalities cannot occur in the "ideal speech" situation of perfect communication considered by Habermas, but, then, this perfection is ideal and notional, and hence, short of the actual and practical solution advocated by this philosophy. In the process of discussion, individuals are led to the consensual view through a learning process that Habermas sees akin to Piaget's and especially Kohlberg's analysis of the formation of moral sentiments of children (this is about the title of Piaget's book of 1932). However, both these authors emphasize progress toward impartiality, and this property in itself is far from defining a specific solution (believing it does is a common mistake among ethicists – Adam Smith's concept and theory of the "impartial spectator" in his *Theory of Moral Sentiments* is a case in point).[3] In the end, this literature of Habermas and Karl-Otto Apel presents interesting philosophical discussions, notably of others' works, but its specific practical conclusion of letting people agree is rather thin.

2. CONSENSUALIZATION

2.1. Overview of issues

The process of influence, generally mutual, and notably through dialog, can be represented by the evolution of individuals' overall or moral preferences. This shows important properties such as the shrinking of the set of Pareto-efficient states (see Section 2.3).[4] For the present problem of global (overall) distributive justice, it is simpler and probably more cogent to directly consider the evolution of individuals' preferred coefficient k. The reasons, preferences, and arguments about the level of k are rather simple and have been considered in previous chapters: apart from

---

[3] For instance, in an ELIE distribution, all values of coeficient k are consistent with impartiality.
[4] And Kolm 2000a.

self-interest, the ethical reason is a balance between an ethic of self-ownership, on the one hand, and a sense of community, solidarity, reciprocity, and mutuality, on the other. Indeed, making this polarized ethical choice clear-cut is precisely the effect of the adoption of the a priori consensual positions (notably about basic rights and Pareto-efficiency) that led to the selection of this particular parameter. Hence, an individual's reasons for preferring a level of k are very largely fully summarized by this level (given her self-interest). We will thus consider the process of interindividual influence on the evolution of the individuals' preferred levels of k. The outcome will depend on the structural properties of this influence and on the initial set of preferred levels. The ideal will be a convergence toward a steady consensus, but one may end up short of that and apply other methods from an outcome of different preferred k which, however, will have been submitted to discussion and argumentation and would hopefully be closer to one another than they initially were.

The structural properties of the influence will manifest the degrees of convincingness of positions and reasons, which can in particular reflect their objective validity after reflection, checking, and pondering. However, other things can happen. In particular, inequalities in convincing capacities and powers may distort the process toward the self-interests or moral prejudices of the more endowed in this respect. Hence, short of a correlation between convincing possibilities and wisdom, this inequality may have to be corrected, either actually as with the Athenian *isēgoria*, or notionally if the analysis of possible influence and consensus is purely conceptual.

The process of influence should normally have the property that it maintains a consensus (if no new external fact intervenes). This should hold a priori and in general, irrespective of which specific consensus this is. Therefore, the fact of being maintained by the process (of being a steady state) will not by itself determine a single consensual k (or reduce the scope of a priori possible consensual levels), and hence, an obtained consensus will depend on the initial preferred k's of the individuals.[5] The initial set of preferred k can in particular be the purely self-interested positions ($k = 0$ or 1 depending on whether $w_i > \overline{w}$ or $w_i < \overline{w}$). Then, individuals' social and moral views about global distribution are formed – or at least become explicit – only in this process of influences. Yet, such views may also be manifested in the initial preferred k's. The minimum consideration may be a lowest level for guaranteeing the satisfaction of basic needs or a highest level for avoiding the "slavery of the talented." We will, for instance, see a simple case where the final consensual k is the arithmetic average of the initial preferred k of the individuals (a property of equal influence accounts for this result).

2.2. The logic of consensualization

Let k_i^θ denote individual i's preferred level of coefficient k at date θ. Time θ can indifferently be taken as continuous or discrete: consider it as discrete here, in

---

[5] That is, there is no "ergodic property" in the sense of the theory of stochastic processes.

taking for θ successive integers from an initial $\theta = 0$ (there also sometimes are successive rounds or stages of dialog which can be labelled as θ). The discussion will be aided by simplifications that keep the essential structure, but all the properties can also be presented with more general models. Individuals' positions will be summarized by their preferred levels of k (if the process describes an evolution of an individual's views from self-interest – or with an important initial influence of her self-interest – to the impartial viewpoint, the effect of self-interest on the preferred k will be taken into account by the initial position). The set of the n k_i^θ's for given θ is denoted as the vector $k^\theta = \{k_i^\theta\}$. An individual's k_i^θ is influenced by her observation of past positions (accompanied by the explicit or implicit justifications or reasons), which is described by the relation $\{k^\tau\}_{\tau \leq \theta} \to k^{\theta+1}$. An individual's $k_i^{\theta+1}$ may depend on her own anterior k_i^τ for $\tau \leq \theta$ because her position may change only relatively slowly, or she compares her position with others' (or she may react against her former views). At time θ, $k_i^{\theta+1} = k_i^\theta$ if individual i's position does not change, and $k_i^{\theta+1} = k_j^\theta$ if individual j fully convinces individual i. The process begins at $\theta = 0$. This may be with the fully self-interested k_i's (0 or 1 if $w_i \neq \bar{w}$). Then, watching this selfish polarization may lead individuals to some moral or socially minded reaction and to the choice of other k_i^θ's. Yet, some moral or social consideration may be present at the onset.

We will consider here the simple case where $k^{\theta+1}$ depends only on k^θ, which is the central case because we consider a process of adjustment for rational individuals having a memory: $k_i^{\theta+1}$ differs from k_i^θ because of the new information received by individual i at time θ, which is k_j^θ for the $j \neq i$ (the information of k_j^τ for $\tau < \theta$ is taken into account in individual i's choice of $k_i^{\tau+1}$, and hence in the subsequent evolution of individual i's preferred k). This "Markov" process is then described by relations $k_i^{\theta+1} = f_i^\theta(k^\theta)$ or $k^{\theta+1} = f^\theta(k^\theta)$ where $f^\theta = \{f_i^\theta\}$. If individual j does not influence individual i at time θ, function f_i^θ does not depend on her argument k_j^θ, and it increases with k_j^θ if this influence is positive. These are normal cases. Function f_i^θ may be decreasing in k_j^θ if individual j's opinion exerts some repulsive influence on individual i, but such a "perverse" effect is not really the process of convincing or imitation we consider here. Moreover, we study the influence process rather than the effects of other events related to time, and hence the functions f_i^θ will be assumed the same at all θ : $k_i^{\theta+1} = f_i(k^\theta)$ or $k^{\theta+1} = f(k^\theta)$ with $f = \{f_i\}$.

Two types of equalities are crucial in this process. One is consensus, the equality of the k_i^θ for all i. The other is steadiness, that is, $k^{\theta+1} = k^\theta$. Steady states last (because function f does not depend on θ): $k^{\theta+1} = k^\theta$ implies $k^{\theta+2} = k^{\theta+1}$ and $k^\tau = k^\theta$ for all $\tau > \theta$. The process may converge to a steady state. Steady states $k^* = \{k_i^*\}$ are solutions of $k^* = f(k^*)$ (the domain of $k = \{k_i\}$ is the n-dimensional unit cube, hence it is closed and bounded, and therefore steady states exist if the function f is continuous). The central a priori property of influence processes is the *steadiness of consensus*: if all individuals agree at a time, the considered process provides no inducement to change to anyone, that is, if $k_i^\theta = c \in [0,1]$

for all i, then $k_i^{\theta+1} = c$ for all i, for any c. A consensus is a steady state. This is a property of the functions $f_i : e$ denoting a vector of n ones, $f_i(ce) = c$ for all i, or $f(ce) = ce$, for all $c \in [0,1]$. With this property, the convergence toward one of these states, and hence the selection of the consensual solution $k = c$, depends a priori on the initial positions k_i^o. The convergence toward consensus can be described by the decrease of a measure of inequality of the k_i^θ for each θ, $J(k^\theta)$. If all functions f_i are identical, consensus is reached in one round. More generally, the more similar they are, the faster the convergence. Sociologically and psychologically, this identity or similarity can result from reason or previous education. However, it should be noted that they imply, in particular, that each f_i is a priori not particularly influenced by the k_i^o of the same i, that is, that individuals consider with impartiality the previous views, including their own, in building their opinion.

The simplest form of the influence functions f_i is the linear form. Its consideration permits a simple illustration of the basic properties of the structure of influence. Then, for each i, $k_i^{\theta+1} = \Sigma_j a_{ij} k_j^\theta$ with constant a_{ij}, or, denoting as $A = \{a_{ij}\}$ the matrix of the a_{ij}, $k^{\theta+1} = Ak^\theta$. The value a_{ij} measures the influence of individual j on individual i. The property of the *steadiness of consensus* is $\Sigma_j a_{ij} = 1$ for all i. It is henceforth assumed. The evolution of opinions is described by $k^{\theta+1} - k^\theta = (A - I)k^\theta$. An individual whose view does not change whatever k^θ is an i such that $a_{ii} = 1$ and $a_{ij} = 0$ for all $j \neq i$. (With a smooth evolution, a_{ii} is closer to 1 when the duration between θ and $\theta + 1$ is shorter.) General *positive* or *nonnegative* influence means $a_{ij} > 0$ or $a_{ij} \geq 0$ for all i, j; they are normal properties of the considered influence process. Steady consensus and nonnegative influence imply that matrix A is row-stochastic. Then, a value $a_{ij} = 1$ means an instant and total influence of individual j on individual i. An opinion leader is an individual j with high a_{ij} for all (or many) individuals $i \neq j$. The limiting case is $a_{ij} = 1$ for all $i \neq j$ (instant total influence on all others), and hence, $a_{i\ell} = 0$ for all i and ℓ that are not j. On the contrary, an individual j influences no other when $a_{ij} = 0$ for all $i \neq j$.

A variation α of k_j^θ induces a variation αa_{ij} in $k_i^{\theta+1}$, the sum of which is $\alpha \Sigma_i a_{ij}$. The number $a_j = \Sigma_i a_{ij}$ can measure the total social influence of individual j. Then, *equal influence* means that the a_j are all equal, $a_j = a$. But, with steadiness of consensus, this implies $a = 1$ since $na = \Sigma_{i,j} a_{ij} = \Sigma_i(\Sigma_j a_{ij}) = n$. Then, $\Sigma_j a_{ij} = 1$. Equal influence is in particular achieved by $a_{ij} = a_{ji}$ for all i, j, that is, equal mutual influence, or balanced *reciprocity* of influence, for each pair of individuals; matrix A then is symmetrical. A particular subcase, for instance, is that where each $k_i^{\theta+1}$ is the same weighted average between k_i^θ and the arithmetic average of the k_j^θ for $j \neq i$, that is, all a_{ij} for $i \neq j$ are equal. Steady consensus, equal influence, and nonnegative influence amount to matrix A being bistochastic.

Equal influence with steady consensus implies

$$\Sigma_i k_i^{\theta+1} = \Sigma_{i,j} a_{ij} k_j^\theta = \Sigma_j(\Sigma_i a_{ij})k_j^\theta = \Sigma_j k_j^\theta.$$

Therefore, $\Sigma k_i^\theta = \Sigma k_i^o$ for all t. Hence, for a consensus level c, $c = (1/n)\Sigma k_i^o$: *the consensus level is unique and is the average of the individuals' initial preferred levels of k.* For instance, if the initial positions reflect only self-interest, $k_i^o = 0$ if $w_i > \overline{w}$ and $k_i^o = 1$ if $w_i < \overline{w}$. Hence, if ν is the number of individuals with $w_i < \overline{w}$ and if $w_i = \overline{w}$ for no i or for a sufficiently small proportion of the individuals, the consensus level is $c = \nu/n$. If this self-interest is mitigated with social or normative considerations demanding a minimum k^- for satisfying basic needs and a maximum k^+ for avoiding the "slavery of the talented," with $0 < k^- < k^+ < 1$, then $k_i^o = k^-$ if $w_i > \overline{w}$ and $k_i^o = k^+$ if $w_i < \overline{w}$, and the final consensus level is (if $w_i = \overline{w}$ for no i or for sufficiently few i)

$$c = (1/n)[\nu k^+ + (n - \nu)k^-] = k^- + (\nu/n)(k^+ - k^-).$$

Steady consensus, equal influence, and nonnegative influence (hence, a bistochastic matrix A) make the successive k_i^θ for each t more equal in the sense that the Lorenz curve of their distribution becomes higher. It diminishes any Schur-convex measure of inequality $J(k^\theta)$.[6]

2.3. Consensualization of preferences

Individuals can derive their preferred level of coefficient k from preferences about the distribution, given the ELIE *structure*. They can also have preferences about more general items. And the process of influence can be described on such sets of individual preferences. This process can result from a dialog of any type (with a possible role for imitation). Then, the final result can be applied for obtaining, notably, coefficient k.

Denote as x, y, etc., states of society, whose set is X. For each individual i and any two $x \in X$ and $y \in X$, either x is preferred to $y(xP_iy)$, or x and y are indifferent $(xI_iy \Leftrightarrow yI_ix)$, or y is preferred to $x(yP_ix)$, and we denote $xR_iy \Leftrightarrow$ not $yP_ix \Leftrightarrow xP_iy$ or xI_iy. R_i suffices to define the ordering since $xP_iy \Leftrightarrow xR_iy$ and not yR_ix, and $xI_iy \Leftrightarrow xR_iy$ and yR_ix.

These preferences evolve in a process of influence (notably a dialog). Let θ denote dates (or rounds of dialogs), and R_i^θ, P_i^θ, and I_i^θ denote R_i, P_i, and I_i at date θ. The process starts at $\theta = 0$. In a dialog, ordering R_i represents the reasons and sentiments that underlie it. R_i^θ a priori depends on all the R_j^τ for $\tau < 0$, but the same reason as that presented for coefficient k_i leads to making R_i^θ depend on the $R_j^{\theta-1}$ only (a Markov process).

The *steadiness of consensus* can apply to orderings R_i globally: if the orderings R_i^θ are the same for all i, the orderings $R_i^{\theta+1}$ all are also the same as these. However, the steadiness of consensus more interestingly applies to each *pairwise* preference. This permits the consideration of the effect of the process on the *domain of consensus*,

---

[6] See *The optimal production of social justice* (Kolm 1966a), Sections 6 and 7, and Kolm 1999a for a full discussion of the underlying concept of inequality.

that is, the set of pairs $(x, y) \in X \times X$ such that all individuals' preferences within the pair coincide.

The following rules of steadiness of pairwise consensus can be considered, for pairs $(x, y) \in X \times X (\forall i$ means: for all $i)$:

1. Strict preference: $x P_i^\theta y, \forall i \Rightarrow x P_i^{\theta+1} y, \forall i.$
2. Indifference: $x I_i^\theta y, \forall i \Rightarrow x I_i^{\theta+1} y, \forall i.$
3. Weak preference: $x R_i^\theta y, \forall i \Rightarrow x R_i^{\theta+1} y, \forall i.$
4. Universal positive influence: $x R_i^\theta y, \forall i$, and $x P_i^\theta y$ for at least one $i \Rightarrow$ $x P_i^{\theta+1} y, \forall i.$

Note that, for condition (3), $x R_i y$ is "not $y P_i x$," and condition (4) adds, to condition (3), that any individual's strict preference entails each individual's strict preference, given that no individual has the opposite strict preference. Condition (4) implies condition (1). Conditions (1), (2), and (3) respectively entail that, in the process, the sets of pairs with consensual (unanimous) strict preference, indifference, and weak preference, lose no element. They may expand (they generally do). These properties express the process of consensualization.

State $x \in X$ is Pareto-efficient when, for no $y \in X$, one has $y R_i x$ for all i and $y P_i x$ for at least one i. Hence, if $x \in X$ is not Pareto-efficient at date (stage)θ, there exists $y \in X$ such that $y R_i^\theta x$ for all i and $y P_i^\theta x$ for at least one i. Then, if condition (4) holds, $y P_i^{\theta+1} x$ for all i. Therefore, x is not Pareto-efficient at date $\theta + 1$ (since $y R_i^{\theta+1} x$ for all i and $y P_i^{\theta+1} x$ for at least one i). Hence, in the process, the set of non-Pareto-efficient states loses no state; therefore, the set of Pareto-efficient states gains no state. This latter set generally shrinks. This again expresses the process of consensualization. Pareto efficiency is, in itself, a more and more efficient (selective) criterion for choosing a solution.

The process may end up with a unique consensual ordering, the same for everyone. If, for instance, the considered states are the income distribution, or the set of transfers $t = \{t_i\}$, this ordering may be representable by an ordinal evaluation function $U(t)$. Then, with the transfers of an ELIE $t_i = k \cdot (\overline{w} - w_i) = k s_i$, the chosen level of coefficient k maximizes $U(t)$. Assume the required differentiabilities and denote $v = \Sigma U_i' s_i$. Then, the chosen k satisfies $0 < k < 1, v = 0$, and $\Sigma U''_{ij} s_i s_j \leq 0$, or $k = 0$ and $v < 0$, or $k = 1$ and $v > 0$.

21

Impartialization to consensus

1. GENERAL OUTLOOK

1.1. Impartialization to consensus

In questions of distribution, individual self-interests are opposed by definition, and this constitutes an intrinsic impediment to consensus. This holds both for individuals' own interests and for those of the people they particularly favour. Individuals' impartial views avoid this impediment, but this raises two problems.

First, individuals may just not have an impartial view. They may, for instance, have no opinion at all when their own interest (or that of the people they favour) is not at stake. One may then try to discuss with these people to make them aware of the issue and induce them to consider some impartial viewpoint (in addition to their self-interest or biased preferences). This, however, may fail or may not suffice. The solution to this problem will consist of theoretically deriving individuals' implicit hypothetical impartial views from their actual purely self-interested or self-centered evaluations. The methods of this derivation are presented, discussed, and applied.

However, the second problem then intervenes: impartiality does not entail consensus, because there are various different impartial moral judgments – contrary to an implicit or explicit belief common among scholars (for instance, an ELIE distribution with any level of coefficient k has a type of impartiality). Yet, impartializations of individuals' views make an important progress toward consensus, because they erase essential causes of disagreements: those due to oppositions among self-interests or self-centered preferences.

Among the solutions to the problem that impartiality does not suffice for consensus, one has a virtue of consistency. This consists of treating individuals' different moral impartial views as their self-interests have been treated in the methods of "impartialization" (described shortly). That is, this is a second-degree impartialization, an impartialization of individuals' impartial views with respect to self-interests. As with the first-degree impartialization, this operation makes

336

individuals' views closer to one another. Yet, it still does not suffice to yield consensus. However, the same method can be further applied, in an infinite regress leading toward consensus. This is the method of *moral regress*.

However, other methods can also solve the problem of the differences between individuals' impartial views. Aggregation of impartial views, or a social contract among them, are possibilities. And in the end, full information, including mutual formative and empathetic information about the causes of others' moral views and the sentiments they raise, provide the deepest answer (see Chapter 15).

1.2. The methods of impartialization

Impartialization consists of deriving impartial views from individuals' self-interested or self-centered evaluations. The methods of impartialization are of two kinds respectively called *extension* and *conjunction*, analyzed in the following sections.

Extension consists of considering that the individual notionally cares for all individuals as she cares for specific individuals she actually and similarly cares for. Indeed, individuals care for individuals who are in a specific relation to them, such as brothers, children, first-degree cousins they see once a year, neighbours, or people belonging to some group that includes the evaluator. This concern, however, generally and a priori depends on this particular type of social relation. A social relation of reference is chosen, and each individual is assumed to evaluate the whole distribution (including her own share) as if it accrued to individuals in this relation with her. The corresponding evaluation of the distribution amounts to that of sharing among people who all are in this same social relation with the evaluator – such as brothers, children, neighbours, cousins, common members of the society, and so on (the individual is in particular assumed to consider her own situation as that of someone in this relation with her).

Apart from its impartiality, an evaluation of justice has two properties. First, it is more or less "integrative": it is more integrative when it is basically concerned with individual's happiness (say) and less when the object of basic concern is more consumption, income, means, or rights. Second, this conception can be more or less in favour of individual equality (*isophily*) as opposed to valuing an aggregate in the considered society (community in an aggregate sense rather than in that of solidarity or mutual concern). Moreover, the conceptions of justice under consideration are those of individuals, even when only notional ones. Hence, this justice is a virtue (this was the sense of the term justice in the Antiquity and until the 16th century). Now, another classical social virtue with respect to individuals' views of others' situations is altruism (possibly benevolence or any of their more specific forms). Altruism is favourable concern for others (possibly particular ones), and it can be more or less intense. Evaluating others' situation can be done with more or less altruistic justice. A more altruistic justice favours more integrative conceptions (the more you like others, the more you are concerned with their happiness rather than with only their income for example). Moreover, altruism tends to increase with the proximity of the social relation. Hence, in the construction under consideration, the solution is more favourable to altruistic justice the closer the social relation of reference. As a limiting case, a particularly close social relation is that of an individual with herself. However, an individual can a priori hardly consider several individuals as being herself since she has only one self. She has a way of sharing among various neighbours or children, not among various "herselfs." The "conjunction" methods face this issue.

Conjunction methods consist in considering that the individual could be the various individuals alternatively in time, as uncertain possibilities, or as the various "selfs" of a "multiple self" personality. They are, respectively, "moral time-sharing," "moral risk" (which includes concepts of the family of the "original position"), and the "multiple self" solution. These evaluations, however, will still depend on the specific individuals considered because preferences about variations in time, about risk, or as concerns various aspects of one's personality, a priori differ from one individual to the other. Moreover, preferences about "being" actual individuals also differ across individuals (although this concept deserves a careful discussion).[1]

Sections 2 and 3 analyze impartialization by extension and by conjunction, respectively. In Section 2.1, individuals' actual concerns for others' situations depend on their specific social relation. This relation is replaced by a uniform notional relation in Section 2.2, and the questions this impartialization of individuals' preferences raises are discussed (Sections 2.3 and 2.4). The general principle and methods of impartialization by conjunction through moral time-sharing, moral risks and the multiple self are considered in Section 3.1, while the rest of Section 2 focuses on the theory of moral risk. This theory is outlined in Section 3.2 and presented in Section 3.3. A particular, limiting case is the theory of the original position where the maximum of features of individuals' situations (notably, allocations and characteristics) is put at stake in considering that each could have others than her own. However, this a priori does not yield unanimity because individuals in the original position have to have their own different preferences as concerns both risk and being alternative various individuals (Section 3.4). This problem is solved by the consistent consideration of an infinite regress of original positions of original positions in the general case (Section 3.5), and when people have a common ordering about being the various individuals (a "fundamental preference," Section 3.6). Section 3.7 shows the corresponding convergence and progressive homogeneization of individuals' preference orderings. These general methods are then applied to the problem of global distributive justice (determination of coefficient k), in a case of a theory of the "partially original position" (Section 3.8). Other ways of solving the incompleteness of theories of the original position are the aggregation of individuals' preferences about risk in the original

---

[1] See the study *Vox populi, vox dei* (Kolm 2001b).

position (Section 3.9), and the use of notional exchanges, in particular in a putative "fundamental insurance" for correcting "brute luck" (Section 3.10). Finally, the question of the validity of theories of justice based on analogies with individual choice in uncertainty is discussed in Section 3.11.

2. IMPARTIALIZATION BY EXTENSION

2.1. Self-centered evaluations

An allocation (possibly a distribution) consists of the allocation of items to the individuals i. Denote as a_i the allocation to individual i. A judgment about the a_i may refer to given characteristics c_i of the individuals. The nature of the a_i and c_i can be varied, and this description can represent many types of judgments, principles, and criteria. For the case of global distributive justice of the previous chapters and an ELIE distribution, we would have $a_i = t_i$ (the tax or subsidy for individual i), and $c_i = w_i$ (individual i's productivity or wage rate). Denote as x_i the pair of a_i and c_i, $x_i = (a_i, c_i)$. Moreover, an individual i's opinion about the allocation a_j of an individual j generally also depends on the social relation of j to i: it generally differs depending on whether individual j is, for individual i, a complete foreigner, a neighbour, a cousin, a member of the same relevant group of any nature, her sister, her daughter, or, indeed, herself. These differences are essentially due to individual i's self-centeredness. Denote as r^i_j this social relation of individual j to individual i. Hence, the r^i_j are particular characteristics, depending on each pair of individuals, and not included in the c_i. Then, individual i's preference ordering for the allocation may be represented by her ordinal utility.

$$u_i \left(\{ a_j, c_j, r^i_j \} \right) = u_i \left(\{ x_j, r^i_j \} \right) . ^2$$

If the set of characteristics c_j is sufficiently exhaustive so as to include all that relevantly differentiates individuals, each function u_i is symmetrical in the triplets $(a_j, c_j, r^i_j) = (x_j, r^i_j)$ – that is, its value is invariant under their permutations. The c_i will be so chosen. The fact that u_i depends on the r^i_j, and the differences in the effects of different r^i_j, manifest individual i's self-centeredness. One of the j is the considered i, an "identity" relation denoted as r^i_i. Since function $u^i(\{x_j, r^i_j\})$

---

2 The brackets { } mean the set for all j of the elements that are within. Note that the utility function u_i may be "direct" or "indirect" in various possible ways. Individual i may care for a_j or c_j directly or for that which individual j does or can do with it. For instance, a_j may be final consumption of individual j, or something that enables individual j to obtain final consumption; and individual i may, in the end, care for individual j's final consumption (in particular when $j = i$). However, individual i can also care directly for other items of individual j than her final consumption, depending on her judgment about proper relevance (for instance, she may hold individual j's use of non-final items a_j or c_j to be her own responsibility). In particular, for global distributive justice, $a_j = t_j$ (transfer) and $c_j = w_j$ (wage rate) are means for individual j to choose her final consumption of goods and leisure, and individual i may directly care for these latter items with u_i then being the corresponding indirect utility function (but individual i may also directly care for individual j's domain of free choice defined by t_j and w_j, or she may have both concerns).

is symmetrical (invariant under permutations) in the pairs (x_j, r_j^i) for all j, by construction (definition of the c_j), then it is symmetrical in the x_j for all j if and only if it is symmetrical in the r_j^i for all j. This symmetry in the x_j or in the r_j^i, for all j, is individual i's impartiality of her evaluation of the distribution of the a_j, $a = \{a_j\}$.

Individuals' evaluations may be so impartial or not. This depends on the individuals, on the nature of the allocated items a_i, and on the considered society constituted by this set of individuals. Individual's actual evaluations are often not impartial: for many issues, people favour themselves and their family (yet, the household, rather than the individual, may be the relevant social unit), they favour their children more than their cousins, their cousins more than their other compatriots, and their compatriots more than foreigners. Yet, justice has to be impartial by nature and definition of the concept, and endogenous social choice has to derive it from individuals' evaluations. This leads to trying to find individuals' implicit impartial evaluations, implied by their actual evaluations. A second step would be to have the consequences accepted at a political level.

2.2. Impartialization by a uniform social relation

The function defined as $U_i(x, \rho) = u_i(\{x_j, \rho\})$ with $x = \{x_j\}$, obtained from the function $u_i(\{x_j, r_j^i\})$ in replacing all social relations r_j^i for this i by a given notional social relation denoted as ρ, constitutes an impartial evaluation. It is symmetrical in the x_i, since it is in the pairs (x_i, ρ). Function U_i shows individual i's evaluation of x – basically, her preference ordering of the x – if all individuals were in the same social relation ρ with her (note that, in particular, r_i^i is replaced by ρ, that is, individual i also sees her own allocation as that of an individual in the reference social relation with her). The transformation of function u_i into function U_i constitutes an impartialization of individual i's evaluation and preference ordering. It depends on the chosen relation of reference ρ. This can be considered for all individuals i, a priori with the same ρ. This is an "impartialization by extension" (of a type of social relation). The chosen social relation ρ is the "social relation of impartialization." The functions U_i and the orderings of x they represent constitute the "ρ-impartialized" individuals' judgments about the distribution.

All functions U_i have in common the property of being symmetrical in the x_j. This is not a priori the case of the u_i as functions of the x_j, for given r_j^i. A function u_i, in particular, is usually very sensitive to some x_j, notably to x_i, and is little sensitive or not sensitive at all to some other x_j. These differences are manifested by the effects of the parameters r_j^i. Then, the evaluations represented by the functions U_i of x for the various individuals i, where these differential effects disappear, are a priori much closer to one another than the evaluations represented by the functions u_i for the various i. These evaluations will be those manifested by the preference orderings of the $x = \{x_i\}$ or $a = \{a_i\}$ represented by these functions (which, therefore, are ordinal functions). For instance, with the assumed sufficiently exhaustive set of characteristics c_i, all the permutations of the x_i are indifferent when compared with the functions U_i (they all give the same value to each U_i for each i and each ρ), but this is generally not the case for the u_i because of the differential effects of the r^i_j on each u_i. Hence, there is at least this domain of identity of the preferences defined by the U_i, which a priori does not exist for the preferences defined by the u_i.

2.3. Social-ethical differences and their erasement

Yet, the preference orderings defined by the U_i are a priori bound to differ from one another: individuals may not evaluate the same way the allocations to a set of individuals in the same social relation with them. However, in a given society, these evaluations may be rather similar because of social norms, a common culture, similar education and examples, and mutual influence. The remaining differences, if any, can be treated in a number of possible ways, given that the consideration of functions U_i for each individual i solves the basic problem of the oppositions among individuals because of their self-interest or self-centeredness. These solutions can consist of some relevant average of solutions preferred with each function U_i, of use of the surplus method with the utility functions U_i, or of some sort of aggregation or notional bargaining based on the U_i. For an ELIE with $a_i = t_i$, the average can be that of the coefficients k that maximize functions U_i, and the use of the surplus method has been shown in Chapter 16. However, the first thing to do for solving this problem, or for further narrowing down interindividual differences, consists in considering communication and dialog about the proper way of evaluating allocations to a set of individuals in the same social relation ρ with the evaluator. This will reinforce the effects of the common culture and of spontaneous interaction. The deepest way of solution, however, consists of considering full formative and empathetic information about the causes, reasons, and sentiments that underlie the social-ethical preferences represented by functions U_i.

Finally, the method of the consistent iteration of moral regress can also be used. This consists of erasing the differences in the preferences represented by the functions U_i as has been done for erasing differences due to self-centeredness for obtaining the U_i. The opinions represented by the U_i are now assumed to be those of individuals in the same social relation to an individual evaluator – a priori the same relation ρ that has been used for defining the U_i. Then, the evaluator arbitrates among these various opinions. The result can depend on which actual individual this evaluator is. However, the resulting views, as judgments about the allocations, will still be closer to one another. Then, possible remaining differences can be treated as noted about differences in the preferences represented by the functions U_i. One of these solutions can consist of a further round of individuals' evaluations of the set of opinions of individuals in the same social relation ρ with them. This will still make individuals' resulting evaluations of the allocation more similar. If necessary, this method can be pursued in further iterations. The logic of such a process is similar to that analyzed in forthcoming Section 3.

2.4. The social relation of impartialization, others as oneself

These solutions a priori depend on the choice of the social relation of impartialization ρ. Closer relations tend to yield more altruistic justice and hence more integrative solutions. For instance, the solution can be extended (and a priori notional) brotherhood (the republican ideal of fraternity), "paternalism," or "nepotism," as distributive justice duplicates judgment or sharing among, respectively, siblings, children, or nephews (the extension to all of society erases the a priori unfairness of preference for family). However, the closest social relation is a priori that of an individual to herself. Moreover, this may permit the application of the extension method to individuals who are purely self-interested (and not only self-centered). Yet, this solution raises the particular problem that an individual, having only one self, has a priori no standard for evaluating distributions among several such "oneselves." The next section faces this problem.

3. IMPARTIALIZATION BY CONJUNCTION

3.1. General principle

Time, uncertainty, and psychology can provide solutions to this question: an individual can be imagined as having properties of several individuals (or even as "being" these individuals) successively in time, as alternative uncertain events, or as the dimensions of a "multiple self" personality. These methods are labelled *moral time-sharing*, *moral risk*, and the *multiple self*, respectively. The basic parameter of these methods is the dichotomy of the aspects of an individual into those that are kept by the evaluating individual and those that are replaced by what they are in all the individuals of the evaluated situation. This replacement is successive for moral time-sharing, it takes the form of a priori uncertain alternative possibilities for moral risk, and of various aspects of a personality for the multiple self. The group of individual aspects or properties that incur this substitution and replacement includes the direct effects of the policy (notably the "allocations") and the particular individual characteristics deemed relevant for the considered evaluation. The other, maintained group of aspects should notably include the individual's characteristics that enable her to evaluate. Given this dichotomy, there a priori is one evaluation for each individual of the society ("external observers" are irrelevant for endogenous social choice). This evaluation is impartial with respect to the substituted aspects if the various substitutions are treated fairly, which will imply equality in time (equal duration),[3] in probability, or in consideration for the multiple self method. These individual evaluations will be more similar to one another than the actual evaluations, and they are more similar when the set of substituted individual properties expands. Hence, these methods extend the domain of consensus. However, they cannot in general produce full consensus because there has to remain an individual evaluator with her specific evaluating preferences, and hence there will remain a different evaluation for each member of the society. Full consensus requires further steps presented shortly.

The theories of moral time-sharing and of moral risk have similar logical structures. One difference is that the additive separability of utilities is, for risk, justified by the classical theory of "rational choice" in uncertainty (von Neumann-Morgenstern, Savage, etc.), while it would have to be a specific assumption in the case of time. The usual psychological theories of the "multiple self" do not add much that is useful here. Indeed, the various selves they consider either correspond to various dates and this is time-sharing, or they consist of very few and very heterogeneous entities, which do not fit our purpose (Freud's distinction between the *id*, the *superego*, and the *ego* is a case in point). Moral risk is the approach taken by the theories of the "original position" (Rawls 1971; Harsanyi 1953, 1955, 1976) or of the partially original position (Kolm 1996d, 1998). However, since the problem concerns distribution among actual individuals, the justified uncertainty should be about having the relevant characteristics or situations of these individuals: any further uncertainty is not justified by the purpose of the theory, and hence, is arbitrary. A case of this uncertainty is provided by the "thin veil of ignorance" used by Harsanyi and so labelled by Rawls. Rawls, however, prefers a larger and very extensive a priori uncertainty (his "thick veil"), while Harsanyi bypasses the fact that the obtained evaluation has to be specific to the evaluator.[4]

3.2. Moral risk: An outline

Let us consider here the theory of moral risk. The theory of moral time-sharing would consist of a similar analysis. An individual considers that she can have some of her properties replaced by the corresponding properties of all the considered individuals with an equal probability. This equality results from the consideration of justice toward these individuals. This artificial uncertainty is the one that can be justified for building a theory of justice among these individuals. More extensive hypothetical uncertainty would lack justification and be arbitrary. The evaluating individuals will be assumed to have a rational evaluation of risk in the classical sense, and hence they maximize the expected value of a specification of their von

---

[3] Classical time discounting is irrelevant here. Hence, the succession of substituted items corresponding to the various individuals should be sufficiently rapid (short durations), but it can be in a revolving rotation. Alternatively, the more distant durations can be longer so as to compensate for time discounting.

[4] See the full discussion in *Vox populi, vox dei* (Kolm 2001b).

Neumann-Morgenstern (VNM) cardinal utility function. There are good classical reasons for this rationality. It is also well known, however, that individuals often behave differently. The reasons are issues of salience and attention, or of emotion. They seem to have to be discarded in this hypothetical risk evaluation for the purpose of building an ethical theory, which should be rational.

A central issue of such an ethical theory consists of the choice of the individual properties that incur the (risky) substitution. They include the allocation and all individual characteristics that are deemed relevant for the choice of this allocation. In one limiting case, there is only the allocation. In the opposite limiting case, all that constitutes the individuals is deemed a priori relevant. This latter case is that of the theories of the "original position" (although Rawls considers a broader uncertainty in the original position: the "thick veil of ignorance" rather than the justifiable "thin veil").

However, in all cases there is one such moral-risk evaluation per individual evaluator. This is, in particular, the case in a theory of the original position, since the evaluator has to evaluate with her own preferences about risk and about "being" particular individuals (this opposes Harsanyi's assumption). Hence, moral risk a priori produces no consensus, although the individuals' moral-risk evaluations are closer to one another than their actual views, as will be shown. Ways of dealing with this plurality will be proposed.

The presentation of the general theory will precede the application to the case of global distributive justice. The cases where the substituted individual items are the allocations (for instance, incomes), or also include characteristics of the individuals, are followed by the rational theory of the original position, where each evaluator considers that she could "be" the various individuals with equal probabilities. Then, the most consistent way of facing the issue of the multiplicity of moral-risk evaluations consists of considering "original positions of original positions" and iterative repetitions of this device in a moral regress that converges to a solution. The case where there is a consensus about the order of desirability of "being" the various individuals (represented by a "fundamental utility") provides a solution with a particularly meaningful structure. It also permits the reduction of solutions by aggregation to the aggregation of individual preferences about risk, which presents remarkable possibilities.

These concepts and results will then be used for answering the question of global (overall) distributive justice. The corresponding moral-risk evaluations take individuals' productivities as individuals' relevant characteristics. The problem of the multiplicity of obtained evaluations can be solved by the consideration of a regress of original positions. It can also be solved by an aggregation of moral-risk evaluations, which reduces to remarkable alternatives when there is a "fundamental utility" because it reduces to aggregating individuals' preferences concerning risk.

Other possible ways of solution consist of exchange agreements among the individuals, possibly with bargaining or arbitrage. The part of arbitrariness in these solutions, due to the a priori irrelevance of facts that determine them, can be reduced if this exchange agreement is assumed to take place among moral-risk evaluations. Then, this agreement can in particular state solutions conditional on the realization of the – assumed – risk, a theory in the family of "fundamental insurance"[5] that will be presented.

Finally, the validity of moral-risk theories of justice will be discussed. The limitations of these theories can be faced with the other methods presented.

3.3. General moral risk

Index u_i will denote a specification of individual i's ordinal utility function. The arguments of this function will be the object of further discussion. Index v_i will denote a specification of individual i's von Neumann-Morgenstern (VNM) cardinal utility, relevant for the evaluation of the considered risks, which the individual ranks as the expected value of v_i. This index is itself an increasing function of u_i, say $v_i = g_i(u_i)$, noted as $v_i = g_i \circ u_i$ when v_i and u_i denote functions (the usual notation for composition of functions). Function g_i denotes individual i's preferences about risk.

If individual i is purely self-interested and only concerned with the allocation a_i she receives, an application of moral risk can consider the notional situation where individual i may receive each of the allocations a_j of the n individuals with an equal probability $1/n$. Then, possible allocations $a = \{a_j\}$ constitute, for individual i, risky prospects that she orders according to the value of the expected utility $n^{-1} \Sigma_j v_i(a_j)$. For instance, Vickrey (1945) and Harsanyi (1953) considered this case where a_i denotes individual i's income. This evaluation is impartial as concerns the allocations, which shows by the fact that it is symmetrical in the a_j (invariant under permutations of the a_j).

If there is a set of individuals' characteristics of any nature, denoted as c_i for individual i, which are deemed relevant for the choice of individual allocations a_i, then, denoting as $x_i = (a_i, c_i)$ the pair of a_i and c_i, one can now rather write $u_i(x_i)$. The case where there are no such individual characteristics can be taken as a particular case (and one could also consider x_i as individual i's "allocation," even though c_i is a priori given). The reason why individual i cares about a_i and c_i incurs no a priori restriction here. The a_i or c_i may have the nature of final consumption in the broad sense (direct concern), or they may not be. When they are not, notably when they are means of individual i's choices or actions, the functions u_i and v_i are the corresponding "indirect" utility functions. Then, the relevant "moral" risky prospect consists of the possibility of having each of the n x_j with the same probability $1/n$. Individual i orders these prospects as the value of the expected utility $n^{-1} \Sigma_j v_i(x_j)$. This evaluation is impartial in the x_j, which shows by its symmetry in these variables.

---

[5] See Kolm 1985a.

3.4. The rational theory of the "original position"

The set of individual characteristics deemed relevant can be more or less extended. It can be very extended in including, notably, all of individuals' capacities, preferences, assets and liabilities, social situation, and so on. The largest extension can be described by the evaluator's consideration that she may "be" any of the actual individuals with the same probability. However, each individual evaluator has to keep the means to make her own evaluation. These means have to be of two types. First, since the evaluation is that of a risky prospect, each evaluator has to keep her preferences concerning risk for this evaluation about the possibility of "being" any individual. However, in considering each of these eventualities, the evaluator considers that she has the preferences of this individual, including her preferences concerning risk for evaluating her situation if this situation involves risk. Second, the notion of preferences about "being" someone else is delicate and rich in pitfalls.[6] However, individuals a priori have different preferences in this respect. Individuals who love glory prefer being Napoleon to anyone else, whereas people particularly keen on charity prefer being Mother Theresa to anyone else. Standard and necessary implications of this "being" will suffice for our purpose.

This consideration of individuals being uncertain about which individual they could be relates to the theories of the "original position." In these theories, the individuals "in the original position" are uncertain about what actual individuals they will "become." However, Rawls considers that the uncertainty in the original position is much larger than only about being the actual individuals in the actual state of the world, whereas only this latter uncertainty seems to be justified by the objective of finding a rule of distributive justice among these actual individuals. The uncertainty considered by Harsanyi (1976) is this latter "thin veil of ignorance," but this author assumes that the evaluating individuals are identical, including in their preferences about risk for evaluating the moral risk, which is not a priori the case if they are the actual individuals. Nevertheless, the intention of these authors, tradition, and illustrative power lead to keeping the name and general concept of the "original position," and then to seeing what can rationally be said about this idea.

What is to be evaluated will be denoted as x. Its nature depends on the specific problem under consideration. It can consist of a whole allocation (set of individual allocations) of any items, along with any other parameters. Let $u_i(x)$ denote a specification of individual i's ordinal utility function evaluating x (if individual i is purely self-interested, u_i depends only on the corresponding part of x, such as individual i's income or consumption). Moreover, it is not uncommon that individuals imagine that they are someone else and have preferences about being various individuals. The object of preference is, more exactly, being such individual when state x holds, since x includes a specification of this individual's situation, allocation,

[6] See *Vox populi, vox dei* (op. cit.).

income, rights, etc. (depending on the definition of state x). Denote as (b_j, x) "being individual j when state x holds." If individual i's such preferences are representable by an ordinal utility function, a specification of this function will be $\widetilde{u}_i(b_j, x)$. Note that "being individual j" implies having individual j's consumption, income, situation, etc., in addition to having individual j's tastes, physical and mental characteristics, etc. Some of these items are described within the variable x.

The function of x $\widetilde{u}_i(b_i, x)$ is ordinally identical to $u_i(x)$, and one can choose, as specification for $u_i(x)$, $u_i(x) = \widetilde{u}_i(b_i, x)$. If individual i's consideration of her being individual j implies that her preference ordering of x is that of individual j, then $\widetilde{u}_i(b_j, x)$ as a function of x is ordinally equivalent to the function $u_j(x)$, which implies that there exists an increasing $\mathcal{R}^1 \to \mathcal{R}^1$ function h_{ij} such that (with the usual notation for composition of functions)

$$\widetilde{u}_i(b_j, x) = h_{ij}[u_j(x)] = h_{ij} \circ u_j(x)$$

(with $h_{ii} = 1$).

Let $g_i(\widetilde{u}_i)$ denote a specification of individual i's VNM cardinal utility. Function g_i is increasing (and, from cardinality, it can be replaced by any $a_i g_i + b_i$ where a_i and b_i are constant and $a_i > 0$). Denote $v_i(x) = g_i \circ u_i(x)$.[7] In the original position, individual i faces the risky prospect of becoming each individual with an equal probability $1/n$ (as a condition of justice and fairness). Her evaluation of this prospect is her expected utility

$$v_i^1(x) = n^{-1} \Sigma_j g_i \circ \widetilde{u}_i(b_j, x) = n^{-1} \Sigma_j g_i \circ h_{ij} \circ u_j(x) = n^{-1} \Sigma_j \gamma_{ij} \circ u_j(x)$$
$$= n^{-1} \Sigma_j g_i \circ h_{ij} \circ g_j^{-1} \circ v_j(x) = n^{-1} \Sigma_j H_{ij} \circ v_j(x),$$

where $\gamma_{ij} = g_i \circ h_{ij}$ and $H_{ij} = g_i \circ h_{ij} \circ g_j^{-1} = \gamma_{ij} \circ g_j^{-1}$ are increasing functions.

These functions represent the n orderings of the x of the individuals in the original position. They are a priori different. However, since the functions γ_{ij} or H_{ij} are increasing, the orderings of the x defined by the v_i^1 are generally more alike than those defined by the v_i in a sense shortly to be made precise and which in general implies a shrinking of the set of Pareto-efficient states – the "Pareto set" – (Section 3.7). Hence, the problem of obtaining a unique ordering unanimously agreed upon is not solved, but a progress has been made in this direction.

---

[7] We can make precise the relation among the various utilities. Denote as $(\beta, \xi) = \{\beta^k, \xi^k; p^k\}$ the risky prospect where (b_j, x) take the values (β^k, ξ^k) with probability $p^k (\Sigma_k p^k = 1$ and $p^k \geq 0$ for all k), where k denotes an index of the occurences. Denote as $U_i(\beta, \xi)$ a specification of individual i's ordinal utility function evaluating (β, ξ), such that $U_i = \widetilde{u}_i(b_j, x)$ when (β, ξ) becomes the sure prospect (b_j, x). With the classical rational evaluation of risk, there are two functions $G_i: \mathcal{R}_1 \to \mathcal{R}_1$ increasing and $\widetilde{v}_i(\beta^k, \xi^k)$ such that $U_i(\beta, \xi) = G_i[\Sigma_k p^k \widetilde{v}_i(\beta^k, \xi^k)]$, where $\widetilde{v}_i$ is a specification of the corresponding VNM cardinal utility of individual i. In particular, when (β, ξ) is the sure (b_j, x), this relation becomes $\widetilde{u}_i(b_j, x) = G_i \circ \widetilde{v}_i(b_j, x)$, or, denoting $g_i = G_i^{-1}$, $\widetilde{v}_i(b_j, x) = g_i \circ \widetilde{u}_i(b_j, x)$. When $j = i$, this becomes $g_i \circ u_i(x) = v_i(x) = \widetilde{v}_i(b_i, x)$, and more generally $\widetilde{v}_i(b_j, x) = g_i \circ \widetilde{u}_i(b_j, x) = g_i \circ h_{ij} \circ u_j(x) = g_i \circ h_{ij} \circ g_j^{-1} \circ v_j(x)$. Then, the theory of the original position considers the uncertain prospect $(\beta, \xi) = \{b_j, x; 1/n\}$, where the indices of the occurences are now the n j (being individual j).

3.5. The moral regress of original positions

Moreover, the problem of having one evaluation per individual in the original position is analogous to the initial problem of having various individual evaluations in the real world. Consistency suggests facing this problem with the same method, especially since it led to some progress. We therefore have to consider an original position of the original position, where the individuals face the risk of having each of the evaluations v_i^1 with the same probability $1/n$. Then, individual i's evaluation in this second-degree original position, $v_i^2(x)$, obtains from the $v_j^1(x)$ as the latter obtained from the $v_\ell(x)$, that is,

$$v_i^2(x) = n^{-1} \Sigma_j H_{ij} \circ v_j^1(x).$$

There still are n evaluations. However, for the same reason as above, the orderings of the x defined by the $v_i^2(x)$ will generally be more alike than those defined by the $v_i^1(x)$. The process then can be repeated, in successively anterior original positions $OP_1, OP_2 \ldots OP_m, \ldots$ with the recurrence relation

$$v_i^{m+1}(x) = n^{-1} \Sigma_j H_{ij} \circ v_j^m(x).$$

Then, the orderings defined by the $v_i^{m+1}(x)$ are generally more alike than those defined by the $v_j^m(x)$, and the Pareto set generally shrinks from one step to the next, in senses and for reasons presented in Section 3.7. When $m \to \infty$, a full convergence of these individual ordering towards the same ordering represented by the ordinal utility $U(x)$ means that there are increasing functions φ_i such that $u_i^\infty(x) = g_i^{-1} \circ v_i^\infty(x) = \varphi_i \circ U(x)$ with $\varphi_i = h_{ij} \circ \varphi_j$ for all i and j. Now, such a solution always satisfies the limit equation $v_i^\infty(x) = n^{-1} \Sigma_j H_{ij} \circ v_j^\infty(x) = n^{-1} \Sigma_j g_i \circ h_{ij} \circ g_j^{-1} \circ v_j^\infty(x)$.

The v_i^m, v_i^∞ and such a reached U are by construction increasing functions of the $u_i(x)$ (and do not depend otherwise on state x). Such a U thus has the form of a classical "social welfare function" $U(x) = W[\{u_i(x)\}]$. It represents the ordering of all individuals in this "*infinite regress*" original position. Hence, the principle of unanimity in this situation demands that it be the social maximand. As a function of the u_i, it has neither an additive utilitarian form (which would be meaningless), nor the structure of additive separability that holds for the v_i^1 (and u_i^1). Unanimity requires more integration of the actual individuals' preferences, so to speak. The increasingness of W in the u_i implies that the final solution is Pareto efficient for individuals' actual preferences.

3.6. The case of a fundamental utility

In important cases, the individuals agree about the ranking of the desirability of being the various individuals. This can result from a common cultural conception of happiness or the good life (this also resolves a numbers of paradoxical situations, such as that raised when each of two individuals prefers to be the other).[8] This common ordering of the pairs (b_i, x) is the "fundamental preference ordering." When it is representable by an ordinal function, this is the "fundamental utility." Let $u(b_i, x)$ denote a specification of this function. Then, for given i, $\widehat{u}_i(x) = u(b_i, x)$ is a specification of individual i's ordinal utility function for evaluating x. The other specifications of the ordinal fundamental utility are $\varphi \circ u(b_i, x) = \varphi \circ \widehat{u}_i(x)$, where φ is any increasing function. Hence, the functions $\widehat{u}_i(x)$ can be replaced by any functions $\varphi \circ \widehat{u}_i(x)$ with the same function φ for all i: that is, they are co-ordinal. However, the other specifications of individual i's ordinal utility are $\varphi_i \circ \widehat{u}_i(x)$ where φ_i is any increasing function (which can depend on individual i).

A specification of individual i's cardinal VNM utility is

$$f_i \circ \widehat{u}_i = f_i \circ u(b_i, x) = f_i \circ \widehat{u}_i(x) = v_i(x),$$

where f_i is an appropriate increasing function (the cardinality says that it can be replaced by any function $a_i f_i + b_i$ where a_i and b_i are constant and $a_i > 0$).[9]

Then, when individual i in the original position considers the prospect of becoming any of the individuals with an equal probability $1/n$, she orders the states of the world x with her VNM expected utility of the corresponding risk:

$$v_i^1(x) = n^{-1} \Sigma_j f_i \circ u(b_j, x) = n^{-1} \Sigma_j f_i \circ \widehat{u}_j(x) = n^{-1} \Sigma_j f_i \circ f_j^{-1} \circ v_j(x).$$

This order is also represented in terms of the fundamental utility levels as

$$\widehat{u}_i^1(x) = f_i^{-1} \circ v_i^1(x) = f_i^{-1}[n^{-1} \Sigma_j f_i \circ \widehat{u}_j(x)],$$

or, denoting as $M[\{\alpha_i\}, \varphi] = \varphi^{-1}[n^{-1} \Sigma \varphi(\alpha_i)]$ the generalized mean of the n numbers α_i with function φ,

$$\widehat{u}_i^1(x) = M[\{\widehat{u}_j(x)\}, f_i].$$

Since this case is a subcase of that of the previous section, the discussion of the general case again applies here. There is a multiplicity of evaluations in the original position, one for each individual. Yet, the orderings of x implied by the

---

[8] For a full discussion of the logical problems raised by preference about being, see Kolm 2001b. The issue of the comparison of happiness will be taken again in Chapter 24.

[9] We can make precise the relations among the various utilities. A specification of individual i's ordinal utility for evaluating the uncertain prospect $(\beta, \xi) = \{\beta^k, \xi^k; p^k\}$ (see note 7) is $U_i(\beta, \xi) = F_i[\Sigma_k p^k \widetilde{v}_i(\beta^k, \xi^k)]$, where v_i is a specification of individual i's VNM cardinal utility and F_i is a $\mathcal{R}_1 \to \mathcal{R}_1$ increasing function. Choose this U_i which is the chosen specification of the fundamental utility when (β, ξ) is certain: when (β, ξ) is the certain (b_j, x), $U_i(b_j, x; 1) = u(b_j, x)$ (this determines the function F_i). Then, $F_i[v_i(b_j, x)] = u(b_j, x) = \widehat{u}_i(x)$, or, denoting $f_i = F_i^{-1}$, $\widetilde{v}_i(b_j, x) = f_i \circ \widehat{u}_i(x)$. One can denote $v_i(x) = \widetilde{v}_i(b_i, x) = f_i \circ \widehat{u}_i(x)$. The theory of the original position takes $(\beta, \xi) = \{b_j, x; 1/n\}$. Note the dual roles of functions $\widehat{u}_i$ (fundamental) and v_i (VNM): functions $\widehat{u}_i$ can meaningfully be compared by $\gtrless$ for different i (and hence, functions $\varphi \circ \widehat{u}_i$ with any increasing function φ also can), but functions v_i cannot; in contrast, values of $\widehat{u}_i$ cannot meaningfully be added, while values of v_i for the same i can. Of course, if another specification of the fundamental utility is chosen, say $\varphi(u)$, functions f_i incur the corresponding contravariant transformation in becoming $f_i \circ \varphi^{-1}$.

$\widehat{u}_i^1$ are more alike than those implied by the $\widehat{u}_i$, and the Pareto set shrinks (with possible limiting cases, see Section 3.7). The solution to the problem raised by the obtained multiplicity that is consistent with a use of an original position in the first place consists of considering an original position of the original position, and so on.

Then, OP_{m+1} obtains from OP_m with the evaluation functions

$$\widehat{u}_i^{m+1}(x) = M[\{\widehat{u}_j^m(x)\},\ f_i]$$

in fundamental utility and

$$v_i^{m+1}(x) = n^{-1} \Sigma_j\, f_i \circ f_j^{-1} \circ v_j^m(x)$$

for the VNM utilities. This constitutes, again, a multiplicity of evaluations, but with implied orderings which are generally more alike, and in general a shrinking of the Pareto set.

If when $m \to \infty$, $\widehat{u}_i^m \to \widehat{u}_i^\infty$ for all i, the $\widehat{u}_i^\infty$ satisfy

$$\widehat{u}_i^\infty(x) = M[\{\widehat{u}_j^\infty(x)\},\ f_i]$$

or

$$n f_i \circ \widehat{u}_i^\infty(x) = \Sigma_j\, f_i \circ \widehat{u}_j^\infty(x),$$

for all i. These conditions are satisfied if and only if the functions $\widehat{u}_i^\infty(x)$ are the same (the levels are the same for each x, given that functions f_i are increasing and $n \geq 2$). Thus, we have for all i the same function $\widehat{u}_i^\infty(x) = U(x)$. This condition of an equal level of happiness or satisfaction (in fundamental utility) is "eudemonistic justice."[10] However, this is for the individuals in the "infinite regress original position," not for the actual individuals.

From its construction, $U(x) = W[\{\widehat{u}_i(x)\}]$. Function W is an increasing symmetrical function of the $\widehat{u}_i$ (at each step, each $\widehat{u}_i^{m+1}$ is an increasing symmetrical function of the $\widehat{u}_i^m$, and each $\widehat{u}_i^1$ is of the $\widehat{u}_i$). This increasingness guarantees Pareto efficiency of the result. The symmetry implies the corresponding impartiality; it is meaningful only because of the existence of a fundamental utility. If all individuals are very risk averse, $\widehat{u}_i^1(x) = \widehat{u}_i^\infty(x) = U(x) = \operatorname{Min}_i \widehat{u}_i(x)$, which is eudemonistic "practical justice."[11] Note that the direct equality of the $\widehat{u}_i(x)$ may have to violate Pareto efficiency, or may not be possible. This was one reason for resorting to practical justice. However, this solution was too extreme for a general solution.[12] If all functions f_i were the same (cardinally, that is, up to an affine increasing function) and were function f (that is, $f_i = a_i\, f + b_i$ with constant a_i and b_i and $a_i > 0$, for all i), then, for all i and $m \geq 1$, $U(x) = \widehat{u}_i^m(x) = \widehat{u}_i^1(x) = M[\{\widehat{u}_i(x)\},\ f]$ and a maximand can be $n f \circ U(x) = \Sigma f \circ \widehat{u}_i(x) = \Sigma v_i(x)$ in calling $f(\widehat{u}_i) = v_i$. This

[10] See Kolm 1971.
[11] Id. Practical justice is more generally the leximin in the $u_i(x)$.
[12] This remark is the last sentence of this work (Kolm 1971).

was the form intended by Harsanyi. It requires both a fundamental utility and identical preferences concerning risk with respect to it. However, there is no a priori reason for this identity of the functions f_i, which describe the various individuals' preferences as concerns risk about the levels of the (comparable) $\widehat{u}_i$.

3.7. Homogeneization and convergence of individual preference orderings

The way to general consensus and unanimity in the sequence of original positions has, more precisely, the following structure. Denote as $\alpha_i(x)$ and $\beta_i(x)$ two sets of n functions of x, each function representing an ordering of the x, and consider n increasing functions A_i defining the α_i from the β_i: $\alpha_i(x) = A_i[\{\beta_j(x)\}]$. The concept to be shown is that the orderings represented by the α_i become more alike, or at least no less alike, than those represented by the β_i. Denote the vectors $\alpha = \{\alpha_i\}$ and $\beta = \{\beta_i\}$. Use the usual vector inequalities: for vectors $\gamma = \{\gamma_i\}$ and $\gamma' = \{\gamma'_i\}$, $\gamma \geqq \gamma'$ is $\gamma_i \geq \gamma'_i$ for all i, $\gamma > \gamma'$ is $\gamma_i > \gamma'_i$ for all i, and $\gamma \geq \gamma'$ is $\gamma_i \geq \gamma'_i$ for all i and $\gamma_i > \gamma'_i$ for at least one i. Then, for x and x', $\beta(x) \geq \beta(x') \Rightarrow \alpha(x) > \alpha(x')$. Hence, $\beta(x) \geqq \beta(x') \Rightarrow \alpha(x) \geqq \alpha(x')$, and $\beta(x) > \beta(x') \Rightarrow \alpha(x) > \alpha(x')$. Also, $\beta(x) \geqq \beta(x') \Rightarrow \alpha(x) \geqq \alpha(x')$. This means that weak unanimity ($\geqq$), strong unanimity ($>$), and "Pareto unanimity" ($\geq$) are maintained in the transformation. That is, the sets of x' that are unanimously preferred to a given x, or to which a given x is unanimously preferred, according to any of these three unanimities, lose no element in the transformation. Generally, they will expand.

Moreover, given a set of orderings represented by functions $\gamma_i(x)$, denote as $P(\gamma)$ the "Pareto set" of the x – the set of Pareto-efficient x –: if Π is the set of possible x, $P(\gamma) \subseteq \Pi$, and $x \in P(\gamma) \Leftrightarrow x \in \Pi$ and $\gamma(x') \geq \gamma(x)$ for no $x' \in \Pi$. Then, $P(\alpha) \subseteq P(\beta)$. Indeed, $x \in \Pi - P(\beta)$ implies that there exists a $x' \in \Pi$ such that $\beta(x') \geq \beta(x)$. But this implies $\alpha(x') > \alpha(x)$ and hence $\alpha(x') \geq \alpha(x)$. Therefore, $x \notin P(\alpha)$. Hence, $P(\alpha) \subseteq P(\beta)$. That is, the Pareto set loses no element in the transformation. It generally shrinks.[13]

These results apply to the successive sets of functions $v^m(x) = \{v_i^m(x)\}$ and $\widehat{u}^m(x) = \{\widehat{u}_i^m(x)\}$ of the two previous sections, in noting respectively $v_i(x) = v_i^o(x)$ and $\widehat{u}_i(x) = \widehat{u}_i^o(x)$, for passing from the set m to the set $m+1$ for all integers m from 0 on. In particular, denoting as P^m the Pareto set for the set of functions of order m in each series, $P^o \supseteq P^1 \supseteq \cdots P^m \supseteq P^{m+1} \supseteq \cdots$.

3.8. Application: Global distributive justice as a regress partially original position

For application to global distributive justice, from the analyses of the previous parts, the relevant evaluated item x will be the set of transfers t_i, or, rather, the set

---

[13] Properties of this type have been noted by Edgeworth (1888) for two individuals, a contract curve and additive combinations, and in general by Kolm (1963) and Archibald and Donaldson (1979).

of pairs (w_i, t_i) since the function of transfers t_i is to compensate for inequalities in the productivities or wage rates w_i. We thus take $x = \{w_i, t_i\}$. If an appropriate maximand evaluation function is obtained, coefficient k to be chosen is that which maximizes this function with $t_i = k \cdot (\overline{w} - w_i)$.

If individual i is solely self-interested, function $u_i(x)$ can be written as $u_i(t_i)$ or, better for the present purpose, as $u_i(w_i, t_i)$. This function is individual i's indirect utility function, derived from her standard utility function $u_i^*(c_i, \lambda_i)$ where c_i and λ_i are individual i's consumption c_i and leisure $\lambda_i = 1 - \ell_i$ where ℓ_i is individual i's labour, as $u_i(w_i, t_i) = \max_{c_i, \ell_i} u_i^*(c_i, \lambda_i)$ under the condition $c_i = w_i \ell_i + t_i$. Then, if $v_i^*(c_i, \lambda_i) = g_i \circ u_i^*(c_i, \lambda_i)$ is a specification of individual i's risk-relevant VNM utility function, $v_i(w_i, t_i) = g_i \circ v_i(w_i, t_i)$ is a specification of this function with the new variables.

A moral evaluation of this individual i can consist of her imagining that she could have the pairs (w_j, t_j) of all considered individuals with the same probability $1/n$ (or that she has these pairs during the same duration for moral time-sharing). These are the relevant items for evaluating global distributive justice. Then, individual i's moral evaluation function is

$$v_i^1(x) = n^{-1} \Sigma_j v_i(w_j, t_j). \tag{1}$$

This function is symmetrical in the pairs (w_j, t_j). It is, of course, no longer solely self-interested. The basic philosophical difference with the presentation of the foregoing sections is a priori self-entitlement ("natural allocation") of eudemonistic capacities represented by functions u_i and v_i. Individuals do not consider that they could have others' "tastes," but only others' pairs (w_i, t_i). This is the case of the "partially original position"[14] relevant for macrojustice.

Let k_i^1 denote the level of coefficient k that maximizes $v_i^1(x)$ with $t_j = k \cdot (\overline{w} - w_j)$ for all j. Then, the k_i^1 will generally have values between 0 and 1, contrary to the purely self-interested levels of k, which are 0 or 1 (except when $w_i = \overline{w}$). The chosen level of k can be derived from the set of the k_i^1 in various ways. It can be their arithmetic average $n^{-1} \Sigma k_i^1$, especially when the k_i^1 are not too dispersed. Or the k_i^1 can provide basic values for an arbitrage, a bargaining, or a dialog exchanging arguments and influencing social and moral sentiments. However, the solution most consistent with the initial consideration of moral risk consists of facing the variety of evaluations v_i^1 with the consideration of original positions evaluating individuals' moral evaluations.

Then, with the notations of the previous sections, one can consider the evaluations

$$v_i^2(x) = n^{-1} \Sigma_j H_{ij} \circ v_j^1(x). \tag{2}$$

The levels of coefficient k that maximize the v_i^2, say k_i^2 for each i, are between the extreme levels of the k_i^1 because functions H_{ij} are increasing. Hence, there

[14] For the general theory of the partially original position, see Kolm 1998b.

still is a best level of k for each individual, but these level are, in this sense, more concentrated than the k_i^1 are. This plurality can then be faced by the consideration of deeper original positions.

Hence, generally and recursively, denote

$$v_i^{m+1}(x) = n^{-1} \Sigma_j H_{ij} \circ v_j^m(x) \tag{3}$$

for all integers m from $m = 1$. If k_i^m is the level of k that maximizes v_i^m (with $x = \{w_i, t_i\}$ and $t_i = k \cdot (\overline{w} - w_i)$), and $k_+^m = \max_i k_i^m$, $k_-^m = \min_i k_i^m$, the k_i^{m+1} satisfy $k_i^{m+1} \in [k_-^m, k_+^m]$ because the functions H_{ij} are increasing. Denoting $k_-^o = 0$ and $k_+^o = 1$, and $K^m = [k_-^m, k_+^m]$ for $m = 0, 1, 2, \ldots$, one has $K^o \supseteq K^1 \supseteq K^2 \supseteq \cdots \supseteq K^m \supseteq K^{m+1} \supseteq \cdots$. In this sense, the set of the k_i^m for each m are more and more concentrated when m increases. As noted in Section 3.5 in the general case, the orderings represented by the functions u_i^m become more alike when m increases, and, with full convergence, when $m \to \infty$, the functions $v_i^m \to v_i^\infty$ satisfying

$$v_i^\infty(x) = n^{-1} \Sigma_j H_{ij} \circ v_j^\infty(x), \tag{4}$$

with $v_i^\infty = \psi_i \circ U(x)$ for functions $\psi_i = g_i \circ \varphi_i$ and $U(x)$, and $U(x)$ is taken as the social maximand. Then, the k_i^∞ that maximize the $v_i^\infty(x)$ are all equal to the k^* that maximizes $U(x)$, $k_i^\infty = k^*$ for all i, which is the consensual solution of the regress original position.

When there is a fundamental utility function $\widehat{u}_i$, equalities (1), (2), (3), and (4) also write, respectively, for all i and x,

$$\widehat{u}_i^1(x) = f_i^{-1}[(n^{-1}\Sigma_j f_i \circ \widehat{u}_i(w_j, t_j)],$$
$$\widehat{u}_i^2(x) = f_i^{-1}[(n^{-1}\Sigma_j f_i \circ \widehat{u}_j^1(x)],$$
$$\widehat{u}_i^{m+1}(x) = f_i^{-1}[(n^{-1}\Sigma_j f_i \circ \widehat{u}_j^m(x)] = M[\{\widehat{u}_j^m(x)\}, f_i],$$
$$\widehat{u}_i^\infty(x) = M[\{\widehat{u}_j^\infty(x)\}, f_i] \text{ or } nf_i \circ \widehat{u}_i^\infty(x) = \Sigma_j f_i \circ \widehat{u}_j^\infty(x),$$

which implies $\widehat{u}_i^\infty(x) = U(x)$ for all i. This means an equal level of happiness or satisfaction, or eudemonistic "justice"[15] for the individuals in the infinite-regress original position. From its construction, function $U(x)$ is symmetrical in the pairs (w_i, t_i), expressing the relevant impartiality.

3.9. The aggregate moral risk

The final maximand obtained by a theory of the regress original position provides a maximand that is an aggregate of the individuals' utilities in the general case, or of individuals' functions u_i^1 or v_i^1 in the foregoing application to macrojustice and an ELIE structure. There can be other aggregations, but the point is to consider justified ones. The theory of the original position when there is a fundamental

---

[15] See Kolm 1971.

utility provides such an opportunity. The reason is that the difference between the $\widehat{u}_i^1$ or v_i^1 in the general case, or the $\widehat{u}_i^2$ or v_i^2 in the application for global distributive justice, reduces to differences in functions f_i, which represent individuals' preferences concerning risk. One can then consider an aggregate evaluator whose corresponding function, say f, depends on the various individuals' functions f_i. All these functions have the particular structure that they are $\mathcal{R}^1 \to \mathcal{R}^1$ cardinal functions depending on one same ordinal variable, the ordinal fundamental utility. This structure implies that the aggregation has specific and remarkable possible forms.

The utility function of the aggregate evaluator will thus be

$$\widehat{v}(x) = n^{-1}\Sigma f \circ \widehat{u}_i(x)$$

for the general theory of the original position, and

$$\widehat{v}(x) = n^{-1}\Sigma f \circ \widehat{u}_i^1(x)$$

for moral risk applied to global distributive justice and ELIE.

The corresponding aggregation then consists of aggregating functions f_i into function f. Hence, function $f(u)$ is a priori a functional of the n functions $f_i(u)$. However, functions f_i and f are cardinal – defined each up to its own arbitrary affine increasing transformation – and function u, here the variable, is ordinal – defined up to an arbitrary increasing transformation, the same for all functions f_i and f. If we find a justified specific form for the relation giving a specification of f from specifications of the f_i, it may not be maintained under these transformations of the f_i, f, and u. Hence, justified forms for this relation are among those that are maintained by these transformations.

First, a cardinal function $\varphi(u)$, which thus can be replaced by any $\lambda\varphi(u) + \mu$ with constant λ and μ (and $\lambda > 0$), is characterized, if it is twice differentiable, by the function $R(u) = \varphi''/\varphi'$, which does not depend on this transformation and integrates into $\lambda\varphi + \mu$ with arbitrary λ and μ: function $R(u)$ is a sufficient functional invariant of cardinal function φ. For functions f_i and f, assumed to be twice differentiable, denote $r_i(u) = -f_i''(u)/f_i'(u)$ and $r(u) = -f''(u)/f'(u)$.[16] The aggregation then should be that of functions r_i into function r. The higher r_i or r, for a given specification of ordinal u, the more egalitarian the corresponding aggregation of the original position.

We now add that the functional $\{r_i\} \to r$ takes the simple form of the same function for each u, $r(u) = \phi[\{r_i(u)\}]$, a "uniform independence of irrelevant alternatives" (an alternative is here a level of u and hence of the $r_i(u)$, and $r(u)$ depends only on these latter levels, and "uniform" means that function ϕ does not depend on u – a normal assumption). Function ϕ will be symmetrical because nothing else relevant differentiates the individuals. It will be increasing for positive sensitivity to individuals' views, or at least nondecreasing and increasing in one

---

[16] The signs of the r_i and r depend on the specification chosen for u and hence have a priori no meaning.

r_i. And if all r_i are equal, their value will also be r, as a respect of individuals' views implying a respect of unanimity.

The ordinality of u means that it can be replaced by any function $\theta(u)$ where θ is an increasing function. Then, a function $\varphi(u)$ becomes $\psi(\theta)$ with $\psi[\theta(u)] = \varphi(u)$. This implies, for twice differentiable functions, $\varphi''/\varphi' = \theta' \cdot (\psi''/\psi') + \theta''/\theta'$. The increasingness of $\theta(u)$, its only required property, permits any positive value for θ' and any value for θ''/θ'. Then, such a change of u simultaneously transforms in this manner functions f_i and f, and hence $r_i(u)$ is transformed into $ar_i + b$, and $r(u)$ is transformed into $ar + b$ with $a = 1/\theta'$ and $b = -\theta''/\theta'^2$. This b can have any value, and this a can have any positive value. If function ϕ is to be independent of the chosen specification of ordinal function u, then any transformation of all r_i into $ar_i + b$ has to transform r into $ar + b$, that is, $\phi(\{ar_i + b\}) = ar + b$ for all b and all $a > 0$.

Then, all the noted properties of function ϕ imply that it is of the form $\phi(\{r_i\}) = \Sigma a_\rho r_\rho$ with constant a_ρ such that $a_\rho \geq 0$ for all ρ, $\Sigma a_\rho = 1$, and $\{r_\rho\}$ is the ordered permutation of the r_i, that is: the set of indexes ρ is a permutation of the set of indexes i, and $\rho > \rho'$ implies $r_\rho \geq r_{\rho'}$.[17] Particular cases are r that are the average, the median, the highest, the lowest, the average in the highest or lowest quantile for some given quantile size, and so on.

3.10. Exchange and risk; fundamental insurance

The theory of moral risk, where each individual has an equal chance of having the relevant allocation and characteristics of each individual, provides impartializations of individuals' judgments and preferences. The obtained individuals' preferences are more alike to one another than the purely self-interested preferences, but they are usually short of consensus. We have seen two ways of facing this multiplicity of judgments: the infinite regress original position, and the aggregation of individuals' preferences concerning risk. Both provide aggregations of individuals' moral-risk evaluations. The former also constitutes a consensus of individuals' views (in the infinite regress original position). Other consensual solutions (without moral risk) were provided by a converging dialog and by full relevant information. There is, however, another way of obtaining an agreement among the individuals, which is to let them agree in an exchange, where each accepts to yield something from her preferred solution under the condition that others behave similarly. This agreement can be actual or notional. The outcome will depend on the conditions of the bargaining, such as: the individuals' preferences, the threat state (the state that prevails in the absence of agreement), individuals' time preferences if the bargaining takes time, possibly individuals' preferences concerning risk, possible arbitration schemes, and so on. These elements, however,

---

[17] This permutation $\{r_i\} \rightarrow \{r_\rho\}$ permits function ϕ to be symmetrical. The other noted property requires that it has the appropriate piecemeal linearity.

may lack ethical relevance and legitimacy. Hence, one may consider applying this exchange agreement in a setting where the relative importance and effect of these morally arbitrary items are reduced. For this purpose, morally relevant aspects can be actual or notionally assumed in individuals' motivations or in the setting of the exchange agreement. These aspects can narrow down the scope of a priori disagreements among the individuals. One of them can be impartiality.

For instance, for the determination of coefficient k of an ELIE, an exchange agreement among purely self-interested individuals, whose preferred levels of k are the extreme values 0 or 1 (when $w_i \neq \overline{w}$), only rests on the circumstances of the bargaining. Each individual i then wants to maximize $u_i(w_i, k \cdot (\overline{w} - w_i))$ (her utility function in indirect form) or its VNM cardinal specification $v_i(w_i, k \cdot (\overline{w} - w_i))$.

The relative importance of these circumstances can be reduced, in keeping the self-interested motivation, by the moral-risk consideration, that is, in considering that the individuals have an equal chance of having the relevant pair (w_i, t_i) of each individual, with $t_i = k \cdot (\overline{w} - w_i)$. Then, individual i wants to maximize the expected value of her VNM utility, that is, $v_i^1 = n^{-1} \Sigma_j v_i(w_j, k \cdot (\overline{w} - w_j))$.

However, the individuals agreeing while facing this risk can all be more satisfied in choosing values of k conditional on the actual realization of the risky event constituted by the allocation of the productivities w_i. In their view, the actual k will be chosen only when the actual allocation of the w_i is observed, but according to a function that they choose *ex ante*. This permits the individuals to make exchanges about the agreed-upon levels of k for the various possible allocations of the w_i, in a kind of mutual insurance scheme respecting the ELIE structure. This is a particular case of a "fundamental insurance" (see Kolm 1985a, and Chapter 25). A fundamental insurance is a theory in compensatory distributive justice that assumes that transfers more or less compensating the distribution of some given characteristics should duplicate the transfers that the individuals would have freely chosen and agreed upon in a notional insurance against the allocation of these characteristics, taken in a hypothetical state where they do not know this allocation. The characteristics here are the productivities w_i. It is moreover assumed that the transfers should have the structure of an ELIE: this is an ELIE-constrained fundamental insurance about productivities. The only choice is that of coefficient k (the equalization labour).

The result, however, depends in particular on the structure of the random "allocation" of the productivities w_i. Since the first purpose of the theory of moral risk is to obtain impartial judgments among actual individuals, the justified (nonarbitrary) uncertainty implies that the individuals could only receive productivities of the actual individuals. For justice, moreover, each individual should receive each of the actual productivities with the same probability. Yet, the agreed-upon levels of coefficient k depend on the considered set of random events, and hence also on the assumed correlation among these individual risks. The considered injustice consists of the inequality of the w_i. If we consider that it is this inequality irrespective of who has which w_i, the moral judgment bears on the pattern of the w_i irrespective of their particular assignment. And this has to be the case for macrojustice where the w_i are the only directly relevant differences among individuals. Now, the problem is to deal with this actual and only relevant injustice, and nothing else. Hence, the random events should consist of these $n!$ assignments. From the principle of insufficient reason, they should be equiprobable. At any rate, since each individual should have the same chance of having each w_i, this generally implies that these assignments should have the same probability $1/n!$.

Each possible assignment is characterized by one of the $n!$ permutations of the w_i among the individuals. Let π denote these permutations; individual i in assignment π receives the productivity $w_{\pi(i)}$. *Ex ante*, these assignments have the same probability $1/n!$. The individuals make the agreement that, if assignment π occurs, the coefficient k of the ELIE rule will be k^π. Then, individual i will face the transfer $t_i^\pi = k^\pi \cdot (\overline{w} - w_{\pi(i)})$, since the average $\overline{w}$ is the same whatever π. The agreement will be about the set of the k^π, the $n!$-vector $K = \{k^\pi\}$. Then, the chosen k will be that which corresponds to the actual assignment, that is, the unit (invariant) permutation where $\pi(i) = i$ for all i, denoted as $\pi = 1$, hence $k = k^1$. In the *ex ante* exchange and agreement, each individual i seeks the highest expected value of her VNM utility,

$$(1/n!)\Sigma_\pi v_i[w_{\pi(i)}, k^\pi \cdot (\overline{w} - w_{\pi(i)})] = \gamma_i(K).$$

We finally have three possible exchange-agreement theories for the determination of the level of coefficient k:

1. The direct agreement, where each individual i seeks to maximize

$$u_i[w_i, k \cdot (\overline{w} - w_i)] \text{ or } v_i[w_i, k \cdot (\overline{w} - w_i)] = \varphi_i(k).$$

2. The direct moral-risk agreement, where each individual i seeks to maximize the expected value

$$n^{-1}\Sigma_j v_i[w_j, k \cdot (\overline{w} - w_j)] = \psi_i(k).$$

3. The fundamental insurance agreement, where each individual i seeks to maximize $\gamma_i(K)$ for vector $K = \{k^\pi\}$, and then k^1 is chosen.

The object of the agreement is number k in the former cases and vector K in the third case. The last two cases manifest the structure obtained for global distributive justice: the individuals are a priori accountable for or entitled to their own preferences, but they are not accountable for or entitled to their productive capacities.

The solution then depends on the modalities of the bargaining, in all three cases. This bargaining can be actual in the former case and it is notional in the other two, and notional bargaining can also be applied to the case of direct agreement. We thus have to rely on theories of bargaining. A complete presentation of the possibilities can be found in Chapter 13, appendix B, of the book *Modern Theories of Justice*.[18] The various concepts of arbitrage related to situations of agreement or bargaining can also be used. Particular values of functions φ_i, ψ_i, or γ_i, or of the object of agreement and bargaining (here, k or K), are often used in these theories, as starting states, threat states (the state realized in the absence of agreement), or reference states used otherwise. Apart from the general definitions of such states or values – such as the k or K that maximize the φ_i, ψ_i, or γ_i – the nature of k provides other specific values, notably full self-ownership $k = 0$ (and, possibly, maximal income equalization $k = 1$). As an example, with $k = 0$ as reference, the "Nash bargaining solutions" maximize $\Pi[\varphi_i(k) - \varphi_i(0)]$, $\Pi[\psi_i(k) - \psi_i(0)]$, or $\Pi[\gamma_i(K) - \gamma_i(0)]$.

3.11. Risk and justice

However, the theories of moral risk as theories of justice have a limited validity (this applies, in particular, to theories of the original position, and similar remarks can apply to moral time-sharing). Theories of moral risk assimilate the choice of justice among several individuals to the individual choice of a self-interested individual who is uncertain about the relevant characteristics and allocation she will have, and, notably, who could have those of the actual individuals with equal chances. These theories provide impartiality (this basically is why Rawls, Harsanyi, or Vickrey considered such schemes). However, impartiality is a necessary property of justice, but it is only one aspect of it. For the rest, the assimilation of justice to individual risk is a priori and in general problematic. One has the right to take a risk for oneself, while no one has the right to commit an injustice. Choices of justice and individual choices in uncertainty have very different natures and rationales. An individual choice in uncertainty is led by tastes about consequences (apart from the particular emotions raised by risk), and is the responsibility of the individual. By contrast, a choice about justice is led by norms and duty, and is accountable toward others, society, or morals. Equality for justice corresponds to certainty for risk, and inequalities are bound to be judged differently in both cases. The relevant items may differ: justice may evaluate incomes (which individuals are free to spend as they want), while the individual choice in uncertainty will consider the resulting welfare. The difference in responsibility is basic. For instance, one has the right to drive fast for gaining ten minutes at the risk of one chance in one million of a fatal accident, whereas one should probably not kill one person for having one million others gain ten minutes. One has the right to bet all one's fortune on one horse for trying one's luck of knowing how it feels to be a millionaire, whereas one should probably not give all the wealth to a single individual in order that there exists a millionaire's experience (assumed to be greatly pleasurable). In all cases, the problem is not the risk per se, but the substitution of an individual

---

[18] Kolm 1996a.

choice and the resulting responsibility to a judgment concerned with a social issue (in the former example, choosing the victim at random is not acceptable either).

Hence, an individual can take the risk of bad situations for herself, while it would be unjust to impose them on particular individuals in the justice interpretation of the structure. There results that justice is bound to be more inequality-averse than individual choice in uncertainty is risk-averse.

However, for endogenous social choice the final criterion for a theory of justice is its consensual endorsement by sufficiently informed, aware, and reflective individuals. Now, differences and inequalities in endowments of given items are often described as if they resulted from a lotterie, in using terms such as chance, and good or bad luck (philosophers coined for this the special term "brute luck"). And this is sometimes seen as an injustice which should be more or less corrected. These views show that there exists a basis for an accepted application of concepts of fundamental insurance. There remains to determine whether putatively free insurance is seen as an appropriate solution, and the scope of relevance and the specific modalities of such theories (choice of the objects so insured, of the hypothetical risk faced, and of the population participating in this mutual insurance). For instance, in analyzing the reasons why Europeans largely favour a public system of health insurance, it seems clear that a main reason is that they favour the part of it that amounts to a fundamental insurance against the propensity to bad health.

All considered, since the difference between risk and justice will be larger, the more there are bad outcomes or individuals' situations, and the larger the inequality, the validity of the analogy may depend on the structure of the problem and of preferences, and on the importance of what is at stake. For global distributive justice, it would be more valid if cases of dire misery are taken care of by another, specific policy. For the determination of coefficient k of an ELIE, the analogy would be more valid when the productivities w_i are closer to one another.

Among normative social theories that historically had a wide audience are the theories of the social contract. Now, a moral-risk theory of justice can be presented as a theory of the social contract where the situation facing the risk is the state of nature. The individuals making a contract among themselves in this situation are impartial as regards the considered items (allocation or characteristics). This agreement can be a direct choice or take the form of a fundamental insurance. Rawls (and Harsanyi) wanted all aspects of individuals' situation and characteristics to be so put at stake, in the "original position." The remaining original individuals would then have to be identical, and hence they would have the same preferences and make the same choice, and therefore there would be no actual exchange. We have seen that this a priori cannot hold because individuals have a priori different preferences toward risk, and, for the case of the "thin veil of ignorance," because they a priori have different preferences for "being" various individuals (some prefer to be Napoleon and others to be mother Theresa). Rawls' "thick veil" of ignorance avoids these obstacles in assuming sufficient chances of sufficiently bad events, so that everyone chooses the maximally cautious so-lution. This has to be justified, though. We have pointed out more consistent solutions to this multiplicity of preferences in the original position, in infinite regress, aggregation of preferences toward risk, and agreements either direct or through fundamental insurance. We have seen that and how these solutions also apply when only the distribution of some of the individual characteristics is at stake (theories of the "partially original position").[19] However, all these concep-tions rest on the parallel between individual risk and social justice, discussed by the foregoing remarks. The validity of this parallel is undoubtedly not universal, and we have proposed directions for evaluating it in specific applications and for delineating its scope.

Finally, the theories of moral risk impartialize individuals' views in introducing a notional ignorance about which characteristics or allocation one has or will have. In contrast, the consideration of formative and empathetic information deals with the problem with full information about others, a situation that can have both notional and actual parts, and that can be promoted by dialog. This provides not only an impartialization of individuals' views, but also a homogeneization of their impartial views, and hence, full consensus. Now, information, rather than ignorance, is a requirement of rationality. However, the considered full informa-tion raises practical difficulties, and hence theories of moral risk are available palliatives if used with caution in verifying their appropriateness in each specific application.

Now, the compensation of given inequalities can be justified by implicit free relations other than selfish exchange (as with fundamental insurance): they can be based on an implicit reciprocity. A reciprocity consists of gifts freely provided given that the receiver also gives to the giver, without these transfers being conditional on each other by an external obligation as in an exchange *stricto sensu*.[20] The motivations differ and are no longer purely selfish. Then, a person aids another in a poor situation, given that the other would have aided her were the situations reversed. If this reversal cannot be actual, this is a putative *fundamental reciprocity*. The result a priori differs from that of a fundamental insurance. It rests on the basic rationales of reciprocity, which are reciprocal fairness and reciprocal altruism. These motives are certainly more appropriate bases of a theory of justice than pure selfishness. Fundamental reciprocity will be further considered in Chapter 25.

---

[19] This issue is fully developed in Kolm 1998b.
[20] See Kolm 1984a, 2000b, 2004b.

PART FIVE

COMPARISON WITH ECONOMICS' SOCIAL ETHICS

22

Related economic values

1. MACROJUSTICE AND MORAL ECONOMICS

The fifth and last part of this study compares the obtained result with normative principles that have been or can be proposed in the framework of economics. These principles are either aspects or cases of the obtained result (e.g., market liberalism, self-ownership, income egalitarianisms, social maximand functions), complements to it (for applications in the fields of microjustice or "mesojustice"), or, possibly, alternative proposals. Hence, the scope of the considered ideas is extensive. The focus here, however, is on their meaning, rather than on technicalities whose relevance fully depends on this meaning in the first place. The resulting survey of meanings of normative economic ideas, principles, or criteria probably has an interest in itself. There is, for instance, a close consideration of the various aspects of freedom (social, defined by a priori domains of choice, "natural" as socially unruly, or as various concepts and types of opportunity, rights, desert or merit from action, or responsibility); of the various meanings, uses, and properties of the concept of "utility" (happiness, satisfaction, lower pain, preference, choice, transitivity, comparabilities of various types); and of the rationally necessary structures of distributive principles (permutability, *prima facie* or ideal equality, lower inequality, benevolence), with their scope of application. Indeed, each principle or criterion should be accompanied by a clear and justified statement of the assumed meaning of the concepts it uses and of their properties, and of the proposed scope of application. Not all principles that have been or could a priori be proposed are explicitly considered. However, each belongs to a family that is considered, discussed, and evaluated. Moreover, many criteria are relevant for issues in microjustice (or mesojustice) rather than macrojustice, and hence, their comparison with the obtained result is not directly relevant. Finally, other surveys of principles need not be duplicated here (in particular, the author's *Modern Theories of Justice* (1996a) can be seen as a complement to the present study).

The structure of macrojustice – social freedom plus ELIE – has been obtained deductively rather than comparatively. It has been derived from the basic principle of endogenous social choice and unanimity. It holds if each step of the derivation holds. Other specific proposals either are in fact particular cases of the result, or do not satisfy some step of the derivation, and in particular have another scope of relevant application. Particular cases of the obtained structure include notably classical process liberalism, the relevant income egalitarianism, and all efficient solutions in between; and the definition of preference-respecting social maximands has proposed solutions, some of which correct or extend classical ones. Moreover, the derivation used reasons of various types. Some relate to the definition of a field of macrojustice, whose existence is unambiguous, but whose role, scope, and properties are considered for each topic. For example, utilitarian-like judgments are relevant for some distributive issues (Chapters 6 and 24), but eudemonistic capacities are not for the income tax and macrojustice in general, from consensual judgment (Chapter 6). Or unsatisfied basic needs should be a foremost public concern, but corresponding aids generally become secondary in volume if the distribution and rights of macrojustice are guaranteed (they can become the main issue if this condition is not satisfied). Or again, concern for specific issues such as health or education are not macrojustice (the question of the relative place of private income spending and of the public sector in their provision will be discussed). And many criteria are for issues in distributive microjustice or arbitration schemes. In addition, a number of criteria or theories need to closely vindicate their conceptual tools and the scope of their validity, as with cardinal utility (see Chapter 24), or the theory of "equivalence" – that is, the replacement of a situation by another that every individual finds as good, for defining justice or optimality (is "as good as just" as just as possible? – see Chapter 26). Finally, the gap may be still larger with worldviews that deny the very relevance of ethical concepts, as James Buchanan's on the ground that ethical motivations necessary for implementing the principles hardly exist.

The obtained result has already been compared with economic proposals when the comparison was obviously necessary, as with the various conceptions of freedom, the welfarist "optimum income tax," various distributive schemes such as the income tax credit or the "universal basic income," and when concepts used for determining the degree of redistribution extended Harsanyi's "original position" or Dupuit's "surplus." Moreover, Part III of this study is devoted to comparisons with ideas from all quarters. Since the macrojustice results are obtained deductively rather than comparatively, these comparisons seemed sufficient. However, readers of a first draft of this study with an economic background practically all demanded further comparisons with economic proposals. The present part constitutes the answer to this demand. Its size and its status led to its presentation as a separate and last part. Inserting it into Part III, along with other comparisons, would probably have delayed too long the analysis of the degree of redistribution in Part IV, which completes the analysis. And it probably was useful to present the other comparisons, with philosophies and distributive schemes, after the derivation of the general structure of the result, for enlightening and situating this result.

Moreover, this brief survey of normative economic ideas emphasizing meaning may be of some use in itself.

From a logical point of view, there is no reason why social ethics, the analysis of freedom, or distributive justice, should constitute two different bodies when seen by economists and by philosophers. However, the fact is that these two corpora of analysis are quite distinct, in spite of decades (or centuries) of dialog – and of the fact that most great economists also were notable philosophers. This may be one of the best proofs of Kuhn's view of science as the sociology of scientific disciplines (which works particularly well for a topic not bound by experience). This also permits enduring biases in both corpora. In economics, this probably is the case of the overvaluation of the formal relative to concerns about meaning and explicit relevance. However, detrimental vagueness or omissions as concerns relations or – for instance – incentives are not uncommon in the philosophical discourse. The suggestion that "all that is important is philosophy and all that is precise is economics" is more caricature – hence, with a grain of truth – than just slander. In the end, one should perhaps dare to suggest, about political philosophy and normative economics, something in the direction of what Jean-Jacques Rousseau wrote about morality and politics: they cannot be separated, and he who wants to study one without the other is bound to misunderstand both.

In the present part, the present chapter is devoted to economic views that are particular cases of the obtained result, or are related to them, from process liberalism to income egalitarianism and the building of overall social ethical maximands. Chapter 23 outlines a general theory of normative principles or criteria. They apply a structure on a substance (such as freedom, happiness, goods, incomes, and so on). The basic necessary properties of the structure are shown, notably the property of permutability of the evaluation, the ensuing *prima facie* or ideal equality, the comparison of inequalities, and the associations of properties or principles. A basic issue concerns the tension between the structural properties of the substance that have an actual meaning and those that are required by the logic of the judgment (equality and comparisons of the items and of their variations, notably across individuals). Chapter 24 focuses on the two families of substance, freedoms or means on the one hand, and happiness, satisfaction, lower pain, or preference on the other hand. It considers their various relevant types and their meaningful relevant properties. Chapter 25 begins with the saga of a strange line of thought, from basic rights to utilitarianism (as a universal principle), to its criticism and its replacement by freedoms and equalities. It then discusses the theory of "fundamental insurance" and recent analyses about needs, capacities, desert, equality of opportunity, and responsibilities. Finally, Chapter 26 presents the theory of equivalence, which applies a principle on a fictive situation that every individual finds as good as the actual one, and its shortcomings and possibilities.

The present chapter discusses economic thoughts that develop aspects of the solutions obtained for macrojustice or that are closely related to them. Social freedom, income egalitarianism, and social maximands are the respective focuses of the three next sections. Section 2 thus considers classical process liberalism with full self-ownership (2.2); its *frères ennemis* constituted by unruly liberty, spontaneous order, constitutional public choice, and "libertarianism" (2.3); the resulting relations between the market and the state (2.4); and Karl Marx's exploitation violating full self-ownership with social freedom (2.5). Income egalitarianism is the focus of Section 3 which considers ELIE in this respect (3.1), the comparison of income inequalities (3.2), the basic comparisons of inequality based on pairwise inclusions (3.3), and the dual evaluation-consistent measures of inequality and inequality-averse evaluation functions (3.4). Section 4 then considers the derivation of preference-respecting social maximands from the theory of endogenous social choice and values which are both individual and social (4.1), thanks to the duality of individuals' interests and values often considered by economic thinkers (4.2), and the extension and adjustment of ideas in the family of Pareto's altruism (4.3), Harsanyi's original position (4.4), or Dupuit's surplus (4.5). Finally, Section 5 remarks that although, in the tripartition of principles of justice respectively concerned with social freedom with self-ownership, income and goods, and preferences or happiness represented by utility, ELIE is only concerned with the former two and their associations, the obtained solution for macrojustice also rests on individuals' preferences of various kinds and in various ways.

2. PROCESS LIBERALISM AND SELF-OWNERSHIP

2.1. Two polar views

The two relevant limiting cases of ELIE are with full self-ownership (the case with a null equalization labour, $k = 0$), and income egalitarianism as ELIE with equalization labour $k = k^e$ close to the lowest normal full labour analyzed in Chapter 11. They correspond to the two basic distributive social ethics in society, also endorsed and analyzed by important positions, schools, and scholars in economics. Income egalitarianism with $k = k^e$ is the relevant limiting case corresponding to the highest relevant value of coefficient k, because of the irrelevance of including incomes that are only potential possibilities in the equalized incomes (see Chapter 11). These two limiting cases of ELIE provide in fact the full and precise theory of these positions (for instance, with the proper income differentials for different labours for a central ideal of income equality, and with the treatment of inefficient "market failures" in the spirit of process-freedom by "liberal social contracts" for classical process liberalism). ELIE also describes intermediate views and compromises between these two polar ethics.

2.2. Classical process liberation: social freedom as full self-ownership

Classical process liberalism, associating social freedom and full self-ownership, is the central social ethics of the modern world, approximately for the last two centuries – although it is much older as part of social systems. It notably is seen as providing the direct legitimacy of the free market. This individualistic legitimacy of the social order succeeded political legitimacies by traditions or by the divine right acknowledging that the divine wants the outcome of pure force since it allows it to win. John Locke (1690), the author of the first scholarly presentation of this philosophy – and one of unrivaled mastery – precisely presented it because he wanted an ideology that could be opposed to those of the absolute monarchy – the French disease of his time (*de morbe gallico*) – whose expansion to England was being checked by the "glorious Revolution." All other social ethics of modern times first or mainly present themselves as an opposition to classical process liberalism. This notably holds for the various brands of socialisms who object to the misery, poverty, and unequal distribution resulting from the market with no transfers, unskilled labour, full self-ownership, full bequest, and business cycles, and to other aspects of the market such as the individualism and selfishness that underlie it. Opposition to classical liberalism is also the position of classical (hence left-wing) political anarchisms who oppose state power as much as classical liberals, but also, no less than classical socialists, big business and the poverty, inequality, individualism, and selfishness resulting from the market they see. Fascisms also present themselves as opposed to classical liberalism, and notably to political freedom and to mental freedom (through propaganda and indoctrination), although their relation to markets is more ambiguous (corporatism). And the strongest opposition to classical liberalism may come from those of communitarianisms whose view of culture, tradition, and solidarity, and aversion for individualism, make them oppose social (and mental) freedom.

Classical process liberalism has recently been joined, in most of its judgments about society, by a small and heterogeneous family of views which, however, deeply differ from it in their foundations, and indeed oppose it as concerns such fundamental issues as the definition of liberty and the status of ethics. They notably include James Buchanan's constitutionalism and "public choice," Friedrich Hayek's "spontaneous order," and Murray Rothbart and David Friedman's "libertarianism." They will shortly be briefly and comparatively considered (economists have held a foremost role in the analyses of these positions).

Process liberalism is a moral view that values social freedom, notably emphasizing its form as process-freedom. Classical process liberalism identifies this freedom with full self-ownership. Now, full self-ownership implies social freedom, from the definitions of ownership and of this liberty. But we have seen, in Chapter 3, that the converse need not be true. The various types of rights in an asset have to be distinguished. Process-freedom implies that individuals are the primary holders of use-rights and benefit-rights in their own capacities. But it is most naturally seen as not implying that they are a priori entitled to all the rent in their own capacities, that they have all these rent-rights in themselves. However, since classical process liberals identify or equate social freedom and full self-ownership, or believe that each implies the other, they do not care to emphasize which of both constitutes their basic value – a question which should be, in their eyes, without consequence if not devoid of meaning. It seems that no answer to this question can be inferred from Locke's writings. In modern times, however, and starting from the late eighteenth century, the corresponding moral discourse emphasizes freedom as the basic value. However, with social freedom not implying full self-ownership, the classical process-liberal stance needs to hold full self-ownership as a primary value. And that is all it needs since full self-ownership implies social freedom. If, on the contrary, social freedom is held as the only basic value, then a sufficiently discriminating analysis of the variety of rights in an asset shows that full self-ownership need not be implied, and this allows for distribution of the rent-rights in capacities and, in the end, leads one to ELIE schemes. Classical process liberalism then is the particular case with a zero equalization labour, $k = 0$.

In any event, classical process liberalism constitutes the praise of the market without redistributive policy for the reason that it respects social freedom as process-freedom, interpreted as full self-ownership, and hence the corresponding rights. It thus sees the resulting incomes as deserved and the resulting distribution as legitimate, and hence, just in this sense. In particular, this justification of the free market and "free enterprise" is not the possible efficiency of the market (and competitive) system which has otherwise been pointed out with a series of arguments. Adam Smith emphasizes that exchange is more efficient than gift-giving because it rests on realistic motivations – but he implicitly rules out the possibility of taking by force, that is, he assumes social freedom in the first place.[1] He also emphasizes the efficiency of the division of labour, but slave labour and planning have also done that. Pareto shows that perfect competition entails Pareto efficiency. Modern economic analyses have emphasized the best use of decentralized information (about desires and local resources – including capacities – and production). More sociological views have pointed out the importance of motivation elicited by the reward of labour, risk-taking, and savings (thus coming back on Adam Smith's ground). This possible performance of the market may rejoice the pure classical process liberal, but it does not motivate her position. This classical process liberal judges according to basic rights, not according to welfare. Her morality is not consequentialist but deontological. For her, the possible efficiency of the market is not its moral justification but only a possible side benefit. It is, in some sort, the immanent reward of virtue.

---

[1] This is the Adam Smith of *The Wealth of Nations*. The very different, much deeper, and more important and original Adam Smith of *The Theory of Moral Sentiments* has been called for assistance in Chapter 17. The idea that selfish motives serve others in the best possible way was the popular thing to say at the eve and in the country of the industrial revolution. However, it was commonplace at this time, and Smith just provided a nice literary wrapping. Smith had in particular read this idea in the *Essays on Morality* of the Jansenist Pierre Nicole, translated into English almost one century earlier by John Locke. The idea in fact dates back at least from the fourth century, when the fathers of the Church wondered whether merchants and businessmen should be excommunicated, since their selfish behaviour opposed Christian charity so much, and eventually decided against because their behaviour served others in the end, leaving the judgment about motivation to a better judge at a later day.

Now, economics has long been very closely associated with classical process liberalism. For most of the nineteenth century and in most of Europe, to be an economist normally implied to be a classical process liberal.[2] And it often just meant to be one – Marx, for instance, puts it this way. Hence, the terms "socialist" and "economist" were commonly seen as the opposite of one another, and the expression "a socialist economist," when it came to be used, was seen as a contradiction in terms (it is therefore fitting that it was probably first used by a poet, as Charles Péguy's title of his review of Léon Walras's work). It is only around the mid-twentieth century that the defense of the market by the efficiency virtue of exchange and competition gained momentum in economics (although this was the line of Adam Smith and Vilfredo Pareto), associated with a distribution derived from a "social welfare function" (utilitarianism of a more general form).

More recently, classical process liberalism has been the ethics of a number of economists or schools of economic thought, such as Maurice Allais, Jacques Rueff, Henry Wallich,[3] Milton Friedman and other "monetarists" (Karl Brunner, Allan Metzler, and others), theoreticians of "property rights" such as Armen Alchian and Pejovich, and many others. Classical process liberalism is also what John Hicks (1959) had in mind in his criticism of "welfarism" – a term he coined. Moreover, these classical process liberals in the strict sense have been joined by a heterogeneous group of renowned and militant scholars, often economists, who are often on the same side of the fence in social debates, but whose more basic philosophy is very different and even opposed. For these scholars, social freedom is more the possible actual outcome of social interaction than an a priori moral value. Friedrich Hayek, James Buchanan, and the self-named "libertarianism" of Murray Rothbart (1973) and David Friedman are barons in this kingdom. The issues these views raise concern the status of ethics, the nature of liberty, the possibilities of the market, and the role of the state.[4]

2.3. Natural freedom, spontaneous order, public choice constitution, and (neo-)libertarians

Process liberalism, the valuation of social freedom, is a type of social ethics. It may seem that social ethics can have an impact on society only if there exist people with sufficient moral motivation for implementing it one way or the other. The classical "economic man," being purely self-interested, cannot be such a person. Hence, if people are actually like that, it may seem that no social ethics can be implemented and thus have an actual effect. Moral views then are just "noise" as holders of this viewpoint sometimes put it. They are judgments, expressions of emotions, or mere postures, with no possible actual consequence. Even people

---

[2] Utilitarianism was uniquely an idea of English scholars (see Chapter 25).

[3] *The Cost of Freedom* (1960).

[4] Note that philosopher Robert Nozick (1974, see Chapter 16), although he claimed to have been inspired by Murray Rothbart, is in fact a moral classical process liberal (as another of his inspirers, John Locke).

who express or even hold such views are not ready to make any actual effort for translating them into facts. Therefore, it would be contradictory, for a scholar, to jointly propose that *homo economicus* is a fair representation of mankind and to hold a moral view about society intended for application. Among others, James Buchanan (1975, 1986) thinks this model of man is a good first approximation.[5] His view of society thus cannot be a moral one. The moral-sounding injunctions he sometimes indulged in thus should be understood as advice about measures that would best serve self-interests (perhaps of everybody). Apart from such statements, his description of society is precisely that: a description, or an explanation, although one may be misled at first sight by the noted injunctions and by the emphasis on concepts that are commonly value loaded, such as freedom or a constitution. For Buchanan, a constitution is but the written or implicit terms of a truce between self-interests.[6] His view implies in particular that it would be sterile and pointless to hold social freedom, basic rights, peace, or nonviolence as values. If social freedom and basic rights are respected, this can only be the factual result of the balance of forces. It can only result from the rational self-interested calculations of people who think that the resources necessary to win a fight and the possible losses they may incur in it, given the others' self-defense, make it profitable for them to stay away or to try to obtain what they desire through exchange. Now, since costs of fighting and losses it entails are sterile in themselves, any outcome involving them is dominated by other peaceful allocations that make everyone better off (discarding the possibly pleasurable consumption of adrenaline produced by fighting and winning). Therefore, Pareto-efficient solutions are peaceful. And peace, the absence of actual violence, social freedom, and basic rights are normally desired by all in themselves, given distribution. The resulting distribution, however, is based on relative willingness to fight and fighting power, and hence, could hardly – and does not – claim to be just. This peace can be *pax romana* with odious domination.

Of course, acknowledging the appallingly frequent selfishness of humans, and discarding the irenic assumption of sufficiently many largely moral-driven people and the irrealistic considerations of devoted politicians, just planners, and counterfactual benevolent dictators, certainly constitute less a cynical vision of society than a sound and fair evaluation. However, the opposite view of an essentially amoral society would no less be overly simplistic and naïve. A main point is that the influence of moral views is most often intricately mixed with motivations, relations, and actions of other types. Some people act morally not because they

---

[5] Hence, a valid scientific assumption (from personal correspondence).

[6] Relatedly, the model of Buchanan's Social Contract is Hobbes' rather than Locke's. Hobbes' compact is a truce among the individuals who give all power to a peacemaker (this elicited Jean de La Fontaine's answer in the fable "The frogs who ask for a king": God sends them as king a crane who eats them all). By contrast, Locke's basic value is process-freedom and full self-ownership, and his Social Contract is only a contract among legitimate owners for establishing a government that will protect their property rights. The Liberal Social Contract (see Chapter 3) could be said to be a Lockean contract after public economics and the analysis of market failures.

are moral but because they care for others' opinions, and so some act morally without intrinsically moral motivations, whereas others judge morally without acting so, and hence, bearing the cost of moral actions.[7] In times and situations of arbitrage, deals, or choice of long-term social rules and constitutions, the search of agreements to propose and of common grounds for discussion require some amount of empathy and impartiality, and rationality then leads to the basis of justice and the relevant equality (see Chapter 23). Fair deals are often preferred to good deals. People commonly have a dual view, one social ethical and political and the other for individual actions, with different modes of implementation. We have capacities for sympathy, empathy, compassion, pity, altruism, and reciprocity, and also for taking Thomas Nagel's "view from nowhere." Adam Smith's view that an "impartial spectator" lies in the breast of each of us has something to it, even though he shares this dwelling with other kinds of creatures. The sense of community does not stop at the household's door but extends with various intensities and types to various groups until the reaches of mankind. And straightforward moral motives and acts are by no means uncommon. Hence, Buchanan's stand constitutes one polar conception worthy of consideration, but certainly not the end of the story.

Friedrich Hayek's "spontaneous order" also seems to be a factual description, although people as he sees them may add, to their self-interested actions in markets, some kind of Alpine communitarian political sentiments. "Social Justice" is an impossible mirage brandished by would-be political exploiters... unless it is the distribution achieved by the *laissez-faire* the author advocates. Indeed, it is hard not to find moral values and commitments in this author's positions, would it only be in his indictment of the "road to serfdom" to totalitarianism. Murray Rothbart's self-named "libertarianism" extends this indictment to any act of any government or public body, and these acts, in his view, both violate freedom and constitute its only violation, and, for this reason, are bad and are the only bad. This school of "thought" sees no difference between the Third Reich and a Swiss canton, or between Gengis Khan and social security. Hayek's view is more moderate: he acknowledges a very limited amount of "market failures" ("roads, externalities"), which, he says, should be dealt with by a government considering welfare. By contrast, Rothbart and "libertarians" hold that the market always does better than a government, a position that sometimes can lead to interesting specific proposals. As for Buchanan, he sees market failures as having a very large extent, exactly that which is actually occupied by politics and the public sector, which "spontaneously" deal with the corresponding issues with "political entrepreneurs" interacting in a "political market" analyzed by the studies of "public choice."

Liberty in social relations is the emphasized principle of the members of this heterogeneous family and of process liberalism. It is ethical or explanatory (with,

---

[7] This kind of situation is fully analyzed in Kolm 1996a, Chapter 13.

then, also slips toward its being felt as a value). It names both liberalism and libertarianism. However, these views use two different, and indeed opposed, conceptions of freedom in social relations: social freedom and what may be called "natural freedom." Social freedom has been defined as the absence of forceful interference among individuals and agents, and process liberalism as the moral valuation of social freedom, hence as the moral indictment of such forceful interference. The opposite is the possibility of these forceful interferences. This defines natural freedom. Natural freedom just bans the ban on violence and force demanded by social freedom. It forbids to forbid.[8] Natural freedom in fact only says that individuals and other agents are allowed to do what they are able to do in any respect. It might be taken as a value by some Nietzschean, Spencerian, or other ego-boosting view. However, it can hardly be a social value since it permits hurting, killing, enslaving, robbing, and so on, when this can be done. Social and natural freedoms differ by the nature of their limit as concerns social relations. By comparison with social freedom, the limit of natural freedom is not right but might, not others' peace but their power compared with the free agent's, not respect but the balance or imbalance of forces, not duty but desire. The "freedom of the free fox in the free poultry yard" is natural freedom, not social freedom. Compared with social freedom, natural freedom extends the domain of freedom of the strong and restricts that of the weak. Buchanan's freedom is natural freedom, and hence its implicit valuation would be unwarranted. Hayek's theory is based on natural freedom, although his indictments are based on the valuation of social freedom from the forceful interference of state power. Libertarianism's (Rothbart's) stand has the merit of being more explicit than the others, and also interestingly bizarre. It values freedom and only freedom, it defines freedom as freedom from government's interference and only that, and it sees government interference as always forceful. Hence, libertarian freedom is in fact natural freedom among private agents and valued social freedom as concerns individuals' submission to public actions. Now, slavery is consistent with Buchanan's freedom if this is the outcome of the confrontation.[9] Stalinism or Nazism can be the outcome of a "spontaneous order" – and what an order! And mafia terror is an instance of the cherished libertarian (Rothbart's) freedom since mafias are not governments but private (and "spontaneous") organizations – one cannot try to be conciliatory with libertarians in admitting that governments are (often) but successful mafias, since mafias have a priori no reason to be bad (but one may perhaps find a common ground in telling them that mafias act like some governments and are prone to call themselves so when they sufficiently win).

---

[8] A motto of the "events" of 1968 in Paris.

[9] John Locke's justification of slavery by freedom of choice is more subtle: the slave chooses to be slave since he could also commit suicide, and he has been brought into slavery as a prisoner in a just war (a point left unexplained). As we know it, Locke wrote the slave-owning constitution of Virginia and owned stocks in a slave-trading company – which also was the basis of Voltaire's fortune (this was the most profitable investment of the time).

2.4. Freedoms, the market, and the state

Both classical process liberals valuing the respectful social freedom and scholars using the unruly natural freedom – and positions that problematically or ambiguously associate both – de facto constitute the defenders of the market for a reason directly based on liberty. They then have to face the problem of "market failures" and of the corresponding role of a public sector. Their answers in this respect are extremely varied, sometimes opposed, and they often give rise to interesting developments. Classical process liberals see the forceful protection of liberal rights – social freedom including its consequences as regards property and other rights – as the task of the government and its only task. This "minarchy," often dubbed the "nightwatchman State," reduced to police (and possibly army), is their historical ideal – and even in present days that of philosopher Nozick,[10] for instance. This view has to face the possible issues of microeconomic and macroeconomic market failures, and of poverty and distribution, which may be reasons for a more extended public sector. Even classical process-liberal governments cared for more than police, for instance as concerns roads or public assistance required by insufficient private or church charity. Any piece of government is too much for libertarians (Rothbart), though. And not only is government identified with evil because it is identified with oppression and unfreedom (by definition); it is, at any rate, always less efficient than markets because it lacks the needed motivation and information. This led to some imaginative and stimulating proposals for replacing classical public actions by market processes. However, the extension to the police in handing out the services of protection to private police firms seems to meet a contradiction. Indeed, with the assumed motivations, these firms have no reason to demand payment: they will just take it, and in fact take more and everything, and the system can only end up in tyranny, gang wars, or syndicated racket.

Buchanan, on the contrary, rather sees very extended market failures, which "spontaneously" elicit the political and public sector, where self-interested political entrepreneurs engage in a particular political market analyzed by "public choice" studies, all in the framework of the "constitutional" balance of forces. A standard view, however, consists in admitting a limited scope for market failures and proposing they be taken care of by a public sector applying criteria of welfare. Both Friedrich Hayek and Milton Friedman hold this stance, for example. Friedman even qualifies his ideal in admitting public transfers. He endorsed public financing of education in proposing that privately managed competing schools be paid by parents with "vouchers" initially allocated to them. In the field of overall income distribution, he imagined and advocated the negative income tax (income tax credit) for replacing income floors in order to diminish inefficiency, induced idleness, and dependency; he should have pursued his thinking to its

---

[10] Nozick incidentally discusses a public good (watching an athlete), but one with possibility of exclusion and hence of pricing.

logical consequences, though, in advocating subsidies and taxes based on items less elastic than incomes, in the family of those obtained here (see Chapter 16). Even in macroeconomic policy, although he condemns fiscal policy and adaptive monetary policy, the money he says should be issued at a steady rate is government issued, contrary to the alternative proposals of purely private moneys (by Hayek, for instance). Finally, "liberal social contracts" (see Chapter 3) strictly follow the process-liberal ethics in their realization as far as allocation and distribution are concerned, with implementers having the necessary power and motivation, possibly politically delegated to them by the people's will.

These freedom-based economists' social philosophies are thus very varied. Freedom is either social or natural (and sometimes praised as social and conceived as natural). The public sector can be the oppressor – the only oppressor – or the protector of basic rights and social freedom, or their substitute or duplicate, or again the outcome of free interaction. The outlook can be moral, or positive, or moral-sounding positive; it may demand "is" from "ought," and it may also derive "ought" from "is" in a way that can be either logically invalid or morally justified (as with endogenous social choice – see Chapter 1). One (minor) conclusion is that a present tendency of referring to all these thoughts by the same name of "libertarians," usually by scholars whose social-ethical conception begins with tangible egalitarianism, blurs essential distinctions and runs the risk of introducing confusion about basic and major issues. Especially so since the term "libertarian" was hijacked by the noted school from its traditional use by classical left-wing anarchists,[11] a group no less cherishing freedom and opposed to State power, but otherwise holding opposite views and values, as it also opposes big business, corporate hierarchies, domination within organizations or through markets, as well as the selfishness of these relations, while praising solidarity, fraternity, and a general federal structure of society, and wanting to believe all this to be within the reach of history and willful action.[12]

2.5. Exploitation and Marx

The indictment of "exploitation" by Marx – and by others such as the "Ricardian socialists" or even Adam Smith – also rests on an assumption of self-ownership because exploitation is seen as theft of workers' labour by capital owners. This thus is theft of workers' free time of life – as in slavery. This stolen labour is the "surplus value" which becomes profit after the sale of the product on the market. The instrument or, rather, the weapon, is the workers' wage (equal to the value of their consumption), which is below the value of labour due to an excess supply of labour: the competition of the "reserve army" of the unemployed permits the "iron

[11] The oldest newspaper in France is *Le Monde Libertaire* (The Libertarian World), the journal of the anarchosyndicalist movement, about one hundred and twenty years old.

[12] The analysis of possibility in the direction of a "directing utopia" of this family is the topic of the volume *The Good Economy, General Reciprocity* (Kolm 1984a).

law of wages" that keeps them at subsistence level[13] without explicit slavery, and the employer keeps the excess product of the inframarginal workers. The present concern is not the analysis of the logic of this theory, but only pointing out a view that had and has a large social importance in the world as a source of social and political indignation and resentment. Marx and Engels denied having views about "justice" (which they saw as a classbound concept) and only asserted they propose "the point of view of the proletariat." Basically, however, they wanted to point out an inconsistency (a "contradiction") in classical process liberalism in showing that "formal" process-freedom can result in violating full self-ownership. This can be compared with ELIE which – with positive equalization labour – departs from full self-ownership within process-freedom, although in transferring from the well-endowed in (given) human capital to the most destitute in this respect. ELIE thus has an aspect of "antiexploitation."

In Marxist eschatology – and following Auguste Blanqui's classification – the Hegelian historical unfolding of liberty would eventually replace exploitation by the distributive principle "to each according to her work" (socialism), and then "to each according to her needs" (communism), while contribution would in all cases be "from each according to her capacities." However, "to each according to her work" can a priori be given two different meanings. One is that the individual receives the product of her labour. The other is according to her labour inputs. The difference rests in the effect of productive capacities, which is assigned to the specific holder in the former case and is not in the latter. The two cases are according to merit or desert, respectively. Now, the meaning retained was the former one, as shown by the fact that the standard antiexploitation expression was that each should receive "the full product of her labour." Hence, this "to each according to her work" a priori means the full self-ownership of the classical process-liberal thurifers of markets and capitalism. This nonexploitation thus hardly is socialism as commonly understood. At least, it opposes the view of the standard egalitarian socialists. Indeed, it gives different incomes, and not only for different labours and efforts, but also for different productive capacities. It is meritarian rather than egalitarian. Socialists rather favoured income equality qualified for incentives or for differences in effort or painfulness. The perceptive and efficient interpretation of this view has been shown to consist of the income-egalitarian ELIE (Chapter 11). A progressive "transition to socialism" should best be seen as an ELIE distribution with a progressive increase in the equalization labour k. This "petit-bourgeois egalitarianism" can well be accompanied by more distribution "according to needs," although this becomes less necessary when sufficient incomes permit people to satisfy their needs as they see them – and the inefficiency of all-powerful state paternalism caring for needs can be a small defect compared with the potential political risk it presents for liberties, autonomy, and

---

[13] Or at the level permitting the worker to satisfy his usual consumption in Marx's writings later in the nineteenth century (see *Wages, Prices and Profits*).

dignity. However, the vanishing of the state (that Marx wishfully foresees), of selfish individualism (the vice he accuses basic rights of), and of crippling specialization (yet with technical progress), draw an all-different picture of the long-range vision. A principle "from each, voluntarily, according to others' needs" requires not only a system of information but also consciousness and self-consciousness of what needs be named a need. The analyses of such psychological and social possibilities are essential exercises, but not the present, more modest, one.[14] Yet it has been noted that the reciprocity structure of ELIE – from each, to each other, the product of the same labour – can provide an efficient egalitarian springboard for a genuine reciprocity of gifts and concerns for others.

3. INCOME EGALITARIANISM

3.1. ELIE and income egalitarianisms

The relevant borderline case of ELIE opposed to full self-ownership is the social-ethical position classically opposed to classical process liberalism: income egalitarianism. The ideal of income equality is a position of the left, and even of the far left short of the more deeply radical positions of theoretical "communism" distributing "according to needs" and of mutuality "anarchism." A number of economists adhered to or favoured this ideal position, such as Oskar Lange and Maurice Dobb, and a number of present-day scholars. It has been proposed, in Chapter 11, that the most standard form of income egalitarianism holds strict income equality to be the ideal only for equal labour and thinks that people who work more (and whose work is more painful) deserve a compensation. It has also been shown that the implementation of this view is ELIE with an equalization labour $k = k^e$ in the neighbourhood of the lowest normal full labour.

However, the theory of ELIE has also considered the equality, equalization, and equal redistribution of other incomes. Maximal income equalization equally redistributes maximal earned incomes $p_i(1)$ or w_i into the averages $\overline{p}(1)$ or $\overline{w}$ thanks to transfers $t_i = \overline{p}(1) - p_i(1)$ or $t_i = \overline{w} - w_i$, which equalize total incomes adding the income value of leisure $w_i \lambda_i$ (with $\lambda_i = 1 - \ell_i$) to earned income $w_i \ell_i$ and transfer t_i, $w_i \ell_i + w_i \lambda_i + t_i = w_i + t_i$, with $\Sigma t_i = 0$. This "Dworkin solution" (in the linear case) is not to be retained for the indicated reasons, notably because it in part equalizes incomes that are only potential, a concept consensually found unjustified.

General ELIE, indeed, consists of the equal redistribution of the generally partial "equalization incomes" $p_i(k)$, where k is the chosen equalization labour, into the average $\overline{p}(k)$, thanks to transfers $t_i = \overline{p}(k) - p_i(k)$, which equalize the

[14] These topics are discussed in other works, notably *The Good Economy, General Reciprocity* (1984a), *Happiness-Freedom* (1982a), *Pluridimensional Man* (1987i), and *The Socialist Transition* (1977b).

partial "compensated equalization incomes" $x_i = p_i(k) + t_i$ given the financial constraint $\Sigma t_i = 0$ (or $\Sigma t_i = b$ with $b < 0$ for providing a budget for other expenditures, or even $b > 0$ for distributing a given global net wealth). Particular cases are with $k = k^e$ and the above $k = 1$. Moreover, individual i's total income in an ELIE with equalization labour k, including earned income $w_i \ell_i$, the income value of leisure $w_i \lambda_i$ (with $\lambda_i = 1 - \ell_i$), and the transfer $t_i = k \cdot (\overline{w} - w_i)$ (in the linear case) is

$$v_i = w_i \ell_i + w_i \lambda_i + t_i = w_i + t_i = w_i + k \cdot (\overline{w} - w_i) = k\overline{w} + (1 - k)w_i.$$

This v_i thus is an average between w_i and the average $\overline{w}$ with weights $1 - k$ and k. This w_i, the wage rate of individual i, is also her productivity, her total "natural wealth," and the income value of her productive capacities. This transformation of the w_i into the v_i is a *concentration* (a linear uniform concentration toward the mean).[15] There are strong reasons for accepting that it makes the v_i be "less unequal" than the w_i are. Finally, we saw in the Appendix of Chapter 10 the possibility of determining "second-best ELIEs" by the maximization of an appropriate function $M(x)$ where x is the set of the x_i.

3.2. Comparing income inequalities

These are applications of the vast field of study of the comparison and measurement of inequalities. This term – rather than "distribution" – suggests that equality is particularly considered. Concerning income, this probably or certainly is for a normative reason. This consideration of inequality can be for judging, or for choosing when reaching equality is not possible or not appropriate, all considered. The reasons for not reaching equality can be of various natures: material, social, political, moral, or mixed. They can in particular be due to reactions of the people to policy measures (taxes and subsidies in particular). These reactions may be due to relations of various types. In particular, the tax base may be an elastic item (that is, it may be influenced by people's actions). These items may in particular be those whose equalization is sought for. Or this situation may result from questions of information, because an estimate uses observations influenced by agents' choices (for instance, their income or their labour). Moreover, there may be other social or ethical ideals interfering with the desired equality. To begin with, there is often a preference for situations where some people gain and no one loses (unanimity), and this may lead one to depart from equality for various possible reasons. There can also more generally be a relevant ideal equality of other items, when the various considered equalities cannot be jointly satisfied. Then, there has to be an association of the various ideals, with some, or all, being satisfied only in a

---

[15] These concentrations were introduced and used for comparing risks in Kolm 1966b. They were later used for the same purpose by J. Stiglitz.

second-best manner. This association can have various possible structures, using, notably, priorities, compromises, or "superimpositions" (that is, the application of one principle from the result of the application of another, such as, for instance, free action or exchange from an equal allocation – an example of which is ELIE).

3.3. Comparisons of inequalities based on pairwise inclusions

Simple as it may seem, the comparison and measure of inequality is in fact a delicate subject, due to the relations between logicomathematical properties and issues of actual meaning which can associate logic and ethics. In fact, for comparing two situations with inequality, about the only case when one can say that inequality certainly is lower in one situation than in another occurs when there are only two items in each distribution, all these items can be meaningfully compared by more or less and hence ordered, and the two items in one situation are between those in the other: inequality then is lower in the former distribution than in the latter. From this comparison one can build comparisons for larger distributions, for instance when this pairwise comparison holds for all unequal pairs that differ, or when the number of pairs whose inequality so increases exceeds that of pairs whose inequality so decreases and other pairs do not change. One can then consider cases where the comparison does not depend on items that do not change, or where these items are measurable by quantities. The most basic properties are outlined here, and in some more detail in the next chapter about the necessary structures of distributive principles.

Consider a distribution of comparable numbers, one for each of the n individuals. A pair of numbers is "included" in another if one of them is between these other two and the other is either between or equal to one of them. A pair is transformed by inclusion when it becomes included in its former values. This probably implies a lower inequality for the pair. Specifying, the inequality of a pair is said to "inclusion-decrease" or decrease by inclusion when the pair is transformed by inclusion (it "inclusion-increases" or increases by inclusion in the converse operation). For any number n of individuals, one can then certainly say that inequality decreases if it inclusion-decreases for all changing pairs of unequal numbers while equal numbers remain equal (a pair changes if at least one of the two numbers changes). Then, considering moreover that two successive decreases in inequality diminish inequality (transitivity of the comparison), this amounts to saying that inequality is diminished by any *truncation*, that is, all numbers above a given number are reduced to it, and/or all numbers below a given number are augmented to its level. This is shown by considering a succession of transformations where the highest number decreases or several equal highest numbers equally decrease, in remaining the highest, and/or the lowest number increases or several equal lowest numbers equally increase, in remaining the lowest. Comparisons by inclusion and truncations only rest on the possibility of ordering the items. More specific meaningful structural properties permit further types of comparisons. When the items are quantities such as incomes, then, after truncations, one of the transformations that certainly should be said to diminish inequality is the concentration previously described.

The effect on inequality of changes by inclusion of only one pair while the other numbers do not change is ambiguous if the increasing number is not the unique lowest, or if the decreasing number is not the unique highest, because the pairwise inequalities inclusion-increase between the increasing number and any other not larger, and between the decreasing number and any other not smaller. However, the property that numbers that do not change are irrelevant for the comparison, which is particular and not necessary, is not meaningless either (the unconcerned individuals are not considered) – this is a property of "independence" or "separability."[16] Then, preferring one number to be higher when there is only one individual because this puts her in a better situation, leads to the same preference when there is a larger number and only one changes – the property of "benevolence" – even though the inequality between this increasing number and each other not higher increases by inclusion. Assuming this preference with priority, preference for lower inequality in a pair in a change by inclusion only has to consider the cases of *full* inclusion where both numbers become between their former values. Now, assuming preference for an increase in only one number (benevolence), indifference to permutations of the numbers (a necessary property when no other difference but these numbers is relevant), and preferences about distributions that are transitive (two successive preferences entail preference), then preference for changes of two numbers only that become less unequal by full inclusion amounts to a preference by leximin, that is: prefer a set of numbers to another when the lowest of the numbers that differ from one to the other is higher.[17] When the lowest numbers of the two sets differ, this choice reduces to maximin: prefer the one with the larger lowest number.

However, this preference refers only to the ordering of the considered numbers. If this is the only relevant structural property, the objection that the considered preference prefers a tiny increase in a lower number at the cost of a large decrease in a higher is irrelevant. However, such an objection is in fact often relevant. It does not, in itself, imply that these numbers measure quantities (see Chapter 24), but it can be valid in particular in this case, which is that of the comparisons of incomes. In this case, a transformation of a pair by inclusion can be achieved by the transfer of an amount from the higher to the lower, of less than the difference or not larger than half the difference (a "progressive transfer"). This is the necessary form of the change by inclusion if the total sum of quantities has to remain constant. Assuming that this diminishes the overall inequality is the "transfer

---

[16] Note 18 will point out the two possible meanings of this property.

[17] There results that leximin amounts to a preference for a change in any two numbers such that all pairs that do not remain identical change by inclusion or the reverse, and they are more numerous in the former category than in the latter. See Appendix A of Chapter 23, and also Kolm (1971) and Hammond (1976a).

principle."[18] Now, the previous remark about changes in only two numbers by pairwise inclusion shows that one cannot a priori say that inequality in the overall distribution is diminished neither by a choice by leximin nor by a progressive transfer (the "transfer principle"), for the same reason. These operations can be said to produce a lower inequality only with the addition of extra properties that imply this conclusion. One possible such property is the noted "independence" or "separability": the evaluation of a change depends on the changing numbers only.[19] This property is particular, by no means necessary, sometimes to be rejected, yet not meaningless either.[20] Finally, basing the comparison of inequalities on that of pairwise inequalities suggests measuring inequalities from inequalities in pairs. For example, the sum of the absolute values of differences in each pair leads to the Gini index, others are possible[21] (and functions of differences to the mean can be expressed in this way).

3.4. Evaluation-consistent measures of inequality

However, reducing inequality is generally not the only value. One may also prefer that some incomes are higher while none is lower, or even that one is slightly lower if this permits a sufficient increase in sufficiently many others. This leads to the consideration of maximands $M(x)$ where $x = \{x_i\}$ is the set of the x_i and x_i is individual i's relevant income. This function will then be increasing (benevolence). If no other characteristics relevantly differentiate the individuals, it has to be symmetrical (invariant under permutations of the x_i). Symmetry plus the transfer principle amounts to "Schur-concavity," which, with preference for higher x_i for all i, is equivalent to a dozen meaningful properties (including preference for higher "concentration curves" – and, when the sum Σx_i is a priori given, for higher Lorenz curves –, and preference for higher sums $\Sigma f(x_i)$ for all increasing concave functions f).[22] Maximin and leximin are limiting

---

[18] The two definitions of a progressive transfer make a difference as properties of measures of inequality or of inequality-averse maximands: "lower than the difference" implies symmetry (invariance under permutations), while this is not the case with "not larger than half the difference." However, the latter also implies symmetry if, moreover, the property of independence-separability holds and the measure is smooth (differentiable) – see Kolm 1966a, 1976a, 1976b. The transfer principle was proposed and discussed notably by Tawney, Taussig, Loria, Pigou, Dalton, and Divisia.

[19] This can in fact mean two things. Either the unchanging numbers are just disregarded, or the judgment is the same whatever they are. In the second interpretation, when two numbers change by inclusion without reversal of their order, if one considers that the others are between the latter values (or equal to them), then all pairs that do not remain identical become less unequal by inclusion. Then, with this independence property, one pair becoming less unequal by inclusion amounts to all changing pairs becoming less unequal by inclusion (this is a truncation with only one increasing and one decreasing number). Similarly, for the derivation of the property of benevolence from independence so interpreted, one can consider the case where all the $n - 1$ fixed numbers are higher than the final level of the unique changing number. Then, all changing pairs become more equal by inclusion (this again is a truncation). Yet, the opposite holds when all fixed numbers are taken to be smaller than the increasing one.

[20] Other possible alternative justifications of the "transfer principle" can be found in Kolm 1999a.

[21] Kolm 1999a.

[22] The set of these properties is presented in Kolm 1966a. The *concentration curve* is the classical name for the sum of the m lowest incomes as a function of m or of m/n, as found in elementary textbooks of statistics. Hence, the Lorenz curve is the concentration curve scaled down by Σx_i. Extraordinarily,

cases. The *equal equivalent income* is the number $\bar{\bar{x}}$ such that function M would have the same value if all x_i were replaced by it, that is, $M(x) = M(\bar{\bar{x}}e)$ where e is the vector of n ones.[23] *Evaluation-consistent* measures of inequality are, denoting as $\bar{x} = (1/n)\Sigma x_i$ the average, the *absolute*, *relative*, and *total* inequalities defined as $I^a = \bar{x} - \bar{\bar{x}}$, $I^r = I^a/\bar{x}$ (or $I^a/\bar{\bar{x}}$), and $I^t = nI^a$, respectively. All these three forms have meaning. The separability property considered above, applied to the ordering of the distributions x by the function M, implies that this M can be taken as the additive form $\Sigma f_i(x_i)$, where functions f_i can be increasing for benevolence, and the same functions $f_i = f$ for symmetry (up to arbitrary added constants), with a strictly concave function f for the transfer principle. The variation of the inequalities when the x_i incur equiproportional or equal variations is considered, including invariances and various types of intermediate cases. Function f can notably be a power function of the augmented incomes $x_i + c$ with a constant $c \geq 0$, which includes, as particular cases, power, logarithmic, and exponential functions.[24] Variations of populations are considered. These properties are then extended to the comparison of multidimensional inequalities, that is, inequalities in bundles of quantities of goods, and, more distantly, of inequalities in freedom as domains of choice.[25, 26]

4. THE PREFERENCE-RESPECTING "SOCIAL WELFARE FUNCTION"

4.1. Social-individual values

Since the mid-twentieth century, a majority view of academic economists simultaneously holds that the social optimum should be derived from a "social welfare" function of individuals' utilities and that no such good function exists (from Arrow 1951). Both terms of this schizophrenic belief are challenged by the present derivation of macrojustice by endogenous social choice. On the one hand, the relevant derivation of the structure of the distribution and of the base and structure of the distributive policy, for macrojustice, do not result from the maximization of a function of individuals' self-interested utilities. This use of utilities would not respect the "natural" self-assignment of eudemonistic capacities for this issue, their irrelevance for this policy, which is an actual consensual ethical judgment (Chapter 6). If, moreover, a redistributive tax-subsidy had to be based on earned income, this "welfarist" ethics would lead to the so-called "optimum

originality has been sought in renaming the concentration curve the "augmented Lorenz curve" (for restating the corresponding results seventeen years after their first printing)!

[23] Kolm 1966a.

[24] See Kolm 1966a, 1966b, 1976a, 1976b, 1999a.

[25] See Kolm 1977a for multidimensional inequalities and 1993d and 1999b for domains of choice.

[26] The literature about the comparison and measure of inequalities is very abundant. Much is gathered in the handbook edited by Jacques Silber (1999). Among several valuable textbooks, the one authored by Peter Lambert (2001) is particularly complete. Most of the main properties were introduced in *The Optimal Production of Social Justice* (Kolm, 1966a). This paper was heard and read by a number of scholars who later presented the topic. However, many students were introduced to the question by those of these properties presented in the very didactic paper by A. Atkinson (1970).

income tax" that has been discussed in Chapters 10 and 15 (and, we have seen, is relevant and had been previously used for issues in microjustice). On the other hand, endogenous social choice does lead to a social preference depending on and "respecting" individuals' preferences (as Part IV of this study has shown), but its implementation has to be through a policy having the obtained structure (this a priori given condition does not impair Pareto efficiency).

Endogenous social choice adds to the classical framework, for obtaining such a solution, both psychological and social realism and a property inherent in the concept of justice, impartiality. Psychological realism acknowledges that individual preferences are of various different types. In particular, individuals have both interests and values, notably values about what society should be. These values can be concerned with the interests of all individuals as they hold relevant to define them, and possibly with others' values. This can include, in particular, a sense or conception of justice. However, does there exist anything like an individual value? Are not values inherently social phenomena? That is, the individuals hold values, but they adopt values that exist and that they observe and hear about in society. This comes from education, influence, imitation, and the like. In particular, social values in the sense of values about society are also social in the sense of being created by society and held by part of it. Tastes are also social phenomena influenced by the social context, of course. But probably less fully so than most values. In addition, the causes of values include, more than is the case for tastes, ingredients of reason, which is by nature transindividual. And yet, the influencing society is made up of individuals, and values can be seen as resulting from influences and interferences among individuals. Moreover, even though an individual does not create her own values ex nihilo, in choosing some rather than others (when this is the case), at any rate in holding, interpreting, and possibly applying them, and in influencing others in this respect (for instance, in education), individuals also more or less participate in the social creation of values. However, given the common complexity of this interactive process, a Durkheimian view of values as holistic social entities is not void of validity, usefulness, and meaning. In any event, endogenous social choice has to rest on these values of the individuals or of society, irrespective of individuals' responsibility in holding them (or satisfaction in having them applied). The only possible qualification concerns the effect of information in considering what these values would be (or will be) with sufficient information about all relevant issues. Several complementary considerations have been used for deriving the solution from individuals' values in Part IV. The deepest one considers the origin of these values and the fact that sufficiently deep mutual information makes them converge (possibly with the help of dialog, and possibly only as a notional effect). Others consider recursive values aggregating values, and another aggregates thanks to the irrelevance of utility levels for macrojustice. The overall social ordering implies the basic structures: social freedom, the distinction of macrojustice, the views about capacities and the ELIE structure, and the degree of redistribution (the equalization labour).

4.2. "Social welfare" and "social choice"

The basis of the solution is the duality of individuals' preferences, which encompass both interests and values. As Blaise Pascal puts it, "man is neither angel nor beast" (he added: "and he who wants to play angel plays beast"). The classical "social welfare function" of economists usually considers individuals' interests only. This results from its being the offspring of utilitarianism, which wants to add individuals' pleasures and pains: this sum was replaced by this more general function of individuals' utilities because of the difficulty of defining concepts of utility (or pleasure, or happiness), that can sufficiently meaningfully be added (by Abram Bergson, Oskar Lange, Maurice Allais, or Paul Samuelson). Most of these authors and the crowd of their epigones are not very explicit about the psychological, social, or political status or meaning of this "social welfare function." Bergson (1938), however, is clear about it and said that his social welfare function represents the social-ethical evaluation of an individual, for instance an official. However, if this maximand should guide policy choices, the selection of this evaluator matters, an issue Bergson does not discuss. Arrow (1951) emphasizes that the social ordering he considers is "society's" view. He uses scores of expressions such as "society prefers." In an early answer, Buchanan (1954) strongly denied that the entity "society" can be said to have such preference orderings. Arrow clearly acknowledges the duality of individuals' views with interests and values. "Individual values" is in the title of his work. However, he says that the individuals' preference orderings he considers can represent either their interests (or welfare) or their value, a versatility that is seen as generality, and hence, as a virtue of the analysis. In contrast, the solution of the social and ethical problem posed (rather than solely of the chosen formal problem)[27] would rather require considering: (1) both individuals' levels of evaluation, interests and values, jointly; (2) the origin of the formation of individual values; (3) variables that can be defined as equal across individuals for considering a requirement of rationality (see Chapter 23); and (4) actual features of values, considered by endogenous social choice.

Indeed, earlier classical apostles of social maximands or orderings explicitly considered the duality of individuals' views, although in quite different ways. This is, for instance, the case of classical utilitarians, of Pareto, and of Condorcet. Classical utilitarians, such as John Stuart Mill or Henry Sidgwick, considered that individuals, in addition to their "utility," hold social-ethical values, but also that these values have to be the utilitarian highest sum of utilities, and hence, are the same for all. This unanimity solves the problem by endogenous social choice (provided one knows what should be added, precisely). These scholars saw this as resulting from the requirement of impartiality for the social-ethical value. In the sum, indeed, "each is to count for one and only for one," according to Mill's famous

---

[27] This formal problem is discussed in Kolm 1996a, Chapter 15. For example, the obtained result (the "impossibility theorem") requires the consideration of sets of individual preferences that certainly cannot exist in reality.

redundancy. However, this evaluative impartiality is, more generally, described by the social evaluation being a symmetric function of the individuals' relevant items (equivalence of permutations). If these items are the (comparable) utilities, the unweighted sum has this property. It is the only linear or affine function having this property (adding a constant makes no difference for the maximization). Yet, if the aggregation can be a more general function, there can be many symmetrical functions, and hence different impartial individual social evaluations. Moreover, the relevant individuals' items can also a priori be of many kinds (welfare, incomes, goods, rights, and so on). Now, the belief that it suffices that individuals hold impartial views for their holding identical views is a classical historical mistake made by the greatest minds. One of them is Adam Smith in his *Theory of Moral Sentiments*.[28] Moreover, individuals actually agree about other kinds of properties of the social ethical solution than impartiality only (this has been shown here as concerns macrojustice).

Condorcet considered voting for aggregating both individuals' interests and individuals' information about an objective good. However, the proper way of solving the latter Platonic question is exchange of information rather than voting (which might only be used after the possibilities of information have been exhausted). Indeed, dialog exchanging information about facts and values, and reasons and arguments, should at any rate also be used for determining the best solution, and voting should possibly intervene only when views no longer converge.

The most explicit joint considerations of the dual self-interested and social preferences of individuals are those proposed by Vilfredo Pareto's distinction of utilities and ophelimities, and by the particular (and problematic) theories of the original position of John Rawls and John Harsanyi. A number of economists' views, such as those of Pareto, Harsanyi, and also Jules Dupuit, can be complemented so as to obtain a social preference from individuals' values (these complements are necessary, though, because Harsanyi's theory fails to do this by itself, Pareto's individuals' social preferences are not impartial, and Dupuit considered efficiency but not justice). The following sections, in some sense, extract the essence or the philosophy of analyses presented in Part IV and summarizes them.

4.3. Pareto's duality extended to justice

Vilfredo Pareto (1913) considered three levels of functions. An individual has an ophelimity function that represents something like her welfare, akin to her interest, and a utility function depending on the ophelimities of various individuals

---

[28] Immanuel Kant is about in the same boat as concerns his Categorical Imperative, which leads him to say that reason alone suffices and to discard moral "sentiments." Indeed, acting as if it could be desired that all others follow the same precept can be justified by considerations of rationality, but it can in general a priori be satisfied by various actions or rules of action, and more specific judgments are required for selecting one.

including herself. Then, social ethics should maximize a utilitarian sum of these utilities. An individual's Paretian utility is thus similar to a Bergson social welfare function. However, although none of these authors is precise about the specific reasons for concern for others' welfare, a Bergson function represents an overall social ethics and, presumably and importantly, a sense of justice, whereas an individual's Paretian utility grasps all reasons an individual has to be concerned by others' ophelimity, with doubtlessly altruism playing an important role – this function is taken to be a weighted sum of individuals' ophelimities (it is a priori not symmetrical). The additive structures of these utilities and of the final sum imply problematic structures of cardinality for the ophelimity and "utility" functions. But these sums can be replaced by more general functions.[29] However, present-day utilitarians would maximize the sum of ophelimities rather than the sum of such utilities. Now, building the social-ethical evaluation function from these utilities, rather than directly from ophelimities, has the advantage that its comparisons of individuals' ophelimities depend on such comparisons performed by the individuals in their own "utility" functions. If these latter comparisons described views about justice, this influence would manifest the principle of endogenous social choice. And the considered individuals' social views can be taken to have this property. Each would be an impartial evaluation of the set of all individuals' interests (including her own). All reasons for particularly favouring some individuals over others that do not belong to the category of justice would be ruled out. Since social relations and social proximity or distance constitute one main cause of such discriminations, each individual evaluation can be assumed to consider the interests of people in the same social relation with the evaluator (for instance, same kin relationship, or belonging to the same social community – and the evaluator's own interest will also be so considered along with others'), and this relation will be assumed to be the same for all individual evaluators. This relation would be sufficiently strong for eliciting altruistic concern, but, being the same for all evaluated interests, the balances among them would represent justice rather than discriminating altruism or indifference. Various considerations, proposed in Chapter 21, can then lead to a convergence of these individual values. A social evaluation can thus be derived from the anthropological data of actual sentiments or actions of distributive justice or sharing.

4.4. The recursive Harsanyi's original position and moral time-sharing

While philosopher John Rawls presented a theory of the "original position" as a device for supplanting utilitarianism, economist John Harsanyi (1976)[30] derived, from this very theory, an additive maximand that many present-day economists

---

[29] Such as in Kolm 1966a and 2000a.
[30] This is the right reference rather than 1953, where the individuals a priori uncertainty bears on their income only.

consider the best case for utilitarianism.[31] The basic idea consists in considering individuals' evaluations "in the original position" where they do not know "who they will be" yet. A social-ethical evaluation can thus be derived from self-interest. Harsanyi seems more rational than Rawls in assuming that this uncertainty is restricted to not knowing which of the actual individuals an individual in the original position will become (with equal chances of becoming any of them) – that is, it is restricted to what Rawls labels the "thin veil of ignorance" rather than being his own very extensive "thick veil" – because the problem is only balancing among the interests of the actual individuals. Then, classical choice in uncertainty (von Neumann-Morgenstern) provides this additive structure. This does not suffice to solve the problem, though, because an evaluation in the original position rests on a preference about being the various actual individuals and on preferences about risk.[32] Hence, the actual individuals, if put in the original position, have these two reasons for having different evaluations. A consistent way of facing this situation consists of considering these individuals in the original position in turn as alternative possible embodiments for individuals in a deeper, more primitive, original position. A multiplicity of evaluations still exists for the same reasons, and the same device can be applied again, with similar considerations. At each step, individuals' evaluations are closer to one another than they were in the previous one because each positively aggregates former individual views (see Chapter 21). A recurrent application of this method makes individuals' views converge toward the same evaluation, a consensual social-ethical ordering (although not one with an additive utilitarian-like structure). This solution is presented and applied in Chapter 21. However, the very assimilation of a choice of justice with an individual self-interested choice in uncertainty is in itself problematic.[33] A parallel method consists of considering individuals who are the various individuals successively in periods of equal duration (the "moral time-sharing" approach presented in Chapter 21).

4.5. Applying Dupuit's surplus to redistributions

The difficulty of measuring utility for the utilitarian sum did not escape Jeremy Bentham. The solution he proposed was to measure utility in money "for lack of a better alternative." This probably means that the utility of an individual in a situation is the money equivalent for her of this situation, or her willingness to pay for it, from another situation taken as reference. These measures can, of course, be logically added (Bentham also expressed doubt about the meaningfulness of adding utilities of different individuals – hence basically about utilitarianism).

---

[31] See the discussion of utilitarianism and "utilitaromorphisms" in Kolm 1996a, Chapter 14.

[32] Risk means uncertainty plus concern for the result (it has a priori nothing to do with using probabilities or not, as an economic literature had it).

[33] This solution is more generally and more fully discussed in the study *Vox populi, vox dei: endogenous social choice and the regress original position* (Kolm 2001b).

Then, the highest sum can be the criterion of the surplus proposed by Jules Dupuit (1844) for choosing public works, and still the standard principle in studies of benefit-cost analysis. This is also akin to the famous "compensation principle" saying that a project should be implemented if the beneficiaries can compensate the losers.[34] If, moreover, majority voting is objected to because it does not take the intensity of individuals' preferences into account, one can weight the votes of individuals by their monetary equivalent or their willingness to pay for having one option rather than the other: the criterion becomes a surplus. The surplus principle also relates to the highest social income – sum of individuals' incomes – with an extensive definition of income including all "psychic incomes." The monetary equivalent or the willingness to pay (or the required compensation for a loss) differ from utility in their discarding the utility of this amount of money provided by the individuals' eudemonistic capacities. Hence, for questions where these capacities are irrelevant, this criterion may well be a first best rather than a second best, as Bentham sees it. However, indifference and hence preference orderings intervene in the definition of the willingness to pay or money equivalent. Hence, the principle depends on this ordinal structure of individuals' preferences, but not on anything that could be a psychological intensity of preferences. This is also the case of individuals' corresponding choices and resulting actions, and of corresponding Pareto efficiency. This separation can therefore rest on the consideration that individuals are concerned by others' actions, whereas any kind of intensity of preference or satisfaction is a psychological private concern that can be circumscribed to a private sphere of the person. The result also depends on the reference state used for measuring willingnesses to pay, a question well known to economists and to which a solution is proposed (see Chapters 19 and 25).

The surplus principle is usually not used for appraising distribution, though, since the money value of a dollar (or the willingness to pay for a dollar) is a dollar, and hence transferring some amount from one person to another provides a zero (extra) surplus. However, this is no longer the case if the individuals care about the distribution not only for their self-interest about their own holdings, but also for other reasons, notably because of social-ethical preferences motivated by a sense of justice. Then, individuals can have willingnesses to pay for – or money equivalents of – others' incomes (or satisfaction), any income for a moral reason, and transfers among any individuals. The surplus principle can thus determine a favoured distribution. This result is obtained from individuals' opinions about the distribution, hence in the spirit of endogenous social choice. This is the theory of the distributive or *moral surplus*, whose application is discussed in Chapter 19.[35] A remarkable property is that, in the surplus of a redistribution, the willingnesses to pay – or money equivalents – for self-interested reasons cancel out and vanish because they are equal to the incomes received or yielded, which balance because

[34] See Chapter 19. The surplus criterion is also a particular application of the theory of "equivalence" presented in Chapter 26 and is discussed there.
[35] The full theory is presented in Kolm 1966a.

income is redistributed and gains equal losses. Hence, the surplus is the (algebraic) sum of willingnesses to pay (or money equivalent) for non-self-interested reasons only. In particular, the method can work even if the individuals are ready to pay only very little for others' incomes (lexical egoism).

5. ELIE IN THE CRITERIA OF JUSTICE

In the tripartition of criteria of justice among full self-ownership and criteria directly concerned with either income and goods or happiness and other concepts representable by utility, the first two cases are particular cases of ELIE which generally consists of the combinations between them. By contrast, the third category seems to be absent. This results from the irrelevance of direct concern for eudemonistic capacities in the policy of macrojustice, discussed in Chapter 6. However, individuals' preferences intervene in three ways. Preferences representing individuals' self-interest intervene through the corresponding free choice and Pareto efficiency. This only entails the acceptance of values and prices (in particular wages) determined by free exchange (implied by process-freedom), and the general conclusion that distributive policy should allocate, and be based on, the given ("natural") resources. However, the income-egalitarian ELIE ($k = k^e$) has the property that most individuals find it almost equivalent to the same allocation of labour k^e and income $\overline{w}k^e$ (this is a case of the principles of "equivalence" discussed in Chapter 26). Individuals' preferences are also used in a more basic way, in the derivation of the solution for macrojustice from endogenous social choice. Yet, this solution uses not only individuals' preferences that represent interests, but also, primarily, preferences that represent individuals' social-ethical values. This was in particular used for determining the degree of redistribution (the equalization labour) in Part IV. Finally, individuals' preferences may be used in estimating individuals' behaviour in applications of the theory of second-best ELIE (see the Appendix to Chapter 10). Moreover, for the sake of completeness and of presenting the largest possible scope of comparison, many other possible allocative criteria that directly rest on individuals' preferences or satisfaction or can be related to them are considered and discussed in forthcoming chapters.

23

The structure and substance of
distributive principles

1. PRESENTATION AND OUTLINE

This chapter presents an analytical summarized overview of the properties of principles of adequate or fair distribution, that these principles hold by necessity created by their topic and by rationality. These principles constitute a rather well-defined set. Only a limited subset has been scholarly considered as yet – and not all fare brilliantly in the test of meaningfulness – while others doubtlessly as useful have not been yet. Logic and morality both entail that no principle can be valid for all questions; hence, each principle should be accompanied by the specification of its scope of application or by sufficient indications about it (as shown in forthcoming Section 2). For instance, ELIE was derived as a solution for overall distribution in macrojustice. A principle is characterized by two aspects, its substance and its structure (Section 4). The substance is the nature of the basic ethical reference of the judgment – this can differ from the direct object of the policy, from its instruments, and from the items whose distribution is observed or discussed. Individualistic principles are considered, and hence the substance is either in the family of freedom or means, or in that of happiness or satisfaction (Section 3) – the meanings and uses of the economic concepts of "utility" will be pointed out. Rationality in the basic and elementary sense of "for a reason," or justified, turns out to imply two basic and related structural properties (Section 5). One is an ideal equality in the sense of a *prima facie* identical treatment of identicals in the relevant characteristics. *Prima facie* means "in the absence of an overpowering reason." Such a reason can be impossibility or the relevance of some other principle (which can be the ideal equality of something else). As very particular cases, the ideal equality can be in the social values of the considered items (for instance, marginal values in the maximization of a sum – for example of incomes into social income, of utilities in utilitarianism, or in aggregate measures of education or health). The second property is the symmetry of the evaluation, in the sense of invariance under permutations in the individuals' items and relevant characteristics. The noted evaluations that favour highest sums (or other aggregates)

389

can also be seen as comparing the variations of individuals' situations across states; yet, such principles are in fact more globally social than individualistic (Section 6). In fact, both the individuals' items and their variation across situations are often jointly considered. Much more generally, several properties or principles are often jointly relevant. Their association can have various types of structure (compromises, priorities, "superimposition," or equivalence theory) (Section 7). The principle can often be represented by an ethical ordering or maximization. This maximand has to be an inequality-averse function (when it is not a sum), which can have various properties – such as benevolence, or "separability" (Section 8). The possible properties, however, depend on the nature of the relevant items (the "substance"). For example, a quantity or income, a bundle of goods, happiness or satisfaction, freedom in any of its definitions and so on, offer very different possibilities for defining, for each individual and across individuals, meaningful concepts of equality and substitution, larger than, variation, addition, transfers, multiplication by scalars, and so on. The resulting tension between the structural properties that are necessary or useful for the choice or comparison, and those that are meaningful for the retained substance, constitutes a major question of the social choice (Section 9). These properties and their relations and consequences are analyzed in the logicoethical field of the comparison of inequalities (Section 10). The most general and basic properties of the comparisons of inequalities are deduced from the decreases of inequality in a pair by inclusion of the new values between the former ones; these properties (truncation, leximin, transfers), are discussed in Appendix A. Finally, Appendix B discusses the general methodology of the derivation of normative principles.

2. THE OBTAINED PRINCIPLE AND THE OTHERS

2.1. The multiplicity of criteria and the essential issue of their scope of application

The obtained structure of macrojustice constitutes a principle of allocation of resources and commodities. Other allocative criteria have been proposed, and many others still a priori are meaningful and can be considered and proposed. The reason for the solution "social freedom with ELIE for overall distributive justice," its justification, stands as it has been proposed rather than comparatively. However, noting the other a priori possible criteria provides an overview of the field of a priori possibilities and of the logical situation of the obtained solution in it. In any event, there is probably an intrinsic interest in the general condensed presentation of these possible criteria, their basic properties, their comparison and classification, their virtues or shortcomings, their meanings and the depth or absence of their meaningfulness, the information they require, their usefulness or absence of it, and their possible scope of application. Indeed, for each a priori possible and meaningful principle or criterion, one of the main questions concerns the type of situations for which it would be the relevant or best judgment. For each principle or criterion, it is straightforward to find examples of situations where it is not the appropriate solution. To begin with, the items considered by the criterion may not be those of the actual problem, or the relevant ones. The criterion's judgment may also be inappropriate, or clearly not the best, in the considered situation. This may in particular be unanimous thoughtful opinion, which leads endogenous social choice to reject this judgment. Moreover, whole families of principles or criteria present basic flaws, sometimes diriment ones, for any, most, or many applications, even if they permit mental exercises that are interesting from the formal, logical, or mathematical point of view. These problems refer to questions of meaningfulness or of the logic of optimality. An example as concerns meaningfulness is the use of cardinal utilities in most normative questions where they should represent satisfaction, happiness, or similar concepts.[1] An example as concerns the logic of optimality is found in applications of the theory of "equivalence" as unanimous indifference: for instance, when some items should be equal, progress in their equalization in a notional, hypothetical situation equivalent in this sense to the actual one may require more inequality in the actual items.[2] Most properties, however, are valid or invalid depending on the specific application (even the noted examples may be valid in particular situations), and hence require a specific discussion in this respect. This holds in particular for other uses of "counterfactuals" (nonexisting, imaginary items or cases, whose consideration can influence actual policy choices and may or may not be relevant). The most general conclusion is that, without a doubt, no principle can be proposed as the universal solution, valid in all possible or actual cases (this is in particular the case for ELIE, obtained for the problem of macrojustice).[3]

2.2. The logical place of ELIE

The obtained solution for macrojustice, and hence ELIE for this application, have been obtained from the basic principle of endogenous social choice and the unanimity it implies. They owe nothing to "intuition." They are by no means

[1] See Chapter 24, and a fuller discussion in Kolm 1996a, Chapter 12.

[2] See Chapter 26. The noted property, called the "reversal syndrome," is but the dramatic manifestation of a more general logical problem.

[3] Universality has sometimes been claimed, for instance, by utilitarianism (which has to know how to add pleasures in the first place). Most commonly, proposals or theories of normative criteria or principles are just silent about their intended field of application or their proposed domain of validity. Of course, studies that focus on actual choices of justice emphasize the presence of various criteria, although they are descriptive rather than normative. They are to be found in all disciplines, such as psychosociology with Leventhal (1976, 1980), Mikula (1980), or Schwinger (1980); economics with Bar Hillel and Yaari (1984); sociology with Elster (1992); law with Zajac (1997); and philosophy with Miller (1999). Walzer (1983), developing Max Weber's assumption about people's sense of justice, is somewhat different because the ideal principle he proposes separates into various "spheres" but is the same in each sphere, an ideal equal sharing of the allocation of services or goods, which disregards issues that may be relevant depending on the case, such as other endowments of individuals, final outcome, particular access, responsibility, or tastes and preferences (see Chapter 16).

some "favoured principles." Technically, they consist of social freedom (as process-freedom) plus something that can be seen either as equal sharing of what is given – with the proper measure for the division – or as an initial equal possible allocation (Chapter 9). These general principles and their association in these ways are in fact very common, because they result from the respect of agency and the rationality of *prima facie* equality.[4] This normative structure thus is very standard with a wide scope of application (for instance, it constitutes the essence of Plato's and Aristotle's presentation of what they see as the common conception of justice). Since the policy respects individuals' choices in social freedom and allocates given resources only, it does not refer to individuals' self-interested preferences, although they of course determine the final allocation of goods, given the resource-sharing policy. Similarly, Pareto efficiency is required, from the principle of consensus or unanimity, but its only relevant consequence is basing the policy on inelastic items – the given resources – (which is also largely implied by process-freedom). Hence, although as a property of the final allocation of goods Pareto efficiency depends on individuals' self-interested preferences, its present use as a general principle for determining the policy does not make this policy depend on the specific preferences of the individuals. Concern about their preferences, information about them and resulting acts are left to the individuals themselves in respecting their social freedom. The basic reason for this property is that this moral philosophy is, in essence, a liberalism, although it is also egalitarian both in the sense of equal social freedom and of equal sharing of given resources properly considered or measured. Of course, information about preferences may yet be made necessary by issues of second best, market failures corrected by liberal social contracts, and microjustice or mesojustice.

3. HOMO ŒCONOMICUS ETHICUS: ACTING AND FEELING, AGENT AND SENTIENT BEING, FREEDOM AND HAPPINESS

The a priori possibly relevant criteria, principles, or methods constitute a well-defined set. Many that have not been proposed in the previous literature make as much sense as some or many that have. The problem is the allocation of goods or resources, or of means with which agents determine this allocation by their actions and interactions, such as incomes and rights, and of any kind of assets, powers, liabilities, or duties (beyond economics proper, the allocation can also concern positions, status, honours, and the like). This allocation is to social entities of various types, notably including individuals. Moral individualism proposes that the relevant issues are the benefits or costs that individuals receive or incur in the end. Most economic criteria thus consider allocation to individuals. Individualism

---

[4] The self-assignment ("natural" allocation) of the value of some capacities can be seen as an equal sharing with measure in availability for individual use (in particular, time of possible use). For macrojustice, it has been obtained that this holds for a part (at least) of productive capacities and all eudemonistic capacities. The issue of the rationality of equality is shortly considered.

also shows by the fact that the reasons and justification exclude reference to social status and corresponding a priori rights: the references are to characteristics of the individuals "as such."

Individuals have faculties, and two categories of them are considered and entail the main differences among the criteria: Individuals are both agents and sentient beings; they act from choice, and they experience feelings of various types which often have an aspect of satisfaction, pleasure or happiness or their opposite. Both their freedom and their happiness may be relevant. The corresponding values thus belong to two broad categories. One concerns individuals' freedom, which can take various forms and refer to various types of reasons, including means, rights, powers, opportunity, and reward, responsibility, and desert or merit from action. The other category of values includes happiness, satisfaction, lower suffering, pleasure, or "felicity" (individual "preference" can refer to satisfaction or to actual or potential free choice). The former values constitute the basis of liberalisms (respecting social freedom), more general "eleutherisms" (basically valuing freedom), and "responsibilisms," whereas the latter underlie eudemonisms, hedonisms, and "welfarism" (Hicks' term), including utilitarianism and "practical justice" (first take care of the most miserable).[5] Choice, implemented by acts, also constitutes a central topic of nonnormative economics, whereas the relevance of happiness is, in economics, practically restricted to moral considerations. A principle most often focuses on a value of one of these two types (although we will meet exceptions).[6] And eudemonisms sometimes rely on free choice and action for their implementation, thanks to the hypothesis that individuals "choose what makes them happier."

Both faculties are commonly represented, for an individual, by her preference ordering of alternatives, often representable by her "utility function" – the banner or totem concept of economics. These concepts are widespread, extremely convenient, and yet, indeed, also intrinsically quite strange. They will be discussed in the next chapter. They are often taken to represent either one or the other of these faculties. The individual chooses an alternative of highest possible rank. And she is happier, or more satisfied, with an alternative of higher rank. The coincidence of both meanings for the same preference ordering or utility function results from the hypothesis that individuals choose the alternative that makes them the happiest. If this is not just a way of speaking, or a quite particular conception – indeed, definition – of the concept of happiness, this relation constitutes a particular psychological assumption about individual behaviour or conduct, the "eudemonistic behavioural hypothesis." Historically, utility was first used both as representing happiness or pleasure and for theorizing consumer's choice. A family of scholars (led by Abraham Wald) then took the preference ordering to describe choice only, although not without some contradiction. Indeed, discarding happiness

---

[5] See Kolm 1971, Part III.
[6] For instance, the theory of "equivalence" considered in Chapter 26.

and considering observable choices only was favoured by many economists for its behaviourist flavour. Yet, the considered ordering structure resulted from a hypothesis about pure "rationality," notably including transitivity (A preferred to B and B preferred to C implies A preferred to C, and the like), whereas this hypothesis does not clearly result from observation and even – as it will be recalled – cannot, in a strict sense, be established by observation. Hence, this view is behaviourist in discarding consideration of mental states of happiness or satisfaction, but not as concerns a hypothesis of individual rationality – as it calls this structure – which is no less about psychology (and even, ultimately, defies observation and falsifiability – as we will see). Moreover, for normative concerns, satisfaction or happiness cannot be bypassed, and hence corresponding uses of utility or preference require these "tangible" meanings.

Hence, in the considered economic criteria, the sentient faculties are restricted to a one-dimensional appreciation meaning satisfaction, happiness, pleasure, "felicity," lower pain, and the like. Only one aspect, property, or dimension of individuals' sentiments, emotions, and feelings is considered – that which psychologists call their "valence" – and, for an individual, these aspects are assumed comparable and are aggregated (there is no consideration of various types of satisfaction, possibly of types that can hardly be compared). This comparability is of course an extraordinary assumption and a drastic simplification. It is also a strong limitation for ethics where the quality of sentiments is an important consideration (the pleasures from playing pushpin or from reading poetry for John Stuart Mill), and notably for social ethics where the nature of sentiments about others is a main value (the problem of comparing, balancing, and possibly "adding" pleasures from sadism, from consumption, or from loving or being loved). Scholars who doubt the meaningfulness of comparing the happiness of various individuals usually forget that it is not easier as concerns the alternative, successive, or simultaneous sentiments of the same individual. The eudemonistic behavioural hypothesis may solve the problem in the latter case in reducing it to observed choices. However, such choices are not available for some applications; in particular, they intrinsically cannot provide the required information when comparisons of preferences for the same individual (and *a fortiori* across individuals) are used in normative applications without the corresponding choice by the individuals; and this behavioural assumption itself needs further consideration of its psychological meaning and validity.

Individuals have, moreover, assets of various kinds that determine their possibilities of action and choice. Rights in capacities are among them. These assets are allocated by the considered normative choice, which can more or less endorse "natural allocations." These goods, resources, rights, capacities, incomes – and the "negative assets" of liabilities – determine individuals' domains of possible choices and actions, which can include interactions of all types with others, including exchanges and other agreements.

4. SUBSTANCE AND STRUCTURE

A distributive principle or criterion has both an ethics and conditions of application (in addition to its field of relevance). These conditions include possibilities, general or about policy instruments, and questions of information. The ethics itself is defined by two aspects, the *nature* of its basic moral concern, that is, its *substance*, and its *structure*.[7] Indeed, its ethical judgment, notably for comparing across individuals, is basically, ultimately concerned with items of the individuals called its *basic concerns* (the expression "individual basic concerns" refers to items of the individuals appraised by the judgment in question). The nature of these items is essential for characterizing the basic ethical nature of the principle. These basic moral concerns need not be direct instrumental or observational concerns. The direct instruments of the policy, or the observed or discussed items, may be other ones, but they relate to the basic concerns that constitute the ultimate reference for the judgment and the choice. Possible judgments of this ethics about such other items are indirect and derived from their relation with the basic concerns. This view may also hold that the ultimate important moral issues are about still other items, influenced by its basic concerns, but that their direct consideration is not relevant for the considered policy.[8] The basic concerns can for instance be about goods, incomes, freedoms, or satisfactions, in various possible specifications. They can be aspects of a state of affairs or variations in comparing two states. The relevance of these considerations is that – as we will see – basic concerns will be the objects of judgments of equivalence of permutations, and hence of ideal equality.

In contrast, the evaluation of the set of individual basic concerns of the judgment is the structure of this principle or criterion. It notably concerns the type of interpersonal comparison of these concerns. For instance, it may favour their equality, or their equality in proportion to or as a function of some characteristics of the individual ("to each according to her . . .", Plato's and Aristotle's "geometric equality"). Or the structure may favour the highest sum, which amounts to comparing variations for the individuals (e.g., utilitarianism, highest social income, highest amount of particular goods). But a noncomparing moral preference for improvement of the basic concerns for each individual is also an aspect of the structure of the principle ("benevolence"), as are other possible particular structures such as "independence" or "separability," assuming that only changing individual items are relevant for comparing various situations. The properties of the comparisons of inequalities in the basic concerns are typical structural properties. The structural properties of a principle – the properties of its structure – intricately associate logic or rationality with moral values (as

---

[7] The term "substance" is borrowed from scholastic philosophy, where it denotes that which is of the same relevant comparable nature in various manifestations or entities.

[8] For example, a judgment basically concerned with incomes or opportunities *may* hold that all that matters, in the end, is individuals' happiness, but that it does not consider it explicitly because obtaining it with the allocated means is the responsibility of the individuals, or because it is mediated by individuals' eudemonistic capacities which it deems to be inappropriate items for its own concern.

it will be emphasized as concerns impartiality, equality, or the comparison of inequalities).

The substance can be a freedom, and the principle is an *eleutherism* (and in particular a *liberalism* if it is social freedom), or happiness, satisfaction, or the like and the criterion is a *eudemonism*. Welfare – a term whose ambiguity will be pointed out – is the direct moral concern of "welfarism" (Hicks' term). Happiness or satisfaction can be described by preferences or utility with such a eudemonistic meaning (see Chapter 24). Freedom and the corresponding possibilities of free choice are determined by means of all kinds in the broadest sense, including goods that are further used (tools in a broad sense), assets (and liabilities), rights of all types (basic rights, specific rights, property rights, etc.), powers of all types (institutional, purchasing power, etc.), acquired or given capacities, and so on. Consumption goods are usually better considered for their own sake – although they are, in a sense, means of the activity of consumption (and for the ensuing satisfaction). Leisure and labour are types of goods which often have to be singled out. Income permits buying, and hence defines a freedom, although it is often directly considered as a synthetic good. It is amenable to several definitions (notably as concerns which earned or earnable income it includes).

The judgments sometimes bear on other items, possibly specifically concerning the individuals, which are not the considered basic concerns, but are related to them. Such judgments are *derived* from the basic moral judgment about the basic concerns, and from the relation between both. They are *indirect* moral judgments in this sense. Their use has several possible reasons: These other evaluated items may be more directly or easily observed – or even defined – than the basic concerns; they may constitute the policy instruments or be directly or clearly related to them; or the relevant structural properties may be more easily defined for them (e.g., in the case of the "equivalence theory" considered in Chapter 26).

An essential topic, belonging to both issues of substance and structure, concerns possible *characteristics* of the individuals, of which the judgment holds that the individual basic concerns should depend on them. These characteristics can for instance describe causes of needs, desert or merit, or previous specific rights. Such characteristics that can differ among the considered individuals have a crucial role for distributive justice. One can then consider jointly the direct concerns and these characteristics, for each individual, for defining the individual *exhaustive basic concern*. There may be no such relevant characteristics different across individuals; then, for the following, the exhaustive basic concerns can just be the basic concerns.

5. SYMMETRY AND EQUALITY

Demands for various kinds of equality are found everywhere. In both *Nicomachean Ethics* and *Eudemian Ethics*, and after Plato, Aristotle states that "Justice is equality, as everybody thinks it is, quite apart from any other consideration." He then categorizes the two great types of equalizands (see Chapter 16). Yet, even a believer in endogenous social choice is entitled to wonder why "everybody" thinks so. The basic point is that equality is required by rationality, at least *prime facie*, that is, in the absence of an overpowering reason such as impossibility or the requirement of something else which may be an ideal equality in something else. Only the weakest of common meaning of the concept of "rationality" is required here. Rational means "for a reason" (or for a valid or good reason), or justified. In fact, a close analysis shows that only the intention of providing a reason suffices for requiring *prima facie* equality.[9]

One aspect of this derivation of equality from rationality is trivial. Indeed, if I give something to someone for some reason that refers to some characteristics of this person, not giving the same thing to someone else who has the same exhaustive set of relevant (influential) characteristics, in the same conditions and possibilities, is irrational, or abitrary, and is resented as unjust for this reason. This is "equal treatment of equals," or, more precisely, "identical treatment of identicals in the relevant characteristics." However, the reason sometimes uses references to characteristics and allocations of other people, notably through comparisons. There also are cases where no specific reason at all is present, which means that the reason only is existence of this person in this situation. Moreover, we should know what to do when the considered equality is not possible, or interferes with other objectives (which may be an ideal equality in other items). For these reasons, the rationality of equality should be considered at a more general and deeper level. This also has the advantage of relating equality to more general logical property, that of the "symmetry" of the evaluation.

Let us thus consider an evaluation that is, to begin with, irrespective of possibilities and impossibilities, which will be introduced only later (this is the standard procedure in economics). However, it is also possible to consider some aspects of possibilities as characteristics of the individuals' situation (an issue that will not be precisely developed here). Similarly, the possible joint relevance of other evaluations will also be introduced later.

The consideration of the elements defined in the previous section leads to the basic property of equivalence of permutations. Indeed, if the exhaustive basic concerns for several individuals were exchanged or permuted among them, the new situation, although it would a priori be different for the individuals, would have no relevant difference with the former one for the considered evaluation or judgment. By construction, there exists no other relevant individual items, different across individuals, and invariant in the permutation, whose presence could induce such a difference – because they would be matched with different permuted items in the permutation. This equivalence under permutations is a logical and necessary property given the choice of the exhaustive basic concerns, hence of the basic concerns (substance) and of the attached relevant individual's characteristics. If the evaluation is representable by a function whose higher value

---

[9] See Kolm 1971 (translation 1998), Foreword, Section 5.

means better, then the considered property is the invariance of this function under permutations of the individual exhaustive basic concern, that is, its symmetry in these variables.

Some individual characteristics, notably among those the basic concerns should depend on, may be shifted into the definition of the basic concerns. For example, if someone should have something in proportion of some specific feature of hers, the basic concern can be directly expressed as this proportion. Consider now individuals such that there are no relevant characteristics left (outside the basic concerns) different from one to the other. Then, these basic concerns are exhaustive. Hence, the foregoing entails that the permutations of the basic concerns among these individuals present no relevant difference for the evaluation (they a priori do for each individual, though).

This absence of relevant difference entails that the present considerations can provide no basis for a reason that would select one situation among all those that are derived from it by such permutations. Now, the alternatives of a choice are defined as mutually exclusive. Hence, a full choice has to select a single one among them. If this choice is rational, the most basic sense of rationality implies that it intends to provide a reason, a justification; that is, it intends not to be arbitrary. This reason should thus point out this single selection. However, we have just seen that no such reason based on the considerations presented so far permits such a selection among states derived from each other by permutations of the basic concerns among the individuals. This constitutes a built-in irrationality, which disappears only when the permuted situations are in fact the same one, that is, when the basic concerns are identical among the considered individuals. This property is "identical treatment of individuals identical in relevant characteristics." It is derived from the minimal property of rationality or providing a reason – whatever it is. This constitutes the basic reason for equality.

One can easily show that selecting one of the permuted situations by a lottery (with equal probabilities) is not a satisfactory solution – although it sometimes constitutes a possible second-best method.[10] This justification of equality elicits a longer and more detailed discussion that need not be repeated here.[11] It should be emphasized, however, that the foregoing concerns only the considered evaluation, irrespective of possibilities and of the possible joint relevance of other principles. For instance, the considered permutations may not be actually possible. The considered equality may not be actually possible. All equalities in the considered basic concerns may be dominated by situations where these concerns are better for all individuals – although unequal – and this unanimous improvement may have to be favoured with priority. And so on. That is, the considered equality is only *ideal* or *prima facie* – that is, again, in the absence of an overpowering reason. The

---

[10] Equality in probabilities should itself be justified. Moreover, this is an inequality *ex ante* while the real world is *ex post*. And is it rational to leave the choice to the irrelevant dynamics of falling bodies – the criterion retained in flipping a coin?

[11] See Kolm 1971 (translation 1998), Foreword, Section 5.

presence of such reasons then leads to considering and defining corresponding second-best egalitarian criteria. The most common form of such criteria consists of choosing the lowest inequality among these basic concerns, subject to actual possibility and to other required or valued properties of the evaluation (maximins or leximins – shortly considered – are limiting cases of this method). Another form consists of obtaining the equality in some situation related to the actual one (as with notional freedoms or with the equivalence theory analyzed in forthcoming chapters).

6. COMPARING DIFFERENCES AND HIGHEST SUM

Even when the relevant equality is possible, or possible along with some other desired property (such as nondomination by other situations better for some individuals and worse for none), one may prefer some other situation if many individuals gain much from the change, while losers lose little and are few in number. In such comparisons, the actual direct concerns are in fact *variations* of the considered individual items between situations. If such comparisons are the only relevant ones, and when adding such items can be given a meaning, the principle generally becomes maximizing their sum.[12] Examples are utilitarianism (for which the question of the meaning of adding is raised in most cases – see next chapter), the highest social income (or its rate of growth), or the highest level of amounts of specific goods (whose quantity is either a priori well defined or results from some specific analysis as with health or education, for instance). Now, such principles raise a particular question about which social entity ultimately matters for them. They consider individual items. They are benevolent in the sense of preferring an improvement for each individual when the others' items do not change. They present the property of symmetry as invariance under permutations, which is a protoegalitarian property. They are "egalitarian" in the particular sense of John Stuart Mill's famous redundant and pleonasmic property: "each is to count for one and only for one." They also are in the other – related – particular sense that one unit more is equally valued whoever receives it. They compare across individuals when they consider variations. However, as concerns the items themselves, the principle of the highest sum (or average) is in itself no longer an individualistic principle. Rather, it is directly concerned about society as a whole. Correspondingly, it no longer favours equality or lower inequality among the individuals' items. This is neatly expressed by Rawls' criticism of utilitarianism on the grounds that "it does not take seriously the division of society in individuals" – although ideal equality among individuals is not very individualistic either, the most individualistic of standard views being, rather, classical liberalism, which

---

[12] When the nature of the items is such that their addition has no meaning, the criterion still provides results, although not so simple ones (see Chapter 24 and Kolm 1996a, 1996h).

only admits peaceful exchange, or even neo-"libertarianism" which does not even require a priori equal protective rights.

However, criteria commonly value both the individual items and their variations. They then qualify an ideal of equality in these items by some relevance in the comparison of their variations. This situation provides the basic material of the analyses of the comparisons and measures of inequalities. For instance, maximizing the sum equally values the same increase, whoever benefits from it; valuing more the same increase if it is received by someone who has less introduces a bias in favour of lower inequality, if the unchanged items can be discarded in the comparison (a critical qualification); and leximin, valuing any increase in a lower endowment more than any increase in a higher one, is still more egalitarian with, however, the same crucial assumption of discarding unchanged items in the comparison.[13]

7. ASSOCIATING CRITERIA OR PROPERTIES

More generally, an evaluation can associate various more elementary principles, criteria, or properties. This association can have various types of structures, which can be used jointly. It can consist of *compromises*, which can be of various types. For instance, compromises between the lowest inequality and the highest sum are found in inequality-averse maximands (and in a theory discussed in Appendix B of Chapter 25). It can also consist of *priorities*. For instance, favouring that one individual be favoured when the others' situation do not change, or *benevolence*, is often held with priority. It is for instance endorsed even if this improvement for one augments the inequality with individuals with worse positions. This secures Pareto efficiency when the individuals' preferences about their items that are the basic concerns of the evaluation coincide with this evaluation's appreciation of these items. The priority of the respect of basic rights is a classical position (formally endorsed by "democratic" regimes and by Rawls' theory, for instance). A third type of association is *superimposition*, whereby a principle is applied from the realization of another. A standard example is social freedom (notably free exchange) from identical individual allocations of goods. ELIE is such a case. Still another type of association is *equivalence*: several principles are applied in different situations that are "equivalent" in the sense that all individuals are indifferent between them (this will be fully analyzed in Chapter 26).

8. ETHICAL ORDERING OR MAXIMIZATION

The considered evaluations often take the form of an ordering of the possibilities, and in particular of a function to be maximized, or maximand. The basic justification is a property of transitivity of the evaluation (*A* better than *B* and *B* better

---

[13] See the Appendix A of this chapter.

than C implies A better than C, and so on), or equivalent properties using choice among more numerous alternatives (the alternative chosen in a set of alternatives does not change if some other, unchosen alternatives are withdrawn from this set). These properties, in the family of consistency, are not a priori necessary. For instance, the actually possible domains of choice may be specific and may not include the noted various choice situations, which may be held irrelevant for this reason. Even when these various domains are considered, the choices may not have the considered properties for quite valid reasons. Indeed, the considered structure is, more precisely, the existence of a preference ordering independent of the domain of choice. Now, it may be, for example, that the alternatives can be a priori ordered by some property (for example more right or more left, possibly in the political sense), and the choice may always be the middle (perhaps the median) of the possibilities, perhaps for a reason of balance, compromise, or following the "middle way" – this is an instance of a "positional choice." Such a choice may entail contradictory or intransitive preferences between pairs.[14] Basically, the consideration of a preference ordering or a maximand implies an a priori strong separation between the evaluation proposed by the principle and the applications to specific cases with particular possibilities. This may not hold in a number of cases where the evaluative discussion is closely related to the actual specific situation met. However, the representation of the evaluation by an ordering or a maximand is acceptable in other cases. It is, then, a particularly convenient analytical tool.

The properties of the principle or criterion then translate as mathematical properties of the maximand function (or ordering). This is a function of the representation of the basic concerns, with representations of the relevant individual characteristics as parameters. Yet, it can also be expressed as a function of other variables related to these, notably the instrumental variables of the policy (for instance, taxes or subsidies). Benevolence translates as this maximand being an increasing function of the proper representation of the basic concerns. Equivalence of permutations of the individual exhaustive basic concerns means that this maximand is a symmetrical function of the representations of these items. Egalitarianism is preference for lower inequality in the exhaustive basic concerns. It translates as the property that the maximand increases when the proper representation of these items become less unequal in some sense. This function then is an "inequality-averse" one. Since "less unequal" can be defined in various possible ways, this inequality aversion consists of a family of possible properties that depends on the possible meaningful structural properties of items in the nature of the considered exhaustive basic concerns. Inequality aversions have both a type

---

[14] If the basic ordering is described by the ordering of letters, if the set of possible alternatives is (a,b,c,d,e), then the middle c is chosen, while if d and e become impossible and the possibility set is reduced to (a,b,c), the middle b is chosen. Then, b and c are possible in both cases, while one is preferred to the other in one case and this "revealed" preference is reversed in the other: there is no a priori preference ordering of the items independent of the possibility set. Other cases of and reasons for not choosing according to an a priori preference ordering or maximand function are shown in Kolm 1992, 1995f, 1996a, Chapter 15, 2000c.

of structure and a relative intensity. Another notable – but not very general – property is that the preference between two states does not depend on the individual concerns that remain the same in both. For example, benevolence results from application of this property when only one individual concern changes, plus a favourable view of improvements in the situation of each individual taken by herself. Assumed for all possible changes, this property of "independence" or "separability" implies that a possible specification of the maximand has the form of a sum of functions of one individual concern each. For example, a sum of representations of the individual concerns display no inequality aversion and satisfies benevolence, and more generally this independence. Maximin and leximin (shortly considered in detail) manifest benevolence (for leximin), independence, and an inequality aversion constrained by these two properties.

9. MEANING AND STRUCTURE OF REPRESENTATIONS AND MEASURES

The foregoing considerations imply a major problem. On the one hand, the basic concerns of the principle or criterion about individuals have been considered with mention of their being notionally exchanged or substituted among individuals, equal among them, larger or smaller for the same individual or across individuals, and added across individuals with interpersonal comparison of their differences. On the other hand, it has been noted that the basic items of individualistic social evaluation were individuals' liberty or happiness (or concepts in the family of these). Can the noted comparisons and operations be applied to such items in a meaningful way? For instance, can one meaningfully add the happiness of various individuals (the answer turns out to be: only for small variations),[15] say that an individual is happier than another (answer: sometimes), say that the same individual is happier in one case than in another (answer: also sometimes), say that an individual is freer in one case than in another or freer than another individual (answer: occasionally), say that an individual is as free as another (same answer), add the freedoms of several individuals (exceptionally)?[16]

However, the case is sometimes better, essentially thanks to the question of assignment of accountability, which can make the individuals accountable for their tastes or eudomonistic capacities, or for their (free) choice. Indeed, if the individuals are accountable for their tastes and eudemonistic capacities, and for that only, the relevant direct concerns of the policy or judgment guided by the principle consist of the individuals' consumption goods represented, in the classical economic model, by the bundles (vectors) of their quantities. These are much handier items than "utilities"; they can unambiguously be added, multiplied by scalars, be equal across individuals in the sense of identical, and compared by "larger than"

---

[15] See Kolm 1996a, Chapters 12 and 14.

[16] For instance with the various situations and hypotheses that make an individual's freedom measurable by an income, the size of a bundle of goods in given proportions she can buy, and so on (see Chapter 24).

if the quantities of all goods of the bundles are in this relation. If, moreover, the individuals buy these goods with their income and are held accountable for this choice (possibly because they are responsible for it), the relevant direct concerns are incomes.[17] Then, all the foregoing operations are possible, and the comparison by larger, smaller, or equal is always possible. The relevant incomes can be of various possible kinds (for instance, ELIE is equal disposable income for some equal notional labour). In fact, income for given prices defines a domain of free choice. For other domains of choice, equality as identity and "smaller than" as inclusion are straightforwardly defined. So is, also, equal full social freedom from a given identical allocation (ELIE is an instance of this) or from allocations with more or less of all goods. And the larger satisfaction of a right or of a set of rights can also be considered. But other comparisons of freedoms and operations involving them raise problems.

In applications, the relevant considered concerns can consist of one quantity of the same given good for each individual. This is the actual field studied by the theory of income inequalities. The concern indeed is often an income. But individuals consume goods. If process-freedom is accepted, the individuals are responsible – and hence generally accountable – for spending their income in buying these goods, and this income can be the right concern. If this is not the case, or not the case for all the considered goods because some goods have no standard market or are "sphered" goods amenable to specific "spheres of justice," the relevant items are bundles of goods, some of which possibly being incomes representing the value of several goods (see Chapter 16; such specific goods can, for instance, be all or part of health, education, security, judicial services, culture, the environment, or the satisfaction of basic needs). Inequalities in bundles of goods are also well studied.[18] More generally, with free choice for which the individuals are responsible – and hence generally accountable – the relevant items become freedoms. This can be defined as domains of choice, or as social freedom from given allocations, with possible further limitations on the domains or scope of this freedom (there can be limits on act-freedom or on aim-freedom – as with taxation of outcomes, for instance). But there can also be, and there are for the general evaluation, concerns of other types, such as power, position, self-respect (three of Rawls' "primary goods"), consideration, dignity, honour, various types of rights and duties, and so on. Even with simply measurable goods, indivisibilities may interfere with issues of equality or equalization, and corresponding compensations require specification (lotteries and the allocation of probabilities may also be used, but they can create an equality *ex ante* only while the relevant allocation may be the resulting one *ex post*, and hence they can only be a last resort). And in strongly consequentialist ethics where the effects of all items are jointly relevant, the considered end-values may have to be happiness, satisfaction, lower suffering,

---

[17] This is the reason given in Kolm 1966a for focusing the analysis of economic inequalities on the logic of income inequalities.

[18] See Kolm 1977a, and the handbook edited by Jacques Silber (1999).

or pleasure. Moreover, there can be the imprecise concept of welfare (is it utility, income, or goods?) or the satisfaction of particular needs, notably the basic ones, with items that can be minimal levels of nutrition, health, housing, education and schooling, culture, and so on (these are not the most difficult of issues, though: general health is classically reduced to the quantity of the duration of life qualified for morbidity, years of schooling are measurable, and so on).[19]

A basic dilemma is then commonly faced as concerns the nature of the chosen variables because they should satisfy two types of requirements that may not be compatible: their properties should be actually meaningful given the nature of the relevant items, and they should have properties needed for the judgment, in particular for the interpersonal aggregation or comparison as concerns these variables or their variations, and for the definition of the relevant equalities and the comparison of inequalities. One can speak of twice richer or richer by ten dollars for one individual or for comparing between individuals. One can say as free or freer when domains of free choice are identical or when one is strictly included in the other, for one individual and for comparing between individuals (but can one still say that if the added possibilities are fully useless, noxious, or identical to former ones?). One can often say that one individual becomes happier, and sometimes unambiguously that one is happier than another. But how can one compare freedoms in other cases? Can one say twice as free or freer by one unit? Or twice as happy or happier by one unit? Should we dare, without shame, to mathematically add quantities of happiness or pleasure as utilitarians have done for a couple of centuries? Which strange hypothesis could lead John Nash (1950, 1953) to consider multiplying my extra happiness by yours – if happiness is what utility means – (the answer is cardinality plus equality in relevant outcomes).[20] Classifications by more or less are often meaningful. But twice happy, free, or honoured, or having one unit more of pleasure, opportunity, or dignity, hardly are. This is the problem of "actual" or "tangible" meaningfulness (as opposed to mathematical, or purely formal, meaningfulness). Meaninglessness in concepts or properties destroys the value of possible convenience in using or assuming them. However, rejecting a philosophical ethical approach because of a lack of

---

[19] This measure of inequality in health raises specific problems. One is the fact that living one year longer may be better at age 35 than both at 5 and at 95 – while receiving one dollar more is generally more appreciated the poorer the receiver is. Other questions are raised by the necessary limitation of life duration. (See Kolm 2002).

[20] See, for instance, the analysis in Kolm 1996a, Chapter 12, Appendix B. This result and utilitarianism are two of the instances of the use of cardinal utilities with a eudemonistic meaning (see Chapter 24). Other cardinal specifications of utility can be meaningful, notably that used for estimating probabilizable uncertainty (von Neumann-Morgenstern). In an early use of this latter concept, Friedman and Savage (1952) pointed out that it is "not for ethics" by which they probably mean not for use in a utilitarian sum intended to add "happinesses." A higher level of the noted utility can describe "more satisfied," and even probably "happier," but a comparison of differences in levels, which is mathematically meaningful for a cardinal utility, cannot have the corresponding meaning about happiness or satisfaction (see Chapter 24).

available concepts that could make it precise can be like looking for a lost object under the lamp because there is more light here even if it was lost elsewhere. Such situations are fields for research. Proxies can be used provided the approximation they provide is fully discussed and evaluated. The considered ethics may have to be reformulated and its role, scope, and possibilities reevaluated.[21]

10. EQUALITY AND INEQUALITIES

The basic properties of equivalence of permutations and equality, even when they remain ideals because of impossibilities or the joint relevance of other values, imply that an individual's item that is the basic concern of the evaluation can notionally be subsituted to that of another individual, and that permutations and equality of these items among individuals can be meaningfully defined. This very basis raises problems for some relevant types of items in the family of satisfaction or liberty. In fact, it is sometimes clear that someone is happier than someone else, but never that they are equally happy. The same can be said for comparing variations in satisfaction (which does not a priori mean mathematical differences). However, equalities may at any rate be impossible, and second-best solutions can consist of focusing on improving the lowest levels, which can sometimes clearly be identified. More generally, impossibility or the joint relevance of other values can lead to relying on second-best egalitarianisms aiming at lowering inequality in the considered items. However, comparing inequalities requires various comparisons of the individual items and of their variations for each individual and across individuals. In the end, the basic issue concerns comparisons of inequalities. This question is not a secondary, or purely technical and statistical, one. It lies at the heart of the social-ethical problem. And the possibility of facing it given the meaningful structural properties of the considered basic concerns is a central issue. Now, the theory of the comparison of inequalities is well developed for items that are the quantity of a good, such as an income; it exists for bundles of goods, for the property of comparing the items by "more or less" for each individual or across them (co-ordinal comparability), and for comparing freedoms – actual or potential ones (see Chapter 24). Properties such as equality, larger than, differences, additions, multiplications, averages, transfers, and so on, are meaningful in some cases, but not in others.

The comparison of inequalities rests on properties that raise a number of types of issues concerning their meaning. A property consists of considering two distributions of the considered items that differ in a certain well-defined way, and in considering that, as a consequence, one distribution is more, less, or as unequal than the other. The first question of meaning consists of the considered comparison,

---

[21] One can thus build an "ordinal utilitarianism" based on valid ordinal comparisons of ordinal comparisons noted in Chapter 24 (see Kolm 1996h).

difference, or transformation being logically meaningful, or not, with respect to the nature of the considered items (the issue of "twice happier," "freer by one unit," and so on). However, a property that is logically meaningful – or possible – in this respect, may have no clear meaning as concerns inequality (or injustice). This may hold either as concerns elaborate consideration or for normal intuition. Moreover, when such a meaning exists, it may concern either the formal aspect of inequality, or its ethical side as distributive injustice. Indeed, apart from any ethical consideration, there can be a kind of intuition about one of the two distributions being more or less unequal than the other, or about the possibility of assuming it. For instance, as concerns pairs of numbers, the pair (1,5) is doubtlessly more unequal than the equal pairs (3,3) or (6,6). It also very likely is more unequal than the pair (2,4) whose numbers 2 and 4 are both between 1 and 5. It even seems more unequal than the pair (11,15) (obtained in adding 10 to both numbers), and possibly less unequal than the pair (2,10) (obtained in doubling both numbers). And possibilities are much expanded for a larger number of items (population) – what about comparing the inequality of triplets (1,1,3) and (1,2,3)? Moreover, for the present issue inequality also means injustice, and not only dispersion, and also has to be appraised under this angle. For instance, it may be fair that all incomes be augmented by the same 10%, or that the overall increase be equally shared.

Any comparison by "more" suggests transitivity and an ordering. This holds for inequality, which can then generally be represented by an index, and possibly a measure. However, the ethical evaluation should encompass all relevant properties, such as, probably, preference for improvement for a single individual (benevolence), and others. The solution then consists of deriving measures of the relevant inequality with an ethical meaning as being distributive injustice implied by inequality-averse social-ethical maximands (see Chapter 22).[22] The analysis of inequality in the quantities of one good, usually taken as income, can use properties of addition, differences, transfers, multiplication by a scalar, averagings, or concavities of functions of which they are arguments. This has been extensively studied and is not further considered here because it is the main object of a recent handbook to which most scholars in the field contributed.[23] This was extended to the comparison of multidimensional inequalities, where the items are vectors of quantities, usually representing bundles of goods.[24] Inequalities for items solely compared by "more," for each individual and across them, have also been considered,[25] as inequalities in freedoms represented by actual or potential domains of possibilities comparable by inclusion.[26] Consideration will be restricted here to the firmest and most general basis for comparing inequalities, which also concern the properties that require the less structure.

---

[22] This approach is introduced and worked out in Kolm 1966a, Sections 6 and 7.
[23] Edited by Jacques Silber (1999).
[24] Kolm 1977a, and same reference.
[25] See Kolm 1971, and Appendix A.
[26] See Chapter 24 and Kolm 1993d, 1999b.

A basic property of the concept of equality is that it is a relation defined for pairs. With the kind of minimal structure where only (strict) equality is defined, for two items there are only two situations (equal and nonequal), but for a larger number there are other possibilities: lower overall inequality relates to clustering only, inequality is fully described by the distribution of the number of elements in clusters, and it can be measured by the fraction of pairs of items whose elements are equal. If, moreover, there is comparability by "more" or "larger than," both for each individual and across individuals, then one can accept more generally that the transformation of a pair by inclusion diminishes the inequality in the pair. But one should then consider the case of a larger number of items. In particular, the case where all pairs are transformed by inclusion, do not change, or have elements that are and remain equal, amounts to a "truncation" of the distribution, and discarding as irrelevant the items that do not change amounts to "leximin" (with other basic properties). Other possibilities appear when changes in items can be compared.[27] If, moreover, these comparisons can be about (mathematical) differences, the effects of transfers and of various types of averagings and concavity can be considered. The next step is the noted field of inequalities among quantities (such as incomes). Appendix A considers the case of preferences about inequalities based on pairwise inclusions.

Appendix A. INEQUALITY COMPARISONS BASED ON PAIRWISE INCLUSION: INCLUSION, TRANSFERS, LEXIMIN, TRUNCATION

A.1. General properties

One can trivially say that an equal distribution (that is, all items are equal or identical) is less unequal than an unequal one. But saying which of two unequal distributions is more or less unequal than the other is a priori elusive and ambiguous. Given two distributions, one can almost always find a priori valid reasons and measures that go both ways. Setting aside the noted case where only equal and unequal are defined, it may be that the only clear case occurs when there are only two items (for example, two individuals holding them), whose specifications can be ranked in order of desirability by numbers, and that vary such as (1,4) becoming (2,3), or, possibly, (1,3) or (2,4). Then inequality would be said to have decreased. The new numbers are *included* in the interval of the former; more precisely, their interval is strictly included in this interval. This comparison of inequality only rests on *ranking* comparisons of the single items. However, if there now are four items (for example, for four individuals), again amenable to ranks of desirability, and two of which are the former ones and vary as just indicated, while the two added are initially equal to the two former and do not change, the distribution passes from (1,1,4,4) to (1,2,3,4). The inequality in the changing pair can be said to decrease, as indicated. However, in contrast, *two equalities have been broken down*, (1,1) and (4,4). Hence, one cannot say a priori that the inequality of the

---

[27] See Chapter 24.

overall distribution has decreased. The comparison depends on further assumptions. If one attaches much importance to strict equality, then the overall inequality has increased. Note that this, again, only depends on the ranking of the numbers, and hence, on the comparability by ordering of the items. But, again in this framework, other assumptions about the concept of inequality can give opposite results. In particular, according to the inclusion criterion for pairs (including the cases where one item of the pair does not change), one can check that while the inequality has increased in two pairs, as noted, it has also decreased in three pairs. Moreover, the normative issue consists of choosing between these two situations or preferring one over the other, rather than comparing their inequality per se. Then, one might add the further assumption that items that do not vary could be discarded in the comparison, as a criterion with priority. This can be because the individuals holding these items are not concerned by the change. This irrelevance of unchanging items is a property of "independence" or "separability" (it is shortly shown that it can have two possible types of justification). Then, in the example, numbers 1 and 4 that do not change are discarded, and the comparison reduces to that of the initial pair of changing items, with a preference for the change if lower inequality is preferred. One does not say that the overall inequality has decreased, but only that the inequality in the pair of changing items has decreased, and the unchanging items are considered irrelevant for the choice or preference (but not a priori for the overall inequality). Moreover, if there is one item only – say one individual holding it – one would prefer this item to be better (for a reason of respect for this individual or benevolence toward her). Then, the irrelevance of unchanging items, applied to the case where one item only varies, leads to preferring a distribution when one item becomes better and the others do not change. This property, moreover, is held with priority in the face of possibly adverse effects by the property of *benevolence*. Of course, this improvement of one item augments the pairwise inequality of this item with all others that are not initially classified above, according to the preceding "inclusion" criterion (for example, (1,2) is preferred to (1,1) even though the pairwise inequality increases by the inclusion criterion).

A particular case occurs when the items have, in addition, the structure of being quantities whose measure provides the ranking. Incomes constitute an example. Then, the transformation of a pair by inclusion that maintains the total quantity is a transfer from the larger to the smaller of an amount lower than the difference or, if one wants not to reverse the ordering, not larger than half the difference. Such transfers may be called, respectively, an "extended progressive transfer" and a "progressive transfer." The preceding examples apply to this case and show that, if such transfers can probably be said to diminish the inequality in the pair, if there are more than two items (say, individuals), they cannot in general be said to diminish the overall inequality without further assumptions which are specific and particular.[28] However, these transformations may be favoured from a possible assumption of irrelevance of unchanged items (separability or independence) applied to these changes in pairs. One other property is indifference to permutations of the items, that is, "symmetry" of the evaluation, which is necessary when no other characteristics of the items (or of the individuals) than the

---

[28] This question is fully analyzed in Kolm 1999a.

considered representation are deemed relevant for the evaluation, and which can exist whatever the nature and structural properties of the items (for instance for ranks). Note that favouring extended progressive transfers implies this symmetry, while this is not the case for favouring progressive transfers. However, favouring progressive transfers implies this symmetry if the noted separability or independence holds for all changes in pairs (and hence also in larger numbers of items).[29] At any rate, both extended and simple progressive transfers amount to the same when this symmetry is assumed a priori. Favouring such transfers with symmetry-permutability and benevolence amounts to a dozen meaningful properties, including preference for a higher concentration curve (or Lorenz curve for a given total amount), Schur-concavity of an evaluation function (that is, a function whose higher level means preferred for the considered overall judgment), and so on.[30]

The property of irrelevance of the unchanging individual items for the overall evaluative preference (separability or independence) depends on which type of changes are considered. The first relevant aspect of changes concerns the number of items that change jointly: the cases of one, two, or any number have to be distinguished. Moreover, for pairwise changes, relevant cases are changes by inclusion when the items can be ranked by an order of value, and this case with constant sum (progressive transfers extended or not) when the items are quantities. Properties of orderings evaluating the overall distribution, or of functions representing them, are in particular considered. Irrelevance of unchanging items for changes of one item only leads to benevolence when improvement for each individual separately is favoured, and to an increasing evaluation function when each considered individual item is represented by a number that denotes its considered value. Consider now changes by pairs, for all pairs. If the items are ranked in an order of value for each considered individual and across them, pairwise changes by inclusion can be taken to imply lower inequality in the pair. A preference for any change in two individual items whose pair changes by inclusion, given benevolence and a continuous domain, amounts to leximin (see below). If, moreover, the items are quantities and changes are restricted to maintaining the sum, preference for extended progressive transfers, or for progressive transfers plus symmetry amounts to a Schur-concave evaluation function – preference for extended progressive transfers imply symmetry. Reverting to any kind of individual items, irrelevance of unchanging items for all changes in pairs, or in any number of items, amount to the same, and occur if and only if an evaluation function can be written as a sum of functions of an individual item each (for a sufficient domain of variation). When, moreover, these items are quantities of the same good (or of income), preference for progressive transfers then imply symmetry,[31] and the added functions of a single item are the same (with possible addition of a constant) and are concave.

[29] See Kolm 1966a, 1976a, 1976b. The properties noted in this paragraph and the next one imply various specific assumptions about domain or smoothness which can be found in the technical literature referred to.

[30] See Kolm 1966a, Sections 6 and 7, and the abundant further literature, notably the recent handbook edited by Jacques Silber (1999) – the concentration curve is statistics textbook name for the sum of the m lowest items as a function of m (or of m/n if n is the total number of items), and hence, the Lorenz curve is derived from it by dividing these sums by the total amount.

[31] See Kolm 1966a, 1976a, 1976b.

A.2. Lower inequality by inclusion in co-rankings

A.2.1. Pairwise inclusions

Let us focus now on comparisons by rankings only. The general notation considers n individuals indexed by the n first integers $i = 1, \ldots n$. Each individual is endowed with one item. The specifications of all these items can be ranked in a unique order of desirability representable by the set of real numbers (or a connected subset of it) and which describes all that is relevant for the considered question as concerns items and individuals. Then, individual i has such a number, x_i. The set or profile of these x_i, one for each individual, is denoted as $x = \{x_i\}$. Other specifications will be denoted as x_i', x', etc. Since only the rank order matters, the x_i can be replaced by $f(x_i)$ where f is any increasing function (the same for all i). The evaluation will be in the form of an ordering of the x, hence with the property of transitivity for comparisons between pairs of these profiles. The fact that the x_i describe all that is relevant implies that any permutation of the x_i among the individuals gives an equivalent set. This is the "symmetry" of the evaluation. Hence, profile x can be represented and replaced by its "ordered permutation", that is, it can be assumed, without loss of generality, that $i > j$ entails $x_i \geq x_j$, or $x_1 \leq x_2 \leq \cdots \leq x_n$.

When x becomes x', the pair (x_i, x_j) (with $i < j$) changes by *inclusion* if $x_i \leq x_i' \leq x_j' < x_j$ or $x_i < x_i' \leq x_j' \leq x_j$ (a strict inclusion of intervals), and by *full inclusion* if $x_i < x_i' \leq x_j' < x_j$. Then, the inequality in this pair can be said to correspondingly decrease.

A preference for a change in only one item by increase of this x_i is *benevolence*. It can be held for $n = 1$. From this case, it can be extended to any n by an assumption of *irrelevance* of unchanging items.

For two items (individuals) i and j, changes by inclusion that are not by full inclusion – that is, only one item changes – are evaluated by benevolence: a preference for an increase in the lowest level and the opposite for a decrease of the highest. Then, given benevolence, only changes by full inclusion need be considered. A *preference for pairwise full inclusion* means a preference for a change in only two levels that change by full inclusion. This can be held for $n = 2$ as a decrease in inequality. From this case, it can be extended to any n by an assumption either of *irrelevance* of unchanging items, or of *independence* of unchanging items and a preference for transformations by inclusion of all pairs that change. This independence means that the judgment about the change does not depend on the unchanging levels. Then, if the change is the pair (x_i, x_j) becoming (x_i', x_j') such that $x_i < x_i' \leq x_j' < x_j$, one can assume that all unchanging x_k for $k \neq i, j$ are such that $x_i' \leq x_k \leq x_j'$. Then, all pairs that change do it by inclusion, and the overall inequality can certainly be said to have decreased.

Preference for pairwise full inclusion implies that any decrease in one x_j to $x_j' < x_j$ is overcompensated by any increase in an x_i such that $x_i < x_i' < x_j$ (if x_i becomes x_i' such that $x_i' > x_j'$, the preference for full inclusion can be applied to x_j becoming the noted x_j' and x_i becoming ξ such that $x_i < \xi \leq x_j'$, and then the sole further increase of ξ to x_i, favoured by benevolence, yields the property). Of course, there generally is something shocking in the discontinuity that says that a decrease in a single x_i is bad while it becomes good if accompanied by a minute increase in a lower x_j. This in fact just shows the severe limitation of an assumption of non-comparability of variations (the adjective "minute" then is meaningless).

A.2.2. Meanings of leximin

For comparing several profiles, maximin is preferring the profile where the lowest level (number) is the highest. And leximin is preferring the profile where the lowest level that differs across profiles is the highest. Specifically, leximin is: of several profiles, prefer the one with the highest of the lowest levels; if the lowest levels are equal, prefer the profile with the smallest number of equal lowest levels; if these numbers are equal, prefer the profile with the highest of the second lowest levels; and so on. When the lowest levels are not different, maximin does not choose and leximin can be seen as its consistent extension in discarding the equal, unchanged lowest levels. Benevolence is preferring one level (for an individual) to be higher. Maximin can be seen as one stage further in preferring the lowest level to be higher irrespective of what happens to the others. And leximin can be seen as still one stage further in preferring any increase in a level to any increase in a higher level. In addition, an increase in a unique lowest level does not increase pairwise inequality with lower or initially equal levels as an increase in another level does (according to the inclusion criterion). In contrast, for leximin that does not reduce to maximin, the lowest level that increases inclusion augments its pairwise inequalities with initially lower or equal fixed levels. For two items (individuals), maximin and leximin amount to benevolence and preference for full inclusion – as shown by the consideration of the various cases.

Given two profiles x and x', denote as α the smallest number such that $x'_\alpha \neq x_\alpha$ (hence, if $\alpha > 1$, $x_i = x'_i$ for all $i < \alpha$). Then, if $x'_\alpha > x_\alpha$ for some $\alpha \leq n$, x' is preferred to x by *leximin*. Leximin implies benevolence and preference for pairwise full inclusion for any pair. For two individuals ($n = 2$), leximin is implied by benevolence and preference for full inclusion. For $n \geq 2$, assume a preference for pairwise full inclusion with benevolence (and symmetry) and consider two profiles x and x' with $x_\alpha < x'_\alpha$. Then, consider $n - \alpha$ numbers ξ_k indexed by the integer k from 1 to $n - \alpha$ such that $x_\alpha < \xi_1 < \xi_2 \ldots \xi_{n-\alpha} = x'_\alpha$. Now, in x replace x_α by ξ_1 and $x_{\alpha+1}$ by $x'_{\alpha+1}$. We have $x_\alpha < \xi_1 \leq x'_{\alpha+1}$ and $x_\alpha \leq x_{\alpha+1}$. If $x'_{\alpha+1} \geq x_{\alpha+1}$, the change is favoured by benevolence. If $x'_{\alpha+1} < x_{\alpha+1}$, and given that $x'_{\alpha+1} \geq \xi_1$, the change is favoured by the preference for pairwise full inclusion. Then, from the obtained profile, replace ξ_1 by ξ_2 and $x_{\alpha+2}$ by $x'_{\alpha+2}$. We have $\xi_1 < \xi_2$ and $\xi_1 < \xi_2 \leq x'_\alpha \leq x'_{\alpha+2}$. Then, if $x'_{\alpha+2} \geq x_{\alpha+2}$, this change is favoured by benevolence. If $x'_{\alpha+2} < x_{\alpha+2}$, and given that $x'_{\alpha+2} \geq \xi_2$, the change is favoured by the preference for pairwise full inclusion. Continuing, one reaches $\xi_{n-\alpha} = x'_\alpha$ and all the x_i for $i > \alpha$ have been replaced by x'_i, that is, the final profile is x'. Then, the transitivity of preference implies that x' is preferred to x. Therefore, with symmetry and benevolence, preference for pairwise full inclusion implies leximin. Conversely, leximin trivially implies preference for any pairwise full inclusion. These two properties thus logically amount to the same, with symmetry, benevolence, transitivity of preferences, and a continuum of possible levels.[32]

---

[32] See Kolm 1971 and Hammond 1976a.

This logical identity reveals the relation between leximin and egalitarianism. For only two individuals ($n = 2$), preference for inclusion clearly has a property of egalitarianism. It is, indeed, about all that can be done for describing lower inequality for items only comparable by ranking. However, a priority of benevolence excludes preferring (x_i', x_j') to (x_i, x_j) if $x_i = x_i' \leq x_j' < x_j$, and implies preferring it if $x_i < x_i' \leq x_j' = x_j$, and hence the egalitarian preference consists of adding a preference for full inclusion. However, with a larger number of individuals, the transformation of x into x' with $x_i < x_i' \leq x_j' < x_j$ and $x_k' = x_k$ for all $k \neq i, j$ entails that the pairs (x_k, x_i) for $x_k \leq x_i$ and (x_j, x_k) for $x_k \geq x_j$ become more unequal with the criterion of inclusion (not necessarily full one). In particular, equalities are broken down for $x_k = x_i$ or $x_k = x_j$. Hence, the effect on the overall inequality is questionable. The properties of irrelevance or independence of the unchanging items (independence or separability) are rather particular. However, the pairs (x_i, x_k) for $x_k \geq x_i'$ and (x_k, x_j) for $x_k \leq x_j'$ become less unequal according to the same criterion. For each $x_k \leq x_i$ and $x_k \geq x_j$, inequality increases with one of the changing items and decreases with the other, in this sense. If the variations are sufficiently small so that none of the changing levels crosses one of the fixed ones, *the number of inequalities that decrease exceeds that of inequalities that increase, according to this inclusion principle.* Indeed, for each level outside the new interval of the changing levels, inequality increases with one of them and decreases with the other; and all the other pairwise inequalities either decrease – between each changing level and both the other one and each fixed level between their initial levels – or are between fixed levels. And a change can always be conceived of as a sequence of changes that respects this noncrossing property. This counting is, in the end, the basic sense in which a change by pairwise inclusion, and hence leximin, is egalitarian. This sense is not direct. Hence, leximin and maximin (when $\alpha = 1$) are much more driven by comparative benevolence and charity than by egalitarianism.

Moreover, in most cases where leximin is considered, one is de facto naturally led to compare situations in comparing variations of individuals' items and levels from one to the other, and differences in individuals' items and levels in each, and in evaluating the set of these individual variations (including comparing the numbers of individuals who gain and who lose) and the variation of these interindividual differences – these comparisons do not imply going as far as resorting to measures by quantities, which may be meaningless. For instance, leximin may lead to choosing a gain for someone only slightly worse off than the others at the cost of losses for very numerous others, or a tiny gain for the worst off at the cost of large losses for many others.[33] These comparisons no longer use only a ranking of the items, but also rank and compare their variations. The meaningful properties in these views have to be extracted and put to applications.[34] If one can go to measures by quantities, one is led to the considerations of previous sections and to the analysis of "income" inequalities.

A.2.3. Truncations

Finally, the criterion of pairwise inclusion certainly leads to a decrease in overall inequality if *all pairs that change either are transformed by pairwise inclusion or remain*

---

[33] This remark is the last sentence of the monograph *Justice and Equity* (1971), the third part of which notably focuses on leximin in ordinal comparable (co-ordinal) utilities.
[34] See Kolm 1996a, Chapter 12 (Appendix A), 1996h, and Chapter 24 below as concerns happiness.

equal. This amounts to a *truncation,* that is, *all levels higher than a certain level are reduced to this level and all levels lower than a certain level are augmented to this level.* Indeed, consider a *continuous progressive* change where, at each time, all the highest levels decrease equally (each remains a highest) and/or all the lowest levels increase equally (each remains a lowest), and the others do not change. Inequality permanently decreases according to the noted principle, no other transformation has this property, and the final result is a truncation. This result more exactly is a *bitruncation,* by higher values and by lower values. It reduces to a *simple truncation* if either the highest levels or the lowest levels do not change (they are a *truncation of lower levels* or a lower truncation, and a *truncation of higher levels* or a higher truncation, respectively). A sequence of truncations is a truncation. A proper bitruncation associates a higher truncation and a lower one, and can result from their sequence. A sequence of truncations where one highest new level is not higher than one lowest new level leads to a complete equalization, which can be at any level. Truncations apply to items that need only be compared by rank order (that is, it is an "ordinal comparison"). Benevolence suffices for favouring a simple lower truncation and for rejecting a simple higher truncation. Bitruncations extend pairwise inclusions to which they reduce when there are only two (unequal) items, and proper bitruncations where both the highest and the lowest levels change to extend full inclusions. When the items are measured as quantities (for example, incomes) one can define "constant-sum (bi)truncations," where the total sum is maintained. Comparability by truncation is a priori particular, as opposed to leximin, for instance, which applies to all profiles. It is used for specific transformations. Of course, it writes as the fact that there are two levels, a and b with $a \geq b$, and x is transformed into x' such that $x'_i = x_i$ if $a \geq x_i \geq b$, $x'_i = a$ if $x_i \geq a$, and $x'_i = b$ if $x_i \leq b$ (this becomes simple truncations for sufficiently high a or low b).

The foregoing has thus shown the two basic comparisons of inequality based on the ordinal comparability of items only, and hence, on the decrease of inequality in a pair due to comparison by inclusion. Benevolence and impartiality (invariance under permutation) are assumed. When all pairs that change do it by inclusion or by the reverse transformation, a preference for the fact that more pairs become more equal by inclusion than incur the reverse transformation amounts to leximin. And a preference for all pairs that change and do not remain equal becoming more equal by inclusion amounts to a preference for truncation. However, truncation cannot compare all distributions, whereas leximin can.

Appendix B. ON METHOD

Economics is defined by its subject matter – say, the allocation of goods – but it is characterized by its concepts, which, in the end, come to constitute a genuine world-view (or underlie or manifest one), no matter how particular and peculiar this picture of man and society is. These concepts are few in number and can be combined for proposing normative properties, criteria, or principles in limited number, although most have not been explicitly stated yet (many of these are no less interesting than some that have already been proposed). The ingredients and their alternative properties will notably be: individuals and other agents (households, firms, government, other group) in various fixed or variable possible numbers; preferences and utility functions; free choice and exchange; domains of choice and their structure; goods (one or several, measurable by a quantity, divisible or with indivisibility, private or "public," etc.); labour and leisure more or less as particular goods; transformation and production with various structures (types of "returns"); prices (including wages); incomes (including the value of leisure or not, earned or not); interactions and "games"; social evaluation functions or orderings and their structure; time; uncertainty. Combinations of these various elements lead to possible criteria in a number that is notable – due to combinatorics – yet limited, say a few hundred (it sometimes is ambiguous whether a property can be called a criterion, and an arbitrary parameter is taken to be a feature of one and the same criterion, except for its particularly meaningful values). As noted, many criteria or principles have not been explicitly stated yet are no less interesting than some that have. The criteria or principles can be classified in categories of various types (such as based on freedom or on utility, simple or combined, maximizing or egalitarian, using such structures of goods or utilities, and so on). The concepts have a mathematical representation. The logical (mathematical) relations between properties and principles or criteria are clear and important.

These principles or criteria have properties.[35] A property has two aspects: a formal or mathematical expression, and its meaning as concerns the real world, its "actual," "real," or "tangible" meaning concerning psychology, technology, sociology, or ethics (or just common sense). The relation between both aspects of properties constitute a fundamental issue. Sometimes, a tangible property has a clear mathematical expression (e.g., increasing utility functions or social-ethical maximand). But it often happens that clear and neat mathematical properties, which are convenient or enticing for this reason, raise problems as concerns their tangible meaning. Indeed, this meaning is sometimes clearly absurd and nonsensical (Chapter 24 will call back to mind examples as concerns measures of utility or freedoms). It sometimes is nonexistent: no tangible meaning can be given to the property which, however, may have important consequences. Then, the property is arbitrary from this point of view. It also happens that the acceptable tangible meaning is restricted to particular domains or cases that, then, should be specified and respected (examples will be provided). And the issue of the tangible meaning sometimes requires a serious analysis on ethical, psychological, or social grounds (for instance, this is often the case for various properties of separability, independence, additivity, homogeneity, invariance to replication or separation, and so on) – this analysis is rarely done, it is sometimes possible, and its conclusion for the property depends on the case. Moreover, a number of relevant and important psychological, social or ethical variables, concepts, or properties have no clear, simple, or obvious mathematical representation (for example, self-respect, honour, social status, many aspects of power or of freedom, and so on) – so representing such concepts can constitute topics of analysis (which may or may not be worthwhile).

The analysis of the logical or mathematical relations between the properties of principles or criteria constitutes a field of study. A school of thought emphasizes the derivation of the principle or criterion as a necessary – in fact, mathematical – consequence of a number of properties that are seen as particularly elementary and basic.

---

[35] Some simple properties are also seen as principles (e.g., Pareto efficiency).

These latter properties are naturally called "axioms," and this approach is labelled "axiomatics." Such presentations rest on the assumption that the value of the principle is justified by that of the axioms that imply it. This epistemic stand is taken as a matter of fact, basically implicitly, without the suggestion that it could need a discussion. Such a discussion is outlined shortly. Whatever its conclusion, such theorems reveal some deep structure and a possible logical meaning of the principle.[36] Whether this relation is important certainly depends on the case. A basic point concerns the "tangible" meaning of the axioms. It is sometimes rather clear and important (e.g., Pareto efficiency, or symmetry which is discussed in Section 5). However, "axioms" are often of the types noted above for which the question of their tangible meaning raises a problem. Many of them are in the category of separabilities, independences, invariances, effects of replication or of partition, and so on, with a clear and neat mathematical meaning but whose ethical, psychological, or sociological significance and meaning require analysis. Others do not have such tangible meanings. Their presence may only manifest convenience or relative simplicity. However, it should then be checked that assuming these properties is sufficiently innocuous. In all cases – notably when there is no pure and clear strong tangible meaning – the various implications or aspects of the property, or ways of seeing it, should be considered.[37] Still other properties may be clearly meaningless, nonsensical, or absurd, as with examples noted in the next chapter about utility or freedom. However, some of them may be valid in a certain domain, for some applications, and then it should be checked that these cases suffice for the derivation, or as convenient approximations (and then it should be proven that their distortion of reality is acceptable).[38]

A frequent question in such studies is the use of counterfactuals. A counterfactual is a case that does not exist but whose idea influences a conclusion or a choice. The use of counterfactuals is frequent and, in a sense, unavoidable, in the statement, derivation or choice of laws of all kinds, principles, rules, or criteria (whether factual, scientific, social, legal, moral, and so on). These uses say: if *a* were the case, then *b* would or should occur. However, the validity of conclusions (such as the choice of a rule or principle) derived from the use of counterfactuals should be carefully considered. Some counterfactuals will undoubtedly never be the case; some are impossible; some are absurd. Others may create a different situation such that the same rule need not apply, or should not apply. The assumed domain of applicability of the considered principle or criterion is crucial. In particular, most "impossibility" results, stating the non-existence of rules (principle, law) with a given set of desired properties, crucially rest on overextensions of the domains of applicability required a priori.[39]

At any rate, however, such "axiomatic" theorems a priori reveal basic structures of the principles, and hence it can be proposed that knowing them is necessary for having

---

[36] We benefit from an outstanding exhaustive presentation of the technique of the axiomatic method and of its achievements with Thomson (2001) – see also Moulin and Thomson (1997).

[37] For example, this is done systematically for the properties of measures of inequality and of inequality-averse maximand functions in Kolm 1999a.

[38] For instance, as concerns domain, it is frequent that properties in the family of linearity are valid for small variations. Another, related example is the meaningfulness of eudemonistic cardinal utility in domains of near indifference (see Chapter 24).

[39] Including Arrow's (1951, 1963). See Kolm 1992, 1995f (and 1996a, Chapter 15), which develop the theory of counterfactuals.

a full understanding of the principles, both if the axioms are sufficiently meaningful on tangible or formal grounds and if they are not. Finally, these theorems can be more or less helpful for judging the principles. Yet, the basic philosophical issue is whether the set of axioms suffices for this evaluation or not. Now, a positive answer turns out to be about the opposite of the most standard methodological position in ethics, which says that a principle has a priori to be evaluated from all its angles. Then, the principle would be evaluated in considering its presentation and definition (or its several equivalent definitions), its properties, the sets of "axioms" that imply it, its possible consequences when it is actually applied, and by comparison with others principles, properties, or cases of application. This evaluation can notably be performed in considering back and forth the various aspects, in consequently iteratively adjusting one's judgment, until an equilibrium is reached. This is about what Plato calls "dialectics" in *The Republic*. Applied to the principle and its consequences in applications, this constitutes John Rawls' "reflective equilibrium." Many scholars have emphasized such an iterative approach in the form of a dialog. This is in particular the case of Jürgen Habermas' and Karl-Otto Apel's "discourse ethics." Although these two approaches – "axiomatics" and "dialectics," say – reflect the structure of main traditions in mathematics and philosophy respectively, they identify with neither of these disciplines, since "axioms" used for ethical conclusions need a "philosophical" discussion, and dialog can be mathematically formalized (see Chapter 20).[40]

The method that has been used here is deductive, deriving its result from a single basic principle, endogenous social choice applied as unanimity of properly considered views, applied to the defined question of macrojustice, and given a number of relevant facts. A first consequence was Pareto-efficiency and social freedom. Then came the ELIE distributive structure, and the methods for determining coefficient k. This deduction, however, is not along the sole lines of formal "axiomatics," although the ELIE structure can be so presented and derived.[41] Various properties and consequences of this distribution have been presented (for example, in Chapters 7, 9, 11, and 14), and this result is compared with other proposals (notably in Parts III and V of this study), but these considerations play no role in the derivation. A theory of dialog has played a role in the determination of coefficient k, but as a consequence of the general property of finding the solution in people's properly informed opinion.

[40] And Kolm 2000a.

[41] A derivation, from such "axioms," of an allocation that amounts to the outcome, after individuals' choice, of an EDIE, has been proposed by F. Maniquet (1998a, 1998b). The previous analyses of ELIE (Kolm 1966b, 1993b, 1996a, 1996b, 1997b) were along the lines presented here. See Appendix A in Chapter 25.

24

Freedom and happiness

1. PRESENTATION: TWO POLAR VALUES AND INTERMEDIATE ONES

Chapter 23 emphasized the general structural properties of distributive principles. The present chapter focuses on issues concerning their "substance," their material, or their basic concern. For individualistic principles, this material belongs to one of two broad families: freedom and possibilities, on the one hand, and happiness, satisfaction, or just preference, on the other hand. Both have held a central place in the normative side of economics for centuries, and, on the whole, freedom, with liberalism, has probably been the most important. Freedom is directly relevant – and, indeed, essential – for macrojustice. It has thus been discussed in Part I of this study for this application, and more broadly in Chapter 22 for comparison with various brands of economic thought. The present chapter is thus restricted, for both fields, to briefly pointing out the main applications, and to discussions of critical points, notably the interpersonal comparisons of freedom and of happiness that are, by logical necessity, required by the corresponding principles.

Indeed, we have seen that principles of justice require the interpersonal comparability of their basic concerns, whether they are the items or their variations, by logical necessity. Equality across individuals has to be considered across states for defining the basic property of nondiscernable permutations, in the same state for defining the ideal equality, and in comparing various states when differences in individual items across states are relevant. Hence, there necessarily exist some – at least one – of the problems of the possible meaning of an individual being as free or as happy as another, or of their having the same extra freedom or extra happiness. However, constraints of the world often prevent the realization of the corresponding first-best justice. One then has to resort to second-best solutions, which replace equalities by criteria using comparisons by more or less. Hence, these constraints that prevent reaching the first-best optimum are commonly welcome from a conceptual point of view, because they permit restricting worries to the possible meaning of individuals being freer or happier than others, or having more extra freedom or happiness than others, which is often clearer than the corresponding

417

equalities. In fact, it is often by no means clear and easy to say when the *same* individual in various situations is as free or as happy, freer or happier, or equally freer or happier. Now, classical theories assume that, as concerns happiness, the comparisons are straightforward for the same individual. Yet, psychological realism shows that this is far from being the case. This is worrisome because it shows a priori the possible difficulties in interpersonal comparisons, but also reassuring since we have at any rate to consider individual improvements in the chosen value.

However, other items, related to these two and more or less intermediate, may be the relevant ones, and they may offer different possibilities for the various comparisons. They are preferences, goods, incomes, and other means of various types. Individual preference orderings, or ordinal utility functions are, in the classical economic model of humans, the structure that fully determines the choices of the individual, and hence her actions. Intensity of preferences, which may have some meaning related to the comparison of happiness or satisfaction for the individual, are irrelevant for this choice and the ensuing action. Hence, the rest of society is actually concerned with these preference orderings (or corresponding ordinal utility functions) only. The intensity – whatever it may mean – can thus be seen as a private concern only. Of course, this discards benevolence, pity, compassion, or envying others' happiness, as irrelevant for the present considerations about justice, and they may just be absent. This provides a possible reason for focusing on individuals' (ordinal) preferences and discarding any consideration of intensity. This is, for instance, met in criteria such as Pareto efficiency, individuals' preferences among their situation and those of others (Section 2.4), and the theory of "equivalence" (discussed in Chapter 26). If, moreover, the whole of satisfaction and preferences is considered a private matter and is discarded as irrelevant for the direct evaluation, the direct concern becomes the bundle of consumption goods. And if the individuals are held accountable (possibly because they are responsible) for the choice of these goods with their income in given markets, the relevant items become incomes. Market prices and conditions may then be accepted as legitimate because they result from free exchange, endorsed as social freedom. At any rate, with given market prices and conditions, income defines a domain of choice, the budget set, and this basic concern is already a case of liberty (specifically analyzed in Section 2.3).

In fact, the relevant qualifications make the two polar values, freedom and happiness, closer to one another and, in the end, identical. We just saw how dropping items from relevance produces a chain of intermediate cases. Moreover, if happiness or satisfaction motivates preference, and hence choice that freedom permits, the two notions imply each other. Indeed, an individual can make choices that satisfy her more when she is relevantly freer, and hence she prefers to be so freer if the costs of choosing, the anguish of choice (emphasized by Jean-Paul Sartre), or the fear of responsibility do not spoil this benefit – sufficient mental freedom permits getting rid of the last two reasons for shunning liberty. And if someone seeking satisfaction or happiness becomes more satisfied, this implies that constraints of some kind have been pushed back (this may be some mental obstacle). Moreover, as concerns mental freedom, the relations with happiness in the deepest sense become very close, intricate, and elaborate, indeed in the direction of identity, but this most important relation of all is beyond the present topic.[1] In contrast, at the core of the economic vision is the close relation between the interpersonal comparisons of the two values when eudemonism is reduced to preference and freedom is extended to potential freedom, expressed by the theorem stating that an overall allocation can result from individuals' free choices in identical domains if and only if no individual prefers any other's allocation to her own (see Section 2).

The next two sections respectively correspond to these two values. The first one, concerned with freedoms, begins with pointing out the polar types of liberty relevant for economic ethics, social freedom defined by the nature of the constraint, and freedom a priori defined by the domains of choice. The corresponding equalities are satisfied by social freedom from an equal allocation in one case, and notably by identical domains of choice in the other. However, these conditions may not be possible or compatible with other required properties such as Pareto efficiency. For social freedom, minimizing the inequality in the initial allocations provides second-best solutions resting on the well-studied comparison of inequalities.[2] For freedom a priori defined by domains of choice, equal freedom provided by different domains can be considered. If this does not suffice, one can base second-best freedom-egalitarian solutions on orderings of the domains of choice, according to the freedom they provide. An example is provided with the case of freedom provided by budget sets (Section 2.2). Moreover, for freedom solely valued for the choice it permits, the respect of individuals' preferences leads one to consider as equivalent domains of choice that lead the individual to the same choice. Then, interpersonal comparison can be made either between the equivalent budget sets (as just noted), or by the inclusion (or identity) of equivalent domains. This latter case provides the theory of general potential freedom. In particular, we have pointed out that the corresponding identity of domains amounts to the principle that no individual prefers any other's allocation to her own; this is the starting point of a whole family of criteria (Section 2.4). More generally, this theory permits the comparison of individuals' situations by the inclusion of domains of choice that would lead them to chose their actual allocation (Section 2.3); then, Pareto efficiency generally implies a corresponding ranking of these individual situations, whence the possibility of defining Pareto-efficient second-best freedom-egalitarian solutions.

---

[1] This is the main topic of the study *Happiness-Freedom* (Kolm 1982a, and 1994).

[2] Income or unidimensional inequalities if the goods are all marketable at the same price for all agents, or, otherwise (including the case of labour and wages), multidimensional inequalities (see Kolm 1977a, and the *Handbook*, edited by Silber 1999). For application to ELIE and the effects of questions of information, see Chapter 10 and notably its Appendix B.

Moreover, a large number of economic principles are directly based on concepts of preferences, utility, satisfaction, happiness, or welfare. Section 2 discusses the possible meanings and basic properties of these notions. All these concepts can have various normative uses, but the justification of the underlying psychological model requires a close scruting (Section 3.1). It is then remarked that cardinal utilities meaning happiness or satisfaction, which are used by many classical economic criteria (utilitarianism is one of them), are clearly devoid of meaning, except in particular circumstances (notably for situations of near indifference). However, there exist psychologically meaningful structural properties of preferences beyond the sole ordering, notably ordering comparisons of pairwise ordering comparisons (Section 3.2). Although the concept of welfare is too ambiguous for scientific use (Section 3.3), that of happiness is unavoidable and the corresponding comparabilities both for the same individual and across individuals are discussed (Section 3.4).

2. FREEDOMS

2.1. Allocative freedoms

Two kinds of characterization of freedom are particularly relevant in the field of allocative criteria. One concerns social freedom (notably as process-freedom) – precisely defined in Chapter 2. The other consists of characterizing freedom by the domain of possible choice, that is, the set of possible alternatives, including the description of the consequences of action. Social freedom implies the relevant freedom of action, possibly including exchanges or free agreements among agents. In such interactions, the domain of possible choice for an individual can depend on others' actions, hence on their preferences, means, information, and expectations, on the expectation of these actions, hence on the full resulting strategic and game-theoretic aspects of the situation, on the possibilities of previous exchange of information, on the various conditions of exchange or bargaining, and on relative bargaining powers. The representation becomes simpler in situations of exchange in perfectly competitive markets. In all cases, the domains of possible choice can often be expressed in several alternative spaces representing more or less final items or means for the chooser. For concerns such as the present one, they are often considered in the space of final consumption (leisure can be one good). They can also – notably here – be expressed in the space of income and leisure or labour, its complement; income then essentially represents the goods it can buy (and, then, it should not include the value of leisure measured at its market price, which is the individuals' wage rate; that is, it should not be "total income").

The difference between these two concepts of freedom appears most clearly when equal freedom has to be considered. With social freedom, the basic principle will be free action or exchange from an equal (identical) allocation. If this equal allocation represents an equal sharing of what is given, then, with process-freedom, such solutions are in the family of the structure of justice pointed out by Plato and Aristotle with "arithmetic" equality for sharing what is given and the "geometric equality" obtained in exchanging. The agents (e.g., individuals) may face the same competitive conditions from this equal allocation. Two cases should then be distinguished. If all the considered goods are transferable among these agents, they face the same competitive prices, and hence, identical domains of choice. However, this is not the case notably when the agents are individuals, leisure is one of the considered goods, and individual productivities differ.

With freedom a priori characterized by the domain of possible choice, equal freedom is achieved by the identity of this domain. In fact, the rational necessity of interpersonal equality (pointed out in Chapter 23) more precisely is "*prima facie* identity of the relevant items for individuals identical in the relevant characteristics." Moreover, inclusion of these domains doubtlessly implies the corresponding comparison "no less free" and "no freer." However, one may have to retain a broader definition of equal freedom and of the corresponding comparison of freedom by more or less, also applicable to domains of freedom that can intersect or be disjoint. A correponding ordering of the domains of choice is considered. Identity of domains imply as free as, and, if a domain is included in another, choice in the latter is no less free than choice in the former and choice in the former is no freer than choice in the latter (strict inclusion may not correspond to strictly less free and freer when the difference does not really correspond to new possible alternatives – when its alternatives are identical to other possible alternatives, or, possibly, when they will certainly not be chosen). This ordering may be representable by an ordinal *freedom function* depending on the domain of choice, although there are also other cases where the ordering has a lexical structure with an order of priority for comparing various aspects of freedom, for instance when basic freedoms with such a priority are considered (but full basic rights are a priori assumed here).

If this ordering compares domains independently of choosers, it constitutes a co-ordering of domains. If domains are the only basic concern, each situation is relevantly constituted, for its evaluation, by a set of n domains, one for each agent. Then, the full logic of co-ordering applies, as in Chapter 23 (and Kolm 1971, Part 3). Possible situations are considered, with possible other required properties, notably Pareto efficiency. Then, cases of equal freedom are considered, and one of them is chosen. If none exists with the required properties, the theory of co-ordinal comparisons provide the concepts and properties of second-best egalitarian solutions with, notably, the concepts and properties of truncations, maximins, and leximins. However, the case is straightforward only when agents' considered possibilities do not depend on the considered choices of other agents. Otherwise, all comparisons across individuals require a particular analysis.[3]

---

[3] See Kolm 1993d. For instance, equal freedom then amounts to the appropriate symmetry in the game-theoretic structure describing the interaction.

The possibilities of comparing freedoms by their domains of choice depend on the specific problem. When the alternatives are bundles of goods and the domains are budget sets, the case where prices and incomes can vary will be considered in Section 2.2. This extends the case considered for the choice of labour and income in Chapter 9, that is, "output-freedom," with a freedom function depending on the transfer and on the wage rate, with the result that ELIE corresponds to freedom functions that can be linear (see Appendix B of Chapter 9). Domains can sometimes be relevantly represented by one comparable parameter while the others are fixed. For instance, for domains of choice of labour-leisure and income-consumption with given, generally different, individual productivities, such a parameter can be disposable income for given labour. Then, interpersonal equality with free redistributive transfers are ELIE schemes. This is, in fact, a case of social freedom. If the relevant equalization is prevented by any kind of constraints (including, possibly, those due to gathering the relevant information), the solution can be the maximization of an increasing, symmetrical, inequality-averse function of these equal-labour disposable incomes with maximin or leximin a limiting case (see the Appendix of Chapter 10).

Freedoms can also be compared by their value. An agent can value her freedom for many different reasons.[4] She can also shun freedom because of the costs of choosing, an aversion for responsibility, and the "anguish of choice." However, the most common value of freedom is that it permits the actualization of the alternative chosen by the agent. This can be called the instrumental value of freedom.[5] For an agent, all domains of choice that lead to choosing the same alternative have the same instrumental value. "Instrumental freedom" denotes freedom whose only value is this instrumental value (there is no other reason for liking or for disliking this freedom). Freedoms can be compared, or possibly "measured," by their value. This may be straightforward for the same sufficiently described agent. Across agents, the possibility depends on the case. One may compare the value for firms by the benefit they can derive. However, across individuals, the issue is akin to interpersonal comparisons of values, utilities, or satisfaction, considered here shortly.

Hence, one possible solution, for a normative evaluation both based on freedom and respecting individuals' own evaluations of their situation, consists of so comparing the liberties for each individual, while across individuals freedoms are only compared by inclusion of domains. For instrumental freedom, this leads to the theory of potential freedom noted in Section 2.3.[6]

---

[4] These values of freedom for an individual are analyzed in Kolm 1996a, Chapter 2 (and 1996g, 1997a).

[5] This is in fact only one of the possible instrumental values of freedom: others may be provided, for instance, by exercising one's capacities in the process of choosing and acting (as emphasized by Aristotle), or by the possible threats offered *ex ante* by the set of possible choices.

[6] See Kolm 1993d, and a more advanced development in 1999b.

2.2. The example of budget freedom

As a matter of example, consider domains of choice constituted by budget sets in a space of quantities of goods. A particular application will be the case, relevant for macrojustice, with two goods, one an aggregate of consumption goods and the other leisure, with the wage rate as price; then the analysis complements and pursues that presented in Appendix B of Chapter 9 (this application with the corresponding notations is not repeated here). For each agent's choice, unit prices and income are given, but various values of them are considered. If x_i and p_i are the quantity and the price of good i, for the m goods, and y is an income, the domain is defined by $\Sigma p_i x_i \leq y$, with nonnegative x_i and p_i for all i and y. It is characterized by y and by the vector $p = \{p_i\}$ of the prices p_i. A freedom function is an ordinal function $\Phi = \Phi(y, p)$. The goods are assumed to be desired in the sense that the agent prefers larger x_i for each i. From the comparison of domains by inclusion or identity, function Φ increases with y, it is a decreasing function of each p_i, and it is homogeneous of degree zero in the set (y, p), and so $\Phi = \Phi(y, p) = \Phi(1, p/y) = \tilde{\Phi}(p/y) = \psi(\eta)$ where $\eta = \{\eta_i\}$ and $\eta_i = y/p_i$ is the ordinate of the intersect of the budget hyperplane $y = \Sigma p_j x_j$ with the axis of the x_i, and the functions $\tilde{\Phi}$ and ψ so defined are respectively decreasing and increasing.

Equal freedom at a certain level Φ corresponds to budget hyperplanes tangent to a particular concave hypersurface (an *equal-freedom envelop hypersurface*). For instance, if Φ is taken to be the value of the corresponding instrumental freedom of the same individual, function Φ is the indirect (Roy) utility function of this individual, and the corresponding envelop hypersurfaces are the indifference loci. If the x_i are inputs for producing an output in quantity $z = F(x)$ where $x = \{x_i\}$, and Φ is taken to be the corresponding instrumental value of freedom, the equal-freedom envelop hypersurfaces are the isoquant $F(x) = $ constant.[7]

Since, when income y is multiplied by a positive number μ, if the bundle $x = \{x_i\}$ was a possible choice, the bundle μx now is one, and your *purchasing power* is multiplied by μ, there is a certain meaning in specifying the measure of freedom in making it proportional to income y for each given price vector p. This *freedom index* then writes $\varphi = y/\pi(p)$ where function $\pi(p)$ is nondecreasing and linearly homogeneous. Hence, $y = \varphi \cdot \pi(p)$.[8] For given prices p, for each x there is a lowest income that permits to choose it, $y = \Sigma p_i x_i$, and hence a lowest freedom that permits to have it, $\varphi = y/\pi(p)$.

Such a function π is a generalized price index. If it has the standard linear form of price indexes, $\pi(p) = \Sigma \alpha_i p_i$ with constant α_i, then $y = \Sigma p_i \varphi \alpha_i$, and equal freedom φ means that the budget hyperplanes pass through the same point $x = \varphi \alpha$ with $\alpha = \{\alpha_i\}$; that is, it is possible to have the bundle $\varphi \alpha$ but not to

---

[7] In both these examples, if a good i can be chosen to be not consumed or not used ($x_i = 0$), then function Φ will a priori be non-increasing in price p_i (with corresponding qualifications for functions $\tilde{\Phi}$ and ψ).

[8] This also writes $\varphi^{-1} = \pi(\{\eta_i^{-1}\})$.

have more of all goods. The equal-freedom envelop hypersurfaces reduce to the points $\varphi\alpha$ of the same ray from the origin (carrying vector α) for each value φ. Hence, the freedom provided by a budget set is proportional to the distance from the origin of its intersect with the ray from the origin of direction α. It can be said to be the amount of a composite good – the volume of a basket of goods – made of the goods in given proportions (the α_i). The α_i can, for instance, be taken as the average consumption of good i in the considered society. ELIE (more exactly EDIE) is a case of such equal freedom with a linear price index, for all individuals' freedoms; the "envelop" point is point K with leisure $1 - k$ and income $k\overline{w}$.

If, however, we choose the particular case $\alpha_j = 0$ for all $j \neq i$ and $\alpha_i = 1$, the price index becomes $\pi = p_i$, the price of a given good i (perhaps of a particular nature such as leisure, or money, or an aggregate of all consumption goods but leisure, or the main staple in this society if there is one). Then, the freedom index φ is the largest amount of this good that the income can buy. And equal-freedom envelop hypersurfaces reduce to the points on the axis of this good.

If instead the price index is of the form $\pi(p) = \min_i\alpha_i p_i$ (or $\max_i\alpha_i p_i$) for given coefficients α_i, then the freedom index is the largest (or smallest) amount of any single good that the income can buy, after the choice of the proper units of the various goods. And the equal-freedom envelop hypersurfaces are constituted, for each φ, by the m points $x_i = \varphi\alpha_i$ and $x_j = 0$ for all $j \neq i$, for all i, and the linear varieties including some of them.

With a logarithmic price index, $\pi(p) = (\Pi p_i)^{1/m}$ where m is the number of goods, then $\varphi = (\Pi\eta_i)^{1/m}$, and freedom becomes measured by a proportion of the mth root of the *volume* of the domain of possible choice (with $x_i \geq 0$ for all i) – and hence ordinally compared by this volume. Each budget hyperplane touches its equal-freedom envelop at a point of coordinates $x_i = \eta_i/m$ for all i. For $m = 2$, the equal-freedom envelops are the equilaterian hyperbolas.[9]

---

[9] Changing the units of goods only multiplies the measure by a constant. One can show that, in this case, the freedom of a society is the product of the freedoms of its members (the sum if this measure of freedom is replaced by its logarithm, which makes freedom be the average of the η_i for each individual). In the case of a countable number of alternatives, Pattanaik and Xu (1990) and Bossert, Pattanaik, and Xu (1994) propose simple axioms that lead to measuring freedom by the number of alternatives (taking as measure the logarithm of the number of alternatives would have the advantage that freedom for only one alternative would be zero, and that, if there are several individuals whose choices do not interfere, social freedom, i.e., the freedom of society, would be the sum of the individual freedoms). Now ethics demands judging principles in looking at them from all angles, including their consequences. This measure of freedom raises problems. First, does adding alternatives that you will absolutely never choose make you freer (the distinction between this case and that of alternatives that you actually cannot choose for some reason is often ambiguous)? Second, does adding alternatives identical to existing ones make you freer? Third, if an option is having an item of which you can drop a part, it in fact constitutes several options, possibly many, possibly infinitely many if the item includes a perfectly divisible good. If these are desired goods, you can discard this difficulty in saying that you will always prefer to choose the whole good or bundle, but then you fall under the spell of the first question. If, when you can choose to have alternative items, a number of them are now joined into a single lot whose possession becomes one alternative, the number of alternatives decreases, but your freedom of choice certainly increases if you can drop some of the items from the lot or abstain from consuming them. As for the second question, it is hard to say that adding an identical option to a single one makes you twice freer (or any freer). But if, now, these options are having items, and the new situation is that you can have

All these forms of the price index are particular or limiting cases of the form $\pi(p) = [\Sigma(p_i\alpha_i)^\beta]^{1/\beta}$. With a weighted logarithmic price index and a proper choice of the units of goods, that is, $\eta = \Pi p_i^{\gamma_i}$ with $\Sigma\gamma_i = 1$, then $\varphi = \Pi\eta_i^{\gamma_i}$ (changing units of goods only multiply this measure by a constant).[10]

For a given price function π (and in particular given α_i for its noted forms), the freedom index φ has the measure of a real income. Hence, freedoms for different y and p can be compared as quantities can be compared. In particular, even when individuals do not face the same prices (in particular wages), the analysis of the comparison and measure of income inequality and of inequality-averse maximand functions can be applied to the comparison and measure of freedom inequality and to maximand functions averse to freedom inequality. Similarly, with such measures, the total freedom in a society can be taken as the sum of these individual freedoms of its members (even if they do not all face the same prices, which can notably be the case for wage rates).[11] However, these operations and measures considering the freedoms of several individuals make sense only if these individuals' choices are independent, that is, the choice of one does not affect the domain of possible choice of another. This is for instance the case in a situation of perfectly competitive equilibrium, where, to begin with, the domains of choice are in fact budget sets with given prices.

For a purely "instrumental freedom," the chooser equally values all domains of choice that lead her to choose the same alternative. Respecting her preferences entails endorsing this equivalence. Then, in the same space of choice as above, an individual's domain of choice of any form can be replaced by the equivalent potential budget set whose budget hyperplane is the supporting hyperplane of the choice of the individual. Then, interpersonal comparison of the corresponding freedom can be performed as in the foregoing analysis. For instance, with different considered price indexes, an individual's instrumental freedom is proportional to the distance from the origin of the intersection of the supporting hyperplane with a given ray from the origin (i.e., to the amount of a composite good with given proportions she could buy with this budget set), or to the amount of a given good she could so buy, or again to the volume below this hyperplane.

(and use) both items jointly, then certainly your freedom of choice has been augmented if you can still have only one item (possibly in taking both and dropping or not consuming one). One might fancy to consider that *then* you have become twice freer (at least if in all cases you can also choose to take nothing since it seems natural to say that your freedom is zero – and not one – if you have no choice at all, that is, only one alternative). Other exciting and surprising proposals for measuring freedom are summarized and discussed in Sugden (2003).

[10] The point of tangency of the budget hyperplane with its equal-freedom envelop is shown to be $x_i = \varphi\pi_i'$ for all i (with $\pi_i' = \partial\pi/\partial p_i$); that is, $x = \varphi$ grad π. The share of good i in the budget then is $p_i x_i/y = p_i\pi_i'/\pi$, the elasticity of the price index for good i's price. For the linear $\pi = \Sigma\alpha_i p_i$, this point is naturally the fixed point $x = \varphi\alpha$. The share of good i in income then is the share of its price in the price index, $p_i x_i/y = \alpha_i p_i/\Sigma\alpha_i p_i$. For the logarithmic or volume case, there comes $p_i x_i = y/m = \varphi\pi/m$; that is, all goods have an equal share of the budget. For the general $\pi = [\Sigma(\alpha_i p_i)^\beta]^{1/\beta}$, $\pi_i = \alpha_i^\beta p_i^{\beta-1}\pi^{1-\beta} = \alpha_i^\beta(\pi/p_i)^{1-\beta} = (p_i\alpha_i/\pi)^\beta(\pi/p_i)$ and the share of good i in income is $p_i x_i/y = (p_i\alpha_i/\pi)^\beta = (p_i\alpha_i)^\beta/\Sigma(p_i\alpha_i)^\beta$. With the weighted logarithmic price index, the share of good i in income is $p_i x_i/y = \gamma_i$.

[11] At least for linear price functions π (see note 9).

2.3. Potential freedom and the freedom ordering of efficiency

However, interpersonal comparisons of freedoms defined by domains of choice require no further hypothesis when these domains are comparable by inclusion. Then, for the particularly important case of instrumental freedom, and a respect of individuals' preferences, this interpersonal comparison by inclusion can be associated with the intrapersonal equivalence of domains conducive to the same choice (including the chosen singleton by itself). In spite of this equivalence, it may be necessary to consider individuals' freedoms (rather than only individuals' allocations), because they are the relevant item of the considered social ethics – notably with an ideal of equal freedom and more generally interpersonal comparisons of freedoms. The following only presents the shortest outline of the ensuing theory.[12]

This approach can start from the basic property that *no individual prefers any other's allocation to her own if and only if their allocations could have been chosen by them from identical domains of choice.* Indeed, choices from identical domains of choice yield the considered preferences since each individual could have chosen an allocation identical to that of any other. Conversely, given this structure of preferences, any set of possibilities constituted by the individuals' allocations and any other that no individual prefers to her own makes each individual's allocation a possible choice of this individual.

Moreover, an individual can certainly be said to be *no less free* than another when her possibility set is included in that of the other (with the possibility of identity). Then, the theory of potential or equivalent freedom holds that an individual is no less free than another when there exist two domains of choice, one for each, which can lead them to choosing their own actual allocations, and such that the domain of the former includes that of the latter (with possible identity). This just is equivalent to the former individual not preferring the other's allocation to her own. Indeed, with such domains, the former individual does not prefer the other's allocation to her own since she could have chosen an allocation identical to it; and conversely, the domains of choice constituted by both individual allocations for the individual who does not prefer the other's allocation to her own, and by her own allocation for the other, present the inclusion condition and can lead to the choice of the considered allocations. The theory then develops in defining "less free" as "no less free," "as free as" as "no less free" both ways (which turns out to amount to the existence of identical potential domains of choice), and "freer" as no less free and not as free as. Then, if allocations are substitutable among individuals (and there is a finite number of individuals), in Pareto-efficient overall allocations, the individuals are ranked by the relation "no less free than" in the sense that there exists a ranking of the individuals such that each is no less free than each other of

---

[12] The full theory is in Kolm 1999b, and a preliminary version in Kolm 1993d. This theory of potential freedom does not present the basic shortcoming of the theory of "equivalence" as unanimous indifference, which will be discussed in Chapter 26.

lower rank, with classes of individuals as free as one another. There results criteria of choice of allocations in the family of maximin or leximin in this potential freedom. They are relevant when the ideal is an equal freedom defined by domain of choice, freedom is valued for the allocation it permits one to have, and Pareto efficiency and benevolence have priority.

2.4. Equity and individuals' preferences among their allocations

The principle that no individual prefers any other's allocation to her own belongs to both the ethics of preferences and the ethics of freedom as equal potential free-dom (it has been called "equity" for "*equal independent liberty*"). It is studied by a very large literature, including early notice by Tinbergen (1946) and Foley (1967), two analyses in book size by Kolm (1971) and Baumol (1986), other early contributions by Schmeidler and Yaari, Schmeidler and Vind (1974), and Varian (1974), and many other important studies that space (and distance from the present topic) precludes mentioning here – a few are noted in the references and they include further references. This principle is but the basic one in a family of criteria based on the individuals' preferences about allocations related to the individuals' allocations. For instance, in "minimal equity" no individual prefers *each* other's allocation to her own (she does not have the worst allocation of all as she sees them), or the same principle can hold with preference or indifference (she feels better than with at least one of the others' allocations) (Kolm 1971). Or each individual's allocation is preferred by at least one other individual to her own (Philippe van Parijs). Or no individual prefers her allocation to the average of the allocations of the others (the "representative other") or of all (Kolm 1971), or of all averages of subsets of individuals including herself or not (William Thomson). Unanimous preference to all weighted averages (linear convex combinations) of all individual allocations ("super-equity") is a particularly meaningful property because it characterizes overall allocations such that all more equal ones are unanimously found worse, with a standard definition of "more equal" for sets of multidimensional bundles of goods (Kolm 1973, 1977a, 1996b). One can also variously use numbers of pairwise preferences (Feldman and Kirman 1974, and full consideration in Kolm 1999b). And so on. Note that such preferences for others' allocations cannot describe a sentiment of envy which implies that the envious person's "utility" jointly depends on both her allocation and that of the person she envies, although a structural relation can be established in deriving individuals' "nonenvious preferences" from their actual preferences.[13]

---

[13] The nonenvious (or envy-free) preferences of a possibly envious individual are her preferences among overall allocations in which other individuals' allocations are identical to her own (and so she can have no envy). These preferences are "laundered" for the sentiment of envy, and this is a case where this operation can be done straightforwardly (this method is applicable to all comparative social sentiments, that is, individuals' sentiments based on comparisons among their allocation and others' – such as jealousy, sentiments of superiority or of inferiority, and preferences for conforming and for distinction). Then, "equity" with these derived nonenvious preferences implies an absence of envy with the actual, possibly envious, preferences. (Kolm 1995a).

3. PREFERENCES, UTILITY, HAPPINESS, WELFARE

3.1. Preferences, choice, and happiness

The obtained structure of macrojustice provides individuals with rights and re-sources (social freedom and ELIE) and makes no reference to their choices, prefer-ences, or happiness, which are private matters for this issue – although it basically refers to unanimity (whence Pareto efficiency), and considers moral views or pref-erences, both for discarding eudemonistic capacities and for its full specification (through the degree of redistribution). In contrast, individuals' utility, preferences, or happiness, and choices, are common in considered or possible economic crite-ria. Choice and action, preferences, tastes and desires, satisfaction, happiness, and suffering – along with the associated information – can encompass an important part of psychology. Economics is used to represent it all by a preference ordering of alternatives, often representable and commonly represented by a utility func-tion. This extraordinarily simplified and summarized representation is also, by the same token, a highly manipulable, versatile, and convenient analytical tool. Hence, such concepts and their use first raise the question of their meaning (and meaningfulness) and of that of their assumed properties.

In fact, there are at least three different types of issues: choice (and action), preference, and happiness or satisfaction (or, more generally, what psychologists call the "valence" of emotions) – plus information. They are related, and all can have both positive (descriptive or explanatory) and normative aspects. The normativity of choice comes through the value of freedom (sometimes also of activity). That of happiness is standard, sometimes seen as necessary (as with Aristotle's *eudemonia*), and sometimes also denied (Nietzsche calls happiness "chewing the cud," Kant sees desires – "inclinations" – as the opposite of morality as reason, Tocqueville despises welfare, *eudemonia* is not pleasure). This value also sometimes requires specification (which kind of happiness, satisfaction, or pleasure is good?), and it is often better replaced by the negative value of suffering (as Buddhism advocates it, for instance). The direct normative use of preferences consists of the "respect of individuals' preferences." This implies finding good what individuals prefer, *ceteris paribus*. This obedience to individuals is a kind of freedom for them, and it is actual freedom when the preference is implemented by letting it guide free choice. And this principle becomes a eudemonism if preferring can be interpreted as "being happier with" (actually so and not only as a way of speaking as is often done).

This psychological model is, of course, highly problematic. So is, for instance, the description of choice by the selection of a highest element, in the set of possibles, of a preexisting "preference ordering" (Wittgenstein and Frege were astounded to see action explained as resulting from preferences "as water flows from a reser-voir"). This hardly describes the choice process. Choices and acts resulting from or manifesting such a maximization are described as "rational choice" or "rational behaviour." Historically, this adjective was introduced in this sense by scholars who did not know how to defend this representation which was so convenient, as a tentative to discard, discourage, or exorcize questioning about it (Hicks, Samuelson). Yet, the various possible senses of the term "rational" hardly apply here. Selecting the most preferred is not a reason, but a tautology when it is true – and it can also be false. Nor does it describe choice resulting from comparison, iterative consideration, and pondering of the alternatives, or it hides it in the darkest of black boxes. "Rational" might also be intended as applied to the underlying properties, notably transitivity: it can then only mean that preferring A to B and B to C would be a "good reason" for preferring A to C. The only defensible idea in this direction is that of describing the preference of A to B, B to C, and C to A as being irrational when this results from focusing attention on different aspects of the alternatives in several pairwise choices and unjustifiably neglecting the other aspects. Moreover, acts resulting from or manifesting such a maximization are often described as "rational behaviour," but rational, in the proper sense of resulting from reason, does not apply to behaviour but to conduct: there is no rational behaviour, only behaviour, on the one hand, and rational conduct, on the other hand.

In fact, individuals commonly have several different preferences, of different types distinguished by their object, their origin, the nature or condition of their application, or their structure (e.g., desires and long-term interest, the *id* and the *superego*, drives and norms, tastes and the reason-driven will).[14] A unique preference may be their synthesis, possibly that "revealed by choice." Yet, such assimilation of choice with preference bypasses issues such as unwanted addiction and *akrasia* or weakness of the will. We have also considered the question of the choice of one's preferences or of changes in them, and the highly ambiguous issue of responsibility for one's preferences and tastes (Chapter 6). The normative endorsement of preferences thus raises problems: which preferences, how are they known, do they exist in the first place? Being more or less happy is clearly often a meaningful relation, and there a priori can be some kind of ordering of imprecise "levels" of happiness. The historical introduction of notions of "utility" meant to describe happiness – or satisfaction– and hence the resulting choice and behaviour were seen as some sort of individual maximization of happiness. This view was later rejected by a number of "positive" economists with behaviourist tendencies. Yet, the consideration of happiness remains crucial for the direct normative uses of this apparatus.

Then, if seeking the highest satisfaction can justify the maximizing model, a discarding of the consideration of sentiments, inspired by behaviourist ideology, undermines this justification. It is in this epistemic mood that the term "rational" was then introduced for denoting this hypothesis of a "maximizing behaviour" – rational choice, rational behaviour – in a rather tongue-in-cheek way (Hicks,

---

[14] See, for instance, the multipreference model of psychoanalytic theory in Kolm 1981 (reprinted 1987i).

Samuelson), for the purpose of shunning discussion and avoiding having to provide a justification that was not in sight, and so for protecting the handy model. This raises two problems, however. First, an agent's rationality of any kind is no less a mental property than satisfaction or pleasure, and hence the behaviourist indictment is not met. Second, why would maximizing behaviour (or conduct) be rational? It was then felt that the answer might lie in the property of transitivity of pairwise preferences – A preferred to B and B preferred to C implies A preferred to C and extensions considering indifference – which is a necessary and sufficient property for the existence of a preference ordering if antisymmetry (A preferred to B excludes B preferred to A) and nonreflexivity (no A preferred to A) are assumed in the first place. This became the starting point of the theoretical presentations (Abraham Wald). However, if antisymmetry is ruling out a contradiction, and hence can be seen as rational as a property of the actor's mind or of the definition of the concept of preference (which also precludes reflexivity), why is transitivity rational, in what sense is it or could it be? In the strict sense of rationality as providing a reason, the answer can only be that preferring A to B and B to C constitutes a good or valid reason for preferring A to C. Why would it be so? There is no direct reason, and this is a bland or empty statement, or a repetition of what it intends to support (a tautology). However, two psychological facts, related to cognition and emotion, can relate these structural properties to rationality. First, cognitive limitations may lead to focusing attention on one aspect of a choice or of its consequences, while there exist others that lead to the opposite choice. This may lead to intransitivity of preferences – as already noted – and even, more directly, to their symmetry (preferring both A to B and B to A). The corresponding lack of equally considering all relevant aspects and of comparing, weighing, and then actually choosing, can be called a lack of rationality. It can be due to cognitive difficulties, and emotions can so impair rational judgment. Second, while people who both prefer A to B and B to A clearly see they are in a contradiction, and have to adjust their preference if they have to manifest them by an actual choice, people who manifest an intransitivity in preferring A to B, B to C, and C to A face no such external obligation. However, if they are clearly aware of these preferences of theirs, they may see this triple of preferences as a kind of cognitive dissonance, and this may make them somewhat ill at ease. As a result, they may reconsider their preferences and modify them in the direction of transitivity. This may suggest some explanation of transitivity or justification for assuming it. Note that equivalent behavioural conditions, such as keeping the same choice in a set of possibilities if some other alternatives are discarded from it (present in economics in Samuelson's theory of "revealed preferences") lead much less or not at all to this kind of reflection, and sometimes for good reasons.[15]

---

[15] Reasons for not satisfying this condition are noted in Chapter 23 (with, in particular, reference to "positional goods") and fully discussed in Kolm 1996a, Chapter 15 (and 1995e, 1995f, 2000c).

Finally, true behaviourism is observing acts. However, checking the transitivity hypothesis requires observing several choice situations of the agent (three for transitivity, two for the other equivalent noted property). Now, the preferences may not be the same in these successive experiments, because time, conditions, and – necessarily – past experience, differ. As with Heraclitus' river baths, one never chooses twice with the same preferences. Hence, this structure of preferences can be tested only with an extra assumption of stability and independence from the noted causes of change, which is something else. In a strict sense, therefore, the hypothesis of an ordering of preferences cannot be tested. In particular, if one assumes it, it cannot be proven false. It is unfalsifiable. That is, this concept is "metaphysical" in Popper's sense of the term (note that Karl Popper sees microeconomics – of which it is a basic assumption – as the example of good social science). However, the next remark should be that holding some metaphysical presuppositions is unavoidable at any rate. And the choice of holding one can certainly put some weight on convenience – since truth is no longer decisive. Now, as concerns preference orderings and utility functions, the other face of economics' psychological dumbness (rather than conscious boldness) is a stroke of genius from the point of view of analytical convenience, power, and versatility. Hence, the final philosophical foundation of preference orderings and utility functions is in the realm of weak pragmatism: for some purposes and applications, it helps. However, this forces one to be all the more careful about the possible meaning or meaninglessness of assumed properties.[16]

3.2. Meaningful and meaningless structures of utility

Normative criteria can be derived from these concepts. They have to be meaningful and nonabsurd. Hence, to begin with, they have to rely on meaningful properties of these concepts. This is a matter of psychology. *Roughly speaking,* pairwise comparisons constitute an ordering when they are transitive (A over B and B over C implies A over C, with extension for equivalences). An ordering may possibly be representable by a function, such as a utility function $u(A)$, and the relation amounts to $u(A) > u(B)$. This function is ordinal, that is, defined up to an arbitrary increasing function in the sense that function u can be replaced by function $f[u(A)]$ where f is any increasing function. Choice cannot mean or reveal structures more specific than such ordinal preferences. However, psychology is richer than that, and this can be relevant for normative uses. The crucial point, however, is what exactly can be meaningful in this respect.[17] If the expressions "I prefer A to B" or "I am happier with A than with B" (or in state A

---

[16] The foregoing psychological and epistemic bases of preference orderings are fully analyzed in Kolm 1986a.

[17] For a full presentation and the establishment of the following properties, see Kolm 1996a Chapter 12, Appendix A.

than in state B) can be meaningful, then comparisons of comparisons of the type "I prefer A to B more than I prefer C to D" or "I am more happier in A than in B than I am happier in C than in D" can also be meaningful. This possibility is unambiguously shown by the cases where either C and D, or B and D, are very similar (since the comparison then reduces to that between A and B or between A and C). Similar comparisons of higher order can also be meaningful. If these comparisons of comparisons are transitive, they imply an ordering of the pairwise comparisons. This ordering may be representable by an ordinal function $U(A, B)$ such that $U(A, B) > U(C, D)$ is meaningful. Moreover, if this relation describes comparison of preference in a "pure" sense, it implies that the same relation holds if A is replaced by A' such that $u(A') = u(A)$, and a similar property for B, C, and D, which implies that function U can be written as $U(A, B) = V[u(A), u(B)]$. Hence, $V[u(A), u(B)] > V[u(C), u(D)]$ can have the noted meaning. If ordinal function V has form $u(A) - u(B)$ as one of its possible specifications, then the relation $u(A) - u(B) > u(C) - u(D)$ can be meaningful. If this holds on a sufficient domain with some purely formal topological conditions of continuity, this amounts to the function u being meaningfully cardinal, that is, defined up to an arbitrary increasing linear (affine) function, $au + b$ with any $a > 0$ and b. However, there is no meaning in function V having this form, hence in a cardinal utility representing a psychological structure of preference or of happiness. However, function V can generally have this structure, for some specification of function u, when $u(A) - u(B)$ and $u(C) - u(D)$ are sufficiently small. Apart from these cases, cardinal utility has no psychological meaning that can refer to preference or happiness.

One consequence is that the many possible normative criteria of distribution or arbitrage based on cardinal utility *assumed to have such a meaning* are *a priori* of no avail. They can be meaningful only with specific vindication of this cardinal utility, which can a priori be of three types: (1) the considered variations in utility are small; (2) the numbers used in fact measure quantities (such as income); and (3) the cardinal structure is shown to be a satisfactory approximation. This is independent of whether these criteria use interpersonal comparisons or not (these comparisons may be acceptable for incomes).[18] Of course, there can be

---

[18] The set of these possible criteria is presented in Kolm 1996a, Chapter 12, Appendix C. They include, among many others, utilitarianism (Bentham [1973], however, chose to measure utility in money "for lack of a better measure," and hence happens to hold a logically valid theory which is in fact a kind of theory of the "surplus"), and theories of such interesting authors as Nash (1950, 1953), Raiffa-Kalai-Smorodinski-Gauthier (1953, 1975, 1986), Binmore and Dasgupta (1987), Samuelson, Herrero, and others, as well as the various other possibilities noted in the indicated reference. This set of criteria is particularly attractive by its clear and simple logic, yet with sufficient richness for being interesting. Hence the importance of presenting one of the three justifications for such uses of cardinal utility. A frequent property is the consideration of a reference state in considering that this reduces the relevant variables to the excess utility above that of this state. These variables – differences in levels of a cardinal utility – are then defined up to a multiplication by any scalar. This logically and interestingly limits the set of possible criteria. The replacement of utilities by quantities introduces, in particular, full interpersonal comparability. Then, some criteria remain meaningful, this structure is necessary for others, but it forbids other exercises. For instance, Nash's axiomatic derivation of his "cooperative bargaining solution" (one

cardinal specifications of the ordinal utility with other meanings, such as the von Neumann-Morgenstern cardinal utility for choices in uncertainty. In presenting this particular function, Friedman and Savage (1952) remarked that "this is not utility to be used for ethics." John Harsanyi took exception to this remark in imagining situations where one does not a priori know whose income one will have (1953), and then which individual one will be (1976, a type of theory Rawls [1971] called the "original position," which has been considered, logically rescued and otherwise discussed in Chapter 21).[19]

3.3. Welfare

Relevant meaningfulness – for instance, psychological rather than merely formal and mathematical – thus is an essential issue. For instance, "welfare" is one of the most used normative notions in economics. However, its uses seem to make its meaning oscillate between goods or income, on the one hand, and happiness, on the other hand. The individuals' eudemonistic characteristics it seems to take into account are quite variable. Hence, this seems to be a highly ambiguous concept and, ultimately, an opaque and mysterious one. This ambiguity is all the more confusing and dangerous in that it is insidious and hypocritical, since welfare evokes mundane images rather than suggesting a metaphysical or scholastic substance. It is not without reason that this term has no translation in other languages (they translate well-being, though). This ambiguity and ambivalence can, however, be a useful and valued property for political and journalistic discourses.

3.4. Happiness

In contrast, the notions of happiness, satisfaction, and, negatively, insatisfaction and suffering, are certainly unavoidable in social-ethical concerns. It is not impossible to hold them to be the only ultimate values – the others then being only means to them – although respect for agency can also lead to directly valuing freedom, including the other mental item that is mental freedom (notably Rousseau-Kant autonomy), and respect for nature or cultures can lead to value corresponding nonindividualistic items. Of course, the noted eudemonistic notions can be ultimate values without being the direct concern of distributive justice and *prima facie* equality, notably because of a self-accountability of eudemonistic capacities, for some issues (as argued for macrojustice). Other related mental and physiological properties, such as joy, pleasure, contentment, etc., and still more specific emotions, sentiments, or states of mind (such as anguish, depression, despair, serenity, equanimity, excitement, ravishment, exhilaration, or again hope, fear,

of the first proposals) is based both on an absence of interpersonal comparability and on the implicit assumption of meaningfulness of such comparability through the consideration of the symmetry of domains in the space of extra utilities.

[19] And is more fully similarly considered in Kolm 2001b.

disappointment, pride, shame, envy, compassion, and so on) are more particular and beyond present consideration.

An essential property of happiness is comparability: "I am happier in state (or with) A than in (with) B" is admitted as a meaningful expression, although not all pairs of states can be so compared – without this noncomparison clearly implying "as happy." Moreover, the corresponding transitivity is certainly also seen as a necessity in the sense that if a person thinks she would be happier in A than in B, in B than in C, and in C than in A, this would imply a focus on different aspects of the situations which would disappear if all aspects are sufficiently and jointly considered (which may not be psychologically easy or even possible). The notion of "as happy in A as in B" is much more elusive, though. At best, it can only be understood as a precise approximation of an imprecise reality. It logically implies the possibility of permuting A and B in the expression (symmetry). But the transitivity of this equality (A as B and B as C, hence A as C) meets the obstacle of the possible presence of thresholds of differentiation: one may feel approximately as happy in A as in B and in B as in C, while a difference appears in comparing A and C. For questions where such difficulties can be bypassed, the noted properties permit the consideration of corresponding relations of "happier" or "as happy" constituting an ordering (a "preordering" or "weak ordering," i.e., with possible equivalence) of the relevant set of states. This ordering may be representable by an ordinal function. They can be called a preference ordering and a utility function with *tangible*, eudemonistic meaning, for distinguishing them from pure preference, or from preference related to choice. These preferences can be identified with those related to choice only if the individual is assumed to chose "what makes her happier" in a literal sense – this is "eudemonistic behaviour or conduct." Finally, there usually are situations that the individual cannot compare with respect to her happiness, for instance because the nature of her sentiments, emotions, and feelings is too different. Hence, the ordering is not complete. However, the individual may have to choose between such states, and this would reveal the ranking if this behaviour can be assumed correspondingly eudemonistic. Other structural properties of these relations have been noted, notably the meaningfulness of ordinal comparisons of pairwise ordinal comparisons, as well as other a priori meaningless structures (for example, there seems to be no meaning in "I am twice happier with A than with B" – a quantity structure – or in "I am twice happier with A rather than B than I am with C rather than D" – possible with a cardinal structure).

3.5. Interpersonal comparisons of happiness

Social-ethical judgments that take, as their basic concerns, individuals' happiness (or satisfaction, pleasure, or suffering), or their variations, are not unfrequent and are, on the whole, rather important (although this does not seem to be relevant for macrojustice, as was pointed out). Now, these judgments should be impartial, by logical necessity (Chapter 23). And this impartiality requires the relevant interpersonal comparability of these items. Hence, this comparability is required by the very existence of such judgments. Moreover, comparison of other aspects or structures of these items may also be required by second-best criteria (for instance, by second-best egalitarian ones). In fact, such comparisons are very frequently made, for this kind of judgment or for any other reason. Yet, precise principles require precise comparisons, about aspects that depend on the principle. Hence, the possibilities of comparing individuals' happiness or their variations should be considered.

An individual may feel miserable and be despaired while this is not the case for another. Or one may be happy and the other unhappy. Then, it can doubtlessly be said that the former is happier than the latter. This can also unambiguously be proposed in a number of other cases, this implying that this judgment would be shared by anyone sufficiently informed, including the two compared persons. When such a comparison cannot be made, it may be possible with more information about these persons. Nothing can be said when one does not know these persons, whereas a common mother or a close friend of both may clearly make such a comparison. Therefore, there is a scope for such interpersonal comparisons. The very use of a comparison by "more" ("happier") suggests transitivity, and, in a set of individuals-in-situation where this pairwise comparison is meaningful and has this property,[20] there is an ordering of happiness that may be representable by an ordinal function – they were called the fundamental eudemonistic preferences and utility function.[21] For the same individual in various situations, this ordering coincides with her own eudemonistic ordering of the preceding section. Of course, this does not imply or suggest that all individuals in all situations can be so compared (the ordering need not be complete in this sense). Indeed, it actually often cannot be said that a single and same individual is happier or more satisfied in one state than in another. For instance, her states of mind in both cases may be of too different types. Hence, whether such comparisons make sense depends on the case and on their actual application. Now, the essential practical application is for acknowledging that some individuals are more miserable than others, or that they are miserable or despaired while the others are not. These are by no means unfrequent occurrences. Their importance is that this may be a reason for helping these people with priority. This maximin in fundamental preference or utility

---

[20] Along with properties that can be taken as definitional properties of the relation: antireflexivity (no "A more than A") and antisymmetry (no both "A more than B and B more than A").

[21] Thus, the domain of definition of the fundamental preference ordering or ordinal utility function is an empirical issue, not a metaphysical one. A priori, even happiness-seeking individuals can have different preferences about being various individuals-in-situation because they have different conceptions of happiness (you prefer to be Napoleon or Mother Theresa depending on whether you are "happier" with glory or with charity). This, however, raises deep problems of consistency (see Chapter 20 and Kolm 2001b). Arrow's (1977) "extended sympathy" assumes that all individuals have the same preference ordering about being various individuals. This is a priori unwarranted. However, it holds for happiness-seeking individuals in the domain of existence of fundamental preferences.

can be extended to a leximin for completeness (and for benevolence and hence Pareto efficiency with regard to these eudemonistic individual evaluations). This requires a more extensive comparability of pairs of individuals, but, de facto, the maximin often suffices for determining the solution. This leximin was called eudemonistic "practical justice," the corresponding eudemonistic "justice" being the case where no individual is clearly less unhappy than another – which is the outcome of the operation of maximin when it can be Pareto efficient in this sense. However, this solution was not proposed as a universal principle for two reasons. First, happiness is often not the relevant criterion of interpersonal comparison. Indeed, the same studies also considered ideal equalities in freedoms, goods, and incomes.[22] Second, it was pointed out that this eudemonistic maximin may lead to sacrificing much happiness of many persons for the sake of eliciting a faint smile on the lips of the most atrabilious individual or of one not really unhappy.[23] Such remarks in fact apply the above noted ordinal comparisons of ordinal comparisons to fundamental utility, a comparability that has also been applied for obtaining other meaningful criteria.[24]

But the simple comparability of orderings or ordinal utility functions (co-ordinality) has led to proposing many other criteria. They are based on the possibility of permuting the individuals when only their happiness or satisfaction matters. To begin with, this restricts substantially the set of Pareto-efficient states, to those where "fundamental efficiency" is satisfied – that is, the absence of possible Pareto domination by a state where the individuals have been permuted.[25] Majorities with such permutations have also been considered. All these criteria are meaningful for, and can be applied to, other cases than comparing individuals' happiness, for instance for comparing the allocation of quantities such as incomes, or freedoms as domains of choice. They are the criteria that use only the property of ordinal interpersonal comparability (co-ordinality), and the compared items can have in addition a structure more specific than an ordering or an ordinal function.

When the happiness of two individuals is not easily comparable, the reason is not only necessarily a lack of information about these persons. It can also result from the fact that happiness is not a sufficiently precisely defined concept in itself. Notably, there are several kinds of happiness, indeed many of them, some of which are very different from one another. For instance, happiness can result from excitement or from serenity. One or the other, or the proper alternance of both, are commonly advocated.[26] Now, one may see that an individual is more joyful than another, or more serene than her, but it may be more difficult to compare the

---

[22] See Kolm 1966a, 1971. See also for instance Chapter 6.

[23] Id., 1971 Part 3.

[24] See Kolm 1996h. Note that variations affecting more than two individuals can be considered.

[25] Kolm 1971, Part III.

[26] For instance, buddhist psychology provides convincing reasons for advising aiming at highly conscious serenity. The economist Tibor Scitovsky is one elaborate advocate of alternating excitement and serenity in *The Joyless Economy* (1976).

serenity of the wise man, the pleasure of the sybarite, and the exhilaration of the sportsman. Yet, it may not be easier, or more significant, to compare the happiness of the same individual in such different states of mind and activities. However, the comparison may then be aided by the observation of the individual's choice, if she is assumed to be a sufficiently informed eudemonist. The interpersonal comparison does not have this possibility, although it sometimes is clear and sufficient. Now, eudemonism – taking happiness or satisfaction as the end value of social ethics and the direct concern of justice – is a very common philosophy including, for instance, utilitarianisms (which needs cardinal utilities in addition) and economists' classical "social welfare functions," and it actually has a scope of valid application. Then, interpersonal comparison of individuals' happiness, about structural aspects that depend on the retained criterion, is required by impartiality and by applications of the considered principle. Hence, although these comparisons are not required for macrojustice, they are for a number of important issues.

25

Freedoms, responsibility, desert, merit, equality of opportunity, capacities, capabilities, basic needs

1. PRESENTATION

Chapter 22 focused on economic ethics that are, one way or the other, closely related to the obtained results as concerns macrojustice. Chapters 23 and 24 considered the general logical and necessary structure of economic ethical principles, and its various specific manifestations as concerns the structure and the "substance" of the families of criteria. This chapter and the next consider specific principles, respectively based on freedom and on preferences. Freedom is the basis of a variety of basic criteria. Among them, responsibility, desert, and merit relate judgment or allocation to the individual's action. Others consist of specifying the relevant meaning of equal freedom – the concepts of equality of opportunity are among them. Other principles propose that what should exist is what the individuals would have chosen in a putative free choice. When this notional choice is a collective free agreement, this is a theory of the social contract. This includes, in particular, "liberal social contracts" (see Chapter 3), and "fundamental insurance" against the occurrence of facts that are in reality given (theories of the "original position" are particular cases). Of course, rights, the scope of opportunities, responsibility, desert, merit, and social contracts have been the object of social-ethical analysis for centuries. They are forms of the most individualistic social ethics. Yet, the vastly unequal wealths that can result from equal social freedom in free markets led to claims of tangible equality or lower inequality, in the outcome. These two positions became the two poles of the debate in society and in social thinking. However, one strand of scholarly thought – whose members tend to think of it as the only one although they are in fact quite few – made an extraordinary detour through utilitarianism, socially launched by Bentham for the purely political purpose of opposing the American and French rights-based revolutionary ideologies, and rejoined the common ethics of liberty and equality, rights and needs, and desert and responsibility, only through late criticisms of utilitarianism or of its basic assumptions. Landmarks of this history will also be pointed out.

The most basic relations of freedom with responsibility, desert, merit, and equality of opportunity are noted in Section 2. Section 3 briefly relates the astounding adventure of scholarly utilitarianism (as universal principle) and of its criticism for rejoining the common path with, however, a number of new proposals. Among the latter, the theory of fundamental insurance, a case of putative liberalism (i.e., a theory based or notional social freedom), of which theories of the original position are particular cases, is summarized in Section 4, which also discusses the related and more justified fundamental reciprocity. Section 5 then considers the vast field of the analysis of basic needs and the formation of capacities (and capabilities), and the central issue of the alternative between macrojustice and catering for specific needs. Finally, remarks about responsibility in Section 6 are completed, in Appendix B, by the discussion of a notable proposal for associating an end-state, consequentialist objective with a deontic moral of equal reward for equal effort. Appendix A situates the obtained result first, for its various elements, in the history of thought, and second, by comparison with a number of recent studies that also rest on concepts of self-accountability of tastes and equal sharing of productive capacities, but are in fact deeply different (they are not liberalisms).

2. FREEDOM AS RESPONSIBILITY, DESERT, MERIT, AND EQUALITY OF OPPORTUNITY

Social freedom, discussed in Chapter 3, about amounts to allocation *according to responsibility*. Indeed, *aim-freedom* means incurring all the consequences of one's action. And *act-freedom* means acting according to one's choice in the sense of acting free from forceful interference; hence, with aim-freedom, it implies incurring the consequences of one's free choice. This allocation according to responsibility holds when these consequences concern *this agent alone*, for *compensating* possible harms to other agents, or as the right of agreeing with others about one's and their acts, including compensations, transfers, and payments. In particular, when several agents freely agree, *the agreement requires the acquiescence of each, and hence each is responsible for the existence of the agreement and therefore for the content and consequences of the agreement*, notably for the part of it *that concerns herself*. This clearly also belongs to what Aristotle means by "geometric equality."

Free agreement, unanimous among the concerned persons, thus solves the problem of *assigning responsibility among persons about items that are joint consequences of their actions*.

However, "according to responsibility" says nothing, in itself, about entitlement to the means of action and to the effects of circumstances and conditions, and it depends on the corresponding rights. These rights can have any origin, but consequences of actions can notably depend on items considered as a priori given. The noted rationality of equality says that, *prima facie*, the benefits (or handicaps) from these items should be allocated equally among individuals that nothing else relevantly differentiates ("arithmetic equality").[1] For capacities, however, these equalities can be measured in possible inputs (e.g., time of use) or in potential output, which makes a difference with different productivities.[2] Equality in input measure is satisfied by the corresponding self-ownership. This relates to a classical distinction in allocations according to action or responsibility: an individual *merits* the consequences of her actions using her given capacities, while she *deserves* the consequences of her actions but not those of the given capacities of hers she uses – then, differences due to the effects of the corresponding capacities should be erased.

This relates to classical discussions about "equality of opportunity." This principle has the extraordinary fate of eliciting two unanimities in opposite evaluations: all politicians favour it, and all philosophers criticize it. Politicians of all sides advocate it... because they would define it in different and opposed ways. And because of this very possibility, philosophers find this notion ambiguous, confusing, unhelpful, hypocritical, or dangerous.[3] The point concerns which of individuals' means, advantages, or handicaps are considered legitimately theirs, and which should ideally be equalized or compensated among them. The issue can be various aspects or effects of social situation, origin, race, gender, culture, education received, and so on. In particular, individuals can be seen as legitimately entitled to their given capacities, or there should be some ideal equalization of their effects. Equality of opportunity has often emphatically meant "the career open to talents" and been conceived as the path to meritocracy, while it often also has aimed at rewarding desert from effort only. And these specifications can apply to various means and conditions in various ways and degrees.

In the framework of labour and income, equality of opportunity based on desert would give the same income y_i to each individual i who provides the same labour or effort ℓ_i, $y_i = f(\ell_i)$ with the same function f for all i. For instance, it can be an equal given wage rate w for all, with income $y_i = w\ell_i$. Individuals are then faced with identical domains of free choice so defined. When individual production functions $p_i()$ or competitive wage rates w_i differ, this solution generally entails Pareto inefficiency. In contrast, full self-ownership $y_i = p_i(\ell_i)$ (possibly $y_i = w_i\ell_i$) for all i is a case of equality of opportunity according to merit and entails no Pareto inefficiency in itself. But this also is the case of the more general remuneration according to *relative merit* where the individuals earn, or lose foregone earnings, from a benchmark of labour k and equal income $\overline{p}(k)$ or $\overline{w}k$ (for financial balance in the equalization), $y_i = p_i(\ell_i) - p_i(k) + \overline{p}(k)$, that is, ELIE. The equalization labour can be zero, yielding full self-ownership. It can also, on the contrary, be the income-egalitarian ELIE with $k = k^e$ (see Chapter 11).

---

[1] Chapter 23.
[2] Chapter 9.
[3] See the references and the discussion in Kolm 2001a.

Hence, ELIE consists of an allocation according to desert restricted to labour (or effort) k, the same for all, or *equal partial desert*, and an allocation according to *relative merit*, for labour relative to this benchmark labour k. It is an allocation according to *merit relative to equal partial desert*. Moreover, since, actually, $\ell_i > k$ for most individuals i and normal equalization labour k, ELIE solutions can also be presented as remuneration according to *desert for labour k* and to *merit for the excess labour $\ell_i - k$*. The principle is full merit for $k = 0$, that is, full self-ownership. It is practically full desert for the income-egalitarian ELIE with $k = k^e$ where most $\ell_i - k^e$ are small (see Chapter 11); then, the principle is, more precisely, desert with marginal merit.

All concepts of equality of opportunity are more deeply criticized by the view that "equality of opportunity is good for horse races, not for people," which sees solidarity and responsibility for others' welfare or fate as more appropriate styles of good human relations. For this reason, "fraternity" qualified the liberty and the equality in rights of the revolutionary motto (yet, the 1789 Declaration understood its central principle of equal freedom as very strongly meritarian, in line with its basic historical reason).[4]

3. A FORTUITOUS HISTORICAL DETOUR THROUGH UTILITARIANISM TO SECOND-BEST EGALITARIANISMS

The hypostasis and enshrinement of individualistic basic rights by the American and French Revolutions came in the context of a political opposition to England. England had been the ideal and model about rights for all European liberals for one century (see, e.g., Voltaire). Yet, this war was waged on all grounds, military, economic, political, and ideological. A foremost fighter in the latter field, Jeremy Bentham set aside his own interest in rights and proclaimed: "rights, nonsense; inalienable rights, nonsense on stilts" ("inalienable" is both in the American Declaration of Independence and in the preamble of the 1789 Declaration). However, a criticism can really be efficient only if backed by an alternative proposal. This could not be the previous legitimations by tradition or the divine will.[5] And since, of the two basic characteristics of individuals that can serve as a basis for social ethics, their being free choosers and "sentient machines," freedom was taken by the ethics of basic rights, happiness alone remained available. Bentham thus put forward utilitarianism, based on pleasure, pain, happiness, utility, or "felicity" in advocating their highest sum over all individuals, along a line suggested by Helvetius, Hume, and Beccaria, among others. However, he also said both that he sees no meaning in adding such items of different individuals (which is "like

---

[4] A protest of young educated bourgeois against the discriminating privileges of the nobility.

[5] Although the other main ideological fighter in the English camp, Edmund Burke, proposed another use of tradition, including an assertion of basic rights supposedly derived from tradition but in fact strangely similar to those of the revolutionary Declarations (in a similar vein, Jellinek later attributed the origin of basic rights to medieval German city-states) – see Kolm 1989a (1991), 1993a.

adding apples and pears"), and that one does not know how to measure the added happiness or the like. That is, he hardly believed in the utilitarianism he so eagerly promoted for a political reason.

Yet, as a result, utilitarianism, understood as a *universal principle to be applied to all issues*, became the dominant (hegemonic) social ethics of English-language scholars, notwithstanding misgivings and qualifications for the best of them, such as John Stuart Mill, who also values private freedom and the quality of pleasure, and Henry Sidgwick, who remarked that his book, *The Method of Ethics*, begins with "ethics" and ends with "failure" and that "where he looked for cosmos he found chaos." Utilitarianism in this sense had no impact in other circles, notably in other cultures where it was seen as an English eccentric idiosyncrasy, and where social ethics rested on rights, freedom, duties, ideal equalities, solidarities, and other views. There were few exceptions, and yet the notable one of Vilfredo Pareto who, however, added his altruistic individual "utilities" rather than the more standardly welfarist "ophelimities."[6] Pareto's position can be seen as an anticipation of the fact that utilitarianism eventually seduced academic economists because of its use of utilities, and its clear mathematical operations of addition and maximization. Academic economists then replaced the sum by a more general function of individuals' utilities because of the difficulty of making sense of cardinal utilities that could meaningfully be added across individuals and mean happiness or the like[7] (Bergson, Lange, Samuelson, Allais). Yet, the individual end values were still individuals' utilities or preferences.

However, a notable part of academic economists did not follow this path. In line with the rest of society, their social ethics rested on process liberalism or other conceptions of freedom, as we have seen,[8] or on ideals of equality in income or other goods (the utilitarian ethics also exists in society, but with a limited scope of application rather than with the universal validity asserted by classical utilitarianism, as noted in Chapter 6). Benefit-cost analysis for public decisions was based on the method of the surplus which adds money equivalents or willingnesses to pay rather than "utilities" (this will be fully discussed in Chapter 26 – see also Chapter 19). Even John Hicks (1959) criticized in passing what he labelled "welfarism." But the criticism clearly gave its reason when it suggested that, for the overall distribution, individuals' eudemonistic capacities should remain in the private sphere and not be considered by the distributive principle. Several proposals advanced reasons for this choice, in the family of freedom or responsibility, and deduced

---

[6] Pareto (1913) considers two levels of individuals' evaluation, their "ophelimities" – says, for short, their individual "welfare" – v_i for individual i, and their "utilities" function of individuals' ophelimities, $u_i = v_i + \Sigma_{j \neq i} a_{ij} v_j$ for individual i. He then proposed the highest Σu_i (modern utilitarians tend to prefer Σv_i, but Bentham had remarked that the pleasure altruistic individuals derive from others' pleasure should be counted, and hence he sides with Pareto). The additive forms of course raise a problem about the cardinality and comultiplicativity of the measures of u_i and v_i. The general acceptable form, including the possibility that u_i depends on the u_j, and a discussion, are presented in Kolm 1966a, 2000a.

[7] This meaning is not the case for the risk-relevant von Neumann-Morgenstern cardinal utility, as Friedman and Savage (1952) suggested in saying that this utility "is not for ethics."

[8] Chapter 22.

from this remark that this overall justice should focus notably on income with some ideal of equality. The idea that "individuals are responsible for their tastes" is found in Kolm (1966a) and Dworkin (1981) – although we have seen in Chapter 6 that the application of the notion of responsibility to such items is in fact quite delicate and demands specific psychological and even ontological distinctions. Rawls (1971) simply emphasized freedom and stated that the proper focus of justice is individuals' means of action: basic freedoms (the classical basic rights) and "primary goods." These authors then concluded that the objective should be an ideal equality in income and other means. However, they saw drawbacks in this equality, and hence, proposed corresponding second-best solutions. The ideally equal objective was income – possibly the "ℓ-equivalent income" and notably the "leisurely equivalent income," that is, the income that, associated with given labour ℓ and notably with zero labour, is as good as the actual situation[9] – and possibly also more specific means, in Kolm (1966a); they were "primary goods" – two of which are income and wealth – in Rawls (1971);[10] and Dworkin (1981) considered the sharing of all given resources including productive capacities measured by their money "total income," which includes the value of leisure at its market price, which is the wage rate. The shortcomings of equality were the possible domination by states better for everyone, or the possible rejection of very high losses for some (possibly many) individuals for very small gains for others (possibly few) who may not fare badly in Kolm (1966a); it was the possible domination by larger amounts of primary goods for all in Rawls (1971); and it was mostly the "slavery of the talented" – see Chapters 7 and 9 – for Dworkin (1981).[11] Note that both the use of leisurely equivalent or more general ℓ-equivalent incomes and that of total incomes are ways of dealing with the questions raised by leisure or labour with different individual productivities and tastes, and, in particular, they avoid the wasteful disincentive effects of the equalization of earned income. However, the equalization of total income gives a situation that can be symmetrically as unequal or unjust as full self-ownership (see Chapters 7 and 9).[12] Rawls' omission of the issue of leisure and labour is the main implicit reason for the disincentive effects of the equalization that are responsible for the noted domination of equality in primary goods by possible states where all individuals have more, due to equalization policies implicitly assumed to be based on earned incomes. The solutions proposed were then the theory of the comparison and measure of inequality and of inequality-averse maximands (Kolm, 1966a); a maximin in an index of "primary goods" – maximin is a particular case of inequality-averse maximands – called the "difference principle" and derived from a theory of the

---

[9] See Chapter 26.

[10] The other "primary goods" are power, position, and self-respect. The problem of finding measures for these items can be superseded by the deeper worry that such an index implies a substitutability between income or wealth and self-respect, that is, it implies that dignity has a price, exactly the opposite of the Kantian stand which Rawls claims inspired him.

[11] Who also discusses substitutes to equal sharing for indivisible items (through auctions).

[12] The case of ℓ-equivalent incomes and in particular leisurely equivalent incomes will be discussed in Chapter 26.

"original position" (Rawls, 1971);[13] and a "fundamental insurance" about productive capacities (Dworkin, 1981) – "fundamental insurance," described in the next section, is a kind of partially original position. Another solution proposed to the same problem was ELIE.[14]

4. UNANIMOUS ETHICS AND FUNDAMENTAL INSURANCE AND RECIPROCITY

These scholarly discardings of utilitarianism correspond to the general opinion of the irrelevance of eudemonistic capacities for redistributive macrojustice (see Chapter 6). This irrelevance is therefore justified by unanimity and the principle of endogenous social choice. The same principle, however, also shows that judgments that amount to utilitarianism are accepted in a number of instances of microjustice. However, the noted studies were about macrojustice (Rawls, Dworkin) or notably about it. Unanimity of various types was also implied by the proposals. It is implied about self-interest in the sense of an absence of unanimous domination, both by evaluation functions increasing functions of incomes, and de facto by Rawls' maximin of an index of "primary goods."[15] Moreover, the inequality-averse structures of evaluation functions of incomes were based on the remark that people agree more than they think about these properties since various people support different properties that happen to be mathematically equivalent.[16] The theories of the "original position," as they were applied, also led to a choice by unanimity in this "position" (see the discussion in Chapter 21, however). But the principle of unanimity also has other applications. In macrojustice, it leads to social freedom, to the ELIE structure (Part I) and, largely, to the selection of the degree of redistribution (Part IV). There is also a practical unanimity for guaranteeing the satisfaction of basic needs when necessary. Unanimity also justifies applications of the theory of "fundamental insurance" and "fundamental reciprocity", in the following sense.

In a community, there generally exists the shared sentiment that members who are favoured by chance should help out those who have bad luck, for certain issues and to some degree. The scope and degree of this aid are a priori the larger the more this set of people constitutes a community (the tighter the communitarian bond is). This sentiment exists even if the risk is not repeated with the possibility that the roles are sometimes reversed, and even in the absence of a previous contract of mutual insurance. The effect of such sentiments is to induce corresponding redistributive transfers, aid, or support. Similar transfers could result from a mutual insurance among the individuals, which can be the exchange of an aid in case of misfortune against a premium paid in any event. However, some risks

[13] See Chapter 21.
[14] Kolm 1966b.
[15] Unanimity *in the index* would be implied by a leximin.
[16] In particular as concerns preference for the dozens of properties equivalent to "progressive transfers," dominance of concentration curves and in particular of Lorenz curves, and so on.

cannot be so insured for a variety of reasons. Then, there can develop the sentiment that the considered aids or transfers should be made, as a substitute for such insurance contracts. The sentiment often consists of internalizing the fairness of the corresponding exchange contract, and people then think "I should help them because they would have helped me, were our situations reversed." The condition in this statement is true if all individuals have this view if they are in the same situation. Among the items individuals cannot take an insurance about are those that occur to them before they are adults capable to write a contract: their innate features, the family they are born in, the education they received, the other consequences of the family such as status, relations, inheritance, and so on. Now, people often speak of such given circumstances of an individual as being a matter of good or bad luck (this probably is what some philosophers have recently called "brute luck"). The corresponding putative, fictive, imaginary insurance is a "fundamental insurance." Such an insurance can notably concern education received, given capacities, the resulting earned income, health, and so on. This corresponds to existing sentiments, for instance for aiding people who receive little family education or family support for education, or concerning health. In this latter domain, the innate characteristic is the propensity to be sick. For instance, such a sentiment seems to be the main reason for favouring public systems of health insurance in Europe. The common argument is that if health insurance were private people more prone to sickness would pay higher premia, and "it is already bad for them to have bad health, and in addition they would have to pay more." The differential between this differentiated private premium and the uniform public premium constitutes the transfers of the fundamental insurance.[17]

The realization of compensations and transfers that would have resulted from some fundamental insurance if it were real is a case of substituting to a missing market. It is putative liberalism rather than direct egalitarianism. The basic implicit equality is that of the (notional) freedom of access to this exchange market rather than that of the considered result. This public substitution to a missing exchange is in a sense a case of a liberal social contract (see Chapter 3). However, while implementing a liberal social contract usually makes all the directly concerned persons better off because it mimics a unanimous free agreement or exchange, a policy replacing a missing insurance agreement, and in particular implementing a fundamental insurance, consists, on the contrary, of interpersonal transfers (because the unanimity would only be about the *ex ante* implicit insurance contract, whereas reality is *ex post*). Now, self-interested individual choice in uncertainty and a parallel interpersonal allocation motivated by direct distributive justice differ, because the individual is a priori responsible for the risks she chooses for herself, whereas the choice of a just allocation is accountable toward ethics and society, and constitutes a duty that has no reason to have the same structure as that of an interest – examples and other reflections clearly show

---

[17] See Kolm 1966b, 1985a, 1987b.

the resulting differences.[18] This affects the position of scholars who have tried to defend an egalitarian ethics through devices of this type, such as Rawls (1971) and Dworkin (1981), whereas others used such reasoning without emphasizing egalitarianism (Kolm 1966b, Harsanyi 1976, Varian 1980). Rawls, Harsanyi, and Varian use the broadest scope about what is so insured (Rawls' "original position").

However, we have seen that the ethics of implementing a fundamental insurance exists in people's mind, with a clear relation to chance and luck and sometimes to insurance, and indeed that it is widespread for some topics in some societies. These topics are also bound to be important – such as health, education, or some capacities – although the view does not extend to the whole scope of individual differences (for instance, to full compensation for beauty or intelligence). Then, if the ethics of fundamental insurance about some issue is shared by everyone in a society when asked and explained, the principle of unanimity demands its implementation.[19]

Moreover, in this case the payers would basically be convinced of the rightfulness of the corresponding distributive taxes or payments. This tends to induce free contributions. Obstacles to such voluntary givings cannot consist of the public good aspect of the "collective gift" from several givers to the same receivers and the corresponding free-riding behaviour, because the motive for giving is the putative two-by-two contract of mutual insurance between each giver and each receiver (I help her because she would have helped me, were the situations reversed) – a general mutual insurance scheme is logically equivalent to a set of two-by-two contracts among members. However, such transfers may have to be publicly implemented for reasons of information about the receivers, and, possibly, because people may adopt the corresponding ethical position and behaviour only if they know the others also similarly contribute. It should also be emphasized that a fundamental insurance does not have to face the issue of "moral hazard" of actual insurances (that is, the insured person takes excessive risks since she is protected), because the "insured" damage has already occurred and the (hypothetical) risk cannot be modified.

Finally, fundamental insurance is an ethical theory in the family of social contracts, because it implements a hypothetical agreement unanimous in a society. More specifically, it can be seen, as suggested, as a case of a liberal social contract (see Chapter 3). The obstacle to spontaneous free exchange would be the "arrow of time," that is, the impossibility of making an agreement of insurance before the occurrence of the insured damage. However, liberal social contracts usually lead to a unanimous (Pareto) improvement for the directly concerned persons. If the

---

[18] See Chapter 21 and Kolm 1985a, 1996a (Chapter 8), 2001b. This also relates to Amiel and Cowell's (1999) findings of differences in people's views about inequality in interpersonal distribution and in risk. Roemer's (1996a) and Fleurbaey's (2003) objection to Dworkin's proposal on the ground that it amounts to a utilitarianism (rather, in fact, to a "partial Harsanyism" in adding risk-relevant von Neumann–Morgenstern utilities) basically has the same source.

[19] See Kolm 1985a, 1987a, 1987b, 1996a, 1998, 2001b, 2002, and Chapter 21.

replaced agreement is an insurance, this unanimous improvement is *ex ante* the insured event. *Ex post*, indeed, the policy consists of sheer transfers. And, for a fundamental insurance, only *ex post* actually exists. But the unanimity is reinstated at the ethical level if the ethics of fundamental insurance is unanimously accepted for the item and among the persons in question.

In addition, people's reference may be to a putative *reciprocity* rather than to a putative *exchange* – an insurance is an exchange. That is, the reasoning may be "I aid people in need, given that they would have aided me if our situations were reversed," without imagining the exchange of an insurance.[20] Then, the fictive reason for aiding is no longer a contractual obligation (transformed into a moral obligation by the idea of a "social contract"). Rather, the fictive item is a gift provided by the other person if the situations were reversed. And the aid is provided in spite of the fact that the reversed situation is known not to be the case. This generally leads to final acts and aids different from those of a fundamental insurance. The basic motive is different since it is the reciprocal fairness and liking of reciprocity rather than pure self-interest. This is not amenable to the objection to fundamental insurance due to the a priori mistaken analogy between a self-interested choice in uncertainty and a choice of justice. The social ethical choice is now derived from motives of social relations more germane to it. This putative reciprocity applied to given characteristics and the corresponding compensation can be called a *fundamental reciprocity*. Note that while a successful purely self-interested exchange is Pareto-efficient (the so-called "Coase theorem") in the space of actions or transfers, this is generally not the case for a reciprocity (for instance, it can be a Cournot-Nash equilibrium, and the theory of reciprocity shows that this is the only case where this solution is justified in a one-shot on two-shot game).[21] However, for a fundamental reciprocity this inefficiency is for a fictive, notional interaction. Only one of the transfers is actualized in each reciprocity between a pair of agents. Hence, this inefficiency in the putative relation entails no inefficiency in the actual one. Finally, the above remarks noting that the transfer motive is about each transfer from one person to the other, rather than about the beneficiary's overall situation (which would be a public good for the payers), and its consequences for implementation, presented for fundamental insurance, also hold for fundamental reciprocity.

5. BASIC NEEDS, "HUMAN CAPITAL", CAPACITIES, CAPABILITIES

We have seen that utilitarianism and other "welfarisms" conceived as universal principles, which fortuitously but durably came to constitute the obvious truth in

---

[20] See Kolm 1984a, 2000b, 2004b.

[21] Each of two actors provides a return gift in answer to the other's gift. Then, a concern for procedural fairness may lead them to desire that the order of giving is of no consequence. Therefore, the first giver provides the gift that would be her return gift if the actual return gift were the initial gift. The outcome thus has a Cournot-Nash structure. In other cases, it has a Stackelberg structure.

specific scholarly circles, were objected to and replaced by freedoms and concerns about inequalities in incomes (and other "primary goods") by a few scholarly studies whose objections merely specified the common view about macrojustice. In addition, there was also a long line of studies emphasizing the satisfaction of *basic needs* and the formation of *human capital*. The field of "development," in particular, often focused on these issues. Human capital notably includes productive and earning capacities. It focuses on education and health. Enhancing capacities provides means and "real" freedom; it can be beneficial both in producing and earning and in other activities; and it affects the final distribution of income in a way that generally entails lower disincentive effects and inefficiencies than redistribution based on earned income does (but not than one based on given "equalization labour").[22] Capacities, which depend on both given characteristics and formation, are means for individuals' free use, as incomes, other "primary goods", and rights are – contrary to happiness or satisfaction –; and they are ingrained in individuals, as happiness, satisfaction, suffering, and the like are – contrary to incomes and other "primary goods." This can make them constitute a kind of "intermediate" focus of considerations of justice. Detailed sectorial studies were accompanied by the joint consideration of the various dimensions of development (such as education, health, general consumption, and so on) with, notably, the comparison of multidimensional inequalities in theory and in applications.[23] However, actual improvement first requires the choice of the appropriate policy given the actual social, political and cultural context.

For instance, the formation of capacities can be chosen by individuals and families or be the object of direct policies – and both can more or less intervene. Now, if productive capacities enable one to earn income, conversely distributed income permits one to freely take care of the formation of one's productive capacities (or of one's children's). More generally, the distributive policy can cater to people's specific needs of any kind, or rather consider and possibly affect their disposable incomes. If people have sufficient income and information, they can freely choose and buy the goods and services that best satisfy their needs as they see them. This sufficient income can result from earning with sufficient productivity and from distribution policy. The latter can be the general overall distribution (as with ELIE, which provides sufficient incomes if the average productivity and the degree of redistribution are sufficient), or result from a specific policy of minimum income. The free buying may also elicit the most efficient supply of these goods or services, in relying on commercial motivations (with the possibility of competition and, if necessary, regulation). Supply includes the possibility of insurance of all kinds (for instance as concerns health) and of borrowing (for instance for education).

---

[22] These disincentive and inefficiencies can for instance result from people making insufficient effort as concerns their education and health because a public policy helps them in this respect.

[23] See Kolm 1959, 1977a. Lowest multidimensional inequality consistent with Pareto efficiency leads to the property of "super-equity" (Kolm 1973a, 1996b).

The conjunction of both free consumer's choice and efficient supply implements Pareto efficiency. The necessity of the public supply of specific goods or services, or of specific income supports, often only results from a failure of the policy of overall distribution. These second-best distributions should not cause forgetting about the first-best which satisfies needs in respecting freedom and efficiency. Or be pretexts for dispensing with overall equity.

Such substitution of public provision of specific goods to an overall just distribution of resources and of the income they provide often results from conflations of interests of the advantaged classes, of administrations at all levels seeking self-justification and power, and of politicians trying both to spare the rich and patronize the poor (notably the voting poor), with the alibi of simple-minded, do-gooder and miserabilist ideologies. Charity is an attempt to escape from justice. When the needs to be satisfied are decided by anybody other than the beneficiaries, paternalism may be the best possible case because it at least implies benevolent intentions. Commonly, the choice of goods distributed obeys a priori views about what people should have and be, derived from a panel of possible influences and models, going from the standard ideology of development to the intent or pretext of creating some kind of "new man." These views also generally happen to favour economic interests in need of workers and consumers, or political interests seeking supporters or forming devotees. Formation, care, or aid are often ways of – or pretexts for – imposing lifestyles, ways of life and of thinking, values, dependencies on administrations or systems, and, indeed, new needs and desires resting more on addiction than on necessity. Moreover, political catering for these needs commonly favours rulers' kin, clan, tribe, party, or supporters. Even in the unfrequent electoral democracies, it has to reward politically correct voters. At any rate, this public or political provision commonly creates a situation of dependency, lack of autonomy, and absence of responsibility and, in the end, of dignity.

Administrative supply is also the source of multiple inefficiencies. The vicarious choice instead of consumers' is one. But even if an administration wanted to follow consumers' desires about their needs, it often could obtain such information only at a cost and imperfectly. Administrative provision also tends to elicit inefficiency-generating disincentives, in inducing people to lower their own efforts for satisfying their needs of all kinds, including through labour, formation, or prevention. And although it should be emphasized that there also exist devoted public services, administrative supply rather often just lacks the motivation to be efficient, as shown by the classical features of bureaucracy, and it provides a field of temptation for political favouritism, as provisioning through public markets provides the main field of temptation for corruption in favour of political parties and public figures. In these respects, efficiency, liberty, dignity, and honesty generally go hand in hand. Of course, as a guarantee against disfunctionings possible in any large society, there should at any rate be a free administrative availability of satisfying, in dignity and with quality, very basic needs in nutrition, health care, education, and so on; but this is not macrojustice.

The formation of capacities raises a particularly deep question as concerns freedom. Capacities are means which provide freedom of choice of actions. They constitute what one is. Choosing them for oneself is choosing what one is. People are freer if they can choose not only what they do but also what they can do in choosing what they are. The possibility of this choice constitutes a liberty which is logically prior to, and in a sense deeper than, that of choosing one's actions with given capacities. Choosing others' capacities, notably through education and formation, constitutes an interference which is more insidious, but in a sense deeper, than interfering with their acts. One should be free and responsible for what one is no less than for what one does (and choosing what one is also implies in part choosing what one will want, in the realm of mental freedom – in a sense, the deepest liberty of all). The availability of the means of formation enhances these particular freedoms, and this can largely consist of general means (income), accompanied by the relevant information and a working supply.

Indeed, free choice requires both means and sufficient information. When information is insufficient, the solution consists of providing it. However, this sufficient transfer of information may not be possible about complex issues such as technologies, aspects of health, or the various aspects of education. This may justify some vicarious choices that would provide what the people would have freely chosen, had they been sufficiently informed (in line with the principle of liberal social contracts – see Chapter 3). Yet, the necessity of such interventions, and the particular choices made, have to be specifically justified in each case.

Education is a particular sector for these issues. It largely consists of information ... which can be fully known only *ex post*. With respect to freedom, education can be the best and the worst of things. It promotes freedom in providing information, mental capacities and, possibly, a sense of criticism, of the value of autonomous reason, and of ways of using it. It generally is necessary for mental freedom. However, it also often inculcates other values, prejudices as concerns proper judgments, good or bad life, or needs, and it is the vehicle of indoctrination. "Modern" education, in the same stroke, both frees from traditions and destroys cultures (and hence, the possibility of living in them), and solving this dilemma – there are ways – is one of the main challenges facing us.

However, all these provisions have other structures that prevent the efficiency and optimality of the result of "spontaneous order," in the classical domains of increasing returns to scale, public goods, and externalities, more or less requiring collective and public interventions, and some of which are specific to the sectors in question. These latter cases include externalities in the fields of health and education. In particular, education faces two of the major externalities in society, which constitute its main interpersonal and intertemporal bonds: the "cultural" and the "parental" externalities. The latter consists of the fact that parents decide for their children and so affect the future adults they will be. This can be in itself good or bad; it creates the continuity of society and culture; but children may have to be freed from part of this influence, and public education has a major role in this respect. The cultural externality is the fact that the culture of individuals benefits other individuals in permitting communication, common understanding, shared values, and their consequences for collective action and general life (languages and respectful attitudes can be parts of this culture). These externalities can provide reasons for public support of education. Moreover, cultural facts are more or less public goods whose efficient provision often also requires support. More deeply, however, the value of cultures transcends their effects for individuals (whether obtained individually, through externalities, or as public goods). Indeed, the preservation and life of cultures, in their variety, certainly is also an end in itself, and a duty for people and societies. Mankind is a family of cultures no less than a conglomeration of individuals, and there is a case for defending that cultures, no less than individuals, have a right to existence and thriving.[24] This, again, sets a meta-individual aim for education.

Yet, important or essential as all these public tasks may be, their aspect as concerns individualistic justice are in the field of microjustice or mesojustice rather than macrojustice (see Chapter 1).

However, in the classical line of reflection about basic needs, human capital and capacities, Amartya Sen (1985, 1993, 1999) and Martha Nussbaum (1986, 1992, 1995a, 1995b, 2000) advocated policies concerned with individuals' "capabilities" which permit their "functionings," and, in spite of the mechanistic connotation of this latter term, deepened the meaning of this viewpoint as concerns economics (Sen) and philosophy (Nussbaum). Capabilities seem to be anything specific that enables one to do or have what one wants. Capacities constitute a very important part of them, but they also include the relevant public goods. A central difference between Sen and Nussbaum is that the latter seems to be satisfied with minimal "thresholds" of capabilities, in line with the studies of "basic needs," while Sen advocates the equality of individuals' capabilities. Nussbaum relates her thinking to Aristotle's considerations about the nature of "the good life." Sen's objective is to focus on a substance intermediate between income and other "primary goods," on the one hand, and "welfare" or happiness, on the other hand. Higher capabilities of an individual extend her possible domain of choice and action, and hence her freedom in this sense (which is not social freedom), but there can also be a functioning for providing happiness (seen as a specific good rather than the all-encompassing evaluator). G. Cohen (1986, 1989) calls this substance the "midfare" level. He also presents the most focused criticism of the objective of equal capabilities in proposing that the choice of this equalizand is arbitrary and that the "currency of equality" (as he nicely puts it) should rather consist of what the individuals are not responsible for. This basically restates an aspect of Plato's and Aristotle's expression of what they see as being the general opinion about justice, and the application to macrojustice leads to the equal

---

[24] See Kolm 1993a.

sharing of the value of given productive capacities properly measured (that is, to ELIE).[25]

This remark is but one aspect of the set of questions suggested by this proposal. Indeed, in relation with this issue of responsibility, the equalization of capabilities elicits queries as concerns liberty, efficiency (as unanimity), and dignity. Individuals can more or less choose not only what they do, but also what they can do and what they are. They can buy various consumption goods and means of action – if they have the income; they can acquire education and formation through effort and sometimes buying; they can acquire health through prudence and sometimes buying; and so on. A number of the means of formation of capabilities are transferable across people and across capabilities. But capabilities themselves are largely non-transferable (this is notably the case of capacities). Now, people have different preferences about what they do, and hence about their capabilities. Therefore, equality in all capabilities a priori implies Pareto-inefficiency. Moreover, the natural endowments (given capacities) of individuals make them differently gifted for the various capabilities, and equality in capabilities may induce waste for this reason also. In addition, the policy of equality will induce people to make lower efforts in forming these capabilities, which also induces waste. And this equality often goes with public provision, which commonly implies inefficient supply for reasons of information and motivation (plus the various possible and common social and political effects noted earlier, some of which finally lead to distributions that are the opposite of equality). This equality is also a restriction of freedom in the choice of one's capabilities. Now capabilities provide freedom of choice when used, but the freedom of choosing them is the deeper freedom about what one is and can do rather than only about what one does. And liberty and responsibility are the two faces of the same coin. One should probably be free and responsible about what one is and can do, and not only about what one does, as much as possible. Finally, since the formed capabilities are not those that the concerned individuals would have chosen if they had the means and the relevant information – these capabilities would not be the same for all in the first place –, the question of the rationale of their choice is raised. Paternalism might be the best case, since it seems to imply that this choice is made with benevolent concern for the people. In fact, such choices commonly result from ideology, political or economic interest, and cultural prejudice with its long history from missions, colonial benevolence, and present-day institutions of development.[26]

However, this kind of issues is bound to occur in the consideration of some of the most important problems, in the questions of "development" and of "poverty".

---

[25] As shown in Part II and Chapter 16.

[26] Moreover, the very notion of "functioning," applied to human beings, is worrisome. Vocabulary may not matter because it is only words, but some people think it matters. Functioning usually applies to machines. Having items in a good state of functioning is the ideal of a garage keeper. The same remark applies to the notion of "human capital" (not long ago, millions of people had to study a pamphlet entitled "Man, the most precious capital").

Now, it seems that the proper approach of such questions should admit four points. A first essential remark is that low income and misery are different things. Balanced traditional life with little modern technology but a rich culture has absolutely no reason to be seen as inferior to the "development" way of integration in the technological world, as an underdog in the working mass, with the ideal prospect to produce modern petits-bourgeois at the fourth generation and the opportunity to generate decultured and stressed executives at the sixth generation. Relevant health care can be introduced, but the merit of "globalized" education is to be carefully questioned. The 19th century ideology of "progress" has for long been unveiled as an ignorant or interested kind of cultural racism, which leads, *per se*, neither to happier or freer lives, nor to superior civilization. Now, the "new" technological world is actually widespread, as is misery in it. But confusing both types of low income life under the heading of "poverty" is a most harmful and dangerous nonsense.

The second central point is that, concerning misery proper in a technological society, the solution consists first of all of securing a minimum income. Specific policies for catering for needs in nutrition, clothing, or housing are doubtlessly inferior to letting people spend their income as they want on these commodities. Specific provision in kind is to be restricted to cases of exceptional and transitory catastrophes. The extra policy should then be restricted to the usual regulation of a competitive market or as concerns safety (with, for housing, urban regulation for location and the environment). Income can also buy insurance, notably health insurance which can finance a part of health care, and part of education, or it can be saved.

The third level of consideration concerns the securing of this minimum income. Chapters 7, 13 and 15 have shown that an ELIE scheme practically dominates all other policies of support to low income (in addition to its rational justification but because of it). The secured income depends on the equalization labour or coefficient k and, indeed, provides a reason for its choice. Then, one of the considerations for choosing k is that the level $k\overline{w}$ be at least sufficient for permitting the satisfaction of basic needs. Basic needs constitute a priori an elusive concept, but they have the remarkable property that they are often more easy to define in practice than in theory. The reason is that, in a given society at a given time, there is, about what basic needs are, if not a consensus, at least a set of conceptions that are not too dispersed.[27] Of course, public policies also include policies that secure economic efficiency, in correcting the various "market failures" by the proper macroeconomic policy, provision of public goods, and regulations and protections.

Yet, the fourth and last level of consideration re-introduces two specific needs. The lower disposable incomes also depend on the productivity of their holders (and possibly of other people through transfers). Education is an essential factor

[27] See Kolm, 1959, 1977b.

of this productivity. It can in part be chosen and financed by families, or by students through borrowing. Yet, the state of means, information and motivation in families, as well as all the various social and external effects of education noted earlier, undoubtedly entail the requirement of a substantial role of the public sector in education. A similar conclusion holds for health, above all because it can be a question of life and death or of handicaps, and for issues of information (health also has its particular externalities and can influence productivity). In the end, only two types of human needs require specific consideration, beyond the sole provision through income and free choice: education and health. Parts of these needs are satisfied by individuals' incomes and choices. Yet, public policy also has an important role to play in them. Relatedly, they raise issues of specific justice that are not solved by income justice alone. They are legitimate domains of "sphered justice" (a term inspired by Waltzer's "spheres of justice") for some items and in part, that is, some allocational choices should not depend, or should depend only little, on allocation in other fields and in particular in income – such as life-saving decisions, basic education and educational opportunities, and so on. Yet, since the issues of education and health include questions and solutions that concern all individuals, they are not well classified in the field of "microjustice" either. They are the main topics of the realm of "mesojustice". Although health and education are, in themselves or by their consequences, essential parts of individuals' overall situation, they raise many more or less specific questions of justice and of application of other values. In fact, most criteria and values intervene in various ways in choices concerning them. Equality is a form that can apply to many items in them with different implications, and various issues concern needs, merit, desert, responsibility, freedom, compensations, Pareto efficiency, efficiency in social output, insurance and risk, fundamental insurance, reciprocity, fundamental reciprocity, culture, comparing sufferings and liberties, social status, the place of the market and of the public and associative sectors, and so on. These important issues are beyond the field of the present study.[28]

6. TO EACH ACCORDING TO HER WORK, RESPONSIBILITY, EQUALITY OF OPPORTUNITY

Although responsibility, the main allocative criterion throughout society (in particular as the aim-freedom part of process-freedom and social freedom), and a main application of Aristotle's principle of "geometric equality," has for long been considered and used by economists – and not only lawyers and philosophers – a few economists a priori prone to value equality in allocations or incomes became aware of its relevance through Cohen's mention of it for replacing the arbitrariness he saw in the principle of the equality of individuals' "capabilities." This led to a

[28] Issues of justice concerning health are notably analyzed in the study *On health and justice* (Kolm 2002) See also the previous remarks about fundamental insurance and fundamental reciprocity.

number of analyses of various types. Some are in tune with the classical view of equalizing what the individuals are not responsible for and letting them receive the full benefit or bear the full cost of what they are responsible for – that is, Plato's and Aristotle's "arithmetic" and "geometric" equality, and Cohen's intent. Others only introduce an ideal of horizontal "responsibilist" equity of equal benefit for equal effort into another ethics, such as the social, aggregate principle of the highest sum of same individual items' (utility, income, education, health) or a more egalitarian objective in end-states. Marc Fleurbaey (a synthesis in 1995) showed logical difficulties in applications of the principle of equality qualified by responsibility, notably due to the question of the assignment of the product of joint causes.[29] In considering applications meeting this kind of issue (for instance, in health policy), John Roemer proposed that the assignment of responsibility be entrusted to the political system – hence, beyond sheer considerations of causality. Roemer (1998) also proposed an elaborate theory – epitomized in a practical formula – for an allocation showing a preference for equal benefit for equal effort and equality of opportunity, but not for equally sharing given resources (or for less unequal outcomes), though; this theory is discussed in Appendix B.[30]

Appendix A. A NOTE ON HISTORY OF THOUGHT

A.1. The elements of the obtained solution

The solution obtained for macrojustice is so straightforward that most of its elements have a long history. This of course is the case for the basis in nonviolence, social freedom, basic rights, or process-freedom – the basis of the social ethics of modernity. *Prima facie* equality is a rational necessity (Chapter 23) and, hence, is everywhere – although in many forms. Process-freedom with equal sharing of given items is a direct application of the two equalities that Plato and Aristotle present as being the common view of justice. For the delineation of macrojustice, the overwhelming importance in volume of the value of labour compared with that of other natural resources has been emphasized notably by Locke (see Chapter 5) and Ricardo (and Marx). The ELIE tax-subsidy structure has been considered and analyzed in Kolm (1966b, 1993e, 1996a, 1996b, 1997b), and the resulting allocation of consumption and labour has been derived from "axioms" by Maniquet (1998a, 1998b) – considered shortly. Although full self-ownership is classical, and usually considered the opposite of egalitarianism, its resource-egalitarian property when individual capacities are measured by their inputs rather than by their outputs is discussed in Kolm 1985a. Its opposite ideal of income equality is a common position of the leftist family (Chapter 11 has shown that its actual implementation should be the income-egalitarian ELIE). Its "wild opposite" of "maximal income equalization" (coefficient $k = 1$), which is unanimously rejected

---

[29] We have seen that unanimous free agreement about the sharing, because of its structure of veto (due to unanimity), makes everyone fully responsible for the outcome and thus constitutes a solution to this question.

[30] A full analysis of this theory and others in similar spirit (for instance, Van de gaer's 1993) is provided in Kolm 2001a.

because it "redistributes" the product of fictive labour, is considered, along with the discussion of its injustice toward the "talented," by Pazner and Schmeidler (1972), Varian (1974, 1975), Pazner (1977), and Dworkin (1981). The self-assignment of eudemonistic capacities and preferences is the common view for macrojustice. It is held by the proponents of both self-ownership and income equality. It is introduced with proposed justifications in scholarly analyses by Kolm (1966a), Rawls (1971), and Dworkin (1981) – see Section 3.

A.2. Other theories of ideal self-accountability of tastes and equal sharing of productive capacities

A number of recent interesting and remarkable studies have in common, with the obtained solution, an intention of self-assignment of eudemonistic capacities, equal sharing of productive capacities, and Pareto efficiency.[31] However, the basic framework, conception, and ethics of these studies are very different from those of the present approach and are, in a deep sense, opposed to it. Let us put aside the fact that these studies refer to self-assignment of preferences as the individuals' "responsibility" for their preferences: although the present author has used this term in this sense in 1966 (Kolm 1966a), better analysis has been made since, and we have seen in Chapter 6 that the issue of responsibility for one's tastes, eudemonistic capacities, or preferences is a very subtle one and that there are other reasons for this self-assignment or "natural" allocation. This relates to a recent but frequent use, in such economic studies, of the term "responsibility" for meaning accountability, whereas responsibility is one reason for accountability, but not the only one; and responsibility requires, to begin with, freedom of choice.

The basic difference, which has important practical consequences, is that the obtained solution is a *liberalism* and not, say, an "authoritarianism" implied by the determination of a best allocation, which then just has to be imposed on people. The individuals have freedom of choice, even in the first-best solution. They are not given an allocation – such as labour and consumption. They freely choose one. Freedom is the basic ethical principle. This thoroughly differs from the freedom the individuals manage to steal away by hiding information about themselves in those of these studies that also belong to the "optimum income tax" family (the authority may be induced to leave to the agents some free choice in order that the realization rests on the value of some relevant parameter unknown to the authority). The obtained solution is a liberalism, although it also is an egalitarianism in equally sharing given resources – with the proper measure – and by its providing equal social freedom. In particular, there is no "social planner" – a concept used in some of these studies, of course as a notional device only, but one that suggests that the consideration of the political

---

[31] See Bossert (1995), Bossert and Fleurbaey (1996), Bossert, Fleurbaey, and Van de gaer (1996), Fleurbaey (1994b, 1995a, 1995b, 1995c), Fleurbaey and Maniquet (1995, 1996), Iturbe and Nieto (1996), Maniquet (1998a, 1998b), Sprumont (1997). The following remarks only show a basic difference with most of these works, and hence a full (and therefore fairer) discussion is not attempted. Studies with a similar intent based on the theory of "equivalence" are considered in Chapter 26. A general theoretical treatment of the ideal equalization of the benefits (or handicaps) from some characteristics while those from others are assigned to the individual is proposed in Kolm 1996d and 1998.

conditions of implementation would be an interesting complement. The position in this respect is described in Chapter 17 (with respect to the classical "benevolent dictator"). The choice of a method or concept of solution is not indifferent, neutral or inocuous. It implies a specific social philosophy which makes a difference when it comes to application (and decentralized implementation through incentives may be adding manipulation to central decision).

A technical consequence is that Pareto efficiency is obtained by individuals' free choice in the proper conditions. It is not obtained by imposing an allocation that has this property. As a consequence, the policy – notwithstanding the ways of its implementation – need not know, consider, or be concerned with individuals' preferences for ascertaining Pareto efficiency. In contrast, the noted studies hold that requiring Pareto efficiency implies a relevance, for the policy, of individuals' preferences. But this is at odds with the hypothesis that the individuals are accountable for their preferences – which, then, should not be a concern for the policy or its analysis. More precisely, Pareto efficiency requires the ordinal structure of the preferences (the preference orderings, the ordered indifference loci, or the ordinal utilities). Hence, self-accountability becomes restricted to the concept of intensity of preferences. Yet, separating both aspects is problematic. Why are the individuals not also accountable for their preference orderings? This is a main aspect of their "tastes" – indeed, they describe all that is needed of their tastes for "positive" economics (they determine choices, demand functions, etc.). Moreover, a standard view with some psychological content is that the preference orderings or indifference loci are derived from satisfaction as function of the consumption: indifference means equal satisfaction. Then, the two aspects cannot be separated. However, some justification for the distinction can be proposed. It rests on the fact that individuals are materially affected by others only through their acts, and, in the classical theory of choice, the agents' choice of their acts results from their preference orderings only (given possibilities), and in no way from any aspect of intensity of these preferences. Hence, individuals are so concerned by others only by their preference ordering, and not by any aspect of preference intensity. In this sense, intensity can be said not to trespass the agent's private sphere. This can be taken as a reason for assigning it to the sole accountability of the agent (a "natural" allocation of preference intensity). Then, public justice could be concerned with the remainder, that is, preference orderings (in addition to other aspects such as productive capacities). However, the basic concept then is external effects (effects on others), and the privacy possibly derived from it, rather than privacy defined in itself or freedom. In contrast, full self-accountability of preferences leads to taking, as the primary public concern, domains and conditions of choice, that is, freedom, and hence it is a liberalism.

Among these studies, one by Maniquet (1998a, 1998b) arrives at a solution that is the final result of an EDIE liberal policy (after individuals' choices). The way this is arrived at, however, is thoroughly different from that presented here (social freedom with equal sharing of the value of the given resources properly measured). This result is deduced from a set of basic formal properties ("axioms"). This shows these properties of EDIE, and a necessary and sufficient set of them. However, for judging EDIE in this way, one should evaluate the interest (or necessity), meaning, significance, or importance of each of these basic formal properties, a discussion that would take us too far away from the present purpose.[32] This contrasts with ELIE as a liberalism primarily based on social freedom.

Appendix B. HORIZONTAL COMPARATIVE RESPONSIBILIST EQUITY IN A GLOBAL AIM

The noted theory of Roemer (1998) is an interesting, imaginative and subtle proposal of an operational solution applicable to important problems. It raises a number of questions, but they can often be answered by appropriate modifications or complements. In this framework, individuals choose to provide effort (this could be labour) and receive a resulting benefit or outcome which could be, for instance, education, health, or utility (one could also add income). This benefit also depends on given "circumstances" and on policy measures. The point is the choice of these measures and the allocation of corresponding resources (although they all remain implicit). This follows two ideal objectives. One is in the field of equity and says that individuals who provide the same effort should ideally receive the same benefit. However, this equity determines neither the difference in benefit of people who provide different efforts, nor, simply, the fair benefit for a given individual effort. It is restricted to *horizontal* (same effort) and *comparative* ideal equity. The other effects of the policy are determined by the second ideal: having the highest sum of individual benefits. This is considered as "efficiency." A highest sum of individuals' benefits is indeed sometime called "efficiency," when society or a sector are considered globally (with also the consideration of the overall resources used). This can relate to more individualistic notions of efficiency (among which Pareto efficiency) when the attainment of this highest sum and its later distribution among the individuals do not interfere. This is not the case here because the policy directly determines individuals' benefits. Hence, this objective is to be considered as an ultimately and irreducibly social, aggregate, and nonindividualistic objective. It might thus be amenable to Rawls' judgment about utilitarianism that "it does not take seriously the division of society into individuals" (and it indeed is utilitarianism when the individual benefits are "utilities"). It might also not obey Kant's injunction of considering persons "in the kingdom of ends." However, the other ideal objective – equal benefit for equal effort – does single individuals out, and with a view of the self that evokes Kant's, because this ideal is explained by a reference to responsibility, an important vector of dignity. The highest sum of individuals' benefits is also amenable to an individualistic interpretation for cases of local and variational justice (see Chapter 6), but this would not fit with the considered applications. At any rate, this use of the term "efficiency" is not economists' most common use of it, Pareto efficiency. Moreover, the consideration of the sum requires that individuals' benefits could meaningfully be added (which notably raises well-known difficulties if these benefits are utilities – but is straightforwardly possible if we choose them to be income).

Now, these two objectives are usually not consistent. The highest sum may require favouring individuals in favourable circumstances (family for education, health, etc.).

---

[32] For instance, these "axioms" include Maskin's "preferences monotonicity," "consistency" (Moulin and Shenker, Thomson), and "replication invariance" (Thomson).

A second-best maximand is then chosen: in the sum, the benefits of individuals who provide the same effort are replaced by the lowest of them. The maximization then pushes this lowest up, which intends to provide a type of tendency toward equalization of the outcomes for the same effort (the limitations of maximin as an egalitarian criterion have been shown in Chapter 23). However, for different efforts, the allocation of the (implicit) policy means is determined by the maximization of the sum (rather than by any attempt to directly relate benefit to effort). Hence, this overall principle has, as an ideal, "to each according to her effort" only for comparing the benefits of individuals who provide the same efforts, and not for different efforts. Using classical vocabulary and concepts, it has an ideal of "horizontal equity" but not one of "vertical equity." As concerns the "vertical" distribution (that is, for individuals who provide different efforts), the allocation is determined by the objective of the highest sum. Moreover, and relatedly, "according to" would not intend to relate benefit to effort, but only to state that people providing the same effort should have the same benefit, whatever it is: this justice is exclusively comparative and not related to intrinsic desert. Formally, in the end, the actual maximand should be the sum of the lowest benefits (outcomes) in each class of individuals providing the same effort, weighted by the number of individuals in this class. In this sense, it is intermediate between the sum and the minimum, and the objective is intermediate between maximizing the sum and the maximin. It is the former if all individuals provide different efforts and the latter if they all provide the same effort. This provides a solution to the question of the choice of the degree of egalitarianism, a justified solution (though not the only possible one, and the application, shortly noted, still demands the further selection of a crucial parameter).

Finally, it is *a priori* assumed that same effort equates same output (benefit), which assumes that the policy actually compensates the effects on outputs of different circumstances for individuals who provide the same effort, while the policy of the model does not guarantee that – hence the use of the maximin. However, this relation is extended to treating as producing the same effort individuals whose output (benefit) is in the same quantile of the statistical description, for some chosen interval size (decile, centile, and so on). Hence, it suffices that each individual's effort and output are in the same quantile of their statistical distribution. This happens whatever the quantile if the rankings of individuals' items are maintained from effort to output. At any rate, it is the more satisfied the larger the quantile (the coarser the statistics).

In the end and summing up, "to each according to her work or effort" is restricted to "equal benefit for equal effort" while benefits for different efforts are determined by the highest sum, and, moreover, "equal effort" is extended to mean effort in the same quantile of benefits (output), and equal benefit is interpreted by the replacement, in the sum, of each individual benefit by the lowest in the same quantile. The resulting formula is convenient for application from given statistics about individuals' outputs. Since there is the same number of individuals in each quantile (by definition and at least for large numbers of individuals), the maximand becomes the sum of the lowest benefits (outputs) in each quantile. When the quantile interval shrinks until including only one item (n intervals), or expands until including all individuals (one interval), the maximand becomes respectively the sum or the lowest of individual outputs (benefits), and the policy becomes maximizing the sum or maximin. The maximand and the principle tend to these cases when the size of the quantile interval shrinks or expands (the number of quantiles expands or shrinks), respectively. Now, the size of the quantile interval is a priori arbitrary. And the maximand and hence the policy depend on it. Moreover, the policy tends to make individuals' benefits more similar when they are in the same quantile interval of efforts and benefits. Hence, the benefits of individuals who receive neighbouring benefits, and hence are assumed to provide neighbouring efforts, tend to be equalized if they fall in the same interval, but they tend to be made more apart if they fall in different intervals. And outputs and efforts in different neighbouring intervals can be closer to one another than outputs and efforts in the same interval, whereas the policy tends to make the latter's outcomes more equal and tends to have an opposite effect on the former's. This is a problem for an ideal policy of similar benefits for similar efforts. These questions could be avoided in taking a more direct measure of effort, but at the cost of losing statistical convenience and having to define and to make operational another measure of effort. With a single interval, the objective is a maximin in individual benefits, which intends to describe an egalitarian ideal with priority to benevolence (limits of this principle in this role have been shown in Chapter 23). If all individuals actually provide different efforts with, a priori, different outputs, the thinnest division singles them out, and the objective is the maximization of the sum of benefits – then, the equity objective vanishes. Now, the interval size can be taken as indicating a degree of the relative importance attached to the two objectives: the coarser the division (larger interval), the more equity would be valued, and the thinner the division (smaller interval), the more this "efficiency" would be valued. However, this measure of relative importance raises the questions previously noted. And the same intent can be realized otherwise, in using other functions than the minimum and the sum, as it is now shown.

Indeed, other meaningful theories can be built in starting from this formula and in considering two transformations. First, if all individuals provide the same effort, or if the considered individual benefits do not depend on individuals' actions, the maximand is the sum of individuals' benefits, which has no overall egalitarian structure whatsoever. Some egalitarian ideal irrespective of effort provided can be introduced in replacing the sum by some increasing inequality-averse function of individuals' benefits. This can also be the limiting case of the maximin or leximin. Second, the replacement of each individual benefit by the lowest benefit obtained with the same effort can again be performed. However, whatever the overall maximand, the theory's replacement of each individual benefit by the lowest with the same effort is not a satisfactory expression of the corresponding egalitarian intent (as shown in Chapter 23). A more adequate and general expression of an ideal of equal benefit for equal effort consists of replacing each individual benefit by a fictive benefit which is an increasing inequality-averse function of the benefits of the individuals providing the same effort. This can in particular be an "equal equivalent" of these benefits computed with some increasing inequality-averse function of them (see Chapter 25), which is a "generalized mean" of these benefits when the evaluation has the property of independence or separability (then, the maximand can be written as a sum of functions of one individual benefit each).[33] The overall maximized function can also be such a mean, and

[33] If x_i is individual i's benefit, $I(e)$ the set of individuals who provide effort e, and $n(e)$ their number, each of the x_i for $i \in I(e)$ is replaced, in the overall maximand, by x^e. This x^e can be such that, replacing each

the maximand becomes a "mean of means" (rather than the original limiting case of a "sum of mins").

One of the two objectives of the considered principle is that individuals who provide the same effort receive the same benefit. This ideal is presented as equality of opportunity. Incidentally, this identification is not the case in general because opportunity is an *ex ante* concept, it refers to agents' possible choices, while the equality of benefits for the same effort is *ex post*. Specifically, if, of two individuals who provide the same effort and enjoy the same benefit, one decides to provide another effort, his new benefit will in general depend on who of the two she is, even after policy adjustments. The new benefit will be the same for both only in particular cases, and notably, in general, in the case of a large number of "small" individuals making independent choices. Now, Roemer considers the case of a large number. Then, equality of opportunity is taken to mean identical domains of choices – individuals receive the same benefit for the same effort, whatever the effort. Since individuals have a priori different capacities, this objective a priori refers to desert rather than to merit, although individual capacities are not explicit – they would be among the "circumstances" whose different effects across the individuals who provide the same effort the policy seeks to compensate. Yet, as we have seen, although this theory would like to provide equal benefits for equal efforts, it does not intend to directly relate benefits to efforts, and hence differences in benefits to differences in effort. It only seeks "horizontal desert." Now, individuals trivially receive according to their contribution to the sum of their benefits, since an individual's action is assumed to directly affect her own benefit only. And since these benefits depend on individuals' capacities, this allocation is according to merit. The policy thus acknowledges "vertical merit." Yet, this benefit also depends on other circumstances, and on the policy which also aims at erasing the differential effects of capacities (and other circumstances) for individuals providing the same effort. The policy finally compromises between horizontal desert and this vertical merit.

Finally, the model of this policy should be considered in its surroundings. This raises various issues, including as concerns Pareto efficiency (and hence, the principle of unanimity). First, the policy's effect on an individual's outcome depends on this individual's effort, which is a base of the policy measures. This base is elastic, since the individual chooses her effort, and hence Pareto inefficiency results. This choice of the individual is the very basis of the underlying philosophy and intent since it entails responsibility and selects an opportunity. This use of an elastic base is not imposed by particular extra constraints, as could be the case when difficulties in information lead one to base estimates of the desired base on observations of items influenced by

---

x_i for $i \in I(e)$ in some increasing inequality-averse function of these x_i by x^e, gives the same value to this function (this x^e is an "equal equivalent" of these x_i – see Kolm 1966a). In particular, if this function can be taken as additively separable $\Sigma_{i \in I(e)} f(x_i)$ for some concave function f, this x^e is the "generalized mean" $x^e = f^{-1}[(1/n(e))\Sigma_{i \in I(e)} f(x_i)]$. Roemer's case is the particular case $x^e = \min_{x \in I(e)} x_i$. Moreover, the first transformation is the replacement of the overall maximand Σx_i by the more general function $F(x)$ where x is the set of the x_i and function F is increasing and inequality averse (it increases when the x_i become more equal in some sense). In particular, $F(x)$ can be $\Sigma\varphi(x_i)$ with some concave function φ. It can then also be the "generalized mean" $\xi = \varphi^{-1}[(1/n)\Sigma\varphi(x_i)]$. In replacing x_i by x^e for $i \in I(e)$, $\Sigma\varphi(x_i)$ becomes $\Sigma n(e)\cdot\varphi(x^e)$. Finally, functions f and φ can be of the type z^α with $0 \le \alpha \le 1$, $\log z$, $1 - e^{-\alpha z}$ with $\alpha > 0$, or the more general $(z+c)^\alpha$ with $c \ge 0$ and $0 \le \alpha \le 1$ (see, for instance, Kolm 1966a, 1966b, 1976a, 1976b, 1999a).

individual choices. It is inherent in the ethical building and meaning of the maximand: Pareto inefficiency is built-in in this ethics.[34] However, the situation will, in the end, be a game-theoretic interaction between the concerned persons and the policy, and the explicit maximand can be useful for analyzing the outcome. Second, for applications to specific fields (education or health, for instance), the consideration and model are only partial and have to be integrated in the complete framework of the economy and society. This has to consider the means and budget of the policy, their overall level, their origin, and the costs in obtaining them. The relation of the considered good and sector with other consumptions and sectors and distributive measures should also influence the best policy. In particular, the relation with overall distribution is crucial. Income distribution can be influenced both by educational, and sometimes health, policies that influence future earned incomes, and by direct income transfers, with some substitutability (but education and health are also more final consumption goods). Conversely, a large part of inequalities in educational circumstances are due to the social situation of the family, which is closely related to income. Inequalities in health circumstances due to information also have such a relation. Moreover, with proper and sufficient overall income distribution, people could freely choose their schooling and health care in more or less paying for them. The virtues and limits of this way of doing have been discussed in previous sections. A number of shortcomings can be met with the provision of information and with policies obeying specific "liberal social contracts" (see Chapter 3).

[34] One way of securing Pareto efficiency is to remunerate according to effort (desert) up to a given effort benchmark, while leaving the person entitled to her extra output. But this is a fully different model: it is in fact ELIE, which can thus be applied to issues of microjustice or mesojustice (education, health) (see Kolm 2001a).

26

The theory of equivalence

1. THE GENERAL THEORY

1.1. Presentation and summary

Two states are "individualistically equivalent," or, for short, "equivalent," when all individuals are indifferent between them (unanimous indifference). The "principle of equivalence" consists of considering properties in states equivalent in this sense to the actual one. Given that the actual state has to be possible, and may be required to have some desired properties, some other properties may be better satisfied in other, equivalent states, or may be satisfied, or even defined, only in such states. These other properties may for instance be lower inequalities in goods or in freedoms, or equalities, or the highest sum of some valued item, and the actual state is often required to be Pareto efficient. The present chapter considers this theory and its applications (and in particular possible applications to global distributive justice). Section 1 presents the general theory and Section 2 the applications.

The philosophy of the equivalence principle, and notably the limit and possibility of its justification, are first considered (Section 1.2). One then notes the previous cases of application of this theory (Section 1.3), and the important property that non-Pareto-efficient states equivalent to a Pareto-efficient one have to be impossible (Section 1.4). The general theory of equivalence is then outlined in Section 1.5 and formally worked out in Section 1.6. The basic idea consists of taking, as specification of the levels of individual ordinal utilities, parameters for which some required properties are meaningful, such as equality, highest sum (in surplus theory), or lower inequality. The maximization of an appropriate increasing function of these "equivalence parameters" yields a Pareto-efficient state equivalent to a property expressed by the structure of this maximand, such as inequality aversion (leximin is a limiting case) or highest sum.

Section 2 then turns to applications of this theory. Their essence is presented in Section 2.1 and the specific models in Section 2.2. The essence is discussed for equivalence parameters that are in the family of incomes, and for the allocation of goods. The case of incomes includes: the classical theory of the surplus, which thus leads to Pareto-efficient choices and can be extended into an egalitarian surplus; the general budget possibility sets as domains of choice; the consideration of equivalent incomes for a given labour, including the "leisurely-equivalent income"; and income transfers or prices and notably wage rates for the latter. The specific models concern the four cases defined by two alternatives for each of two characteristics: the basically valued items are individuals' allocations or freedom, and the considered space is general or is the two-dimensional space of labour-leisure and income-consumption (relevant for macrojustice). The various possible meaningful equivalence parameters are shown in all cases. The case of freedom with labour and income is particularly rich (and related to freedom-based macrojustice). Finally, two Appendices consider particularly proposals in this latter field (Appendix A), and the evaluation of an allocation by the comparisons by inclusion of the notional domains of choice of the individuals that can lead them to choosing this allocation (a case where the basic philosophical difficulty of equivalence theory does not appear, Appendix B).

1.2. The moral philosophy of individualistic equivalence

1.2.1. The basic problem

If all individuals are as satisfied with what they have as with what they would have in some just situation, is this as good as justice (or as just), is this just? In a sense, surrogate justice is not justice; justice is here and now, not in dreamtime, wonderland, or the next life. However, if all individuals find both situations as good as each other, and if one respects their preferences – and hence, their unanimity in this judgment – shouldn't one accept this equivalence? If one does, justice, or any other optimality principle, can a priori be better realized. Indeed, it only need be satisfied in any situation that all the individuals find as good as the same possible one. This includes the possible situations as particular cases. The actual chosen situation will be a corresponding equivalent possible situation. This extends the domain of optimization of the considered property from the possible situations to the situations the individuals all find as good as any same possible one. This extension is usually extremely large (for instance, for only self-concerned individuals, each individual allocation or domain of choice can be replaced by any that she finds as good, irrespective of possibilities). Hence, the normative principle will generally be better satisfied (at least it cannot be satisfied less well). In particular, some criterion – for instance some equality – may be actually impossible, and yet be satisfied in some situation that all individuals find as good as a possible one.

Yet, *the actual situation that all individuals find as good as this best notional situation is generally not the best possible actual situation according to the same optimality criterion*, since it is not chosen so as to be it. There generally is a domain where an improvement of the criterion in a notional unanimously equivalent situation is necessarily accompanied by a worsening of this criterion in the corresponding equivalent actual situation. For instance, diminishing inequality in the notional situation may augment it in the actual one. Making the poorest less poor or the least free freer in the notional situation may not affect the individuals who hold these relative positions in the actual situation. It may instead favour the already richer or freer. Indeed, the poorest or least free in the notional situation may be the richest or freest in the actual situation. Even though each individual finds both situations as good as each other. This depends on the relative structure of individuals' indifference sets or *loci*. For instance, two situations may be as good as each other for two individuals, whereas one individual has more of all goods than the other in one situation and the converse holds in the other, or one individual's domain of choice strictly includes that of the other in one situation, and the converse holds in the other. These cases constitute instances of the property of *reversal*, a conspicuous syndrome of the basic problem.[1] And the change may in the end even make the actually poorest still poorer, or the actually least free still less free.

Moreover, if the individuals are indifferent between the actual situation and another one where the considered social-ethical property is better satisfied, they generally are also indifferent between them and other situations where the property is in a worse state than in the actual situation. *Why retain indifference with better rather than with worse?*

However, the valued property may be impossible with any possible actual situation, while it is possible with some notional situation that all individuals find as good as some possible one. This can, for instance, be equality in some items. At any rate, this impossibility in the possible situations forces one to resort to a second-best satisfaction of this property, and hence to define such a corresponding second-best criterion in the first place. Might not the satisfaction of the property in a situation unanimously found as good constitute such a second best? Yet, if one also defines otherwise a corresponding second-best criterion (for instance, the lowest value of some relevant measure of inequality), then the foregoing problem is here again: this criterion is a priori better satisfied in some possible situation than in the actual (hence possible) situation that everyone finds as good as the notional situation where it is satisfied at best (notably with full, first-best satisfaction of the property).

More generally, it may be possible to define, in notional situations, degrees of quality more in tune with some ethical view than those that can be defined in the possible situations. With the definition in the possible situations, however, the noted problem still occurs. It can be discarded only if the best description of the desired value in the possible situations is sufficiently less satisfactory than that possible in notional situations unanimously found as good as possible ones.

---

[1] A straightforward diagrammatic illustration is shortly pointed out.

The noted quality of the description of the satisfaction of a desired property can refer to both ethics and logic. For instance, the ideal may be an equality in individuals' allocations of one or several goods, or an identity in individuals' freedoms, which may be clearly defined while the definition of corresponding degrees of inequality raises a number of problems and additional ethical choices. In other cases, the ethics wants a highest aggregate, which again may be hard to define, whereas the equivalence concept may offer an answer (we will see that the classical theory of the surplus belongs to this category). A notable point, in this respect, is that equivalence theory leads to considering a one-parameter variable for each individual in the equivalent situation. This parameter can in addition often be a quantity. Then, equality and sum are defined, and degrees of inequality constitute a well-studied field.

All the foregoing holds if "possible" stands for possible plus some property or properties other than the discussed one. For example, the following applications will require Pareto efficiency – which in itself requires possibility – as an application of the general principle of optimality. Then, the discussed other property will most of the time be equality in some items such as allocations or freedoms (defined as social freedom or by a priori given domains of choice). The equivalence theory can then try to solve manifestations of the frequent and classical dilemma of inconsistency between efficiency and equality.[2] The actual situation would be efficient and all individuals may find it as good as some other social situation with equality in the considered items. Or, if some comparison of the considered inequalities can be defined, the actual situation would be efficient and all individuals would find it as good as some notional social situation with inequality lower than in any efficient situation and in any other notional situation that all find as good as any same efficient situation (full equality is a particular case). Then, however, this obtained actual situation will not be the efficient situation with the lowest inequality. Other applications are also considered, such as the classical theory of the "surplus" where the ideal is the highest sum of individuals' money equivalent of changing to another situation (this can also lead to other criteria, such as equal individual surpluses).

1.2.2. Possible justification by endogenous social choice and moral unanimity

However, this use of unanimous indifference may provide a good answer to the problem of second-best when other answers are hard to find or bad, only if it can be considered as constituting such an answer in the first place. Now, who is entitled to judge this validity, that of other second-best solutions, and the comparison among these solutions, and, indeed, to propose the normative criterion in the first place, which are all moral choices? If all the individuals have such

---

[2] For example, equal allocations in several goods for individuals with different tastes, equalization of earned incomes with the resulting disincentives, equal wage rates with free choice of labour for individuals with different productivities, or taxation with elastic bases and positive marginal rates.

judgments and agree about them, unanimity – again – can provide the answer. Such opinions are, of course, something else than the individuals' preferences and equivalences previously considered. Indeed, there are two levels of evaluations: the considered individuals' indifference and the overall normative judgment. Now, the individuals commonly have overall normative views in addition to the considered preferences and indifferences, above them in a sense. Then, if they all accept that some property is satisfied, or satisfied at best, only in a situation that is equivalent for them all for the considered preferences (at the "lower level"), this can – or should – be accepted for the social-ethical evaluation from the principle of unanimity considered at this "higher," social-ethical level.

Practically, this may happen when the individuals are well aware of the notional "equivalent" situation for which the property is considered. Issues of information may be irrelevant for the theoretical ethical choice, but individuals are commonly not even aware of their preferences (hence of their indifferences) in domains distant from the actual situations. This awareness is bound to occur either when the notional situation is *close* to the actual one, or when it is *conspicuous* because of some remarkable property. For example, the theory of the surplus, which is the standard normative principle in benefit-cost analysis (starting with Jules Dupuit in 1844) is based on individuals' indifference between two situations that differ by two items only, the realization of some project, and individuals' money holdings, which determine their "money equivalents" of the project, whose net sum is maximized for choosing the project; the notional equivalent situation is only the present one plus the "money equivalent" for each individual; the conditions of closeness and awareness are often satisfied; moreover, the application in the theory of the "marginal surplus" (see Kolm 1966a and an example in Chapter 19) only considers surpluses for neighbouring situations. Another example of proximate equivalence is that of the income-egalitarian ELIE (see Chapter 11), where most individuals are practically indifferent between their actual labour and income and the nearby common intersection of their budget lines, hence to a situation of equal income with equal labour – a case indeed close to a suggestion of Oskar Lange in 1937, as will be noted. A case of conspicuous equivalence is that of the lower inequality or equality of the "leisurely equivalent incomes," that is, incomes that, associated with zero labour, are deemed equivalent by the individuals to their actual income and labour pair.[3]

1.2.3. Information

Moreover, application of the concept may require knowing individuals' indifference and hence preferences (or ordinal utility functions) in a domain including the considered situations. Practically, this may be manageable when the notional situations are not too far away from actual ones, where choices can be observed.

---

[3] See Kolm 1966a, Sections 5, 6, and 7.

Questionnaires may permit a wider scope, but with serious limits (the individuals themselves are not aware of their preferences when they involve unusual situations). Now, the surplus method considers rather proximate situations. Proximity is also the case for the income-egalitarian ELIE; in this case, in fact, the relevant rates of substitution of preferences amount to the wage rates; and, indeed, this solution requires no information at all about preferences since it results from individuals' free choice given the ELIE transfers.

For situations distant from actual ones, the problem about individuals' comparisons and indifference may be deeper than knowing given individuals' preferences, and reach issues concerning their meaningfulness. This can thus affect not only practical applications, but also theoretical issues. This can indeed occur for comparisons with situations that the individuals have never faced, cannot consider facing, or even cannot face, for instance for some consumptions, labours, or domains of choice. In fact, we will see that when one property is Pareto efficiency, the situation having the other property has to be impossible – although this impossibility is for the overall situation of all the individuals rather than for each separately independently of the others' situation.

A property such as Pareto efficiency also rests on individuals' preference orderings. However, this property can result from social freedom in individual or collective choices and notably exchange, and hence a liberal policy that relies on such freedom can secure this property without being informed about these preferences. The property obtains whatever these preferences. Preferences are relevant but their specificity is not, for the policy, contrary to what is the case for the method of equivalence considered here. This is in particular the case of ELIE schemes.[4]

1.2.4. Relevant items

This relates to the question of the relevant items. Three types of properties will be considered: individuals' indifferences, Pareto efficiency, and other normative properties such as equalities, lower inequalities, or highest sum. The considered use of indifferences makes sense if the latter properties involve other items than individuals' preferences – such as allocations, incomes, or freedoms – since the individuals are indifferent between the two situations, and hence a property that refers to preferences only is the same in both situations (Pareto efficiency also considers possibilities). However, if these equalized or added items are the basically ethically relevant ones (the basic concerns of Chapter 23), this implies a priori that individuals' preferences and indifferences do not have this basic ethical relevance. Assuming that they also are so relevant is the basic reason of the noted difficulty (exemplified by the reversal syndrome). The only way out of this dilemma again consists of resorting to higher-order ethical judgments of the individuals, that would endorse this association. Pareto efficiency rests on individuals'

---

[4] And when more specific information is needed, for second-best policies for instance (see Chapter 10, Appendix), it concerns preferences not far from domains of observation.

preferences, but it also considers actual possibilities, it directly relates to endogenous social choice, it can be endorsed by higher-order ethical judgments, and, with a liberal policy, it may result from individuals' free actions and interactions without explicit consideration of individuals' specific preferences.

1.2.5. Equivalent situations

The considered "situations" are a priori of any type with any specification. They can consist of or include: allocations of goods; labours; incomes; prices; wages; freedoms of any type such as, notably, social freedom or free exchange from some given allocation, or freedom solely defined by some a priori given domain of free choice (this can notably make a difference when equal freedom is considered); rights; powers; statuses; and so on.

Two situations will be said to be *equivalent* for an individual when she is indifferent between them for the explicitly considered preferences. These are the individuals' preferences of "lower order" just considered, not their "higher-order" judgments (if they have any). These preferences will include individuals' self-interest. They may also encompass some moral or social judgments, but this will not be met in the particular applications that will be considered here. At any rate, we will see that the simplest form of the general theory of equivalence requires that there exists, for each individual, one parameter that concerns herself only, and even that these parameters be unidimensional (i.e., the manifestations of each can be ordered) and have some kind of comparability across the individuals. If two situations are equivalent for all individuals, they are "individualistically equivalent": this means that they are not a priori equivalent as concerns their other, "metaindividualistic" properties, notably those that are the base of the social judgment – such as equality or lower inequality across individuals, or a total sum of individual items for the whole of society. Individuals' possible judgments at this higher level are not considered. We will, for short, say that two situations are *equivalent* when they are equivalent for all individuals. *Equivalence* will thus stand for *unanimous indifference*. A semantic shift from equivalence so defined to the idea that the situations are also morally equivalent as concerns their other properties would be a conceptual mistake and confusion. Equivalence as defined entails no moral equivalence as concerns the other properties by logical or synthetic necessity. Assuming that it implies such an equivalence constitutes a specific moral hypothesis that should be justified. The foregoing discussion suggests that, in the appropriate circumstances, there may be some ground for that, based on the overall evaluations of individuals and society.

This theory of equivalence permits the consideration of impossible properties, in considering them in impossible situations equivalent to the actual ones. This can for instance, be the case of some equalities. The theory permits the joint consideration of several incompatible properties, in considering them to hold in different situations all equivalent to the actual one – which can be one of them: the incompatibility is thus solved by a kind of "division of labour" among equivalent situations. These properties can, for instance, be efficiencies and equalities of various possible types – such incompatibilities constitute one of the most frequent dilemmas in social ethics. This efficiency can refer to some total amount in society (the overall social income or more specific goods) or to Pareto efficiency. For instance, equalization can induce disincentives that can impair efficiency of both types; an identical allocation of several transferable goods to individuals with different tastes generally is Pareto inefficient; identical domains of choice of labour and income (for example equal wage rates) generally entail Pareto inefficiency when individuals' productivities differ. The satisfaction of a property may be its full attainment, or the possibility to define some degree of its satisfaction and to reach good levels in it. The following will consider jointly only two properties. One is always Pareto efficiency for the actual situation, with the actual possibilities and constraints. The other can be of various types. Pareto efficiency, attained in full, is required by the principle of unanimity (it will sometimes be abbreviated as efficiency and efficient).[5] We will see that a non-Pareto-efficient situation equivalent to a Pareto-efficient one has to be impossible, because a possible situation equivalent to a Pareto-efficient one is Pareto-efficient. Hence, the second property belongs to an impossible situation. This other situation is called the equivalent situation.

The other considered property will be of two kinds. The main focus will be on equalities, or lower inequalities, in allocations or in freedoms of choice. This freedom will itself be of two types, social freedom and a priori given domains of choice, with, notably, equalities in social freedom from identical allocations, and identical domains of choice. These equivalences to equalities of any type will be referred to by the general expression of equivalence to equality or *equality equivalence*. More generally, when the obtained property in the equivalent situation can only be some lower inequality of any type, the reference will be to "egalitarian equivalence." The problem will thus be one of characterizing efficient equality or egalitarian equivalence. However, the property of the highest level of a sum will also be considered, notably for the classical theory of the surplus – the most common principle in applied normative economics and "benefit-cost analysis."

1.3. Presentation, applications, history, alternatives

1.3.1. The general theory

The rest of this section considers the general theory of efficient equivalence, while the specific applications are the object of the second section. In the present section 1.3, former applications are pointed out (Section 1.3.2), while the next Section 1.4 focuses on the relations between the principles of equivalence and

---

[5] This property is considered for the standard preferences, its relation to preferences of higher order if any are considered is discussed in Part IV of this study.

of Pareto efficiency, with the conclusion that the equivalent situation not only is notional, but also has to be impossible. Section 1.5 then outlines the essence of the general theory which Section 1.6 presents with precision. Pareto-efficiency turns out to amount to the maximization of any increasing function (including the limiting case of the leximin) of comparable one-dimensional parameters of individuals' situations in the equivalent situation. This function can notably be inequality-averse, including leximin as limiting case, and then it may lead to some equality, or else it can be a sum. The other parameters of the equivalent situation can be chosen a priori, for instance for satisfying some equality. Section 1.7 presents the various types of applications and examples of the basic difficulty (reversal).

1.3.2. The applications

These applications, analyzed in Section 2, include the surplus and the equivalence to less unequal allocations or freedoms – defined either as social freedom or by a priori domains of choice (a difference relevant for defining equal freedom). Among the various particular cases are the theory of the surplus, considered by Dupuit (1844) and innumerable followers, related to the "symmetrical" classical "principle of compensation" (the beneficiaries can compensate the losers). The highest surplus is thus shown to lead to a Pareto-efficient choice – this has not yet been shown so far. An egalitarian efficient surplus can also be considered. Equivalence to an equal allocation is suggested by Lange (1937) for income and labour, although without consideration of efficiency or maximization. It is considered by equality in "given-labour-equivalent income" and in particular "leisurely equivalent income," with the analysis of their lower inequality, and with efficiency in all cases, in Kolm (1966a). Rather than such an equalizing of income or of a quantity of a good in taking the quantities of the other goods as equal a priori, Pazner and Schmeidler (1978) study efficient equivalence in proportionally increasing a bundle of all goods equally allocated to all individuals, and in assuming that the limit in an equivalent allocation corresponds to a Pareto-efficient actual allocation (see Section 2.1.2). The set of the equal allocations equivalent to efficient ones is analyzed in Kolm (1996b). Efficient equivalence to social freedom from an equal allocation leads to the concept of equivalence to "generalized ELIE" and other concepts, considered shortly. Efficient equivalence to equal (identical) or less unequal domains of choice includes the case where this domain is a budget set with given supply functions or prices, or these plus labour, and highest equal incomes or an inequality-averse maximand function of incomes (Kolm 1966a). It also includes a general analysis with interpersonal comparison of equivalent domains by inclusion (Kolm 1993d, see Appendix B).[6] It equally includes the consideration

---

[6] Equivalence and efficient equivalence to identical domains of choice and to "equity" (no individual prefers any other's allocation to her own) amount to the same (see also Kolm 1971). Pazner (1977) notes equivalence to equity (without mention of domain of choice).

of the highest equal income with given prices which can be notional by Thomson (1994). And it includes efficient equivalence to equal or less unequal productivities or wage rates from an equal allocation which can be, in particular, full self-ownership, maximal income equalization, or the income-egalitarian ELIE; and efficient equivalence to equal or less unequal possible disposable incomes for given equal labour – such as no labour (transfers), maximal labour or the income-egalitarian equalization labour –, with given equal productivities or wage rates – such as the average, the median, the lowest, or the highest of the actual levels. In other cases, the equivalent productivities depend on the actual ones, which is another way of expressing partial self-ownership. For determining an "optimum income tax," Fleurbaey and Maniquet (2001, 2002a) interestingly chose cases of leximin in wage rates for full self-ownership and in transfers for a wage rate equal to the official minimum. Still other applications are proposed. For all types of objective, the framework is sometimes general; or it consists of quantities of goods in any number; or it concerns labour and income with a priori possible application to the question of macrojustice; or again it consists of public goods and money or income for the surplus principle and the compensation principle.

1.4. Pareto-efficient equivalence: A basic property

Pareto efficiency refers here to this property in the actual situation, not only with the actual individuals' preferences, but also with the actual possibilities and constraints. The case where Pareto efficiency is one of the valued properties yields a remarkable property: *non-Pareto-efficient situations equivalent to a Pareto-efficient situation are impossible.* Indeed, a possible situation equivalent to a Pareto-efficient situation is Pareto-efficient. The reason is that Pareto efficiency means possibility plus the nonexistence of a possible situation preferred by some individuals and found worse by none. And if this nonexistence holds for one situation, it also holds for all equivalent situations (since equivalence means indifference for all individuals).

Hence if, facing an impossibility of jointly having Pareto efficiency and another property, we choose to allocate these properties to different but equivalent situations, the non-Pareto-efficient one is impossible. Therefore, if we want the actual situation, which must be possible, to have at least one of these properties, it has to be Pareto efficient. In fact, if the actual situation were another situation equivalent to these two, it would be Pareto-efficient because, being actual, it must be possible, and a possible situation equivalent to a Pareto-efficient situation is itself Pareto efficient (because no possible situation is better than any of these equivalent situations for any individual and worse for none). The problem thus consists of finding impossible situations having the required property and being equivalent to Pareto-efficient ones. Note that this impossibility is for the overall situation rather than for one individual situation taken separately irrespective of the others.

1.5. The general method of solution

The general solution consists of taking, as specification of each individual's ordinal utility index, the level of a variable one-dimensional (real number) parameter that this individual prefers to be higher and that concerns this individual alone, in a situation whose aspects other than these parameters remain the same. These parameters are chosen as being relevantly analogous and comparable across the individuals, so that the required comparisons among them are logically meaningful (such as equality, lower inequality, highest sum, and so on). If another situation has, for an individual, a level of utility measured in this way, this means that this individual is indifferent between this situation and the former one where the parameters are defined and where the individual's parameter has this level. Now, with any specification of individuals' ordinal utility functions, the Pareto efficient situations are the possible ones that maximize the increasing functions of these utility levels for all individuals, in adding the particular limiting cases of the orders of priority that can be described as the leximins for all possible specifications of the ordinal utility functions. This holds with the considered parameters taken as specifications of the utility levels. The new thing is that the relevant interpersonal comparisons of these parameters are logically meaningful (which is not true for any specification of these ordinal functions). For example, these parameters can be: quantities of a given good for each individual, while the quantities of the other goods remain constant; in particular, "monetary or money equivalents" or "willingnesses to pay" whose sum is a "surplus"; individuals' incomes, while prices remain constant (these are the arguments of utility functions written as René Roy's "indirect" utility functions); lump-sum subsidies or taxes; these plus income obtainable for given labour; wage rates; and so on. This gives possible logical meaning to some structures of the maximand, such as: the sum if the parameters are comparable quantities (including incomes); the leximin or maximin, which often lead to equality, if these parameters are comparable by the relations larger, lower, or equal across individuals; or, if they are comparable quantities, inequality-averse maximands which increase when these quantities become more equal in some sense.[7] When an equality across the individuals is so reached, this is only for *one* unidimensional parameter, that chosen as the variable specifying the utility levels, but one can a priori introduce equalities among other interpersonally comparable parameters for the various individuals in the reference equivalent situation. A number of examples, probably constituting the most important applications, are considered shortly.

Then, the policy acts on the actual situation so as to maximize the considered function; the actual situation becomes Pareto efficient, while the considered

---

[7] See, for instance, the handbook on income inequality measurement edited by Jacques Silber (1999), or, among several other books, that of Peter Lambert (2001), which is particularly complete, or the early presentation – which happens to use equivalent incomes – in Kolm (1966a).

parameters in the equivalent notional situation acquire the desired structure (such as equality, lower inequality, or the highest sum).

The situation taken as reference, with the values of the variable parameters that correspond to the actual situation, is the equivalent situation of the theory. For the values of the parameters that maximize the considered function (possibly leximin), hence with Pareto efficiency of the actual situation, this equivalent situation is impossible from the previous section (except if the actual situation happens to coincide with it, but, in this case, it presents the final disposition of the variable parameters and of the other aspects of the chosen reference, which, then, are consistent with Pareto efficiency). Since this equivalent situation is finally impossible at any rate, its various aspects are not a priori bound by any possibility, reality, or realism. The only principle of their choice is meaningfulness. This holds both for the chosen variable parameters and for the other aspects of the equivalent reference situation. For instance, the variable parameters can be incomes whose sum exceeds society's possibilities. Or individuals' productivities in the equivalent situation, either a priori given or taken as these variable parameters, can be different from what they actually are; they may not depend on these actual values at all, or they may be related to them for expressing some kind and degree of entitlement of the individuals to their productive capacities.

1.6. A formal presentation of the general theory of efficient equivalence

Some readers may be used to thinking more easily with signs than with sentences. Let us therefore denote situations by sufficient sets of parameters, X for the actual situation and x for the other, equivalent, situation. These parameters can describe anything that directly or indirectly concerns the individuals, such as the quantities of goods they have, or of labour they provide, their incomes, prices, wage rates, domains of their free choice, and so on. An individual need not be concerned by all these parameters; for instance, she may not be concerned by others' consumption, income, labour, or domain of free choice. Individual i has an ordinal utility function u^i; number u^i is any specification of its value; by definition of ordinalism, any increasing function $g_i(u^i)$ can replace u^i. Situations x and X are equivalent when $u^i(x) = u^i(X)$ for all i (this writing needs some caution because x and X need not be defined with the same items – for instance, there may be allocations of goods in one and domains of free choice in the other – but this is a technicality easily faced).

Denote as z_i a one-dimensional (real number) parameter of situation x that concerns individual i only, for each i; as $z = \{z_i\}$ the set of parameters z_i; and as $x \backslash z$ the set of parameters x except the parameters z. One can write $u^i(x) = u^i(x \backslash z, z_i)$ (since individual i is not concerned by parameters z_j for $j \neq i$). Choose the parameters z_i such that individual i prefers z_i to be larger (function u^i is increasing in z_i), and assume all the necessary continuity. Then, when the set of parameters $x \backslash z$ is a priori given and remains the same, level u^i is an increasing function of parameter z_i. Hence, since utility function u^i is *ordinal*, z_i is another specification of this function, and hence, it can replace the specification denoted as u^i. Specifically, if situations x and X are equivalent, this can be written (with a noted caution) as $u^i(x \backslash z, z_i) = u^i(X)$. Solving this equation for z_i gives a function $z_i = \varphi_i(X)$, which is a particular specification of individual i's ordinal utility function. Function φ_i depends on the a priori choice of the set of parameters $x \backslash z$. These parameters z_i are called the *equivalence parameters*.

Then, Pareto-efficient situations are those that maximize increasing functions $M(z) = M[\{\varphi_i(X)\}]$, plus the limiting cases noted above, on the set of possible situations $X \in P$.

Coming back to the definition of parameters z_i, one can choose parameters of the same nature for the various individuals, hence comparable in some sense across individuals. They can for instance be: incomes with given prices (which are in the set of parameters $x \backslash z$); incomes for given labour; quantities of the same good; money equivalent or willingness to pay for variations in the actual situation described by X; prices of some good; in particular wage rates (which permit the individuals to choose more or less labour and income from given benchmark amounts of them), or their relation to some given level or to the individuals' actual own wage rates; and so on. The most a priori meaningful cases will be considered in the applications. In fact, these z_i will have the nature of comparable quantities (some as rates).

This nature and comparability of the z_i permits giving function M specific structures. Sums Σz_i are sometimes meaningful (this is in the nature of a "surplus" if the z_i are individual i's money equivalent or willingnesses to pay). The leximin often reduces to maximin, which commonly leads to equal z_i. With z_i being comparable quantities, function $M(z)$ can be an inequality-averse function of some sort. But it may also depend on some relevant characteristics of individuals such as needs, family size of the household, and so on.

When the policy maximizes $M(z) = M[\{\varphi_i(X)\}]$, the constraints bear on the actual situation X, not on the z_i themselves in situation x. Equivalent situation x is at any rate an impossible one for the Pareto-efficient maximum (Section 1.3). For instance, if the z_i are transfers, or are related to transfers, they need not be restricted by a budget constraint; if they are quantities of a good, their sum may exceed the available quantity of this good; if they are incomes, their sum may exceed the highest possible social income; if they are individuals' productivities, they can differ from the actual ones. Relations with actual data only result from considerations of meaningfulness.

Finally, the z_i are unidimensional parameters (real numbers). This is crucial in the theory because it takes the z_i as specification of the (unidimensional) ordinal utility functions (which had u^i as an a priori arbitrary specification). In particular, their equality, or lower inequality, refer to only one dimension of the situation x. The other parameters of x, the set $x \backslash z$, have to be chosen a priori. They may or may not refer to actual situations. They have no logical requirement to do so.

Such references or identities can only result from considerations of significance, meaningfulness, or ethical relevance. Of course, they can a priori have impossible values. The a priori choice of these parameters offers possibilities. For instance, if one wants some multidimensional equality – interindividual equality for parameters of each type of a set of types (for example, identical bundles of quantities of goods) – it suffices to set these parameters equal for all individuals for all types but one, and to take the parameters of this latter type as the parameters z_i. Then, a leximin of the z_i may lead to their equality, and hence to this multidimensional equality in the equivalent situation while the actual one is Pareto efficient. Or the z_i can maximize some inequality-averse maximand $M(z)$.

1.7. Types of applications, and representation

1.7.1. Types of application

We will first point out that the theory of the surplus, which is the standard criterion in benefit-cost analyses, is an instance of the theory of equivalence. There results that the standard principle of the highest surplus yields a Pareto-efficient solution (even if lump-sum transfers are not possible), a property that had not been explicitly pointed out. A different, egalitarian, use of the surplus concept will also be considered.

The other cases will consider equality of some sort as the ideal property. These cases are referred to as *egalitarian equivalence* (extending this term that was used for full equality in quantities of all goods – a case of equality equivalence – to cases of equalities in other items – various types of freedom, for instance – and of lower inequalities). *Equality equivalence* denotes equivalence to some strict equality. Two distinctions structure the field. On the one hand, the items can be either allocations of goods or freedoms. On the other hand, either the general space of goods is considered, or the analysis is specified to the case of income and labour or leisure (notably relevant for macrojustice). Ideal equal freedoms can notably be either identical domains of choice – equivalent to the "equity" principle that no individual prefers any other's allocation to her own (Chapter 24) – or social freedom from an equal allocation, which, for the case of income and labour, differs from the former case when individual wages differ and is akin to ELIE distributions.

1.7.2. Diagrammatic representation; reversal

An easy and fast grasp of all the cases considered can be obtained with a two-dimensional diagram of the quantities of two goods (a particular case being labour or leisure and income or consumption), with two individuals concerned by their own allocation only, and two indifference curves, one for each individual. Individual allocations are represented by points of this diagram, where individual domains of choice can also be represented. An individual's choice in a domain of possible choice is represented by a point of tangency of this domain with an indifference curve.[8]

As an example, this permits the representation of dramatic instances of the reversal syndrome. Consider two indifference curves, one for each of the two individuals, that intersect once. The considered allocations of each individual will be represented by points on her indifference curve. She is thus indifferent between the considered situations. A situation consists of an allocation or a domain of choice for each individual. Consider two situations such that the individual allocations in each are on the same side of the intersection, these sides being opposite for the two situations. Then, one straightforwardly sees that an individual can have more of both goods than the other in one situation and less of both goods than her in the other situation (more of the good leisure means lower labour). And that an individuals' domain of choice can strictly include that of the other in one situation, while the converse holds in the other. Although both situations are equivalent. And they also are equivalent to the identical individual allocations of the point of intersection of the indifference curves. If one situation is the actual one, favouring the least endowed or least free individual in the other situation requires favouring the individual actually better endowed or freer, and diminishing the relevant inequality in the notional equivalent situation requires increasing this inequality in the actual situation.

However, the dramatic form of the basic problem of equivalence theory shown by such reversal properties need not be the case. It is a priori less likely to occur if the actual and equivalent situations are sufficiently close to one another. Moreover, an equivalent situation may display an equality that happens to be actually impossible, such as identical allocations or domains of choice. And – short of reversal – it is possible to consider, in the equivalent situation, equal quantities of one good for both individuals (in the case of two goods), and hence to reduce the inequality to that in a unique quantity, that of the other good, which is conceptually more easily manageable and provides the one-dimensional parameters required by the theory of efficient egalitarian equivalence.

2. APPLICATIONS

We will first consider the essence of the applications of the theory of equivalence (Section 2.1), and then the corresponding precise models (Section 2.2). Apart from the theory of the surplus, the applications will consider egalitarian equivalences with equivalent situations that are either allocations of goods or freedoms, for labour (leisure) and income (consumption) or in a general space of quantities of goods, with freedoms that can refer to social freedom or to a priori given domains

---

[8]   In this section, and in the forthcoming ones discussing cases in two-dimensional spaces, the description is sufficient for not presenting a diagram, although the reader may want to draw one for visualizing the issues.

of choice, and that can notably be free choice in budget sets with the relevant incomes, prices, and productivities.

2.1. Philosophy of applied equivalence

In most applications, the equivalent parameters z_i are and have been incomes. However, income entities can be conceived of and applied in several ways. Income is sometimes a money equivalent or surplus, sometimes the limitation of free choice in a budget set, sometimes an earning, sometimes a transfer (possibly plus some earning), and it is sometimes considered as an aggregate good along with leisure or labour. More general allocations will then be considered.

2.1.1. Incomes

1) Surplus theory

1.1) The classical surpluses and the compensation principle

First, income may be "income equivalent" or "monetary or money equivalent," or else "willingness to pay." This is notably the case in the theory of the surplus, which maximizes the sum of these money equivalents for all individuals. This theory is the standard principle in benefit-cost analysis, the oldest and most common rational principle in applied normative economics (Jules Dupuit 1844). It constitutes an application of equivalence theory in the following way. Various alternative projects, or variants of a project, are considered. Abstention may be an alternative. An individual's *money equivalent* of a project is the amount of received money that she would find as good as the project. Her *willingness to pay* for the project is the amount of money she would have to yield for making the accompanying realization of the project a matter of indifference for her. It is equal to the money equivalent in a domain if and only if the individual's preferences have the particular classical property of "constant marginal utility of money" in this domain. These amounts are negative if the individual dislikes the project. The project includes its financing with the corresponding evaluation by payers. The surplus is the (algebraic) sum of the individuals' money equivalents. The standard principle holds that the chosen project should be that which makes this surplus as high as possible. This is a case of equivalence theory. The individuals' money equivalents are the parameters z_i. The actual situation is the present situation plus the project (including actual payments that are attached to it). The equivalent situation is the present situation plus her money equivalent of the project for each individual z_i. The maximand is Σz_i. From the general theory of equivalence, the chosen project is Pareto efficient (a property that had not been shown yet).

Replacing money equivalents by willingnesses to pay gives something different (when they differ, which is the general case), yet meaningful and interesting.

However, this is no longer a case of equivalence theory, and the result (giving the highest sum, or also the highest level of any increasing function of these amounts, or a leximin among them) is in general no longer Pareto-efficient. The reason is that an individual generally has different willingnesses to pay for possible projects among which she is indifferent, as it is easily checked. Hence, an individual's willingness to pay cannot in general be taken as an index of utility. Exceptions occur when there is "constant marginal utility of money," or when the individuals have strict preference (no indifference) among the considered projects. The latter case occurs for instance when the choice concerns a single parameter with monotonic preferences.

Yet, replacing money equivalent by willingnesses to pay has some meaning and has attracted some attention. It amounts to inverting the roles of the situations without and with the project: given the realized project, the willingness to pay becomes the money equivalent of not having the project any longer. A criterion built with these magnitudes thus constitutes a *regret* equivalence principle. This *ex post* view, considering the sum of willingnesses to pay and applied to the question of realizing a specified project or not, also amounts to the celebrated "compensation principle," whereby a project should be realized if "the beneficiaries can compensate the losers." A famous debate opposed economists who insisted that this compensation should be actual, thus in fact only advocating a unanimous ("Pareto") improvement (Ezra Mishan, Nicholas Kaldor), and those who argued that the compensation can remain notional (John Hicks), probably both from a utilitarian ethics where utility is approximated by money value – as proposed by Bentham himself – and because distribution can be the concern of other, specific, policies. The economist Tibor Scitovsky noted in 1941 that these two *ex post* and *ex ante* principles can lead to opposite conclusions, because the sums of money equivalents and of willingnesses to pay may have opposite signs (in counting the cost of financing the project – that is, the cost of the project is between these two sums for the project itself): then, the willingness-to-pay criterion leads to regretting the choice advocated by the money-equivalent criterion. Such possibilities are related to the general possible property of "reversal" of equivalence theory.[9] However, upon reflection the Scitovsky problem turned out to constitute a favourable property for the theory of the surplus, in using, as principle, the dual relative surplus noted in Chapter 19 – both do not leave the chosen solution and return to it if you do – and its marginal application (where this pair of conditions also provides the second-order conditions) also used there.[10]

---

[9] The noted effect is due to a structure of preferences involving some "intersecting indifference curves," as noted above. Assume, for instance, that the project has a given cost between the money equivalent and the willingness to pay of a beneficiary assumed to be the only one, or between the sum of these two entities not counting contributions for financing for all the beneficiaries.

[10] From Kolm 1966a, which also shows the surplus principle considering the effects of the choice on allocations, prices, and distribution, which may concern the individuals for various reasons.

1.2) The egalitarian surplus

Equivalence theory also suggests a different normative use of the concept of the surplus. The highest sum of money equivalents constitutes an aggregate social criterion that sees no difference among individuals for counting their money values – as Rawls says of utilitarianism, it "does not take seriously the separation of society into individuals." Another possible criterion is having equal individual money equivalents, and, then, at the highest possible level. This may be Pareto efficient, and it will often be. If not, and more generally, the individual money values can be the arguments of an increasing inequality-averse maximand function, adding, as a possibility, the limiting case of the leximin. The project that achieves this maximization is then chosen. It is Pareto efficient. This *egalitarian surplus* can be more or less egalitarian, depending on the corresponding structure of the maximand. Note that the considered project includes the individuals' payments related to it, notably for its financing (as well as possible money benefits or other costs). Hence, this equality can effect the realization but is notably likely to affect the financing. Such egalitarian properties make this criterion for a limited project a case of individualistic local justice. This may be justified, notably if the project satisfies needs for which such specific justice seems adequate, and in particular if this moral view is widely shared – the project can then be said to provide a "sphered good," a term inspired by Walzer's view of "spheres of justice" (although his "spheres" consist of sectors rather than single projects). This can, for instance, implement a Pareto-efficient egalitarian provision of a public good: the individuals' excesses of their money equivalent for the good over the specific payment they provide for it are equal or not too unequal.

2) The general budget possibility set

The most standard income-related conception, however, is that of income that individuals spend in buying various goods (possibly in the future through savings). With given prices, this income defines the set of bundles of goods the individual can buy, a set of possible choices that is the budget possibility set. The corresponding utility function is René Roy's indirect utility function of the individual's income and prices. These incomes at given prices can be taken as the parameters z_i of the equivalence theory. The maximand is an increasing function of these incomes, with leximin often reducible to maximin as a limiting case. In particular, maximizing the sum of incomes is classically considered a meaningful social principle (it often takes the form of aiming at the highest growth of national income). But lowering income inequality is a standard value, justifiable for incomes that are the basic concerns (see Chapter 23). This is represented by inequality-averse increasing maximands whose theory was specifically developed in application to equivalent incomes, with any structure of costs and prices.[11] A particular limiting

---

[11] See Kolm 1966a, Sections 5, 6, and 7.

case is leximin, often actually reduced to maximin. This may in particular lead to equal equivalent incomes – then with a Pareto-efficient actual situation. Then, if the considered cost functions and prices are the same for all individuals, this equivalent situation presents identical budget sets, a particular case of identical individual domains of free choice. Note that in these equivalent situations, which are at any rate impossible in the end, cost functions and prices need not be the actual ones. Hence, they can be taken as the same for all individuals, even if this is not actually the case (as an application, notional wage rates buying leisure, or individual productivities, can be taken as identical). The general case of equivalence to identical domains of choice is considered in Kolm (1993d). It amounts to equivalence to situations such that no individual prefers any other's allocation to her own.[12] Thomson (1994) obtains efficient equivalence to equal incomes in increasing equivalent equal incomes until the Pareto-frontier is reached (as it is shortly discussed as concerns allocations).

3) Income and labour

The nonscholarly conception of income does not include the money value of some leisure. Both ordinary income and income taking account of leisure or labour were used in equivalence theory. However, when the problem concerns the whole economy rather than a more restricted issue, with individuals providing various labours, and an evaluation with more or less inequality aversion, evaluating the set of incomes requires taking care of the inequalities in labour and leisure. A solution consists of considering a situation equivalent to the actual one, where all individuals provide the same labour (and hence, enjoy the same leisure). The *ℓ-equivalent income* of an individual is the income that, associated with labour ℓ, is equivalent, for this individual, to her actual pair of labour and income (Section 5 in Kolm 1966a). In particular, for $\ell = 0$, the *leisurely equivalent income* of an individual is the income that, associated with zero labour, is equivalent to the actual situation for this individual (idem). Another case can be a ℓ equal to the official or standard duration of labour in countries where there is one.

This was given two interpretations. In one, the case is considered as describing two goods, specifically consumption goods, one being measured by its amount or value which is taken to be the income, and the other being leisure or labour measured by a quantity (see Chapter 7). Yet, a more refined analysis was also presented as concerns both these items. Labour can be mutidimensional (duration, intensity, formation and training, and so on – see Chapter 7) – although, for the leisurely equivalent income, dimensions other than the zero duration are

---

[12] Unanimous equivalence to the same domain of choice (valued only for the item it permits one to choose) implies unanimous equivalence to the chosen allocations, which constitute such an "equitable" overall allocation. And unanimous equivalence to an equitable overall allocation implies unanimous equivalence to any possibility set constituted by these individual allocations plus any other that no individual prefers to her own. Pazner (1977) notes equivalence to this "equity" but does not mention the relation with this equal free choice.

irrelevant. Moreover, the income considered was the lowest value of bundles of (nonleisure) consumption goods that, with labour ℓ, provide a situation equivalent to the actual one (the lowest budget that permits buying goods with this equivalence). The increasing maximands, notably inequality-averse ones, with the limiting cases of the sum and of the maximin or leximin which may lead to equal and maximal incomes, were then analyzed with any of these definitions of income (1966a, Sections 6 and 7).

A case of equivalence to equal income for a given equal labour had indeed been considered by Oskar Lange (1937), although not with the consideration of the highest such income for the given labour, which might lead to a Pareto-efficient solution, and, indeed, without explicit consideration of this efficiency. As a socialist of some sort, Lange favoured equal incomes. This equality should be completed by equal labour, and hence he considered everyone working eight hours per day. However, as an economist, Lange was aware that individuals have different tastes and preferences as concerns labour and income, possibly also that this equality generally implies Pareto inefficiency, and he might also have been sensitive to the lack of individual free choice this equality entails. He thus suggested that individuals earn incomes that, with their actual labours, are for them equivalent to the same income for all with eight hours work, that is, equal eight-hour-equivalent incomes.

In fact, the income-egalitarian ELIE considered in Chapter 11 is an equality equivalent that is not far from Lange's intent, plus Pareto efficiency. Indeed, all individuals providing normal full labour freely choose a labour in the neighbourhood of the corresponding equalization labour k^e. Since the choice of the individuals is free (and the scheme is Pareto efficient), each individual's indifference curve passing through her chosen pair (point) of labour and income is tangent to her budget line and locally coincides with it – normally assuming smooth preferences. Hence, these indifference curves practically pass through the same point, the common intersection of these budget lines at labour k^e and leisure $\overline{w}k^e$.

4) Transfers and prices

Considering both the pair labour (or leisure) and income, and free choices in budget sets, leads to the core framework of macrojustice, and hence to its core problem: the degree of self-ownership or equalizing redistribution concerning individuals' productive capacities. With actual social freedom (as process-freedom) and Pareto efficiency, the only possible distributive parameter is the sharing of rent-rights in individuals' productive capacities, and hence, with logical equality and the question of the measure of values, the solutions are ELIE schemes whose coefficients k denote degrees of redistribution. The individuals are fully entitled to the income value of their capacities with $k = 0$ (full self-ownership), and the relevant opposite case is the income-egalitarian ELIE with $k = k^e$ (rather than

$k = 1$). This latter case – it was just seen – practically amounts to an equivalence to identical allocations (of labour-leisure and income). However, one can also consider equivalence to fictive situations of freedom of choice. This opens another structural possibility for sharing the benefits of productive capacities. Indeed, the equivalent situation is fictive, notional, and even impossible when the actual situation is Pareto efficient. Hence, a priori, one can consider individual productivities and wages rates in it that differ from the actual ones. Each individual's fictive productivity or wage rate can depend positively on the actual ones of this individual in a degree that is a degree of self-ownership. This relation can be full identity, or be partial, or absent. When this relation exists, it constitutes a second way of describing degrees of self-ownership and of equal sharing of the advantages (or handicaps) of productive capacities, which can be used jointly with the one described by ELIE schemes (as is shortly shown precisely). When these fictive equivalent productivities or wage rates do not depend on the actual ones, they can be taken as equal for all individuals, or their lower inequality may be favoured.

The relevant parameters in the equivalent notional situations will thus be of two types. Some are incomes for a given labour that is the same for all individuals, equal to transfers (positive or negative) plus income earned by this labour (with the considered productivities). The other parameters determine the considered notional productivities or wages. Parameters of either type can be chosen as the equivalence parameters z_i, while those of the other type are chosen a priori. Since this equivalent situation is notional – and at any rate ultimately impossible – these variables are not a priori bound by the actual values, which only intervene for reasons of meaning and of ethical considerations. This applies not only to the productivities or wages, but also to transfers which need not a priori balance. The reference labour, denoted as k, can correspond to full self-ownership $k = 0$, to its opposites (the logical extreme $k = 1$ or the actually relevant $k = k^e$), or to other values that are salient or determined by the considerations of Part IV of this study for the equalization labour. The notional productivities or wage rates can be, as limiting cases, the actual ones or the same for all. In this latter case, natural values can be derived from the actual ones and be the lowest, the highest, the average or the median. These notional individual productivities and wage rates can also be proportional to the actual ones for expressing some degree of self-entitlement. Then, the efficient actual solution is determined by the maximization of an increasing function of the chosen equivalence parameters z_i, possibly an inequality-averse one with the possible limiting case of a leximin. As examples, for determining an "optimum income tax" based on actual income for Mirrlees' "informational" reason (see Chapters 10 and 15), while holding individuals fully "responsible" for the intensity of their preferences but neither for their indifferences nor for their productive capacities, Fleurbaey and Maniquet (2001, 2002a) use an equivalence with full self-ownership reference but ideally equal wage rates, and choose leximins in either the wage rates or transfers with wage rates equal to the the minimum official level – an interesting association of two basic tools of distributive policy.[13]

2.1.2. Allocations

For allocations of quantities of goods, an instance of which is the allocation of a consumption good measured by income and of leisure (or labour), the obvious one-dimensional equivalence parameter z_i is the quantity of one good (as in Kolm 1966a). For example, if one wants an equivalent situation where all individuals have the same quantity of each good, one takes a reference equivalent situation where this is the case for all goods but one; the quantities of the remaining good held by the individuals are taken as the equivalence parameters z_i; and the maximand is an inequality-averse increasing function of these quantities, including the limiting case of leximin which yields equality in this good – and hence in all goods – if this is consistent with Pareto efficiency of the actual allocation. Applied to the case of labour-leisure and income, this is the efficient equality or lower inequality in ℓ-equivalent incomes (same reference).

In contrast, Pazner and Schmeidler's (1978) presentation rather amounts to the choice, as equivalent parameter, of the length of a vector of quantities of divisible goods in given proportions (in a given direction in the space of quantities, the unit length being that of any given such vector). One could then choose one such length for each individual as equivalence parameter z_i, and obtain a Pareto-efficient solution in maximizing any increasing function of these measures, notably an inequality-averse one, including the limiting case of the leximin. This leximin would lead to equal such lengths, vectors, and allocations of quantities, if there exists one such equal solution with these proportions compatible with Pareto efficiency of the actual equivalent allocation. However, these authors rather a priori consider equal such lengths for all individuals, and hence the corresponding identical equivalent individual allocations for all individuals, and progressively increase this length. This a priori correspondingly augments all individuals' utilities, until the point in utility space reaches a limit of the actual possibilities in this space. The obtained utilities are yielded by a possible actual allocation that gives, to each individual, the same utility level as that provided by the obtained same bundle of quantities. Thus, this actual allocation is equivalent to the reached allocation with identical bundles for all individuals. If the obtained point in the space of utilities corresponds to Pareto efficiency, then the corresponding actual allocation is both Pareto efficient and equivalent to this constructed allocation where all individuals have the same quantities of all goods. However, it may be that, at the reached point in utility space, some (at least one) of the individuals' utilities can be increased while the others remain the same. Such a point does

[13] See Appendix A of this chapter.

not correspond to a Pareto-efficient allocation (it is not on the "Pareto frontier"). Then, there is no Pareto-efficient allocation equivalent to an equal allocation (i.e., an overall allocation constituted of identical individual allocations) with goods in the a priori considered proportions. This may be the effect of all the constraints of the problem (plus, possibly, of some satiation of some individuals). However, there may exist Pareto-efficient allocations equivalent to equal allocations with other proportions of the quantities of the various goods. There may finally be many such Pareto-efficient equality equivalents. Pazner and Schmeidler then consider sharing given total quantities of goods, and suggest taking an equivalent allocation with the same proportions of the goods as these given quantities. This solution, however, is more distinguished by salience than by ethical or logical reasons. If the sharing meets no other constraints than the total quantities, the goods are perfectly transferable and divisible, and the individuals display no satiety, these authors' reasoning actually leads to Pareto-efficient solutions equivalent to identical allocations for all individuals.[14] Other specific solutions have been proposed, including in the more general case where there can be transformations among these goods (see Section 2.2.2 and Kolm 1996b).

2.2. A more detailed presentation

2.2.1. The question and its cases

Let us consider more precisely main cases of Pareto-efficient situations with an equivalent situation generally manifesting some preference for equality, by application of the general theory of efficient egalitarian equivalence. There are n individuals with given preference orderings. Two equivalent (unanimously indifferent) situations are considered. One is actual. It has to comply with the constraints of the real world. The considered policy instruments and all issues concerning them – such as information about bases – should be seen as included in the definition of these actual constraints and possibilities. These constraints determine the set of possibilities and that of the Pareto efficient solutions. The other situation is a conceptual construct built for the purpose of the normative judgment. One should define this situation, the selection of the equivalence one-dimensional individual parameters z_i in it, and also, relatedly, the maximand function. This determines the selection of a Pareto-efficient actual situation. The ethical and logical issues concerning the choice of increasing inequality-averse maximand functions of comparable individual

---

[14] However, their initial motivation concerned the other problem, where there are individual labours with different productivities and which are nontransferable, since they wanted to find a criterion for replacing the "equity" principle (see Chapter 24) which they had shown could be incompatible with Pareto efficiency in this case (Pazner and Schmeidler 1974). Yet, the solution also applies to this case with nontransferability in one good – leisure – with equal total "amount" of labour plus leisure for each individual.

one-dimensional parameters (often quantities) are by now well analyzed.[15] There remains to define the equivalent situation and the equivalence parameters. The items, variables, facts, and constraints in the two situations have completely different meanings. They are actual for the actual situation, while, in the equivalent situation, they are notional constructs and assumptions exclusively chosen from considerations of meaningfulness and ethics. In particular, the properties of the notional equivalent situation need not be possible ones. Indeed, this situation is in fact impossible when the actual situation is Pareto efficient. The only logical requirement about this equivalent situation is that individuals' preferences about it exist (with comparison with the actual situation). For the rest, relations of the properties of this situation with real facts can only be chosen for reasons of meaning and ethical significance. Both situations can be of various types, they can associate different types, and they need not even be of the same type(s). The types are essentially the consideration of allocations of goods and of freedoms – notably, of social freedom and of freedom a priori defined by domains of choice. The present concern will only be the ethical criterion, rather than the full optimization. Hence, the explicitly considered situation will be the notional equivalent one. And since the issues concerning the choice of the maximand are well studied, the focus will be on the nature of the situation and of the chosen equivalence parameter.

The cases are separated by two dichotomies, hence into four families. First, the equivalence can be with allocations of goods or with domains of free choice. Second, the problem can be set for any goods or is specified for the case of labour or leisure and income (the domain relevant for macrojustice). Equal freedom is notably achieved, for the two relevant types of freedom, by the two polar cases of full social freedom from an equal allocation, and identical domains of free choice.

2.2.2. General allocation

With n individuals and m divisible goods, individual i has quantities x_j^i of each good j. She thus has the bundle (m-vector) of quantities of goods $x^i = \{x_j^i\}_j$, which is her individual allocation. The set of these individual allocations is the (overall) allocation $x = \{x^i\} = \{x_j^i\}$, (a $n \times m$ matrix). The allocation x is said to be equal when all its individual allocations x^i are identical (for each j, x_j^i is the same for all i; all vectors x^i are equal). The actual allocation will be denoted with primes and the equivalent one without them. Equivalence between allocations x and x' means $u^i(x^i) = u^i(x^{i'})$ for all i, where u^i is individual i's utility function. The total quantity of good j is $X_j = \Sigma_i x_j^{i'}$, and $X = \{X_j\}$ is the m-vector of these quantities. The domain of possible X is denoted as P. A noted method consists of taking, as one-dimensional parameters of the equivalence theory, $z_i = x_j^i$ for some good j for all i, while the x_k^i for $k \neq j$ are a priori given, possibly equal for all

---

[15] See notably the *Handbook on Income Inequality Measurement*, ed. by Jacques Silber (1999).

individuals i: $x_k^i = \alpha_k$ for all i and all $k \neq j$. The other method consists of taking $x^i = z_i \beta$ for each i, $\beta = \{\beta_j\}$ being a given vector of goods. The maximand is an increasing function $M(z)$ where $z = \{z_i\}$, possibly inequality-averse including the limiting case of the leximin. The result may be equal z_i, which are then the equal and maximal z_i (Pazner and Schmeidler use the second form in setting a priori all z_i equal, $z_i = \zeta$ for all i and $x^i = \zeta \beta$ for all i, and in maximizing ζ). Without any other constraint than $\Sigma x_j^{i'} = X \in P$ and no satiation, equality is a possible result in all cases, notably given by the leximin. The obtained actual allocation, which is an *efficient egalitarian-equivalent allocation* for any inequality-averse increasing maximand M (included leximin), becomes an *efficient equality-equivalent allocation* when the obtained equivalent allocation is equal, and the latter allocation is an *equal efficient-equivalent allocation*. Denote as $\xi = x^i$ for all i the obtained equal x^i. The ξ that can be so obtained constitute a hypersurface in the space of goods, denoted as E.[16] If an equal allocation with such a ξ as individual allocations were possible, it would jointly be equal and Pareto efficient. If this result is not possible, so are the obtained equal equivalent allocations. That is, $n\xi \notin P$, or $\xi \notin P/n$ where P/n is the set of possible X/n, the homothetic reduction of P by $1/n$ from the origin. If allocation x' is Pareto efficient, the average allocation $\bar{x}' = (1/n)\Sigma x^{i'}$ is on the efficient frontier of domain P/n, and this frontier at this point and individuals' indifference hypersurfaces at the individual allocations $x^{i'}$ have parallel tangent hyperplanes (normal to the "efficiency prices"). If this allocation is also equality-equivalent, all these indifferent hypersurfaces intersect at a common point ξ of hypersurface E.

Various specific solutions can be suggested. One is such that ξ and $\bar{x}'$ are colinear: $\xi = \gamma \bar{x}'$. If the p_j are the efficiency prices, other solutions are the *equal-valued equivalent* or *average* (or *total*) ones, such that $p_j \xi_j$, or $p_j \bar{x}'_j$ (or $p_j X_j$), are the same for all goods j. Other solutions would choose the ratio of values $p\xi / p\bar{x}'$ as small (or large) as possible.[17] And so on.

2.2.3. Allocation of labour and income

Consider the case of two goods, income y aggregating the goods it buys (excluding leisure) and playing the role of a consumption good, and leisure λ or labour ℓ taken in their unidimensional normalized measure with $\ell + \lambda = 1$ (see Chapter 8). These variables are y_i, ℓ_i, and λ_i for individual i. Moreover, individual i's production function is $p_i(\ell_i)$, increasing with $p_i(0) = 0$, which take the form $w_i \ell_i$ in the linear case.

Since there are only two dimensions, an individual allocation is defined by two independent relations. The choice of the equivalence parameter z_i constitutes one,

---

[16] This geometry is presented in more detail, with diagrammatic illustrations for the case of $m = 2$ goods, in Kolm 1996b.

[17] With $p\xi = \Sigma p_j \xi_j$ and $p\bar{x}' = \Sigma p_j \bar{x}'_j$.

and hence there need and can be only one other given a priori. With an egalitarian intent, the latter expresses an equality across individuals. The pair of this relation and of z_i can notably be the following (it may be enlightening to consider the geometrical representation of the proposed concepts in a plane with axes ℓ_i (or λ_i) and y_i).

If $u^i(y_i, \lambda_i)$ is individual i's utility function, individual i's ℓ-*equivalent income* is y_i^ℓ defined by $u^i(y_i, \lambda_i) = u^i(y_i^\ell, 1 - \ell)$. Taking the ℓ- equivalent income y_i^ℓ as equivalence parameter z_i leads to taking, as the given relation, $\ell_i = \ell$ with a given ℓ, the same for all i. This also amounts to taking the same given leisure λ_i for all i. Levels of ℓ can notably be $\ell = 0, 1, k^e$ (the income-egalitarian equalization labour of Chapter 11), or $1/2$. More generally, the discussion of the level of coefficient k presented in Part IV of this study is in part relevant for choosing this level ℓ. Moreover, with given constant wage rates w_i, other solutions measure labour or leisure in income value and consider equal given $w_i\ell_i$, or equal given $w_i\lambda_i$, for all i (these two cases are now different). The case $\ell = 0$, yielding leisurely equivalent incomes as equivalence parameters z_i, is the same for the cases of equal ℓ_i or equal $w_i\ell_i$. Parameters z_i can also be $(1/2)(y_i^o + y_i^1)$ or $z_i = y_i^o + k^e \cdot (y_i^1 - y_i^o) = k^e y_i^1 + (1 - k^e)y_i^o$.[18] For all these cases, the incomes y_i^ℓ can be replaced by their labour value y_i^ℓ / w_i for defining z_i. The roles of the two coordinates can also be inverted. Then, the y_i, or the y_i / w_i, are taken as equal and given, and the equivalence parameters z_i can be the corresponding λ_i or $w_i\lambda_i$, or ℓ_i or $w_i\ell_i$ with a decreasing maximand. Furthermore, either the given equal parameters, or the z_i, can be ratios such as y_i/λ_i or $y_i/w_i\lambda_i$ and the other parameter can be any of those just considered. Finally, the *equal-value equivalent* parameter is defined as $z_i = y_i = w_i\lambda_i$, or as $z_i = y_i/w_i = \lambda_i$.

Consider the ℓ-equivalent incomes as equivalence parameters, $y_i^\ell = z_i$ for all i. With a distributive policy that can perform lump-sum transfers among individuals (and no satiation), equal and maximal y_i^ℓ for any given ℓ provide equal labour-income pairs equivalent to Pareto-efficient actual situations. These values are $y_i^\ell = \zeta(\ell)$ for all i. Then, each individual i has a possibility frontier $y_i = p_i(\ell_i) + t_i$, where t_i, of any sign, is the transfer, with $\Sigma t_i = 0$. Her indifference curve tangent to this frontier at her actual efficient allocation also passes through point $[\ell, \zeta(\ell)]$, the same for all i. If all individuals i worked the same labour ℓ, they would produce a total income $\Sigma p_i(\ell) = n\overline{p}(\ell)$, which can be equally redistributed by transfers in giving $\overline{p}(\ell)$ to each. Hence, $\overline{p}(\ell)$ is the highest income of the possible equal allocations with labour ℓ (such an equal allocation is possible, but it would generally neither be Pareto efficient nor respect process-freedom). If the equivalent equal allocation with $\ell_i = \ell$ and $y_i = \zeta(\ell)$ for all individuals were possible, it would be Pareto efficient because it is equivalent to a Pareto-efficient allocation (see Section 1.3). If no Pareto-efficient equal allocation is possible, $\zeta(\ell) > \overline{p}(\ell)$, for all ℓ. In the diagram with coordinates ℓ and y, the curve of equal efficient-equivalents

---

[18] These possible solutions constitute an extension of the equivalence theory as presented.

$\zeta(\ell)$ is above that of average production curve $\overline{p}(\ell)$. A point common to these two curves would constitute an equal Pareto-efficient allocation. Hence, from previous remarks, these two curves come very close to one another for $\ell = k^e$, the income-egalitarian equalization labour of ELIE theory, and then, with $\zeta(\ell) > \overline{p}(\ell)$ for other ℓ, they are practically tangent for this labour. Function $\zeta(\ell)$ is univalued by construction, and its inverse is also as can be shown in inverting the role of the coordinates ℓ and y (take the equivalent leisure λ_i for each same income $y_i = y$ as equivalence parameters z_i). Hence, function $\zeta(\ell)$ is monotonic, and, since its representative curve is tangent to the increasing curve of equation $y = \overline{p}(\ell)$, it is increasing. For the leisurely equivalent incomes, efficient-equivalent equality is with $\zeta(0) > 0$. If individuals freely choose labour and income with a lump-sum transfer t_i for individual i (positive or negative) – hence with budget constraints $y_i = p_i(\ell_i) + t_i$ –, with the constraint $\Sigma t_i = 0$ of the distributive public budget, a situation where all individuals' indifference curves have a common point with labour ℓ and income $\zeta(\ell)$ is not in general an ELIE (where the budget curves have a common point) – although it often is one when there are only two individuals, $n = 2$.

2.2.4. General freedom

When the equivalent situation refers to freedom of choice, the parameters z_i of the general theory of efficient equivalence are parameters of the individuals' domains of choice D_i from which the individuals choose their allocation. An income, a transfer, a price are standard examples in applications. These domains a priori need not obey the requirements of reality since they concern the fictive equivalent situation (even an impossible one when the actual situation is Pareto efficient). Their relation with reality is a question of meaningfulness that characterizes the ethical choice. It will be sufficient, in the following, to consider that these fictive choices of the individuals do not interfere (the possibilities of one do not depend on others' choices, as in perfectly competitive markets for instance). Individual i's corresponding utility function and level is

$$v_i(D_i) = \max_{x^i \in D_i} u^i(x^i).$$

For instance, if η_i is individual i's income and $c^i(x^i)$ is the cost of obtaining x^i for individual i, the domain D_i is defined by $c^i(x^i) \leq \eta_i$. This income η_i is a possible equivalence parameter z_i. In particular, one can have $c^i(x^i) = \Sigma_j \pi^i_j x^i_j$, where π^i_j is the given price of good j for individual i. These π^i_j, for a j, may be the same for all i or they may not be (for instance, if one good is some leisure and the corresponding price is the wage rate). One good may be labour provided and the corresponding prices π^i_j be wage rates, and then the corresponding x^i_j is taken as negative. Possible equivalence parameters z_i are the π^i_j for some given good j. Other possible choices of z_i, generalizing the choice of η_i, are $z_i = \eta_i - \Sigma_j \pi^i_j \xi^i_j$

for some given quantities ξ^i_j (and prices π^i_j). If a good j is labour, $\xi^i_j < 0$ and the corresponding amount $-\pi^i_j \xi^i_j$ is added to income η_i.

2.2.5. Freedom equivalences with leisure-labour and income

1) General philosophy

The general theory of equivalence, in particular applied to equivalent freedoms, can be applied to the case where the allocations are those of income and leisure or labour. Income stands for the value of nonleisure consumption, which can be obtained by a suboptimization using this income.[19] The theory can be applied to cases of microjustice, but both the items (labour-leisure and income) and the emphasis on freedom constitute the framework of the question of overall distributive justice in macrojustice (see Part I of this study). This could provide a large number of a priori possible solutions, depending on the chosen nature of three things: the type and specifics of freedom; the equivalence one-dimensional parameters z_i of the general theory of equivalence; and the choice of a set z of z_i corresponding to a Pareto-efficient actual situation, possibly through that of a maximizing criterion. In particular, the considered freedom can be social freedom, or freedom solely defined by the domain of choice irrespective of the individual and her capacities. Then, for cases of equality equivalence, the equality is in particular respectively satisfied by full social freedom from identical allocations (ELIE schemes are such cases), and by identical domains of choice.[20] The parameters z_i can notably be incomes that it is possible to have for a given labour, such as lump-sum transfers with zero labour, total incomes for maximal labour, and intermediate others; or they can be productivities or wage rates, or relations with the actual ones, from some equal benchmark allocation of income and leisure (labour); other meaningful alternatives are shortly noted. The objective is the maximization of a function $M(z)$ where $z = \{z_i\}$. It can notably be an inequality-averse maximand. The limiting case of the leximin has been shown to present a notable shortcoming as an egalitarian criterion when it does not yield equality (this is a logical consequence of its property of "independence" – see Chapter 23). Now, all these solutions meet the general problem of equivalence theory: the actual situation that yields the best equivalent situation for the considered property is not the best actual situation for this property if a degree of satisfaction of this property in actual situations is defined. In particular, the *reversal* syndrome of this issue can be met, notably for egalitarian intentions: the policy, acting on

---

[19] See Kolm 1966a, Section 5.

[20] There have been studies of efficient equivalence to general identical domains of choice (Kolm 1993d), and, for budget sets with given cost or supply functions or prices, to less unequal or equal incomes (Kolm 1966a) and to equal incomes with given prices (Thomson 1994). The various recent applied specifications of this principle include applications to general theories of the income tax – hence as alternative proposals for overall distributive justice – by Fleurbaey and Maniquet (2001, 2002a), just noted and which are discussed in full in Appendix A.

the actual situation for making the equivalent situation less unequal, may well make the actual situation more unequal in the items considered relevant (see Section 1.6.2). Moreover, other situations equivalent to the chosen actual one fare worse than it for the property (if degrees are defined). Answers to these possible shortcomings have been suggested. Finally, solutions based on the concept of equivalence face, for practical applications, the major information problem of knowing the individuals' indifference loci, and hence preference orderings or ordinal utility functions, in a domain which is sometimes large, sometimes far beyond observed choices (and indeed, necessarily for impossible overall situations). This informational difficulty is of a much higher order of magnitude than any that can be met in only knowing the relevant wage rates used by policies of ELIE.

2) The framework and the four families of solutions

The equivalent situation is considered, with individual labour ℓ, leisure λ, and income y which is seen either as a consumption good or as the value of (nonleisure) consumption goods that can be bought with it in an implicit choice. Labour and leisure are taken in their unidimensional normalized measures (see Chapter 8), hence with $\ell + \lambda = 1, 0 \leq \ell \leq 1, 0 \leq \lambda \leq 1$. An individual's domain of choice is described by a possibility function P such that the individual can choose ℓ, λ, and y satisfying $y \leq P(\ell)$. For a specific individual i, these items are ℓ_i, λ_i, y_i, and P_i. In a diagram of coordinates ℓ and y, the actual allocation of individual i is represented by a point of her indifference curve tangent to the curve $P_i(\ell)$, as a result of her fictive choice in this equivalent situation. The *actual* production possibilities of individual i are described by her production function p_i, stating that she can earn income $y_i = p_i(\ell_i)$ in providing labour ℓ_i. Function p_i is increasing (or nondecreasing), with $p_i(0) = 0$. A particular case is the linear form $y_i = w_i \ell_i$ with a given wage rate w_i.

A solution of the considered family is determined by three choices: (1) the possibility functions P_i; (2) the equivalence parameters z_i; and (3) the selection of one Pareto-efficient set $z = \{z_i\}$, possibly by the maximization of an increasing function $M(z)$ (leximin being a limiting case).

For each of the two first choices, of the P_i and of the z_i, there are two particularly a priori meaningful families of possibilities, which make four families of cases. Either P_i for individual i specifically depends on her actual specific production function p_i, or this is not the case. And either z_i describes income for given labour (zero, full, or anything justified in between), or z_i affects the slopes of function P_i, the variational, marginal, or unit possibilities (possibly seen as fictive productivities). The fact that function P_i specifically depends on individual i's production function p_i is justified by the notion that individual i is attributed some entitlement or accountability as concerns her own productivity (hence, the relation is a positive one); this constitutes, after ELIE structures, another, different way of expressing such an entitlement-accountability. In the other case, any such entitlement or accountability is a priori denied. The corresponding ideal equalities are respectively in the family of social freedom from an equal allocation and ELIE when P_i specifically depends on p_i, and of identical domains of choice when it does not (in the case of ELIE, the effects of different productivities are equalized for the equalization labour k and are "naturally" allocated to the individuals only for variations of labour from k).

The two noted types of choice can be distinguished first in choosing functions $\widehat{p}_i(\ell)$ specifically depending or not on the corresponding production functions p_i; and second, in taking for functions P_i affine forms

$$P_i(\ell) = a_i \cdot \widehat{p}_i(\ell) + b_i \tag{1}$$

and relating the one-dimensional equivalence parameters z_i to parameters a_i or b_i.

If parameters z_i concern variational possibilities seen as fictive productivities, functions $P_i(\ell)$ represented by curves passing through the same point $\ell = k$ and $P_i(k) = \pi$ for all i are chosen, and, from equation (1),

$$P_1(\ell) - \pi = a_i \cdot [\widehat{p}_i(\ell) - \widehat{p}_i(k)] \tag{2}$$

and one can take $z_i = a_i$.[21] One can in particular choose $\pi = \overline{p}(k)$ where $\overline{p}(\ell) = (1/n)\Sigma\, p_i(\ell)$.

If parameters z_i are affected by notional lump-sum transfers, one can take $a_i = 1$, and hence, from equation (1),

$$P_i(\ell) = \widehat{p}_i(\ell) + b_i, \tag{3}$$

and one can take $z_i = P_i(k) = \widehat{p}_i(k) + b_i$ for some benchmark labour k.

3) Equivalent social freedom

3.1) Transfers

As regards functions $\widehat{p}_i(\ell)$, the first case chooses $\widehat{p}_i(\ell) = p_i(\ell)$ for all i and ℓ.
Then, form (3) becomes

$$P_i(\ell) = p_i(\ell) + b_i, \tag{4}$$

and in particular

$$P_i(\ell) = w_i\ell + b_i \tag{4'}$$

if $p_i(\ell) = w_i\ell$, and the equivalence parameter is $z_i = p_i(k) + b_i$, and, with (4'), $z_i = w_i k + b_i$. If all z_i are equal, $z_i = \zeta$ for all i, all curves $P_i(\ell)$ pass through the same point $\ell = k$ and $P_i(k) = \zeta$ for all i, and the considered equivalent situation has the form of a *generalized ELIE*, the generalization coming from the fact

---

[21] Such curves passing through the same point constitute a "pencil" of curves. Other possible solutions, such as, when $\widehat{p}_i(\ell) = p_i(\ell)$, $P_i(\ell) - p_i(k) = a_i \cdot [p_i(\ell) - p_i(k)]$, seem less meaningful.

that the algebraic sum of transfers Σb_i need not be zero because this equivalent situation is fictive. The actual situation then is *generalized ELIE equivalent*. Then, $\zeta = \overline{p}(k) + \overline{b}$ where $\overline{p}$ and $\overline{b} = (1/n)\Sigma b_i$ are the average p_i and b_i. In the most common case, there can be a *Pareto-efficient generalized ELIE equivalent*, corresponding to the highest level of ζ, ζ^*, under the constraints of the equivalent actual situation. If lump-sum transfers are possible in the actual situation, then generally $\overline{b}^* = \zeta^* - \overline{p}(k) > 0$ in this equivalent fictive situation. More generally, a Pareto-efficient solution results from the maximization of any increasing function $M(z)$ with $z = \{z_i\}$. Such a function can in particular be inequality-averse, with the limiting case of leximin in the z_i. Coefficient k can notably be 0, 1, k^e, 1/2, where k^e is the k of the income-egalitarian ELIE presented in Chapter 11. With $k = 0$, the equivalent situation is full self-ownership plus transfers – equal transfers if $z_i = \zeta$ is the same for all i. More generally, the choice of k can result from the considerations developed in Part IV of this study.

3.2) Productivity adjustments

With $\widehat{p}_i(\ell) = p_i(\ell)$ for all i and ℓ, form (2) becomes

$$P_i(\ell) - \pi = a_i \cdot [\, p_i(\ell) - p_i(k)] \tag{5}$$

and, in the linear case where $p_i(\ell) = w_i \ell$,

$$P_i(\ell) - \pi = a_i w_i \cdot (\ell - k) \tag{5'}$$

(in this latter case, choosing $z_i = a_i w_i$ amounts to choosing $z_i = a_i$ with $\widehat{p}_i(\ell) = \ell$, shortly considered). If $a_i = 1$ and $P_i(k) = \pi = \overline{p}(k)$ for all i, this equivalent situation is an ELIE with equalization labour k. The situation described by form (5) and any a_i, for all i, and $\pi = \overline{p}(k)$, thus is a *productivity-adjusted ELIE*, and a *uniformly productivity-adjusted ELIE* if all a_i are equal. Note that $\pi = \overline{p}(k)$ is the same for all a_i. If individual i chooses labour ℓ_i under the constraint $y_i = P_i(\ell_i)$, she prefers a higher a_i if $\ell_i > k$ and a lower a_i if $\ell_i < k$. One has $\ell_i \geq k$ for $k \leq k^e$ for most full labours ℓ_i, and necessarily for $k = 0$. Then, the a_i can be taken as the z_i of the general theory. The case $k = 0$ corresponds to full self-ownership. The level of k can be chosen from the considerations of Part IV of this study. The equal and maximal z_i most often correspond to a Pareto-efficient actual situation. More generally, however, this Pareto efficiency results from the maximization of an increasing function $M(z)$ which can be inequality averse, with the leximin as limiting case. However, the case of $k = 1$ and $\pi = \overline{p}(1)$ can also be chosen, as can more generally any k such that $\ell_i \leq k$ for all i, with individuals preferring lower a_i. If these a_i are taken as z_i, Pareto efficiency of the actual situation most often results from equal and minimal z_i, and it more generally results from the maximization of a decreasing function, or the minimization of an increasing function, $M(z)$, which can be inequality averse, with the "leximax" (converse of the leximin) as limiting case.

4) Irrelevant individual productivities

4.1) The common reference productivity

In the foregoing cases, the obtained or ideal egalitarian equivalence is with social freedom from an equal allocation. The degree of equalization of individual productivities (of the income value of individuals' productive capacities) is coefficient k. This equalization is practically full with $k = k^e$. The alternative view of freedom as solely determined by the domain of possible choices without consideration of the nature and cause of the constraint entails that equal freedom holds, in particular, when these domains are identical. This leads to considering functions $\widehat{p}_i(\ell)$ that are the same for all k, $\widehat{p}_i(\ell) = p(\ell)$ for all i and ℓ.

If $p(\ell)$ is a constant, $p(\ell) = c$, if the individuals prefer a lower labour for each income they choose $\ell_i = 0$, and the equivalent situation amounts to that of the leisurely equivalent income (for instance, with form (1) this income is $a_i c + b_i$ and one can take it as z_i – for example in taking $a_i = 0$ and $z_i = b_i$ or $b_i = 0$ and $z_i = a_i c$). Conversely, if the curve $p(\ell)$ is sufficiently steep, individuals faced with the corresponding constraint choose $\ell_i = 1$, and $P_i(1)$ can be taken as z_i for all i.

A normal uniform function is $p(\ell) = \overline{p}(\ell)$, the average of individuals' production function. Other natural possibilities are $p(\ell) = \min_i p_i(\ell)$ or $p_i(\ell) = \max_i p_i(\ell)$ for all ℓ. They seem particularly significant when this minimum is given by the same i for all ℓ. Similarly, if the same i gives the median $p_i(\ell)$ for all ℓ, this $p_i(\ell)$ can meaningfully be taken as $p(\ell)$. If all individuals have linear production functions $w_i \ell$, these cases lead to taking a linear $p(\ell) = w\ell$ with a constant notional wage rate w, with, for w, the average $\overline{w}$, the median, the lowest or the highest of the w_i. In a case of an application of structure (3) with identical linear functions $\widehat{p}_i(\ell) = p(\ell) = w\ell$, Fleurbaey and Maniquet (2002a) propose to choose, as w, the official minimum wage rate – in a country where there exists one.

4.2) Transfers

With

$$P_i(\ell) = p(\ell) + b_i, \qquad (6)$$

parameters $z_i = p(k) + b_i$, give a result that does not depend on k, and is the same as that given with the (fictive) transfers b_i, for operations of equality, maximum with equality, the highest sum, maximin, and leximin. For other increasing maximands $M(z)$, this independence of the result from k and the equivalence with maximizing $M(b)$ with $b = \{b_i\}$, hold in all cases if and only if hypersurfaces $M(z) = $ constant in the n-dimensional space of the z_i transform into one another by translations in the direction of the vector of n ones. If, moreover, maximand M has the property of "independence" or "separability" meaning that the choice is the same whatever the specific levels of the z_i that do not change, then this ordinal function has a specification of the form $-\Sigma e^{-\alpha z_i}$ where $\alpha > 0$ gives both increasingness and inequality aversion (Σz_i and min z_i are two limiting cases).

4.3) Productivity adjustments

With $\widehat{p}_i(\ell) = p(\ell)$, form (2) becomes

$$P_i(\ell) - \pi = a_i \cdot [p(\ell) - p(k)] \tag{7}$$

with $\pi = P_i(k)$ for all i, and notably $\pi = \overline{p}(k)$ or $\pi = p(k)$. This is an ELIE-like structure where individuals have proportional productivities, $a_i \cdot p(\ell)$ for individual i. Equal a_i taken as z_i give an identical possibility function $P_i(\ell)$ for all individuals i. If ℓ_i is labour chosen by individual i under the constraint $y_i \leq P_i(\ell_i)$, individual i prefers a higher a_i if $\ell_i > k$ and a lower a_i if $\ell_i < k$. If $k \leq k^e$ (the income-egalitarian equalization labour of Chapter 11), $\ell_i \geq k$ for all individuals providing normal full labour. This is in particular the case for the income-egalitarian level $k = k^e$. And $\ell_i \geq k$ for all i for $k = 0$, which corresponds to the classical liberal *full self-ownership*. Conversely, $\ell_i \leq k$ for all i for some k, notably for the maximal $k = 1$, for which one can take $\pi = \overline{p}(1)$ – the maximal income equalization – or $\pi = p(1)$. Then, lower parameters a_i are preferred and, if one takes $z_i = a_i$ for all i, function $M(z)$ should be either increasing and minimized, or decreasing and maximized (with the limiting case of "leximax"). In the linear case $p(\ell) = w\ell$, $P_i(\ell) - \pi = a_i w \cdot (\ell - k)$, and one can also take $z_i = a_i w$ and have $P_i(\ell) - \pi = z_i \cdot (\ell - k)$ and notably $P_i(\ell) = \overline{p}(k) + z_i \cdot (\ell - k)$, with notable particular reference to full self-ownership with $k = 0$ and $P_i(\ell) = z_i \ell$, maximal income equalization with $k = 1$ and $P_i(\ell) = \overline{p}(1) - z_i \cdot (1 - \ell)$, and income-egalitarian equalization with $k = k^e$ and $P_i(\ell) = \overline{p}(k^e) + z_i \cdot (\ell - k^e)$. With $p_i(\ell) = w_i \ell$ for given w_i for all i, the last two cases are $P_i(\ell) = \overline{w} - z_i \cdot (1 - \ell)$ and $P_i(\ell) = \overline{w}k^e + z_i \cdot (\ell - k^e)$. With $p(\ell) = w\ell$ and $z_i = a_i$ for all i, the result does not depend on w and is the same as with $z_i = a_i w$ for all i, for: equal z_i; maximal or minimal equal z_i; maximin or minimax; leximin or "leximax"; any increasing or decreasing ordinal function M that has a homogeneous specification (the hypersurfaces $M = $ constant in the space of the z_i are homothetic among themselves from the origin); and in particular, for an "independent" or "separable" evaluation where the choice does not depend on the specific value of the z_i that do not vary, a specification of the form Σz_i^α with $\alpha > 0$ for increasingness, $\alpha < 0$ for decreasingness, and $\alpha < 1$ for inequality aversion, or $\Sigma \log z_i$ or $-\Sigma \log z_i$. The general choice of coefficient k can result from the considerations of Part IV of this study. This choice very much influences the result. A diagram with labour ℓ and income y as coordinates shows straightforwardly that, for given indifference curves, which individual has the lowest (or highest) a_i can depend on the level of k (and she is the individual favoured by the policy for a leximin or maximin, possibly leading to an equalization).

Given these choices of k, $p(\ell)$, and z_i, the method of the general theory of Pareto-efficient egalitarian equivalence applies. The z_i can be equal. Then their highest or lowest value (depending on the chosen k) most often corresponds to a Pareto-efficient actual situation. More generally, Pareto efficiency results from maximizing or minimizing – depending on the chosen k – under the constraints and with the policy tools of the actual situation, an increasing function $M(z)$, which can be inequality averse. A possible limiting case is leximin or leximax.

Appendix A. APPLICATIONS TO DISTRIBUTIVE INCOME TAXATION

Two interesting and rare specific applications of equivalence theory with a practical intent are provided by Fleurbaey and Maniquet (2001, 2002a). They want to determine an "optimum income tax" based on income for Mirrlees' (1971) reason of taking income as a proxy for presumably unobservable individual productive capacities. Their basic ethics stems from the notion that individuals are not responsible for their (productive) capacities. Yet, they hold them "responsible for their tastes." However, the considered policy, which is not a liberalism in the sense that it does not a priori aim at social freedom, would have to explicitly consider indifference loci because it wants Pareto efficiency. The authors then resort to leximins in equivalent transfers with wage rates equal to the minimum official rate, and in equivalent wage rates without transfers. These applications of the equivalence principle interestingly raise a number of crucial questions. In short, one is the general handicap of equivalence theory and its syndrome in the property of "reversal." Another is the fact that, although the maximand does not depend on individuals' productivities, they make a difference for the individuals when the maximization is performed. There is also the general vast informational requirement of equivalence concepts, about individuals' preferences. This contrasts with the problematic informational reason for taxing earned income. Moreover, many other equivalence parameters could be chosen. And the leximin criterion has problems as an egalitarian principle (Chapter 23). Furthermore, can the individuals be "responsible" for the intensity of preferences but not for the corresponding preference orderings? Finally, Pareto efficiency does not require explicit consideration by the policy if it results from free choices.

(1) A first problem is the basic and foundational handicap of the equivalence principle: the obtained solution does not satisfy at best any index of the considered ethical objective, function of properties of the actual situation (see the discussion in Section 1). In particular, phenomena of *reversal* have a priori a fair probability of occurence. For egalitarian equivalence, the decrease in inequality or favouring the least endowed in the fictive (and ultimately impossible) equivalent situation may entail, on the contrary, increasing inequality or worsening the situation of the least endowed (or favouring the most endowed) – in the relevant items – in the actual situation.

(2) Individual productivities do not appear in the considered criteria. This is for the basic chosen ethical reason that "individuals are not responsible for their productive capacities," which is assumed to imply that their final situation should not be differentiated according to their specific productivities. However, the chosen

solution only states that the overall criterion is not so differentiated. Now, in applying the obtained "optimum income tax," the outcome for each individual will depend on her productivities (such as her competitive wage rate). The basic ethical stand requires that these effects be erased or compensated as much as possible. Yet, the considered objective does not do that. It is unconcerned with productivities, whereas the retained ethics and tax structure demand a kind of compensatory discrimination with respect to them.

(3) The second general problem of egalitarian equivalence is informational. Applications indeed require extensive information about individuals' indifference loci, that is, ordinal utility, in domains generally away from observed choices (and, indeed, in overall impossible situations). This is vastly more demanding than knowing, observing, or estimating wage rates.

(4) In the present case, moreover, this informational difficulty may raise an issue of consistency with the basic aim and the reason given for it: devising an income-based tax for the reason proposed by Mirrlees (1971) that individuals' productivities are unobservable and should be replaced by earned income as a proxy. Mirrlees himself, however, concluded his article by the remark that labour duration can also be observed and the wage rate results. Indeed, wage rates are still more often directly observable. This question has been discussed in Chapters 10 and 16. It was pointed out that, apart from raising public revenue, the main actual reason for the base and structure of present progressive taxes based on incomes is ethical rather than informational in nature: this intends to constitute some compromise between ideals of income equality, on the one hand, and full self-ownership, on the other hand. It was also proposed that this objective is better achieved by some ELIE scheme. Then, the vanishing of the disincentive effect of the income-based tax changes the whole structure of the issue.

(5) Other questions relate to the specific choices of the egalitarian-equivalence principle. As we just noted, the basic underlying ethical view presented is that, since the individuals are not responsible for their productive capacities, they are not accountable for them. This leads to solutions in the family of those with identical functions $\widehat{p}_i(\ell) = p(\ell)$ for all individuals i. However, this ethics can also be expressed otherwise, such as by the income-egalitarian ELIE with $k = k^e$. Moreover, most people think that individuals have at least some partial entitlement in their own productive capacities. This is the first reason for the limitation in the equalization of incomes. But this ethics is better implemented by general ELIE schemes.

(6) The two considered relations are particular forms of the general structure $P_i(\ell) = a_i \widehat{p}_i(\ell) + b_i$ of Section 2.2.5 of the chapter. They choose to express the irrelevance of production functions p_i in choosing $\widehat{p}_i(\ell) = p(\ell)$, the same for all i (rather than as ELIE does, for instance). More precisely, they choose linear functions $p(\ell)$. These chosen solutions are natural, but a number of others are too. One of these proposals chooses z_i such that $P_i(\ell) = z_i \ell$, a case of full self-ownership (with notional productivities z_i). However, other choices than this full self-ownership $k = 0$ are possible for $P_i(\ell) - \pi = z_i \cdot (\ell - k)$, such as, for instance, $P_i(\ell) - \overline{p}(k^e) = z_i \cdot (\ell - k^e)$, $P_i(\ell) - \overline{p_i}(1) = z_i \cdot (1 - \ell)$, and others. The other solution takes z_i such that $P_i(\ell) = w\ell + z_i$ with, for w, the official minimum

wage rate. Yet, other w are possible (such as the average, median, lowest, or highest of the w_i), as well as nonlinear forms of function $p(\ell)$ (this may for instance be $\overline{p}(\ell)$, among others noted).

(7) Moreover, the formal criterion of leximin has particular limitations as an egalitarian principle (see Chapter 23).

(8) The basic moral reason presented for resorting to concepts of equivalence is that the individuals are "responsible" for the intensity of their preferences but not for the corresponding indifference loci (and preference orderings). Now, for such moral applications, indifference means equal satisfaction (rather than only hesitation or indeterminacy in choice). And if an individual is responsible for how high her satisfaction, happiness, or the like is for each of her possible allocations, she also is for her indifference loci and preference ordering which are fully determined by this property. However, we have seen (Chapter 6) that the concept of responsibility about one's tastes is highly ambiguous. One could then replace it by the a priori moral concept of *accountability*. Then, a ground for making individuals accountable for the intensity of their preferences but not for their preference ordering may be found in the fact that others are concerned with the acts chosen by the individual, which relate to her preference ordering only, whereas intensity of satisfaction is a purely private concern (and one for the family and compassion). This assumes the eudemonistic psychological theory of choice (people choose what makes them more satisfied or happier). Yet, the criterion discriminating between private and public concern is no longer responsibility but is externality.

(9) Finally, a reason proposed for considering indifference loci and preference orderings – but not necessarily intensities of preferences – is the reference to Pareto efficiency. However, Pareto efficiency can be secured without explicit and specific consideration of individuals' preference orderings by the policy, by freedom of choice under actual constraints or in the relevant exchanges or agreements. Then, it suffices, for securing it, that the policy does not interfere in a way that distorts these choices, and the policy has no need to explicitly consider individuals' preferences and final choice. This is notably the case with ELIE policies.

Appendix B. POTENTIAL FREEDOM

The noted general logical shortcoming of equivalence theory, whereby improving a quality of the equivalent situation can worsen it in the actual situation, dramatically instantiated by the reversal syndrome, is due to the differences in the relative situations of the individuals in the actual and equivalent situations, and hence to the relative positions of the sets of equivalent situations for each individual between the considered situations.[22] This shortcoming is generally less serious – and the reversal less likely – the closer these situations, *ceteris paribus*, as it was noted. It disappears when the two overall allocations in both situations are the same. Then, the concept of equivalence can only be among freedoms provided by domains of choice that lead to choosing this allocation, or this allocation itself. For an individual, all domains of choice that lead her to choose the same individual allocation are said to be equivalent,

[22] For instance, intersecting indifference curves for reversal with two goods.

and they are equivalent to this allocation, which is the case where the domain of choice shrinks to this single alternative.[23] The reason for considering this equivalence is to resort to a moral concept of equal liberty, interpersonal comparisons of liberty, and maximin in liberty. Then, with this equivalence, a number of individuals are equally free when they have one identical equivalent domain of choice; and one is no less free than another when one of her equivalent domains of choice includes one of the other's equivalent domains. These definitions are shown to imply that, for two individuals, no less free both ways amounts to as free. This equivalent equal freedom, for any number of individuals, amounts to no individual preferring any other's allocation to her own (Kolm 1971, 1973, and Chapter 24). When the overall allocation is Pareto efficient, permutations of individuals' allocations are possible, and the number of individuals is finite, this comparison by no less free is shown to provide a ranking of individuals such that each is no less free than all of lower ranks (Kolm 1993d, 1999b). Then, when no such equal freedom "equivalent" is Pareto efficient (or possible), this ranking permits solutions by maximin or leximin in these equivalent freedoms (idem).

---

[23] That is, reasons for valuing or disliking freedom other than the chosen alternative it permits are not considered (freedom may be disliked because of the triad of reasons of cost of choosing, responsibility aversion, and anguish of choice).

27

Conclusion

1. PRESENTATION

This concluding chapter begins with a recapitulation of the general method, line of argument, and result. It then proposes practical strategies for introducing the obtained structure of distribution in actual distributive policies by more or less progressive transformations of present-day fiscal tools, possibly with unanimous, consensual approval at each step. The chapter then takes a look at the field of social improvement beyond macrojustice, in a chain of influences where one improvement paves the way for the next. Distributive justice is favourable to freely peaceful social relations and then to positive, other-regarding ones: the appropriate liberty and equality favour fraternity – which is hampered by the use of force and by envy, resentment, and sentiments that others benefit from what should be one's own. Sentiments favourable to other persons constitute a lowering of the importance of the ego, which can favour this lowering in the personal field, thus reducing acquisitiveness, greed, and unwarranted attachments and desires. This, by the way, will in turn reduce the effects and importance of imperfections in distributive justice. This may also free attention and energy for knowledge and appreciation of the cultural heritage of civilizations, and, possibly, for contributing to it. But these will be other stories.

Section 2 recapitulates the essential of the central derivation of macrojustice in society. Section 3 shows how the result can be implemented by progressive transformations of the present fiscal policies. Finally, Section 4 shows how this can lead the rest of the improvement of society, in the rest of justice and beyond justice.

2. RECAPITULATION OF THE CENTRAL DERIVATION

We all would be happier and freer if we manage not to want more than we can have, more than we really need, and more than leaves enough for others. Since one can hardly hope that this self formation reaches fast a sufficient scale in a large society, distributive justice has to be considered. Why, however, would my conception of justice be better than yours? Have I the right to impose it, even as a proposal? Would not this be arbitrary, paternalistic, and intrusive? Then, where else could one find the definition of what is just but in the considered society itself? Respect, and possibly rationality, suggest defining what is just as what society thinks is just. Ethics then becomes a positive science, by nature a part of anthropology. In application, it becomes the servant of society, giving it indications about how to realize what it wants, possibly about how to express and formalize its aspirations. This is the opposite of the usual attitude of ethics, playing teacher and judge, assertive, supposedly omniscient, inherently arrogant, but confined to sterile ratiocinations if the philosopher is not also king or a dictator's advisor, and hence basically undemocratic if it wants to have any actual effect.

Finding out what should be done solely from society's opinions is "endogenous social choice." What, however, if several different and opposed opinions exist in society? What if individuals' views differ (or if the same individual has several different views, is of several minds, which is not unfrequent)? It turns out that unanimity, properly conceived and applied, suffices for solving most of the problem of justice. And the result it gives is remarkably simple and meaningful. Endorsing unanimous views is the "unanimity principle." The considered opinions will, of course, have to be sufficiently reflective and informed. Then, ordinary judgments in a society coincide about certain questions, topics, or domains. This happens in two types of ways. One consists of formally considering all comparisons or choices about which there is unanimity. This leads to the requirement of Pareto efficiency, by definition – and this alone can have far-reaching consequences in choices of policies. More specifically, everybody agrees about some particular issues. This corresponds to Rawls' attractive label of "overlapping consensus." One might think, however, that distributive justice is precisely the field where this approach would lead nowhere because, by definition, it deals with opposed individual interests. However, the question considered is justice, and hence the corresponding relevant views of the individuals are their views about justice and not their interests. Individuals do have such views (although they most often are shared views of groups in the society rather than specifically their own). Moreover, if necessary, an individual's views about justice can be notionally constructed from her self-interested or self-centered views and from properties intrinsic to the very concept of justice, notably impartiality (see Chapter 21). Indeed, justice has to be impartial from the very concept and meaning of the term (impartiality is an "a priori" property of justice). This does not by itself a priori fully solve the problem, since there can be various types of impartial opinions. However, individuals' impartial judgments have much larger overlap than their self-interested or self-centered views. Moreover, along with further considerations, this finally leads to the solution.

Macrojustice is the main and first field of application of these considerations. It consists of the basic rules of society and their application to the distribution of the main resources in global (overall) distributive justice. It is logically and commonly distinguished from the other distributive issues. Unanimity, possibly with the requirement of impartiality, leads to choosing social freedom – the absence of forceful interference – or the classical basic rights as the general rule (Chapters 2 and 4). Pareto efficiency or the process-freedom aspect of social freedom leads to restricting distribution to given resources. Among these, considerations of relative importance, possible policies, and commonly accepted criteria lead to focusing on the allocation of given capacities (Chapter 4). Moreover, consensus considers that comparing eudemonistic capacities is irrelevant for the policy implementing global distributive justice (Chapter 6). Finally, social freedom in using one's capacities reduces what is to be distributed to the value of given productive capacities. Then, equality, a consequence of rationality (Chapter 23), leads to the distributive structure of equal labour income equalization or ELIE (Chapter 9). This necessary structure compensates lower given productivities by transfers proportionately higher. It has a number of highly meaningful properties such as, partially, equal pay for equal work, self-ownership, labour reciprocity, income equalization, solidarity, mutual obligation, and commonality; it also implies a given minimum income for a minimum labour (or for involuntary unemployment); and so on. However, this distribution can go from full self-ownership to the most faithful implementation of the income-egalitarian ideal. This depends on the degree of income equalization, solidarity, reciprocity, or community. The social, ethical, and political debate in society can focus on this coefficient, helped by comparisons with actual degrees of redistribution. However, it can be helped by the deepest methods of determining the distributional consensus (Part IV).

Macrojustice is then fully determined by the applications of the general methods of endogenous social choice. It should first be pointed out that judgments about the proper or just organization of society are, in nature, no less social than they are individual, since individuals usually adopt some existing view and are influenced by education, contact, dialog, and social experience. Yet, the methods will rest on the consideration of consensus or unanimity, in line with the general consequence of basic rights or of democracy, which holds that social or cultural views should be taken into account solely through their expression by individuals who alone can be responsible (the individualistic filter).

There are two ways for individuals to agree about an issue: in a "preference agreement," they have the same preferences about the issue; in an "exchange agreement," they agree about a specific choice as a result of an agreement where each yields something in exchange for concessions by others (these yieldings can be payments, the exchange can consist in mutual contributions or restraints, and so on). Preference agreements are more complete solutions because exchange agreements depend on items that have to be justified, first of all a "starting state," which may be the "disagreement state" prevailing in case of failure to agree, and possibly also the rules of the agreement (game) and relative bargaining powers. Moreover, these agreements can be actual or fictional, or reality can go some way and theoretical constructs can complete the attainment of the consensus. These two distinctions, preference agreement vs. exchange and actual vs. fictional, lead to four types of methods of endogenous social choice, and there are mixed solutions. A number of classical theories are so described. For instance, free exchange solutions use exchange agreement. Agreement through convincing, argument, or rhetoric, notably in dialog, is preference agreement. Social contracts are putative exchange agreements. And both the notional "ideal speech" in Habermas's "discourse ethics," and an "original position" as conceived by Rawls are hypothetical preference agreements.

An important class of preference-agreement solutions consists of considering that each individual equally takes the views of all the individuals, actually, notionally, or as a mix of both. This can be done in two types of ways. In one, which can be called "fusional," each individual takes all views, reasons, causes of views, and sentiments that accompany these judgments, all together, jointly, hence in inherently producing a synthesis when she has to evaluate. In the other category, which can be labelled "substitution," each individual considers she is all the individuals – for the relevant items – successively in time, as uncertain possibilities, or as the dimensions of a "multiple self": the first of these methods is "moral time-sharing," and the second is "moral risk," a concept in the family of theories of the "original position." In all cases, each individual should be fully informed of others' views. Full relevant information is, indeed, a general requirement, since ethics cannot be based on ignorance, confusion, or misunderstanding. This information should include knowing "how it feels" to hold such views, and the complete and full knowledge of this item implies fully sharing and experiencing this feeling: this is "empathetic information." It can be helped by knowing the causes of these views, such as reasons, influences received, and life experiences ("formative information") – including the corresponding empathetic information. This information and a resulting narrowing down of differences toward a fusion of views can result from a dialog which can be actual, notional, or both (Chapter 20).

The substitution methods do not directly lead to unanimity, because individuals have a priori different preferences about being the various individuals, and also different preferences about risk or variability in time (with equal probabilities or durations for impartiality). Yet, the new individual views are closer to one another than the initial ones. The most consistent way of facing the obtained plurality consists of repeating the same operation with the obtained views (there can for instance be "original positions of original positions"), and in continuing in a converging infinite regress (Chapter 21). One can also build a social contract (a notional exchange agreement) from the obtained views, and some structures permit a solution by a meaningful aggregation of individuals' preferences toward risk (ibid.).

However, the limit to full individual relevant information, and limits to assimilating justice to choice in uncertainty (and time-sharing), lead one to also use other methods. The "extension" method estimates individuals' objective evaluations in considering that they care for all individuals in the society as they actually care for individuals in a particular social relation with them (Chapter 21).

Finally, the consensus about the irrelevance of comparative eudemonistic capacities leads an aggregative solution to weight and measure individuals' comparisons between two states by their willingness to pay for there being one rather than the other. For judging a redistribution, the values representing self-interest cancel out, and only those representing moral preferences remain: this leads to the choice of a distribution by the "distributive surplus" (Chapter 19). Other methods focus on the various ways of knowing individuals' moral distributive preferences (ibid.).

3. STRATEGY OF IMPLEMENTATION

The general principle applied here, endogenous social choice, basically means implementing what people want. This *prima facie* favours a large social acceptance of its implementation, or even support for it. However, this desire may be hidden by psychological or social circumstances, such as insufficiency of information (notably of individuals about others), awareness, reflexion, or communication, or the various aspects of interaction (see Chapter 17). Yet, such obstacles are lowered by information, explaining and dialog. We have also noted that the reasons for desired coercion may elicit apparent oppositions that are not actual ones. Moreover, there are a number of ways of transforming actual distributive policies into the obtained scheme by more or less progressive transformations with, possibly, consensus (or almost so) at each step. Major instances of these strategies have been shown in previous chapters, and a few important ones are added.

The Presentation has considered ways of dealing with the fact that present practice does not abide by functional finance – in particular, large and general taxes mix all functions of public finance and, notably, do not distinguish the distributive function from the others. It was pointed out that this confusion necessarily constitutes a major source of waste and injustice in society. It was then suggested that one way toward optimality was to introduce taxation according to capacities in the form of "equal labour contribution." This was taken again in Chapter 11 about the classical principles of public finance. On the subsidy side, it was shown in Chapter 7, in a numerical example, how the introduction of an ELIE distributive scheme can render classical supports of low incomes obsolete, and hence, can replace them in making everyone better off. The question of estimating the information used in ELIE schemes has been discussed at length in Chapter 10, notably in the Appendix. It has also been noted that optimizing the gathering of information and facing the circumstances and constraints (in the gathering of information and elsewhere) that force resorting to a second-best policy can be achieved by the maximization of an increasing, symmetrical and inequality-averse function of individuals' "corrected equalization incomes." The following other strategies of realization can also be used.

A classical proposal consists of the "universal allocation" of the same "basic income" to everyone. The financing of this scheme is both its drawback – since a sufficient universal basic income implies an impossible cost and a realistic cost implies an insufficient universal basic income – and the way in which it has a distributive effect. Now, if one proposes a financing "according to ability to earn, to earning capacities," the whole of the universal basic income and its financing is but an ELIE distribution. Indeed, using notations of previous chapters (w_i is individual i's competitive wage rate and their average is $\overline{w} = (1/n)\Sigma w_i$), each individual i pays kw_i and all receive the basic income $k\overline{w}$, and so each receives (or yields) the net transfer $t_i = k\overline{w} - kw_i = k\cdot(\overline{w} - w_i)$. One can then say that the universal basic income is financed by the value of the productive capacities (given ones for the appropriate definition of the w_i – see Chapter 8) in proportion to this value. Taking this financing into account, some individuals receive and others pay. However, one feature is at odds with a property emphasized by the proponents of universal basic incomes: not all individuals receive something when they choose not to work, and those more productive than average ($w_i > \overline{w}$) even have to work for paying the tax. In contrast, with an ELIE scheme, all individuals can have the same disposable income $k\overline{w}$), but when they provide the same work (k), which is not zero (except in the limiting case of full self-ownership where this income also is zero).

One can also start from aid to low incomes. An individual i who works ℓ_i for wage rate w_i earns the income $\ell_i w_i$. If this income is deemed too low, it may be replaced by the minimum income y, thanks to the subsidy $y - \ell_i w_i$, with maximal disincentive effect for labour. This disincentive effect is reduced, and the individual's responsibility is taken into account, if the subsidy is only a fraction of this gap, $\alpha\cdot(y - \ell_i w_i)$ with $0 < \alpha < 1$: this is a usual negative income tax or income tax credit. The first step then consists of replacing actual labour ℓ_i by the same notional labour ℓ, the same for all – for instance, the official labour duration if there is one. The subsidy becomes $\alpha\cdot(y - \ell w_i)$, and the disincentive price effect vanishes altogether, along with the waste it induces (with the proper definition of w_i and ℓ_i – see Chapter 8). This finally becomes an ELIE subsidy when y is chosen as $y = \ell\overline{w}$. This subsidy is with $k = \alpha\ell$. Finally, a full ELIE scheme is obtained if the financing of these expenditures is chosen to be according to earning capacities for individuals who do not receive this aid, that is, such that $w_i > \overline{w}$, each paying, symmetrically, the same fraction k of the excess $w_i - \overline{w}$ as the fraction subsidized of $\overline{w} - w_i$ when $w_i < \overline{w}$.

A more general starting point can be the income tax. Its transformation into an ELIE scheme results from a series of simple operations:

- Complete the income tax by the subsidies of a negative income tax or income tax credit.
- Distinguish, notionally or actually, the financing of redistribution from that of other public expenditures, and consider the former.
- In the tax base, replace actual labours by a notional labour, the same for all. This can, for instance, be the official duration of labour if there is one.

- Require financial balance.
- Flatten the tax schedule.

Then, the outcome is an ELIE distribution.

Formally, if individual i pays $f(w_i\ell_i)$, set $f(w_i\ell_i) < 0$ for $w_i\ell_i < y$ for some income y, that is, these individuals receive the tax credit $-f(w_i\ell_i)$. Focus now on taxes for redistribution, or on this part of the tax. Then, replace, in the base, actual labour ℓ_i by the same notional labour ℓ (possibly the official labour duration). The tax becomes $f(w_i\ell)$. If, then, the function f is taken as linear (affine), it is $\alpha \cdot (w_i\ell - y)$ for some given α and y. And if the distributive financial balance is required, parameters y and ℓ are such that $y = \overline{w}\ell$. The resulting scheme is an ELIE with subsidy or tax $t_i = k \cdot (\overline{w} - w_i)$, with $k = \alpha\ell$ as equalization labour.

The introduction of an ELIE distribution can be more or less rapid or progressive. This will notably depend on political demand and possibility. One possibility consists of introducing an ELIE scheme with a very low coefficient k, superimposed to all existing taxes and subsidies, and of letting the level of k progressively increase, in modifying or suppressing other aids or taxes when their role becomes replaced by the corresponding effect of the ELIE scheme. The example given in Chapter 7 suggests that this can be done in better satisfying everyone's interest throughout the process, hence with unanimous support (although habit may still lead to favouring progressiveness).

4. THE REST OF OPTIMALITY

Overall distributive justice, and more generally – along with basic rights and social freedom – macrojustice, describe an important part of the optimality of society. Among the other aspects, the closest one in nature concerns the rest of justice. Although the central topic of this volume concerns macrojustice, much has been said about issues of microjustice (and mesojustice) along the way, in the analyses of general properties, comparisons, applications, or complements: the general structure of criteria of justice (Chapter 23); the substances of justice and their problems (Chapter 24); the correlation between principles and types of social relations (Chapter 16); the allocation of nonhuman natural resources (Chapter 5); the theory of equivalence (Chapter 26); and issues of surplus theory (Chapters 19 and 26), principles of compensation (Chapter 26), fundamental insurance (Chapters 16, 21 and 25), utilitarianism (Chapter 6), eudemonistic practical justice (Chapter 24), liberalisms (Chapters 3 and 22), liberal social contracts (Chapter 3), partially original positions (Chapter 21), potential freedom (Chapters 24 and 26), comparing inequalities (Chapter 23), and desert, merit, need, responsibility, and equality of opportunity (Chapter 25). The interface between macrojustice and microjustice notably concerns the scope of allocative issues that can be solved by exchange, markets, or compensations using incomes whose allocation is an issue in macrojustice. Such uses of income can be prevented by practical considerations, but also for reasons of moral appropriateness for goods whose allocation constitutes a "sphere" distinct from income and exchange, for reasons that can also be related to the importance of the issue, its interference with dignity, its cultural aspects, or the social relations it involves. A field of "mesojustice" can also be distinguished, concerned with issues that are specific and yet are important and concern everyone, such as education and health.[1]

The rest of the quality of society is beyond justice. However, justice itself is largely to be seen as a means for other things that it can favour – if not imply – such as peaceful social relations without domination, an absence of resentment, envy, and anger from injustice, and quietness of the mind. These effects are in the fields of social relations, social sentiments, and mental states. People accept social distribution (of any items) if they are sufficiently convinced that it is just, or if they think it is just and this sufficiently dominates, as motive, their self-interested or self-centered impulses. Indeed and conversely, sentiments of injustice commonly lead to more eager conflicts than do self-interest alone. Hence, justice, so acknowledged by people, can lead them to abstain from forceful acts toward others intending to change the distribution. It thus favours social freedom and diminishes the need of its enforcement by a protective force. People can also directly be convinced by the value of social freedom – a dimension of macrojustice – to the point of voluntarily abstaining from using force against others. The resulting absence of forceful prevention of forceful interference leads to the most complete form of social freedom. This, of course, can be a matter of degree (the police can be, if not absent, at least light or symbolic).

However, good social relations are not only a neutral absence of force, but also positive relations, attitudes, and sentiments toward others. Now, the types of social relations constitute one of the most important aspects of the quality of a society. They constitute among the most important and valuable "goods" consumed by people. However, these goods are intrinsically not commodities, they are not marketable, they cannot be bought and sold. For instance, the paragons of such relations are altruism, and giving and receiving as a gift. Now, one cannot buy gift-giving by the very nature and definition of giving (just as a gift cannot be taken by force). One can induce giving, notably by a previous gift that induces a return gift. However, this relation is not an exchange in the ordinary sense of the term, like a market exchange, which consists of transfers that are mutually conditional by external obligation (or promise keeping or later punishment). "I freely give you" – possibly induced by having received a gift – deeply differs from "I give you this if you give me that," where the term "give" is here a misnomer and merely means handing out, transferring. Such relations are "reciprocities." The main point is that relations of genuine giving and reciprocity generally go

---

[1] See *On health and justice*, Kolm 2002, WHO, and 2003.

along with positive, other-regarding, and "good" attitudes and sentiments toward others – although gift-giving by itself can be of very various types some of which with quite negative aspects.[2]

The particular distributive structure obtained can be favourable to such positive social relations in various ways. The necessity and rationality of its derivation are bound to make it convincing as a just scheme. Moreover, this derivation is based on unanimity at each step. Some of these unanimities, however, are for individuals' conceptions of justice, which may be constructed or inferred rather than actually held by the individuals. In these cases, however, there is the best possible ground for trying to convince these individuals about the just solution. A second aspect concerns the specific structure of ELIE obtained. Indeed, we have seen that ELIE is equivalent to a "general equal labour reciprocity" in the sense that each individual yields to each other the product of the same amount of labour. This balance of bilateral mutual transfers in labour or leisure value may be favourable to seeing it as a fair reciprocity, where the positive social sentiments that characterize reciprocities in the strict sense would also develop.

In a region of Southern France, people have set up a network of relations, called Local Exchange System (SEL in French), where persons provide others with services of their speciality, and the accounting is made in hours of labour rather than in the market value of these services. Individuals should finally provide others with the same number of hours of labour they receive from them, globally. The members of this network emphasize that this is accompanied by particularly good and valuable social relations among participants. Each makes the others benefit from what she can best do, from the best of her characteristic capacities, and of her self in this sense, without demanding the market value of this work, but in receiving, from any others, work in the same amount, in the various specialities she needs. In addition, for part of their needs and income, members have recourse to ordinary market buying and selling. For the part within the SEL, the particular productivities and capacities of the individuals have no influence on the amount of services they can receive (measured in labour time). This principle is exactly that of ELIE schemes for the equalization labour.[3]

[2] There are givings intending to humiliate, to show or enforce a domination or, on the contrary, to assert a subjection, or abiding by a constraining social norm. The point, however, is that there are also givings carrying the best of pro-other and prosocial attitudes and sentiments, and most givings are in this case (an exhaustive analysis of this issue, and more generally of the quality of social relations, is provided in *The Good Economy, General Reciprocity*, Kolm 1984a – see also 2000a, 2000b, 2000d, 2004b).

[3] Labour time is used as unit of account (since SEL also means "salt," the units are called "grains of salt"). This system is now under the scrutiny of the fiscal administration who is at a loss about how to treat it. It performs a redistribution that is in various ways better than that achieved by the actual public budget.

References and bibliography

Ackerman, B. A. 1980. *Social Justice in the Liberal State.* New Haven, CT: Yale University Press.

Alexander, J. M. 2002. Capability egalitarianism and moral selfhood. Paper prepared for the Conference *Promoting Women's Capabilities: Examining Nussbaum's Approach,* University of Cambridge, UK, 9–10 September, Mimeo.

Allingham, M. G. 1973. Towards an ability tax. *Journal of Public Economics* 4: 361–76.

Amiel, Y. and F. Cowell. 1999. *Thinking About Inequality.* Cambridge: Cambridge University Press.

Anderson, E. 1999. What is the point of equality? *Ethics* 109: 287–337.

Apel, K.-O. 1980. *Towards a Transformation of Philosophy.* London: Routledge and Kegan Paul.

Archibald, G. C. and Donaldson, D. 1979. Notes on economic inequality. *Journal of Public Economics* 12: 205–14.

Aristotle. *Eudemian Ethics.* Any edition.

Aristotle. *Nicomachean Ethics.* Any edition.

Aristotle. *Politics.* English trans. by E. Barker. 1946. Oxford: Oxford University Press.

Arneson, R. J. 1989. Equality and equal opportunity for welfare. *Philosophical Studies* 56: 77–93.

Arneson, R. J. 1990. Liberalism, distributive subjectivism, and equal opportunity for welfare. *Philosophy and Public Affairs* 19: 158–94.

Arnsperger, C. 1994. Envy-freeness and distributive justice: A survey of the literature. *Journal of Economic Surveys* 8: 155–86.

Arrow, K. J. 1951. *Social Choice and Individual Values.* New York: Wiley.

Arrow, K. J. 1963. *Social Choice and Individual Values,* 2nd ed. New Haven, CT: Yale University Press.

Arrow, K. J. 1973. Some ordinalist-utilitarian notes on Rawls's Theory of Justice. *Journal of Philosophy* 70: 245–63.

Arrow, K. J. 1977. Extended sympathy and the possibility of social choice. *American Economic Review* 67: 219–25.

Arrow, K. J. and T. Scitowsky, eds. 1969. *Readings in Welfare Economics.* Homewood, IL: Irwin.

Arthur, J. and W. H. Shaw, eds. 1978. *Justice and Economic Distribution.* Englewood Cliffs, NJ: Prentice-Hall.

d'Aspremont, C. and L. Gevers. 1977. Equity and the informational basis of collective choice. *Review of Economic Studies* 46: 199–209.

Atkinson, A. B. 1970. On the measurement of inequality. *Journal of Economic Theory* 2: 244–63.

Atkinson, A. B. 1973. How progressive should income tax be? In *Essays on Modern Economics,* ed. by M. Parkin and R. Nobay. London: Longman.

Atkinson, A. B. 1983a. *Social Justice and Public Policy.* Cambridge, MA: MIT Press.

Atkinson, A. B. 1983b. *The Economics of Inequality*. Oxford: Oxford University Press.

Baker, J. 1987. *Arguing for Equality*. London: Verso.

Barry, B. 1989. *A Treatise on Social Justice. Vol. 1: Theories of Justice*. Hemel Hempstead: Harvester-Wheatsheaf.

Barry, B. 1995. *Justice as Impartiality*. Oxford: Clarendon Press.

Barry, B., R. Barber, J. S. Fishkin and R. C. Flathman. 1983. Symposium on Justice. *Ethics*, 93.

Baumol, W. 1986. *Superfairness*. Cambridge, MA: MIT Press.

Benhabib, S. and F. Dallmayr, eds. 1990. *The Communicative Ethics Controversy*. Cambridge, MA: MIT Press.

Benn, S. 1988. *A Theory of Freedom*. Cambridge: Cambridge University Press.

Bentham, J. 1843. *The Works of Jeremy Bentham*, 11 vols., ed. by John Bowring. Edinburgh: William Tait.

Bentham, J. 1973. *Bentham's Political Thought*, ed. by Bikhu Parekh. London: Croom Helm.

Bergson, A. 1938. A reformulation of certain aspects of welfare economics. *Quarterly Journal of Economics* 52: 310–34.

Bergson, A 1966. *Essays in Normative Economics*. Cambridge, MA: Harvard University Press.

Berlin, I. 1956. Equality. *Proceedings of the Aristotelian Society*. London: Harrison, new series, Vol. LVI, 301–26.

Berlin, I. 1958. *Two Concepts of Freedom*. Oxford: Clarendon Press.

Berlin, I. 1969. *Four Essays on Liberty*. Oxford: Oxford University Press.

Binmore, K. 1994. *Game Theory and the Social Contract, Vol. 1: Playing Fair*. Cambridge, MA: MIT Press.

Binmore, K. and P. Dasgupta, eds. 1987. *The Economics of Bargaining*. Oxford: Basil Blackwell.

Blackorby, C., D. Donaldson and J. A. Weymark. 1984. Social choice with interpersonal utility comparisons: A diagrammatic introduction. *International Economic Review* 25: 327–56.

Bossert, W. 1995. Redistribution mechanisms based on individual characteristics. *Mathematical Social Sciences* 29: 1–17.

Bossert, W. and M. Fleurbaey. 1996. Redistribution and compensation. *Social Choice and Welfare* 13: 343–55.

Bossert, W., M. Fleurbaey and D. Van de gaer. 1996. On second best compensation. Mimeo.

Bossert, W., M. Fleurbaey and D. Van de gaer. 1999 Responsibility, talent, and compensations: A second-best analysis. *Review of Economic Design* 4: 35–55.

Bossert, W., P. Pattanaik and Y. Xu. 1994. Ranking opportunity sets: An axiomatic approach. *Journal of Economic Theory* 63: 326–45.

Boudon, R. 1999. Vox populi, vox dei? Le "spectateur impartial" et la théorie des opinions. GEMAS working papers, Paris.

Brams, S. J. and A. Taylor. 1996. *Fair Division, from Cake Cutting to Dispute Resolution*. Cambridge: Cambridge University Press.

Brandt, R. B. 1979. *A Theory of the Good and the Right*. Oxford: Oxford University Press.

Brandt, R. B. 1986. The future of ethics. In J. P. de Manco and R. M. Fox (eds), *New Directions in Ethics, The Challenge of Applied Ethics*. New York, London: Routledge and Kegan Paul.

Braybrooke, D. 1987. *Meeting Needs*. Princeton, NJ: Princeton University Press.

Broome, J. 1991. *Weighting Goods*. Oxford: Basil Blackwell.

Buchanan, J. M. 1954. Individual choice in voting and the market. *Journal of Political Economy* 62: 334–43.

Buchanan, J. M. 1975. *The Limits of Liberty*. Chicago: University of Chicago Press.

Buchanan, J. M. 1986. *Liberty, Market and the State*. Brighton: Wheatsheaf Books.

Buchanan, J. M. 1991. *The Economics and the Ethics of Constitutional Order*. Ann Arbor: University of Michigan Press.

Buchanan, J. and G. Tullock. 1962. *The Calculus of Consent*. Ann Arbor: University of Michigan Press.

Burke, E. [1790] 1989. *Reflexions on the Revolution in France*. Paris: Hachette.

Campbell, D. 1992. *Equity, Efficiency and Social Choice*. New York: Oxford University Press.

Champsaur, P. and G. Laroque. 1981. Fair allocations in large economies. *Journal of Economic Theory* 25: 269–82.

Chipmann, J. S. 1987. Compensation principle. In *New Palgrave Dictionary in Economics*, ed. by J. Eatwell et al. London: MacMillan, pp. 524–31.

Coase, R. H. 1960. The problem of social cost. *Journal of Law and Economics* 3: 1–44.

Cohen, G. A. 1986. Self-ownership, world-ownership and equality. In *Justice, Equality, Here, Now*, ed. by F. S. Lucash. Ithaca, NY: Cornell University Press, pp. 108–35; and *Social Philosophy and Policy* (Spring 1986)3: 77–96.

Cohen, G. A. 1989. On the currency of egalitarian justice. *Ethics* 99: 906–44.

Cohen, G. A. 1995. *Self-Ownership, Freedom and Equality*. Cambridge: Cambridge University Press.

Condorcet, J.-A.-N. Caritat de. 1785. *Essai sur l'application de l'analyse à la probabilité des décisions rendues à la pluralité des voix*. Paris.

Condorcet, J.-A.-N. Caritat de. 1847–1849. *Oeuvres complètes*, ed. by F. Arago and Mme O'Connor. 12 volumes. Paris: F. Didot.

Cook, K. and K. Hegtvedt. 1985. *Distributive Justice*. New Haven, CT: Yale University Press.

Daniel, T. E. 1975. A revised concept of distributional equity. *Journal of Economic Theory* 11: 94–109.

Daniels, N. 1996. *Justice and Justification, Reflective Equilibrium in Theory and Practice*. Cambridge: Cambridge University Press.

Dasgupta, P., and P. J. Hammond. 1980. Fully progressive taxation. *Journal of Public Economics* 13: 141–54.

Deutsch, M. 1985. *Distributive Justice: A Social-Psychological Perspective*. New Haven, CT: Yale University Press.

Diamantaras, D. and W. Thomson. 1990. An extension and refinement of the no-envy concept. *Economic Letters* 30: 103–7.

Diamantaras, D. and W. Thomson. 1991. A refinement and extension of the no-envy concept. *Economic Letters* 33: 217–22.

Doyal, L. and I. Gough. 1991. *A Theory of Human Need*. London: Macmillan.

Dupuit, J. 1844. De la mesure de l'utilité des travaux publics. *Annales des Ponts et Chaussées*. Séries 2, 2, 2ème semestre, pp. 332–75. English translation (1969): On the measurement of the utility of public works. In *Readings in Welfare Economics*, ed. by K. J. Arrow and T. Scitovsky. Homewood, IL: Irwin, pp. 255–83.

Dworkin, R. 1981. What is equality? Part I : Equality of welfare; Part II: Equality of resources. *Philosophy and Public Affairs* 10: 185–246, 283–345.

Dworkin, R. 2000. *Sovereign Virtue*. Cambridge, MA: Harvard University Press.

Edel, A. 1986. Ethical theory and moral practice: On the term of their relation. In de Manco and Fox (eds), *New Directions in Ethics*.

Edgeworth, F. Y. [1881] 1888. *Mathematical Psychics*. London: C. Kegan Paul.

Eichhorn, W., ed. 1994. *Models and Measurement of Welfare and Inequality*. Heidelberg: Springer-Verlag.

Elster, J. 1992. *Local Justice*. Cambridge: Cambridge University Press.

Fauré, C. 1988. *Les déclarations des droits de l'homme de 1789*. Paris: Payot.

Feinberg, J. 1970. *Doing and Deserving: Essays in the Theory of Responsibility*. Princeton, NJ: Princeton University Press.

Feinberg, J. 1980. *Rights, Justice and the Bounds of Liberty*. Princeton, NJ: Princeton University Press.

Feldman, A. 1987. Equity. In *New Palgrave Dictionary in Economics*, ed. by J. Eatwell. London: Mondane, Macmillan.

Feldman, A. 1987. Fairness. In *New Palgrave Dictionary in Economics*, ed. by J. Eatwell. London: Mondane, Macmillan.

Feldman, A. and A. Kirman. 1974. Fairness and envy. *American Economic Review* 64, 6: 995–1005.

Fishkin, J. 1983. *Justice, Equal Opportunity and the Family*. New Haven, CT: Yale University Press.

Fleming, M. 1952. A cardinal concept of welfare. *Quarterly Journal of Economics* 66: 366–84.

Fleurbaey, M. 1994a. On fair compensations. *Theory and Decision* 36: 277–307.

Fleurbaey, M. 1994b. L'absence d'envie dans une problématique post-welfariste. *Recherches Economiques de Louvain* 60: 9–41.

Fleurbaey, M. 1995a. Equality and responsibility. *European Economic Review* 39: 683–89.

Fleurbaey, M. 1995b. Three solutions for the compensation problem. *Journal of Economic Theory* 65: 505–21.

Fleurbaey, M. 1995c. The requisites of equal opportunity. In *Advances in Social Choice Theory and Comparative Games*, ed. by W. Barnett, H. Moulin, M. Salles and N. Schofield. Cambridge: Cambridge University Press.

Fleurbaey, M. 1995d. Equal opportunity or equal social outcome? *Economics and Philosophy* 11: 25–55.

Fleurbaey, M. 1995e. Equality and responsibility. *European Economic Review* 39: 683–89.

Fleurbaey, M. 1996. *Théories Economiques de la Justice*. Paris: Economica.

Fleurbaey, M. 1998. Equality among responsible individuals. In J. F. Laslier, M. Fleurbaey, N. Gravel and A. Trannoy (eds), *Freedom in Economics: New Perspective in Normative Analysis*. London: Routledge.

Fleurbaey, M. 2003. Symposium on Dworkin. *Journal of Political Philosophy*.

Fleurbaey, M. and F. Maniquet. 1995. Fair allocation with unequal production skills: The solidarity approach to compensation. University of Cergy-Pontoise Discussion Paper.

Fleurbaey, M. and F. Maniquet. 1996. Fair allocation with unequal production skills: The no-envy approach to compensation. *Mathematical Social Sciences* 32: 71–93.

Fleurbaey, M. and F. Maniquet. 1997. Optimal income taxation: An ordinal approach. Mimeo.

Fleurbaey, M. and F. Maniquet. 1999. Cooperative production with unequal skills: The solidarity approach to compensation. *Social Choice and Welfare* 16: 569–83.

Fleurbaey, M. and F. Maniquet. 2001. Fair social orderings when agents have unequal production skills. Mimeo.

Fleurbaey, M. and F. Maniquet. 2002a. Fair income tax. Mimeo.

Fleurbaey, M. and F. Maniquet. 2002b. Help the low-skilled or let the hardworking thrive? A study of fairness in optimal income taxation. Mimeo.

Foley, D. K. 1967. Resource allocation and the public sector. *Yale Economic Essays* 7: 45–98.

Friedman, D. 1978. *The Machinery of Freedom*, 2nd ed. La Salle, IL: Open Court Press.

Friedman, M. 1962. *Capitalism and Freedom*. Chicago: University of Chicago Press.

Friedman, M. and R. Friedman. 1981. *Free to choose*. New York: Avon.

Friedman, M. and L. J. Savage. 1952. The expected utility hypothesis and the measurability of utility. *Journal of Political Economy* 60: 463–74.

Gaertner, W. and M. Klemisch-Ahlert. 1992. *Social Choice and Bargaining Perspectives on Distributive Justice*. Bonn: Springer-Verlag.

Gallie, W. 1956. Liberal morality and socialist morality. In Laslett, *Philosophy, Politics and Society*. Oxford: Oxford University Press.

Gauthier, D. 1986. *Morals By Agreement*. Oxford: Clarendon Press.

Gauthier, D. and R. Sugden. 1993. *Rationality, Justice and the Social Contract*. Ann Arbor: University of Michigan Press.

Gewirth, A. 1982. *Human Rights: Essays on Justification and Applications*. Chicago: University of Chicago Press.

Goodin, R. E. 1976. *The Politics of Rational Man*. New York: Wiley.

Goodin, R. E. 1986. Laundering preferences. In *Foundations of Social Choice Theory*, ed. by J. Elster and A. Hylland. Cambridge: Cambridge University Press.

Gravel, N., J.-F Laslier and A. Trannoy. 2000. Consistency between tastes and values: A universalization approach. *Social Choice and Welfare*.

Griffin, J. 1986. *Well-Being: Its Meaning, Measurement, and Moral Importance*. Oxford: Clarendon Press.

Gutmann, A. 1980. *Liberal Equality*. Cambridge: Cambridge University Press.

Habermas, J. 1981. *Theorie des Kommunikativen Handelns*. Frankfurt: Suhrkamp.

Habermas, J. 1983. *Moralbewusstein und Kommunikatives Handeln*. Frankfurt: Suhrkamp.

Hammond, P. 1976a. Equity, Arrow's conditions, and Rawls' difference principle. *Econometrica* 44: 793–804.

Hammond, P. 1976b. Why ethical measures of inequality need interpersonal comparisons. *Theory and Decision* 7: 263–74.

Hammond, P. 1977. Dual interpersonal comparison of utility and the welfare economics of income distribution. *Journal of Public Economics* 7: 51–71.

Harsanyi, J. C. 1953. Cardinal utility in welfare economics and in the theory of risk-taking. *Journal of Political Economy* 61: 434–35.

Harsanyi, J. 1955. Cardinal welfare, individualistic ethics and interpersonal comparisons of utility. *Journal of Poltical Economy* XLIII: 309–21.

Harsanyi, J. C. 1976. *Essays in Ethics, Social Behaviour and Scientific Explanation*. Dordrecht: Reidel.

Hausman, D. M., and M. S. MacPherson. 1996. *Economic Analysis and Moral Philosophy*. Cambridge: Cambridge University Press.

Havelock, E. A. 1978. *The Greek Concept of Justice: From Its Shadow in Homer to Its Substance in Plato*. Cambridge, MA: Harvard University Press.

Hayek, F. A. 1976a. *The Mirage of Social Justice, Law, Legislation and Liberty*. London: Routledge and Kegan Paul.

Hayek, F. A. 1976b. *Law, Legislation and Liberty*, Vol. 2. Chicago: University of Chicago Press.

Herrero, C., I. Iturbe-Ormaetxe and J. Nieto. 1998. Ranking opportunity profiles on the basis of the common opportunities. *Mathematical Social Sciences* 35: 273–89.

Hicks, J. 1959. *Essays in World Economy*. Oxford: Basil Blackwell. Preface, reprinted as "A Manifesto." In *Wealth and Welfare*. Oxford: Basil Blackwell, 1981, pp. 135–41.

Iturbe-Ormaetxe, I. 1997. Redistribution and individual factors. *Review of Economic Design* 3: 45–55.

Iturbe, I. and J. Nieto. 1996. On fair allocations and monetary compensations. *Economic Theory* 7: 125–38.

Jellineck, G. 1895. *Die Erklärung der Menschen und Bürgerrechte*.

Johansen, L. 1981. Review and comments. *Journal of Public Economics* 16: 123–8.

Kalai, E., and M. Smorodinski. 1975. Other solutions to Nash bargaining problem. *Econometrica* 43: 513–8.

Kaldor, N. 1939. Welfare propositions of economics and interpersonal comparisons of utility. *Economic Journal* 49: 549–52.

Kamenka, E. and A. Erh-Soon Tay. 1979. *Justice.* London: Edward Arnold.

Kant, I. 1959. *Foundations of the Metaphysics of Morals.* New York: Liberal Art Press.

Kant, I. [1785] 1969. *Fundamental Principles of the Metaphysics of Morals,* 1785, or *Foundations of the Metaphysics of Morals,* ed. R. Wolff. Indianapolis: Bobbs-Merrill.

Kant, I. [1797] 1981. *Metaphysics of Morals,* II, 1797, trans. by J. W. Ellington. New York: Harper.

Kant, I. 1997. *Groundwork of the Mataphysics of Morals.* Ed. Mary Gregor, Cambridge: Cambridge University Press.

Kohlberg, L. 1963. The development of children's orientations towards moral order: I. Sequence in the development of moral thought. *Vita Humana* 6: 11–33.

Kolm, S.-Ch. 1959. *Les Hommes du Fouta-Toro.* Saint-Louis: MAS.

Kolm, S.-Ch. 1963. *Les Fondements de l'économie publique: Introduction à la théorie du rôle économique de l'état.* Paris: IFP.

Kolm, S.-Ch. 1966a. *The Optimal Production of Social Justice.* In International Economic Association Conference on Public Economics, Biarritz. Proceedings ed. by H. Guitton and J. Margolis. *Economie Publique,* Paris: CNRS, 1968, pp. 109–77. *Public Economics,* London: Macmillan, 1969, pp. 145–200. Reprinted in *Landmark Papers in General Equilibrium Theory, Social Choice and Welfare, The Foundation of the 20th Century Economics,* selected by K. J. Arrow and G. Debreu, 2001, Cheltenham: Edward Elgar.

Kolm, S.-Ch. 1966b. *Les Choix financiers et monétaires (Théorie et technique modernes).* Paris: Dunod.

Kolm, S.-Ch. 1969a. Théorie démocratique de la justice sociale. *Revue d'Economie Politique* 1: 138–41.

Kolm, S.-Ch. 1969b. *Prix publics optimaux.* Paris: CNRS.

Kolm, S.-Ch. 1970a. *La Valeur publique.* Paris: Dunod-CNRS.

Kolm, S.-Ch. 1970b. *L'Etat et le système des prix.* Paris: Dunod-CNRS.

Kolm, S.-Ch. 1970c. *Le Service des masses.* Paris: Dunod-CNRS.

Kolm, S.-Ch. 1970d. L'inégalité des valeurs des vies humaines. *Cahiers du Séminaire d'Econométrie,* ed. by R. Roy, 18: 40–62.

Kolm, S.-Ch. 1971. *Justice et équité.* Paris: CEPREMAP. Reprinted Paris: CNRS, 1972. English translation by H. See: *Justice and Equity.* 1998. Cambridge, MA: MIT Press.

Kolm, S.-Ch. 1973a. Super-équité. *Kyklos* XXVI, fasc.4: 841–43.

Kolm, S.-Ch. 1973b. A note on optimum tax evasion. *Journal of Public Economics* 2.

Kolm, S.-Ch. 1974. Sur les conséquences économiques des principes de justice et de justice pratique. *Revue d'Economie Politique* 1: 80–107.

Kolm, S.-Ch. 1976a. Unequal inequalities: I. *Journal of Economic Theory* 12: 416–42.

Kolm, S.-Ch. 1976b. Unequal inequalities: II. *Journal of Economic Theory* 13: 82–111.

Kolm, S.-Ch. 1976c. Public safety. *American Economic review* 66:382–87, and in *Essays in Public Economics,* ed. by A. Sandmo. Lexington: Lexington Books, 1978, pp. 1–9.

Kolm, S.-Ch. 1977a. Multidimensional egalitarianism. *Quarterly Journal of Economics* 91: 1–13.

Kolm, S.-Ch. 1977b. *La Transition socialiste.* Paris: Editions du Cerf.

Kolm, S.-Ch. 1977c. *Les Elections sont-elles la démocratie ?* Paris: Editions du Cerf.

Kolm, S.-Ch., ed. 1978. *Solutions socialistes.* Paris: Editions Ramsay.

Kolm, S.-Ch. 1980. La philosophie bouddhiste et les hommes économiques. *Social Science Information* 3: 489–588.

Kolm, S.-Ch. 1981. Psychanalyse et théorie des choix. *Social Science Information.* 19(2): 269–340, and Proceedings of the 5th Congress of Economic Psychology, *Revue de psychologie économique.*

Kolm, S.-Ch. 1982a. *Le Bonheur-Liberté (Bouddhisme profond et modernité).* Paris: Presses Universitaires de France. New edition 1994.

Kolm, S.-Ch. 1982b. La théorie bouddhique de la liberté. *Critique.*

Kolm, S.-Ch. 1982c. Les logiques du libéralisme moderne. *Commentaires.*

Kolm, S.-Ch. 1983a. Altruism and efficiency. *Ethics* 94: 18–65.

Kolm, S.-Ch. 1983b. Introduction à la Réciprocité Générale. *Social Science Information* 22: 569–621.

Kolm, S.-Ch. 1983c. Problèmes du libéralisme économique. *Commentaires.* 6: 49–56.

Kolm, S.-Ch. 1983d. Au deuxième siècle après Marx. *Commentaires* 6: 521–5.

Kolm, S.-Ch. 1984a. *La Bonne Économie, La Réciprocité Générale.* Paris: Presses Universitaires de France.

Kolm, S.-Ch. 1984b. *Le Libéralisme moderne.* Paris: Presses Universitaires de France.

Kolm, S.-Ch. 1985a. *Le Contrat social libéral (Théorie et pratique du libéralisme).* Paris: Presses Universitaires de France.

Kolm, S.-Ch. 1985b. Le raisonnement d'éthique sociale. Paris: CERAS, 41.

Kolm, S.-Ch. 1986a. *Philosophie de l'Economie.* Paris: Editions du Seuil.

Kolm, S.-Ch. 1986b. L'allocation des ressources naturelles et le libéralisme. *Revue Economique* 37: 207–41.

Kolm, S.-Ch. 1986c. Alternative ethical foundations of fiscal systems. Paris: CERAS, 50.

Kolm, S.-Ch. 1986d. The Buddhist theory of "no-self". In *The Multiple Self,* ed. by J. Elster. Cambridge: Cambridge University Press, pp. 133–263.

Kolm, S.-Ch. 1987a. Public Economics. In *New Palgrave Dictionary in Economics,* ed. by J. Eatwell et al. London: Macmillan, pp. 1047–55.

Kolm, S.-Ch. 1987b. The freedom and consensus normative theory of the state: The liberal social contract. In *Individual Liberty and Democratic Decision-Making: The Ethics, Economics and Politics of Democracy,* ed. by P. Koslowski. Tübingen: J. C. B. Mohr, pp. 97–127.

Kolm, S.-Ch. 1987c. Libéralismes classiques et renouvelés. In *Nouvelle histoire des idées politiques,* ed. by Pascal Ory. Paris: Hachette, pp. 575–87.

Kolm, S.-Ch. 1987d. Liberty-based public economics: Its foundations, principle, method, application and structural results. Paris: CERAS, 60.

Kolm, S.-Ch. 1987e. Free-riding and voluntary contributions in large numbers. Paris: CERAS, 63.

Kolm, S.-Ch. 1987f. Freedoms, cores and public goods. Paris: CERAS, 66.

Kolm, S.-Ch. 1987g. Freedom and the provision of public goods with all degrees of exclusion. Paris: CERAS, 67.

Kolm, S.-Ch. 1987h. Freedom, core, efficiency with public goods in general interdependence. Paris: CERAS, 68.

Kolm, S.-Ch. 1987i. *L'Homme pluridimensionnel (bouddhisme, marxisme, psychanalyse pour une économie de l'esprit).* Paris: Albin Michel.

Kolm, S.-Ch. 1987j. Adequation, equity and fundamental analysis. Paris: CERAS,59.

Kolm, S.-Ch. 1988. Adequacy, equity and fundamental dominance. Paris: CERAS, 76.

Kolm, S.-Ch. 1989a. Free and equal in rights: The philosophies of the 1789 Declaration of the Rights of Man and of the Citizen. Bicentennial Conference, Canadian Political Science Association, Québec. *Journal of Regional Policy* 11–1 (1991): 5–62.

Kolm, S.-Ch. 1989b. The psychology of happiness and of liberty. *The Journal of Oriental Studies,* The Institute of Oriental Philosophy, 2: 11–20; and in *Buddhism Today,* Tokyo: The Institute of Oriental Philosophy, 1990, pp. 34–45.

Kolm, S.-Ch. 1989c. Cooperative-game properties of international coordination. Paris: CERAS, 77.

Kolm, S.-Ch. 1990a. *The General Theory of Justice.* Paris: CERAS.

Kolm, S.-Ch. 1990b. Employment and fiscal policy with a realistic view of the social role of wages. In *Essays in Honor of Edmond Malinvaud*. Cambridge, MA: MIT Press, pp. 226–86.

Kolm, S.-Ch. 1991a. The normative economics of unanimity and equality: Equity, adequacy and fundamental dominance. In *Markets and Welfare*, ed. by K. J. Arrow. London: Macmillan, pp. 243–86.

Kolm, S.-Ch. 1991b. Full process liberalism. IMF Working paper (Fiscal Affairs), and Paris: CGPC.

Kolm, S.-Ch. 1991c. Super-equity. German Bernacer Lecture, University of Alicante. Paris: CERAS, 90.

Kolm, S.-Ch. 1992. What sense social choice? Paris: CGPC.

Kolm, S.-Ch. 1993a. Free and equal in rights: The philosophies of the 1789 Declaration of the Rights of Man and of the Citizen. *Journal of Political Philosophy* 1: 158–83.

Kolm, S.-Ch. 1993b. Distributive justice. In *A Companion to Political Philosophy*, ed. by R. Goodin and P. Pettit. Oxford: Blackwell, pp. 438–61.

Kolm, S.-Ch. 1993c. The impossibility of utilitarianism. In *The Good and the Economical*, ed. by P. Koslowski and Y. Shionoya. Berlin: Springer-Verlag, pp. 30–66.

Kolm, S.-Ch. 1993d. *Equal Liberty*. Paris: CGPC.

Kolm, S.-Ch. 1993e. *Efficient Economic Justice*. Paris: CGPC.

Kolm, S.-Ch. 1993f. *Inequalities and Super-Equity*. Paris: CGPC.

Kolm, S.-Ch. 1994a. Rational justice and equality. In *Models and Measurement of Welfare and Inequality*, ed. by W. Eichhorn. Berlin: Springer-Verlag, pp. 970–92.

Kolm, S.-Ch. 1994b. The meaning of fundamental preferences. *Social Choice and Welfare* 11: 193–8.

Kolm, S.-Ch. 1994c. L'égalité de la liberté. *Recherches Economiques de Louvain* 1: 81–6.

Kolm, S.-Ch. 1995a. The economics of social sentiments: The case of envy. *Japanese Economic Review* 46: 63–87.

Kolm, S.-Ch. 1995b. Economic justice: The central problem. *European Economic Review* 39: 661–73.

Kolm, S.-Ch. 1995c. Sens ou non-sens du calcul économique public: Le principe de compensation. *Entreprise Ethique* 2: 1–9.

Kolm, S.-Ch. 1995d. The modern theory of justice. *L'Année Sociologique* 5: 297–315.

Kolm, S.-Ch. 1995e. Income justice: Its reason and optimum policy. Paris: CGPC.

Kolm, S.-Ch. 1995f. Meanings and rationalities in Social Choice Theory. In *Faces of Rationality*, ed. by D. Andler, P. Banerjee, M. Chaudhury, and O. Guillaume. New Delhi, London: Sage, pp. 79–103.

Kolm, S.-Ch. 1996a. *Modern Theories of Justice*. Cambridge, MA: MIT Press.

Kolm, S.-Ch. 1996b. The theory of justice. *Social Choice and Welfare* 13: 151–82.

Kolm, S.-Ch. 1996c. Rational just social choice. In *Social Choice Re-examined*, ed. by K. Arrow, A. Sen and K. Suzumura. London: Macmillan, Vol. 2, pp. 167–95.

Kolm, S.-Ch. 1996d. Risk, justice, and social policy. In *Restructuring the Welfare State: Ethical Issues of Social Policy in an International Perspective*, ed. by P. Koslowski and A. Føllesdal. Berlin: Springer-Verlag, pp. 287–318.

Kolm, S.-Ch. 1996e. Moral public choice. *Public Choice* 87: 117–41.

Kolm, S.-Ch. 1996f. Playing fair with fairness. *Journal of Economic Survey* 10(2).

Kolm, S.-Ch. 1996g. The values of liberty. *The Nordic Journal of Political Economy* 23, 1: 25–46.

Kolm, S.-Ch. 1996h. The comparison of pairwise preferences and its normative consequences. Paris: CGPC.

Kolm, S.-Ch. 1997a. The values of freedom. In *The Economics and Philosophy of Liberty*, ed. by M. Fleurbaey, N. Gravel, J.-F. Laslier, and A. Trannoy. London: Routledge, pp. 17–44.

Kolm, S.-Ch. 1997b. *Macrojustice*. Paris: CGPC.

Kolm, S.-Ch. 1998. Chance and justice: Social policy and the Harsanyi-Vickrey-Rawls problem. *European Economic Review* 42: 1393–416.

Kolm, S.-Ch. 1999a. Rational foundations of income inequality measurement. In *Handbook of Income Inequality Measurement*, ed. by J. Silber. Dordrecht: Kluwer, pp. 19–94.

Kolm, S.-Ch. 1999b. Freedom Justice. CREME, University of Caen.

Kolm, S.-Ch. 2000a. Introduction: The economics of reciprocity, giving and altruism. Chapter 1 in *The Economics of Reciprocity, Giving and Altruism*, ed. by L.-A. Gérard-Varet, S.-Ch. Kolm and J. Mercier-Ythier, International Economic Association, Houndsmill: Macmillan, pp. 1–44.

Kolm, S.-Ch. 2000b. The theory of reciprocity. Chapter 5 in *The Economics of Reciprocity, Giving and Altruism*, ed. by L.-A. Gérard-Varet, S.-Ch. Kolm and J. Mercier-Ythier, International Economic Association, Houndsmill: Macmillan, pp. 115–52.

Kolm, S.-Ch. 2000c. A historical introduction to normative economics. *Social Choice and Welfare* 17, 4: 707–38.

Kolm, S.-Ch. 2000d. The logic of good social relations. *Annals of Public and Cooperative Economics* 72: 171–89.

Kolm, S.-Ch. 2001a. To each according to her work? Just entitlement from action: Desert, merit, responsibility and equal opportunities. IDEP (01–07).

Kolm, S.-Ch. 2001b. Vox populi, vox dei: Endogenous social choice and the rational original position. IDEP.

Kolm, S.-Ch. 2002. On health and justice. Genève: WHO. IDEP working paper. In *Global Health: From Goodness to Fairness*, ed. by D. Wikler, 2004.

Kolm, S.-Ch. 2003. Quelques souvenirs de John Rawls. *Revue de Philosophie Economique* 7: 21–32.

Kolm, S.-Ch. 2003. Logique at usage du contrat social. *Revue de Philosophie Economique* 8: 3–17.

Kolm, S.-Ch. 2004a. Liberty and distribution: Macrojustice from social freedom. *Social Choice and Welfare* 22: 1–33.

Kolm, S.-Ch. 2004b. Reciprocity: its scope, rationales, and consequences. In S.-Ch. Kolm and J. Mercier Ythier (eds.), *Handbook on the Economics of Giving, Reciprocity, and Altruism*, Amsterdam: North-Holland.

Konow, J. 2003. Which is the fairest of all? A positive analysis of justice theories. *Journal of Economic Literature* XLI: 1186–237.

Konow, J. 2004. Blind spots: The effects of information and stakes on justice biases. Draft, Loyola Marymount University.

Kortian, G. 1980. *Metacritique: The Philosophical Argument of Jürgen Habermas*. Cambridge: Cambridge University Press.

Kymlicka, W. 1989. *Liberalism, Community and Culture*. Oxford: Clarendon Press.

Lambert, P. 2001. *The Distribution and Redistribution of Income*. Oxford: Basil Blackwell.

Lange, O. 1937. On the economic theory of socialism, Part II. *Review of Economic Studies* 4, 2: 123–42.

Lange, O. 1942. The foundations of welfare economics. *Econometrica* 10: 215–28.

Larmore, C. 1987. *Patterns of Moral Complexity*. Cambridge: Cambridge University Press.

Le Breton, M. 1997. Arrovian social choice on economic domains. In K. J. Arrow, A. Sen and K. Suzumura (eds), *Social Choice Re-examined*, Vol. 1. London: Macmillan, and New York: St. Martin's Press, pp. 72–96.

Leonard, H. 1983. Elicitation of honest preferences for the assignment of individuals to positions. *Journal of Political Economy* 91: 461–90.

Leventhal, G. S. 1976. The distribution of rewards and resources in groups and organisations. In L. Bertowitz and E. Walster (eds), *Advances in Experimental Social Psychology*, Vol. 9. New York: Academic Press.

Leventhal, G. S. 1980. What should be done with equity theory? New approaches to the study of fairness in social relationships. In K. J. Gergen, M. S. Greenberg and R. H. Willis (eds), *Social Exchange: Advances in Theory and Research*. New York: Plenum Press.

Leventhal, G. S. and D. Anderson. 1970. Self-interest and the maintenance of equity. *Journal of Personality and Social Psychology* 15: 57–62.

Lindbeck, A. 1985. Redistribution policies and the expansion of the public sector. *Journal of Public Economics* 28: 309–28.

Locke, J. [1690] 1960. *Second Treatise of Government*, ed. by P. Laslett. Cambridge: Cambridge University Press.

Lucas, J. 1993. *Responsibility*. Oxford: Oxford University Press.

Maasoumi, E. 1986. The measurement and decomposability of multidimensional inequality. *Econometrica* 54: 991–8.

MacCormick, N. and O. Weinberger. 1986. *An Institutional Theory of Law, New Approaches to Legal Positivism*. Dordrecht, Boston, Lancaster, Tokyo: D. Reidel, Kluwer Academic Publishers.

Machan, T. 1982. *The Libertarian Reader*. Totowa, NJ: Rowman and Littlefield.

MacIntyre, A. 1985. *After Virtue: A Study in Moral Theory*. London: Duckworth.

MacIntyre, A. 1988. *Whose Justice? Which Rationality?* London: Duckworth.

Macpherson, C. B. 1985. *The Rise and Fall of Economic Justice*. Oxford: Oxford University Press.

Maniquet, F. 1998a. An equal right solution to the compensation-responsibility dilemma. *Mathematical Social Sciences* 35: 185–202.

Maniquet, F. 1998b. An axiomatic characterization of the equal labor income equalization. Mimeo.

Marx, K. [1867] 1976. *Das Kapital*, Vol. 1, trans. by B. Fowlkes. Harmondsworth: Penguin Books.

Marx, K. [1875] 1972. Critique of the Gotha Programme. Reprinted in *The Marx-Engels Reader*, ed. by R. C. Tucker. New York: Norton, pp. 363–98.

Maskin, E. 1980. On first-best taxation. In *Income Distribution: The Limits to Redistribution*, ed. by D. Collard, R. Lecomber and M. Slater. Dorchester: Wright and Sons.

Meade, J. E. 1964. *Efficiency, Equality and the Ownership of Property*. London: Allen and Unwin.

Meade, J. E. 1976. *The Just Economy*. London: Allen and Unwin.

Melden, A. I., ed. 1970. *Human Rights*. Belmont, CA: Wadsworth.

Mikula, G., ed. 1980. *Justice and Social Interaction: Experimental and Theoretical Contribution from Psychological Research*. New York: Springer-Verlag.

Mill, J. S. [1859a]. *On Liberty*, ed. by R. B. Mc Callum. Oxford: Basil Blackwell.

Mill, J. S. [1859b]. *On Liberty and Considerations on Representative Government*, ed. by R. B. Mc Callum. Oxford: Basil Blackwell.

Mill, J. S. 1962. *Utilitarianism, On Liberty, Essay on Bentham*, ed. by M. Warnock. London: Fontana Library.

Mill, J. S. 1963. *On Liberty*. In *Essays on Politics and Society, Collected Works*, Vol. XVIII.

Miller, D. 1976. *Social Justice*. Oxford: Clarendon Press.

Miller, D. 1999. *Principles of Social Justice*. Cambridge, MA: Harvard University Press.

Mirrlees, J. 1971. An exploration in the theory of optimum income taxation. *Review of Economic Studies* 38: 175–208.

Mirrlees, J. 1974. Notes on welfare economics, information and uncertainty. In *Essays on Economic Behaviour Under Uncertainty*, ed. by M. S. Balch, D. McFadden and S. Y. Wu. Amsterdam: North-Holland.

Mirrlees, J. 1986. The theory of optimal taxation. In *Handbook of Mathematical Economics*, Vol. 3 ed. by K. J. Arrow and M. D. Intriligator. Amsterdam: North-Holland.

Mishan, E. J. 1960. A survey of welfare economics, 1939–59. *Economic Journal* 70: 247.

Mongin, P. and C. d'Aspremont. 1998. Utility theory in ethics. In S. Barberá, P. Hammond and C. Seidl, eds. *Handbook in Utility Theory*, Vol. 1. Boston: Kluwer Academic Press.

Moulin, H. 1987. Egalitarian equivalent cost-sharing of a public good. *Econometrica* 55: 963–77.

Moulin, H. 1988. *Axioms of Cooperative Decision Making*. Cambridge: Cambridge University Press.

Moulin, H. 1990. Joint ownership of a convex technology: Comparison of three solutions. *Review of Economic Studies* 57: 439–52.

Moulin, H. 1995. *Cooperative Microeconomics*. Princeton, NJ: Princeton University Press.

Moulin, H. and J. Roemer. 1989. Public ownership of the external world and private ownership of self. *Journal of Political Economy* 97: 347–67.

Moulin, H. and S. Shenker. 1994. Average cost pricing vs serial cost sharing: An axiomatic comparison. *Journal of Economic Theory* 64: 178–201.

Moulin, H. and W. Thomson. 1997. Axiomatic analysis of resource allocation problems. In K. J. Arrow, A. Sen and K. Suzumura (eds), *Social Choice Re-Examined*, Vol. 1. London: Macmillan, and New York: St. Martin's Press, pp. 101–20.

Mueller, D. 1979. *Public Choice*. Cambridge: Cambridge University Press.

Musgrave, R. A. 1959. *The Theory of Public Finance*. New York: McGraw-Hill.

Musgrave, R. A. 1974. Maxima, uncertainty and the leisure trade-off. *Quarterly Journal of Economics* 86: 625–32.

Musgrave, R. A. and A. T. Peacock, eds. 1962. *Classics in the Theory of Public Finance*. London: Macmillan.

Nagel, T. 1986. *The View from Nowhere*. Oxford: Clarendon Press.

Nagel, T. 1991. *Equality and Partiality*. Oxford: Oxford University Press.

Narveson, J. 1976. A puzzle about economic justice in Rawls' theory. *Social Theory and Practice* 4: 1–27.

Narveson, J. 1983. On Dworkinian equality. *Social Philosophy and Policy* 1: 1–23.

Nash, J. F. 1950. The bargaining problem. *Econometrica* 18: 155–62.

Nash, J. F. 1953. Two-person cooperative games. *Econometrica* 21: 128–40.

Ng, Y. K. 1979. *Welfare Economics*. London: MacMillan.

Nicole, P. 1671. *Essais de Morale* [1857]. Paris: Silvestre de Saci.

Norman, R. 1987. *Free and Equal: A Philosophical Examination of Political Values*. Oxford: Oxford University Press.

Nozick, R. 1974. *Anarchy, State and Utopia*. New York: Basic Books.

Nussbaum, M. C. 1986 (2001). *The Fragility of Goodness*. (Updated edition). Cambridge: Cambridge University Press.

Nussbaum, M. C. 1992. Human functioning and social justice: In defense of Aristotelian essentialism. *Political Theory* 20 (2): 202–46.

Nussbaum, M. C. 1995a. *Poetics of Justice*. Boston: Beacon Press.

Nussbaum, M. C. 1995b. Aristotle on human nature and the foundation of Ethics. In J. A. Altham and R. Harrison (eds), *World, Mind and Ethics*. Cambridge: Cambridge University Press.

Nussbaum, M. C. 2000. Aristotle, politics and human capabilities. *Ethics* 111: 102–40.

Ooghe, E., E. Schokkaert and D. Van de gaer. 2003. Equality of opportunity versus equality of opportunity sets. Mimeo.

Pareto, V. 1913. Il massimo di utilità per una collettività in sociologia. *Giornali degli economisti*, 3rd serie, 337–41 (also in *Trattato di Sociologia Generale* and *Mind and Society*).

Pareto, V. 1916. *A Treatise on General Sociology*. New York: Dover.

Pattanaik, P. 1971. *Voting and Collective Choice*. Cambridge: Cambridge University Press.

Pattanaik, P. K. and M. Salles, eds. 1983. *Social Choice and Welfare*. Amsterdam: North-Holland.

Pattanaik, P. and Y. Xu. 1990. On ranking opportunity sets in terms of freedom of choice. *Recherches Economiques de Louvain* 56: 383–90.

Paul, E. F., F. D. Miller and J. Paul, eds. 1985. *Ethics and Economics.* Oxford: Basil Blackwell.

Paul, E. F., F. D. Miller and J. Paul. 1985. *Liberty and Equality.* Oxford: Basil Blackwell.

Pazner, E. A. 1977. Pitfalls in the theory of fairness. *Journal of Economic Theory* 14: 458–66.

Pazner, E. and D. Schmeidler. 1972. Decentralization, income distribution and the role of money in socialist economies. *Economic Inquiry.*

Pazner, E. and D. Schmeidler. 1974. A difficulty in the concept of fairness. *Review of Economic Studies* 41: 441–3.

Pazner, E. and D. Schmeidler. 1978. Egalitarian-equivalent allocations : A new concept of economic equity. *Quarterly Journal of Economics* 92: 671–87.

Pazner, E. and D. Schmeidler. 1978. Decentralization and income distribution in socialist economies. *Economic Inquiry* XVI: 257–64.

Péguy, C. 1897. Un économiste socialiste: M. Léon Walras. *Revue Socialiste* 25, 146: 174–86.

Pen, J. 1971a. *Income Distribution.* London: Allen Lane.

Pen, J. 1971b. *Income Distribution: Facts, Theories, Policies.* London: Routledge and Kegan Paul.

Perelman, C. 1963. *The Idea of Justice and the Problem of Argument.* London: Routledge and Kegan Paul.

Perelman, C. 1972. *Justice et raison,* 2nd ed. Brussels: Bruylant.

Pettit, P. 1980. *Judging Justice.* London: Routledge and Kegan Paul.

Phelps, E. S. 1973. *Economic Justice.* Harmondsworth: Penguin Books.

Phelps, E. S. 1977. Recent developments in welfare economics: Justice et équité. In *Frontiers of Quantitative Economics,* Vol. 3, ed. by M. D. Intriligator. Amsterdam: North-Holland. Reprinted in E. Phelps, *Studies in Macroeconomic Theory,* Vol. 2. New York: Academic Press.

Phillips, D. L. 1979. *Equality, Justice and Rectification.* London: Academic Press.

Piaget, J. 1932. *The Moral Judgment of the Child.* London: Routledge and Kegan Paul.

Piggins, A. 1999. Review of books. *Economic Journal.*

Pigou, A. C. 1928. *A Study in Public Finance.* London: Macmillan.

Piketty, T. 1994. *Introduction à la Théorie de la Redistribution des Richesses.* Paris: Editions Economica.

Plato. *The Laws.* Any edition.

Plato. *The Republic.* Any edition.

Pojman, L., and O. McLeod. 1999. *What Do We Deserve? A Reader on Justice and Desert.* Oxford: Oxford University Press.

Posner, R. 1977. *The Economic Analysis of Law,* 2nd ed. Boston: Little Brown.

Posner, R.1981. *The Economics of Justice.* Cambridge, MA: Harvard University Press.

Raiffa, H. 1953. Arbitration schemes for generalized two-person games. In *Contributions to the Theory of Games II,* ed. by H. W. Kuhn and A. W. Tucker. Princeton, NJ: Princeton University Press.

Raphael, D. D. 1980. *Justice and Liberty.* London: Athlone Press.

Rawls, J. 1971. *A Theory of Justice.* Cambridge, MA: Harvard University Press.

Rawls, J. 1980. Kantian constructivism in moral theory. *The Journal of Philosophy* LXXVII/9: 515–72.

Rawls, J. 1982a. Social unity and primary goods. In *Utilitarianism and Beyond,* ed. by A. Sen and B. Williams. Cambridge: Cambridge University Press, pp. 159–85.

Rawls, J. 1982b. The basic liberties and their priority. *The Tanner Lectures on Human Values,* Vol. 3, ed. by S. MacMurrin. Cambridge: Cambridge University Press, pp. 1–89.

Rawls, J. 1985. Justice as fairness: Political not metaphysical. *Philosophy and Public Affairs* 14 (3): 223–51.

Rawls, J. 1987. The idea of an overlapping consensus. *Oxford Journal of Legal Studies* 7: 1–25.

Rawls, J. 1989. The domain of the political and overlapping consensus. *New York University Law Review* 64: 233–55.

Raz, J. 1986. *The Morality of Freedom.* Oxford: Oxford University Press.

Rials, S., ed. 1989. *La Déclaration de 1789.* Paris: Presses Universitaires de France.

Roemer, J. 1982. *A General Theory of Exploitation and Class.* Cambridge, MA: Harvard University Press.

Roemer, J. 1985. Equality of talent. *Economics and Philosophy* 1: 151–87.

Roemer, J. 1986a. Equality of resources implies equality of welfare. *Quarterly Journal of Economics* 101: 751–84.

Roemer, J. 1986b. The mismarriage of bargaining theory and distributive justice. *Ethics* 97: 88–110.

Roemer, J. 1986c. *Value, Exploitation and Class.* Chur: Harwood.

Roemer, J. 1993. A pragmatic theory of responsibility for the egalitaran planner. *Philosophy and Public Affairs* 22: 146–66.

Roemer, J. 1996. *Theories of Distributive Justice.* Cambridge, MA: Harvard University Press.

Roemer, J. 1998. *Equality of Opportunity.* Cambridge, MA: Harvard University Press.

Roemer, J. and J. Silvestre. 1989. Public ownership: Three proposals for resource allocation. University of California, Davis, mimeo.

Ross, W. D. 1930. *The Right and the Good.* Oxford: Clarendon Press.

Ross, W. D. 1939. *Foundations of Ethics.* Oxford: Oxford University Press.

Rothbart, M. 1973. *For a New Liberty.* New York: Macmillan.

Rousseau, J. J. [1755] 1973. *A Discourse on the Origin of Inequality.* In *The Social Contract and Discourses.* London: Dent and Sons.

Rousseau, J. J. [1762] 1913. *Du Contrat Social,* trans. by G. D. H. Cole. London: Dent.

Sandel, M. 1982. *Liberalism and the Limits of Justice.* Cambridge: Cambridge University Press.

Scanlon, T. M. 1986. Equality of resources and equality of welfare: A forced marriage. *Ethics* 97: 111–8.

Scherer, K. 1992. *Justice, Interdisciplinary Perspectives.* Cambridge: Cambridge University Press.

Schmeidler, D. and K. Vind. 1974. Fair net trades. *Econometrica* 40: 637–42.

Schoeman, F. D. 1992. *Privacy and Social Freedom.* Cambridge: Cambridge University Press.

Schokkaert, E. and L. Lagrou. 1983. An empirical approach to distributive justice. *Journal of Public Economics* 21: 33–52.

Schokkaert, E. and B. Overlaet. 1989. Moral intuitions and economic models of distributive justice. *Social Choice and Welfare* 6: 19–31.

Schwinger, T. 1980. Just allocation of goods: Decisions among three principles. In Mikula (ed).

Schwinger, T., W. Nährer and E. Kayser. 1982. *Prinzipien der gerechten Vergabe von Zuneigung und Geld in Verschiedenen Sozialbeziehungen.* Bericht aus dem Sonderforschungsbereich 24: Universität Mannheim.

Scitovsky, T. 1941. A note on welfare propositions in economics. *Review of Economic Studies* 9: 77–88. Reprinted in *Readings in Welfare Economics,* ed. by K. J. Arrow and T. Scitowsky. Homewood, IL: Irwin, 1969, pp. 390–401.

Scitovsky, T. 1976. *The Joyless Economy: An Inquiry Into Human Satisfaction and Consumer Dissatisfaction.* New York: Oxford University Press.

Seade, J. 1977. On the shape of optimal tax schedules. *Journal of Public Economics* 7: 203–36.

Seidler, V. J. 1986. *Kant, Respect and Injustice: The Limits of Liberal Moral Theory.* London: Routledge.

Sen, A. K. 1985. *Commodities and Capabilities.* Amsterdam: North-Holland.

Sen, A. K. 1993. Well-being and capability. In M. Nussbaum and A. Sen (eds), *The Quality of Life.* Oxford: Oxford University Press.

Sen, A. K. 1999. *Development as Freedom.* Oxford: Oxford University Press.

Sen, A. K. and B. Williams. 1982. *Utilitarianism and Beyond.* Cambridge: Cambridge University Press.

Sher, G. 1987. *Desert.* Princeton, NJ: Princeton University Press.

Sheshinski, E. 1971. On the theory of optimal income taxation. Harvard Institute of Economic Research. Discussion Paper 172.

Sidgwick, H. 1874. *The Methods of Ethics.* London: Macmillan.

Silber, J., ed. 1999. *Handbook on Income Inequality Measurement.* Boston, Dordrecht, London: Kluwer Academic Publishers.

Slemrod, J. 2002. Tax systems. *NBER Reporter,* Summer 2002, NBER, pp. 8–13.

Smith, A. [1759] 1976. *The Theory of Moral Sentiments.* Oxford: Oxford University Press.

Soltan, K. E. 1982. Empirical studies of distributive justice. *Ethics* 92: 673–91.

Spinoza, B. 1675/1677. *Ethics.* Any edition.

Sprumont, Y. 1997. Balanced egalitarian redistribution of income. *Mathematical Social Sciences*: 185–201.

Steedman, I. 1989. *From Exploitation to Altruism.* Cambridge: Polity Press.

Steiner, H. 1982. Justice and entitlement. In *Reading Nozick,* ed. by J. Paul. Oxford: Basil Blackwell.

Steiner, H. 1994. *An Essay on Rights.* Oxford: Blackwell.

Stoljar, S. J. 1984. *An Analysis of Rights.* London: Macmillan.

Sugden, R. 1981. *The Political Economy of Public Choice.* Oxford: Martin Robertson.

Sugden, R. 1998. The metric of opportunity. *Economics and Philosophy* 14: 307–337.

Sugden, R. 2003. Opportunity as a space for individuality: its value and the impossibility of measuring it. *Ethics* 113: 783–809.

Sugden, R. 2004. Living with unfairness: the limits of opportunity in a market economy. *Social Choice and Welfare* 22: 211–237.

Summer, L. W. 1987. *The Moral Foundation of Rights.* Oxford: Oxford University Press.

Suppes, P. 1966. Some formal models of grading principles. *Synthèse* 16: 284–306.

Suzumura, K. 1983. *Rational Choice, Collective Decisions, and Social Welfare.* Cambridge: Cambridge University Press.

Suzumura, K. 1983. Resolving conflicting views of justice in social choice. In *Social Choice and Welfare,* ed. by P. K. Pattanaik and M. Salles. Amsterdam: North-Holland.

Taylor, C. 1985. The nature and scope of distributive justice. In *Philosophical Papers,* Vol. 2. Cambridge: Cambridge University Press, pp. 289–317.

Taylor, M. 1982. *Community, Anarchy and Liberty.* New York: Cambridge University Press.

Temkin, L. 1993. *Inequality.* New York: Oxford University Press.

Thomson, G. 1987. *Needs.* London: Routledge and Kegan Paul.

Thomson, W. 1983. Equity in exchange economies. *Journal of Economic Theory* 29: 217–44.

Thomson, W. 1988. A study of choice correspondences in economies with a variable number of agents. *Journal of Economic Theory* 46: 237–54.

Thomson, W. 1994. *Bargaining Theory: The Axiomatic Approach.* San Diego: Academic Press.

Thomson, W. 2001. On the axiomatic method and its recent applications to game theory and resource allocation. *Social Choice and Welfare.*

Thomson, W. Forthcoming. *The Theory of Fair Allocation.* Princeton, NJ: Princeton University Press.

Thomson, W. and H. Varian. 1985. Theories of justice based on symmetry. Chapter 4 in *Social Goals and Social Organization. Essays in Memory of E. Pazner,* ed. by L. Hurwicz, D. Schmeidler and H. Sonnenshein. Cambridge: Cambridge University Press, pp. 107–29.

Tinbergen, J. 1946. *Redelijke Inkomensverdeling.* Haarlem: De Gulden Pers.

Tinbergen, J. 1953. *Redelijke inkomensverdeling,* 2nd ed. Haarlem: N. De Gulden Pers.

Tinbergen, J. 1957. Welfare economics and income distribution. *American Economic Review* XLVII: 490–503.

Tinbergen, J. 1975. *Income Distribution.* Amsterdam: North-Holland.

Tobin, J. 1970. On limiting the domain of inequality. *Journal of Law and Economics* 13: 363–78.

Törnblom, K. Y. and W. L. Griffith. 1992. *Beyond Equity Theory: Emerging Approaches to the Social Psychological Study of Justice in Resource Allocations.* New York: Plenum Press.

Tuck, R. 1979. *Natural Rights Theories: Their Origin and Development.* Cambridge: Cambridge University Press.

Van de gaer, D. 1993. *Equality of Opportunity and Investments in Human Capital.* Ph.D. Thesis, KULeuven.

Van der Veen, R. 1988. *Social Policy and Social Justice.* Leiden.

Van Parijs, P. 1990. Equal endowments as undominated diversity. *Recherches Economiques de Louvain* 56: 327–55.

Van Parijs, P. 1995. *Real Freedom for All. What (if Anything) Can Justify Capitalism?* Oxford: Oxford University Press.

Varian, H. 1974. Equity, envy, and efficiency. *Journal of Economic Theory* 19: 63–91.

Varian, H. 1975. Distributive justice, welfare economics, and the theory of fairness. *Philosophy and Public Affairs* 4: 223–47.

Varian, H. 1976. Two problems in the theory of fairness. *Journal of Public Economics* 5: 249–60.

Varian, H. 1980. Redistributive taxation as social insurance. *Journal of Public Economics* 14: 49–68.

Vickrey, W. 1945. Measuring marginal utilities by reactions to risk. *Econometrica* 13: 319–33.

Vickrey, W. 1960. Utility, strategy and social decision rules. *Quarterly Journal of Economics* 74: 507–35.

Vickrey, W. 1961. Risk, utility and social policy. *Social Research* 28: 205–17.

Vlastos, G. 1962. Justice and equality. In *Social Justice,* ed. by R. Brandt. Prentice-Hall; and in *Equality,* ed. by L. Pojman and R. Westmoreland. Oxford: Oxford University Press.

Waldron, J., ed. 1984. *Theories of Rights.* Oxford: Oxford University Press.

Waldron, J. 1988. *The Rights to Private Property.* Oxford: Clarendon Press.

Wallich, H. 1960. *Cost of Freedom.* Greenwood Press.

Walras, L. [1898] 1936. *Études d'Economie sociale.* Lausane: F. Rouge and Paris: F. Pichon; new edition: 1936.

Walzer, M. 1983. *Spheres of Justice.* Oxford: Blackwell.

Weber, M. 1962. *Basic Concepts in Sociology.* New York: Citadel Press.

Weymark, J. 1994. Harsanyi's social aggregation theorem with alternative Pareto principles. In *Models and Measurement of Welfare and Inequality,* ed. by W. Eichhorn. Heidelberg: Springer-Verlag.

Wicksteed, P. H. 1888. *The Alphabet of Economic Science.* London: R. H. Hutton.

Wicksteed, P. H. 1933. *The Common Sense of Political Economy.* London: Robbins.

Yaari, M. E. and Bar-Hillel, M. 1984. On dividing justly. *Social Choice and Welfare* 1.

Yaari, M. E. 1993. Judgments of distributive justice. In *Psychological Perspectives on Justice,* ed. by B. Mellers and J. Baron, Chapter 4. Cambridge, MA: Cambridge University Press.

Young, H. P., ed. 1985. *Fair Allocation.* AMS Short Course Lecture Notes, Vol. 33. Providence: American Mathematical Society.

Young, H. P. 1992. *Equity.* Princeton, NJ: Princeton University Press.

Zajac, E. 1997. *The Political Economy of Fairness.* Cambridge, MA: MIT Press.

Index

happiness (*cont.*)
  Pareto-efficient states, 436
  preferences, 428, 434
  See also eudemonistic capacities
Harsanyi, John, 343, 344, 345, 351, 358, 364, 366, 384, 385, 433
Hayek, Friedrich, 253, 367, 369, 371, 373
health, 27, 445, 453, 454
Hegel, G. F. W., 375
Hicks, John, 312, 369, 442
history, 28, 329
Hobbes, Thomas, 370
holism, 287–288
homogeneization, 351
horizontal equity, 458, 459

id, 343
idleness, 123, 124
impartiality, 14, 33, 280, 300, 342
  coefficient *k* and, 285
  coercion and, 292
  conjunction and, 337, 342
  consensus and, 289–290, 336
  equalities and, 13
  extension and, 337, 339
  individuals and, 288, 336
  information and, 298
  justice and, 13, 501
  methods of, 337
  self-centeredness and, 319
  social relations and, 340
  unanimity and, 13, 501–502
incentives, 3–4, 22, 179, 202, 229, 236. *See also* disincentives
inclusion, 407, 410
income, 23, 146, 160, 200, 478
  allocation function, 4, 88, 199, 486, 487
  basic, 119, 224–225, 235, 238, 240, 242, 504
  budget possibility set, 480–481
  disincentives and, 194
  distribution and, 185
  ELIE and. *See* ELIE
  equal equivalent (income), 381
  equalization of. *See* income equalization
  extremes of, 122
  gaps in, 162
  goods and, 145
  guaranteed, 119, 124, 240
  highest, 122, 156
  inequalities, 377, 473
  justice and, 185
  labour, 440
  labour and, 23, 149, 153, 156, 185, 189, 207, 481–482
  leisure and, 116, 490
  leisurely-equivalent (income), 443, 481
  ℓ-equivalent (income), 443, 481, 488
  lowest, 122, 125

  marginal utility of, 98
  minimum, 3, 117, 279, 285–286, 453
  opportunity and, 440
  productive capacities and, 23
  purchasing power and, 1–2
  self-ownership and, 148, 162
  tax on. *See* income tax
  unemployment income, 212, 213, 215, 216
  work and, 188
income equalization, 28, 129, 187, 188, 191, 194, 202, 205, 207, 253, 257
  defined, 130–131
  Dworkin on, 253, 443
  ELIE and, 376. *See* ELIE
  income and, 114, 253
  labour and, 149, 153. *See also* ELIE
  necessary and sufficient conditions, 130
  self-ownership and, 129, 156
  unequal outcome freedoms, 131
income tax, 490, 496, 497
  ELIE and, 195, 505
  financing, 236
  functions of, 195
  general, 15
  macrojustice and, 178
  negative, 66, 119, 124, 204, 226, 234, 240, 242
  optimum, 175–176, 187, 197
  price effects, 203–204
  progressive, 196
  tax credit, 119, 124, 204
  utilitarianism and, 178
incommensurability, 101
independence, 380
indifference curves, 477, 479, 498
individualism, 117, 393, 396
  basic rights and, 24, 25, 75, 78
  communitarianism and, 367
  community and, 272
  conjunction and, 289
  endogenous social choice and, 288
  extension and, 289
  fraternity and, 269
  impartiality and, 288, 291, 336
  integration and, 268
  interindividual rights, 169
  justice and, 299
  leisure and, 253
  moral views and, 283, 293
  opinion and, 288, 336
  ordinal utility and, 183
  others and, 34–35
  preferences, 306, 307, 317, 318
  properties of, 342
  self-interest and, 304, 306
  society and, 280, 281
  values, 382, 393
inequalities, 378, 380